PHYSICAL ANTHROPOLOGY AND ARCHAEOLOGY

WORLD COUNTRIES

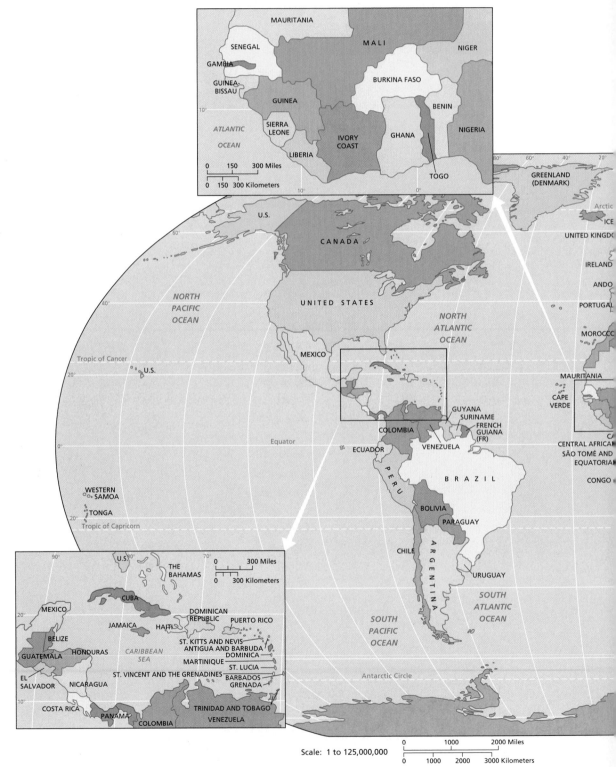

MAURITANIA
SENEGAL
GAMBIA
GUINEA-BISSAU
GUINEA
SIERRA LEONE
LIBERIA
ATLANTIC OCEAN
MALI
BURKINA FASO
IVORY COAST
GHANA
TOGO
BENIN
NIGER
NIGERIA

0   150   300 Miles
0   150   300 Kilometers

GREENLAND (DENMARK)
Arctic
ICE
UNITED KINGDO
IRELAND
ANDO
PORTUGAL
MOROCCO
MAURITANIA
CAPE VERDE
CA
CENTRAL AFRICA
SÃO TOMÉ AND
EQUATORIA
CONGO

U.S.
CANADA
UNITED STATES
NORTH PACIFIC OCEAN
Tropic of Cancer
U.S.
MEXICO
NORTH ATLANTIC OCEAN
GUYANA
SURINAME
FRENCH GUIANA (FR)
COLOMBIA
VENEZUELA
ECUADOR
Equator
PERU
BRAZIL
BOLIVIA
PARAGUAY
CHILE
ARGENTINA
URUGUAY
WESTERN SAMOA
TONGA
Tropic of Capricorn
SOUTH PACIFIC OCEAN
SOUTH ATLANTIC OCEAN
Antarctic Circle

U.S.
THE BAHAMAS
0   300 Miles
0   300 Kilometers
MEXICO
CUBA
JAMAICA
HAITI
DOMINICAN REPUBLIC
PUERTO RICO
BELIZE
GUATEMALA
HONDURAS
CARIBBEAN SEA
ST. KITTS AND NEVIS
ANTIGUA AND BARBUDA
DOMINICA
MARTINIQUE
ST. LUCIA
EL SALVADOR
NICARAGUA
ST. VINCENT AND THE GRENADINES
BARBADOS
GRENADA
COSTA RICA
PANAMA
COLOMBIA
TRINIDAD AND TOBAGO
VENEZUELA

Scale: 1 to 125,000,000

0   1000   2000 Miles
0   1000   2000   3000 Kilometers

Note: All world maps are Robinson projection.

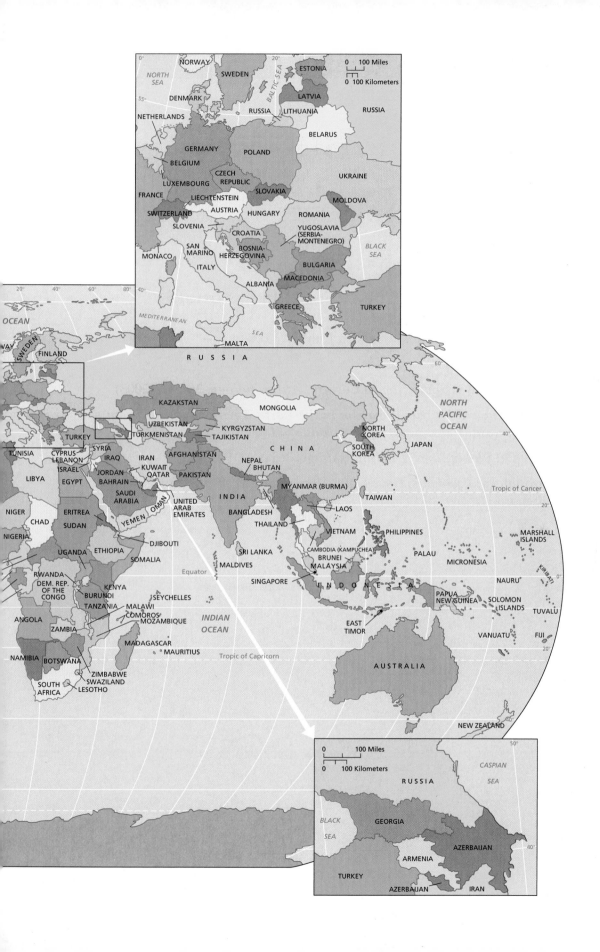

LIST OF BOOKS

PHYSICAL ANTHROPOLOGY AND ARCHAEOLOGY

Conrad Phillip Kottak

University of Michigan

McGraw Hill

Boston   Burr Ridge, IL   Dubuque, IA   Madison, WI   New York   San Francisco   St. Louis
Bangkok   Bogotá   Caracas   Kuala Lumpur   Lisbon   London   Madrid   Mexico City
Milan   Montreal   New Delhi   Santiago   Seoul   Singapore   Sydney   Taipei   Toronto

The McGraw·Hill Companies

 Higher Education

PHYSICAL ANTHROPOLOGY AND ARCHAEOLOGY

Published by McGraw-Hill, a business unit of The McGraw-Hill Companies, Inc. 1221 Avenue of the Americas, New York, NY, 10020. Copyright © 2004, by The McGraw-Hill Companies, Inc. All rights reserved. No part of this publication may be reproduced or distributed in any form or by any means, or stored in a database or retrieval system, without the prior written consent of The McGraw-Hill Companies, Inc., including, but not limited to, in any network or other electronic storage or transmission, or broadcast for distance learning.
Some ancillaries, including electronic and print components, may not be available to customers outside the United States.

This book is printed on acid-free paper.

1 2 3 4 5 6 7 8 9 0 DOW/DOW 0 9 8 7 6 5 4 3

ISBN 0–07-286366-8

Publisher: *Phillip A. Butcher*
Sponsoring editor: *Kevin Witt*
Developmental editor: *Pam Gordon*
Marketing manager: *Dan Loch*
Media producer: *Shannon Gattens*
Project Manager: *Jean R. Starr*
Production Supervisor: *Carol A. Bielski*
Designer: *Mary E. Kazak*
Media PM/Supplement producer: *Marc Mattson*
Photo research coordinator: *Alexandra Ambrose*
Photo researcher: *Barbara Salz*
Cover design: *Cassandra Chu*
Interior design: *Kay Fulton*
Typeface: *10/12 Palatino*
Compositor: *Precision Graphics*
Printer: *R. R. Donnelley/Willard*

Library of Congress Cataloging-in-Publication Data
Kottak, Conrad Phillip.
    Physical anthropology and archaeology / Conrad Phillip Kottak.
        p. cm.
    Includes bibliographical references and index.
        ISBN 0-07-286366-8 (softcover : alk. paper)
        1. Physical anthropology. 2. Archaeology. 3. Anthropology, Prehistoric. I. Title.
    GN60.K68 2004
    599.9—dc21
                                                                2003048749

www.mhhe.com

For my grandchildren,
Lucas and Elena—
sweet boy, sweet girl

BRIEF CONTENTS

CONTENTS

Part One   THE DIMENSIONS OF ANTHROPOLOGY   1

Part Two   PHYSICAL ANTHROPOLOGY
                 AND ARCHAEOLOGY   57

LIST OF BOXES

ABOUT THE AUTHOR

Conrad Phillip Kottak (A.B. Columbia College, 1963; Ph.D. Columbia University, 1966) is a Professor and Chair of the Department of Anthropology at the University of Michigan, where he has taught since 1968. In 1991 he was honored for his teaching by the university and the state of Michigan. In 1992 he received an excellence in teaching award from the College of Literature, Sciences, and the Arts of the University of Michigan. And in 1999 the American Anthropological Association (AAA) awarded Professor Kottak the AAA/Mayfield Award for Excellence in the Undergraduate Teaching of Anthropology.

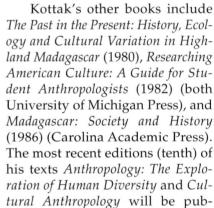

Professor Kottak has done ethnographic field work in Brazil (since 1962), Madagascar (since 1966), and the United States. His general interests are in the processes by which local cultures are incorporated—and resist incorporation—into larger systems. This interest links his earlier work on ecology and state formation in Africa and Madagascar to his more recent research on global change, national and international culture, and the mass media.

The third edition of Kottak's popular case study *Assault on Paradise: Social Change in a Brazilian Village,* based on his field work in Arembepe, Bahia, Brazil, was published in 1999 by McGraw-Hill. In a research project during the 1980s, Kottak blended ethnography and survey research in studying "Television's Behavioral Effects in Brazil." That research is the basis of Kottak's book *Prime-Time Society: An Anthropological Analysis of Television and Culture* (Wadsworth 1990)—a comparative study of the nature and impact of television in Brazil and the United States.

Kottak's other books include *The Past in the Present: History, Ecology and Cultural Variation in Highland Madagascar* (1980), *Researching American Culture: A Guide for Student Anthropologists* (1982) (both University of Michigan Press), and *Madagascar: Society and History* (1986) (Carolina Academic Press). The most recent editions (tenth) of his texts *Anthropology: The Exploration of Human Diversity* and *Cultural Anthropology* will be published by McGraw-Hill in summer 2003. He is also the author of *Mirror for Humanity: A Concise Introduction to Cultural Anthropology* (3rd ed., McGraw-Hill, 2003) and (with Kathryn A. Kozaitis) *On Being Different: Diversity* and *Multiculturalism in the North American Mainstream* (2nd ed., McGraw-Hill, 2003).

Conrad Kottak's articles have appeared in academic journals, including *American Anthropologist, Journal of Anthropological Research, American Ethnologist, Ethnology, Human Organization,* and *Luso-Brazilian Review.* He has also written for more popular journals, including *Transaction/SOCIETY, Natural History, Psychology Today,* and *General Anthropology.*

In recent research projects, Kottak and his colleagues have investigated the emergence of ecological awareness in Brazil, the social context of deforestation and biodiversity conservation in Madagascar, and popular participation in economic development planning in northeastern Brazil. Since 1999 Professor Kottak has been active in the University of Michigan's Center for the Ethnography of Everyday Life, supported by the Alfred P. Sloan Foundation. In that capacity, for a research project entitled "Media, Family, and Work in a Middle-Class Midwestern Town," Kottak has investigated how middle-class families draw on various media in planning, managing, and evaluating their choices and solutions with respect to the competing demands of work and family.

Conrad Kottak appreciates comments about his books from professors and students. He can be readily reached by e-mail at the following Internet address:

ckottak@umich.edu

PREFACE

Since 1968, I've regularly taught physical anthropology and archaeology, as the first half of a four-field introduction to anthropology, to a class of 375 to 550 students. Constant feedback from students, teaching assistants, fellow instructors, and my colleagues in physical anthropology and archaeology keeps me up to date on the interests, needs, and views of the people for whom this text is written. I continue to believe that effective textbooks are rooted in enthusiasm for and enjoyment of one's own teaching experience.

My graduate training in anthropology at Columbia University in the 1960s was far broader than what most anthropology departments offer today. Fascinated with the entire field of anthropology, I took as many courses in physical anthropology and archaeology as I did in ethnology. In that less specialized time, when a broader vision of anthropology—which I still share—prevailed, I had to pass prelims in all four subfields. I've never lost my fascination with physical anthropology and archaeology, and how they relate to research in the other subfields, such as my own work on biodiversity conservation and the origin of the state.

As a college student, I was drawn to anthropology by its breadth and because of what it could tell me about the human condition, present and past. Since then, I've been fortunate in spending my teaching career at a university that values and unites anthropology's four subdisciplines. I have daily contact with members of all the subfields, and as a regular teacher of the four-field introductory anthropology course, I'm happy to keep up with the four subfields. I love anthropology's breadth. I believe strongly in anthropology's capacity to enlighten and inform. The subject matter is intrinsically fascinating, and the focus on diversity helps students understand and interact with their fellow human beings in an increasingly interconnected world and an increasingly diverse North America.

When I wrote my first textbook three decades ago, anthropology had far fewer texts than it does today. They were less specialized than today's texts, but they were still encyclopedic, as they tried to cover all of anthropology rather than its individual subfields. I found them too long and too unfocused to fit my course and my image of contemporary anthroplogy—which was changing rapidly. Anthroplogists were writing about a "new archaeology" and a "new ethnography." Fresh fossil finds and biochemical studies were challenging our understanding of human primate evolution. Studies of monkeys and apes in their natural settings were contradicting conclusions that were based on work in zoos. Today there are new issues and approaches, such as molecular anthropology and new forms of spatial analysis. The fossil and archaeological records expand every day. Anthropology hasn't lost its excitement. But the texts that present the field seem to grow ever more specialized, longer, and more detailed—again reaching lengths that surpass what it's possible to cover easily in a mere semester. I offer this book as an antidote—with what I see as a unique set of goals and themes.

Goals and Themes

My book has three main goals. My first goal was to make this book both a serious scientific introduction to physical anthropology and archaeology and a holistic book that systematically approaches the course from a four-field perspective. Anthropology is a *science*—a "systematic field of study or body of knowledge that aims, through experiment, observation, and deduction, to produce reliable explanations of phenomena, with reference to the material and physical world" (*Webster's New World Encyclopedia*, 1993, p. 937). Clyde Kluckhohn (1944, p. 9) called anthropology "the science of human similarities and differences," and his statement of the need for such a science still stands: "Anthropology provides a scientific basis for dealing with the crucial dilemma of the world today: how can peoples of different appearance, mutually unintelligible languages, and dissimilar ways of life get along peaceably together?" (Kluckhohn 1944, p. 9). Physical anthropology and archaeology have compiled an impressive body of scientific knowledge, which this book attempts to encapsulate.

My second goal was to write a book that would be good for students. This book would be user-friendly in approach and pedagogy. It would stress to students why anthropology should matter to them, how they can use anthropology to understand themselves. By discussing current events, it would show how anthropology affects their lives. Through the unique "Beyond the Classroom boxes" (see below), the book would also highlight the work that students just like them are doing in anthropology.

My third goal was to write a book that professors (who often complain that existing texts are too long), as well as students, could easily read and master. *Physical Anthropology and Archaeology* is intended to provide a manageable, yet amply illustrated, introduction to those subfields of anthropology. I sought to create a book that is manageable in size and up to date with the latest finds and that features an extraordinary support package. The shorter length increases the instructor's options for assigning lab work or additional reading—case studies, readers, and other supplements. The supplements benefit both student and professor.

This book has two themes, which mirror my three goals: "Bringing It All Together" and "Understanding Ourselves."

Bringing It All Together: Most texts give lip service to the fact that anthropology is an integrated, comparative, four-field approach to human similarities and differences. This book, however, takes a truly holistic approach through the "Bringing it All Together" essays that come after Chapters

5, 8, and 11. These essays show how anthropology's subfields and dimensions combine to interpret and explain a common topic. The topics that are "brought together" are (1) deforestation, as a threat to biological and cultural diversity, which applied anthropologists have attempted to mitigate; (2) the matter of when *Homo sapiens* became fully human, behaviorally as well as biologically, and the kinds of cultural (archaeological) evidence we have for this emergence; and (3) the biological and cultural dimensions of the peopling of Polynesia, one of the last major areas to be settled by humans.

Understanding Ourselves: It's common and proper for texts to present facts and theories prominent in the field of study, but often such material seems irrelevant to the student. In anthropology particularly, facts and theories should be presented not just to be read and remembered, but because they help us understand ourselves. "Understanding Ourselves" paragraphs, found in each chapter, answer the question "So what?" For example, we see how the unique human combination of upright bipedalism and large brain size affects the birthing, maturation, and socialization of human children. These discussions also serve to "bring together" the biological and cultural dimensions of anthropology, and so the overall theme of this book may be stated as "Understanding Ourselves by Bringing It All Together through Anthropology's Unique Four-Field Approach."

Pedagogy

Working closely together, the author, editors, designer, and photo researcher have developed a format for this text that supports the goal of a readable, practical, up-to-date, and attractive book. I tried to follow through with my goal of making the book student-friendly.

Here's a summary of the pedagogical features of *Physical Anthropology and Archaelogy*:

- **Part openers**—These features provide descriptions of what is to come in the part and how part chapters work together.
- **Chapter-opening previews**—Succinct chapter-opening outlines and concise overviews help students focus on the chapter's critical concepts and main points. They help students understand what they

should get when they read the chapter and offer a road map of what is to come.

- **Chapter-opening vignettes**—"In the News" vignettes open every chapter, highlighting the relevance of anthropology in today's world. These vignettes serve as a bridge between the world we live in and the chapter content. They show how anthropology is relevant to our world and how, specifically, the content of every chapter can be found in today's headlines.

- **In-text icons**—Marginal icons tell students when more information on a particular topic is available at the Online Learning Center (see below).

- **Intriguing *Interesting Issues* Boxes**—Coverage of current issues in Anthropology, many with maps and photos, raise students' awareness of some of the more provocative aspects of anthropology today.

- **"Beyond the Classroom" Boxes**—These thematic boxes highlighting student research in anthropology enable students to read about the work their peers at other schools are doing, further highlighting the relevance of anthropology in the real world.

- **Easy-to-use end-of-chapter reviews**—Clear, concise *numbered* chapter summaries facilitate chapter concept review, while end-of-chapter glossaries enable students to go over the chapter's key terms.

- **Critical Thinking, Internet, and Atlas exercises**—Chapter-ending exercises challenge students to use their critical thinking skills to apply what they have read about in the chapter, to explore chapter concepts in greater detail via Web research, and to explore the geographic and visual dimensions of anthropology using our unique atlas.

- **Suggested Readings**—An up-to-date list of additional reading materials, briefly annotated, comes at the end of each chapter to help guide student research.

- **End-of-book glossary**—This feature brings together all the key terms defined at the end of each chapter for easy access and review.

- **A Spanish glossary**—This feature defines key terms in Spanish to help students for whom Spanish is the primary language.

Visuals

When writing this book, I was committed to creating a text with an outstanding visual program. A wealth of illustrations, including photos with thought-provoking captions, make the chapter material clear, understandable, and inviting. Maps, figures, charts, and tables are also plentiful.

Since anthropology examines and explains human diversity across space and time, students need help to conceptualize the places and time spans discussed in the book. Where in the world do people live today, and where have they lived at various times in the past? This text has an unusually rich map program. Orientation globes help students figure out where in the world the places under discussion are located.

In addition to the book's internal maps, a separate atlas is shrink-wrapped with every copy of the text. The "Interpret the World" feature, found in every chapter, ties the running text to material in the atlas. Also, end-of-chapter atlas questions allow students to apply atlas content.

Content and Organization

Physical Anthropology and Archaeology, guided by very thoughtful reviewers, covers the core and basics of those subfields, as well as prominent current issues and approaches.

Part I ("The Dimensions of Anthropology") introduces anthropology as a four-field integrated discipline, with academic and applied dimensions, that examines human biological and cultural diversity in time and space. Anthropology is discussed as a comparative and holistic science, featuring biological, social, cultural, linguistic, and historical approaches. Part I explores links between anthropology and other fields—other natural sciences as well as social sciences and the humanities. Examples of applied anthropology from the various subfields are provided. This part was designed with one of my goals (as mentioned previously) for the text in mind—introducing a holistic field consisting of four subfields and two dimensions.

Part II ("Physical Anthropology and Archaeology") begins with a chapter (Chapter 3) devoted to ethics and methods in the two subfields, including the controversy surrounding the discovery and disposition of "Kennewick Man." Part II poses and answers several key questions: When did we originate, and how did we become what we are? What role do genes, the environment, society, and culture play in human variation and diversity? What can we tell about our origins and nature from the study of our nearest relatives—nonhuman primates? When and how did the primates originate? What key features of their early adaptations are still basic to our abilities, behavior, and perceptions? How did hominids develop from our primate ancestors? When, where, and how did the first hominids emerge and expand? What about the earliest real humans? How do we explain biological diversity in our own species, *Homo Sapiens?* How does such diversity relate to the idea of race? What major transitions have taken place since the emergence of *Homo sapiens?* The origin of food production (the domestication of plants and animals) was a major change in human adaptation, with profound implications for society and culture. The spread and intensification of food production are tied to the appearance of the first towns, cities, and states, and the emergence of social stratification and major inequalities.

Here are specific content features, chapter by chapter:

Chapter 1 introduces anthropology as a four-field integrated discipline, with academic and applied dimensions, that focuses on human biological and cultural diversity in time and space. Anthropology is discussed as a comparative and holistic science, with links to the natural and social sciences and the humanities. Chapter 1 concludes with a section titled "Science, Explanation, and Hypothesis Testing."

In Chapter 2 ("Applying Anthropology") applied anthropology is presented as a second dimension, rather than a fifth subfield, of anthropology. Examples of applied anthropology from the various subfields are provided. There is a major section on ethics and anthropology.

The focus of Chapter 3 is ethical issues and research methods in physical anthropology and archaeology. Also discussed are dating techniques. In this chapter, I wanted to highlight the ethical issues that anthropologists increasingly confront, such as those surrounding NAGPRA and "Kennewick Man." I also wanted to show students how

anthropologists do their work and how that work is relevant in understanding ourselves.

Chapter 4 ("Evolution and Genetics") discusses natural selection and other evolutionary principles, along with genetics and biological adaptation, including genes and disease. I hoped to provide a gentle, yet complete, introduction to these difficult topics. I wanted to give enough information for basic anthropology students but to avoid the medical student coverage that some other books include. This approach again illustrates my goal of creating a student-friendly text.

Chapter 5 ("The Primates") surveys primate traits, trends in primate evolution, and the major primate groups. Also included is the most recent information on endangered primates and on hunting and tool use by chimpanzees. Again, I tried to cover the basics—what's interesting and relevant about primates—while avoiding the more elaborate terminology and more detailed classifications that other texts introduce.

Chapter 6 ("Primate Evolution") explores primate evolution, including the latest theories on how and when the primates emerged. Its photos compare fossil primates with their most similar living relatives. The discussion of Miocene apes, based on the latest research, examines several possible common ancestors for humans and the apes as well as the recent Toumai discovery in Chad.

Chapter 7 considers early hominids—their fossils and tool making—from *Ardipithecus* and the australopithecines to *Homo habilis, rudolfensis,* and *erectus.* The latest finds and interpretations are covered.

Based on the most recent discoveries confirming the expansion of early *Homo erectus* (sometimes known as *Homo ergaster*) out of Africa, Chapter 8 ("Modern Humans") describes recent fossil finds in Europe. This chapter also includes the latest information on the various theories for the origin of *Homo sapiens.*

Chapter 9 ("Human Diversity and 'Race'") surveys ways of understanding human biological diversity. The concept of race has been abandoned in favor of an approach focusing on *explaining* specific aspects of human biological diversity. This chapter, which uniquely (compared with other physical and archaeology texts) discusses both the biological and social components of the race concept, includes data from U.S. Census 2000 and a section on interracial, biracial, and multiracial identity.

Chapter 10 ("The First Farmers") examines the origin and implications, and the costs and benefits, of food production (the domestication of plants and animals). The seven world centers of domestication are identified and discussed, with a focus on the first farmers and herders in the Middle East and the first farmers in Mexico and adjacent areas.

Chapter 11 ("The First Cities and States") examines, and introduces theories about, the emergence of towns, cities, chiefdoms, and states. Its examples include the Middle East, India/Pakistan, China, Mesoamerica, and Peru. Students learn how archaeologists make inferences about ancient societies from contemporary ethnographic studies. This again illustrates the texts's overall focus on anthropology as a four-field discipline in which findings from one subfield are integral to the others.

Supplements

As a full-service publisher of quality educational products, McGraw-Hill does much more than just sell textbooks: It creates and publishes an extensive array of print, video, and digital supplements for students and instructors. *Physical Anthropology and Archaeology* boasts an extensive, comprehensive supplements package. Orders of new (versus used) textbooks help defray the cost of developing such supplements, which is substantial. Please consult your local McGraw-Hill representative for more information on any of the supplements.

FOR THE STUDENT

The Kottak Anthropology Atlas (by John Allen and Audrey Shalinsky)—Shrink-wrapped and free with every copy of the text, the *Kottak Anthropology Atlas* offers 26 large-scale, global, full-color anthropology-related reference maps. The atlas maps are specifically tied to the content of each chapter in the text through corresponding in-text features. These features, "Interpret the World" and "Atlas Questions," ask students to consider the relationship between the topics they are studying and the world we live in. Designed specifically to help students who struggle with a lack of knowledge of geography, the *Atlas* will give students a stronger understanding of the world we live in today as well as the world of our ancestors.

The Student's Online Learning Center (by Chris Glew and Patrick Livingood)—This free Web-based, partially password-protected student supplement features a large number of helpful tools, interactive exercises and activities, links, and useful information at www.mhhe.com/kottak. To access the password-protected areas of the site, students must purchase a new copy of the text. Designed specifically to complement the individual chapters of the text, this feature gives students access to material by text chapter.

Exciting Interactivity includes:

- Virtual Explorations—Offer students the opportunity to view short film clips from *The Films from the Humanities and Sciences* on chapter-related topics and complete critical thinking activities based on the films and to work with fascinating simulations and animations which show complex processes and phenomena.

- Interactive Exercises—Allow students to engage and work interactively with visuals, maps, and line drawings and explore chapter content.

- Internet Exercises—Offer chapter-related links to World Wide Web–related sites and activities for students to complete based on the sites.

- Atlas Exercises—Offer interactive activities based on *Kottak Anthropology Atlas* maps.

- Interactive Globe—Offers helpful geographic support.

Useful study tools include:

- Chapter objectives, outlines, and overviews—Designed to give students signposts for understanding and recognizing key chapter content.

- PowerPoint lecture notes—Offer point-by-point lecture notes on chapter sections.

- Multiple choice, true/false, and short answer questions—Give students the opportunity to quiz themselves on chapter content with feedback indicating why an answer is correct or incorrect.

- Essay questions—Allow students to explore key chapter concepts through their own writing.

- Glossary—Illustrates key terms.
- Audio Glossary—Helps students with difficult-to-pronounce words through audio pronunciation help.
- Vocabulary flashcards—Allow students to test their mastery of key vocabulary.
- Chapter-related readings—Give students the opportunity to explore topics of interest through additional readings on chapter-related topics.

  Helpful links include:

- General Web links—Offer chapter-by-chapter links for further research.
- Links to *New York Times* articles—Give students immediate access to articles on chapter-related content.
- Bringing It all Together links—Offer students links related to the "Bringing It All Together" text features.
- Information on Anthropology links—Provides useful links to anthropology information.
- Study break links—Give students fun links on related topics.

  Useful Information includes:

- FAQ's—Give students answers to typical chapter-related questions.
- Career opportunities—Offer students related links to useful information on careers in anthropology.
- How to Ace This Course—Offers students useful study tips for success.

PowerWeb—This resource is offered free with the purchase of a new copy of the text and is available via a link on the Student's Online Learning Center. PowerWeb helps students with online research by providing access to high-quality academic sources. PowerWeb is a password-protected site that provides students with the full text of course-specific, peer-reviewed articles from the scholarly and popular press, as well as Web links, student study tools, weekly updates, and additional resources. For further information about PowerWeb, visit www.dushkin.com/powerweb/pwwt1.mhtml.

The McGraw-Hill Anthropology Supersite—Available at http://www.mhhe.com/anthrosupersite,

this comprehensive, one-stop supersite provides links to book-specific McGraw-Hill websites, anthropology Web links, student tutorials, breaking news in anthropology, and timely chapter-by-chapter updates of selected McGraw-Hill anthropology textbooks.

Reflections on Anthropology: A Four-Field Reader (by Katherine A. Dettwyler and Vaughn M. Bryant)—Designed specifically to complement and follow the organization of *Physical Anthropology and Archaeology*, this reader provides many varied and exciting articles that will motivate and capture a student's interest in anthropology.

FOR THE INSTRUCTOR

The Instructor's Resource Binder (by Chris Glew and Patrick Livingood)—This indispensable instructor supplement features a three-ring binder with tabbed sections that allows professors to integrate McGraw-Hill–provided instructor support items with their own customized course materials. The flexible format of the binder allows professors to store all indispensable course items in one handy place. McGraw-Hill–provided items include:

- Chapter outlines—Offer comprehensive reviews of chapter material for easy reference.
- Lecture topics—Provide ideas for classroom discussion sections and lectures.
- Atlas advice—Offers ideas for how to integrate and use *Kottak Anthropology Atlas*–related chapter maps in class.
- Suggested films—Provide an annotated list of useful films for classroom use.
- A complete test bank—Offers numerous multiple choice, true/false, and essay questions.
- A guide to the visual supplements—Offers guidance for using the Lecture Launcher VHS tape and the Image Library (both described below) successfully in class and includes a directory of the VHS tape.
- A correlation guide to popular anthologies and supplements—Offers chapter-by-chapter suggestions for integrating specific, useful salable supplements with the text.

The Instructor's Resource CD-ROM (by Chris Glew and Patrick Livingood)—This easy-to-use disk provides:

- PowerPoint lecture slides—Give professors ready-made chapter-by-chapter presentation notes.

- A computerized test bank—Offers numerous multiple choice, true/false, and essay questions in an easy-to-use program that is available for both Windows and Macintosh computers.

- An electronic version of the McGraw-Hill–provided resources in the Instructor's Resource Binder—Gives professors the ability to customize these useful aids.

- Atlas maps—Provides electronic versions of all of the maps in the *Kottak Anthropology Atlas* ready to be used in any applicable teaching tool.

The Lecture Launcher VHS Tape—This supplement offers professors a dynamic way to kick off lectures or illustrate key concepts by providing short (two- to four- minute) clips pulled from full-length, anthropology-related films from the *Films from the Humanities and Sciences,* each tied to a chapter in the text. The Instructor's Resource Binder offers a complete guide to the Lecture Launcher VHS Tape, including a chapter-by-chapter description of each clip, the length of each clip so that instructors can queue up the tape easily, useful suggestions for incorporating the film clips in class, and discussion questions.

The Instructor's Online Learning Center (by Chris Glew and Patrick Livingood)—This password-protected site offers access to all the student online materials plus important instructor support materials and downloadable supplements such as:

- An image library—Offers professors the opportunity to create custom-made, professional-looking presentations and handouts by providing electronic versions of many of the maps, charts, line art, and photos in the text along with additional relevant images not included in the text. All images are ready to be used in any applicable teaching tools, including a professor's own lecture materials and McGraw-Hill–provided PowerPoint lecture slides. The Instructor's Resource Binder offers a complete guide to the Image Library and useful suggestions

for incorporating the images into teaching materials.

- Atlas Maps—Provide electronic versions of all the maps in the *Kottak Anthropology Atlas* ready to be used in any applicable teaching tool.

- An electronic version of the McGraw-Hill–provided resources in the Instructor's Resource Binder—Gives professors the ability to customize these useful aids.

- PowerPoint lecture slides—Give professors ready-made chapter-by-chapter presentation notes.

- Links to professional resources—Provide useful links to professional anthropological sites on the World Wide Web.

PowerWeb—This resource is available via a link on the Instructor's Online Learning Center. PowerWeb helps with online research by providing access to high-quality academic sources. PowerWeb is a password-protected site that provides instructors with the full text of course-specific, peer-reviewed articles from the scholarly and popular press, as well as Web links, weekly updates, and additional resources. For further information about PowerWeb, visit www.dushkin.com/powerweb/pwwt1.mhtml.

The McGraw-Hill Anthropology Supersite—Available at http://www.mhhe.com/anthrosupersite, this comprehensive, one-stop supersite provides links to book-specific McGraw-Hill websites, anthropology Web links, instructor downloads, breaking news in anthropology, and timely chapter-by-chapter updates of selected McGraw-Hill anthropology textbooks.

PageOut: The Course Website Development Center—All online content for the text is supported by WebCT, Blackboard, eCollege.com, and other course management systems. Additionally, McGraw-Hill's PageOut service is available to get professors and their courses up and running online in a matter of hours at no cost. PageOut was designed for instructors just beginning to explore Web options. Even a novice computer user can create a course website with a template provided by McGraw-Hill (no programming knowledge necessary). To learn more about PageOut, visit www.mhhe.com/pageout.

Videotapes—A wide variety of full-length videotapes from the *Films for the Humanities and Sciences* series is available to adopters of the text.

Acknowledgments

I'm grateful to many colleagues at McGraw-Hill. I thank Pam Gordon, freelance development editor, for her excellent ideas, suggestions, guidance, timetables, and work behind the scenes involving five books, including *Physical Anthropology and Archaeology*. I continue to enjoy working with Phil Butcher, McGraw-Hill's editorial director for social sciences and humanities. I thank him for his unflagging support as our association has entered its second decade. I'm also delighted to be working with Kevin Witt, McGraw-Hill's sponsoring editor for anthropology.

I thank Jean Starr for her work as project manager, guiding the manuscript through production and (along with Pam Gordon) keeping everything moving on schedule. Carol Bielski, production supervisor, worked with the compositor and printer to make sure everything came out right. It's always a pleasure to work with Barbara Salz, photo researcher, with whom I've worked for more than a decade. I want to thank Patrick Livingood and especially Chris Glew for their work on the supplements for, and Internet features of, this book. I thank Chris especially for his hard and creative work on the last two editions of my longer texts. I also thank Eric Lowenkron for his copyediting, Kay Fulton and Mary Kazak for conceiving and executing the design, and Dan Loch, a knowledgeable, creative, and enthusiastic marketing manager. Robin Mouat and Alex Ambrose also deserve thanks as art editor and photo research coordinator, as does Kathleen Cowan, McGraw-Hill's editorial assistant for anthropology.

Thanks, too, to Shannon Gattens, media producer, for creating the OLC and VHS tape, and to Marc Mattson, supplements producer, who created all the other supplements.

I also thank Wes Hall, who has handled the literary permissions and Marty Granahan, McGraw-Hill's permissions coordinator. For their work on the atlas, I thank Ted Knight and Ava Suntoke at Dushkin and John Allen and Audrey Shalinsky,

authors of the atlas. Finally, I thank Pablo Nepomnaschy for doing the Spanish glossary.

I'm especially indebted to Bill Engelbrecht, Buffalo State College, who reviewed this first edition manuscript.

I'm also grateful to the reviewers of the seventh, eighth, and ninth editions of *Anthropology: The Exploration of Human Diversity*. Their comments have also helped me plan *Physical Anthropology and Archaeology*.

Their names are as follows:

Reviewers

Julianna Acheson
Green Mountain College

Mohamad Al-Madani
Seattle Central Community College

Robert Bee
University of Connecticut

Daniel Boxberger
Western Washington University

Ned Breschel
Morehead State University

Peter J. Brown
Emory University

Margaret Bruchez
Blinn College

Karen Burns
University of Georgia

Richard Burns
Arkansas State University

Mary Cameron
Auburn University

Dianne Chidester
University of South Dakota

Inne Choi
California Polytechnic State University–San Luis Obispo

Jeffrey Cohen
Penn State University

Barbara Cook
California Polytechnic State University–San Luis Obispo

Norbert Dannhaeuser
Texas A&M University

Michael Davis
Truman State University

Robert Dirks
Illinois State University

Bill Donner
Kutztown University of Pennsylvania

Paul Durrenberger
Pennsylvania State University

George Esber
Miami University of Ohio

Grace Fraser
Plymouth State College

Laurie Godfrey
University of Massachusetts–Amherst

Bob Goodby
Franklin Pierce College

Tom Greaves
Bucknell University

Mark Grey
University of Northern Iowa

Homes Hogue
Mississippi State University

Alice James
Shippensburg University of Pennsylvania

Richard King
Drake University

Eric Lassiter
Ball State University

Jill Leonard
University of Illinois–Urbana–Champaign

David Lipset
University of Minnesota

Jonathan Marks
University of North Carolina–Charlotte

Barbara Miller
George Washington University

John Nass, Jr.
California University of Pennsylvania

Frank Ng
California State University–Fresno

Martin Ottenheimer
Kansas State University

Leonard Plotnicov
University of Pittburgh

Janet Pollak
William Patterson College

Howard Prince
CUNY–Borough of Manhattan Community College

Steven Rubenstein
Ohio University

Mary Scott
San Francisco State University

Brian Siegel
Furman University

Esther Skirboll
Slippery Rock University of Pennsylvania

Gregory Starrett
University of North Carolina–Charlotte

Karl Steinen
State University of West Georgia

Noelle Stout
Foothill and Skyline Colleges

Susan Trencher
George Mason University

Mark Tromans
Broward Community College

Christina Turner
Virginia Commonwealth University

Donald Tyler
University of Idaho

Daniel Varisco
Hofstra University

Albert Wahrhaftig
Sonoma State University

David Webb
Kutztown University of Pennsylvania

George Westermark
Santa Clara University

Nancy White
University of South Florida

I was delighted by the enthusiasm expressed in their comments.

Students, too, regularly share their insights about my longer anthropology text via e-mail and thus have contributed to this book. Anyone—student or instructor—with access to e-mail can reach me at the following address: ckottak@umich.edu.

As usual, my family has offered me understanding, support, and inspiration during the preparation of this book. This book is dedicated to my grandchildren, Lucas and Elena, in the hope that they, too, like my own children, will continue a family tradition of exploring human diversity and diagnosing and treating the human condition.

After 35 years of teaching, I've benefited from the knowledge, help, and advice of so many friends, colleagues, teaching assistants, and students that I can no longer fit their names into a short preface. I hope they know who they are and accept my thanks.

I especially thank Joyce Marcus for her careful reading of Chapter 11. I've tried to do justice to her extensive knowledge, comments, and suggestions. Throughout my career at Michigan, I've been privileged to work with scholars such as Kent Flannery, Joyce Marcus, Jeff Parsons, and Henry Wright, who share my interest in chiefdoms and states and thus have contributed directly and indi-rectly to this book. I also thank Milford Wolpoff, Roberto Frisancho, John Mitani, and Rachel Caspari, who are always willing to answer my questions about biological anthropology.

Since 1968 I've regularly taught Anthropology 101 ("Introduction to Anthropology"), with the help of several teaching assistants each time. Feedback from students and teaching assistants keeps me up to date on the interests, needs, and views of the people for whom this book is written. I continue to believe that effective textbooks are based in enthusiasm and in practice—in the enjoyment of teaching. I hope this product of my experience will be helpful to others.

Conrad Phillip Kottak
Ann Arbor, Michigan
ckottak@umich.edu

WALKTHROUGH

Comparative "Bringing It All Together" Essays

Unique thematic essays—which appear after groups of related chapters—show how anthropology's subfields combine to interpret and explain a common topic. The essays offer a truly integrated, comparative, and holistic introduction to anthropology. Through multiple and diverse perspectives, they offer students a fuller understanding of what it means to be human.

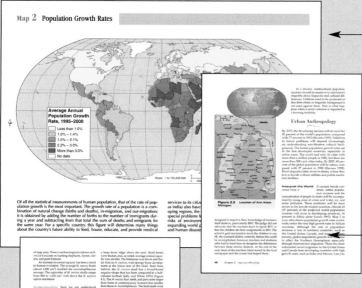

Unique Anthropology Atlas and In Text Atlas Features

A separate atlas, offering important reference maps, is shrink-wrapped with every copy of the text purchased new from the publisher. Designed specifically to help students who struggle with a lack of knowledge of geography, the atlas will bring a stronger understanding of the world we live in today as well as the world of our ancestors. The "Interpret the World" feature and end-of-chapter atlas questions tie the text to the maps in the atlas.

Relevant "Understanding Ourselves" Paragraphs

"Understanding Ourselves" paragraphs help students see why anthropology should matter to them and how anthropology is relevant to their own lives.

Unique Chapter on Ethics and Methods

An important chapter on ethics and methods in physical anthropology and archaeology highlights these essential topics.

Helpful Chapter-Opening Previews

Succinct chapter-opening outlines and concise overviews help students focus on the chapter's critical concepts and main points.

Current Chapter-Opening Vignettes

"In the News" vignettes open each chapter and show how anthropology is relevant to our world and how specifically the content of every chapter can be found in today's headlines.

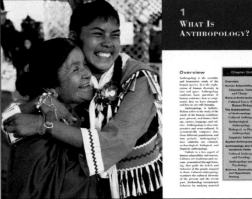

Unique *Beyond the Classroom* Boxes

Beyond the Classroom boxes highlight undergraduate student research in anthropology and enable students to read about the work that their counterparts are doing in anthropology.

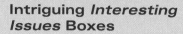

Intriguing *Interesting Issues* Boxes

Interesting Issues boxes feature discussions of provocative aspects of anthropology today and promote critical thinking.

Helpful Part Openers

Part opening pages describe what is to come in the part and how chapters in the part work together.

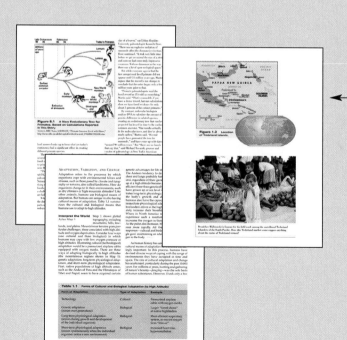

Outstanding and Plentiful Visuals

The text features a wealth of photos, maps, figures, charts, and tables. Intuitive orientation globes help students figure out where in the world places under discussion are located.

Easy-to-Use End-of-Chapter Reviews and Questions

Clear summaries, end-of-chapter glossaries, and suggested readings facilitate chapter concept review and help guide student research, while Critical Thinking, Internet, and Atlas Exercises challenge students to test themselves and apply what they have read in the chapter.

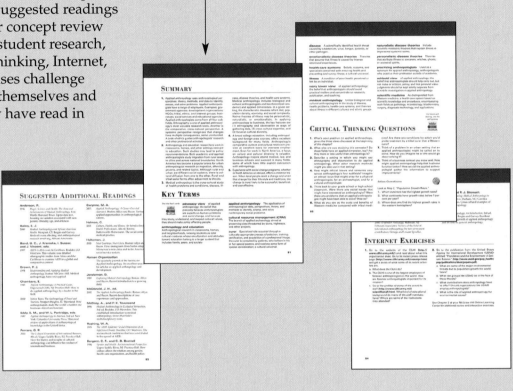

Useful Spanish Glossary

A unique Spanish glossary defines key terms in Spanish to help students for whom Spanish is the primary language.

Customizable Instructor's Resource Binder

This indispensable instructor supplement features a three-ring binder with tabbed sections allowing professors to integrate McGraw-Hill provided instructor support items with their own customized course materials. The flexible format of the binder allows professors to store all essential course items in one handy place.

Exciting Lecture Launcher VHS Videotape

This supplement offers professors a dynamic way to begin lectures or illustrate key concepts, by providing short (2–to–4 minute) video segments taken from full length, anthropology-related films from *Films from the Humanities and Sciences.* Each video segment is tied to a text chapter.

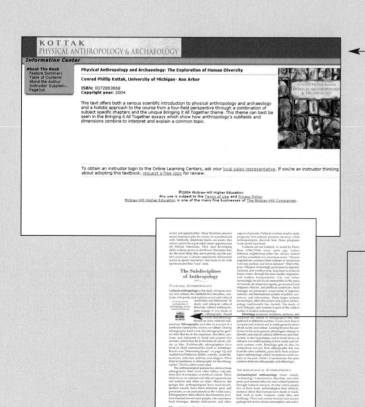

A New Generation of Anthropology Technology

A fully integrated Kottak Online Learning Center offers richer and more dynamic technology than any previously available book specific CD-ROMs. The website provides professors with an Image Bank and other valuable resources, and gives students all of their book-specific technology-based resources and activities in one convenient place. In text icons clearly guide students to information on a particular topic that is available on the Online Learning Center. See the heavy-stock password card at the start of this book for highlights of the instructor and student resources on the Online Learning Center.

Part One

The Dimensions of Anthropology

In Part 1 we'll explore the two different dimensions of anthropology. Those dimensions are academic (theoretical) and applied (practical) anthropology. Anthropology is the scientific and humanistic study of the human species. It is the academic field that most systematically explores biological and cultural diversity in time and space. Anthropologists explore every aspect of human diversity: past, present, and future; biology, society, language, and culture. Anthropology compares ways of life, and the people who lived them, from radically different times and places. Anthropologists work in varied contexts, including colleges, universities, museums, government agencies, businesses, and organizations.

The academic field of anthropology as a whole is known as "general" or "four-field" anthropology. The latter name is based on its four subfields: physical (biological), archaeological, cultural, and linguistic anthropology. Cultural anthropology examines the cultural diversity of the present and the recent past. Archaeology reconstructs behavior and social life by studying material remains. Physical anthropologists study human fossils, genetics, and bodily form and growth. They also study nonhuman primates (monkeys and apes). Linguistic anthropology considers how speech varies with social factors and over time.

Besides its four subfields, anthropology has the two dimensions mentioned above: academic and applied anthropology. Applying anthropology in the world beyond anthropology entails identifying, assessing, and solving problems that affect human beings in North America and abroad. The knowledge and methods of all four subfields, alone and in combination, are used to apply anthropology. Key aspects of anthropology, whether academic or applied, include its distinctive observation-based approach to gathering data, its comparative approach, and its focus on cultural diversity.

1

WHAT IS ANTHROPOLOGY?

Overview

Anthropology is the scientific and humanistic study of the human species. It is the exploration of human diversity in time and space. Anthropology confronts basic questions of human existence: how we originated, how we have changed, and how we are still changing.

Anthropology is holistic. Holism refers to the study of the whole of the human condition: past, present, and future; biology, society, language, and culture. Anthropology is also comparative and cross-cultural. It systematically compares data from different populations and time periods. Anthropology's four subfields are cultural, archaeological, biological, and linguistic anthropology.

Culture is a key aspect of human adaptability and success. Cultures are traditions and customs, transmitted through learning, that guide the beliefs and behavior of the people exposed to them. Cultural anthropology examines the cultural diversity of the present and the recent past. Archaeology reconstructs behavior by studying material

remains. Biological anthropologists study human fossils, genetics, and bodily growth and development. They also study nonhuman primates (monkeys and apes). Linguistic anthropology considers how speech varies with social factors and over time. Anthropology's two dimensions are academic and applied. Applied anthropology uses anthropological knowledge to identify and solve social problems.

Anthropology is related to many other fields, including the sciences and the humanities. There are links to both the natural sciences (e.g., biology) and the social sciences (e.g., sociology). Anthropologists bring their distinctive cross-cultural perspective to the study of economics, politics, psychology, art, music, literature—and society in general. As scientists, anthropologists attempt to identify and explain cultural differences and similarities and to build theory about how social and cultural systems work.

For a multimedia presentation of this Overview, see the Virtual Exploration

mhhe ●com /kottak

Hot Asset in Corporate: Anthropology Degrees

USA Today News Brief

by Del Jones

February 18, 1999

"Been on any digs lately?" Anthropologists are used to hearing that question after announcing their profession. People often confuse anthropology with archaeology, which is one—but only one—of anthropology's subfields. Many anthropologists do dig in the ground, but others dig into the intricacies of cultural diversity and everyday behavior. More and more businesses are hiring anthropologists because they like its characteristic observation of behavior in natural settings and its focus on cultural diversity. Thus, as we see in this article, Hallmark Cards has hired anthropologists to observe parties, holidays, and celebrations of ethnic groups to improve its ability to design cards for targeted audiences. Anthropologists go into people's homes to see how they actually use products. This permits better product design and more effective advertising.

Don't throw away the MBA degree yet.

But as companies go global and crave leaders for a diverse workforce, a new hot degree is emerging for aspiring executives: anthropology.

The study of man is no longer a degree for museum directors. Citicorp created a vice presidency for anthropologist Steve Barnett, who discovered early warning signs to identify people who don't pay credit card bills.

Not satisfied with consumer surveys, Hallmark is sending anthropologists into the homes of immigrants, attending holidays and birthday parties to design cards they'll want.

No survey can tell engineers what women really want in a razor, so marketing consultant Hauser Design sends anthropologists into bathrooms to watch them shave their legs.

Unlike MBAs, anthropology degrees are rare: one undergraduate degree for every 26 in business and one anthropology Ph.D. for every 235 MBAs.

Textbooks now have chapters on business applications. The University of South Florida has created a course of study for anthropologists headed for commerce.

Motorola corporate lawyer Robert Faulkner got his anthropology degree before going to law school. He says it becomes increasingly valuable.

Corporate anthropologists employ varied techniques, including ethnographic observation and focus groups, such as the one shown here, which is being videotaped through a two-way mirror in California.

"When you go into business, the only problems you'll have are people problems," was the advice given to teenager Michael Koss by his father in the early 1970s.

Koss, now 44, heeded the advice, earned an anthropology degree from Beloit College in 1976, and is today CEO of the Koss headphone manufacturer.

Katherine Burr, CEO of The Hanseatic Group, has masters in both anthropology and business from the University of New Mexico. Hanseatic was among the first money management programs to predict the Asian crisis and last year produced a total return of 315% for investors.

"My competitive edge came completely out of anthropology," she says. "The world is so unknown, changes so rapidly. Preconceptions can kill you."

Companies are starving to know how people use the Internet or why some pickups, even though they are more powerful, are perceived by consumers as less powerful, says Ken Erickson, of the Center for Ethnographic Research.

It takes trained observation, Erickson says. Observation is what anthropologists are trained to do.

Source: Del Jones, "Hot Asset in Corporate: Anthropology Degrees," *USA Today,* February 18, 1999, p. B1.

Many anthropologists are educators, working in colleges, universities, and museums. Many other anthropologists, like the ones discussed in this news article, work outside of academia, for example, in business. Cultural anthropologists focus on cultural diversity and the intricacies of everyday behavior and social life. A more biologically oriented anthropologist might advise an engineering team in designing accommodations, such as spacecraft seating, that have optimal fits with human anatomy. Anthropologists study human beings wherever and whenever they find them—in the Australian outback, a Turkish café, a Mesopotamian tomb, or a North American shopping mall. Anthropology is the exploration of human diversity in time and space. Anthropology studies the whole of the human condition: past, present, and future; biology, society, language, and culture. Of particular interest is the diversity that comes through human adaptability.

Human Adaptability

Humans are among the world's most adaptable animals. In the Andes of South America, people wake up in villages 16,000 feet above sea level and then trek 1,500 feet higher to work in tin mines. Tribes in the Australian desert worship animals and discuss philosophy. People survive malaria in the tropics. Men have walked on the moon. The model of the *Starship Enterprise* in Washington's Smithsonian Institution symbolizes the desire to "seek out new life and civilizations, to boldly go where no one has gone before." Wishes to know the unknown, control the uncontrollable, and bring order to chaos find expression among all peoples. Adaptability and flexibility are basic human attributes, and human diversity is the subject matter of anthropology.

Students are often surprised by the breadth of **anthropology,** which is the study of the human species and its immediate ancestors. Anthropology is a uniquely comparative and **holistic** science. Holism refers to the study of the whole of the human condition: past, present, and future; biology, society, language, and culture. Most people think that anthropologists study fossils and nonindustrial, non-Western cultures, and many of them

do. But anthropology is much more than the study of nonindustrial peoples: It is a comparative field that examines all societies, ancient and modern, simple and complex. The other social sciences tend to focus on a single society, usually an industrial nation like the United States or Canada. Anthropology, however, offers a unique cross-cultural perspective by constantly comparing the customs of one society with those of others.

People share society—organized life in groups—with other animals, including baboons, wolves, and even ants. Culture, however, is distinctly human. **Cultures** are traditions and customs, transmitted through learning, that govern the beliefs and behavior of the people exposed to them. Children learn such a tradition by growing up in a particular society, through a process called *enculturation.* Cultural traditions include customs and opinions, developed over the generations, about proper and improper behavior. These traditions answer such questions as: How should we do things? How do we make sense of the world? How do we tell right from wrong? What is right, and what is wrong? A culture produces a degree of consistency in behavior and thought among the people who live in a particular society.

The most critical element of cultural traditions is their transmission through learning rather than through biological inheritance. Culture is not itself biological, but it rests on certain features of human biology. For more than a million years, humans have had at least some of the biological capacities on which culture depends. These abilities are to learn, to think symbolically, to use language, and to employ tools and other products in organizing their lives and adapting to their environments.

Anthropology confronts and ponders major questions of human existence as it explores human biological and cultural diversity in time and space. By examining ancient bones and tools, we unravel the mysteries of human origins. When did our ancestors separate from those remote great-aunts and great-uncles whose descendants are the apes? Where and when did *Homo sapiens* originate? How has our species changed? What are we now and where are we going? How have changes in culture and society influenced biological change? Our genus, *Homo,* has been changing for more than one million years. Humans continue to adapt and change both biologically and culturally.

ADAPTATION, VARIATION, AND CHANGE

Adaptation refers to the processes by which organisms cope with environmental forces and stresses, such as those posed by climate and *topography* or terrains, also called landforms. How do organisms change to fit their environments, such as dry climates or high mountain altitudes? Like other animals, humans use biological means of adaptation. But humans are unique in also having cultural means of adaptation. Table 1.1 summarizes the cultural and biological means that humans use to adapt to high altitudes.

Interpret the World
Atlas Map 1

Map 1 shows global topography, including mountains, hills, lowlands, and plains. Mountainous terrains pose particular challenges, those associated with high altitude and oxygen deprivation. Consider four ways (one cultural and three biological) in which humans may cope with low oxygen pressure at high altitudes. Illustrating cultural (technological) adaptation would be a pressurized airplane cabin equipped with oxygen masks. There are three ways of adapting biologically to high altitudes (the mountainous regions shows in Map 1): genetic adaptation, long-term physiological adaptation, and short-term physiological adaptation. First, native populations of high altitude areas, such as the Andes of Peru and the Himalayas of Tibet and Nepal, seem to have acquired certain genetic advantages for life at very high altitudes. The Andean tendency to develop a voluminous chest and lungs probably has a genetic basis. Second, regardless of their genes, people who grow up at a high altitude become physiologically more efficient there than genetically similar people who have grown up at sea level would be. This illustrates long-term physiological adaptation during the body's growth and development. Third, humans also have the capacity for short-term or immediate physiological adaptation. Thus, when lowlanders arrive in the highlands, they immediately increase their breathing and heart rates. Where in North America would you expect to experience such a reaction? Hyperventilation increases the oxygen in their lungs and arteries. As the pulse also increases, blood reaches their tissues more rapidly. All these varied adaptive responses—cultural and biological—achieve a single goal: maintaining an adequate supply of oxygen to the body.

As human history has unfolded, the social and cultural means of adaptation have become increasingly important. In this process, humans have devised diverse ways of coping with the range of environments they have occupied in time and space. The rate of cultural adaptation and change has accelerated, particularly during the past 10,000 years. For millions of years, hunting and gathering of nature's bounty—*foraging*—was the sole basis of human subsistence. However, it took only a few

---

Table 1.1 Forms of Cultural and Biological Adaptation (to High Altitude)

Form of Adaptation	Type of Adaptation	Example
Technology	Cultural	Pressurized airplane cabin with oxygen masks
Genetic adaptation (occurs over generations)	Biological	Larger "barrel chests" of native highlanders
Long-term physiological adaptation (occurs during growth and development of the individual organism)	Biological	More efficient respiratory system, to extract oxygen from "thin air"
Short-term physiological adaptation (occurs spontaneously when the individual organism enters a new environment)	Biological	Increased heart rate, hyperventilation

thousand years for **food production** (the cultivation of plants and domestication of animals), which originated some 12,000–10,000 years ago, to replace foraging in most areas.

Between 6000 and 5000 B.P. (before the present), the first civilizations arose. These were large, powerful, and complex societies, such as ancient Egypt, that conquered and governed large geographic areas. Much more recently, the spread of industrial production has profoundly affected human life. Throughout human history, major innovations have spread at the expense of earlier ones. Each economic revolution has had social and cultural repercussions. Today's global economy and communications link all contemporary people, directly or indirectly, in the modern world system. People must cope with forces generated by progressively larger systems—region, nation, and world. The study of such contemporary adaptations generates new challenges for anthropology: "The cultures of world peoples need to be constantly rediscovered as these people reinvent them in changing historical circumstances" (Marcus and Fischer 1986, p. 24).

American anthropology arose out of concern for the history and cultures of Native North Americans. Ely S. Parker, or Ha-sa-no-an-da, was a Seneca Indian who made important contributions to early anthropology. Parker also served as Commissioner of Indian Affairs for the United States.

General Anthropology

The academic discipline of anthropology, also known as **general anthropology** or "four-field" anthropology, includes four main subdisciplines or subfields. They are sociocultural, archaeological, biological, and linguistic anthropology. (From here on, the shorter term *cultural anthropology* will be used as a synonym for "sociocultural anthropology.") Of the subfields, cultural anthropology has the largest membership. Most departments of anthropology teach courses in all four subfields.

For current news about anthropology, see the OLC Internet Exercises

mhhe
●**com**
/kottak

There are historical reasons for the inclusion of four subfields in a single discipline. American anthropology arose more than a century ago out of concern for the history and cultures of the native peoples of North America. Interest in the origins and diversity of Native Americans brought together studies of customs, social life, language, and physical traits. Anthropologists are still pondering such questions as: Where did Native Americans come from? How many waves of migration brought them to the New World? What are the linguistic, cultural, and biological links among Native Americans and between them and Asia? Another reason for anthropology's inclusion of four subfields was an interest in the relation between biology (e.g., "race") and culture. More than 50 years ago, the anthropologist Ruth Benedict realized that "In World history, those who have helped to build the same culture are not necessarily of one race, and those of the same race have not all participated in one culture. In scientific language, culture is not a function of race" (Benedict 1940, Ch 2). (Note that a unified four-field anthropology did not develop in Europe, where the subdisciplines tend to exist separately.)

There are also logical reasons for the unity of American anthropology. Each subfield considers variation in time and space (that is, in different geographic areas). Cultural and archaeological anthropologists study (among many other topics) changes in social life and customs. Archaeologists have used studies of living societies and behavior patterns to imagine what life might have been like in the past. Biological anthropologists examine evolutionary changes in physical form, for example, anatomical changes that might have been associated with the origin of tool use or language. Linguistic anthropologists may reconstruct the basics of ancient languages by studying modern ones.

The subdisciplines influence each other as anthropologists talk to each other, read books and journals, and associate in professional organizations. General anthropology explores the basics of human biology, society, and culture and considers their interrelations. Anthropologists share certain key assumptions. Perhaps the most fundamental is the idea that sound conclusions about "human nature" cannot be derived from studying a single nation or cultural tradition. A comparative, cross-cultural approach is essential.

We often hear "nature versus nurture" and "genetics versus environment" questions. Consider gender differences. To what extent do male and female capacities, attitudes, and behavior reflect biological, or cultural, variation? Are there universal emotional and intellectual contrasts between the sexes? Are females less aggressive than males? Is male dominance a human universal? By examining diverse cultures, anthropology shows that many contrasts between men and women reflect cultural training rather than biology.

CULTURAL FORCES SHAPE HUMAN BIOLOGY

Cultural forces constantly mold human biology. For example, culture is a key environmental force in determining how human bodies grow and develop. Cultural traditions promote certain activities and abilities, discourage others, and set standards of physical well-being and attractiveness. Physical activities, including sports, which are influenced by culture, help build the body. For example, North American girls are encouraged to pursue, and therefore do well in, competitive track and field, swimming, diving, and many other sports. Brazilian girls, by contrast, have not fared nearly as well in international athletic competition involving individual sports as have their American and Canadian counterparts. Why are girls encouraged to excel as athletes in some nations but discouraged from engaging in physical activities in others? Why don't Brazilian women, and Latin American women generally, do better in most athletic categories? Does it have to do with "racial" differences or cultural training?

Years of swimming sculpt a distinctive physique: an enlarged upper torso, a massive neck, and powerful shoulders and back. Shown here is the Dutch swimmer Inge de Bruijn, who won multiple medals at the 2000 summer Olympics in Sydney.

Cultural standards of attractiveness and propriety influence participation and achievement in sports. Americans run or swim not just to compete but to keep trim and fit. Brazil's beauty standards accept more fat, especially in female buttocks and hips. Brazilian men have had some international success in swimming and running, but Brazil rarely sends female swimmers or runners to the Olympics. One reason Brazilian women avoid competitive swimming in particular is that sport's effects on the body. Years of swimming sculpt a distinctive physique: an enlarged upper torso, a massive neck, and powerful shoulders and back. Successful female swimmers tend to be big, strong, and bulky. The countries that produce them most consistently are the United States, Canada, Australia, Germany, the Scandinavian nations, the Netherlands, and the former Soviet Union, where this body type isn't as stigmatized as it is in Latin countries. Swimmers develop hard bodies, but Brazilian culture says that women should be soft, with big hips and buttocks, not big shoulders. Many young female swimmers in Latin America choose to abandon the sport rather than the "feminine" body ideal.

Understanding Ourselves   Our parents may tell us that drinking milk and eating vegetables promote healthy growth, but they don't as readily recognize the role that culture plays in shaping our bodies. Our genetic attributes provide a foundation for our growth and development, but human biology is fairly plastic. That is, it is malleable; the environment influences how we grow. Identical twins raised from birth in radically different environments—e.g., one in the high Andes and one at sea level—will not, as adults, be physically identical. Nutrition matters in growth; so do cultural guidelines about what is proper for boys and girls to do. Culture is an environmental force that affects our development as much as do nutrition, heat, cold, and altitude. One aspect of culture is how it provides opportunities and assigns space for various activities. We get to be good at sports by practicing them. When you grew up, which was it easiest for you to engage in— baseball, golf, mountain climbing, or fencing? Think about why.

Cultural factors help explain why African Americans excel in certain sports and whites excel in others. A key factor is degree of public access to sports facilities. In our public schools, parks, sandlots, and city playgrounds, African Americans have access to baseball diamonds, basketball courts, football fields, and running tracks. However, because of restricted economic opportunities, many black families can't afford to buy hockey gear or ski equipment, take ski vacations, pay for tennis lessons, or belong to clubs with tennis courts, pools, or golf courses. In the United States, mainly white suburban boys (and, increasingly, girls) play soccer, the most popular sport in the world. In Brazil, however, soccer is the national pastime for all males—black and white, rich and poor. There is wide public access. Brazilians play soccer on the beach and in streets, squares, parks, and playgrounds. Many of Brazil's best soccer players, including the world-famous Pelé, have dark skins. When blacks have opportunities to do well in soccer, tennis, golf, or any other sport, they are physically capable of doing as well as whites.

Why does the United States have so many black football and basketball players and so few black swimmers and hockey players? The answer lies mainly in cultural factors, including variable

This Brazilian soccer team won the 2002 World Cup, defeating the German team shown on the right. What contrasts do you notice between the two teams? How do you explain them?

The 2002 German National Soccer Team.

access and opportunities. Many Brazilians practice soccer, hoping to play for money for a professional club. Similarly, American blacks are aware that certain sports have provided career opportunities for African Americans. They start developing skills in those sports in childhood. The better they do, the more likely they are to persist, and the pattern continues. Culture—specifically differential access to sports resources—has more to do with sports success than "race" does.

The Subdisciplines of Anthropology

CULTURAL ANTHROPOLOGY

Cultural anthropology is the study of human society and culture, the subfield that describes, analyzes, interprets, and explains social and cultural similarities and differences. To study and interpret cultural diversity, cultural anthropologists engage in two kinds of activity: ethnography (based on field work) and ethnology (based on cross-cultural comparison). **Ethnography** provides an account of a particular community, society, or culture. During ethnographic field work, the ethnographer gathers data that he or she organizes, describes, analyzes, and interprets to build and present that account, which may be in the form of a book, article, or film. Traditionally, ethnographers have lived in small communities (such as Arembepe, Brazil—see "Interesting Issues" on page 12) and studied local behavior, beliefs, customs, social life, economic activities, politics, and religion. What kind of experience is ethnography for the ethnographer? The box offers some clues.

For a quiz on the subdisciplines of anthropology, see the Interactive Exercise

mhhe
●com
/kottak

The anthropological perspective derived from ethnographic field work often differs radically from that of economics or political science. Those fields focus on national and official organizations and policies and often on elites. However, the groups that anthropologists have traditionally studied usually have been relatively poor and powerless, as are most people in the world today. Ethnographers often observe discriminatory practices directed toward such people, who experience food shortages, dietary deficiencies, and other

aspects of poverty. Political scientists tend to study programs that national planners develop, while anthropologists discover how these programs work on the local level.

Cultures are not isolated. As noted by Franz Boas (1940/1966) many years ago, contact between neighboring tribes has always existed and has extended over enormous areas. "Human populations construct their cultures in interaction with one another, and not in isolation" (Wolf 1982, p.ix). Villagers increasingly participate in regional, national, and world events. Exposure to external forces comes through the mass media, migration, and modern transportation. City and nation increasingly invade local communities in the guise of tourists, development agents, government and religious officials, and political candidates. Such linkages are prominent components of regional, national, and international systems of politics, economics, and information. These larger systems increasingly affect the people and places anthropology traditionally has studied. The study of such linkages and systems is part of the subject matter of modern anthropology.

Ethnology examines, interprets, analyzes, and compares the results of ethnography—the data gathered in different societies. It uses such data to compare and contrast and to make generalizations about society and culture. Looking beyond the particular to the more general, ethnologists attempt to identify and explain cultural differences and similarities, to test hypotheses, and to build theory to enhance our understanding of how social and cultural systems work. Ethnology gets its data for comparison not just from ethnography but also from the other subfields, particularly from archaeological anthropology, which reconstructs social systems of the past. (Table 1.2 summarizes the main contrasts between ethnography and ethnology.)

ARCHAEOLOGICAL ANTHROPOLOGY

Archaeological anthropology (more simply, "archaeology") reconstructs, describes, and interprets past human behavior and cultural patterns through material remains. At sites where people live or have lived, archaeologists find artifacts, material items that humans have made or modified, such as tools, weapons, camp sites, and buildings. Plant and animal remains and ancient garbage tell stories about consumption and activi-

Table 1.2   Ethnography and Ethnology—Two Dimensions of Cultural Anthropology

Ethnography	Ethnology
Requires field work to collect data	Uses data collected by a series of researchers
Often descriptive	Usually synthetic
Group/community specific	Comparative/cross-cultural

ties. Wild and domesticated grains have different characteristics, which allow archaeologists to distinguish between gathering and cultivation. Examination of animal bones reveals the ages of slaughtered animals and provides other information useful in determining whether species were wild or domesticated.

Analyzing such data, archaeologists answer several questions about ancient economies. Did the group get its meat from hunting, or did it domesticate and breed animals, killing only those of a certain age and sex? Did plant food come from wild plants or from sowing, tending, and harvesting crops? Did the residents make, trade for, or buy particular items? Were raw materials available locally? If not, where did they come from? From such information, archaeologists reconstruct patterns of production, trade, and consumption.

Archaeologists have spent much time studying potsherds, fragments of earthenware. Potsherds are more durable than many other artifacts, such as textiles and wood. The quantity of pottery fragments allows estimates of population size and density. The discovery that potters used materials that were not locally available suggests systems of trade. Similarities in manufacture and decoration at different sites may be proof of cultural connections. Groups with similar pots may be historically related. Perhaps they shared common cultural ancestors, traded with each other, or belonged to the same political system.

Many archaeologists examine paleoecology. Ecology is the study of interrelations among living things in an environment. The organisms and environment together constitute an ecosystem, a patterned arrangement of energy flows and exchanges. Human ecology studies ecosystems that include people, focusing on the ways in which human use "of nature influences and is influenced

by social organization and cultural values" (Bennett 1969, pp. 10–11). Paleoecology looks at the ecosystems of the past.

In addition to reconstructing ecological patterns, archaeologists may infer cultural transformations, for example, by observing changes in the size and type of sites and the distance between them. A city develops in a region where only towns, villages, and hamlets existed a few centuries earlier. The number of settlement levels (city, town, village, hamlet) in a society is a measure of social complexity. Buildings offer clues about political and religious features. Temples and pyramids suggest that an ancient society had an authority structure capable of marshaling the labor needed to build such monuments. The presence or absence of certain structures, like the pyramids of ancient Egypt and Mexico, reveals differences in function between settlements. For example, some towns were places where people came to attend ceremonies. Others were burial sites; still others were farming communities.

Archaeologists also reconstruct behavior patterns and life styles of the past by excavating. This involves digging through a succession of levels at a particular site. In a given area, through time, settlements may change in form and purpose, as may the connections between settlements. Excavation can document changes in economic, social, and political activities.

Although archaeologists are best known for studying prehistory, that is, the period before the invention of writing, they also study the cultures of historical and even living peoples. Studying sunken ships off the Florida coast, underwater archaeologists have been able to verify the living conditions on the vessels that brought ancestral African Americans to the New World as enslaved people. Another, even more contemporary, illustration of archaeology is a research project begun

I first lived in Arembepe (Brazil) during the (North American) summer of 1962. That was between my junior and senior years at New York City's Columbia College, where I was majoring in anthropology. I went to Arembepe as a participant in a now defunct program designed to provide undergraduates with experience doing ethnography—firsthand study of an alien society's culture and social life.

Brought up in one culture, intensely curious about others, anthropologists nevertheless experience culture shock, particularly on their first field trip. Culture shock refers to the whole set of feelings about being in an alien setting, and the ensuing reactions. It is a chilly, creepy feeling of alienation, of being without some of the most ordinary, trivial (and therefore basic) cues of one's culture of origin.

As I planned my departure for Brazil in 1962, I could not know just how naked I would feel without the cloak of my own language and culture. My sojourn in Arembepe would be my first trip outside the United States. I was an urban boy who had grown up in Atlanta, Georgia, and New York City. I had little experience with rural life in my own country, none with Latin America, and I had received only minimal training in the Portuguese language.

New York City direct to Salvador, Bahia, Brazil. Just a brief stopover in Rio de Janeiro; a longer visit would be a reward at the end of field work. As our prop jet approached tropical Salvador, I couldn't believe the whiteness of the sand. "That's not snow, is it?" I remarked to a fellow field team member . . .

My first impressions of Bahia were of smells—alien odors of ripe and decaying mangoes, bananas, and passion fruit—and of swatting the ubiquitous fruit flies I had never seen before, although I had read extensively about their reproductive behavior in genetics classes. There were strange concoctions of rice, black beans, and gelatinous gobs of unidentifiable meats and floating pieces of skin. Coffee was strong and sugar crude, and every tabletop had

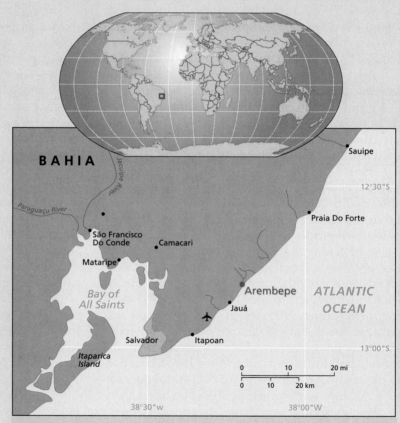

Figure 1.1   **Location of Arembepe, Bahia, Brazil.**

in 1973 in Tucson, Arizona. Archaeologist William Rathje has learned about contemporary life by studying modern garbage. The value of "garbology," as Rathje calls it, is that it provides "evidence of what people did, not what they think they did, what they think they should have done, or what the interviewer thinks they should have done" (Harrison, Rathje, and Hughes 1994, p. 108). What people report may contrast strongly with their real behavior as revealed by garbology. For example,

containers for toothpicks and for manioc (cassava) flour to sprinkle, like Parmesan cheese, on anything one might eat. I remember oatmeal soup and a slimy stew of beef tongue in tomatoes. At one meal a disintegrating fish head, eyes still attached, but barely, stared up at me as the rest of its body floated in a bowl of bright orange palm oil . . .

I only vaguely remember my first day in Arembepe (Figure 1.1). Unlike ethnographers who have studied remote tribes in the tropical forests of interior South America or the highlands of Papua New Guinea, I did not have to hike or ride a canoe for days to arrive at my field site. Arembepe was not isolated relative to such places, only relative to every other place I had ever been . . .

I do recall what happened when we arrived. There was no formal road into the village. Entering through southern Arembepe, vehicles simply threaded their way around coconut trees, following tracks left by automobiles that had passed previously. A crowd of children had heard us coming, and they pursued our car through the village streets until we parked in front of our house, near the central square. Our first few days in Arembepe were spent with children following us everywhere. For weeks we had few moments of privacy. Children watched our every move through our living room window. Occasionally one made an incompre-

An ethnographer at work. During a 1980 visit, the author, Conrad Kottak, catches up on the news in Arembepe, a coastal community in Bahia state, northeastern Brazil, that he has been studying since 1962. How might culture shock influence one's research?

hensible remark. Usually they just stood there . . .

The sounds, sensations, sights, smells, and tastes of life in northeastern Brazil, and in Arembepe, slowly grew familiar . . . I grew accustomed to this world without Kleenex, in which globs of mucus habitually drooped from the noses of village children whenever a cold passed through Arembepe. A world where, seemingly without effort, women . . . carried 18-liter kerosene cans of water on their heads, where boys sailed kites and sported at catching houseflies in their bare hands, where

old women smoked pipes, storekeepers offered *cachaça* (common rum) at nine in the morning, and men played dominoes on lazy afternoons when there was no fishing. I was visiting a world where human life was oriented toward water—the sea, where men fished, and the lagoon, where women communally washed clothing, dishes, and their own bodies.

This description is adapted from my ethnographic study *Assault on Paradise: Social Change in a Brazilian Village*, 3rd ed. (New York: McGraw-Hill, 1999).

the garbologists discovered that the three Tucson neighborhoods that reported the lowest beer consumption actually had the highest number of discarded beer cans per household (Podolefsky and Brown 1992, p. 100)!

BIOLOGICAL, OR PHYSICAL, ANTHROPOLOGY

The subject matter of **biological,** or **physical, anthropology** is human biological diversity in time and space. The focus on biological variation

Archaeological anthropology reconstructs, describes, and interprets human behavior through material remains. In Grosse Point Park, Michigan, these high school students have made pottery using online information from an archaeological dig in Egypt.

unites five special interests within biological anthropology:

1. Human evolution as revealed by the fossil record (paleoanthropology).

2. Human genetics.

3. Human growth and development.

4. Human biological plasticity (the body's ability to change as it copes with stresses, such as heat, cold, and altitude).

5. The biology, evolution, behavior, and social life of monkeys, apes, and other nonhuman primates.

These interests link physical anthropology to other fields: biology, zoology, geology, anatomy, physiology, medicine, and public health. Osteology—the study of bones—helps paleoanthropologists, who examine skulls, teeth, and bones, to identify human ancestors and to chart changes in anatomy over time. A paleontologist is a scientist who studies fossils. A paleoanthropologist is one sort of paleontologist, one who studies the fossil record of *human* evolution. Paleoanthropologists often collaborate with archaeologists, who study artifacts, in reconstructing biological and cultural aspects of human evolution. Fossils and tools are often found together. Different types of tools provide information about the habits, customs, and life styles of the ancestral humans who used them.

More than a century ago, Charles Darwin noticed that the variety that exists within any population permits some individuals (those with the favored, or adaptive, characteristics) to do better than others at surviving and reproducing. Genetics, which developed later, enlightens us about the causes and transmission of this variety. However, it isn't just genes that cause variety. During any individual's lifetime, the environment works along with heredity to determine biological features. For example, people with a genetic tendency to be tall will be shorter if they are poorly nourished during childhood. Thus, biological anthropology also investigates the influence of environment on the body as it grows and matures. Among the environmental factors that influence the body as it develops are nutrition, altitude, temperature, and disease, as well as

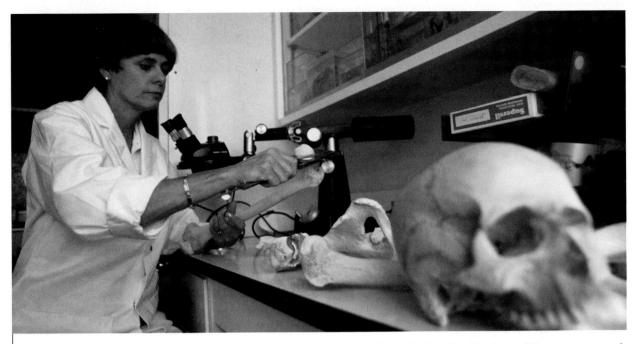

Forensic anthropologist Kathy Reichs at work. Like other forensic anthropologists, Dr. Reichs, and her mystery novel alter ego, Temperance Brennan, work with the police, medical examiners, the courts, and international organizations to identify victims of crimes, accidents, wars, and terrorism.

cultural factors, such as the standards of attractiveness we considered previously.

Biological anthropology (along with zoology) also includes primatology. The primates include our closest relatives—apes and monkeys. Primatologists study their biology, evolution, behavior, and social life, often in their natural environments. Primatology assists paleoanthropology, because primate behavior may shed light on early human behavior and human nature.

LINGUISTIC ANTHROPOLOGY

We don't know (and probably never will) when our ancestors acquired the ability to speak, although biological anthropologists have looked to the anatomy of the face and the skull to speculate about the origin of language. And primatologists have described the communication systems of monkeys and apes. We do know that well-developed, grammatically complex languages have existed for thousands of years. Linguistic anthropology offers further illustration of anthropology's interest in comparison, variation, and change. **Linguistic anthropology** studies language in its social and cultural context, across space and over time. Some linguistic anthropologists make inferences about universal features of language, linked perhaps to uniformities in the human brain. Others reconstruct ancient languages by comparing their contemporary descendants and in so doing make discoveries about history. Still others study linguistic differences to discover varied perceptions and patterns of thought in different cultures.

Historical linguistics considers variation in time, such as the changes in sounds, grammar, and vocabulary between Middle English (spoken from approximately AD 1050 to 1550) and modern English. **Sociolinguistics** investigates relationships between social and linguistic variation. No language is a homogeneous system in which everyone speaks just like everyone else. How do different speakers use a given language? How do linguistic features correlate with social factors, including class and gender differences (Tannen 1990)? One reason for variation is geography, as in regional dialects and accents. Linguistic variation also is expressed in the bilingualism of ethnic groups. Linguistic and cultural anthropologists collaborate in

Beyond the *Classroom*
The Utility of Hand and Foot Bones for Problems in Biological Anthropology

Background Information

STUDENT: Alicia Wilbur
SUPERVISING PROFESSOR: Della Collins Cook
SCHOOL: Indiana University
YEAR IN SCHOOL/MAJOR: Junior and Senior/ Anthropology
FUTURE PLANS: Ph.D. in Biological Anthropology
PROJECT TITLE: The Utility of Hand and Foot Bones for Problems in Bioanthropology

How does this account suggest common problems of interest to more than one subfield of anthropology? Does the research have implications for cultural and applied anthropology as well as for biological and archaeological anthropology?

The large, well-preserved skeletal series from west-central Illinois, housed in the Department of Anthropology at Indiana University, has been the focus of many archaeological and bioanthropological research projects over the years. I became interested in the use of hand and foot bones to determine the stature and sex of the individuals buried in those mounds. This information is important for both archaeological and biological studies of past peoples and their cultures, but is also relevant to modern forensic and mass disaster situations. In both archaeological and modern situations, the human remains recovered may be extremely fragmentary. A single hand or foot can play an important role in identifying modern victims of crime or mass disasters.

Most equations used for estimating adult stature or determining sex from skeletal material are constructed from data on modern Europeans or modern Americans of European or African extraction. Because body proportions differ between populations, applying these equations to skeletal remains of other groups may give inaccurate results. A benefit of my study was that it was constructed on Native American remains and thus could be used for modern Native Americans' remains in forensic cases or mass disasters.

I measured femurs (the thigh bone) and hand and foot bones for 410 adult skeletons and used statistical methods to predict the sex of the individuals, with accuracies exceeding 87 percent. Stature estimation also was found to be possible with hand and foot bones, although the range given was too large to be

studying links between language and many other aspects of culture, such as how people reckon kinship and how they perceive and classify colors.

Applied Anthropology

Anthropology is not a science of the exotic carried on by quaint scholars in ivory towers. Rather, it is a holistic, comparative, biocultural field with a lot to tell the public. Anthropology's foremost professional organization, the American Anthropological Association, has formally acknowledged a public service role by recognizing that anthropology has two dimensions: (1) academic anthropology and (2) practicing or **applied anthropology.**

The latter refers to the application of anthropological data, perspectives, theory, and methods to identify, assess, and solve contemporary social problems. More and more anthropologists from the four subfields now work in such "applied" areas as public health, family planning, and economic development.

In its most general sense, applied anthropology includes any use of the knowledge and/or techniques of the four subfields to identify, assess, and solve practical problems. Because of anthropology's breadth, it has many applications. For example, the growing field of medical anthropology considers both the sociocultural and the biological contexts and implications of disease and illness. Perceptions of good and bad health, along with actual health

useful in a court of law. Still, estimates resulting from these equations may be useful for delimiting a range of possible heights for preliminary identification purposes.

The project was published in the *International Journal of Osteoarchaeology* in 1998. While running statistical analyses on the hand and foot data, I noticed a discrepancy in the body proportions of one female adult. Upon carefully examining the rest of her skeleton, I discovered a suite of skeletal anomalies that suggest a rare genetic syndrome called Rubinstein-Taybi Syndrome that affects many organs. Symptoms include delayed growth, mental retardation, and abnormalities of the head and face, including widely spaced eyes and an abnormally large nose. Affected individuals also may have abnormally large big toes and thumbs. There also may be breathing and swallowing difficulties.

It may yet prove possible to analyze DNA from this sample to determine if my diagnosis is correct. If so, it would be the earliest known case of this syndrome. Knowing that this individual lived to mid- to late adulthood with several physical and mental disabilities tells us something about her culture.

These types of studies on skeletal material are important for the information they give us about the past and also for their relevance to modern problems. Future research will focus on genetic and infectious diseases that beset ancient peoples as well as application of this work to modern problems.

threats and problems, differ among cultures. Various societies and ethnic groups recognize different illnesses, symptoms, and causes and have developed different health-care systems and treatment strategies. Medical anthropologists are both biological and cultural, and both academic and applied. Applied medical anthropologists, for example, have served as cultural interpreters in public health programs, which must fit into local culture and be accepted by local people.

Other applied anthropologists work for international development agencies, such as the World Bank and USAID (the United States Agency for International Development). The job of such development anthropologists is to assess the social and cultural dimensions of economic development. Anthropologists are experts on local cultures. Working with and drawing on the knowledge of local people, anthropologists can identify specific social conditions and needs that must be addressed and that influence the failure or success of development schemes. Planners in Washington or Paris often know little about, say, the labor necessary for crop cultivation in rural Africa. Development funds are often wasted if an anthropologist is not asked to work with the local people to identify local needs, demands, priorities, and constraints.

Projects routinely fail when planners ignore the cultural dimension of development. Problems arise from lack of attention to, and consequent lack of fit with, existing sociocultural conditions. One example is a very naive and culturally incompatible

Medical anthropology studies health conditions from a cross-cultural perspective. In Uganda's Mwiri primary school, children are taught about HIV. Can you imagine a similar lesson in the primary school you attended?

project in East Africa. The major fallacy was to attempt to convert nomadic herders into farmers. The planners had absolutely no evidence that the herders, on whose land the project was to be implemented, wanted to change their economy. The herders' territory was to be used for new commercial farms, and the herders, converted into small farmers and sharecroppers. The project, whose planners included no anthropologists, totally neglected social issues. The obstacles would have been evident to any anthropologist. The herders were expected readily to give up a generations-old way of life in order to work three times harder growing rice and picking cotton. What could possibly motivate them to give up their freedom and mobility to work as sharecroppers for commercial farmers? Certainly not the meager financial return the project planners estimated for the herders—an average of $300 annually versus more than $10,000 for their new bosses, the commercial farmers.

To avoid such unrealistic projects, and to make development schemes more socially sensitive and culturally appropriate, development organizations now regularly include anthropolo-

gists on planning teams. Their team colleagues may include agronomists, economists, veterinarians, geologists, engineers, and health specialists. Applied anthropologists also apply their skills in studying the human dimension of environmental degradation (e.g., deforestation, pollution). Anthropologists examine how the environment influences humans and how human activities affect the biosphere and the earth itself.

Applied anthropologists also work in North America. Garbologists help the Environmental Protection Agency, the paper industry, and packaging and trade associations. Many archaeologists now work in cultural resource management. They apply their knowledge and skills to interpret, inventory, and preserve historic resources for local, state (provincial), and federal governments. Forensic (physical) anthropologists work with the police, medical examiners, the courts, and international organizations to identify victims of crimes, accidents, wars, and terrorism. From skeletal remains they may determine age, sex, size, ethnic origin, and number of victims. Applied physical anthropologists link injury patterns to design flaws in aircraft and vehicles.

Table 1.3   The Four Subfields and Two Dimensions of Anthropology

Anthropology's Subfields (General Anthropology)	Examples of Application (Applied Anthropology)
Cultural anthropology	Development anthropology
Archaeological anthropology	Cultural resource management (CRM)
Biological or physical anthropology	Forensic anthropology
Linguistic anthropology	Study of linguistic diversity in classrooms

Ethnographers have influenced social policy by showing that strong kin ties exist in city neighborhoods whose social organization was previously considered "fragmented" or "pathological." Suggestions for improving education emerge from ethnographic studies of classrooms and surrounding communities. Linguistic anthropologists show the influence of dialect differences on classroom learning. In general, applied anthropology aims to find humane and effective ways of helping the people whom anthropologists have traditionally studied. Table 1.3 shows the four subfields and two dimensions of anthropology.

Anthropology and Other Academic Fields

As mentioned previously, one of the main differences between anthropology and the other fields that study people is holism, anthropology's unique blend of biological, social, cultural, linguistic, historical, and contemporary perspectives. Paradoxically, while distinguishing anthropology, this breadth is what also links it to many other disciplines. Techniques used to date fossils and artifacts have come to anthropology from physics, chemistry, and geology. Because plant and animal remains often are found with human bones and artifacts, anthropologists collaborate with botanists, zoologists, and paleontologists.

As a discipline that is both scientific and humanistic, anthropology has links with many other academic fields. Anthropology is a **science**— a "systematic field of study or body of knowledge that aims, through experiment, observation, and deduction, to produce reliable explanations of phenomena, with reference to the material and physical world" (*Webster's New World Encyclopedia* 1993, p. 937). Clyde Kluckhohn (1944, p. 9) called anthropology "the science of human similarities and differences." His statement of the need for such a science still stands: "Anthropology provides a scientific basis for dealing with the crucial dilemma of the world today: how can peoples of different appearance, mutually unintelligible languages, and dissimilar ways of life get along peaceably together?" (p. 9). Anthropology has compiled an impressive body of knowledge that this textbook attempts to encapsulate.

Anthropology also has strong links to the humanities. The humanities include English, comparative literature, classics, folklore, philosophy, and the arts. These fields study languages, texts, philosophies, arts, music, performances, and other forms of creative expression. Ethnomusicology, which studies forms of musical expression on a worldwide basis, is especially closely related to anthropology. Also linked is folklore, the systematic study of tales, myths, and legends from a variety of cultures. One might well argue that anthropology is among the most humanistic of all academic fields because of its fundamental respect for human diversity. Anthropologists listen to, record, and represent voices from a multitude of nations and cultures. Anthropology values local knowledge, diverse worldviews, and alternative philosophies. Cultural anthropology and linguistic anthropology in particular bring a comparative and nonelitist perspective to forms of creative expression, including language, art, narratives, music, and dance, viewed in their social and cultural context.

CULTURAL ANTHROPOLOGY AND SOCIOLOGY

Cultural anthropology and sociology share an interest in social relations, organization, and behavior. However, important differences between these disciplines arose from the kinds of societies each traditionally studied. Initially sociologists focused on the industrial West; anthropologists, on nonindustrial societies. Different methods of data collection and analysis emerged to deal with those different kinds of societies. To study large-scale, complex nations, sociologists came to rely on questionnaires and other means of gathering masses of quantifiable data. For many years, sampling and statistical techniques have been basic to sociology, whereas statistical training has been less common in anthropology (although this is changing as anthropologists increasingly work in modern nations).

Traditional ethnographers studied small and nonliterate (without writing) populations and relied on methods appropriate to that context. "Ethnography is a research process in which the anthropologist closely observes, records, and engages in the daily life of another culture—an experience labeled as the fieldwork method—and then writes accounts of this culture, emphasizing descriptive detail" (Marcus and Fischer 1986, p. 18). One key method described in this quote is participant observation—taking part in the events one is observing, describing, and analyzing.

In many areas and topics, anthropology and sociology now are converging. As the modern world system grows, sociologists now do research in developing countries and in other places that were once mainly within the anthropological orbit. As industrialization spreads, many anthropologists now work in industrial nations, where they study diverse topics, including rural decline, inner-city life, and the role of the mass media in creating national cultural patterns.

ANTHROPOLOGY AND PSYCHOLOGY

Like sociologists, most psychologists do research in their own society. But statements about "human" psychology cannot be based solely on observations made in one society or in a single type of society. The area of cultural anthropology known as psychological anthropology studies cross-cultural variation in psychological traits.

Societies instill different values by training children differently. Adult personalities reflect a culture's child-rearing practices.

Bronislaw Malinowski, an early contributor to the cross-cultural study of human psychology, is famous for his field work among the Trobriand Islanders of the South Pacific (Figure 1.2). The Trobrianders reckon kinship matrilineally. They consider themselves related to the mother and her relatives, but not to the father. The relative who disciplines the child is not the father but the mother's brother, the maternal uncle. One inherits from the uncle rather than the father. Trobrianders show a marked respect for the uncle, with whom a boy usually has a cool and distant relationship. In contrast, the Trobriand father–son relationship is friendly and affectionate.

Malinowski's work among the Trobrianders suggested modifications in Sigmund Freud's famous theory of the universality of the Oedipus complex (Malinowski 1927). According to Freud (1918/1950), boys around the age of five become sexually attracted to their mothers. The Oedipus complex is resolved, in Freud's view, when the boy overcomes his sexual jealousy of, and identifies with, his father. Freud lived in patriarchal Austria during the late 19th and early 20th centuries—a social milieu in which the father was a strong authoritarian figure. The Austrian father was the child's primary authority figure and the mother's sexual partner. In the Trobriands, the father had only the sexual role.

If, as Freud contended, the Oedipus complex always creates social distance based on jealousy toward the mother's sexual partner, this would have shown up in Trobriand society. It *did not*. Malinowski concluded that the authority structure did more to influence the father–son relationship than did sexual jealousy. Like many later anthropologists, Malinowski showed that individual psychology depends on its cultural context. Anthropologists continue to provide cross-cultural perspectives on psychoanalytic propositions (Paul 1989) as well as on issues of developmental and cognitive psychology (Shore 1996).

Understanding Ourselves How much would we know about human behavior, thought, and feeling if we studied only our own kind? What if our entire understanding of human

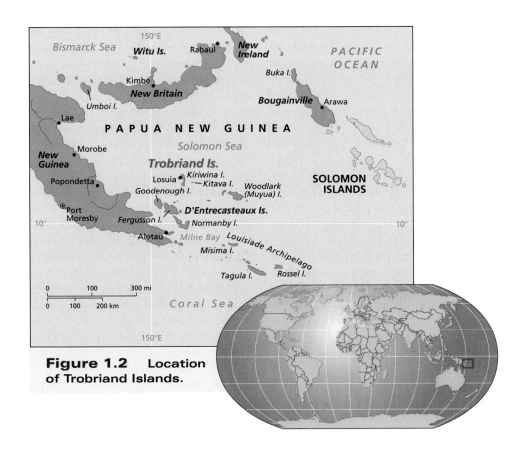

Figure 1.2 Location of Trobriand Islands.

Bronislaw Malinowski is famous for his field work among the matrilineal Trobriand Islanders of the South Pacific. Does this Trobriand market scene suggest anything about the status of Trobriand women?

behavior were based on analysis of questionnaires filled out by college students in Oregon? A radical question but one that should make you think about the basis for statements about what humans are like. A primary reason why anthropology helps us understand ourselves is the cross-cultural perspective. One culture can't tell us everything we need to know about what it means to be human. Earlier we saw how cultural forces influence our physical growth. Culture also guides our emotional and cognitive growth and helps determine the kinds of personalities we have as adults. Among scholarly disciplines, anthropology stands out as the field that provides the cross-cultural test. How does television affect us? To answer that question, study not just North America in 2003 but some other place—and perhaps also some other time (such as Brazil in the 1980s; see Kottak 1990). Anthropology specializes in the study of human variation in space and time.

Science, Explanation, and Hypothesis Testing

A key feature of anthropology is its comparative, cross-cultural dimension. As was stated previously (see p. 10), *ethnology* draws on ethnographic, as well as archaeological, data to compare and contrast, and to make generalizations about, societies and cultures. As a scientific pursuit, ethnology attempts to identify and explain cultural differences and similarities, test hypotheses, and build theory to enhance our understanding of how social and cultural systems work.

In their 1996 article "Science in Anthropology," Melvin Ember and Carol R. Ember stress a key feature of science as a way of viewing the world: Science recognizes the tentativeness and uncertainty of our knowledge and understanding. Scientists strive to improve understanding by testing *hypotheses*— suggested explanations of things and events. In science, understanding means *explaining*—showing how and why the thing to be understood (the explicandum) is related to other things in some known way. Explanations rely on associations and theories. An association is an observed relationship between two or more variables. A theory is more general, suggesting or implying associations and attempting to explain them (Ember and Ember 1996).

A thing or event, for example, the freezing of water, is explained if it illustrates a general principle or association. "Water solidifies at 32 degrees" states an association between two variables: the state of the water and the air temperature. The truth of the statement is confirmed by repeated observations. In the physical sciences, such relationships are called "laws." Explanations based on such laws allow us to understand the past and predict the future.

In the social sciences, associations usually are stated probabilistically: Two or more variables *tend to be* related in a predictable way, but there are exceptions (Ember and Ember 1996). For example, in a worldwide sample of societies, the anthropologist John Whiting (1964) found a strong (but not 100 percent) association or correlation between a low-protein diet and a long postpartum sex taboo—a prohibition against sexual intercourse between husband and wife for a year or more after the birth of a child.

Laws and statistical associations explain by relating the explicandum (e.g., the postpartum sex taboo) to one or more other variables (e.g., a low-protein diet). We also want to know why such associations exist. Why do societies with low-protein diets have long postpartum sex taboos? Scientists formulate theories to explain the correlations they observe.

A **theory** is an explanatory framework that helps us understand *why* (something exists). Returning to the postpartum sex taboo, why might societies with low-protein diets develop this taboo? Whiting's theory is that the taboo is adaptive; it helps people survive and reproduce in certain environments. With too little protein in their diets, babies may develop a protein-deficiency disease called kwashiorkor. But if the mother delays her next pregnancy, her current baby, by breastfeeding longer, has a better chance to survive. Whiting suggests that parents may be unconsciously or consciously aware that having another baby too soon might jeopardize the survival of the first one. Thus, they avoid sex for more than a year after the birth of the first baby. When such abstinence becomes institutionalized, everyone is expected to respect the taboo.

A theory is an explanatory framework containing a series of statements. An association simply states an observed relationship between two or more known variables. Parts of a theory, by con-

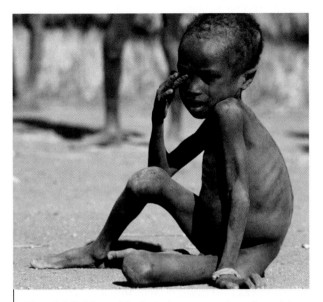

This child's bloated body is due to protein malnutrition. This condition, known as *kwashiorkor*, comes from a West African word meaning "one-two." This refers to the practice in some societies of abruptly weaning one infant when a second one is born. With no mother's milk, the first baby may get no protein at all. What are some cultural ways of fending off kwashiorkor?

trast, may be difficult or impossible to observe or to know directly. With Whiting's theory, for example, it would be hard to determine whether people developed the sex taboo because they recognized that it would give babies a better chance to survive. Typically, some elements of a theory are unobservable (at least at present). In contrast, statistical associations are based entirely on observations (Ember and Ember 1996).

If an association is tested and found to recur again and again, we may consider it proved. Theories, by contrast, are unprovable. Although much evidence may support them, their truth isn't established with certainty. Many of the concepts and ideas in theories aren't directly observable or verifiable. Thus, scientists may try to explain how light behaves by postulating that it consists of "photons," which can't be observed even with the most powerful microscope. The photon is a "theoretical construct," something that can't be seen or verified directly (Ember and Ember 1996).

Why should we bother with theories if we can't prove them? According to the Embers, the main value of a theory is to promote new understanding. A theory can suggest patterns, connections, or relationships that may be confirmed by new research. Whiting's theory, for example, suggests hypotheses for future researchers to test. Because the theory proposes that the postpartum taboo is adaptive under certain conditions, one might hypothesize that certain changes would lead the taboo to disappear. By adopting birth control, for instance, families could space births without avoiding intercourse. So, too, might the taboo disappear if babies started receiving protein supplements, which would reduce the threat of kwashiorkor.

Although theories can't be proved, they can be rejected. The method of *falsification* (showing a theory to be wrong) is our main way of evaluating theories. If a theory is true, certain predictions should stand up to tests designed to disprove them. Theories that haven't been disproved are accepted (for the time being at least) because the available evidence seems to support them.

What is acceptable evidence that an explanation is probably right? Cases that have been personally selected by a researcher don't provide an acceptable test of a hypothesis or theory. (Imagine that Whiting had combed the ethnographic literature and chosen to cite only those societies that supported his theory.) Ideally, hypothesis testing should be done using a sample of cases that have been selected randomly from some statistical universe. (Whiting did this in choosing his cross-cultural sample.) The relevant variables should be measured reliably, and the strength and significance of the results should be evaluated by using legitimate statistical methods (Bernard 1994).

Understanding Ourselves Science is a powerful tool for understanding ourselves. Properly, science isn't rigid or dogmatic; scientists recognize the tentativeness and uncertainty of knowledge and understanding, which they try to improve and enhance. Working to confirm laws, refine theories, and provide accurate explanations, scientists strive to be objective. Science relies on unbiased methods, such as random sampling, impartial analytic techniques, and standard statistical tests. But complete objectivity is impossible. There is always observer bias—that is, the presence of the scientist and his or her tools and methods always affects the outcome of an experiment, observation, or analysis. Through their very presence, anthropologists influence the living people and social conditions they study, as do survey researchers when they phrase questions in certain ways. Statisticians have designed techniques to measure and control for observer bias, but observer bias can't be eliminated totally. As scientists, we can only strive for objectivity and impartiality. Science, which has many limitations, certainly is not the only way we have to understand ourselves. Nevertheless, its goals of objectivity and impartiality help distinguish science from ways of knowing that are more biased, more rigid, and more dogmatic.

SUMMARY

1. Anthropology is the holistic and comparative study of humanity. It is the systematic exploration of human biological and cultural diversity. Examining the origins of, and changes in, human biology and culture, anthropology provides explanations for similarities and differences. The four subfields of general anthropology are (socio)cultural, archaeological, biological, and linguistic. All consider variation in time and space. Each also examines adaptation—the process by which organisms cope with environmental stresses.

2. Cultural forces mold human biology, including our body types and images. Societies have particular standards of physical attractiveness. They also have specific ideas about what activities, for example, various sports, are appropriate for males and females.

3. Cultural anthropology explores the cultural diversity of the present and the recent past. Archaeology reconstructs cultural patterns, often of prehistoric populations. Biological anthropology documents diversity involving fossils, genetics, growth and development, bodily responses, and nonhuman primates. Linguistic anthropology considers diversity among languages. It also studies how speech changes in social situations and over time. Anthropology has two dimensions: academic and applied. The latter uses anthropological knowledge and methods to identify and solve social problems.

4. Concerns with biology, society, culture, and language link anthropology to many other fields—sciences and humanities. Anthropologists study art, music, and literature across cultures. But their concern is more with the creative expressions of common people than with arts designed for elites. Anthropologists examine creators and products in their social context. Sociologists traditionally study urban and industrial populations, whereas anthropologists have focused on rural, nonindustrial peoples. Psychological anthropology views human psychology in the context of social and cultural variation.

5. As scientists, anthropologists attempt to identify and explain cultural differences and similarities and to build theory about how social and cultural systems work. Scientists strive to improve understanding by testing hypotheses—suggested explanations. Explanations rely on associations and theories. An association is an observed relationship between variables. A theory is more general, suggesting or implying associations and attempting to explain them.

KEY TERMS

See the flash cards
mhhe
.com
/kottak

anthropology The study of the human species and its immediate ancestors.

applied anthropology The application of anthropological data, perspectives, theory, and methods to identify, assess, and solve contemporary social problems.

archaeological anthropology The study of human behavior and cultural patterns and processes through the culture's material remains.

biological anthropology The study of human biological variation in time and space; includes evolution, genetics, growth and development, and primatology.

cultural anthropology The study of human society and culture; describes, analyzes, interprets, and explains social and cultural similarities and differences.

culture Distinctly human; transmitted through learning; traditions and customs that govern behavior and beliefs.

ethnography Field work in a particular culture.

ethnology Cross-cultural comparison; the comparative study of ethnographic data, of society, and of culture.

food production Cultivation of plants and domestication (stockbreeding) of animals; first developed 10,000 to 12,000 years ago.

general anthropology The field of anthropology as a whole, consisting of cultural, archaeological, biological, and linguistic anthropology.

holistic Interested in the whole of the human condition: past, present, and future; biology, society, language, and culture.

linguistic anthropology The descriptive, comparative, and historical study of language and of linguistic similarities and differences in time, space, and society.

physical anthropology See biological anthropology.

science A systematic field of study or body of knowledge that aims, through experiment, observation, and deduction, to produce reliable explanations of phenomena, with reference to the material and physical world.

sociolinguistics Investigates relationships between social and linguistic variations.

theory An explanatory framework, containing a series of statements, that helps us understand *why* (something exists); theories suggest patterns, connections, and relationships that may be confirmed by new research.

CRITICAL THINKING QUESTIONS

For more self testing, see the self quizzes

mhhe
com
/kottak

1. Which do you think is more unique about anthropology: its holism or its comparative perspective? Can you think of other fields that are holistic and/or comparative?
2. Besides race and gender, what are some other areas in which anthropology's biocultural, four-field approach might shed light on current issues and debates? Would sexuality be such an area?
3. Many other disciplines are limited by their focus on powerful people and elites. How have your professors in other classes tried to justify, or compensate for, such limitations?
4. Besides the examples given in this chapter, think of some other problems or issues in the modern world to which applied anthropology might contribute.

5. What are some theories, as defined here, that you routinely use to understand the world?

Atlas Questions

Look at Map 1, "World Topography."
1. Which continent is most mountainous?
2. What are plateaus, and where are they located?
3. Which continent is least diverse in terms of terrains?

Suggested Additional Readings

Clifford, J.

1988   *The Predicament of Culture: Twentieth-Century Ethnography, Literature, and Art.* Cambridge, MA: Harvard University Press. Literary evaluation of classic and modern anthropologists and discussion of issues of ethnographic authority.

Endicott, K. M., and R. Welsch

2001   *Taking Sides: Clashing Views on Controversial Issues in Anthropology.* Guilford, CT: McGraw-Hill/Dushkin. Thirty-eight anthropologists offer opposing viewpoints on 19 polarizing issues, including ethical dilemmas.

Fagan, B. M.

2001   *People of the Earth: An Introduction to World Prehistory,* 11th ed. Upper Saddle River, NJ: Prentice-Hall. Introduction to the archaeological study of prehistoric societies, using examples from all areas.

2002   *Archeology: A Brief Introduction,* 8th ed. Upper Saddle River, NJ: Prentice-Hall. Introduction to archaeological theory, techniques, and approaches, including field survey, excavation, and analysis of materials.

Geertz, C.

1995   *After the Fact: Two Countries, Four Decades, One Anthropologist.* Cambridge, MA: Harvard University Press. A prominent cultural anthropologist reflects on his work in Morocco and Indonesia.

Harris, M.

1989   *Our Kind: Who We Are, Where We Came From, Where We Are Going.* New York: HarperCollins. Clearly written survey of the origins of humans, culture, and major sociopolitical institutions.

Marcus, G. E., and M. M. J. Fischer

1999   *Anthropology as Cultural Critique: An Experimental Moment in the Human Sciences,* 2nd ed. Chicago: University of Chicago Press. Different types of ethnographic accounts as forms of writing, a vision of modern anthropology, and a consideration of anthropologists' public and professional roles.

Nash, D.

1999   *A Little Anthropology,* 3rd ed. Upper Saddle River, NJ: Prentice-Hall. Short introduction to societies and cultures, with comments on developing nations and modern America.

Podolefsky, A., and P. J. Brown, eds.

2002   *Applying Anthropology: An Introductory Reader,* 7th ed. Boston: McGraw-Hill. Essays focusing on anthropology's relevance to contemporary life; a readable survey of the current range of activities in applied anthropology.

Wolf, E. R.

1982   *Europe and the People without History.* Berkeley: University of California Press. Influential and award-winning study of the relation between Europe and various nonindustrial populations.

INTERNET EXERCISES

1. News in Anthropology: Look at Texas A&M University's "Anthropology in the News," **http://www.tamu.edu/anthropology/news.html,** which contains links to articles relevant to anthropology.

   a. After reading the chapter in the textbook and reading some recent news articles, do you think anthropology is more or less relevant to your life?

   b. Look at the variety of topics discussed. Are the connections between the articles and anthropology clear to you? Were they clear to you before you read this chapter?

   c. Examine the first 10 articles. Which subfield of anthropology does each article relate to most closely?

   d. Browse the list of article titles. What are some of the current hot topics in the news about anthropology?

2. Careers in Anthropology: Go to the American Anthropological Association's Jobs Page (**http://aaanet.jobcontrolcenter.com/search/results/**) and Northern Kentucky's list of organizations in their area hiring anthropologists (**http://www.nku.edu/~anthro/careers.html**).

   a. What kinds of organizations are hiring anthropologists?

   b. What kinds of qualifications are these employers looking for? Do they require a graduate degree, or are they seeking people with an undergraduate degree in anthropology?

   c. What subfields are being sought by employers?

Note that these are just two job listing pages on the Web, and there are many others. If you have an interest in a field of anthropology that is not listed on these pages, use a web search engine to research what kinds of jobs are available. A good place to start is **http://www.aaanet.org/careers.htm** for more information on careers in anthropology.

See Chapter 1 at your McGraw-Hill Online Learning Center for additional review and interactive exercises.

2

APPLYING ANTHROPOLOGY?

Overview

In what ways is anthropology useful? What kind of public service role should it play? In a host of different settings anthropology is "applied" every day—used to identify and solve social problems. Applied anthropologists work for governments, agencies, and businesses. One goal of applied anthropology is to identify needs for change that local people perceive. A second goal is to work with those people to design culturally appropriate change. A third goal is to protect local people and cultural resources from harmful policies, including destructive development schemes.

An anthropologist's foremost ethical responsibility is to the people, species, and materials he or she studies. This responsibility, anthropology's "prime directive," entails respecting the well-being of humans and nonhuman primates, avoiding harm to them, and working for the conservation of the archaeological, fossil, and historical records.

Applied anthropology proceeds in all four subfields. Medical anthropology links biological and

cultural anthropology. Other domains of applied anthropology include educational, urban, and business anthropology. These domains have theoretical as well as applied dimensions. Medical anthropologists study disease and health-care systems cross-culturally. Although modern Western medicine has a scientific basis, it is also a cultural system with many elements based on custom rather than science. Educational anthropologists work in classrooms, homes, neighborhoods, and other settings relevant to education. Urban anthropologists study problems and policies involving city life and urbanization.

For business, key aspects of anthropology include ethnography and observation as ways of gathering data, cross-cultural expertise, and a focus on cultural diversity. Anthropology's comparative outlook, long-standing Third World focus, and cultural relativism offer a background for overseas work. A focus on culture and diversity is also valuable for work in North America.

Buried on a Hillside, Clues to Terror

NEW YORK TIMES NEWS BRIEF

by Malcolm W. Browne

February 23, 1999

The news account that opened Chapter 1 described ways in which anthropology can be applied in a business context. Anthropology has many other "applications"—playing a public service role and being used to identify and solve various kinds of social problems. Applied anthropologists work for governments, agencies, and local communities, as well as for businesses. Some of anthropology's applications, while useful, can be very grim. This article describes research in Guatemala by biological and archaeological anthropologists, who also have been able to draw on the knowledge of cultural and linguistic anthropologists working in the same area. In 1982, some 376 villagers were massacred in the village of San Francisco de Nenton (Figure 2.1). Seventeen years later, scientific inquiry began to expose material evidence of that atrocity. This village's fate was common throughout Guatemala in the 1980s, as the government, with the support of the United States, sought to crush rebel guerrilla groups.

SAN FRANCISCO DE NENTON, Guatemala—On the morning of July 17, 1982, a convoy of army trucks made its way up a nearly impassable trail to this remote Mayan Indian hamlet and unloaded a company of troops . . . What happened next was a butchery that left all but four of the village's inhabitants dead and all the buildings razed . . . The rampaging troops killed all they found, shooting some villagers, blowing some up with grenades, hacking some to death, burning some or crushing them under the walls of falling buildings.

Relatives and acquaintances of the victims compiled a list of 376 villagers believed to have perished. For 17 years there had been no serious effort to check this list or details of the massacre by independent means, but finally the light of scientific inquiry has begun to expose material evidence of the atrocity . . .

But the tally of dead and missing victims of Guatemala's reign of terror is far from complete, and a band of volunteer forensic anthropologists, acting with the government's blessing, has set out to decipher a few of the massacre sites, gathering

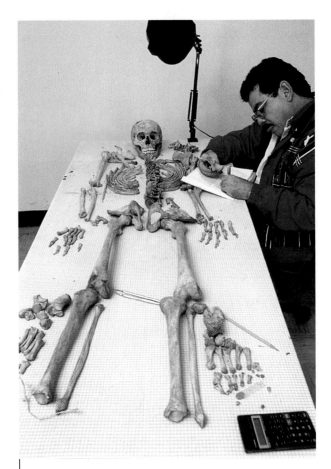

One applied anthropology career is in forensics, as in Guatemala City's Institute for Forensic Anthropology. Identification of war victims, such as those uncovered at San Francisco de Nenton, proceeds here in 1997.

evidence from shattered bones, spent bullets and domestic objects including the pitiful remnants of children's clothing.

"We have absolutely no political objectives," said Fredy A. Peccerelli, a forensic anthropologist who heads the Foundation for Forensic Anthropology of Guatemala. "What we're attempting to do is check the accounts of witnesses and wherever possible to apply the techniques of forensic science to set the record straight. We examine massacre sites using many of the same techniques police use at crime scenes." . . .

In the San Francisco project as in dozens of other projects involving massacre sites in Guatemala, the group has had support and guidance from Dr. Clyde Collins Snow, a 71-year-old forensic anthropologist who lives in Norman, Okla. Dr. Snow, virtually a

Figure 2.1 Location of San Francisco de Nenton.

legend among forensic experts, has investigated massacres in 20 countries in Latin America, Africa, the Balkans and Asia . . .

The place where San Francisco de Nenton stood covers a cluster of picturesque hills a few miles south of the Mexican border. Adorned by an ancient Mayan pyramid, the site would make a lovely picnic ground.

But just beneath the grassy surface lies the horror the forensic team is unearthing, as it measures,

photographs, and catalogues the grim remnants before transporting them to Mr. Peccerelli's combination home and laboratory in Guatemala City. There, the bones will be X-rayed and further examined.

At one of a half-dozen burial sites discovered at San Francisco de Nenton so far, Renaldo Acevedo, a Guatemalan anthropologist, paused to look into a shallow pit where he and several colleagues had been digging . . .

A cluster of little bones covered by the faded but still colorful clothing of an adult Indian woman lay exposed.

Dr. Snow carefully dislodged one of several jawbones in the pit and held it close to his glasses. Speaking carefully in a slow Texas drawl as if addressing a tape recorder in the Oklahoma City morgue where he often works, he said:

"This is the site of a house said to have belonged to one Felipe Sylvestre. We have here a juvenile skull with several fractures, probably post-mortem. Two of the teeth are deciduous but one molar has erupted. This child was between 6 and 7 years old. Sex undetermined, but may be inferred from laboratory measurements and a statistical computer program called discriminant function analysis." . . .

A hundred yards away, working with a dental pick and toothbrush, Claudia Rivera and several other Guatemalan archeologists were excavating the village magistrate's office. So far, they had found skull parts and jaws of 11 bodies.

After a painstaking process of sorting and matching, the first batches of bones and artifacts were packed in plastic bags and cardboard cartons. The team's pickup truck doubles as a hearse, transporting the forensic treasure through the bandit-infested Guatemalan highlands to Mr. Peccerelli's laboratory in Guatemala City. There the skeletons are being laid out on tables for closer scrutiny and measurement.

"It's much the same as excavating an archeological site," Ms. Rivera said. "As the years pass, everything in a site like this decays, and it gets harder to interpret, just as ancient sites are hard to interpret. But for us this is not academic archeology. This place—how shall I say?—it has special meaning for us."

Forensic teams sometimes make as many as 200 skeletal measurements in pursuing identities. For example, slight disparities in the length of the radius and ulna arm bones can reveal a person's handedness. Another useful gauge is the degree of fusion between two adjoining pelvic bones (the pubic symphysis), which indicates an adult's age quite accurately. The ratio of an eye socket's width to its height, the distance between brow ridges, the width of nose bridges and many other facial characteristics can suggest kinships that help in tracing relatives.

In cases where relatives (and money) are available, DNA analysis is a powerful identification tool, Dr. Snow said. Even in badly decayed skeletons,

hard shells of dentine usually protect the pulp cavities of teeth, preserving the DNA inside.

SOURCE: "Buried on a Hillside, Clues to Terror," by Malcolm W. Browne, February 23, 1999, www.nytimes.com.

See the OLC Internet Exercises

/kottak

Forensic anthropology, as discussed in this article, is one form of **applied anthropology**—the application of anthropological perspectives, theory, methods, and data—in this case from all four subfields—to identify, assess, and solve social problems. As Erve Chambers (1987, p. 309) states it, applied anthropology is the "field of inquiry concerned with the relationships between anthropological knowledge and the uses of that knowledge in the world beyond anthropology." As was mentioned in Chapter 1, anthropology's foremost professional organization, the American Anthropological Association (AAA), recognizes that anthropology has two dimensions: (1) academic anthropology and (2) practicing or applied anthropology.

There are two important professional groups of applied anthropologists (also called **practicing anthropologists**). The older is the independent Society for Applied Anthropology (SfAA), founded in 1941. The second, the National Association for the Practice of Anthropology (NAPA), was established as a unit of the American Anthropological Association in 1983. (Many people belong to both groups.) Practicing anthropologists work (regularly or occasionally, full or part time) for nonacademic clients. These clients include governments, development agencies, nongovernmental organizations (NGOs), tribal and ethnic associations, interest groups, businesses, and social-service and educational agencies. Applied anthropologists work for groups that promote, manage, and assess programs aimed at influencing human social conditions. The scope of applied anthropology includes change and development abroad and social problems and policies in North America.

Applied anthropologists come from all four subfields. Biological anthropologists work in public health, nutrition, genetic counseling, substance abuse, epidemiology, aging, and mental illness. They apply their knowledge of human anatomy and physiology to the improvement of automobile

Supervised by archaeologists from India, with funding from the United Nations, these workers are cleaning and restoring the front facade of Cambodia's historic Angkor Wat temple. To decide what needs saving, and to preserve significant information about the past even when sites cannot be saved, is the work of cultural resource management (CRM).

tural resource managers typically work for federal, state, or county agencies. Applied cultural anthropologists sometimes work with the public archaeologists, assessing the human problems generated by the proposed change and determining how they can be reduced.

Cultural anthropologists work with social workers, businesspeople, advertising professionals, factory workers, nurses, physicians, gerontologists, mental-health professionals, school personnel, and economic development experts. Linguistic anthropology, particularly sociolinguistics, aids education. Knowledge of linguistic differences is important in an increasingly multicultural society whose populace grows up speaking many languages and dialects. Because linguistic differences may affect children's schoolwork and teachers' evaluations, many schools of education now require courses in sociolinguistics.

The Role of the Applied Anthropologist

By instilling an appreciation for human diversity, anthropology combats *ethnocentrism*—the tendency to view one's own culture as superior and to apply one's own cultural values in judging the behavior and beliefs of people raised in other cultures. This broadening, educational role affects the knowledge, values, and attitudes of people exposed to anthropology. Now we focus on the question: What contributions can anthropology make in identifying and solving problems stirred up by contemporary currents of economic, social, and cultural change?

Anthropologists have held three different positions about applying anthropology—using it to identify and solve social problems. People who hold the **ivory tower view** contend that anthropologists should avoid practical matters and concentrate on research, publication, and teaching. Those who favor what Ralph Piddington (1970) has called the **schizoid view** think that anthropologists should help carry out, but not make or criticize, policy. In this view, personal "value judgments" should be kept strictly separate from scientific investigation. The third view is **advocacy.** Its proponents assert that precisely because anthropologists are experts on human problems and social

safety standards and to the design of airplanes and spacecraft. In forensic work, biological anthropologists help the police identify skeletal remains. The account you just read shows how forensic biological and archaeological anthropologists reconstruct crimes by analyzing physical evidence.

Applied archaeology, usually called *public archaeology,* includes such activities as cultural resource management, contract archaeology, public educational programs, and historic preservation. An important role for public archaeology has been created by legislation requiring evaluation of sites threatened by dams, highways, and other construction activities. To decide what needs saving, and to preserve significant information about the past when sites cannot be saved, is the work of **cultural resource management** (CRM). CRM involves not only preserving sites but allowing their destruction if they are not significant. The "management" part of the term refers to the evaluation and decision-making process. If additional information is needed to make decisions, then survey or excavation may be done. CRM funding comes from federal, state, and local governments and from developers who must comply with preservation regulations. Cul-

change and because they study, understand, and respect cultural values, they should make policy affecting people. In this view, proper roles for applied anthropologists include (1) identifying needs for change that local people perceive, (2) working with those people to design culturally appropriate and socially sensitive change, and (3) protecting local people from harmful policies and projects that threaten them.

I join many other anthropologists in favoring advocacy. I share the belief that no one is better qualified to propose and evaluate guidelines for society than are those who study anthropology. To be effective advocates, anthropologists must present their views clearly, thoughtfully, and forcefully to policy makers and the public. Many anthropologists do serve as social commentators and problem solvers, and as policy makers, advisers, and evaluators. We express our policy views in publications and lectures and through professional associations such as the Society for Applied Anthropology and the National Association of Practicing Anthropologists.

In this 1985 photo, Robert Goizueta (on the left), who then chaired the Board and served as CEO of the Coca-Cola Company, toasts New Coke. Despite what we read and hear frequently, "new" isn't necessarily "improved." Have you sipped any New Coke lately?

Understanding Ourselves Is change good? American culture seems to think so. "New and improved" is a slogan we hear all the time—a lot more often than "old reliable." But new isn't always improved. People often resist change, as the Coca Cola Company (TCCC) discovered several years ago when it changed the formula of its premium soft drink and introduced "New Coke." When hordes of customers protested, TCCC brought back old, familiar, reliable Coke under the name "Coca Cola Classic," which thrives today. New Coke is history.

TCCC tried a *top-down change* (a change decided and initiated at the top of a hierarchy rather than by the communities affected by the change). The people, that is, customers, didn't ask TCCC to change its product; executives made the decision to change Coke's taste. Executives are to business decisions as policy makers are to social change programs; both stand at the top of organizations that provide goods and services to people. Smart executives and policy makers listen to people to try to determine *locally-based demand*—what the people want. What's working well (assuming it's not discriminatory or illegal) should be maintained, encouraged, and strengthened. What's

wrong, and how can it be fixed? What changes do the people—and which people—want? How can conflicting wishes and needs be accommodated? Applied anthropologists help answer these questions, which are crucial in understanding whether change is needed, and how it will work.

There was a time—the 1940s in particular—when most anthropologists focused on the application of their knowledge. During World War II, American anthropologists studied Japanese and German "culture at a distance" in an attempt to predict the behavior of the enemies of the United States. After the war, Americans did applied anthropology in the Pacific, working to gain native cooperation with American policies in various trust territories.

Modern applied anthropology differs from an earlier version that mainly served the goals of colonial regimes. Application was a central concern of early anthropology in Great Britain (in the context of colonialism) and the United States (in the context of Native American policy). Before turning to the new, we should consider some dangers of the old.

In the context of the British empire, specifically its African colonies, Malinowski (1929a) proposed that "practical anthropology" (his term for colonial applied anthropology) should focus on westernization, the diffusion of European culture into tribal societies. He contended that anthropologists should and could avoid politics by concentrating on facts and processes. However, he was actually expressing his own political views, because he questioned neither the legitimacy of colonialism nor the anthropologist's role in making it work. For instance, Malinowski saw nothing wrong with aiding colonial regimes by studying land tenure and land use, to decide how much of their land natives should keep and how much Europeans should get. Malinowski's views exemplify a historical association between anthropology, particularly in Europe, and colonialism (Maquet 1964).

Colonial anthropologists faced, as do some of their modern counterparts (Escobar 1991, 1994), problems posed by their inability to set or influence policy and the difficulty of criticizing programs in which they have participated. Anthropology's professional organizations have addressed some of these problems by establishing codes of ethics and ethics committees. Also, as Tice (1997) notes, attention to such ethical issues is paramount in the teaching of applied anthropology today.

Ethics and Anthropology

As the main organization representing the breadth of anthropology (all four subfields, academic and applied dimensions), the American Anthropological Association believes that generating and appropriately using knowledge of the peoples of the world, past and present, is a worthy goal. The production of anthropological knowledge is a dynamic process involving different and ever-evolving approaches. The mission of the AAA is to advance anthropological research and encourage the spread of anthropological knowledge through publications, teaching, public education, and application. Part of that mission is to help educate AAA members about ethical obligations and challenges (http://www.aaanet.org).

As anthropologists conduct research and engage in other professional activities, ethical issues inevitably arise. Anthropologists have typically worked abroad, outside their own society. In the context of international contacts and cultural diversity, different value systems will meet, and often compete. To guide its members in making decisions involving ethics and values, the AAA offers a Code of Ethics. The most recent Code was approved in June 1998 and updated on March 31, 1999. The Code's preamble states that anthropologists have obligations to their scholarly field, to the wider society and culture, and to the human species, other species, and the environment. This Code's aim is to offer guidelines and to promote discussion and education. Although the AAA has investigated allegations of misconduct by anthropologists, it does not adjudicate such claims. The AAA also recognizes that anthropologists belong to multiple groups—including, perhaps, a family, a community, a religion, and other organizations—each of which may have its own ethical and moral rules. Because anthropologists can find themselves in complex situations and subject to more than one ethical code, the AAA Code provides a framework, not an ironclad formula, for making decisions.

The AAA wants its members to be attentive to ethical issues, and it urges anthropology departments to include ethical training in their curricula. The AAA Code addresses several contexts in which anthropologists work. Its main points about the ethical dimensions of research may be summarized.

Anthropologists should be open and honest about all dimensions of their research projects with funding agencies, colleagues, and all parties affected by the research. These parties should be informed about the purpose(s), potential impacts, and source(s) of support for the research. Anthropologists should disseminate the results of their research in an appropriate and timely way.

Researchers should not compromise anthropological ethics in order to conduct research. They should also pay attention to proper relations between themselves as guests and the host nations and communities where they work. The AAA does not advise anthropologists to avoid taking stands on issues. Indeed, the Code states that leadership in seeking to shape actions and policies may be as ethically justifiable as inaction.

Here are some of the headings and subheadings of the Code:

A. Responsibility to people and animals

1. The primary ethical obligation of the anthropologist is to the people, species, and materials they study. This obligation takes precedence over the goal of seeking new knowledge. It can also lead to the decision not to undertake, or to discontinue, research when ethical conflicts arise. This primary ethical obligation—anthropology's "prime directive"—entails:

   Avoiding harm or wrong.

   Understanding that the production of knowledge can have positive or negative effects on the people or animals worked with or studied.

   Respecting the well-being of humans and nonhuman primates.

   Working for the long-term conservation of the archaeological, fossil, and historical records.

   Consulting actively with the affected individuals or group(s), with the goal of establishing a working relationship that will benefit all parties.

2. Researchers must do all they can to preserve the safety, dignity, and privacy of the people with whom they work. Anthropologists working with animals should not endanger their safety, psychological well-being, or survival.

3. Anthropologists should determine whether their hosts wish to remain anonymous or to receive recognition, and should try to comply with those wishes. Researchers should make clear to research participants that, despite the best efforts of the anthropologist, anonymity may be compromised or recognition fail to materialize.

4. Researchers must obtain the *informed consent* of affected parties. That is, prior to their agreement to participate, people should be told about the purpose, nature, and procedures of the research and its potential impact on them. Informed consent (agreement to take part in the research) should be obtained from anyone providing information, owning materials being studied, or otherwise having an interest that might be impacted by the research.

Margaret Mead talks with a mother and child during a revisit to the Manus of the Admiralty Islands, one of the South Pacific societies where she worked and established long-term, ongoing relationships. Mead was known for her research on the impact of cultural diversity on childhood, adolescence, and gender roles.

Informed consent does not necessarily imply or require a written or signed form.

5. Researchers who develop ongoing relationships with individuals providing information or with hosts must continue to respect the obligations of openness and informed consent.

6. Anthropologists may gain personally from their work, but they should not exploit individuals, groups, animals, or cultural or biological materials. They should recognize their debt to the communities and societies in which they work and to the people with whom they work. They should reciprocate in appropriate ways.

B. Responsibility to scholarship and science

1. Anthropologists should attempt to identify potential ethical conflicts and dilemmas when preparing proposals, and as projects proceed.

2. Anthropologists are responsible for the integrity and reputation of their field, of

scholarship, and of science. They are subject to the general moral rules of scientific and scholarly conduct. They should not deceive or knowingly misrepresent (i.e., fabricate evidence, falsify, plagiarize). They should not attempt to prevent reporting of misconduct, or obstruct the scholarly research of others.

3. Anthropologists should do all they can to preserve opportunities for future researchers to follow them to the field.

4. To the extent possible, anthropologists should disseminate their findings to the scientific and scholarly community.

5. Anthropologists should consider all reasonable requests for access to their data and materials for purposes of research. They should preserve their data for use by posterity.

C. Responsibility to the public
1. Anthropologists should strive to ensure that their findings are contextualized properly and used responsibly. Anthropologists should also consider the social and political implications of their conclusions. They should be honest about their qualifications and philosophical and political biases. They must be alert to possible harm their information might cause people with whom they work, or colleagues.

2. Anthropologists may move beyond disseminating research results to a position of advocacy. This is an individual decision, but not an ethical responsibility.

D. Ethics Pertaining to Applied Anthropology
1. The same ethical guidelines apply to all anthropological work—academic and applied. Applied anthropologists should use their results appropriately (i.e., publication, teaching, program and policy development) within a reasonable time. Applied anthropologists should be honest about their skills and intentions. They should monitor the effects of their work on everyone affected.

2. In dealings with employers, applied anthropologists should be honest about their qualifications, abilities, and goals. The applied anthropologist should review the aims and interests of the prospective employer, taking into consideration the employer's past activities and future goals. Applied anthropologists should not accept conditions contrary to professional ethics.

The full Code of Ethics, which is abbreviated and paraphrased here, is available at the AAA website (http://www.aaanet.org).

Academic and Applied Anthropology

Previously, we examined the role of applied anthropology during and immediately after World War II. Applied anthropology did not disappear during the 1950s and 1960s, but academic anthropology did most of the growing after World War II. The baby boom, which began in 1946 and peaked in 1957, fueled expansion of the American educational system and thus of academic jobs. New junior, community, and four-year colleges opened, and anthropology became a standard part of the college curriculum. During the 1950s and 1960s, most American anthropologists were college professors, although some still worked in agencies and museums.

This era of academic anthropology continued through the early 1970s. Especially during the Vietnam War, undergraduates flocked to anthropology classes to learn about other cultures. Students were especially interested in Southeast Asia, whose indigenous societies were being disrupted by war. Many anthropologists protested the superpowers' apparent disregard for non-Western lives, values, customs, and social systems.

During the 1970s, and increasingly thereafter, although most anthropologists still worked in academia, others found jobs with international organizations, government, business, hospitals, and schools. This shift toward application, though only partial, has benefited the profession. It has forced anthropologists to consider the wider social value and implications of their research.

THEORY AND PRACTICE

One of the most valuable tools in applying anthropology is the ethnographic method. Ethnographers study societies firsthand, living with and

During the Vietnam War, many anthropologists protested the superpowers' disregard for the values, customs, social systems, and lives of Third World peoples. Several anthropologists (including the author) attended this all-night Columbia University "teach-in" against the war in 1965.

learning from ordinary people. Ethnographers are participant-observers, taking part in the events they study in order to understand local thought and behavior. Applied anthropologists use ethnographic techniques in both foreign and domestic settings. Other "expert" participants in social-change programs may be content to converse with officials, read reports, and copy statistics. However, the applied anthropologist's likely early request is some variant of "take me to the local people." We know that people must play an active role in the changes that affect them and that "the people" have information that "the experts" lack.

Anthropological theory—the body of findings and generalizations of the subdisciplines—also guides applied anthropology. Anthropology's holistic perspective—its interest in biology, society, culture, and language—permits the evaluation of many issues that affect people. Theory aids practice, and application fuels theory. As we compare social-change policy and programs, our understanding of cause and effect increases. We add new generalizations about culture change to those discovered in traditional and ancient cultures.

Anthropology's systemic perspective recognizes that changes don't occur in a vacuum. A pro-

gram or project always has multiple effects, some of which are unforeseen. For example, dozens of economic development projects intended to increase productivity through irrigation have worsened public health by creating waterways where diseases thrive. In an American example of unintended consequences, a program aimed at enhancing teachers' appreciation of cultural differences led to ethnic stereotyping (Kleinfeld 1975). Specifically, Native American students did not welcome teachers' frequent comments about their Indian heritage. The students felt set apart from their classmates and saw this attention to their ethnicity as patronizing and demeaning.

Anthropology and Education

Anthropology and education refers to anthropological research in classrooms, homes, and neighborhoods (see Spindler 2000). Some of the most interesting research has been done in classrooms, where anthropologists observe interactions among teachers, students, parents, and visitors. Jules Henry's classic account of the American elementary school classroom (1955) shows how students learn to conform to and compete with their peers. Anthropologists also follow students from classrooms into their homes and neighborhoods, viewing children as total cultural creatures whose enculturation and attitudes toward education belong to a context that includes family and peers.

Sociolinguists and cultural anthropologists work side by side in education research, for example, in a study of Puerto Rican seventh-graders in the urban Midwest (Hill-Burnett 1978). In classrooms, neighborhoods, and homes, anthropologists uncovered some misconceptions by teachers. For example, the teachers had mistakenly assumed that Puerto Rican parents valued education less than did non-Hispanics. However, in-depth interviews revealed that the Puerto Rican parents valued it more.

Researchers also found that certain practices were preventing Hispanics from being adequately educated. For example, the teachers' union and the board of education had agreed to teach "English as a foreign language." However, they had not provided bilingual teachers to work with Spanish-

These kids get a basic education in Cite Soleil, a slum of Port-au-Prince, Haiti. What do you see here that differs from classrooms in your country? Do you think these differences would affect how you would do research in Haiti? Assume this classroom would be part of your study.

speaking students. The school started assigning all students (including non-Hispanics) with low reading scores and behavior problems to the English-as-a-foreign-language classroom.

This educational disaster brought together a teacher who spoke no Spanish, children who barely spoke English, and a group of English-speaking students with reading and behavior problems. The Spanish speakers were falling behind not just in reading but in all subjects. They could at least have kept up in the other subjects if a Spanish speaker had been teaching them science, social studies, and math until they were ready for English-language instruction in those areas.

A dramatic illustration of the relevance of applied sociolinguistics to education comes from Ann Arbor, Michigan (Figure 2.2). In 1979, the parents of several black students at the predominantly white Dr. Martin Luther King Jr. Elementary School sued the Board of Education. They claimed that their children faced linguistic discrimination in the classroom.

The children, who lived in a neighborhood housing project, spoke Black English Vernacular

See the OLC
Internet Exercises

mhhe
com
/kottak

(BEV) at home. At school, most had encountered problems with their classwork. Some had been labeled "learning-impaired" and placed in remedial reading courses. (Consider the embarrassment that children suffer and the effect on self-image of such labeling.)

The African-American parents and their attorney contended that the children had no intrinsic learning disabilities but simply did not understand everything their teachers said. Nor did their teachers always understand them. The lawyer argued that because BEV and Standard English (SE) are so similar, teachers often misinterpreted a child's correct pronunciation (in BEV) of an SE word as a reading error.

The children's attorney recruited several sociolinguists to testify on their behalf. The school board, by contrast, could not find a single qualified linguist to support its argument that there was no linguistic discrimination.

The judge ruled in favor of the children and ordered the following solution: Teachers at the King School had to attend a full-year course

In a diverse, multicultural populace, teachers should be sensitive to and knowledgeable about linguistic and cultural differences. Children need to be protected so that their ethnic or linguistic background is not used against them. That is what happens when a social variation is regarded as a learning disability.

Urban Anthropology

By 2025, the developing nations will account for 85 percent of the world's population, compared with 77 percent in 1992 (Stevens 1992). Solutions to future problems will depend increasingly on understanding non-Western cultural backgrounds. The fastest population growth rates are in the less developed countries, especially in urban areas. The world had only 16 cities with more than a million people in 1900, but there are more than 300 such cities today. By 2025, 60 percent of the global population will be urban, compared with 37 percent in 1990 (Stevens 1992). Rural migrants often move to slums, where they live in hovels without utilities and public sanitation facilities.

Interpret the World If current trends continue, urban population increase and the concentration of people in slums will be accompanied by rising rates of crime and water, air, and noise pollution. These problems will be most severe in the less-developed countries. Almost all (97 percent) of the projected world population increase will occur in developing countries, 34 percent in Africa alone (Lewis 1992). Map 2 in your atlas shows population growth rates worldwide; notice the very high growth rates in African countries. Although the rate of population increase is low in northern countries, such as the United States, Canada, and most European nations, global population growth will continue to affect the Northern Hemisphere, especially through international migration. There has been substantial recent migration to the United States and Canada from developing countries with high growth rates, such as India and Mexico. Can you

Figure 2.2 **Location of Ann Arbor, Michigan.**

designed to improve their knowledge of nonstandard dialects, particularly BEV. The judge did not advocate that the teachers learn to speak BEV or that the children do their assignments in BEV. The school's goal remained to teach the children to use SE, the standard dialect, correctly. Before this could be accomplished, however, teachers and students alike had to learn how to recognize the differences between these similar dialects. At the end of the year, most of the teachers interviewed in the local newspaper said the course had helped them.

identify other such countries (that is, those with high growth rates and significant out-migration) on Map 2?

As industrialization and urbanization spread globally, anthropologists increasingly study these processes and the social and health problems they create. Urban anthropology, which has theoretical (basic research) and applied dimensions, is the cross-cultural and ethnographic study of global urbanization and life in cities. The United States and Canada also have become popular arenas for urban anthropological research on topics such as ethnicity, poverty, class, and subcultural variations (Mullings 1987).

URBAN VERSUS RURAL

Recognizing that a city is a social context that is very different from a rural community, an early student of Third World urbanization, the anthropologist Robert Redfield, focused on contrasts between rural and urban life. He contrasted rural communities, whose social relations are on a face-to-face basis, with cities, where impersonality characterizes many aspects of life. Redfield (1941) proposed that urbanization be studied along a rural-urban continuum. He described differences in values and social relations in four sites that spanned such a continuum. In Mexico's Yucatán peninsula, Redfield compared an isolated Maya-speaking Indian community, a rural peasant village, a small provincial city, and a large capital. Several studies in Africa (Little 1971) and Asia were influenced by Redfield's view that cities are centers through which cultural innovations spread to rural and tribal areas.

In any nation, urban and rural represent different social systems. However, migrants bring rural social forms, practices, and beliefs to town. They also take back urban and national patterns when they visit, or move back permanently to, their villages of origin. Inevitably, the experiences and social units of rural areas affect adaptation to city life. Social organization based on *descent*

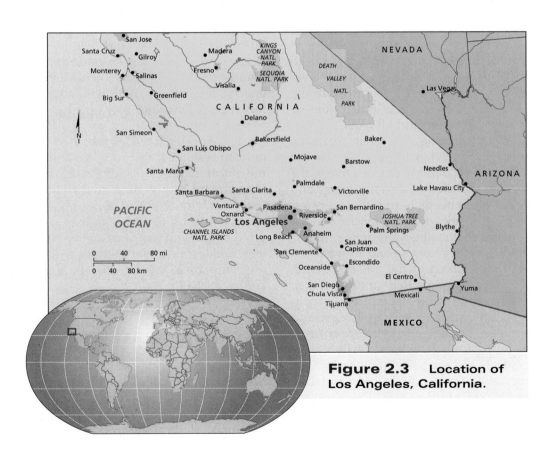

Figure 2.3 Location of Los Angeles, California.

A Samoan mother adjusts the tassel of her daughter's cap as the teenager graduates from high school in Long Beach, California. California—Los Angeles specifically—has the largest Samoan immigrant community in the United States. Did your immigrant parents or grandparents settle in a city or a rural area?

The ideology of such associations is that of a gigantic kin group. The members call one another "brother" and "sister." As in an extended family, rich members help their poor relatives. When members fight among themselves, the group acts as judge. A member's improper behavior can lead to expulsion-an unhappy fate for a migrant in a large ethnically heterogeneous city.

Modern North American cities also have kin-based ethnic associations. One example comes from Los Angeles (Figure 2.3), which has the largest Samoan immigrant community (12,000 people) in the United States. Samoans in Los Angeles draw on their traditional system of *matai* (*matai* means chief; the *matai* system now refers to respect for elders) to deal with modern urban problems. One example: In 1992, a white policeman shot and killed two unarmed Samoan brothers. When a judge dismissed charges against the officer, local leaders used the *matai* system to calm angry youths (who have formed gangs, like other ethnic groups in the Los Angeles area). Clan leaders and elders organized a well-attended community meeting, in which they urged young members to be patient.

Los Angeles Samoans also used the American judicial system. They brought a civil case against the officer in question and pressed the U.S. Justice Department to initiate a civil-rights case in the matter (Mydans 1992b). One role for the urban applied anthropologist is to help relevant social groups deal with larger urban institutions, such as legal and social-service agencies with which recent migrants, in particular, may be unfamiliar (see Holtzman 2000).

groups—cohesive units whose members claim common ancestry—is fundamental to many rural African societies. Such organizing principles as descent provide migrants to African cities with coping mechanisms, for example, when they reside with or near extended kin already in the city. City folk also develop new institutions to meet specific urban needs (Mitchell 1966).

Applying anthropology to urban planning starts by identifying the key social groups in the urban context. After identifying those groups, the anthropologist elicits their wishes for change and helps translate those needs to funding agencies. The next step is to work with the agencies and the people to ensure that changes are implemented correctly and that they correspond to what the people said they wanted at the outset. African urban groups that an applied anthropologist would consult include ethnic associations, occupational groups, social clubs, religious groups, and burial societies. Through membership in these groups, urban Africans have wide networks of personal contacts and support. Ethnic or "tribal" associations are common both in West and East Africa (Banton 1957; Little 1965). These groups maintain links with, and provide cash support and urban lodging for, their rural relatives.

Medical Anthropology

Medical anthropology is both academic/ theoretical and applied/practical. It is a field that includes both biological and sociocultural anthropologists. Medical anthropology is discussed in

*See the
Virtual Exploration*

**mhhe
●com
/kottak**

this chapter because of its many applications. Medical anthropologists examine such questions as: Which diseases affect different populations? How is illness socially constructed? How does one treat illness in effective and culturally appropriate ways?

This growing field considers the sociocultural context and implications of disease and illness (Helman 2001; Strathern and Stewart 1999). **Disease** refers to a scientifically identified health threat caused by a bacterium, virus, fungus, parasite, or other pathogen. Illness is a condition of poor health perceived or felt by an individual (Inhorn and Brown 1990). Cross-cultural research shows that perceptions of good and bad health, along with health threats and problems, are culturally constructed. Different ethnic groups and cultures recognize different illnesses, symptoms, and causes and have developed different healthcare systems and treatment strategies.

Disease also varies among cultures. Traditional and ancient foragers, because of their small numbers, mobility, and relative isolation from other groups, were not subject to most of the epidemic infectious diseases that affect agrarian and urban societies (Cohen and Armelagos 1984; Inhorn and Brown 1990). Epidemic diseases such as cholera, typhoid, and bubonic plague thrive in dense populations, and thus among farmers and city dwellers. The spread of malaria has been linked to population growth and deforestation associated with food production.

Certain diseases have spread with economic development. *Schistosomiasis* or bilharzia (liver flukes) is probably the fastest-spreading and most dangerous parasitic infection now known (Heyneman 1984). It is propagated by snails that live in ponds, lakes, and waterways, usually ones created by irrigation projects. A study done in a Nile Delta village in Egypt (Farooq 1966) illustrated the role of culture (religion) in the spread of schistosomiasis. The disease was more common among Muslims than among Christians because of an Islamic practice called *wudu*, ritual ablution (bathing) before prayer. The applied anthropology approach to reducing such diseases is to see if natives perceive a connection between the vector (e.g., snails in the water) and the disease, which can take years to develop. If they do not, such information

may be spread by enlisting active local groups and schools. With the worldwide diffusion of the electronic mass media, culturally appropriate public information campaigns have increased awareness and modified behavior that has public health consequences.

In eastern Africa, AIDS and other sexually transmitted diseases (STDs) have spread along highways, via encounters between male truckers and female prostitutes. STDs also are spread

Schistosomiasis (liver flukes) is among the fastest spreading and most dangerous parasitic infections now known. It is propagated by snails that live in ponds, lakes, and waterways (often ones created by irrigation projects) such as this one in Luxor, Egypt. As an applied anthropologist, what would you do to cut the rate of infection?

through prostitution as young men from rural areas seek wage work in cities, labor camps, and mines. When the men return to their natal villages, they infect their wives (Larson 1989; Miller and Rockwell 1988). Cities are also prime sites of STD transmission in Europe, Asia, and North and South America (French 2002).

The kind and incidence of disease vary among societies, and cultures interpret and treat illness differently. Standards for sick and healthy bodies are cultural constructions that vary in time and space (Martin 1992). Still, all societies have what George Foster and Barbara Anderson (1978) call "disease-theory systems" to identify, classify, and explain illness. According to Foster and Anderson (1978), there are three basic theories about the causes of illness: personalistic, naturalistic, and emotionalistic. **Personalistic disease theories** blame illness on agents (often malicious), such as sorcerers, witches, ghosts, or ancestral spirits. **Naturalistic disease theories** explain illness in impersonal terms. One example is Western medicine or *biomedicine*, which aims to link illness to scientifically demonstrated agents that bear no personal malice toward their victims. Thus, Western medicine attributes illness to organisms (e.g., bacteria, viruses, fungi, or parasites), accidents, or toxic materials. Other naturalistic ethnomedical systems blame poor health on unbalanced body fluids. Many Latin cultures classify food, drink, and environmental conditions as "hot" or "cold." People believe their health suffers when they eat or drink hot or cold substances together or under inappropriate conditions. For example, one shouldn't drink something cold after a hot bath or eat a pineapple (a "cold" fruit) when one is menstruating (a "hot" condition).

Emotionalistic disease theories assume that emotional experiences cause illness. For example, Latin Americans may develop *susto*, or soul loss, an illness caused by anxiety or fright (Bolton 1981; Finkler 1985). Its symptoms include lethargy, vagueness, and distraction. Of course, modern psychoanalysis also focuses on the role of the emotions in physical and psychological well-being.

All societies have **health-care systems.** These consist of beliefs, customs, specialists, and techniques aimed at ensuring health and preventing, diagnosing, and curing illness. A society's illness-causation theory is important for treatment. When illness has a personalistic cause, shamans and other magico-religious specialists may be good curers. They draw on varied techniques (occult and practical) that comprise their special expertise. A shaman may cure soul loss by enticing the spirit back into the body. Shamans may ease difficult childbirths by asking spirits to travel up the birth canal to guide the baby out (Lévi-Strauss 1967). A shaman may cure a cough by counteracting a curse or removing a substance introduced by a sorcerer.

All cultures have health-care specialists. If there is a "world's oldest profession" besides hunter and gatherer, it is curer, often a shaman. The curer's role has some universal features (Foster and Anderson 1978). Thus, curers emerge through a culturally defined process of selection (parental prodding, inheritance, visions, dream instructions) and training (apprentice shamanship, medical school). Eventually, the curer is certified by older practitioners and acquires a professional image. Patients believe in the skills of the curer, whom they consult and compensate.

Non-Western systems (traditional medicine) offer some lessons for Western medicine. For example, traditional practitioners may have more success treating certain forms of mental illness than psychotherapists do. Non-Western systems may explain mental illness by causes that are easier to identify and combat. Thus, it may be simpler to rid a body of a spirit possessor than to undo all the damage that a Freudian might attribute to an unresolved Oedipus complex.

Another reason non-Western therapy may succeed is that the mentally ill are diagnosed and treated in cohesive groups with the full support of their kin. Curing may be an intense community ritual in which the shaman heals by temporarily taking on and then rejecting the patient's illness (Lévi-Strauss 1967). In modern mental institutions, by contrast, no prior social ties link patients to each other or to doctors and nurses. Mental illness is viewed as the patient's individual burden. Psychotropic drugs are increasingly used, often effectively, to treat and control psychological disorders. However, for severe mental illness, the context of treatment may be one of isolation and alienation—separation of the afflicted person from society—rather than participation by a group in a common ritual.

What makes us sick? Maybe we can agree that germs, allergens, poor nutrition, advanced age, accidents, poisons, and environmental hazards contribute to poor health. But what about heat, cold, drafts, dryness, and humidity? What about physical activity or the lack thereof? And foods that don't go together, such as ice cream and vinegar or Coca Cola and tomato juice? How about spirits, ghosts, witches, and sorcerers?

If we're feeling sick, we often feel better once a label (diagnosis) is attached to our illness. In contemporary society, it's usually a physician who provides us with such a label—and maybe with a medicine that cures it or alleviates our suffering. In other contexts, a shaman or magico-religious specialist provides the diagnosis and treatment plan. We live in a world where alternative health-care systems coexist, sometimes competing, sometimes complementing, one another. Never have people had access to such a wide range of choices in health care. In seeking good health and survival, it may be only natural for people to draw on alternative systems—acupuncture for one problem, chiropractic for another, medicine for a third, psychotherapy for a fourth, spiritual healing for a fifth. Think about the alternative treatment systems you may have used in the last year.

We should not lose sight, ethnocentrically, of the difference between **scientific medicine** and Western medicine per se (Lieban 1977). Despite advances in pathology, microbiology, biochemistry, surgery, diagnostic technology, and applications, many Western medical procedures have little justification in logic or fact. Overprescription of tranquilizers and drugs, unnecessary surgery, and the impersonality and inequality of the physician-patient relationship are questionable features of Western medical systems. Also, overuse of antibiotics, not just for people, but also in animal feed and antibacterial soaps, seems to be triggering an explosion of resistant microrganisms, which may pose a long-term global public health hazard.

Still, western medicine surpasses tribal treatment in many ways. Although medicines like quinine, coca, opium, ephedrine, and rauwolfia were discovered in nonindustrial societies, thousands of effective drugs are available today to treat myriad diseases. Preventive health care improved during the 20th century. Today's surgical procedures are safer and more effective than those of traditional societies.

But industrialization has spawned its own health problems. Modern stressors include noise, air, and water pollution; poor nutrition; dangerous machinery; impersonal work; isolation; poverty; homelessness; and substance abuse. Health problems in industrial nations are due as much to economic, social, political, and cultural factors as to pathogens. In modern North America, for example, poverty contributes to many illnesses. These include arthritis, heart conditions, back problems, and hearing and vision impairment. Poverty is also a factor in the differential spread of infectious diseases.

Medical anthropologists have served as cultural interpreters in public health programs, which must pay attention to native theories about the nature, causes, and treatment of illness. Successful health interventions cannot simply be forced on communities. They must fit into local cultures and be accepted by local people. When Western medicine is introduced, people usually retain many of their old methods while also accepting new ones (see Green 1987/1992). Native curers may go on treating certain conditions (like spirit possession), whereas M.D.s may deal with others. If both modern and traditional specialists are consulted and the patient is cured, the native

A traditional healer at work in Malaysia. What does this remind you of?

Background Information

STUDENT:	Ann L. Bretnall
SUPERVISING PROFESSOR:	David Himmelgreen
SCHOOL:	University of South Florida
YEAR IN SCHOOL/MAJOR:	Senior/Anthropology
FUTURE PLANS:	After completion of master's in applied anthropology, work with the local social service agencies in community outreach projects
PROJECT TITLE:	Establishing a Farmers Market for the Local Hispanic Community

Note how this essay links the worlds of commerce, nutrition, health, and social interaction. The comfortable and convivial atmosphere of the local farmers' market is an appropriate setting for applying anthropology—aimed at culturally appropriate education and innovation. As immigration has increased, work demands and ready access to fast foods have changed the nature of meals and diet among Latinos in the Tampa area. Ann Bretnall discusses her work organizing educational events and the participation of local community members in the farmer's market.

The Applied Anthropology program at the University of South Florida, in Tampa, gives students practical experience with community projects. The Project New Life-Good Health (Nueva Vida-Buena Salud) is one of many projects the Anthropology Department is currently working on. This project is designed to develop and implement a community-engaged nutrition and health education program targeting recently arrived Latino immigrant families. My project is to develop a church-based farmer's market for the local Hispanic community.

In recent years the Hispanic population of Hillsborough County, which includes Tampa, has significantly increased. Immigrants have arrived from Central and South America and from the Caribbean. According to U.S. Census Bureau data, the 1990 Hispanic population of Hillsborough County was 106,908, rising to 179,692 in 2000.

Project New Life-Good Health rests on two previous projects focusing on the local Hispanic community. Those projects were called "Acculturation and Nutritional Needs Assessment of Tampa" (ANNA-T) and "Promoting Adequate Nutrition" (PAN). The ANNA-T project investigated food consumption and physical activity patterns of recently arrived Latino immigrants. The research of ANNA-T helped to develop project PAN. PAN was a series of culturally tailored nutrition-education and disease-prevention seminars targeting low-income Latino families. Projects ANNA-T and PAN found there had been a significant change in diet, with a new emphasis on fast food and sodas and a reduced consumption of fresh fruits and vegetables. ANNA-T also discovered that lack of time and of social support were barriers to traditional family meals.

curer may get as much credit as or more credit than the physician.

A more personal treatment of illness that emulates the non-Western curer-patient-community relationship could probably benefit Western systems. Western medicine has tended to draw a rigid line between biological and psychological causation. Non-Western theories usually lack this sharp distinction, recognizing that poor health has intertwined physical, emotional, and social causes. The mind-body opposition is part of Western folk taxonomy, not of science.

Non-Western practitioners often treat symptoms, instead of seeking causes. Their aim—and often their result—is an immediate cure. Traditional curers often succeed with health problems that

vendors, unlike the sometimes uncomfortable interactions with employees in a grocery store.

My work with the Project New Life-Good Health farmers' market involves organizing the resources necessary to implement farmers' market events. In interviews and observations, I have found genuine interest among community members and vendors. The literature I reviewed also confirms advantages to individuals involved in local farmers' markets. Efforts by community members to organize and establish the farmers' market as their own will be crucial to the success of the market as a permanent institution in their community.

To summarize, the goal of the farmers' market is to provide a venue to understand community needs, to educate, and to improve the nutrition and health of the local Hispanic community. This can be accomplished by ensuring the availability of some culturally specific foods and by introducing other healthful foods into the Hispanic diet. Our ongoing research will provide the local community with the resources to continue and manage the farmers' market as a positive and sustainable alternative within their local economy.

The goals of project New Life-Good Health are to: 1) develop a culturally appropriate nutrition-education and disease-prevention curriculum, 2) conduct a series of healthy-eating and disease-prevention seminars, and 3) develop a church-based farmers' market that includes nutrition-education and health-promotion activities for the larger community. Local farmers' markets have an open and informal setting, which provides a unique ambiance to the shopping experience. This social setting allows customers to converse easily with

western medicine classifies as psychosomatic (not a disease, therefore not an illness) and dismisses as not requiring treatment—despite the feelings of the ill patient. Non-Western medical systems tell us that patients can be treated effectively as whole beings, using any combination of methods that prove beneficial. Indeed there is a growing related field known as *holistic medicine* in contemporary North America.

Anthropology and Business

Carol Taylor (1987) discusses the value of an "anthropologist-in-residence" in a large, complex organization such as a hospital or a business. A free-ranging ethnographer can be a perceptive oddball when information and decisions usually move through a rigid hierarchy. If allowed to observe and converse freely with all types and levels of personnel, the anthropologist may acquire a unique perspective on organizational conditions and problems. For many years, anthropologists have used ethnography to study business settings (Arensberg 1987). For example, ethnographic research in an auto factory may view workers, managers, and executives as different social categories participating in a common social system. Each group has characteristic attitudes, values, and behavior patterns. These are transmitted through *microenculturation,* the process by which people learn particular roles in a limited social system. The free-ranging nature of ethnography takes the anthropologist from worker to executive. Each of these people is both an individual with a personal viewpoint and a cultural creature whose perspective is, to some extent, shared with other members of a group. Applied anthropologists have acted as "cultural brokers," translating managers' goals or workers' concerns to the other group.

Closely observing how people actually use products, anthropologists work with engineers to design products that are more user-friendly. Increasingly, anthropologists are working with high-tech companies, where they use their observational skills to study how people work, live, and use technology. Such studies can be traced to 1979, when the Xerox Palo Alto (California) Research Center (PARC) hired the anthropologist Lucy Suchman. She worked in a laboratory where researchers were trying to build artificial intelligence to help people use complicated copiers. Suchman observed and filmed people having trouble with a copying job. From her research came the realization that simplicity is more important than fancy features. That's why all Xerox copiers, no matter how complex, now include a single green copy button for when someone wants an uncomplicated copy (Weise 1999).

"[Our] graduate students keep getting snatched up by companies," says Marietta Baba (now of Michigan State University), former chair of the anthropology department at Wayne State University (WSU) in Detroit (quoted in Weise 1999). WSU trains anthropology students to observe social interactions so as to understand the underlying structures of a culture, and to apply those methods to industry. Baba estimates that about 9,000 American anthropologists work in

Professor Marietta Baba of Michigan State University is also a prominent applied anthropologist known for her studies of the automobile industry.

academia and that about 2,200 hold applied anthropology positions in industry. "But the proportions are shifting, so you're getting more and more applied ones," she says (quoted in Weise 1999). Companies hire anthropologists to gain a better understanding of their customers and to find new products and markets that engineers and marketers might never imagine. Andrea Saveri, a director at the Institute for the Future in Menlo Park, California, contends that traditional market research is limited by its question-and-answer format. "In the case of surveys, you're telling the respondent how to answer and you're not giving them any room for anything else" (quoted in Weise 1999). Saveri, who thinks ethnography is more precise and powerful than surveys, employs anthropologists to investigate the consequences of technology (Weise 1999).

For business, key features of anthropology include (1) ethnography and observation as ways of gathering data, (2) cross-cultural expertise, and (3) a focus on cultural diversity. The cross-cultural perspective enters the picture when businesses seek to know why other nations have higher (or lower) productivity than we do (Ferraro 2001). Reasons for differential productivity are cultural, social, and economic. To find them, anthropologists must focus on key features in the organization of production. Subtle but potentially important differences can emerge from workplace ethnography—close observation of workers and managers in their natural (workplace) setting.

Careers in Anthropology

Many college students find anthropology interesting and consider majoring in it. However, their parents or friends may discourage them by asking, "What kind of job are you going to get with an anthropology major?" The purpose of this section is to answer that question. The first step in answering "What do you do with an anthropology major?" is to consider the more general question "What do you do with any college major?" The answer is "Not much, without a good bit of effort, thought, and planning." A survey of graduates of the literary college of the University of Michigan showed that few had jobs that were clearly linked to their majors. Medicine, law, and many other professions require advanced degrees. Although many colleges offer bachelor's degrees in engineering, business, accounting, and social work, master's degrees are often needed to get the best jobs in those fields. Anthropologists, too, need an advanced degree, most typically a Ph.D., to find gainful employment in academic, museum, or applied anthropology.

The following discussion is aimed mainly at undergraduates who are considering an anthropology major—not at students who are considering advanced degrees in anthropology, although there are some comments for them, too. A broad college education, and even a major in anthropology, can be an excellent foundation for success in many fields. Many University of Michigan undergraduates who are planning careers in medicine, public health, or dentistry choose a joint major in anthropology and zoology. A recent survey of women executives showed that most had not majored in business but in the social sciences or humanities. Only after graduating did they study business, obtaining a master's degree in business administration. These executives felt that the breadth of their college educations had contributed to their business careers. Anthropology majors go on to medical, law, and business schools and find success in many professions that often have little explicit connection to anthropology.

Anthropology's breadth provides knowledge and an outlook on the world that are useful in many kinds of work. For example, an anthropology major combined with a master's degree in business is excellent preparation for work in international business. However, job seekers must always convince employers that they have a special and valuable "skillset."

Breadth is anthropology's hallmark. Anthropologists study people biologically, culturally, socially, and linguistically, in time and space, in developed and underdeveloped nations, in simple and complex settings. Physical anthropologists teach about human biology in time and space, including our origins and evolution. Most colleges have cultural anthropology courses that compare cultures and others that focus on particular world areas, such as Latin America, Asia, and Native North America. The knowledge of geographic areas acquired in such courses can be useful in many jobs. Anthropology's comparative outlook, its long-standing Third World focus, and its appreciation of diverse life styles combine to provide an excellent foundation for overseas employment.

Even for work in North America, the focus on culture is valuable. Every day we hear about cultural differences and about social problems whose solutions require a multicultural viewpoint—an ability to recognize and reconcile ethnic differences. Government, schools, and private firms constantly deal with people from different social classes, ethnic groups, and tribal backgrounds. Physicians, attorneys, social workers, police officers, judges, teachers, and students can all do a better job if they understand social differences in a part of the world that is one of the most ethnically diverse in history.

What if you want more than an undergraduate degree in anthropology? What if you do decide to pursue an advanced degree? Although some practicing anthropologists find jobs with only the master's degree, the more typical credential for gainful employment in anthropology is the doctorate, the Ph.D. Traditionally, most people with Ph.D.s in anthropology have expected to find employment as college teachers or in museums. Things are changing today. The American Anthropological Association has estimated that at least half of future anthropology Ph.D.s will not find work in academia. One reason for this shift is that academic jobs have become harder to get and are not clearly expanding. Another reason is that the production of Ph.D.s in anthropology has increased faster than the number of academic jobs available. A final reason is that many anthropology Ph.D.s actually prefer applied work to work in academia. Whatever the reason, there is no doubt that more and more anthropologists will be doing applied anthropology.

One place they'll be doing it is business. The cross-cultural perspective and the focus on diversity are two reasons why some North American businesses have become interested in anthropology, as we saw in the news vignette that opened Chapter 1. Also, an ethnographic focus on behavior in the daily social setting can help locate problems that plague American businesses, which tend to be overly hierarchical. Attention to the social dimension of business can only gain importance. More and more executives recognize that proper human relations are as important as economic forecasts in maximizing productivity. Contemporary applied anthropologists devise ways to deploy employees more effectively and to increase job satisfaction.

Applied anthropologists also work to help communities threatened by external systems. As highways and power-supply systems cross tribal boundaries, the "modern" world comes into conflict with historic land claims and traditions. An anthropological study is often considered necessary before permission is granted to extend a public works system across native lands.

Because construction, dams, reservoirs, and other public works may threaten archaeological sites, fields such as cultural resource management have developed. Government agencies, engineering firms, and construction companies now have jobs for people with an anthropological background because of federal legislation to protect historic and prehistoric sites.

Knowledge about the traditions and beliefs of the many social groups within a modern nation is important in planning and carrying out programs that affect those groups. Attention to social background and cultural categories helps ensure the welfare of affected ethnic groups, communities, and neighborhoods. Experience in planned social change—whether community organization in North America or economic development overseas—shows that a proper social study should be done before a project or policy is implemented. When local people want the change and it fits their lifestyle and traditions, it will be more successful, beneficial, and cost-effective. There will be not

only a more humane but a more economical solution to a real social problem.

Some agencies working overseas place particular value on anthropological training. Others seek employees with certain skills without caring much about specific academic backgrounds. Among the government agencies that hire anthropologists are USAID (the United States Agency for International Development) and USDA (the United States Department of Agriculture). These organizations hire anthropologists both full-time and as short-term consultants.

Private voluntary organizations working overseas offer other opportunities. These PVOs (a kind of NGO) include Care, Save the Children, Catholic Relief Services, Foster Parents Plan International, and Oxfam (a hunger relief organization operating out of Boston and Oxford). Some of these groups employ anthropologists full-time.

Anthropologists apply their expertise in surprisingly diverse areas. They negotiate business deals, suggest and implement organizational changes, and testify as expert witnesses. Physical anthropologist Kathy Reichs applies anthropology in her forensic work for the Office of the Chief Medical Examiner of North Carolina and for the Laboratoire de Sciences Judiciares et de Médecine Légale in Montreal, Quebec. Dr. Reichs is also a professor of anthropology at the University of North Carolina, Charlotte, a frequent expert witness in criminal trials, and the author of several mystery novels featuring the heroine Temperance Brennan—also a forensic anthropologist. Anthropologists also have worked for pharmaceutical firms interested in potential conflicts between traditional and Western medicine, and in culturally appropriate marketing of their products (e.g., Viagra) in new settings. Other anthropologists are working to help native peoples get a share of the profits when their traditional remedies, including medicinal plants, are marketed by drug companies.

People with anthropology backgrounds are doing well in many fields. Furthermore, even if the job has little or nothing to do with anthropology in a formal or obvious sense, anthropology is always useful when we work with fellow human beings. For most of us, this means every day of our lives.

SUMMARY

1. Applied anthropology uses anthropological perspectives, theory, methods, and data to identify, assess, and solve problems. Applied anthropologists have a range of employers. Examples: government agencies; development organizations; NGOs; tribal, ethnic, and interest groups; businesses; social services and educational agencies. Applied anthropologists come from all four subfields. Ethnography is one of applied anthropology's most valuable research tools. Another is the comparative, cross-cultural perspective. A systemic perspective recognizes that changes have multiple consequences, some unintended. A code of ethics guides anthropologists' research and other professional activities.

2. Anthropology and education researchers work in classrooms, homes, and other settings relevant to education. Such studies may lead to policy recommendations. Both academic and applied anthropologists study migration from rural areas to cities and across national boundaries. North America has become a popular arena for urban anthropological research on migration, ethnicity, poverty, and related topics. Although rural and urban are different social systems, there is cultural diffusion from one to the other. Rural and tribal social forms affect adjustment to the city.

3. Medical anthropology is the cross-cultural study of health problems and conditions, disease, illness, disease theories, and health-care systems. Medical anthropology includes biological and cultural anthropologists and has theoretical (academic) and applied dimensions. In a given setting, the characteristic diseases reflect diet, population density, economy, and social complexity. Native theories of illness may be personalistic, naturalistic, or emotionalistic. In applying anthropology to business, the key features are (1) ethnography and observation as ways of gathering data, (2) cross-cultural expertise, and (3) focus on cultural diversity.

4. A broad college education, including anthropology and foreign-area courses, offers excellent background for many fields. Anthropology's comparative outlook and cultural relativism provide an excellent basis for overseas employment. Even for work in North America, a focus on culture and cultural diversity is valuable. Anthropology majors attend medical, law, and business schools and succeed in many fields, some of which have little explicit connection with anthropology.

5. Experience with social-change programs, whether in North America or abroad, offers a common lesson. When local people want a change and when that change fits their life style and traditions, the change is most likely to be successful, beneficial, and cost-effective.

KEY TERMS

See the flash cards

advocacy view of applied anthropology; the belief that precisely because anthropologists are experts on human problems and social change, and because they study, understand, and respect cultural values, they should make policy affecting people.

anthropology and education
Anthropological research in classrooms, homes, and neighborhoods, viewing students as total cultural creatures whose enculturation and attitudes toward education belong to a larger context that includes family, peers, and society.

applied anthropology The application of anthropological data, perspectives, theory, and methods to identify, assess, and solve contemporary social problems.

cultural resource management (CRM)
The branch of applied archaeology aimed at preserving sites threatened by dams, highways, and other projects.

curer Specialized role acquired through a culturally appropriate process of selection, training, certification, and acquisition of a professional image; the curer is consulted by patients, who believe in his or her special powers, and receives some form of special consideration; a cultural universal.

disease A scientifically identified health threat caused by a bacterium, virus, fungus, parasite, or other pathogen.

emotionalistic disease theories Theories that assume that illness is caused by intense emotional experiences.

health-care systems Beliefs, customs, and specialists concerned with ensuring health and preventing and curing illness; a cultural universal.

illness A condition of poor health perceived or felt by an individual.

ivory tower view of applied anthropology; the belief that anthropologists should avoid practical matters and concentrate on research, publication, and teaching.

medical anthropology Unites biological and cultural anthropologists in the study of disease, health problems, health-care systems, and theories about illness in different cultures and ethnic groups.

naturalistic disease theories Include scientific medicine; theories that explain illness in impersonal systemic terms.

personalistic disease theories Theories that attribute illness to sorcerers, witches, ghosts, or ancestral spirits.

practicing anthropologists Used as a synonym for applied anthropology; anthropologists who practice their profession outside of academia.

schizoid view of applied anthropology; the belief that anthropologists should help carry out, but not make or criticize, policy, and that personal value judgments should be kept strictly separate from scientific investigation in applied anthropology.

scientific medicine As distinguished from Western medicine, a health-care system based on scientific knowledge and procedures, encompassing such fields as pathology, microbiology, biochemistry, surgery, diagnostic technology, and applications.

For more self testing, see the self quizzes

CRITICAL THINKING QUESTIONS

mhhe
com
/kottak

1. What's your position on applied anthropology, given the three views discussed at the beginning of this chapter?

2. What else are you studying this semester? Do those fields have an applied dimension, too? Are they more or less useful than anthropology is?

3. Describe a setting in which you might use ethnography and observation to do applied anthropology. What other research methods might you also use in that setting?

4. How might ethical issues and concerns vary across anthropology's four subfields? Imagine an ethical issue that might arise for a physical anthropologist, for an archaeologist, and for a cultural anthropologist.

5. Think back to your grade school or high school classroom. Were there any social issues that might have interested an anthropologist? Were there any problems that an applied anthropologist might have been able to solve? How so?

6. What do you see as the costs and benefits of Western medicine compared with tribal medi-

cine? Are there any conditions for which you'd prefer treatment by a tribal curer than a Western curer?

7. Think of a problem in an urban setting that an applied anthropologist might be called on to solve. How do you imagine he or she would go about solving it?

8. Think of a business context you know well. How might applied anthropology help that business function better? How would the applied anthropologist gather the information to suggest improvements?

Atlas Questions

Look at Map 2, "Population Growth Rates."

1. Which continent has the highest growth rates?

2. What continents have growth rates below 1 percent per year?

3. Where does one find the highest growth rates in the western hemisphere?

SUGGESTED ADDITIONAL READINGS

Anderson, R.

1996 *Magic, Science, and Health: The Aims and Achievements of Medical Anthropology.* Fort Worth: Harcourt Brace. Up-to-date text, focusing on variation associated with race, gender, ethnicity, age, and ableness.

Bailey, E. J.

2000 *Medical Anthropology and African American Health.* Westport, CT: Bergin and Garvey. Medical issues affecting, and anthropological research involving, African Americans.

Bond, G. C., J. Kreniske, I. Susser, and J. Vincent, eds.

1997 *AIDS in Africa and the Caribbean.* Boulder, CO: Westview. This volume uses detailed ethnographic studies from Africa and the Caribbean to examine AIDS in a global and comparative context.

Brown, P. J.

1998 *Understanding and Applying Medical Anthropology.* Boston: McGraw-Hill. Medical anthropology, basic and applied.

Chambers, E.

1985 *Applied Anthropology: A Practical Guide.* Englewood Cliffs, NJ: Prentice-Hall. How to do applied anthropology, by a leader in the field.

2000 *Native Tours: The Anthropology of Travel and Tourism.* Prospect Heights, IL: Waveland. How anthropologists study the world's number one business—travel and tourism.

Eddy, E. M., and W. L. Partridge, eds.

1987 *Applied Anthropology in America,* 2nd ed. New York: Columbia University Press. Historical review of applications of anthropological knowledge in the United States.

Ferraro, G. P.

2002 *The Cultural Dimension of International Business,* 4th ed. Upper Saddle River, NJ: Prentice-Hall. How the theory and insights of cultural anthropology can influence the conduct of international business.

Gwynne, M. A.

2003 *Applied Anthropology: A Career-Oriented Approach.* Boston: Allyn and Bacon. Various applied opportunities in anthropological careers.

Helman, C.

2001 *Culture, Health, and Illness: An Introduction for Health Professionals,* 4th ed. Boston: Butterworth-Heinemann. The social context of medical practice.

Holtzman, J.

2000 *Nuer Journeys, Nuer Lives.* Boston: Allyn and Bacon. How immigrants from Sudan adapt to Minnesota's twin cities and to the American social service system.

Human Organization

The quarterly journal of the Society for Applied Anthropology. An excellent source for articles on applied anthropology and development.

Joralemon, D.

1999 *Exploring Medical Anthropology.* Boston: Allyn and Bacon. Recent introduction to a growing field.

McDonald, J. H., ed.

2002 *The Applied Anthropology Reader.* Boston: Allyn and Bacon. Recent descriptions of case experiences and approaches.

McElroy, A., and P. K. Townsend

1996 *Medical Anthropology in Ecological Perspective,* 3rd ed. Boulder, CO: Westview. This established introduction to medical anthropology shows that field's multidisciplinary roots.

Rushing, W. A.

1995 *The AIDS Epidemic: Social Dimensions of an Infectious Disease.* Boulder, CO: Westview. The sociocultural conditions that have contributed to the spread of AIDS.

Sargent, C. F., and C. B. Brettell

1996 *Gender and Health: An International Perspective.* Upper Saddle River, NJ: Prentice-Hall. How culture affects the relation among gender, health-care organization, and health policy.

Sargent, C. F., and T. J. Johnson, eds.

1996   *Medical Anthropology: A Handbook of Theory and Method,* rev. ed. Westport, CT: Praeger Press. Articles cover theoretical perspectives, medical systems, health issues, methods in medical anthropology, and issues of policy and advocacy.

Spindler, G. D., ed.

2000   *Fifty Years of Anthropology and Education, 1950-2000: A Spindler Anthology.* Mahwah, NJ: Erlbaum Associates. Survey of the field of educational anthropology by two prominent contributors, George and Louise Spindler.

Strathern, A., and P. J. Stewart

1999   *Curing and Healing: Medical Anthropology in Global Perspective.* Durham, NC: Carolina Academic Press. Cross-cultural examples of medical anthropology.

Van Willigen, J.

2002   *Applied Anthropology: An Introduction,* 3rd ed. Westport, CT: Bergin and Garvey. Excellent review of the growth of applied anthropology and its links to general anthropology.

INTERNET EXERCISES

1. Go to the website of the CILHI **(http://www.cilhi.army.mil/)** and read about what this organization does. Go to its recent press release page **(http://www.cilhi.army.mil/recentpr.htm)** and get a sense of what some of its recent activities are.

   a. What does the CILHI do?

   b. The CILHI is one of the largest employers of forensic anthropologists in the world. How are forensic anthropologists important for its mission?

   c. Go to the profiles of some of the scientific staff **(http://www.cilhi.army.mil/scientificstaff.htm)**. What kind of educational background do many of the staff members have? Where are some of the institutions they attended?

2. Go to the publication from the United States Agency for International Development (USAID) entitled "Population and the Environment: A Delicate Balance" **(http://www.usaid.gov/pop_health/pop/publications/docs/popenv.pdf)**.

   a. What are some of the major environmental threats due to population growth the world faces?

   b. What can groups like USAID do in the face of these threats?

   c. What contributions does anthropology have to offer? Should organizations like USAID employ anthropologists?

   d. What is the role of applied anthropology for environmental issues?

See Chapter 2 at your McGraw-Hill Online Learning Center for additional review and interactive exercises.

Part Two

Physical Anthropology and Archaeology

In Part 2, we'll explore physical (or biological) anthropology and archaeology, two of anthropology's four subfields. Although some physical anthropologists and even archaeologists work with living people, a common interest in the past and in change—in evolution—unites physical anthropology and archaeology. Physical anthropologists and archaeologists frequently work abroad, and in teams. In Chapter 3 we'll consider some of the ethical contexts in which physical anthropologists and archaeologists operate, along with the research methods they employ. Physical anthropology and archaeology are united by their common interest in evolution, which we'll examine from a biological perspective and as a genetic process in Chapter 4.

Evolutionary principles also are illustrated by our nearest relatives—nonhuman primates, such as monkeys and apes. Chapter 5 considers traits and trends in primate anatomy, along with primate behavior and social organization. Chapter 6 examines the evolution of the primates, from their remote origins to the last common ancestor shared by humans and apes. In Chapters 7 and 8 we turn to hominid and human evolution. In Chapter 7, we'll learn about when, where, why, and how the first members of the hominid family, which includes modern humans, originated. We'll also examine (mainly in Chapter 8) the origins of physical and behavioral modernity in *Homo sapiens*. Spanning time and space, Chapter 9 considers contemporary human biological variation, its nature and causes,

while also exposing weaknesses in traditional ideas—both scientific and popular—about race and human races. The chapters in Part 2 tend to emphasize a particular subfield, such as physical anthropology in Chapters 4 through 9 and archaeology in Chapters 10 and 11. But all the chapters in Part 2 also draw on knowledge and techniques from other subfields, including cultural anthropology.

Chapters 10 and 11 focus on what archaeologists have reconstructed about the origins of food production and the state. Food production was a major innovation in human adaptation as humans began to influence, and then control, the reproduction of plants and animals. The earliest food producers, who lived in the Middle East, became the world's first farmers and herders. The changes triggered by food production, including poplulation growth and increasing economic and social complexity, paved the way for the first states or civilizations. These were literate societies with central governments. States featured highly evolved class structures, authority systems, and patterns of exploitation unlike anything seen previously in human evolution. Archaeologists and physical anthropologists have investigated the origins and consequences of food production and state formation in both the Eastern Hemisphere (e.g., the ancient Middle East) and the Western Hemisphere (e.g., Mexico, Peru, and other parts of the Americas). Part 2 explores this panorama of origins and change—biological and cultural—across millions of years and thousands of miles.

3

ETHICS AND METHODS IN PHYSICAL ANTHROPOLOGY AND ARCHAEOLOGY

Overview

Because science exists in society, and in the context of law and ethics, anthropologists can't study things simply because they have potential scientific value. Anthropologists have obligations to the field of anthropology, to the wider society, and to the human species, other species, and the environment. The anthropologist's most fundamental ethical obligation is to the people, species, and materials he or she studies.

Physical anthropologists and archaeologists pursue diverse research topics, using varied methods and often working together. At an archaeological site, a physical anthropologist may complement the picture of ancient life by examining skeletons to reconstruct their physical traits, health status, and diet. Within physical anthropology, studies of nonhuman primates suggest hypotheses about behavior that humans do or do not share with our nearest relatives and with our hominid ancestors. Various methods have been used to show that humans are unusually social, compared with nonhuman primates.

Physical anthropologists also study the biology of bone—its genetics; cell structure; growth, development, and decay; and patterns of movement. Paleopathologists examine disease and injury in skeletons from archaeological sites. Molecular anthropology uses genetic analysis (of DNA sequences) to assess evolutionary relationships among ancient and contemporary populations and among species.

Archaeologists typically work in teams and across time and space. Like paleoanthropologists and paleontologists, they combine both local (excavation) and regional (systematic survey) perspectives. Sites are excavated because they are in danger of being destroyed or because they address specific research interests.

Anthropologists and paleontologists use stratigraphy and radiometric techniques to date fossils. Carbon-14 (^{14}C) dating is most effective with remains less than 40,000 years old. Potassium-argon (K/A) dating can be used for fossils older than 500,000 years.

Museums and Tribes: A Tricky Truce

NEW YORK TIMES NEWS BRIEF

by Stephen Kinzer

December 24, 2000

In this 1999 photo, Dr. Francis McManamon, chief archaeologist of the National Park Service and chief consulting archaeologist for the Department of the Interior, announces his readiness to launch the nondestructive scientific study of Kennewick Man.

When bones and artifacts are discovered, who should own them? Should they belong to the owner of the land where they are found, to the discoverer, to some public entity, or to people who claim rights to that land from time immemorial? The Native American Graves Protection and Repatriation Act (NAGPRA) gives ownership of Native American physical and archaeological remains to Indians. NAGPRA requires museums to return remains and artifacts to any tribe that requests them and that can prove a "cultural affiliation" with the tribe from which they came. The 1996 discovery in Washington state of a skeleton dubbed "Kennewick Man" eventually led to a legal case between anthropologists and five Indian tribes with ancestral homelands in the area where Kennewick Man was found. The anthropologists wanted to conduct a thorough study of the 9,000-year-old fossil to see what its anatomy and DNA might tell us about the early settlement of the Western Hemisphere. The Umatilla Indians and their allies in four other Indian Nations believe they have always occupied the region where the skeleton was found. In their view, Kennewick Man was an ancestor, whom they want to rebury with dignity and without contamination from scientific testing. On August 30, 2002 U.S. Magistrate Judge John Jelderks ruled that the Kennewick remains could be subjected to scientific study.

. . . The Native American Graves Protection and Repatriation Act, was signed by President George [H. W.] Bush in November 1990 after years of discussion among scientists, museum curators and Indian groups. It seeks to reconcile two profoundly different value systems, one based on the primacy of reason and science and the other revolving around spiritual and religious values.

In the decade since the law was passed, it has had a profound effect on museums and the philosophy on which they are based. At the same time, it has had incalculable emotional and social impact on Indian tribes across the country that have recovered long-lost artifacts, many of which have enormous spiritual significance, as well as the remains of thousands of their ancestors.

When the law was first enacted, some Indian leaders feared that they were about to begin a period of bitter clashes with defiant museum curators. Some curators feared that their collections would be gutted as they were forced to return huge numbers of artifacts. Ten years later, however, both sides agree that their fears were exaggerated, and many say the law has actually increased understanding between tribes and museum administrators . . .

There are still some areas of conflict, especially over efforts by some tribes to recover remains that are many thousands of years old and that scientists say should be studied for vital clues about the history of human migration to the American continent. But many curators have come to agree that Indians have a right to recover their sacred artifacts and the bones of those they can legitimately claim as ancestors . . .

The 1990 law affects every museum and federal agency that owns "Native American human remains and associated funerary objects" as well as "unassociated funerary objects, sacred objects or objects of cultural patrimony." It requires each museum and agency to compile an inventory of its holdings, identify them by tribal origin and notify existing tribes of objects that appear to come from that tribe's tradition.

Under the law, museums must return all remains and artifacts to any tribe that requests them and that can prove a "cultural affiliation" with the tribe from which they came . . .

Some Indian leaders maintain that all objects from all non-European cultures in North America belong in the hands of Indians, regardless of whether those alive today can claim kinship with the cultures that produced the objects. The 1990 law, however, rejects that so-called "pan-Indian" argument. It requires that the claimant tribe prove it is a "lineal descendant" of the tribe from which the artifacts or remains came.

As a result of this provision, the law has served some tribes better than others. Southwestern tribes like the Hopi and Navajo, for example, have maintained cultural continuity over centuries and therefore have strong claims to objects in museum collections. Other tribes, including many in the Eastern United States that were decimated by successive waves of European settlement, have more trouble proving their descent from tribes that existed long ago . . .

One apparently unintended consequence of the law has been that Indian tribes have laid claim to several sets of very old human remains that have been found in the United States since the mid-1990's. Indians claim these as remains of their ancestors, since their religious tradition tells them that they were always present on the North American continent. Many scientists say that claim is dubious at best, and complain that potentially thrilling discoveries about the early peopling of the Americas may never be made if they do not have the chance to study the remains they unearth.

This issue has come into public view largely because of an intensifying legal controversy over the skeleton of a man, apparently about 9,000 years old, that was found in 1996 in Kennewick, Washington.

Five Indian tribes in the Northwest have collectively claimed Kennewick Man as an ancestor and want to rebury his remains. Scientists are protesting. They say the skeleton has features suggesting that it may be of Japanese or Polynesian origin, and that in any case no tribe or ethnic group in the world can trace its ancestry back 9,000 years. In September [2000], Interior Secretary Bruce Babbit ruled in favor of the tribes, saying he believed they were "culturally affiliated" with the Kennewick skeleton. A group of anthropologists, however, has filed a lawsuit seeking to block the reburial . . .

Despite this debate and a handful of others like it, many scientists, museum curators and tribal leaders, more than a few of whom had expected to be locked in bitter battles over ownership of valuable artifacts, say the opposite has happened . . .

"We have a collection of 800,000 objects, so in a quantitative sense the law has had a very small impact," said Rick West [director of the Smithsonian Institute's Museum of the American Indian], who is a Cheyenne Indian. "But from a qualitative standpoint I do think it has an impact, and that impact is absolutely positive.

"As institutions of culture, museums that house these materials have a vital interest in buttressing those cultures and supporting them into the future," Mr. West said. "To the extent that we believe maintenance of these cultures is important, and I think it is, museums have an obligation to support that cultural diversity . . ."

For current information on Kennewick Man see the OLC Internet Exercises

/kottak

Source: Excerpted from Stephen Kinzer, "Museums and Tribes: A Tricky Truce," *New York Times*, December 24, 2000, late edition, final, section 2, p. 1, column 1; www.nytimes.com.

Anthropologists could draw on various methods and theories to study and interpret Kennewick Man. Analysis of anatomy and DNA might suggest connections with similarly dated fossils in Asia or elsewhere in North or South America. (**Fossils** are remains [e.g., bones, teeth, skulls], traces, or impressions [e.g., footprints] of ancient life.) Skull form, teeth, and bones might reveal something about diet. The skeleton might be marked by evidence of fractures or disease. Anthropological theory recognizes that change, in culture and biology, is constant and ongoing. Given biological and cultural evolution, we would expect significant differences in the anatomy and artifacts of people living in the Pacific Northwest now versus people who lived 9,000 years ago. Anthropological theory and methods could be applied productively in the scientific study of Kennewick Man and similarly dated fossils found in North and South America. But science exists in society, and in the context of law and ethics. Anthropologists can't study things simply because they happen to be interesting or of value to science. Anthropologists are increasingly aware of the ethical and legal contexts in which their work proceeds. This chapter examines ethics and methods in physical anthropology and archaeology.

Ethics

Anthropologists frequently do research outside their nations of origin. As in the Guatemalan forensic anthropology study discussed in Chapter 2, physical anthropologists and archaeologists often work as members of international teams. These teams include researchers from several countries, including the *host country*—the place (e.g., Guatemala) where the research takes place. In **paleoanthropology** (a.k.a. *human paleontology*)— the study of human evolution through the fossil record—physical anthropologists and archaeologists often work together. The physical anthropologists are more interested in the bones; the archaeologists, in the artifacts. But their work may proceed jointly, as they try to infer the relation between the physical and cultural features of the remains they are examining. Much of our knowledge of early human evolution comes from Africa, where international collaboration is common.

International work exposes physical anthropologists and archaeologists to varying national and cultural procedures, value systems, and ethical and legal codes. In such contexts, the American Anthropological Association (AAA) advises anthropologists to be guided by its Code of Ethics. How do specific guidelines in the AAA Code of Ethics, which was discussed in Chapter 2, apply to physical anthropology and archaeology? To gain permission and collaboration in the host country, anthropologists need to inform officials and colleagues there about the purpose, funding, and likely results, products, and impacts of their research. They need to negotiate the matter of where the materials produced by the research will be analyzed and stored—in the host country or in the anthropologists' country—and for how long. To whom do research materials, such as bones, artifacts, and blood samples, belong? What kinds of restrictions will apply to their use?

It's crucial for anthropologists to establish and maintain proper relations between themselves as guests and the host nations, regions, and communities where they work. Remember that the anthropologist's primary ethical obliga-

Scientists designing zoo displays of primates (and other animals) need to pay special attention to ethical issues. Living conditions should be humane, ideally suggesting a natural setting. Shown here is Opening Day at the Henry Doorly Zoo in Omaha, Nebraska, whose Lied Jungle is the largest tropical rain forest exhibit in a North American zoo. What animals live in tropical forests?

tion is to the people, species, and materials he or she studies. Although nonhuman primates can't give informed consent, primatologists still must take steps to ensure that their research doesn't endanger the animals. Either government agencies or nongovernmental organizations (NGOs) may be entrusted with protecting primates. If this is the case, the anthropologist will need their permission and informed consent to conduct research.

With living humans, informed consent is a necessity—for example, in obtaining biological samples, such as blood or urine. The research subjects must be told how the samples will be collected, used, and identified, and about the potential costs and benefits to them. Informed consent is needed from anyone providing data or information, owning materials being studied, or otherwise having an interest that might be affected by the research.

The AAA Code says that anthropologists should not exploit individuals, groups, animals, or cultural or biological materials. They should recognize their debt to the people with whom they work and should reciprocate in appropriate ways. For example, it is highly appropriate for North

American anthropologists working in another country to (1) include host country colleagues in their research planning and requests for funding, (2) establish truly collaborative relationships with those colleagues and their institutions before, during, and after field work, (3) include host country colleagues in dissemination, including publication, of the research results, and (4) ensure that something is "given back" to host country colleagues. For example, research equipment and technology are allowed to remain in the host country. Or funding is provided for host country colleagues to do research, attend international meetings, or visit foreign institutions—especially those where their international collaborators work.

Physical anthropologists and archaeologists, more often than cultural anthropologists, work as members of teams. Teams include host country collaborators; typically, they also include students—graduate and undergraduate. Training students in the value of long-term collaboration is one way of preserving opportunities for future field workers to follow current researchers to the field.

Methods

There are all sorts of specialized research interests, topics, and methods within both physical anthropology and archaeology. (Given space limitations only some of them can be covered here.) Remember that physical anthropologists and archaeologists often collaborate. In the study of human evolution, the physical anthropologists focus on the fossil remains—and what they tell us about ancient human biology. The archaeologists focus on the artifacts—and what they tell us about past cultures. Often their work proceeds jointly as they try to infer the relation between the physical features and cultural features of the remains they are examining. What are some of the methods and techniques used by physical anthropologists and archaeologists?

MULTIDISCIPLINARY APPROACHES

Scientists from diverse fields, for example, soil science and **paleontology** (the study of ancient life through the fossil record), using varied techniques, collaborate with physical anthropologists and archaeologists in the study of sites where fos-

sils and/or artifacts have been found. **Palynology,** the study of ancient plants through pollen samples taken from such sites, is used to determine a site's environment at the time of occupation. Physical anthropologists and archaeologists turn to physicists and chemists for help with dating techniques. Physical anthropologists representing a subspeciality known as *bioarchaeology* may complement the picture of ancient life at a particular site by examining skeletons to reconstruct their physical traits, health status, and diet (Larson 2000). Evidence for social status may endure in hard materials—bones, jewels, buildings—through the ages. During life, bone growth and stature are influenced by diet. Genetic differences aside, taller people are often that way because they eat better than shorter people do. Differences in the stature and chemical (e.g., strontium) composition of groups of bones at a site may help distinguish privileged nobles from less fortunate commoners. To reconstruct ancient biology and ways of life, physical anthropologists, archaeologists, and their collaborators analyze the remains of humans, plants, and animals, as well as such artifacts (manufactured items) as ceramics, tiles, casts, and metals.

Physical anthropologists and archaeologists draw on low-tech as well as high-tech tools and methods. Small hand-held tools are used at excavation sites, where photos, maps, drawings, and measurements record where every find stands in relation to the site as a whole. Data are entered in field notebooks and computers.

Illustrating more sophisticated technology, sites, such a system of ancient canals, may be located and defined from the air. Aerial photos (taken from airplanes) and satellite images are forms of **remote sensing** used in site location. For example, ancient buried footpaths visible not to the naked eye but only in satellite imagery have been studied in Costa Rica by University of Colorado and National Aeronautics and Space Administration (NASA) archaeologists (Scott 2002). Up to six feet of volcanic ash, sediment, and vegetation had covered and obscured the footpaths. Images of the paths, some dating to 2,500 years ago, were first made in 1984 by a NASA aircraft using instruments that could "see" in the electromagnetic spectrum invisible to humans. In 2001 a commercial satellite took additional images of the buried footpaths, which showed up as thin red lines, reflecting the dense vegetation growing

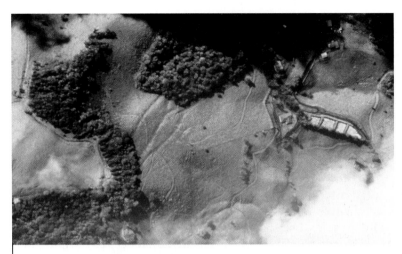

Costa Rican footpaths as revealed from space. Footpaths up to 2,500 years old were visible in satellite imagery but not to the naked eye. The paths had been buried by volcanic ash, sediment, and vegetation. What other archeological features might be visible from space?

over them. The footpaths were dated on the basis of the stratigraphy (layers of geological deposits) of the Arenal volcano, which has erupted 10 times in the last 4,000 years.

Village life was established around Arenal some 4,000 years ago, and endured through the Spanish Conquest around 1500. Villagers periodically fled volcanic eruptions, returning when it was safe to resume farming of corn and beans in the nutrient-rich volcanic soil. According to team leader Payson Sheets of the University of Colorado, "they inhabited a very large region and seemed to avoid conflict, conquest and serious disease . . . They led comfortable lives, relying on an abundance of natural resources and a stable culture" (quoted in Scott 2002).

Excavation of the footpaths uncovered stone tools, pottery, and floors of ancient houses. The paths once linked a cemetery to a spring and quarries where construction stone was mined. A primary goal of a 2002 field team led by Sheets was to understand ancient activities at the cemetery, where bodies were laid to rest in stone coffins. Funerary ceramics and meal vessels, plus cooking stones, indicate that people camped, cooked, and feasted at the cemetery for long time periods (Scott 2002).

Anthropologists work with geologists, geographers, and other scientists in using satellite images to find not just ancient footpaths, roads, canals, and irrigation systems but also patterns and sites of, say, flooding or deforestation, which can then be investigated on the ground. Anthropologists have used satellite imagery to identify, and then investigate on the ground, regions where deforestation is especially severe and where people and biodiversity, including non-human primates, may be at risk (Green and Sussman 1990; Kottak, Gezon, and Green 1994; Kottak 1999).

PRIMATOLOGY

Primatologists are like ethnographers in their close observation of a group of primates, in this case, non-human. Primate behavior has been observed in zoos (e.g., de Waal 1998) and through experimentation (e.g., Harlow 1966), but the most significant studies have been done in natural settings, among free-ranging apes, monkeys, and lemurs. You, as an anthropology student, may be given an assignment to observe primates in zoos. Try to avoid nocturnal primates, which probably will be sleeping when you visit the zoo, unless you visit the Hall of Night Animals at New York's Bronx Zoo—or a similar zoo habitat in which animals, through lighting, are fooled into switching night and day. Some primatologists have studied free-ranging nocturnal primates, such as tarsiers, owl monkeys, and the aye-aye of Madagascar. But most primates are active during the day (*diurnal*), as are humans, and are easier to study for that reason. It's also easier for humans to study terrestrial than arboreal species. In Madagascar I've raced down hills following lemurs moving rapidly through the trees. As a college student I made the mistake of studying the slow loris in New York's Central Park Zoo. That loris, a prosimian, or lemur-like animal, catches insects by staying still, then suddenly snaring bugs that land nearby. Unless there are insects in the cage, observing the slow loris (like observing the South American sloth, which is *not* a primate) is only slightly more interesting than watching an egg.

Since the 1950s, when primatologists began their shift from zoos to natural settings, numerous studies have been done of apes (chimps, gorillas, orangutans, and gibbons), monkeys (e.g., baboons,

This slow loris, a nocturnal primate, grasps a bug. What problems might you encounter in studying such an animal?

macaques), and lemurs (e.g., Madagascar's indrii, sifaka, and ring-tailed lemurs). *Arboreal* primates (those which spend most of their time in the trees— e.g., howler monkeys and gibbons) may be difficult to see and follow, but they typically make a lot of noise. Their communication systems, including howls and calls, can be studied and teach us about how primates communicate. Studies of primate social systems and behavior, including their mating patterns, infant care, and patterns of contact and dispersal, suggest hypotheses about behavior that humans do or do not share with our nearest relatives—and also with our hominid ancestors.

Like ethnographers, primatologists have to establish rapport (a "friendly" working relationship) with the individuals they are studying. Since language can't be used with nonhuman primates, rapport involves gradual habituation; the animals have to get used to the researcher. Animals must be identified and observed over time. Often a fledgling primatologist will join a longitudinal team that has been observing a group of monkeys or apes for years, even decades. Identification of the animals and close attention to their behavior and interactions are necessary to understand primate behavior and social organization. Particular animals may be followed for set periods of time—with each episode of behavior and interaction systematically recorded on film or in a notebook. Or the researcher can focus on certain scenes, for example, a particular tree or

water source where primates congregate at particular times. Or individuals and/or places can be chosen randomly for study at particular times.

Although *Homo sapiens,* unlike most other primates, is neither a "threatened" nor an "endangered" species, many humans live in areas of poverty and overpopulation. The pressure of human activities on scarce resources, such as forested lands, creates threats for primates and animals sharing their habitat. People hunt or buy primates for food and for their assumed medicinal properties. People also clear land from, and build roads through, forested habitats where primates once thrived. Deforestation is a major threat to primates. Many cultural anthropologists work with people whose activities pose threats to primates. Working in the same areas, primatologists are experts on the precise habitat, needs, and behavior patterns of the nonhuman primates. Working together and with conservation groups and governments, cultural and physical anthropologists can apply their knowledge in devising plans to conserve forests and their animal dwellers, while also allowing people to meet their basic needs.

Interpret the World
Atlas Map 3

Map 3 in your atlas shows annual change in forest cover between 1990 and 1995. Name two countries where the forest cover has stayed the same or increased. We frequently hear about threats to Brazil's Amazon rainforest, but is Brazil one of the countries in which forests are retreating most rapidly? On what continent do you see deforestation as posing the greatest threat? Is it likely that this threat is related to high rates of population increase, as discussed in Chapter 2, and shown on Map 2 in your atlas?

ANTHROPOMETRY

Physical anthropologists use various techniques to study nutrition, growth, and development. **Anthropometry** is the measurement of human body parts and dimensions, including skeletal parts (*osteometry*). Anthropometry is done on living people as well as on skeletal remains from sites. Body mass and composition provide measures of nutritional status in living people. Body mass is calculated from height and weight. The *body mass index* (kg/m^2) is the ratio of weight in kilograms divided by height in meters squared. An adult body mass above 30 is considered at risk of overweight, while one below 18 is at risk of underweight or malnutrition. To assess body composition, subcutaneous (below the surface) fat is estimated from skin fold thickness (measured with calipers) and body circumference. These values are compared to anthropometric standards (Frisancho 1990). For a given gender and age group, values above the 85th percentile are associated with excess fat, and values below the 15th percentile are associated with leanness.

Joe Zias, a curator at Rockefeller Museum, measures an ancient skull. Anthropometry is done on skeletal remains from sites as well as on living people. Has anyone ever done anthropometry on you?

A machine called a *calorimeter* is used to measure resting metabolic rates, based on the amount of oxygen consumed and carbon dioxide produced when an individual rests for 30 minutes. The instrument calculates the body's minimum energy needs (in calories) at rest. Based on daily calories consumed, used at rest, and used in activities, scientists can determine whether conditions favor weight gain or loss. Measurement of the resting metabolic rate also reveals the extent to which weight gains or losses may reflect metabolism versus eating patterns.

Knowledge about how contemporary humans adapt (e.g., to heat and cold) and use energy (e.g., in metabolism) can be used to understand human evolution. For example, during hominid evolution brain size has increased. In contemporary humans, the brain represents just 5 percent of body weight, yet brain activity consumes 20 percent of the resting metabolic rate. During human evolution, the adaptive advantages of having a large brain must have outweighed the high cost in energy. However, increased activity would have been necessary to feed growing human bodies and brains.

Understanding Ourselves Humans are really social compared with our primate relatives. Even chimps, our closest relatives, don't cooperate nearly to the extent that we do. Apparently apes aren't wired for cooperation and altruism as we are (see "Interesting Issues," p. 68). We'll never know all the causes of human sociality, but some are based in human anatomy—from the brain to the pelvis. Consider the female pelvis, whose evolution has been guided by these facts: (1) Humans walk upright, (2) babies are born with big brains, and (3) babies have to negotiate a complicated birth canal during childbirth.

There are striking and significant contrasts between primates and humans in anatomy and in the birthing process. Nonhuman primates aren't bipedal; compared with humans, they have smaller brains, simpler birth canals, and more independent infants. As they move through the birth canal, human babies must make several turns, so that their heads and shoulders, the two body parts with the largest dimensions, are consistently aligned with the widest parts of the birth canal. Monkeys and apes don't have this problem.

Birthing assistance is almost universal in human societies. Shown here, an Uzbeki midwife uses a traditional instrument to listen to a baby's heartbeat. Locate Uzbekistan (Central Asia) in your atlas.

Unlike those of humans, primate birth canals have a constant shape.

Also, the primate infant emerges facing forward. The mother can grasp it, even pull it straight to her nipple. Human babies are born facing backward, away from the mother, and so she has trouble assisting in the birth. The presence of someone else (e.g., a midwife) to help with delivery reduces the mortality risk for human infants and their mothers.

Birthing assistance is almost universal among human societies. According to Karen Rosenberg and Wenda Trevathan (2001), our wish to have supportive, familiar people around at childbirth goes way back. On the basis of pelvic openings, and estimated infant skull sizes, of extinct hominids, Rosenberg and Trevathan (2001) conclude that such assistance may date back millions of years. Nonhuman primate mothers seek seclusion when they give birth, and act as their own midwives in the birthing process. Not so humans—social as ever. Midwives, obstetricians, baby showers—all are expressions of human sociality with deep evolutionary roots.

BONE BIOLOGY

Central to physical anthropology is **bone biology** (or skeletal biology)—the study of bone as a biological tissue, including its genetics; cell structure;

growth, development, and decay; and patterns of movement (*biomechanics*) (Katzenberg and Saunders, eds. 2000). Within bone biology, *osteology* is the study of skeletal variation and its biological and social causes. Osteologists study such variables as stature in living and ancient populations (White and Folkens 2000). The interpretation of fossil remains relies on understanding the structure and function of the skeleton. **Paleopathology** is the study of disease and injury in skeletons from archaeological sites. Some forms of cancer leave evidence in the bone. Breast cancer, for example, may spread (metastasize) skeletally, leaving holes or lesions in bones and skull. Certain infectious diseases (e.g., syphilis and tuberculosis) also mark bone, as do injuries and nutritional deficiencies (e.g., rickets, a vitamin D deficiency that deforms the bones).

In forensic anthropology, as discussed in Chapter 2, physical anthropologists work in a legal context, assisting coroners, medical examiners, and law enforcement agencies in recovering, analyzing, and identifying human remains and determining the cause of death (Nafte 2000; Prag and Neave 1997). For example, when unknown skeletal remains are found, the police and the Delaware Medical Examiner's Office call on University of Delaware physical anthropologist Karen Rosenberg to help identify the body. By examining the bones, Rosenberg can determine characteristics, such as the height, age, and sex of the person. She notes that "the police authorities always ask for the race of an unidentified person. But racial categories are, in part, culturally defined and in any case are not closed biological 'types.' Recently I identified a skeleton as possibly being Caucasian, then on subsequent examinations thought he might be African American. In actuality, when the identification was made, he turned out to be Hispanic" (Rosenberg, quoted in Moncure 1998).

MOLECULAR ANTHROPOLOGY

Molecular anthropology uses genetic analysis (of DNA sequences) to assess evolutionary links. Through molecular comparison, evolutionary

Using a novel method of scanning neural activity in people playing games, scientists have discovered that cooperation triggers pleasure in the brain. Anthropologist James Rilling and five other scientists monitored brain activity in young women playing a laboratory game called Prisoner's Dilemma. Players select greedy or cooperative strategies as they pursue financial gain. The researchers found that the choice to cooperate stimulated areas of the brain associated with pleasure and reward-seeking behavior—the same areas that respond to desserts, pictures of pretty faces, money, and cocaine (Rilling et al. 2002; Angier 2002). According to coauthor Gregory S. Berns, "In some ways, it says that we're wired to cooperate with each other" (quoted in Angier 2002).

The researchers studied 36 women age 20 to 60. Why women? Some previous studies had found male–male pairs to be more cooperative than female–female pairs, and others had found the opposite. Rilling and his colleagues didn't want to mix more cooperative and less cooperative pairs, and so they restricted their sample to one gender to control for possible differences in tendencies toward cooperation. The choice to use women rather than men was an arbitrary one.

In the experiment two women would meet each other briefly ahead of time. One was then placed in the scanner, while the other remained outside the scanning room. The two interacted by computer, playing about 20 rounds of the game. In every round, each player pressed a button to indicate whether she would "cooperate" or "defect." Her answer would be shown on-screen to the other player. Money was awarded after each round. When one player defected and the other cooperated, the defector earned $3, and the cooperator earned nothing. When both cooperated, each earned $2. If both defected, each earned $1. Mutual cooperation from start to finish was a more profitable strategy, at $40 a woman, than complete mutual defection, which yielded only $20 to each woman.

If one woman got greedy, she took the risk that the cooperative strategy might fall apart and that both players would lose money as a result. Most of the time, the women cooperated. Even occasional defections weren't always fatal to an alliance, although the woman who had been "betrayed' once might be suspicious after that. Because of occasional defections, the average per-experiment take for the participants was in the range of $30.

The scans showed that two broad areas of the brain were activated by cooperation. Both areas are rich in neurons that respond to dopamine, a brain chemical that plays a well-known role in addictive behaviors. One is the anteroventral striatum in the midbrain, just above the spinal cord. Experiments have shown that when electrodes are placed in this area, rats will repeatedly press a bar to stimulate the electrodes. They apparently receive such pleasurable feedback that they will starve to death rather than stop pressing the bar (Angier 2002).

Another brain region activated during cooperation was the orbitofrontal cortex, just above the eyes. Besides being part of the reward-processing system, this area is involved in impulse control. According to Rilling, "Every round, you're confronted with the possibility of getting an extra dollar by defecting. The choice to cooperate requires impulse control" (quoted in Angier 2002).

In some cases, the woman in the scanner played a computer and knew her partner was a machine. In other tests, women played a computer but thought it was a human. The reward circuitry of the women was considerably less responsive when they knew they were playing against a computer. The thought of a human bond, not mere monetary gain, was the source of contentment. Also, the women were asked afterward to summarize their feelings during the games. They often described feeling good when they cooperated and expressed feelings of camaraderie toward their playing partners.

Assuming the urge to cooperate is to some extent innate among humans, and is reinforced by our neural circuitry, why did it arise? Anthropologists generally assume that it took teamwork and altrism for our ancestors to hunt large game, share food, and engage in other social activities, including raising children. A neural tendency to cooperate and to share would have conferred a survival advantage on our ancestors. Instead of "Why can't we all get along," these researchers were exploring why we get along so well.

SOURCE: Information from Angier 2002; Rilling et al. 2002; and Rilling, personal communication.

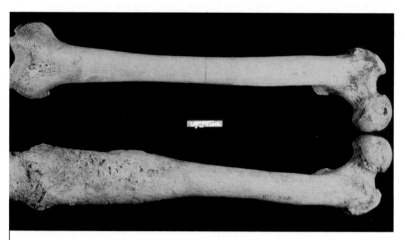

Two adult femora. The top one is normal in size and shape. The bottom one shows swelling and a ragged surface resulting from the chronic bacterial infection called osteomyelitis. These thigh bones are from the Mississippian period Hazel site in Arkansas.

related people) defined by a specific cluster of genetic traits that occur together. Native Americans have four major haplogroups, which are also linked to East Asia. Among the many sorts of questions that molecular anthropology may answer: How can DNA sequences be used to trace migration routes during the peopling of North America and the Pacific? Are there tribal-specific genetic markers among Native Americans or Pacific Islanders? Which genes influence susceptibility to which diseases? For nonhuman primates, molecular anthropologists use DNA sequences to identify parentage, and to calculate kinship and degree of inbreeding within primate colonies. We'll see later that molecular anthropologists also use "genetic clocks" to estimate divergence time (date of most recent common ancestry) among species (e.g., humans, chimps, and gorillas—5 million to 8 million years ago) and of various human groups (e.g., Neandertals and modern humans).

PALEOANTHROPOLOGY

Paleoanthropologists study early hominids through fossil remains. Typically, a team composed of scientists, students, and local workers, representing diverse backgrounds and academic fields, participates in a paleoanthropological study. Such teams may include physical anthropologists, archaeologists, paleontologists, geologists, palynologists, paleoecologists, physicists, and chemists. Their common goal is to date and reconstruct the structure, behavior, and ecology of early hominids. The geologists and paleontologists may be called in during early surveying—perhaps using remote sensing—to locate potential early hominid sites. Paleontologists help locate fossil beds containing remains of animals that can be dated and that are known to have coexisted with hominids at various time periods. Good preservation of faunal remains may suggest that hominid fossils have survived as well. Sometimes it's impossible to date the hominid fossils and artifacts found at a given site by using the most accurate and direct (radiometric) methods. In this

distance among living species, along with dates of most recent common ancestry, can be estimated. Molecular studies also have been used to assess and date the origins of modern humans and to examine their relation to extinct human groups such as the Neandertals, which thrived in Europe between 130,000 and 30,000 years ago. The scientists who successfully filed suit to examine Kennewick Man, as discussed at the beginning of this chapter, wished to compare his DNA with that of more recent and living Native Americans, and with that of Asians and Pacific Islanders, to measure evolutionary links and distances.

In 1997, ancient DNA was extracted from a Neandertal bone originally found in Germany's Neander Valley in 1856. This was the first time the DNA of a premodern human had been recovered. This DNA, from an upper arm bone (humerus), was compared with the DNA of modern humans. There were 27 differences between the Neandertal DNA and modern DNA; by contrast, samples of modern DNA show only 5 to 8 differences among the samples.

Molecular anthropologists examine relationships among ancient and contemporary populations and among species. It's well established, for example, that humans and chimpanzees have more than 98 percent of their DNA in common. Molecular anthropologists also reconstruct waves and patterns of migration and settlement. A *haplogroup* is a biological lineage (a large group of

case, comparison of the faunal remains at that site with similar, but more securely dated, fauna at another site may suggest a date for those animal fossils and the hominids and artifacts associated with them.

Once potential sites have been identified, more intensive surveying begins. Archaeologists take over and search for hominid traces—bones or tools. Only hominids work rock to make tools and move rock fragments over long distances. Some early hominid sites are strewn with thousands of tools. If a site is shown to be a hominid site, much more concentrated work begins. Financial support may come from private donations and government agencies. The research project usually is headed by an archaeologist or a physical anthropologist. The field crew will continue to survey and map the area and start searching carefully for bones and artifacts eroding out of the soil. Also, they will take pollen and soil samples for ecological analysis and rock samples for use in various dating techniques. Analysis is done in laboratories, where specimens are cleaned, sorted, labeled, and identified.

Consideration of the animal habitats suggested by the site (e.g., forest, woodland, or open country) will assist the reconstruction of the paleoecological settings in which early hominids lived. Pollen samples help reveal diet. Sediments and other geological samples will suggest climatic conditions at the time of deposition. Sometimes fossils are embedded in rock, from which they must be extracted carefully. Once recovered and cleaned, fossils may be made into casts to permit wider study.

Survey and Excavation

Archaeologists and paleoanthropologists typically work in teams and across time and space. Typically, archaeologists, paleoanthropologists, and paleontologists combine both local (excavation) and regional (systematic survey) perspectives. They recognize that sites may not be discrete and isolated, but parts of larger social systems. Let's examine some of the main techniques that anthropologists use to study patterns of behavior in ancient societies, based on their material remains. Archaeologists recover remains from a series of contexts, such as pits, sites, and regions. The archaeologist also integrates data about different social units of the past, such as the household, the village, and the regional system.

SYSTEMATIC SURVEY

Archaeologists and paleoanthropologists have two basic fieldwork strategies: systematic survey and excavation. **Systematic survey** provides a regional perspective by gathering information on settlement patterns over a large area. *Settlement pattern* refers to the distribution of sites within a particular region. Regional surveys reconstruct settlement patterns by addressing several questions: Where were sites located? How big were they? What kinds of buildings did they have? How old are the sites? Ideally, a systematic survey involves walking over the entire survey area and recording the location and size of all sites. From artifacts found on the surface, the surveyor estimates when each site was occupied. A full-coverage survey isn't always possible. The ground cover may be impenetrable (e.g., thick jungle), or certain parts of the survey area may be inaccessible. Permission to survey may be denied by landowners. Surveyors may have to rely on remote sensing to help locate and map sites.

With regional data, scientists can address many questions about the prehistoric communities that lived in a given area. Archaeologists use settlement pattern information to make population estimates and to assess levels of social complexity. Among hunter-gatherers and simple farmers, there are generally low numbers of people living in small camp sites or hamlets with little variation in the architecture. Such sites are scattered fairly evenly across the landscape. With increasing social complexity, the settlement patterns become more elaborate. Population levels rise. Such social factors as trade and warfare have played a more important role in determining the location of sites (on hilltops, waterways, trade routes). In complex societies, a settlement hierarchy of sites emerges. Certain sites are larger, with greater architectural differentiation, than others. Large sites with specialized architecture (elite residences, temples, administrative buildings, meeting places) are generally interpreted as regional centers that exerted control over the smaller sites with less architectural differentiation.

See the OLC
Internet
Exercises

mhhe
com
/kottak

EXCAVATION

Paleontologists, paleoanthropologists, and archaeologists also gather information about the past by excavating sites. During an **excavation,** scientists recover remains by digging through the cultural and natural stratigraphy—the layers of deposits that make up a site. These layers or strata are used to establish the relative time order of the materials encountered during the dig. This relative chronology is based on the principle of *superposition*: In an undisturbed sequence of strata, the oldest layer is on the bottom. Each successive layer above is younger than the one below. Thus, artifacts and fossils from lower strata are older than those recovered from higher strata in the same deposit. This relative time ordering of material remains lies at the heart of archaeological, paleoanthropological, and paleontological research.

The archaeological and fossil records are so rich, and excavation is so labor-intensive and expensive, that nobody digs a site without a good reason. Sites are excavated because they are endangered, or because they answer specific research questions. Cultural resource management (CRM), as discussed in Chapter 2, focuses on managing the preservation of archaeological sites that are threatened by modern development. Many countries require archaeological impact studies before construction can take place. If a site is at risk and the development cannot be stopped, CRM archaeologists are called in to salvage what information they can from the site. Another reason a site may be chosen for excavation is that it is well suited to answer specific research questions. For example, an archaeologist studying the origins of agriculture wouldn't want to excavate a large, fortified hilltop city with a series of buildings dating to a period well after the first appearance of farming communities. Rather, he or she would look for a small hamlet-size site located on or near good farmland and near a water source. Such a site would have evidence of an early occupation dating to the period when farming communities first appeared in that region.

Before a site is excavated, it is mapped and surface collected so that the researchers can make an informed decision about where exactly to dig. The collecting of surface materials at a given site is similar to what is done over a much larger area in a regional survey. A grid is drawn to represent and subdivide the site. Then collection units, which are equal-size sections of the grid, are marked off on the actual site. This grid enables the researchers to record the exact location of any artifact, fossil, or feature found at the site. By examining all the materials on the surface of the site, archaeologists can direct their excavations toward the areas of the site that are most likely to yield information that will address their research interests. Once an area is selected, digging begins, and the location of every artifact or feature is recorded in three dimensions.

Digging may be done according to arbitrary levels. Thus, starting from the surface, consistent amounts of soil (usually 10 or 20 centimeters) are systematically removed from the excavation unit. This technique of excavation is a quick way of digging, since everything within a certain depth is removed at once. This kind of excavation usually is done in test pits, which are used to determine how deep the deposits of a site go and to establish a rough chronology for that site.

A more labor-intensive and refined way of excavating is to dig through the stratigraphy one layer at a time. The strata, which are separated by differences in color and texture, are studied one by one. This technique provides more information about the context of the artifacts, fossils, or features because the scientist works more slowly and in meaningful layers. A given 10 centimeter level may include within it a series of successive house floors, each with artifacts. If this deposit is excavated according to arbitrary levels, all the artifacts are mixed together. But if it is excavated according to the natural stratigraphy, with each house floor excavated separately, the resulting picture is much more detailed. The procedure here is for the archaeologist to remove and bag all the artifacts from each house floor before proceeding to the level below that one.

Any excavation recovers varied material remains, such as ceramics, stone artifacts (lithics), human and animal bones, and plant remains. Such remains may be small and fragmented. To increase the likelihood that small remains will be recovered, the soil is passed through screens. To recover very small remains, such as fish bones and carbonized plant remains, archaeologists use a technique called *flotation*. Soil samples are sorted using

An archaeologist drives in another stake for a large grid at an excavation site in Teotihuacan, Mexico. Such a grid enables the researchers to record the exact location of any artifact or feature found at the site.

water and a series of very fine meshes. When the water dissolves the soil, the carbonized plant remains float to the top. The fish bones and other heavier remains sink to the bottom. Flotation requires considerable time and labor. This makes it inappropriate to use on all the soil that is excavated from a site. Flotation samples are taken from a limited number of deposits, such as house floors, trash pits, and hearths.

Kinds of Archaeology

Archaeologists pursue diverse research topics, using a wide variety of methods. Experimental archaeologists try to replicate ancient techniques and processes (e.g., tool making) under controlled conditions. Historical archaeologists use written records as guides and supplements to archaeological research. They work with remains more recent—often much more recent—than the advent of writing. Colonial archaeologists, for instance, use historical records as guides to locate and excavate postcontact sites in North and South America,

and to verify or question written accounts. Classical archaeologists usually are affiliated with university departments of classics or the history of art, rather than with anthropology departments. These classical scholars focus on the literate civilizations of the Old World, such as Greece, Rome, and Egypt. Classical archaeologists are often as (or more) interested in art—styles of architecture and sculpture—as in the social, political, and economic variables that typically interest the anthropologist. Underwater archaeology is a growing field that investigates submerged sites, most often shipwrecks. Special techniques, including remotely operated vehicles like the one shown in the movie *Titanic,* are used, but divers also do underwater survey and excavation.

In Chapter 2, cultural resource management was discussed as a form of applied (or public) anthropology, as archaeologists apply their techniques of data gathering and analysis to manage sites that are threatened by development, public works, and road building. Some CRM archaeologists are *contract archaeologists,* who typically negotiate specific contracts (rather than applying for

Scuba divers at an underwater archaeology site. Graduate degrees in underwater, or nautical, archaeology are available at East Carolina University, Florida State University, and Texas A&M University. This growing field of study investigates submerged sites, most often shipwrecks.

areas have a better chance to be preserved than do animals that live in other habitats. Fossilization is also favored in areas with volcanic ash, or where rock fragments eroding from rising highlands are accumulating in valleys or lake basins. Once remains do get buried, chemical conditions must be right for fossilization to occur. If the sediment is too acidic, even bone and teeth will dissolve. The study of the processes that affect the remains of dead animals is called **taphonomy,** from the greek *taphos,* which means "tomb." Such processes include scattering by carnivores and scavengers, distortion by various forces, and the possible fossilization of the remains.

The conditions under which fossils are found also influence the fossil record. For example, fossils are more likely to be uncovered through erosion in arid areas than in wet areas. Sparse vegetation allows wind to scour the landscape and uncover fossils. The fossil record has been accumulating longer and is more extensive in Europe than in Africa because civil engineering projects and fossil hunting have been going on longer in Europe than in Africa. A world map showing where fossils have been found does not indicate the true range of ancient animals. Such a map tells us more about ancient geological activity, modern erosion, or recent human activity—such as paleontological research or road building. In considering the primate and hominid fossil records in later chapters, we'll see that different areas provide more abundant fossil evidence for different time periods. This doesn't necessarily mean that primates or hominids were not living elsewhere at the same time. What dating techniques are used to determine *when* animals that have been fossilized actually lived?

We've seen that *paleontology* is the study of ancient life through the fossil record and that *paleoanthropology* is the study of ancient humans and their immediate ancestors. These fields have established a time frame, or *chronology,* for the evolution of life. Scientists use several techniques to date fossils. These methods offer different degrees of precision and are applicable to different periods of the past.

research grants) for their studies, which often must be done rapidly, for example, when an immediate threat to archaeological materials becomes known. Based on a membership study done for the Society of American Archaeology in 1994, Melinda Zeder (1997) found that 40 percent of the respondents worked as contract archaeologists—for firms in the private sector, state and federal agencies, and educational institutions. An equivalent 40 percent held academic positions.

Dating the Past

The archaeological record hasn't revealed every ancient society that has existed on earth; nor is the fossil record a representative sample of all the plants and animals that have ever lived. Some species and body parts are better represented than others are, for many reasons. Hard parts, such as bones and teeth, preserve better than do soft parts, such as flesh and skin. The chances of fossilization increase when remains are buried in a newly forming sediment, such as silt, gravel, or sand. Good places for bones to be buried in sediments include swamps, floodplains, river deltas, lakes, and caves. The species that inhabit such

A swamp is a good place for bones to be buried in sediments. Here a female mammoth is represented sinking into the La Brea Tarpits in Los Angeles, California. What other locales and conditions favor fossilization?

RELATIVE DATING

Chronology is established by assigning dates to geologic layers (strata) and to the material remains, such as fossils and artifacts, within them. Dating may be relative or absolute. **Relative dating** establishes a time frame in relation to other strata or materials rather than absolute dates in numbers. Many dating methods are based on the geological study of **stratigraphy,** the science that examines the ways in which earth sediments accumulate in layers known as *strata* (singular, *stratum*). As was noted previously, in an undisturbed sequence of strata, age increases with depth. Soil that erodes from a hillside into a valley covers, and is younger than, the soil deposited there previously. Stratigraphy permits relative dating. That is, the fossils in a given stratum are younger than those in the layers below and older than those in the layers above. We may not know the exact or absolute dates of the fossils, but we can place them in time relative to remains in other layers. Changing environmental forces, such as lava flows and the alternation of land and sea, cause different materials to be deposited in a given sequence of strata; this allows scientists to distinguish between the strata.

Remains of animals and plants that lived at the same time are found in the same stratum. When fossils are found within a stratigraphic sequence, scientists know their dates relative to fossils in other strata; this is relative dating. When fossils are found in a particular stratum, the associated geological features (such as frost patterning) and remains of particular plants and animals offer clues about the climate at the time of deposition.

Besides stratigraphic placement, another technique of relative dating is fluorine absorption analysis. Bones fossilizing in the same ground for the same length of time absorb the same proportion of fluorine from the local groundwater. Fluorine analysis uncovered a famous hoax involving the so-called Piltdown man, once considered an unusual and perplexing human ancestor (Winslow and Meyer 1983). The Piltdown "find," from England, turned out to be the jaw of a young orangutan attached to a *Homo sapiens* skull. Fluorine analysis showed the association to be false. The skull had much more fluorine than the jaw—impossible if they had come from the same individual and had been deposited in the same place at the same time. Someone had fabricated Piltdown man in an attempt to muddle the interpretation of the fossil record. (The attempt was partially successful—it did fool some scientists.)

ABSOLUTE DATING

The previous section reviewed relative dating based on stratigraphy and fluorine absorption analysis. Fossils also can be dated more precisely, with dates in numbers (**absolute dating**), by using several methods. For example, the ^{14}C, or carbon-14, technique is used to date organic remains. This is a *radiometric* technique (so called because it measures radioactive decay). ^{14}C is an unstable radioactive isotope of normal carbon, ^{12}C. Cosmic radiation entering the earth's atmosphere produces ^{14}C, and plants take in ^{14}C as they absorb carbon dioxide. ^{14}C moves up the food chain as animals eat plants and as predators eat other animals.

With death, the absorption of ^{14}C stops. This unstable isotope starts to break down into nitrogen (^{14}N). It takes 5,730 years for half the ^{14}C to change to nitrogen; this is the half-life of ^{14}C. After another 5,730 years only one-quarter of the original ^{14}C will remain. After yet another 5,730 years only one-eighth will be left. By measuring the proportion of ^{14}C in organic material, scientists can determine a fossil's date of death, or the date of an ancient campfire. However, because the half-life of ^{14}C is short, this dating technique is less dependable for specimens older than 40,000 years than it is for more recent remains.

For more information on radiocarbon dating, see the Virtual Exploration

mhhe
com
/kottak

Fortunately, other radiometric dating techniques are available for earlier periods. One of the most widely used is the potassium-argon (K/A) technique. ^{40}K is a radioactive isotope of potassium that breaks down into argon-40, a gas. The half-life of ^{40}K is far longer than that of ^{14}C—1.3 *billion* years. With this method, the *older* the specimen, the more reliable the dating. Furthermore, whereas ^{14}C dating can be done only on organic remains, K/A dating can be used only for inorganic substances: rocks and minerals.

^{40}K in rocks gradually breaks down into argon-40. That gas is trapped in the rock until the rock is heated intensely (as with volcanic activity), at which point it may escape. When the rock cools, the breakdown of potassium into argon resumes. Dating is done by reheating the rock and measuring the escaping gas.

In Africa's Great Rift Valley, which runs down eastern Africa and in which early hominid fossils abound, past volcanic activity permits K/A dating.

East Africa's Great Rift Valley runs through Ethiopia, Kenya (shown here), and Tanzania. What dating technique(s) can be used in this volcanic region?

Table 3.1 Absolute Dating Techniques

Technique	Abbreviation	Materials Dated	Effective Time Range
Carbon-14	^{14}C	Organic materials	Up to 40,000 years
Potassium-argon	K/A and ^{40}K	Volcanic rock	Older than 500,000 years
Uranium series	^{238}U	Minerals	Between 1,000 and 1,000,000 years
Thermoluminescence	TL	Rocks and minerals	Between 5,000 and 1,000,000 years
Electron spin resonance	ESR	Rocks and minerals	Between 1,000 and 1,000,000 years

In studies of strata containing fossils, scientists find out how much argon has accumulated in rocks since they were last heated. They then determine, using the standard ^{40}K deterioration rate, the date of that heating. Considering volcanic rocks at the top of a stratum with fossil remains, scientists establish that the fossils are *older than*, say, 1.8 million years. By dating the volcanic rocks below the fossil remains, they determine that the fossils are *younger than*, say, 2 million years. Thus, the age of the fossils and of associated material is set at between 2 million and 1.8 million years. Note that absolute dating is that in name only; it may give ranges of numbers rather than exact dates.

Many fossils were discovered before the advent of modern stratigraphy. Often we can no longer determine their original stratigraphic placement. Furthermore, fossils aren't always discovered in volcanic layers. Like ^{14}C dating, the K/A technique applies to a limited period of the fossil record. Because the half-life of ^{40}K is so long, the technique cannot be used with materials less than 500,000 years old.

Other radiometric dating techniques can be used to cross-check K/A dates, again by using minerals surrounding the fossils. One such method, *uranium series dating*, measures fission tracks produced during the decay of radioactive uranium (^{238}U) into lead. Two other radiometric techniques are especially useful for fossils that cannot be dated by ^{14}C (up to 40,000 B.P.) or ^{40}K (more than 500,000 B.P.). These methods are *thermoluminescence* (TL) and *electron spin resonance* (ESR). Both TL and ESR measure the electrons that are constantly being trapped in rocks and minerals (Shreeve 1992). Once a date is obtained for a rock found associated with a fossil, that date also can be applied to that fossil. The time spans for which the various absolute dating techniques are applicable are summarized in Table 3.1.

MOLECULAR DATING

In 1987, in a very influential study, researchers at the University of California at Berkeley used DNA analysis to advance the idea that anatomically modern humans (AMHs) arose fairly recently (around 130,000 years ago) in Africa. Rebecca Cann, Mark Stoneking, and Allan C. Wilson (1987) analyzed genetic traits in placentas donated by 147 women whose ancestors came from various parts of the world. The researchers focused on mitochondrial DNA (mtDNA), which only the mother contributes to the fertilized egg, and thus to the child. To establish a "genetic clock," the researchers measured the variation in mtDNA in their 147 tissue samples. They cut each sample into segments to compare with the others. By estimating the number of mutations (spontaneous changes in DNA) that had taken place in each sample since its common origin with the 146 others, the researchers drew an evolutionary tree with the help of a computer. That tree started in Africa, then branched in two. One group stayed in Africa. The other one left Africa and carried its mtDNA to the rest of the world. Assuming a constant mutation rate (e.g., one mutation per 25,000 years), and counting the number of mutations in each sample, molecular anthropologists estimate the time period of the most recent common ancestor. Note that such estimates of divergence dates based on a constant mutation rate are not as widely accepted as is radiometric dating.

SUMMARY

1. Because science exists in society, and in the context of law and ethics, anthropologists can't study things simply because they happen to be interesting or of scientific value. Anthropologists have obligations to their scholarly field, to the wider society and culture (including that of the host country), and to the human species, other species, and the environment. The anthropologist's primary ethical obligation is to the people, species, and materials he or she studies.

2. Physical anthropologists and archaeologists pursue diverse research topics, using varied methods and often working together. At an archaeological site, physical anthropologists may complement the picture of ancient life by examining skeletons to reconstruct their physical traits, health status, and diet. Remote sensing may be used to locate ancient footpaths, roads, canals, and irrigation systems, which can then be investigated on the ground.

3. Studies of primates suggest hypotheses about behavior that humans do or do not share with our nearest relatives—and also with our hominid ancestors. Anthropometry, the measurement of human body parts and dimensions, is done on living people and on skeletal remains from sites. Humans are unusually social, compared with nonhuman primates. Unlike other primate babies, humans are born facing backward, away from the mother, and so she has trouble assisting in the birth. The presence of someone else (e.g., a midwife) to help with delivery reduces the mortality risk for human infants and their mothers.

4. Central to physical anthropology is bone biology—the study of bone genetics; cell structure; growth, development, and decay; and patterns of movement. Osteologists study skeletal variation and its biological and social causes. Paleopathology is the study of disease and injury in skeletons from archaeological sites. Molecular anthropology uses genetic analysis (of DNA sequences) to assess evolutionary relationships among ancient and contemporary populations and among species.

5. Archaeologists, who typically work in teams and across time and space, combine both local (excavation) and regional (systematic survey) perspectives. Archaeologists use settlement pattern information to make population estimates and to assess levels of social complexity. Sites are excavated because they are in danger of being destroyed or because they address specific research interests. There are many kinds of archaeology, such as historical, classical, and underwater archaeology.

6. The fossil record is not a representative sample of all the plants and animals that have ever lived. Hard parts, such as bones and teeth, preserve better than soft parts, such as flesh and skin, do. Anthropologists and paleontologists use stratigraphy and radiometric techniques to date fossils. Carbon-14 (^{14}C) dating is most effective with fossils less than 40,000 years old. Potassium-argon (K/A) dating can be used for fossils older than 500,000 years. ^{14}C dating is done on organic matter, whereas the K/A, ^{238}U, TL, and ESR dating techniques are used to analyze minerals that lie below and above fossils. Molecular anthropology has also been used as a dating technique, based on the assumption of a constant mutation rate.

KEY TERMS

absolute dating Dating techniques that establish dates in numbers or ranges of numbers; examples include the radiometric methods of ^{14}C, K/A, ^{238}U, TL, and ESR dating.

anthropometry The measurement of human body parts and dimensions, including skeletal parts (*osteometry*).

bone biology The study of bone as a biological tissue, including its genetics; cell structure; growth, development, and decay; and patterns of movement (*biomechanics*).

excavation Digging through the layers of deposits that make up an archaeological or fossil site.

fossils Remains (e.g., bones), traces, or impressions (e.g., footprints) of ancient life.

molecular anthropology Genetic analysis, involving comparison of DNA sequences, to determine evolutionary links and distances among species and among ancient and modern populations.

paleoanthropology Study of hominid and human life through the fossil record.

paleontology Study of ancient life through the fossil record.

paleopathology Study of disease and injury in skeletons from archaeological sites.

palynology Study of ancient plants through pollen samples from archaeological or fossil sites in order to determine the site's environment at the time of occupation.

relative dating Dating technique, for example, stratigraphy, that establishes a time frame in relation to other strata or materials, rather than absolute dates in numbers.

remote sensing Use of aerial photos and satellite images to locate sites on the ground.

stratigraphy Science that examines the ways in which earth sediments are deposited in demarcated layers known as strata (singular, stratum).

systematic survey Information gathered on patterns of settlement over a large area; provides a regional perspective on the archaeological record.

taphonomy The study of the processes that affect the remains of dead animals, such as their scattering by carnivores and scavengers, their distortion by various forces, and their possible fossilization.

CRITICAL THINKING QUESTIONS

1. Considering anthropology's four subfields, are some more likely to use a team approach than others are? What about the equipment needs of the different subfields?
2. How might ethical issues and concerns differently affect cultural, physical, and archaeological anthropologists?
3. Name three factors that might influence an anthropologist's plans to study, or not to study, a particular topic in a particular place.
4. In practical terms, what does it mean to say that anthropologists have obligations to their scholarly field and to the wider society and culture? How might they abuse those responsibilities?
5. What three archaeological topics seem most interesting to you?
6. What three topics in physical anthropology seem most interesting to you?
7. Give two examples of how a physical anthropologist and an archaeologist might collaborate.

8. Imagine a scenario in which an archaeologist or physical anthropologist might use remote sensing.

9. What's your body mass index?

10. What are two examples of social tendencies you have that may have a deep evolutionary history?

11. Who assisted your mother in your birthing process?

12. Name two problems that might interest a bone biologist.

13. What are the strengths and limitations of relative dating? Of absolute dating?

Atlas Questions

Look at Map 3, "Annual Change in Forest Cover, 1990–1995."

1. Also consult Map 2, "Population Growth Rates." Name two countries in which deforestation is correlated with high population growth rates and two countries in which it is not.

2. On what continents do you find stable or increased forest cover? Does this surprise you given the population growth rates on those continents?

3. Is the greatest deforestation in the western hemisphere associated with the highest population growth rates?

SUGGESTED ADDITIONAL READINGS

Boaz, N. T., and A. J. Almquist

2002 *Biological Anthropology: A Synthetic Approach to Human Evolution*, 2nd ed. Upper Saddle River, NJ: Prentice-Hall. Basic text in physical anthropology; includes discussion of methods.

Katzenberg, M. A., and S. R. Saunders, eds.

2000 *Biological Anthropology of the Human Skeleton*. New York: Wiley. Analysis of skeletal and dental remains, including use of new technology.

Larsen, C. S.

2000 *Skeletons in Our Closet: Revealing Our Past through Bioarchaeology*. Princeton, NJ: Princeton University Press. How human remains from archaeological sites help us interpret lifetime events such as disease, injury, tool use, and diet.

Nafte, M.

2000 *Flesh and Bone: An Introduction to Forensic Anthropology*. Durham, NC: Carolina Academic Press. Methods and procedures, avoiding technical terminology.

Park, M. A.

2002 *Biological Anthropology*, 3rd ed. Boston: McGraw-Hill. A concise introduction, with a focus on scientific inquiry.

Prag, J., and R. Neave

1997 *Making Faces: Using Forensic and Archaeological Evidence*. College Station, TX: Texas A&M University Press. How ancient faces are reconstructed.

Renfrew, C., and P. Bahn

2000 *Archaeology: Theories, Methods, and Practice*, 3rd ed. London: Thames and Hudson. Most useful treatment of methods in archaeological anthropology.

Turnbaugh, W. A., R. Jurmain, L. Kilgore, and H. Nelson

2000 *Understanding Physical Anthropology and Archaeology*. 8th ed. Belmont, CA: Wadsworth. Introduction to these two subfields, with a discussion of methods in each.

White, T. D., and P. A. Folkens

2000 *Human Osteology*, 2nd ed. San Diego: Academic Press. Includes case studies and discussion of molecular osteology, with life-size photos of skeletal parts.

INTERNET EXERCISES

1. Dating Techniques: Go to the USGS website on Fossils, Rocks, and Time (**http://pubs.usgs.gov/gip/fossils/contents.html**) and read through all the sections.

    a. How do researchers use the law of superposition to date fossils?

    b. What are isotopes? How are they used by researchers to calculate numeric dates for fossils?

    c. How do relative and absolute/numeric dating techniques complement each other?

2. Go to the on-line field journal for the 2002 Warren Wilson College Field School (**http://www.warren-wilson.edu/~arch/fs2002/main.html**). Read the introduction and then click on Day 1. Browse through each day of the field school to get a sense of what the archaeological research was like.

    a. What are some of the investigative techniques that the archaeologists used?

    b. What were some of the significant discoveries? Why were they important?

3. Archaeological Fieldwork: Visit the Dust Cave Field School website (**http://www.dustcave.ua.edu/**) and read the History of Dust Cave (**http://www.dustcave.ua.edu/history.htm**).

    a. Watch the video prepared by CNN of the work done at Dust Cave (**http://www.dustcave.ua.edu/dccnn.ram**); the video is in RealPlayer format. (If you do not have a player, go to www.realplayer.com). Based on the video, is this portrayal of archaeology what you expected? Is there more to conducting field work than just digging? Was it important for the participants to be able to work as a team?

    b. Go to the "Student Research 1999" page (**http://www.dustcave.ua.edu/99/stud99.htm**). These are papers written by undergraduate participants at Dust Cave during the summer of 1999. Read through at least one student paper (by clicking on the photograph of that student). What did the student research? What were the conclusions? How does it contribute to the overall understanding of prehistoric life, in Dust Cave?

See Chapter 3 at your McGraw-Hill Online Learning Center for additional review and interactive exercises.

4

EVOLUTION AND GENETICS

Overview

Charles Darwin and Alfred Russel Wallace proposed that natural selection could explain the origin of species, as well as many biological differences and similarities among life forms. For natural selection to work, there needs to be (and there always is) variety within the population undergoing selection.

Darwin didn't know the precise genetic mechanisms that allowed natural selection to work. It was his contemporary Gregor Mendel who discovered that genetic traits are inherited as discrete units, now called chromosomes and genes. Mendel also discovered that hereditary traits may be inherited independently of each other, rather than as a bundle. Such traits may then reunite in new combinations. This genetic recombination supplies some of the variety on which natural selection depends.

The adaptive value of particular traits depends on the environment. If the environment changes, nature can only select from traits that are already present in the population. If there isn't enough variety to permit adaptation to the environmental change, extinction is likely. New types don't appear just because they are needed.

Other evolutionary mechanisms work along with natural selection. Genetic drift operates most obviously in small populations, where pure chance can easily change gene frequencies. Gene flow and interbreeding keep subgroups of the same species connected genetically and thus work against speciation—the formation of new species.

There are links between genetically determined traits, such as hemoglobins in the blood, and selective forces, such as malaria. Selection through differential resistance to disease has influenced the distribution of human blood groups. Natural selection also has operated on facial features, body size and shape, and many other expressions of human biological diversity.

DNA Backs a Tribe's Tradition of Early Descent from the Jews

NEW YORK TIMES NEWS BRIEF (BOOK REVIEW)

by Nicholas Wade

May 9, 1999

Geneticists have discovered that Lemba men living in southern Africa have a set of DNA sequences that is distinctive of the cohanim, Jewish priests believed to be the descendants of Aaron, elder brother of Moses.

Note in this account how different lines of evidence come together to solve a problem. The Lemba of southern Africa assert remote Jewish ancestry. They retain customs believed to have survived from a distant time when they lived closer to the Jewish homeland. Yet the Lemba now live thousands of miles from that homeland, among people from whom they are physically, linguistically, and, in many ways, culturally indistinguishable. Biology, language, and culture don't go together in neat bundles. It's possible for people who look different from each other to share more genetic attributes with each other than they do with people who look much more like them. Also, people can look the same, or (in this case) share genetic traits, while speaking different languages and engaging in different cultural traditions.

The Lemba, a Bantu-speaking people of southern Africa, have a tradition that they were led out of Judea by a man named Buba. They practice circumcision, keep one day a week holy and avoid eating pork or piglike animals . . .

The . . . Lemba tradition . . . may be exactly right. A team of geneticists has found that many Lemba men carry in their male [Y] chromosome a set of DNA sequences that is distinctive of the cohanim, the Jewish priests believed to be the descendants of Aaron, [the elder brother of Moses]. This genetic signature [called the cohen genetic signature] . . . is particularly common among Lemba men who belong to the senior of their 12 groups, known as the Buba clan.

Y chromosomes are bequeathed from father to son, more or less unchanged apart from the occasional mutation. The mutations are particularly helpful for reconstructing population history because each lineage of men has its own distinctive pattern of mutations . . .

David B. Goldstein, a population geneticist at Oxford University in England, . . . tested DNA samples collected from the Lemba . . . Dr. Goldstein reported that 9 percent of Lemba men carried the cohen genetic signature, and of those who said they belonged to the Buba clan, 53 percent had the distinctive sequences. These proportions are similar to those found among the major Jewish populations.

Because the cohen genetic signature is rare or absent in all non-Jewish populations tested so far, the findings strongly support the Lemba tradition of Jewish ancestry . . .

How did a Jewish priestly male chromosome come to be found in a black, Bantu-speaking people that looks very much like its southern African neighbors? [Dr. Tudor Parfitt, director of the Center for Jewish Studies at the School of Oriental and African Studies in London,] . . . who says he believes he has found the answer, first came across the Lemba while giving a lecture in Johannesburg about Ethiopian Jews. Some people in the audience wearing yarmulkes told him they, too, were Jewish.

Dr. Parfitt visited their homes, which are in northern South Africa and Zimbabwe. Many of the Lemba, who number more than 50,000 people, are Christians, but they see no contradiction in professing Judaism, too. He learned that they had an enigmatic tradition about their origin: "We came from the north, from a place called Senna. We left Senna, we crossed Pusela, we came to Africa and there we rebuilt Senna."

Dr. Parfitt said that he was later traveling in the Hadramawt region, a former site of Jewish communities in Yemen, and mentioned the Lemba tradition of Senna to the religious leader of the holy city of Tarim. The leader was surprised to hear it because, he told Dr. Parfitt, there was a nearby village called Senna.

"So I went off to find Senna," Dr. Parfitt said. "It's very remote and had never been visited by anyone before. The local tradition is that centuries ago the valley had been very fertile, irrigated by a dam, the ruins of which are still there. And then the dam burst, they think about a thousand years ago, and the people fled."

There is a valley that leads from Senna to a port on the Yemeni coast called Sayhut. If the winds are right, a ship from Sayhut could reach southern Africa in nine days, Dr. Parfitt said. And the valley that leads from Senna to Sayhut is called the Wadi al-Masilah. Dr. Parfitt believes that Masilah may be the "Pusela" of the Lemba oral tradition . . .

Dr. Parfitt . . . said he had been excited to hear of Dr. Goldstein's genetic results confirming the Lemba tradition . . .

Dr. Parfitt said that in collecting samples from the Lemba—a swab of cells scraped from inside the cheek—he had first explained the purpose of the research to local chiefs and obtained their permission. He then told each individual what was involved, sometimes saying "your blood carries important history, the footprints of your ancestors," if he could not explain the genetics.

Being very keen to know where they came from, the Lemba lined up to give samples, Dr. Parfitt said. They were so pleased to learn the results that Dr. Parfitt was made an honorary Lemba.

Dr. Parfitt said he was particularly appreciative of the honor because Lemba tradition prohibits outside men from becoming Lembas . . . This exclusion of outside males . . . would explain why the cohen genetic signature has been preserved at high frequency among the Lemba for so many centuries.

Source: *New York Times*, May 9, 1999, late edition—final, section 1, p. 1, column 5.

When the Valley of Senna could no longer sustain its people, they fled, eventually reaching southern Africa, where, over the generations, they have assimilated both biologically and culturally. In appearance, the Lemba are indistinguishable from their African neighbors; like them, they speak a Bantu language. Biology, however, is more than meets the eye; biology extends to genetic characteristics. The Lemba retain genetic markers of a Jewish ancestry that dates back a thousand years. Genetic patterns may remain fairly stable over time, as in this case, or may change substantially. Indeed, we'll see in this chapter that genetic change is the basis of biological evolution. Although they retain both biological and cultural markers of their remote Jewish heritage, the Lemba have adapted and changed both biologically and culturally.

Compared with most other animals, humans have uniquely varied ways—cultural and biological—of evolving, of adapting to environmental stresses. Exemplifying cultural adaptation, we manipulate our artifacts and behavior in response to environmental conditions. The ancestors of the Lemba migrated after their irrigation system failed. Contemporary North Americans turn up thermostats or travel to Florida in the winter. We turn on fire hydrants, swim, or ride in air-conditioned cars from New York City to Maine to escape the summer's heat. Although such reliance on culture has increased in the course of human evolution, people haven't stopped adapting biologically. As in other species, human populations adapt genetically in response to environmental forces, and individuals react physiologically to stresses. Thus, when we work in the midday sun, sweating occurs spontaneously, cooling the skin and reducing the temperature of subsurface blood vessels.

We are ready now for a more detailed look at the principles that determine human biological adaptation, variation, and change.

Creationism and Evolution

During the 18th century, many scholars became interested in human origins, biological diversity, and our position within the classification of plants and animals. At that time, the commonly accepted explanation for the origin of species came from

According to creationism all life originated during the six days of creation described in the Bible. Catastrophism proposed that fires and floods, including the biblical deluge involving Noah's ark (depicted in this painting by the American artist Edward Hicks), destroyed certain species. How might a creationist account for differences and similarities between fossils and contemporary life forms?

Genesis, the first book of the Bible: God had created all life during six days of Creation. According to **creationism,** biological similarities and differences originated at the Creation. Characteristics of life forms were seen as immutable; they could not change. Through calculations based on genealogies in the Bible, the biblical scholars James Ussher and John Lightfoot even managed to trace the Creation to a very specific time: October 23, 4004 BC, at 9 AM.

Carolus Linnaeus (1707–1778), who accepted the biblical account of Creation, developed the first comprehensive and still influential classification, or taxonomy, of plants and animals. He grouped life forms on the basis of similarities and differences in their physical characteristics. He used traits such as the presence of a backbone to distinguish vertebrates from invertebrates and the presence of mammary glands to distinguish mammals from birds. Linnaeus viewed the differences between life forms as part of the Creator's orderly plan. Biological sim-

ilarities and differences had been established at the time of Creation and had not changed.

Fossil discoveries during the 18th and 19th centuries raised doubts about creationism. Fossils showed that different kinds of life had once existed. If all life had originated at the same time, why weren't ancient species still around? Why weren't contemporary plants and animals found in the fossil record? A modified explanation combining creationism with **catastrophism** replaced the original doctrine. In this view, fires, floods, and other catastrophes, including the biblical flood involving Noah's ark, had destroyed ancient species. After each destructive event, God had created again, leading to contemporary species. How did the catastrophists explain certain clear similarities between fossils and modern animals? They argued that some ancient species had managed to survive in isolated areas. For example, after the biblical flood, the progeny of the animals saved on Noah's ark spread throughout the world.

The alternative to creationism and catastrophism was *transformism,* also called **evolution.** Evolutionists believed that species arose from others through a long and gradual process of transformation, or descent with modification. Charles Darwin became the best known of the evolutionists. However, he was influenced by earlier scholars, including his own grandfather. Erasmus Darwin, in a book called *Zoonomia* published in 1794, had proclaimed the common ancestry of all animal species.

Charles Darwin also was influenced by Sir Charles Lyell, the father of geology. During Darwin's famous voyage to South America aboard the *Beagle,* he read Lyell's influential book *Principles of Geology* (1837/1969), which exposed him to Lyell's principle of **uniformitarianism.** Uniformitarianism states that the present is the key to the past. Explanations for past events should be sought in the long-term action of ordinary forces that still work today. Thus, natural forces (rainfall, soil deposition, earthquakes, and volcanic action) have gradually built and modified geological features such as mountain ranges. The earth's structure has been transformed gradually through natural forces operating for millions of years (see Weiner 1994).

Uniformitarianism was a necessary building block for evolutionary theory. It cast serious doubt on the belief that the world was only 6,000 years old. It would take much longer for such ordinary forces as rain and wind to produce major geological changes. The longer time span also allowed enough time for the biological changes that fossil discoveries were revealing. Darwin applied the ideas of uniformitarianism and long-term transformation through natural forces to living things. Like other evolutionists, he argued that all life forms are ultimately related. In opposition to the creationists, Darwin argued that the number of species is not immutable but has increased over time. (For more on science, evolution, and creationism, see Futuyma 1995; Gould 1999; Wilson 2002.)

Darwin offered natural selection as a principle that could explain the origin of species, biological diversity, and similarities among related life forms. His major contribution was not the theory of evolution, as most people believe, but the idea that natural selection explains evolutionary change. Natural selection wasn't Darwin's unique discovery. Working independently, the naturalist Alfred Russel Wallace had reached a similar conclusion (Shermer 2002). In a joint paper read to London's Linnaean Society in 1858, Darwin and Wallace made their discovery public. Darwin's book *On the Origin of Species* (1859/1958) offered fuller documentation but created great controversy.

For information about common misconceptions about evolution, see your OLC Internet Exercises

mhhe ● **com** **/kottak**

Natural selection is the process by which nature selects the forms most fit to survive and reproduce in a given environment. For natural selection to work on a particular population, there must be variety within that population, as there always is. Natural selection operates when there is competition for *strategic resources* (those necessary for life), such as food and space, between members of the population. Organisms whose attributes render them most fit to survive and reproduce in their environment do so in greater numbers than others do. Over the years, the less fit organisms gradually die out and the favored types survive.

The giraffe's neck can be used to illustrate how natural selection works on variety within a population. In any group of giraffes, there is always variation in neck length. When food is adequate, the animals have no problem feeding themselves with foliage. But in times when there is pressure on strategic resources, so that dietary foliage is not as abundant as usual, giraffes with longer necks have an advantage. They can feed off the higher branches. If this feeding advantage permits longer-necked giraffes to survive and reproduce even slightly more effectively than shorter-necked ones, the trait will be favored by natural selection. The giraffes with longer necks will be more likely to transmit their genetic material to future generations than will giraffes with shorter necks.

An incorrect alternative to this (Darwinian) explanation would be the inheritance of acquired characteristics. That is the idea that in each generation, individual giraffes strain their necks to reach just a bit higher. This straining somehow modifies their genetic material. Over generations of strain, the average neck gradually gets longer through the accumulation of small increments of neck length acquired during the lifetime of each generation of giraffes. This is not how evolution works. If it did work in this way, weight lifters could expect to produce especially muscular babies. Workouts that promise no gain without the pain apply to the physical development of individuals, not species. Instead, evolution works as the process of natural selection takes advantage of the variety that is already present in a population. That's how giraffes got their necks.

The process of natural selection continues as long as the relationship between the population and its environment remains the same. However, if emigration, or some change in the environment, occurs, natural selection will begin to favor types that are more likely to survive and reproduce in the new environment. This new selection will continue until an equilibrium is reached. Environmental change or migration may then occur again. Through such a gradual, branching process, involving adaptation to thousands of environments, natural selection has produced the diverse plants and animals found in the world today.

Genetics

Darwin recognized that for natural selection to operate, there must be variety in the population undergoing selection. Documenting and explaining human variation is a major concern of modern biological anthropology. Genetics, a science that emerged after Darwin, helps us understand the causes of biological variation. We now know that DNA (deoxyribonucleic acid) molecules make up genes and chromosomes, which are the basic hereditary units. Biochemical changes (mutations) in DNA provide much of the variety on which natural selection operates. (See the section on mutation on page 94.) Through sexual reproduction, recombination of the genetic traits of mother and father in each generation leads to new arrangements of the hereditary units received from each parent. Such genetic recombination also adds variety on which natural selection may operate.

Mendelian genetics studies the ways in which chromosomes transmit genes across the generations. *Biochemical genetics* examines structure, function, and changes in DNA. (Our website provides additional information on biochemical genetics.) **Population genetics** investigates natural selection and other causes of genetic variation, stability, and change in breeding populations.

MENDEL'S EXPERIMENTS

In 1856, in a monastery garden, the Austrian monk Gregor Mendel began a series of experiments that were to reveal the basic principles of genetics. Mendel studied the inheritance of seven contrasting traits in pea plants. For each trait there were only two forms. For example, plants were either tall (6 to 7 feet) or short (9 to 18 inches), with no intermediate forms. Similarly, seeds were either smooth or wrinkled, and pea color was either yellow or green.

Mendel discovered that heredity is determined by discrete particles or units. Although traits could disappear in one generation, they reemerged in their original form in later generations. For example, Mendel crossbred pure strains of tall and short plants. Their offspring were all tall. This was the first descending, or first filial, generation, designated F_1. Mendel then interbred the plants of the F_1 generation to produce a gener-

ation of grandchildren, the F_2 generation (Figure 4.1). In this generation, short plants reappeared. Among thousands of plants in the F_2 generation, there was approximately one short plant for every three tall ones.

From similar results with the other six traits, Mendel concluded that although a **dominant** form could mask the other form in *hybrid*, or mixed, individuals, the dominated trait—the **recessive**—was not destroyed; it wasn't even changed. Recessive traits would appear in unaltered form in later generations because genetic traits were inherited as discrete units.

These basic genetic units that Mendel described were factors (now called genes or alleles) located on **chromosomes.** Chromosomes are arranged in matching (homologous) pairs. Humans have 46 chromosomes, arranged in 23 pairs, one in each pair from the father and the other from the mother.

For simplicity, a chromosome may be pictured as a surface (see Figure 4.2) with several positions, to each of which we assign a lowercase letter. Each position is a **gene.** Each gene determines, wholly or partially, a particular biological trait, such as whether one's blood is A, B, or O. **Alleles** (for example, b^1 and b^2 in Figure 4.2) are biochemically different forms of a given gene. In humans, A, B, AB, and O blood types reflect different combinations of alleles of a particular gene.

In Mendel's experiments, the seven contrasting traits were determined by genes located on seven different pairs of chromosomes. The gene for height occurred in one of the seven pairs. When Mendel crossbred pure tall and pure short plants to produce his F_1 generation, each of the offspring received an allele for tallness (T) from one parent and one for shortness (t) from the other. These offspring were mixed, or **heterozygous,** with respect to height; each had two dissimilar alleles of that gene. Their parents, in contrast, had been **homozygous,** possessing two identical alleles of that gene (see Hartl and Jones 2002).

In the next generation (F_2), after the mixed plants were interbred, short plants reappeared in the ratio of one short to three talls. Knowing that shorts only produced shorts, Mendel could assume that they were genetically pure. Another fourth of the F_2 plants produced only talls. The remaining half, like the F_1 generation, were heterozygous; when interbred, they produced three talls for each short. (See Figure 4.3.)

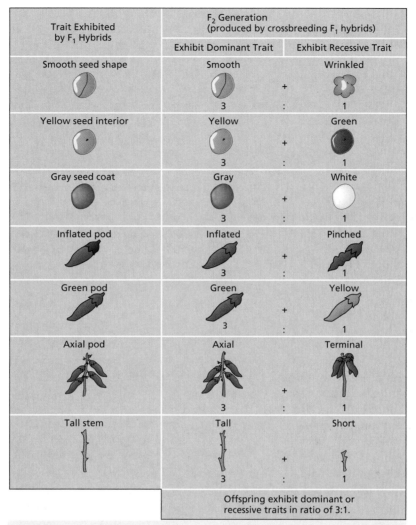

Trait Exhibited by F₁ Hybrids	F₂ Generation (produced by crossbreeding F₁ hybrids)	
	Exhibit Dominant Trait	Exhibit Recessive Trait
Smooth seed shape	Smooth 3	Wrinkled 1
Yellow seed interior	Yellow 3	Green 1
Gray seed coat	Gray 3	White 1
Inflated pod	Inflated 3	Pinched 1
Green pod	Green 3	Yellow 1
Axial pod	Axial 3	Terminal 1
Tall stem	Tall 3	Short 1

Offspring exhibit dominant or recessive traits in ratio of 3:1.

Figure 4.1   Mendel's Second Set of Experiments with Pea Plants.
Dominant colors are shown unless otherwise indicated.

Dominance produces a distinction between **genotype,** or hereditary makeup, and *phenotype,* or expressed physical characteristics. Genotype is what you really are genetically; phenotype is what you appear as. Mendel's peas had three genotypes—TT, Tt, and tt—but only two phenotypes—tall and short. Because of dominance, the heterozygous plants were just as tall as the genetically pure tall ones. How do Mendel's discoveries apply to humans? Although some of our genetic traits follow Mendelian laws, with only two forms—dominant and recessive—other traits are determined differently. For instance, three alleles determine whether our blood type is A, B, AB, or O. People with two alleles for type O have that blood type. However, if they received a gene for either A or B from one parent and one for O from the other, they will have blood type A or B. In other words, A and B are both dominant over O. A and B are said to be *codominant.* If people inherit a gene for A from one parent and one for B from the other, they will have type AB blood, which is chemically different from the other varieties, A, B, and O.

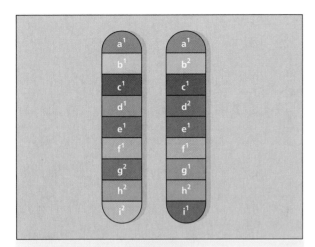

Figure 4.2 Simplified Representation of a Normal Chromosome Pair.
Letters indicate genes; superscripts indicate alleles.

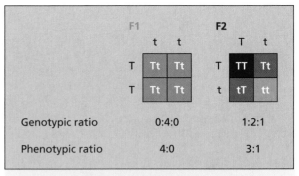

	F1		F2	
	t	t	T	t
T	Tt	Tt	TT	Tt
T	Tt	Tt	tT	tt
Genotypic ratio	0:4:0		1:2:1	
Phenotypic ratio	4:0		3:1	

Figure 4.3 Punnett Squares of a Homozygous Cross and a Heterozygous Cross.
These squares show how phenotypic ratios of the F$_1$ and F$_2$ generation are generated. Colors show genotypes.

These three alleles produce four phenotypes— A, B, AB, and O—and six different genotypes— OO, AO, BO, AA, BB, and AB (Figure 4.4). There are fewer phenotypes than genotypes because O is recessive to both A and B.

INDEPENDENT ASSORTMENT AND RECOMBINATION

Through additional experiments, Mendel also formulated his law of **independent assortment.** He discovered that traits are inherited independently of one another. For example, he bred pure round yellow peas with pure wrinkled green ones. All the F$_1$ generation peas were round and yellow, the dominant forms. But when Mendel interbred the F$_1$ generation to produce the F$_2$, four phenotypes turned up. Round greens and wrinkled yellows had been added to the original round yellows and wrinkled greens.

The independent assortment and recombination of genetic traits provide one of the main ways by which variety is produced in any population. **Recombination** is important in biological evolution because it creates new types on which natural selection can operate.

An organism develops from a fertilized egg, or *zygote,* created by the union of two sex cells, one from each parent. The zygote grows rapidly

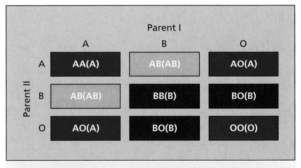

Figure 4.4 Determinants of Phenotypes (Blood Groups) in the ABO System.
The four phenotypes—A, B, AB, and O—are indicated in parentheses and by color.

through **mitosis,** or ordinary cell division, which continues as the organism grows. The special process by which sex cells are produced is called **meiosis.** Unlike ordinary cell division, in which two cells emerge from one, in meiosis four cells are produced from one. Each has half the genetic material of the original cell. In human meiosis, four cells, each with 23 individual chromosomes, are produced from an original cell with 23 pairs.

With fertilization of egg by sperm, the father's 23 chromosomes combine with the mother's 23 to re-create the pairs in every generation. However, the chromosomes sort independently, so that a

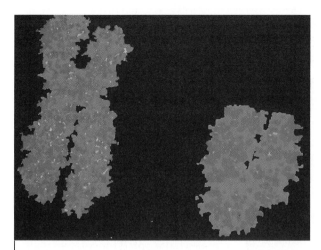

The chromosomes that determine sex in humans. The X chromosome (left) is clearly larger than the Y chromosome (right). What are the genotypes of males and females in terms of these chromosomes?

child's genotype is a random combination of the DNA of its four grandparents. It is conceivable that one grandparent will contribute very little to its grandchild's heredity. Independent assortment of chromosomes is a major source of variety, because the parents' genotypes can be assorted in 2^{23}, or more than 8 million, different ways.

Population Genetics

Population genetics studies stable and changing populations in which most breeding normally takes place (see Gillespie 1998; Hartl 2000). The term **gene pool** refers to all the alleles and genotypes within a breeding population—the "pool" of genetic material available. When population geneticists use the term *evolution,* they have a more specific definition in mind than the one given earlier ("descent with modification over the generations"). For geneticists, **genetic evolution** is defined as change in gene frequency, that is, in the frequency of alleles in a breeding population from generation to generation. Any factor that contributes to such a change can be considered a mechanism of genetic evolution. Those mechanisms include natural selection, mutation, random genetic drift, and gene flow (see Mayr 2001).

Mechanisms of Genetic Evolution

NATURAL SELECTION

The first mechanism of genetic evolution is natural selection, which remains the best explanation for evolution. Essential to understanding evolution through natural selection is the distinction between genotype and phenotype. Genotype refers just to hereditary factors—genes and chromosomes. Phenotype—the organism's evident biological characteristics—develops over the years as the organism is influenced by particular environmental forces. (See the photo of the identical twins on the next page. Identical twins have exactly the same genotype, but their actual biology, their phenotypes, may differ as a result of variation in the environments in which they have been raised.) Also, because of dominance, individuals with different genotypes may have identical phenotypes (like Mendel's tall pea plants). Natural selection can operate only on phenotype—on what is exposed, not on what is hidden. For example, a harmful recessive gene can't be eliminated from the gene pool if it is masked by a favored dominant.

Phenotype includes not only outward physical appearance, but also internal organs, tissues, and cells and physiological processes and systems. Many biological reactions to foods, disease, heat, cold, sunlight, and other environmental factors are not automatic, genetically programmed responses but the product of years of exposure to particular environmental stresses. Human biology is not set at birth but has considerable *plasticity.* That is, it is changeable, being affected by the environmental forces, such as diet and altitude, that we experience as we grow up (see Bogin 2001).

The environment works on the genotype to build the phenotype, and certain phenotypes do better in some environments than other phenotypes do. However, remember that favored phenotypes can be produced by different genotypes. Because natural selection works only on genes that are expressed, maladaptive recessives can be removed only when they occur in homozygous form. When a heterozygote carries a maladaptive

For an example of natural selection, see your OLC Internet Exercises

mhhe
●com
/kottak

Twin Wade on the left is bigger and taller than his brother Wyatt. How can this be if they are identical?

Selection also operates through competition for mates in a breeding population. Males may openly compete for females, or females may choose to mate with particular males because they have desirable traits. Obviously, such traits vary from species to species. Familiar examples include color in birds; male birds, such as cardinals, tend to be more brightly colored than females are. Colorful males have a selective advantage because females like them better. As, over the generations, females have opted for colorful mates, the alleles responsible for color have built up in the species. **Sexual selection,** based on differential success in mating, is the term for this process in which certain traits of one sex are selected because of advantages they confer in winning mates.

recessive, its effects are masked by the favored dominant. The process of perfecting the fit between organisms and their environment is gradual.

Directional Selection   After several generations of selection, gene frequencies will change. Adaptation through natural selection will have occurred. Once that happens, those traits that have proved to be the most **adaptive** (favored by natural selection) in that environment will be selected again and again from generation to generation. Given such *directional selection,* or long-term selection of the same trait(s), maladaptive recessive alleles will be removed from the gene pool.

Directional selection will continue as long as environmental forces stay the same. However, if the environment changes, new selective forces start working, favoring different phenotypes. This also happens when part of the population colonizes a new environment. Selection in the changed, or new, environment continues until a new equilibrium is reached. Then there is directional selection until another environmental change or migration takes place. Over millions of years, such a process of successive adaptation to a series of environments has led to biological modification and branching. The process of natural selection has led to the tremendous array of plant and animal forms found in the world today.

Selection operates *only* on traits that are present in a population. A favorable mutation *may* occur, but a population doesn't normally come up with a new genotype or phenotype just because one is needed or desirable. Many species have become extinct because they weren't sufficiently varied to adapt to environmental shifts.

There are also differences in the amount of environmental stress that organisms' genetic potential enables them to tolerate. Some species are adapted to a narrow range of environments. They are especially endangered by environmental fluctuation. Others—*Homo sapiens* among them—tolerate much more environmental variation because their genetic potential permits many adaptive possibilities. Humans can adapt rapidly to changing conditions by modifying both biological responses and learned behavior. We don't have to delay adaptation until a favorable mutation appears.

Sickle-Cell Anemia   We see that natural selection can *reduce* variety in a population through directional selection—by favoring one allele or trait over another. Selective forces also can work to *maintain* genetic variety by favoring a situation in which the frequencies of two or more alleles of a gene remain constant from generation to generation. This may be because the phenotypes they produce are neutral, equally favored, or equally opposed by selective forces. Sometimes a particular force favors (or opposes) one allele while a different but equally effective force favors (or opposes) the other allele.

One well-studied example involves two alleles, Hb^A and Hb^S, that affect the production of the beta strain (Hb) of human hemoglobin. Hemoglobin, which is located in our red blood cells, carries oxygen from our lungs to the rest of the body via the circulatory system. The allele that produces normal hemoglobin is Hb^A. Another allele, Hb^S, produces a different hemoglobin. Individuals who are homozygous for Hb^S suffer from *sickle-cell anemia*. Such anemia, in which the red blood cells are shaped like crescents or sickles, is associated with a disease that is usually fatal. This condition interferes with the blood's ability to store oxygen. It increases the heart's burden by clogging the small blood vessels.

Given the fatal disease associated with Hb^S, geneticists were surprised to discover that certain populations in Africa, India, and the Mediterranean had very high frequencies of Hb^S (Figure 4.5). In some West African populations, that frequency is around 20 percent. Researchers eventually discovered that both Hb^A and Hb^S are maintained because selective forces in certain environments favor the heterozygote over either homozygote.

Initially, scientists wondered why, if most Hb^S homozygotes died before they reached reproductive age, the harmful allele hadn't been eliminated. Why was its frequency so high? The answer turned out to lie in the heterozygote's greater fitness. Only people who were homozygous for Hb^S died from sickle-cell anemia. Heterozygotes suffered very mild anemia, if any. On the other hand, although people homozygous for Hb^A did not suffer from anemia, they were much more susceptible to *malaria*—a killer disease that continues to plague *Homo sapiens* in the tropics.

The heterozygote, with one sickle-cell allele and one normal one, was the fittest phenotype for a malarial environment. Heterozygotes have enough abnormal hemoglobin, in which malaria parasites cannot thrive, to protect against malaria. They also have enough normal hemoglobin to fend off sickle-cell anemia. The Hb^S allele has been maintained in these populations because the heterozygotes survived and reproduced in greater numbers than did people with any other phenotype.

The sickle-cell allele spread in the tropics as a result of certain economic and cultural changes—specifically, a shift from hunting and gathering to farming (Livingstone 1958). Many societies in West Africa took up a form of cultivation known as *slash and burn*. With this system, trees were cut down and burned to provide ashes for fertilizing the soil. After the land was farmed for one or two years, yields began to drop, and farmers chose another plot to slash and burn.

Slash-and-burn cultivation created breeding areas for *Anopheles* mosquitoes, which carry the malarial parasites and transmit them to people. Farming eroded and hardened the topsoil, increasing rain runoff to pools of stagnant water. The destruction of the forest promoted an increase in malarial mosquitoes, which bred more effectively in water exposed to the sun than in shaded areas. Rare in the forest, mosquitoes became common in the new environment.

Simultaneously, the new economy produced more food than the old one had. This fueled population

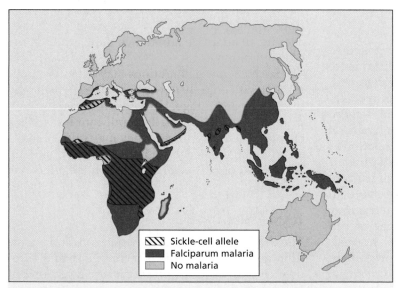

Figure 4.5 **Distribution of Sickle-Cell Allele and Falciparum Malaria in the Old World.**

Legend:
- Sickle-cell allele
- Falciparum malaria
- No malaria

Source: Adapted from *Human Evolution: An Introduction to the New Physical Anthropology* by Joseph B. Birdsell. Copyright © 1975, 1981 by HarperCollins, Publishers, Inc. Reprinted by permission of the publisher.

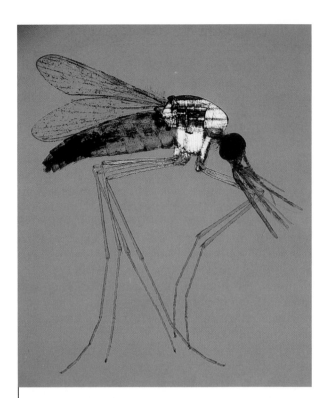

Beware the *Anopheles* mosquito, vector of malaria. An adult female is shown here. What is a genetic antimalarial?

growth. Villages became larger and closer together. Population density increased, providing more hosts for parasites. In this changed environment, the sickle-cell allele began to play an adaptive role.

The example of the sickle-cell allele demonstrates the relativity of evolution through natural selection: Adaptation and fitness are in relation to specific environments. Traits are not adaptive or maladaptive for all times and places. Even harmful alleles can be selected if heterozygotes have an advantage. Moreover, as the environment changes, favored phenotypes and gene frequencies can change. In malaria-free environments, normal-hemoglobin homozygotes reproduce more effectively than heterozygotes do. With no malaria, the frequency of Hb^S declines, because Hb^S homozygotes can't compete in survival and reproduction with the other types. This has happened in areas of West Africa where malaria has

For an introduction to evolution, see the Virtual Exploration

mhhe
●com
/kottak

been reduced through drainage programs and insecticides. Selection against Hb^S also has occurred in the United States among Americans descended from West Africans (Diamond 1997).

MUTATION

The second mechanism of genetic evolution is mutation. Mutations, which occur spontaneously and regularly, provide new biochemical forms—variety—on which natural selection may operate. **Mutations** are changes in the DNA molecules of which genes and chromosomes are built. If a mutation occurs in a sex cell that combines with another as a fertilized egg, the new organism will carry the mutation in every cell. This may result in a biochemical difference between the mutant child and the parent. The abnormal protein associated with sickle-cell anemia is caused by just such a difference in a single allele between normal individuals and those with the disease.

Mutations occur in about 5 percent of sex cells. The rate varies from gene to gene. Many geneticists believe that most mutations are neutral, conferring neither advantage nor disadvantage. Others argue that most mutations are harmful and will be weeded out because they deviate from the types that have been selected over the generations. However, if the selective forces affecting a population change, mutations in its gene pool may acquire an adaptive advantage they lacked in the old environment.

Such chemical alterations may provide a population with entirely new phenotypes, which may offer some advantage. Variants produced through mutation can be especially significant if there is a change in selective forces. They may prove to have an advantage they lacked in the old environment. The spread of Hb^S as farming expanded offers one example.

RANDOM GENETIC DRIFT

The third mechanism of genetic evolution is **random genetic drift.** This is a change in allele frequency that results not from natural selection but from chance. Since random genetic drift is most common in small populations, it has probably been important in human evolution, because humans have lived in small groups during much of our history. In a small population, alleles are likely to be lost by chance.

To understand why, compare the sorting of alleles to a game involving a bag of 12 marbles, 6 red and 6 blue. In step 1, you draw six marbles from the bag. Statistically, your chances of drawing three reds and three blues are less than those of getting four of one color and two of the other. Step 2 is to fill a new bag with 12 marbles on the basis of the ratio of marbles you drew in step 1. Assume that you drew four reds and two blues: The new bag will have eight red marbles and four blue ones. Step 3 is to draw six marbles from the new bag. Your chances of drawing blues in step 3 are lower than they were in step 1, and the probability of drawing all reds increases. If you do draw all reds, the next bag (step 4) will have only red marbles.

This game is analogous to random genetic drift operating over the generations. The blue marbles were lost purely by chance. Alleles, too, can be lost by chance rather than because of any disadvantage they confer. Lost alleles can reappear in a gene pool only through mutation.

GENE FLOW

The fourth mechanism of genetic evolution is **gene flow,** the exchange of genetic material between populations of the same species. Gene flow, like mutation, works in conjunction with natural selection by providing variety on which selection can work. Gene flow may consist of direct interbreeding between formerly separated populations of the same species (e.g., Europeans, Africans, and Native Americans in the United States), or it may be indirect.

Consider the following hypothetical case (Figure 4.6). In a certain part of the world live six local populations of a certain species. P_1 is the westernmost of these populations. P_2, which interbreeds with P_1, is located 50 miles to the east. P_2 also interbreeds with P_3, located 50 miles east of P_2. Assume that each population interbreeds with, and only with, the adjacent populations. P_6 is located 250 miles from P_1 and does not directly interbreed with P_1, but it is tied to P_1 through the chain of interbreeding that ultimately links all six populations.

Assume further that some allele exists in P_1 that isn't particularly advantageous in its environment. Because of gene flow, this allele may be passed on to P_2, by it to P_3, and so on, until it eventually reaches P_6. In P_6 or along the way, the allele may encounter an environment in which it does

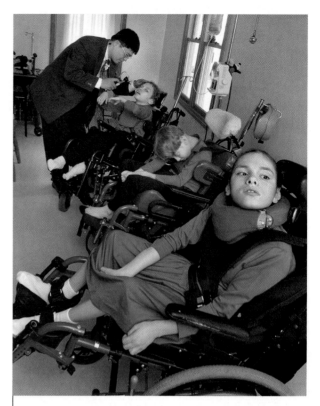

Dr. Heng Wang of the Deutsch Center for Special Needs Children in Middlefield, Ohio works with three siblings (in wheelchairs) at an Amish farm. These children suffer from a genetic disorder, as yet undiagnosed. Intermarriage within small groups, such as the Old Order Amish, increases the likelihood that harmful genes will be expressed in phenotype.

have a selective advantage. If this happens, it may serve, like a new mutation, as raw material on which natural selection can operate.

Alleles are spread through gene flow even when selection is not operating on the allele. In the long run, natural selection works on the variety within a population, whatever its source: mutation, drift, or gene flow. Selection and gene flow have worked together to spread the Hb^S allele in Central Africa. Frequencies of Hb^S in Africa reflect not only the intensity of malaria but also the length of time gene flow has been going on (Livingstone 1969).

Gene flow is important in the study of the origin of species. A **species** is a group of related organisms whose members can interbreed to produce offspring that can live and reproduce. A species has to

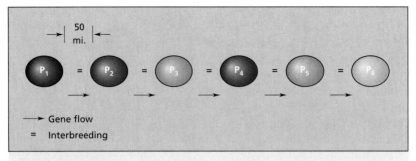

Figure 4.6   Gene Flow between Local Populations.
P_1–P_6 are six local populations of the same species. Each interbreeds
(=) only with its neighbor(s). Although members of P_6 never
interbreed with P_1, P_6 and P_1 are linked through gene flow. Genetic
material that originates in P_1 eventually will reach P_6, and vice versa,
as it is passed from one neighboring population to the next. Because
they share genetic material in this way, P_1–P_6 remain members of the
same species. In many species, local populations distributed
throughout a larger territory than the 250 miles depicted here are
linked through gene flow.

be able to reproduce itself through time. We know
that horses and donkeys belong to different species
because their offspring cannot meet the test of long-
term survival. A horse and a donkey may breed to
produce a mule, but mules are sterile. So are the offspring of lions with tigers. Gene flow tends to prevent **speciation**—the formation of new species—
unless subgroups of the same species are separated
for a sufficient length of time.

When gene flow is interrupted, and isolated
subgroups are maintained, new species may arise.
Imagine that an environmental barrier arises
between P_3 and P_4, so that they no longer interbreed. If over time, as a result of isolation, P_1, P_2,
and P_3 become incapable of interbreeding with
the other three populations, speciation will have
occurred.

Human Biological Adaptation

This section considers several examples of human
biological diversity that reflect adaptation to environmental stresses, such as disease, diet, and climate. There is abundant evidence for human
genetic adaptation and thus for evolution (change

in gene frequency) through selection working in
specific environments. One example is the adaptive value of the Hb^S heterozygote and its spread
in malarial environments. Adaptation and evolution go on in specific environments. There is no
generally or ideally adaptive allele and no perfect
phenotype. Nor can an allele be assumed to be
maladaptive for all times and all places. We have
seen that even Hb^S, which produces a lethal anemia, has a selective advantage in the heterozygous
form in malarial environments.

Also, alleles that were once maladaptive may
lose their disadvantage if the environment shifts.
Color blindness (disadvantageous for hunters and
forest dwellers) and a form of genetically determined diabetes are examples. Today's environment contains medical techniques that allow people with such conditions to live fairly normal lives.
Formerly maladaptive alleles have thus become
neutral with respect to selection. With thousands
of human genes now known, new genetic traits
are discovered almost every day. Such studies
tend to focus on genetic abnormalities, because of
their medical and treatment implications.

In June 2000 scientists announced completion of
a first draft of a map of the human genome—all our
genes and chromosomes—some 3 billion genetic letters in human DNA. One of the two main groups

behind this discovery is the National Institutes of Health's Human Genome Project, whose website is worth a visit: **http://www.ornl.gov/hgmis/.**

Given current knowledge about genetically transmitted diseases, people with a family history of such a disease can be advised about their children's chances of being affected. Many currently incurable hereditary illnesses are destined to become neutral traits in tomorrow's medical environment. However, genetic testing raises many ethical questions. Given possible discrimination in employment and in obtaining health insurance, some members of the medical community have advised people not to be tested for genetic markers that might indicate a tendency to develop, say, Alzheimer's disease. Laws to forbid genetic discrimination are not yet fully in place. Alzheimer's is likely to become much more prevalent, and costly to treat as a public health problem, as the baby-boomer cohort ages.

Genetic discrimination isn't new. Some of its most virulent manifestations occurred in Adolph Hitler's Third Reich. More surprisingly, in 1997 it was revealed that, through the 1970s, some 60,000 people were sterilized in Sweden, and 11,000 in Finland, as part of government policies designed to weed out traits such as poor eyesight and Gypsy features (Wade 1997). This is an example of **eugenics,** a highly controversial movement aimed at genetic improvement by encouraging the reproduction of individuals with favored features and discouraging that of individuals with features deemed undesirable. Should past crimes committed in the name of eugenics prevent people from being allowed to choose benefits that genetic engineering may offer in the future? A related question: What ethical questions are raised by the cloning of human beings? Cloning can be combined with genetic enhancement—adding genes to produce desired traits. Genetic enhancement has been the main reason for cloning animals, such as Dolly the lamb, introduced in 1997 as the world's first mammal cloned from an adult donor cell.

In cloning, a cell is taken from a donor animal and inserted into an egg cell (of the same species) whose genetic material has been removed. This allows the donor's genetic material to direct the development of a new embryo, then fetus, then live animal, which will be the donor's identical twin. Successful animal cloning has made it possible to think seriously about using cloning for the genetic enhancement of human beings (Kolata 1997). Scientists could grow a person's cells in sheets in the laboratory and sprinkle those cells with genes. The cells that take up the genes could be used as donor cells to make human clones, which would contain the added genes in every cell of their bodies. With humans the first genetic enhancements would probably be genes to protect against diseases. Genes to counter AIDS and Alzheimer's disease have already been identified. Some scientists see this process as no different morally from vaccinating a child. Here are some ethical questions to consider: Who would raise human clones: scientists or families? What would be the legal status of clones? Would they be people

DNA specialist Craig Venter of Celera Genomics, Inc. looks at a computer monitor showing genome sequencing. On June 26, 2000 Celera announced the completion of a draft of the human genome—all our genes and chromosomes.

or products? Would they be free human beings or entities designed to satisfy wishes, whims, and medical needs of others? What do you think about the ethics of human cloning?

GENES AND DISEASE

According to the *World Health Report*, published by the World Health Organization (WHO) in Geneva, Switzerland, tropical diseases affect more than 10 percent of the world's population. Malaria, the most widespread of these diseases, afflicts between 300 million and 500 million people annually. Schistosomiasis (snail fever), a waterborne parasitic disease, affects more than 200 million. Some 120 million people have filariasis, which causes elephantiasis—lymphatic obstruction leading to the enlargement of body parts, particularly the legs and scrotum (check out the website of the World Health Organization at http://www.who.int/home/).

The malaria threat is spreading. Brazil had 560,000 cases in 1988, versus 100,000 in 1977. Worldwide, the number of malaria cases rose from 270 million in 1990 to over 400 million in 1997 (*New York Times* 1990; World Health Organization 1997). Contributing to this rise is the increasing resistance of parasites to drugs used to treat malaria. However, hundreds of millions of people are genetically resistant. Sickle-cell hemoglobin is the best known of the genetic antimalarials (Diamond 1997).

Microbes have been major selective agents for humans, particularly before the arrival of modern medicine. Some people are genetically more susceptible to certain diseases than others are, and the distribution of human blood types continues to change in response to natural selection.

After food production emerged around 10,000 years ago, infectious diseases posed a mounting risk and eventually became the foremost cause of human mortality. Food production favors infection for several reasons. Cultivation sustains larger, denser populations and a more sedentary life style than does hunting and gathering. People live closer to each other and to their own wastes, making it easier for microbes to survive and to find hosts. Domesticated animals also transmit diseases to people.

Until 1977, when the last case of smallpox was reported, smallpox had been a major threat to humans and a determinant of blood group fre-

quencies (Diamond 1990, 1997). The smallpox virus is a mutation from one of the pox viruses that plague such domesticated animals as cows, sheep, goats, horses, and pigs. Smallpox appeared in human beings after people and animals started living together. Smallpox epidemics have played important roles in world history, often killing one-fourth to one-half of the affected populations. Smallpox contributed to Sparta's defeat of Athens in 430 BC and to the decline of the Roman empire after AD 160.

The ABO blood groups have figured in human resistance to smallpox. Blood is typed according to the protein and sugar compounds on the surface of the red blood cells. Different substances (compounds) distinguish between type A and type B blood. Type A cells trigger the production of *antibodies* in B blood, so that A cells clot in B blood. The different substances work like chemical passwords; they help us distinguish our own cells from invading cells, including microbes, we ought to destroy. The surfaces of some microbes have substances similar to ABO blood group substances. We don't produce antibodies to substances similar to

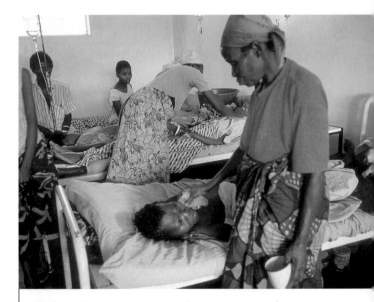

AIDS is widespread in many African nations such as Rwanda—shown here—as well as in the United States, France, Thailand, Brazil, and many other countries. What would be evidence for genetic variation in susceptibility to the HIV virus?

those on our own blood cells. We can think of this as a clever evolutionary trick by the microbes to deceive their hosts, because we don't normally develop antibodies against our own biochemistry.

People with A or AB blood are more susceptible to smallpox than are people with type B or type O. Presumably this is because a substance on the smallpox virus mimics the type A substance, permitting the virus to slip by the defenses of the type A individual. By contrast, type B and type O individuals produce antibodies against smallpox because they recognize it as a foreign substance.

The relation between type A blood and susceptibility to smallpox was first suggested by the low frequencies of the A allele in areas of India and Africa where smallpox had been endemic. A comparative study done in rural India in 1965–66, during a virulent smallpox epidemic, did much to confirm this relationship. Drs. F. Vogel and M. R. Chakravartti analyzed blood samples from smallpox victims and their uninfected siblings (Diamond 1990). The researchers found 415 infected children, none ever vaccinated against smallpox. All but eight of the infected children had an uninfected (also unvaccinated) sibling.

The results of the study were clear: Susceptibility to smallpox varied with ABO type. Of the 415 infected children, 261 had the A allele; 154 lacked it. Among their 407 uninfected siblings, the ratio was reversed. Only 80 had the A allele; 327 lacked it. The researchers calculated that a type A or type AB person had a seven times greater chance of getting smallpox than did an O or B person.

In most human populations, the O allele is more common than A and B combined. A is most common in Europe; B frequencies are highest in Asia. Since smallpox was once widespread in the Old World, we might wonder why natural selection didn't eliminate the A allele entirely. The answer appears to be this: Other diseases spared the type A people and penalized those with other blood groups.

For example, type O people seem to be especially susceptible to the bubonic plague—the "Black Death" that killed a third of the population of medieval Europe. Type O people are also more likely to get cholera, which has killed as many people in India as smallpox has. On the other hand, blood group O may increase resistance to syphilis. The ravages of that venereal disease,

which may have originated in the New World, may explain the very high frequency of type O blood among the natives of Central and South America. The distribution of human blood groups appears to represent a compromise among the selective effects of many diseases.

Associations between ABO blood type and noninfectious disorders also have been noted. Type O individuals are most susceptible to duodenal and gastric ulcers. Type A individuals seem most prone to stomach and cervical cancer and ovarian tumors. However, since these noninfectious disorders tend to occur after reproduction has ended, their relevance to adaptation and evolution through natural selection is doubtful (see also Weiss 1993).

Understanding Ourselves In the weeks and months after September 11, 2001, millions of Americans started worrying about anthrax—and more generally about biological terrorism. Anthrax, we learned, is easily treated with antibiotics such as Cipro and doxycycline. But what about other diseases—ones whose cure isn't as easy and risk-free? What about smallpox, a viral disease that had been eradicated in nature? Could evildoers seize smallpox samples stored in labs and unleash an epidemic? The U.S. government started preparing for a possible smallpox attack. The plan was to increase the supply and availability of smallpox vaccine. But who would receive it? Although it is a highly effective vaccine, a smallpox inoculation has been known to kill people who otherwise would never have been exposed to the disease. Knowing what you now know about blood groups and smallpox, would you want to pay attention to an individual's ABO blood type before administering smallpox vaccine? Which recipients probably would be at greatest risk?

In the case of diseases for which there are no effective drugs, genetic resistance maintains its significance. There is probably genetic variation in susceptibility to the HIV virus, for example. We know that people exposed to HIV vary in their risk of developing AIDS and in the rate at which the disease progresses. AIDS is widespread in many African nations (and in the United States, France, and Brazil). Particularly in Africa, where treatment strategies now used in the industrial nations are not widely available, the death rate from AIDS could eventually (let us hope it does not) rival that of past epidemics of smallpox and plague. If so, AIDS could cause large shifts in human gene frequencies—again illustrating the ongoing operation of natural selection.

Facial Features

Natural selection also affects facial features. For instance, long noses seem to be adaptive in arid areas (Brace 1964; Weiner 1954), because membranes and blood vessels inside the nose moisten the air as it is breathed in. Long noses are also adaptive in cold environments, because blood vessels warm the air as it is breathed in. This nose form distances the brain, which is sensitive to bitter cold, from raw outer air. These were adaptive biological features for humans who lived in cold climates before the invention of central heating.

The association between nose form and temperature is recognized as **Thomson's nose rule** (Thomson and Buxton 1923), which shows up statistically. In plotting the geographic distribution of nose length among human populations, the average nose does tend to be longer in areas with lower mean annual temperatures.

Other facial features also illustrate adaptation to selective forces. Among contemporary humans, average tooth size is largest among Native Australian hunters and gatherers, for whom large teeth had an adaptive advantage, given a diet based on foods with a considerable amount of sand and grit. People with small teeth—if false teeth and sand-free foods are unavailable—can't feed themselves as effectively as people with more massive dentition can (see Brace 2000).

Size and Body Build

Certain body builds have adaptive advantages for particular environments. The relation between body weight and temperature is summarized in **Bergmann's rule:** The smaller of two bodies similar in shape has more surface area per unit of weight. Therefore, it sheds heat more efficiently. (Heat loss occurs on the body's surface—the skin perspires.) Average body size tends to increase in cold areas and to decrease in hot ones because big bodies hold heat better than small ones do. To be more precise, in a large sample of native populations, average adult male weight increased by 0.66 pound (0.3 kilogram) for every 1 degree Fahrenheit fall in mean annual temperature (Roberts 1953; Steegman 1975). The "pygmies" and the San, who live in hot climates and weigh only 90 pounds on the average, illustrate this relation in reverse.

Body shape differences also reflect adaptation to temperature through natural selection. The relationship between temperature and body shape in animals and birds was first recognized in 1877 by the zoologist J. A. Allen. **Allen's rule** states that the relative size of protruding body parts—ears, tails, bills, fingers, toes, limbs, and so on—increases with temperature. Among humans, slender bodies with long digits and limbs are advantageous in tropical climates. Such bodies increase body surface relative to mass and allow for more efficient heat dissipation. Among the cold-adapted Eskimos, the opposite phenotype is found. Short limbs and stocky bodies serve to conserve heat. Cold area populations tend to have larger chests and shorter arms than do people from warm areas (Roberts 1953).

This discussion of adaptive relationships between climate and body size and shape illustrates that natural selection may achieve the same effect in different ways. East African Nilotes, who live in a hot area, have tall, linear bodies with elongated extremities that increase surface area relative to mass and thus maximize heat dissipation (illustrating Allen's rule). Among the "pygmies," the reduction of body size achieves the same result (illustrating Bergmann's rule). Similarly, the large bodies of northern Europeans and the compact stockiness of the Eskimos serve the same function of heat conservation.

Interpret the World
Atlas Map 4
Map 4 in your atlas shows the relation between body mass index and mean annual temperature. People adapt both culturally and biologically, and some human groups haven't lived in their current habitats long enough for long-term biological adaptation to have occurred. Nevertheless, try to locate areas on the map where Bergmann's and Allen's rules are illustrated with respect to cold adaptation (big or compact bodies) and heat adaptation (small or elongated bodies).

This Nilotic man, a Nuer herder from Sudan, has a tall linear body with elongated extremities (note his fingers). Such proportioning increases the surface area relative to mass and thus dissipates heat (Allen's rule). What other body form can achieve the same result?

Cold weather populations tend to have relatively larger chests and shorter arms than do people from warm areas. Among the cold-adapted Inuit, such as this Alaskan woman, short limbs and stocky bodies help to conserve heat. How important is biology to cold adaptation today?

LACTOSE TOLERANCE

Many biological traits that illustrate human adaptation are not under simple genetic control. Genetic determination of such traits may be likely but unconfirmed, or several genes may interact to influence the trait in question. Sometimes there is a genetic component, but the trait also responds to stresses encountered during growth. We speak of **phenotypical adaptation** when adaptive changes occur during the individual's lifetime. Phenotypical adaptation is made possible by biological plasticity—our ability to change in response to the environments we encounter as we grow (see Frisancho 1993; Bogin 2001). Recall the discussion of physiological adaptation to high altitude in Chapter 1.

Genes and phenotypical adaptation work together to produce a biochemical difference between human groups in the ability to digest large amounts of milk—an adaptive advantage when other foods are scarce and milk is available, as it is in dairying societies. All milk, whatever its source, contains a complex sugar called *lactose*. The digestion of milk depends on an enzyme called *lactase*, which works in the small intestine. Among all mammals except humans and some of their pets, lactase production ceases after weaning, so that these animals can no longer digest milk.

Lactase production and the ability to tolerate milk vary between populations. About 90 percent of northern Europeans and their descendants are lactose tolerant; they can digest several glasses of milk with no difficulty. Similarly, about 80 percent of two African populations, the Tutsi of Rwanda and Burundi in East Africa and the Fulani of Nigeria in West Africa, produce lactase and digest milk easily. Both these groups traditionally have been herders. However, such nonherders as the Yoruba and Igbo in Nigeria, the Baganda in Uganda, the Japanese and other Asians, Eskimos, South American Indians, and many Israelis cannot digest lactose (Kretchmer 1972/1975).

However, the variable human ability to digest milk seems to be a difference of degree. Some populations can tolerate very little or no milk, but others are able to metabolize much greater quantities. Studies show that people who move from no-milk or low-milk diets to high-milk diets increase their lactose tolerance; this suggests some phenotypical adaptation. We can conclude that no simple genetic trait accounts for the ability to digest milk. Lactose tolerance appears to be one of many aspects of human biology governed both by genes and by phenotypical adaptation to environmental conditions.

Understanding Ourselves "Hey, it's all in the genes." When did you last hear a statement like that? We routinely use assumptions about genetic determination to explain, say, why tall parents have tall kids or why obesity runs in families. But how true is the statement? How much do our genes influence our bodies? The genetic causes of some of our physical traits are clear. This is true with the ABO blood group system, and with other blood factors, such as whether we are Rh positive or negative and whether we are sickle-cell carriers. But the genetic roots of other physical traits aren't so clear. A grandmother may assert that her inability to digest milk runs in her family—so they never bought milk. What would have happened if they had consumed small quantities of milk over the years? Would they gradually have become habituated to lactose? There's evidence that such habituation is possible because of the plasticity of human genotypes. Can you crease or fold your tongue by raising its sides? Some people can; some people never can; some people who never thought they could can after practice. Again, an apparent genetic limitation turns out to be more plastic.

Human biology is plastic, but only to a degree. If you're born with blood group O, you've got it for the rest of your life. The same applies to disorders due to harmful genes, such as those that cause hemophilia (transmitted on the X chromosome) and sickle-cell anemia. Still, if there's no genetic solution, there may be a cultural one. Modern medicine now treats effectively a variety of genetic disorders that once would have been much more life-threatening. Fortunately for us, plasticity through culture steps in to complement human biological plasticity.

We see that human biology changes constantly, even without genetic change. In this chapter we've considered ways in which humans adapt biologically to their environments, and the effects of such adaptation on human biological diversity. Modern biological anthropology seeks to *explain* specific aspects of human biological variation. The explanatory framework encompasses the same mechanisms—selection, mutation, drift, gene flow, and plasticity—that govern adaptation, variation, and evolution among other life forms (see Futuyma 1998; Mayr 2001).

SUMMARY

1. In the 18th century, Carolus Linnaeus developed biological taxonomy. He viewed differences and similarities among organisms as part of God's orderly plan rather than as evidence for evolution. Charles Darwin and Alfred Russel Wallace proposed that natural selection could explain the origin of species, biological diversity, and similarities among related life forms. Natural selection requires variety in the population undergoing selection.

2. Through breeding experiments with peas in 1856, Gregor Mendel discovered that genetic traits pass on as units. These are now known to be chromosomes, which occur in homologous pairs. Alleles, some dominant, some recessive, are the chemically different forms that occur at a

given genetic locus. Mendel also formulated the law of independent assortment. Each of the seven traits he studied in peas was inherited independently of all the others. Independent assortment of chromosomes and their recombination provide some of the variety needed for natural selection. But the major source of such variety is mutation, a chemical change in the DNA molecules of which genes are made.

3. Population genetics studies gene frequencies in stable and changing populations. Natural selection is the most important mechanism of evolutionary change. Others are mutation, random genetic drift, and gene flow. Given environmental change, nature selects traits already present in the population. If variety is insufficient to permit adaptation to the change, extinction is likely. New types don't appear just because they are needed.

4. One well-documented case of natural selection in contemporary human populations is that of the sickle-cell allele. In homozygous form, the sickle-cell allele, Hb^s, produces an abnormal hemoglobin. This clogs the small blood vessels, impairing the blood's capacity to store oxygen. The result is sickle-cell anemia, which is usually fatal. The distribution of Hb^s has been linked to that of malaria. Homozygotes for normal hemo-

globin are susceptible to malaria and die in great numbers. Homozygotes for the sickle-cell allele die from anemia. Heterozygotes get only mild anemia and are resistant to malaria. In a malarial environment, the heterozygote has the advantage. This explains why an apparently maladaptive allele is preserved.

5. Other mechanisms of genetic evolution complement natural selection. Random genetic drift operates most obviously in small populations, where pure chance can easily change allele frequencies. Gene flow and interbreeding keep subgroups of the same species genetically connected and thus impede speciation.

6. Differential resistance to infectious diseases has influenced the distribution of human blood groups. Natural selection also has operated on facial features and body size and shape. Phenotypical adaptation refers to adaptive changes that occur in the individual's lifetime, in response to the environment the organism encounters as it grows. Biological similarities between geographically distant populations may be due to similar but independent genetic changes, rather than to common ancestry. Or they may reflect similar physiological responses to common stresses during growth.

KEY TERMS

adaptive   Favored by natural selection in a particular environment.

allele   A biochemical variant of a particular gene.

Allen's rule   Rule stating that the relative size of protruding body parts (such as ears, tails, bills, fingers, toes, and limbs) tends to increase in warmer climates.

Bergmann's rule   Rule stating that the smaller of two bodies similar in shape has more surface area per unit of weight and can therefore dissipate heat more efficiently; hence, large bodies tend to be found in colder areas and small bodies in warmer ones.

catastrophism   View that extinct species were destroyed by fires, floods, and other catastrophes. After each destructive event, God created again, leading to contemporary species.

chromosomes   Basic genetic units, occurring in matching (homologous) pairs; lengths of DNA made up of multiple genes.

creationism   Explanation for the origin of species given in Genesis: God created the species during the original six days of Creation.

dominant   Allele that masks another allele in a heterozygote.

eugenics   Controversial movement aimed at genetic improvement by encouraging the reproduction of individuals with favored features and discouraging that of individuals with features deemed undesirable.

evolution Belief that species arose from others through a long and gradual process of transformation, or descent with modification.

gene Area in a chromosome pair that determines, wholly or partially, a particular biological trait, such as whether one's blood type is A, B, or O.

gene flow Exchange of genetic material between populations of the same species through direct or indirect interbreeding.

gene pool All the alleles and genotypes within a breeding population—the "pool" of genetic material available.

genetic evolution Change in gene frequency within a breeding population.

genotype An organism's hereditary makeup.

heterozygous Having dissimilar alleles of a given gene.

homozygous Possessing identical alleles of a particular gene.

independent assortment Mendel's law of; chromosomes are inherited independently of one another.

meiosis Special process by which sex cells are produced; four cells are produced from one, each with half the genetic material of the original cell.

Mendelian genetics Studies ways in which chromosomes transmit genes across the generations.

mitosis Ordinary cell division; DNA molecules copy themselves, creating two identical cells out of one.

mutation Change in the DNA molecules of which genes and chromosomes are built.

natural selection Originally formulated by Charles Darwin and Alfred Russel Wallace; the process by which nature selects the forms most fit to survive and reproduce in a given environment, such as the tropics.

phenotypical adaptation Adaptive biological changes that occur during the individual's lifetime, made possible by biological plasticity.

population genetics Field that studies causes of genetic variation, maintenance, and change in breeding populations.

random genetic drift Change in gene frequency that results not from natural selection but from chance; most common in small populations.

recessive Genetic trait masked by a dominant trait.

recombination Following independent assortment of chromosomes, new arrangements of hereditary units produced through bisexual reproduction.

sexual selection Based on differential success in mating, the process in which certain traits of one sex (e.g., color in male birds) are selected because of advantages they confer in winning mates.

speciation Formation of new species; occurs when subgroups of the same species are separated for a sufficient length of time.

species Population whose members can interbreed to produce offspring that can live and reproduce.

Thomson's nose rule Rule stating that the average nose tends to be longer in areas with lower mean annual temperatures; based on the geographic distribution of nose length among human populations.

uniformitarianism Belief that explanations for past events should be sought in ordinary forces that continue to work today.

CRITICAL THINKING
QUESTIONS

For more self testing, see the self quizzes

/kottak

1. If you are (or are pretending you are) a creationist, what do you see as the most convincing evidence for evolution?

2. If you are (or are pretending you are) an evolutionist, what do you see as the least convincing evidence for evolution?

3. Which of the examples of natural selection mentioned in the book most surprised you? Can you think of examples of natural selection other than those mentioned in the book?

4. Choose five people in your classroom who illustrate a range of phenotypical diversity. Which of their features vary most evidently? How do you explain this variation? Is some of the variation due to culture rather than to biology?

5. Imagine that some of the seven traits that Mendel studied in pea plants were determined by genes on the same chromosome. How might his results have differed?

6. Give three examples of how and why identical genotypes might develop different phenotypes. (Identical twins and clones have identical genotypes.)

7. Is *Homo sapiens* more or less adaptable than other species? What makes us so adaptable? Can you think of some species that are more adaptable than we are?

8. What are two important lessons to be learned from the case of the sickle-cell allele (Hb^S)?

9. Which of the mechanisms of genetic evolution acts to prevent speciation?

10. Did anything stated in this chapter about your ABO blood type give you cause for alarm? Why?

11. How would you design the ideal body for a very cold climate? How about for a very hot one?

12. Besides those mentioned in the book, give an example of a biological trait that depends on physiological adaptation.

Atlas Questions

Look at Map 4, "Human Variations: Height and Weight."

1. Which areas have the biggest (heaviest) people? Does this illustrate Bergmann's or Allen's rule?

2. Which areas have populations with compact builds? Does this illustrate Bergmann's or Allen's rule?

3. Where are the world's smallest indigenous populations located? Which rule does this illustrate?

SUGGESTED ADDITIONAL
READINGS

Bogin, B.
2001   *The Growth of Humanity.* New York: Wiley-Liss. Up-to-date perspective on human growth and development.

Cavalli-Sforza, L. L., P. Menozzi, and A. Piazza
1994   *The History and Geography of Human Genes.* Princeton, NJ: Princeton University Press. Comprehensive look at the geographic spread of human genes.

Eiseley, L.
1961   *Darwin's Century.* Garden City, NY: Doubleday, Anchor Books. Discussion of Lyell, Darwin, Wallace, and other major contributors to natural selection and transformation.

Frisancho, A. R.
1993   *Human Adaptation and Accommodation.* Ann Arbor: University of Michigan Press. Influence of the environment on phenotype, particularly during growth and development; a basic text.

Futuyma, D. J.

1995   *Science on Trial,* updated ed. Sunderland, MA: Sinauer Associates. The case of evolution versus creationism—favoring the former.

1998   *Evolutionary Biology.* Sunderland, MA: Sinauer Associates. Basic text.

Gillespie, J. H.

1998   *Population Genetics: A Concise Guide.* Baltimore: Johns Hopkins University Press. Good introduction to population genetics.

Gould, S. J.

1999   *Rock of Ages: Science and Religion in the Fullness of Life.* New York: Ballantine Books. Evolution, science, and religion by the well-known naturalist and science writer.

Hartl, D. L.

2000   *A Primer of Population Genetics,* 3rd ed. Sunderland, MA: Sinauer Associates. Short introduction to the field.

Hartl, D. L., and E. W. Jones

2002   *Essential Genetics,* 3rd ed. Sudbury, MA: Jones and Bartlett. Basic introduction to genetics.

Lewontin, R.

2000   *It Ain't Necessarily So: The Dream of the Human Genome and Other Illusions.* New York: New York Review of Books. Questions about nature, nurture, and contemporary genetic research.

Mayr, E.

2001   *What Evolution Is.* New York: Basic Books. A master scholar sums it all up.

Roberts, D. F.

1986   *Genetic Variation and Its Maintenance: With Particular Reference to Tropical Populations.* New York: Cambridge University Press. Evidence for human genetic evolution, with a focus on tropical populations.

Shermer, M.

2002   *In Darwin's Shadow: The Life and Science of Alfred Russel Wallace.* New York: Oxford University Press. The other inventor of natural selection.

Stinson, S., ed.

2000   *Human Biology: An Evolutionary and Biocultural Perspective.* New York: Wiley. Articles on physical anthropology and human biology.

Weiner, J.

1994   *The Beak of the Finch: A Story of Evolution in Our Time.* New York: Alfred A. Knopf. An excellent introduction to Darwin and to evolutionary theory.

Weiss, K. M.

1993   *Genetic Variation and Human Disease: Principles and Evolutionary Approaches.* New York: Cambridge University Press. Selection connected with human diseases.

Wilson, D. S.

2002   *Darwin's Cathedral: Evolution, Religion, and the Nature of Society.* Chicago: University of Chicago Press. Religion, sociology, and evolution.

INTERNET EXERCISES

1. Creationism: Look at the CreationWise cartoon website, **http://members.aol.com/dwr51055/humor.htm**. This site uses cartoons to express the concerns creationists have about evolution.

   a. What is the creationist version of the origin of life? What evidence do they use to support their claims? According to these cartoons, what are some of the problems that creationists have with evolution?

   b. What would be the response to these questions from a scientist who studies evolution?

2. Adaptation to Environment: Read Dennis O'Neil's page on "Adapting to Climate Extremes" (**http://anthro.palomar.edu/adapt/adapt_2.htm**).

   a. What is Bergmann's rule? What is Allen's rule?

   b. How do the !Kung and Australian Aborigines respond to cold differently from the Inuit and groups from Tierra del Fuego? Is there an adaptive reason why these groups have different responses to cold?

   c. What are the advantages of evaporative cooling? What are the disadvantages?

See Chapter 4 at your McGraw-Hill Online Learning Center for additional review and interactive exercises.

5

THE PRIMATES

Overview

Humans, apes, monkeys, and prosimians all belong to the zoological order known as primates. The apes are our closest relatives. Humans share more than 98 percent of our DNA with chimpanzees and gorillas.

Early primates, like many contemporary ones, lived in the trees. Reflecting our arboreal heritage, primates share certain anatomical features. These include grasping hands with opposable thumbs, depth and color vision, and use of the fingertip pads as the main organs of touch. With large and complex brains, humans, apes, and monkeys rely extensively on learning. Primates live in social groups and invest considerable time and energy in their offspring and kin.

Gorillas, the least arboreal apes, are vegetarians confined to equatorial Africa. Two species of chimpanzees live in the forests and woodlands of tropical Africa. All the apes and many other primate species are endangered, mainly by deforestation and human hunting. Some important developments in human evolution, such as hunting and tool making, are foreshadowed in other primates, particularly chimpanzees. It is likely that for millions of years sharing and cooperation have been basic features of human social life. Other primates show affection with their kin, but only humans have systems of kinship and marriage that permit us to maintain lifelong ties with relatives in different local groups.

Chimp Tool Sites Show Evidence of Human-like Behavior

CBC NEWS BRIEF

May 26, 2002

Primatologists study nonhuman primates, such as apes, monkeys, and lemurs. The study of monkeys, and particularly of apes, our nearest zoological relatives, is of interest to anthropology mainly because their attributes and their behavior tell us something about human nature and origins. To what extent are we distinct, especially from chimpanzees, which share more than 98 percent of our DNA? What about tool making, a key ingredient in human cultural adaptation, permitting our survival and expansion? More than any other primate, chimps share the human capacity for deliberate tool manufacture, as the following news story demonstrates. As you read this account, think about how primatology and archaeology can be combined to shed light on early human behavior.

WASHINGTON—Chimpanzees in a remote West African rainforest use crude stone tools to crack open nuts, a skill which they teach to their young, researchers have found.

The chimpanzees used hammer stones to break open hard, golfball-sized nuts from panda trees.

Melissa Panger of George Washington University studies primate tool use and is a co-author of the nut cracking report, which appears in Friday's issue of the journal *Science*.

Panger said the chimps showed precise control over the force needed to break open the nuts. It takes a lot of pressure, but if too much is applied then the nuts shatter into inedible pieces, she said.

Panger's colleagues on the study were Christophe Boesch, an expert on chimpanzee behavior at the Max Planck Institute for Evolutionary Anthropology in Germany and Julio Mercader, a specialist in rainforest archaeology at the George Washington University Department of Anthropology.

The team found the nut shells and remains were concentrated in a nut cracking area called Panda 100 in Ivory Coast's Tai National Park.

The area is what archeologists call a site, and the researchers say their study is the first time archeology has been successfully applied to past chimpanzee behavior.

At Tai National Park (Ivory Coast), young chimps learn from their mothers how to use stone tools to crack nuts. Is this cultural behavior?

At the nut cracking sites, the chimps gather their nuts, put them on trees which are used as anvils, and pound the nuts with heavy stones.

Mothers showed their young how to crack the nuts, the same way humans teach their children.

The nut cracking behavior is limited to chimps living in Ivory Coast, Liberia and Guinea-Conakry, even though the nuts and stones are available to chimps in central Africa. Experts say the difference may mean it is a cultural, learned behavior.

The chimps must also select hammer stones suited to smashing nuts and carry them to where the nut trees grow — sophisticated behavior for an animal.

The unearthed materials included more than 470 stone pieces that may have flaked off when smashed against the anvils. The flakes resemble those used by early humans as knives and other tools.

"Some of the stone by-products of chimpanzee nut-cracking are similar to what we see left behind by some of our ancestors in East Africa during a period called the 'Oldowan,'" said Mercader, the lead author of the study.

Source: http://cbc.ca/stories/2002/05/23/chimp_tools020523.

Primatology is the study of nonhuman primates—fossil and living apes, monkeys, and prosimians—including their behavior and social life. Primatology is fascinating in itself, but it also helps anthropologists make inferences about the early social organization of *hominids* (members of the zoological family that includes fossil and living humans) and untangle issues of human nature and the origins of culture, such as early tool making—its nature and value. Of particular relevance to humans are two kinds of primates:

1. Those whose ecological adaptations are similar to our own: **terrestrial monkeys** and apes—that is, primates that live on the ground rather than in the trees.

2. Those that are most closely related to us: the great apes, specifically the chimpanzees and gorillas.

Our Place among Primates

Similarities between humans and apes are evident in anatomy, brain structure, genetics, and biochemistry. The physical similarities between humans and apes are recognized in zoological taxonomy—the assignment of organisms to categories (*taxa*; singular, *taxon*) according to their relationship and resemblance. Many similarities between organisms reflect their common *phylogeny*—their genetic relatedness based on common ancestry. In other words, organisms share features they have inherited from the same ancestor. Humans and apes belong to the same taxonomic superfamily, *Hominoidea* (hominoids). Monkeys are placed in two others (Ceboidea and Cercopithecoidea). This means that humans and apes are more closely related to each other than either is to monkeys.

Figure 5.1 summarizes the various levels of classification used in zoological taxonomy. Each lower-level unit belongs to the higher-level unit above it. Thus, looking toward the bottom of Figure 5.1, similar species belong to the same genus (plural, *genera*). Similar genera make up the same family, and so on through the top of Figure 5.1, where similar phyla (plural of *phylum*) are included in the same kingdom.

We see that the highest (most inclusive) taxonomic level is the *kingdom*. At that level, animals are distinguished from plants. The lowest-level taxa are species and subspecies. A *species* is a group

Compare the human and the gorilla. What similarities do you notice? What differences? Humans, gorillas, and chimps have more than 98 percent of their DNA in common.

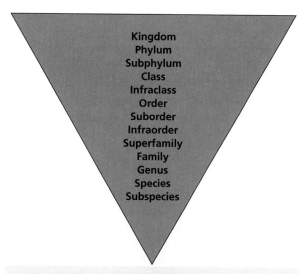

Figure 5.1 The Principal Classificatory Units of Zoological Taxonomy. Moving down the figure, the classificatory units become more exclusive, so that "Kingdom" at the top is the most inclusive unit and "Subspecies" at the bottom is the most exclusive.

Kingdom
Phylum
Subphylum
Class
Infraclass
Order
Suborder
Infraorder
Superfamily
Family
Genus
Species
Subspecies

of organisms that can mate and give birth to *viable* (capable of living) and *fertile* (capable of reproducing) offspring whose own offspring are viable and fertile. *Speciation* (the formation of a new species) occurs when groups that once belonged to the same species can no longer interbreed. After a sufficiently long period of reproductive isolation, two closely related species assigned to the same genus will have evolved out of one.

At the lowest level of taxonomy, a species may have subspecies. These are its more or less, but not yet totally, isolated subgroups. Subspecies can coexist in time and space. For example, the Neandertals, who thrived between 130,000 and 30,000 years ago, often are assigned not to a separate species but merely to a different subspecies of *Homo sapiens*. Just one subspecies of *Homo sapiens* survives today.

The similarities used to assign organisms to the same taxon are called homologies, similarities they have jointly inherited from a common ancestor. Table 5.1 summarizes the place of humans in zoological taxonomy. We see in Table 5.1 that we are mammals, members of the class Mammalia. This is a major subdivision of the kingdom Animalia. Mammals share certain traits, including mammary

glands, that set them apart from other taxa, such as birds, reptiles, amphibians, and insects. Mammalian homologies indicate that all mammals share more recent common ancestry with each other than they do with any bird, reptile, or insect.

Humans are mammals that, at a lower taxonomic level, belong to the *order* Primates. Another mammalian order is Carnivora: the carnivores (dogs, cats, foxes, wolves, badgers, weasels). Rodentia (rats, mice, beavers, squirrels) form yet another mammalian order. The primates share structural and biochemical homologies that distinguish them from other mammals. These resemblances were inherited from their common early primate ancestors after those early primates became reproductively isolated from the ancestors of the other mammals.

Homologies and Analogies

Organisms should be assigned to the same taxon on the basis of homologies. The extensive biochemical homologies between apes and humans confirm our common ancestry and support our traditional joint classification as hominoids. For example, it is estimated that humans, chimpanzees, and gorillas have more than 98 percent of their DNA in common.

However, common ancestry isn't the only reason for similarities between species. Similar traits also can arise if species experience similar selective forces and adapt to them in similar ways. We call such similarities **analogies.** The process by which analogies are produced is called **convergent evolution.** For example, fish and porpoises share many analogies resulting from convergent evolution to life in the water. Like fish, porpoises, which are mammals, have fins. They are also hairless and streamlined for efficient locomotion. Analogies between birds and bats (wings, small size, light bones) illustrate convergent evolution to flying (see Angier 1998).

In theory, only homologies should be used in taxonomy. With reference to the hominoids, there is no doubt that humans, gorillas, and chimpanzees are more closely related to each other than any of the three is to orangutans, which are Asiatic apes (Ciochon 1983). Humans, chimps, and gorillas share a more recent ancestor with each other

Table 5.1 The Place of Humans (*Homo sapiens*) in Zoological Taxonomy

Homo sapiens is an Animal, Chordate, Vertebrate, Mammal, Primate, Anthropoid, Catarrhine, Hominoid, and Hominid. (Table 5.2 shows the taxonomic placement of the other primates.)

Taxon	Scientific (Latin) Name	Common (English) Name
Kingdom	Animalia	Animals
Phylum	Chordata	Chordates
Subphylum	Vertebrata	Vertebrates
Class	Mammalia	Mammals
Infraclass	Eutheria	Eutherians
Order	Primates	Primates
Suborder	Anthropoidea	Anthropoids
Infraorder	Catarrhini	Catarrhines
Superfamily	Hominoidea	Hominoids
Family	Hominidae	Hominids
Genus	*Homo*	Humans
Species	*Homo sapiens*	Recent humans
Subspecies	*Homo sapiens sapiens*	Anatomically modern humans

than they do with orangs. The *Hominidae* family is the zoological family that includes hominids—fossil and living humans. Many scientists now also place gorillas and chimps in that same family. This leaves the orangutan (genus *Pongo*) as the only member of the pongid family (Pongidae). Table 5.2 and Figure 5.2 illustrate our degree of relatedness to other primates.

Primate Tendencies

Primates are varied because they have adapted to diverse ecological niches. Some primates are active during the day; others, at night. Some eat insects; others, fruits; others, shoots, leaves, and bulk vegetation; and others, seeds or roots. Some primates live on the ground, others live in trees, and there are

See the Virtual Exploration

mhhe
●com
/kottak

intermediate adaptations. However, because the earliest primates were tree dwellers, modern primates share homologies reflecting their common **arboreal** heritage.

Many trends in primate evolution are best exemplified by the anthropoids: monkeys, apes, and humans, which constitute the suborder *Anthropoidea*. The other primate suborder, Prosimii, includes lemurs, lorises, and tarsiers. These prosimians are more distant relatives of humans than are monkeys and apes. The primate trends—most developed in the anthropoids—can be summarized briefly. Together they constitute an anthropoid heritage that humans share with monkeys and apes.

1. **Grasping.** Primates have five-digited feet and hands that are suited for grasping. Certain features of hands and feet that were originally adaptive for arboreal life have been transmitted across the generations to contemporary primates. Flexible hands and feet that could encircle branches were important features in the early primates' arboreal life. Thumb opposability might have been favored by the inclusion of insects in the early primate diet. Manual dexterity makes it easier to catch insects attracted to abundant arboreal flowers and fruits. Humans and many other primates have

Table 5.2   **Primate Taxonomy**

The subdivisions of the two primate suborders: Prosimii (Prosimians) and Anthropoidea (Anthropoids). Humans (see also Table 5.1) are anthropoids who belong to the superfamily Hominoidea (the hominoids), along with the apes.

Suborder	Infraorder	Superfamily	Family	Subfamily
Prosimii (Prosimians)	Lemuriformes	Lemuroidea	Daubentoniidae (Aye-aye)	
			Indridae (Indri)	
			Lemuridae (Lemurs)	
	Lorisiformes	Lorisoidea	Lorisidae	Galaginae (Bushbabies)
				Lorisinae (Lorises)
	Tarsiiformes	Tarsioidea	Tarsiidae (Tarsiers)	
Anthropoidea (Anthropoids)	Platyrrhini	Ceboidea	Callitrichidae (Tamarins and marmosets)	
			Cebidae	Atelinae (Spider monkeys and woolly monkeys)
	Catarrhini	Cercopithecoidea	Cercopithecidae	Cercopithecinae (Macaques, guenons, and baboons)
				Colobinae (Colobines)
		Hominoidea	Hylobatidae (Gibbons and siamangs)	
			Pongidae (Orangutans)	
			Hominidae (Gorillas, chimpanzees, and humans)	

SOURCE: Adapted from R. Martin, "Classification of Primates," in S. Jones, R. Martin, and D. Pilbeam, eds., *The Cambridge Encyclopedia of Human Evolution* (Cambridge, England: Cambridge University Press, 1992), pp. 20–21.

opposable thumbs: The thumb can touch the other fingers. Some primates also have grasping feet. However, in adapting to the bipedal (two-footed) locomotion, humans eliminated most of the foot's grasping ability.

2. **Smell to Sight.** Several anatomic changes reflect the shift from smell to sight as the primates' most important means of obtaining information. Monkeys, apes, and humans have excellent *stereoscopic* (able to see in

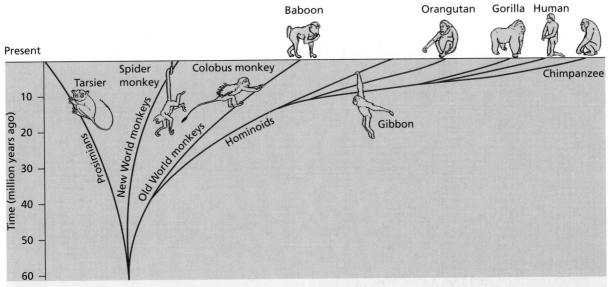

Figure 5.2 **Primate Family Tree.** When did the common ancestors of all the Primates live?

SOURCE: From Roger Lewin, *Human Evolution: An Illustrated Introduction*, 3rd ed. (Boston: Blackwell Scientific Publications, 1993), p. 44.

depth) and color vision. The portion of the brain devoted to vision expanded, while the area concerned with smell shrank.

3. **Nose to Hand.** Sensations of touch, conveyed by *tactile* organs, also provide information. The tactile skin on a dog's or cat's nose transmits information. Cats' tactile hairs, or whiskers, also serve this function. In primates, however, the main touch organ is the hand, specifically the sensitive pads of the "fingerprint" region.

4. **Brain Complexity.** The proportion of brain tissue concerned with memory, thought, and association has increased in primates. The primate ratio of brain size to body size exceeds that of most mammals.

5. **Parental Investment.** Most primates give birth to a single offspring rather than a litter. Because of this, growing primates receive more attention and have more learning opportunities than do other mammals. Learned behavior is an important part of primate adaptation.

6. **Sociality.** Primates tend to be social animals that live with others of their species. The need for longer and more attentive care of offspring places a selective value on support by a social group.

Prosimians

The primate order has two suborders: prosimians and anthropoids. The early history of the primates is limited to prosimian-like animals known through the fossil record. (See Chapter 6.) The first anthropoids, ancestral to monkeys, apes, and humans, appeared more than 40 million years ago. Some prosimians managed to survive in Africa and Asia because they were adapted to nocturnal life. As such, they did not compete with anthropoids, which are active during the day. Prosimians (lemurs) in Madagascar had no anthropoid competitors until people colonized that island some 1,500 years ago.

In their behavior and biology, Madagascar's *lemurs*, with 33 species, show adaptations to an array of environments or ecological niches. Their diets and times of activity differ. Lemurs eat fruits, other plant foods, eggs, and insects. Some are nocturnal; others are active during the day. Some are totally arboreal; others spend some time in the trees and some on the ground. Another kind of prosimian is the *tarsier*, today confined to Indonesia, Malaysia, and the Philippines. From the fossil record, we know that 50 million years ago, several genera of tarsier-like prosimians lived in North

Primates have five-digited feet and hands, well suited for grasping. Flexible hands and feet that could encircle branches were important features in the early primates' arboreal life. In adapting to bipedal (two-footed) locomotion, hominids eliminated most of the foot's grasping ability—illustrated here by the chimpanzee.

A crown lemur. Because these prosimians were confined to Madagascar, lemurs had no anthropoid competitors until people colonized that island some 1,500 years ago. Most lemur species are now endangered by human encroachment on their forest habitat.

America and Europe, which were much warmer then than they are now (Boaz 1997). The one genus of tarsier that survived is totally nocturnal. Active at night, tarsiers don't directly compete with anthropoids, which are active during the day. Lorises are other nocturnal prosimians found in Africa and Asia.

Anthropoids

All anthropoids share resemblances that can be considered trends in primate evolution in the sense that these traits are fully developed neither in the fossils of primates that lived prior to 45 million years ago nor among contemporary prosimians.

All anthropoids have overlapping fields of vision, permitting them to see things in depth. With reduction of the snout, anthropoid eyes are placed forward in the skull and look directly ahead. The fields of vision of our eyes overlap. Depth perception, impossible without overlapping visual fields, proved adaptive in the trees. Tree-dwelling primates that could judge distance better because of depth perception survived and reproduced in greater numbers than did those that could not.

The abilities to see in depth and in color may have developed together. Both helped early anthropoids interpret their arboreal world. Superior vision made it easier to distinguish edible insects, fruits, berries, and leaves. Furthermore, having color and depth vision makes it easier to groom—to remove burrs, insects, and other small objects from other primates' hair. Grooming is one way of forming and maintaining social bonds.

Visual and tactile changes have been interrelated. Monkeys, apes, and humans have neither tactile muzzle skin nor "cat's whiskers." Instead, fingers are the main touch organs. The ends of the fingers and toes are sensitive tactile pads. Forward placement of the eyes and depth vision allow anthropoids to pick up small objects, hold them in

Beyond the *Classroom*
A Behavioral Ecology Study of Two Lemur Species

Background Information

STUDENT 1:	Jennifer Burns
YEAR IN SCHOOL/MAJOR:	Senior/Anthropology
FUTURE PLANS:	Field work/graduate school
STUDENT 2:	Chris Howard
YEAR IN SCHOOL/MAJOR:	Post-undergraduate/ Anthropology
FUTURE PLANS:	Graduate school
SUPERVISING PROFESSORS:	Dr. Deborah Overdorff, Dr. Beth Erhart
DEPARTMENT:	Anthropology
SCHOOL:	University of Texas at Austin
PROJECT TITLE:	A Behavioral Ecology Study of Two Lemur Species

---

Lemurs are endangered prosimians confined to the island of Madagascar. In this account, pay attention to the problems and pitfalls of primatological research. How would the logistics of studying a baboon or gorilla troop differ from the field methods described here?

Simply the word "Madagascar" conjures up brilliant images of an exotic land. Having broken off from Africa approximately 165 million years ago, this magical island mesmerizes the scientific community as 85–90 percent of its flora and fauna is endemic.

Within the heart of southeastern Madagascar, Ranomafana National Park protects 41,600 hectares of montane rain forest. The park was established at the close of the 1980s and has done a remarkable job of integrating the needs of the Malagasy people with this segment of rain forests' need for protection from further destruction. A developed infrastructure helps the park to balance local and foreign tourist groups as well as scientific research. With one main research site and two bush camp research sites, many fruitful studies are conducted over a wide variety of flora and fauna.

The aims of our project are to better understand the social dynamics and feeding ecology of two of the twelve species of lemurs living within Ranomafana National Park: the red-fronted lemur, *Eulemur fulvus rufus*, and sifaka species, *Propithecus diadema edwardsi*. For five days each week over a six-month period, behavioral and ecological data were collected on one group from each species. To aid with individual distinction and recognition, the members of each group were fitted with colored identification necklaces, with one collar of each group containing a radio transmitter. This radio-tracking device made it possible to locate the groups each morning. While these classic techniques are tremendously helpful, problems can often occur with the radio equipment. Heavy rainfall can waterlog the gear, and the rugged mountainous terrain adds strong echoes to the signal, making group location more difficult. When the radio fails, finding the groups can be nearly impossible, as they cover a tremendous area, and can easily take days, if they are found at all.

These two species are of particular interest because of their many contrasts both physically and socially. In trying to more fully define and understand the implications of terms like "dominance," "leadership," "competition," "reproductive stress," and "male versus female roles" within varying lemur species, this study hopes to not only provide new insights, but also open the door to new questions.

front of their eyes, and appraise them. Our ability to thread a needle reflects an intricate interplay of hands and eyes that took millions of years to achieve. Manual dexterity, including the opposable thumb, confers a tremendous advantage in examining and manipulating objects and is essential to a major human adaptive capacity: tool making. Among monkeys, thumb opposability is indispensable for feeding and grooming.

Another trend is increased size of the *cranium* (skull) to fit a larger brain. The brain/body size ratio is greater among anthropoids than among prosimians. Even more important, the brain's outer layer—concerned with memory, association, and integration—is relatively larger. Monkeys, apes, and humans store an array of visual images in their memories, which permits them to learn more. The ability to learn from experience and from other group members is a major reason for the success of the anthropoids compared to most other mammals.

Understanding Ourselves Think about our senses—vision, hearing, touch, smell, and taste. Where have we suffered sensory loss during our evolutionary history? Like almost all the anthropoids, humans are diurnal, active during the day. If we were night animals, we'd sense things differently. Maybe our eyes would be bigger, like those of an owl or a tarsier. Maybe we'd have biological radar systems, as bats do. Perhaps we'd develop a more acute sense of hearing or smell to penetrate the shield of the dark. As animals, humans are programmed to rise at dawn and to sleep when the sun disappears. As cultural creatures, we venture into the night with torches, lanterns, and flashlights, and we shut the dark out of our dwellings by using artificial light.

Which is most debilitating—loss of vision, hearing, or smell? Among our senses, we seem to value hearing, and above all vision, most. The anthropoids as a group are preeminently visual animals. Whole industries exist to improve our sight and hearing. But how often do you hear of a product designed to improve your ability to smell, taste, or touch things? Other animals can detect all kinds of scents and odors that help them interpret the world. Humans, by contrast, use an array of products designed *not* to improve our sense of smell, but to eliminate even the faint odors our limited olfactory apparatus permits us to smell. *Blindness* and *deafness* are common words that indicate the senses whose loss we deem most significant. The rarity of the word *anosmia*, the inability to smell, tells us something about our senses and our values. The sensory shifts that occurred in primate evolution, especially the one from smell to sight, explain something fundamental about ourselves.

Monkeys

The anthropoid suborder has two infraorders: *platyrrhines* (New World monkeys) and *catarrhines* (Old World monkeys, apes, and humans). The catarrhines (sharp-nosed) and platyrrhines (flatnosed) take their names from Latin terms that describe the placement of the nostrils (Figure 5.3). Old World monkeys, apes, and humans are all catarrhines. Being placed in the same taxon (infraorder in this case) means that Old World monkeys, apes, and humans are more closely related to each other than to New World monkeys. In other words, one kind of monkey (Old World) is more like a human than it is like another kind of monkey (New World). The New World monkeys were reproductively isolated from the catarrhines before the latter diverged into the Old World monkeys, apes, and humans. This is why New World monkeys are assigned to a different infraorder.

All New World monkeys and many Old World monkeys are arboreal. Whether in the trees or on the ground, however, monkeys move differently from apes and humans. Their arms and legs move parallel to one another, as dogs' legs do. This contrasts with the tendency toward *orthograde posture*, the straight and upright stance of apes and humans. Unlike apes, which have longer arms than legs, and humans, who have longer legs than arms, monkeys have arms and legs of about the same length. Most monkeys also have tails, which help them maintain balance in the trees. Apes and humans lack tails. The apes' tendency toward orthograde posture is most evident when they sit down. When they move about, chimps, gorillas, and orangutans habitually use all four limbs.

NEW WORLD MONKEYS

New World monkeys live in the forests of Central and South America. There are interesting parallels between New World monkeys and some arboreal

Figure 5.3   Nostril Structure of Catarrhines and Platyrrhines. Above: narrow septum and "sharp nose" of a guenon, a catarrhine (Old World monkey). Below: broad septum and "flat nose" of Humboldt's woolly monkey, a platyrrhine (New World monkey). Which nose is more like your own? What does that similarity suggest?

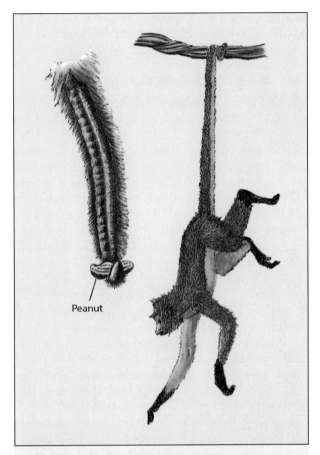

Figure 5.4   The Prehensile Tail of the Spider Monkey, a New World Monkey. Such a tail can be used to grasp a branch, or to pick up small objects, such as the peanut. Do any of the apes have grasping tails?

primates of the Old World. These analogies exhibit convergent evolution—that is, they have developed as a result of adaptation to a similar arboreal niche. Like the gibbon, a small Asiatic ape, some New World monkeys have developed a form of **brachiation**—under-the-branch swinging. Most monkeys run and jump from branch to branch, but gibbons and some New World monkeys swing through the trees, using their hands as hooks. Hand over hand, they move from branch to branch, propelled onward by the thrust of their bodies.

Unlike Old World monkeys, many New World monkeys have *prehensile*, or grasping, tails (Figure 5.4). Sometimes the prehensile tail has tactile skin, which permits it to work like a hand, for instance, in conveying food to the mouth. Old World monkeys, however, have developed their own characteristic anatomic specializations. They have rough patches of skin on the buttocks, adapted to sitting on hard rocky ground and rough branches. If the primate you see in the zoo has such patches, it's from the Old World. If it has a prehensile tail, it's a New World monkey. Among the anthropoids, there's only one nocturnal animal, a New World monkey called the night monkey or owl monkey. All other monkeys and apes, and humans, too, of course, are diurnal—active during the day.

OLD WORLD MONKEYS

The Old World monkeys have both terrestrial and arboreal species. Baboons and many macaques are terrestrial monkeys. Certain traits differentiate terrestrial and arboreal primates. Arboreal primates tend to be smaller. Smaller animals can reach a greater variety of foods in trees and shrubs, where the most abundant foods are located at the ends of branches. Low weight is adaptive for end-of-branch feeding. Arboreal monkeys are typically lithe and agile. They escape from the few predators in their environment—snakes and monkey-eating eagles—through alertness and speed. Large size, by contrast, is advantageous for terrestrial primates in dealing with their predators, which are more numerous on the ground.

Another contrast between arboreal and terrestrial primates is in sexual dimorphism—marked differences in male and female anatomy and temperament (see Fedigan 1992). Sexual dimorphism tends to be more marked in terrestrial than in arboreal species. Baboon and macaque males are larger and fiercer than are females of the same species. However, it's hard to tell, without close inspection, the sex of an arboreal monkey.

Of the terrestrial monkeys, the baboons of Africa and the (mainly Asiatic) macaques have been the subjects of many studies. Why do you think there have been more studies of terrestrial than of arboreal primates? Terrestrial monkeys have specializations in anatomy, psychology, and social behavior that enable them to cope with terrestrial life. Adult male baboons, for example, are fierce-looking animals that can weigh 100 pounds (45 kilograms). They display their long, projecting canines to intimidate predators and when confronting other baboons. Faced with a predator, a male baboon can puff up his ample mane of shoulder hair, so that the would-be aggressor perceives the baboon as larger than he actually is.

Longitudinal field research shows that, near the time of puberty, baboon and macaque males typically leave their home troop for another. Because males move in and out, females form the stable core of the terrestrial monkey troop (Cheney and Seyfarth 1990; Hinde 1983). By contrast, among

Hamadryas baboons. The male grooms the female. How does this photo illustrate sexual dimorphism?

chimpanzees and gorillas, females are more likely to emigrate and seek mates outside their natal social groups (Rodseth et al. 1991; van Schaik and van Hooff 1983; Wrangham 1980). Among terrestrial monkeys, then, the core group consists of females; among apes it is made up of males.

Apes

The Old World monkeys have their own separate superfamily (Cercopithecoidea), while humans and the apes together compose the hominoid superfamily (Hominoidea). Among the hominoids, the so-called great apes are orangutans, gorillas, and chimpanzees. Humans could be included here, too; we are sometimes called "the third African ape." The lesser (smaller) apes are the gibbons and siamangs of Southeast Asia and Indonesia.

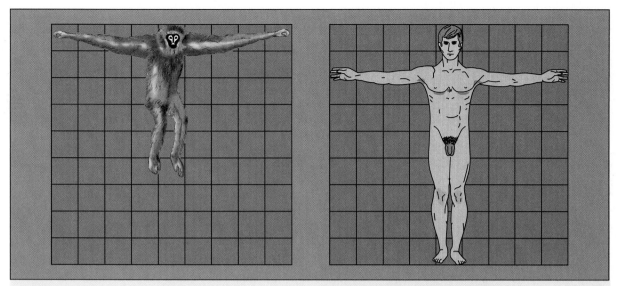

Figure 5.5 **The Limb Ratio of the Arboreal Gibbon and Terrestrial *Homo*.**
How does this anatomical difference fit the modes of locomotion used by gibbons and humans?

Apes live in forests and woodlands. The light and agile gibbons, which are skilled brachiators, are completely arboreal. The heavier gorillas, chimpanzees, and adult male orangutans spend considerable time on the ground. Nevertheless, ape behavior and anatomy reveal past and present adaptation to arboreal life. For example, apes still build nests to sleep in trees. Apes have longer arms than legs, which is adaptive for brachiation (see Figure 5.5). The structure of the shoulder and clavicle (collarbone) of the apes and humans suggests that we had a brachiating ancestor. In fact, young apes still do brachiate. Adult apes tend to be too heavy to brachiate safely. Their weight is more than many branches can withstand. Gorillas and chimps now use the long arms they have inherited from their more arboreal ancestors for life on the ground. The terrestrial locomotion of chimps and gorillas is called *knuckle-walking*. In it, long arms and callused knuckles support the trunk as the apes amble around, leaning forward.

Understanding Ourselves Do you remember the "monkey bars" in your school playground and how you used them? It wasn't like a monkey. The human shoulder bone, like that of the apes, is adapted for brachiation—swinging hand over hand through the trees. Monkeys move about on four feet—whether in the trees or on the ground. Apes can stand and walk on two feet, as humans habitually do, but in the trees, and otherwise when climbing, apes and humans don't jump around as monkeys do. In climbing we extend our arms and pull up, and when we use monkey bars, we hang and move hand over hand rather than getting on top and running across, as a monkey would. Maybe the name should be changed to human bars.

A brachiator's shoulder is one clue to an arboreal heritage we share with the apes. What about nest building? Based on what we know about the habitats of early hominids, it's a good bet they took refuge in, and may even have slept in, trees. Are blankets, sheets, pillows, and mattresses the modern-day equivalent of ancestral nests made of leaves and twigs? And when we dream of falling, are we experiencing an evolutionary consciousness shared with the African apes, which build nests but occasionally wake up on the ground? Another lesson for the field primatologist—don't set up camp under a gorilla's nest.

GIBBONS

Gibbons are widespread in the forests of Southeast Asia, especially in Malaysia. Smallest of the apes, male and female gibbons have about the same

With long arms and fingers, the gibbon is the most agile of the apes. Gibbons occasionally walk upright on the ground, using their long arms as balancers. Shown here, a white-handed gibbon strolls through the forest.

firmed by their numbers and range. Hundreds of thousands of gibbons span a wide area of Southeast Asia.

ORANGUTANS

There are two existing species of orangutan, Asiatic apes that belong to the genus *Pongo*. The range of the orangutan once extended into China, but contemporary orangs are confined to two Indonesian islands. Sexual dimorphism is marked, with the adult male weighing more than twice as much as the female. The orangutan male, like his human counterpart, is intermediate in size between chimps and gorillas. Some orang males exceed 200 pounds (90 kilograms). With only half the gorilla's bulk, male orangs can be more arboreal, although they typically climb, rather than swing through, the trees. The smaller size of females and young permits them to make fuller use of the trees. Orangutans have a varied diet of fruit, bark, leaves, and insects. Because orangutans live in jungles and feed in trees, they are especially difficult to study. However, field reports about orangutans in their natural setting (MacKinnon 1974) have clarified their behavior and social organization. Orangs tend to be solitary animals. Their tightest social units consist of females and preadolescent young. Males forage alone.

GORILLAS

With just one species, *Gorilla gorilla*, there are three subspecies of gorillas. The western lowland gorilla is the animal you normally see in zoos. This, the smallest subspecies of gorilla, lives mainly in forests in the Central African Republic, Congo, Cameroon, Gabon, Equatorial Guinea, and Nigeria. The eastern lowland gorilla, of which there are only four in captivity, is slightly larger and lives in eastern Congo. There are no mountain gorillas, the third subspecies, in captivity, and it's estimated that no more than 650 of these animals survive in the wild. These are the largest gorillas with the longest hair (to keep them warm in their mountainous habitat). They are also the rarest gorillas, which Dian Fossey and other scientists have studied in Rwanda, Uganda, and eastern Congo.

Full-grown male gorillas may weigh 400 pounds (180 kilograms) and stand six feet tall (183 centimeters). Like most terrestrial primates, gorillas show marked sexual dimorphism. The average

average height (3 feet, or 1 meter) and weight (12 to 25 pounds, or 5 to 10 kilograms). Gibbons spend most of their time just below the forest canopy (treetops). For efficient brachiation, gibbons have long arms and fingers, with short thumbs. Slenderly built, gibbons are the most agile apes. Unlike knuckle-walkers, they use their long arms for balance when they occasionally walk erect on the ground or along a branch. Gibbons are the preeminent arboreal specialists among the apes. They subsist on a diet mainly of fruits, with occasional insects and small animals. Gibbons and siamangs, their slightly larger relatives, tend to live in *primary groups*, which are composed of a permanently bonded male and female and their preadolescent offspring. Gibbon evolutionary success is con-

adult female weighs half as much as the male. Gorillas spend little time in the trees. It's particularly cumbersome for an adult male to move his bulk about in a tree. When gorillas sleep in trees, they build nests, which are usually no more than 10 feet (3 meters) off the ground. By contrast, the nests of chimps and female orangs may be 100 feet (30 meters) above the ground.

Most of the gorilla's day is spent feeding. Gorillas move through jungle undergrowth eating ground plants, leaves, bark, fruits, and other vegetation. Like most primates, gorillas live in social groups. The troop is a common unit of primate social organization, consisting of multiple males and females and their offspring. Although troops with up to 30 gorillas have been observed, most gorillas live in groups of from 10 to 20. Gorilla troops tend to have fairly stable memberships, with little shifting between troops (Fossey 1983). Each troop has a silver-back male, so designated because of the strip of white hair that extends down his back. This is the physical sign of full maturity among the male gorillas. The silverback is usually the only breeding male in the troop, which is why gorilla troops are sometimes called "one-male groups." However, a few younger, subordinate males may also adhere to such a one-male group (Harcourt et al. 1981; Schaller 1963).

For a quiz on primate types, see the Interactive Exercises

mhhe
●com
/kottak

CHIMPANZEES

Chimpanzees belong to the genus *Pan*, which has two species: *Pan troglodytes* (the common chimpanzee) and *Pan paniscus* (the bonobo or "pygmy" chimpanzee) (de Waal 1997; Susman 1987). Like humans, chimps are closely related to the gorilla, although there are some obvious differences. Like gorillas, chimps live in tropical Africa, but they range over a larger area and more varied environments than gorillas do (Figure 5.6). The common chimp, *Pan troglodytes*, lives in western central Africa (Gabon, Congo, Cameroon), as well as in western Africa (Sierra Leone, Liberia, The Gambia) and eastern Africa (Congo, Uganda, and Tanzania). Bonobos live in remote and densely forested areas of just one country—the Democratic Republic of Congo. Common chimps live mainly in tropical rain forests but also in woodlands and mixed forest-woodland-grassland areas, such as the

Gombe Stream National Park, Tanzania, where Jane Goodall (1996) and other researchers began to study them in 1960.

There are dietary differences between chimps and gorillas. Gorillas eat large quantities of green bulk vegetation, but chimps, like orangutans and gibbons, prefer fruits. Chimps are actually omnivorous, adding animal protein to their diet by capturing small mammals, birds' eggs, and insects.

Chimps are lighter and more arboreal than gorillas are. The adult male's weight—between

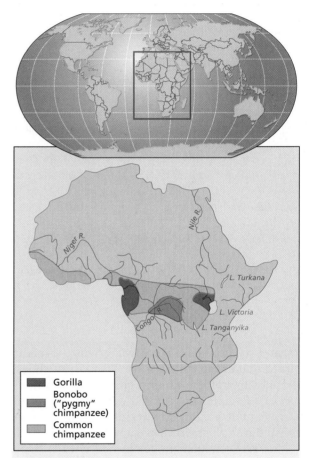

Figure 5.6 **Geographic Distribution of African Apes.**

Chimpanzees and gorillas are primarily rain forest dwellers. However, some chimpanzee populations live in woodland environments. This map shows the ranges of the three species of African apes.

SOURCE: From C. J. Jolly and F. Plog, *Physical Anthropology and Archeology*, 4th ed. (New York: McGraw-Hill, 1986), p. 115.

Most endangered of the apes, the orangutan has the most restricted habitat. The colorful orang is also the least social of the apes. What are the main threats to nonhuman primates such as the orang? What would it take to save the orang from extinction?

Of the three young women recruited in the 1960s by the paleontologist Louis Leakey to study great apes, Dr. Birutá Galdikas, now 53, is the least known. Dr. Leakey's first disciple, Dr. Jane Goodall, who discovered that chimpanzees made tools, has become an international scientific celebrity, and Dr. Dian Fossey, who lived among the gorillas of Rwanda and was killed there in 1985, was played by Sigourney Weaver in the movie *Gorillas in the Mist*.

But the story of Dr. Galdikas, who quietly devoted herself to the study and preservation of the Indonesian orangutan, remains largely unknown. "That's because I have a name nobody can pronounce and because I've been in Borneo all these years, tracking an elusive and solitary animal," Dr. Galdikas, whose name is Lithuanian (pronounced bi-ROO-tay GALD-i-kus), said on a recent morning . . .

Still a resident of Borneo, Dr. Galdikas recently became an Indonesian citizen because "the orangutans are Indonesian and because someone in the government suggested it would be helpful.". . .

Q. Give us a report on the state of the world's orangutans?

A. They are poised on the edge of extinction. It's that simple. We're still seeing orangutans in the forest; they are coming into captivity in enormous numbers. You just know that there can't be that many left in the wild.

Q. How did the orangutans come to be so threatened?

A. The main factor was that until 1988, Indonesia had a forestry minister who was a real forester. In 1988, he was replaced by a forestry minister who was an agriculturist, a

100 and 200 pounds (45 to 90 kilograms)—is about a third that of the male gorilla. There is much less sexual dimorphism among chimps than among gorillas. Females approximate 88 percent of the average male height. This is similar to the ratio of sexual dimorphism in *Homo sapiens*.

Several scientists have studied wild chimps, and we know more about the full range of their behavior and social organization than we do about the other apes (see Wrangham et al. 1994). The long-term research of Jane Goodall and others at Gombe provides especially useful information. Approximately 150 chimpanzees range over Gombe's 30 square miles (80 square kilometers). Goodall (1986, 1996) has described communities of about 50 chimps, all of which know one another and interact from time to time. Communities regularly split up into smaller groups: a mother and her offspring; a few males; males, females, and young; and occasionally solitary animals. Chimp communities are semiclosed. The social networks of males are more closed than are those of females, which are more likely to migrate and mate outside their natal group than males are (Wrangham 1994).

When chimps, which are very vocal, meet, they greet one another with gestures, facial expressions, and calls. They hoot to maintain contact during their daily rounds. Like baboons and macaques, chimps exhibit dominance relationships through attacks and displacement. Some adult females outrank younger adult males, although females do not display as strong dominance relationships among themselves as males do. Males occasionally cooperate in hunting parties.

promoter of plantations. That signaled a shift in government policy from selective logging to clear-cutting of the forest . . . If you selectively log, some animals will survive. But with clear-cutting, the habitat is gone. If that weren't enough, in 1997, there were these horrendous fires that devastated the forests. Moreover, the last three years have been a period of intense political upheaval . . .

After President Suharto stepped down in 1998, there was a vacuum of power in the center. Once people in the provinces understood that, some felt they could do whatever they wanted . . .

At first, only local loggers came in. When nobody stopped them, the bigger commercial loggers followed. Suddenly, there were no more protected parks . . .

We're trying to set up patrols of local men to go out with park rangers so that when they come across illegal loggers, they don't feel totally intimidated. We're working with the Indonesian government to set up new wildlife reserves at expired logging concessions . . .

We have a hospital for 130 orangutans. We have an orphanage for the babies. Eventually, they are released to the wild, though with the fast-disappearing habitat, it's always tough to find a safe place for them.

Q. Tell us what you've learned about orangutans in the nearly 30 years you've been studying them?

A. Well, we've gotten a picture of a very long-lived primate who probably lives 60 to 70 years in the wild. They use a wide variety of foods in the wild, about 400 different kinds, because food is generally scarce for them. The males come and go. They're very, very competitive. Probably very few males are successful at actually impregnating females.

And the females seem to get pregnant about once every eight years. Also, they're very smart. When orangutans have interactions with humans, they use tools at an incredibly rapid pace . . .

SOURCE: http://www.nytimes.com/library/national/science/032100sci-animal-orangutan.html.

BONOBOS

Ancestral chimps, and especially humans, eventually spread out of the forests and into woodlands and more open habitats. Bonobos, which belong to the species *Pan paniscus*, apparently never left the protection of the trees. Up to 10,000 bonobos survive in the humid forests south of the Zaire River, in the Democratic Republic of Congo (DRC). Despite their common name—the pygmy chimpanzee—bonobos can't be distinguished from chimpanzees by size. Adult males of the smallest subspecies of chimpanzee average 43 kilograms (95 pounds), and females average 33 kilograms (73 pounds). These figures are about the same for bonobos (de Waal 1995, 1997).

Although much smaller than the males, female bonobos seem to rule. De Waal (1995, 1997) characterizes bonobo communities as female-centered, peace-loving, and egalitarian. The strongest social bonds are among females, although females also bond with males. The male bonobo's status reflects that of his mother, to whom he remains closely bonded for life.

The frequency with which bonobos have sex—and use it to avoid conflict—makes them exceptional among the primates. Despite frequent sex, the bonobo reproductive rate doesn't exceed that of the chimpanzee. A female bonobo gives birth every five or six years. Then, like chimps, female bonobos nurse and carry around their young for up to five years. Bonobos reach adolescence around seven years of age. Females, which first give birth at age 13 or 14, are full-grown by 15 years.

This photo from the San Diego zoo shows sexual activity involving a male bonobo and a younger female, as two other bonobos embrace. Among bonobos, the strongest social bonds are among females, although females do also bond with males.

It was once thought that face-to-face copulation was a cultural innovation that needed to be taught to nonindustrial peoples (hence the term "missionary position"). Not so—even bonobos engage in face-to-face sex in about one-third of their sexual encounters. This makes them more human-like than are chimpanzees, which rarely have sex face to face. As in human females, the bonobo vulva and clitoris face the front, making the anatomy of their female genitalia adapted for face-to-face activity.

Like baboons and chimps, bonobo females have an estrus cycle. Periodically, females "go into heat" or enter estrus, a period of heightened sexual receptivity. Estrus is signaled by swelling and coloration of the vaginal skin. Female bonobos are receptive during a longer portion of their estrus cycle than female chimps are. This increased sexual receptivity is another similarity with humans. Bonobos have sex in virtually every partner combination imaginable (although they appear to avoid incest). The bonobo's most typical sexual pattern, undocumented in any other primate, is genito-genital rubbing (or GG rubbing) between adult females. Two females embrace in a face-to-face position and rub their genital swellings together, emitting grins and squeals that probably reflect

orgasmic experiences (de Waal 1995, 1997). What about males? Standing back to back, one male may rub his scrotum against the buttocks of another male. Males also practice so-called penis-fencing: Two males hang face to face from a branch while rubbing their erect penises together. Bonobos also engage in occasional oral sex, massage of another individual's genitals, and intense tongue-kissing.

How do we know that bonobos use all this sexual activity to avoid conflict? According to de Waal:

> First, anything, including food, that arouses the interest of more than one bonobo at a time tends to result in sexual contact. If two bonobos approach a cardboard box thrown into their enclosure, they will briefly mount each other before playing with the box. Such situations lead to squabbles in most other species. But bonobos are quite tolerant, perhaps because they use sex to divert attention and to diffuse tension. Second, bonobo sex often occurs in aggressive contexts totally unrelated to food. A jealous male might chase another away from a female, after which the two males reunite and engage in scrotal rubbing. Or after a female hits a juvenile, the latter's mother may lunge at the aggressor, an action that is immediately followed by genital rubbing between the two adults (De Waal 1995, p. 87).

De Waal sees bonobo sexual behavior as a mechanism to displace aggression. Because of this, bonobos' sexual behavior is indistinguishable from their overall social behavior. Given its roles in peacemaking and appeasement, it's not surprising that bonobo sex has so many manifestations.

For more information on bonobos, see the Internet Exercise at your OLC

/kottak

Endangered Primates

Deforestation poses a special risk for the primates, because 90 percent of the 190 living primate species live in tropical forests—in Africa, Asia, South America, and Central America. Figure 5.7 is a map showing the distribution of primates today. As the earth's human population swells, the populations of the nonhuman primates are shrinking. Accord-

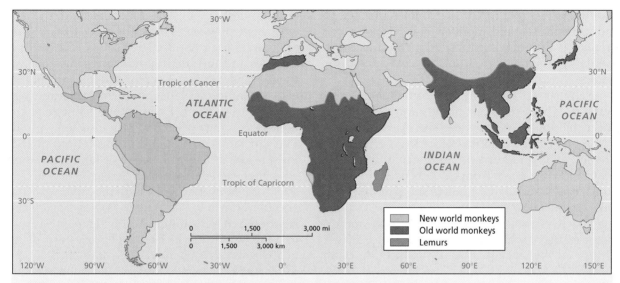

Figure 5.7 **Geographic Distribution of Living Primates.**
SOURCE: From Roger Lewin, *Human Evolution: An Illustrated Introduction*, 3rd ed. (Boston: Blackwell Scientific Publications, 1993), p. 45.

ing to the Convention on International Trade in Endangered Species (ratified in 1973), all nonhuman primates are now endangered or soon to be endangered. The apes (gibbons, gorillas, orangutans, and chimps) are in the "most endangered" category. Mountain gorillas, which once ranged widely in the forested mountains of East Africa, are now limited to a small area near the war-ravaged borders of Rwanda, the DRC, and Uganda. Other severely threatened species include the golden lion tamarin monkey of southeastern Brazil, the cotton-top tamarin of Colombia, the lion-tailed macaque of southern India, the woolly monkeys of Amazonia, and the orangutan of Southeast Asia.

See the Internet Exercise at your OLC

mhhe
com
/kottak

A combination of forestry and forest fires has been deadly to orangutans in Sumatra and Borneo in Indonesia. Sumatra, which is losing 1,000 orangs a year, has an estimated population of 6,000 left. A road for loggers and miners that penetrated the orangutan range in Sumatra led to contact with humans that proved fatal to hundreds of the animals. Borneo was devastated by fires in 1997–98, leaving some 10,000–15,000 orangs, compared with 60,000 in 1980. Habitat destruction and fragmentation can isolate small groups of animals, leaving them vulnerable to extinction due to loss of genetic diversity. Primate populations are slow

to recover from such threats. Ape species, for example, are slow reproducers, rarely having more than three to four offspring over a lifetime (Stern 2000).

Interpret the World
Atlas Map 5

Map 5 in your atlas shows the world geographic distribution of nonhuman primates. Both surviving and extinct primate species are displayed. These include prosimians, New World monkeys, Old World monkeys, gibbons and siamangs, and the Great Apes. Note that primates (what kind?) once thrived in North America, when that continent was warmer and more forested than it is now. Compare maps 3 and 5 to see how primate distribution is related to deforestation. Primates are among the world's most endangered animals. What are some areas of deforestation where you can detect threats to specific primates, such as lemurs or apes (based on maps 3 and 5)?

Although the destruction of their forest habitats is the main reason the primates are disappearing, it isn't the only reason. Another threat is human hunting of primates for bush meat (Viegas 2000). In Amazonia, West Africa, and Central Africa, primates are a major source of food. People kill thousands of monkeys each year. Human hunting is less of a threat to primates in Asia. In India, Hindus avoid monkey meat because the monkey is sacred, while Moslems avoid it because monkeys are considered unclean and not fit for human consumption.

People also hunt primates for their skins and pelts; poachers sell their body parts as trophies and ornaments. Africans use the skins of black-and-white colobus monkeys for cloaks and head-dresses, and American and European tourists buy coats and rugs made from colobus pelts. In Amazonia, ocelot and jaguar hunters shoot monkeys to bait the traps they set for the cats.

Poachers pose the greatest threat to the mountain gorillas, of which there were as few as 250 left in the wild when Fossey started studying them

In Africa, poachers shoot apes with high-powered rifles, then decapitate them and cut off their hands. They sell gorilla heads as trophies and turn the hands into grotesque ashtrays. Is killing a gorilla murder?

(Fossey 1981, 1983). The poachers shoot the apes with high-powered rifles, then decapitate them and cut off their hands. They sell gorilla heads as trophies and turn their hands into grotesque ash-trays. Traps and snares set for antelope and buffalo also endanger gorillas, which sometimes get caught in the traps. Even if they manage to free themselves, they often die from infected wounds. The sad fate (murder and decapitation) of Dian Fossey's favorite gorilla, Digit, is familiar to those who have seen the 1988 film *Gorillas in the Mist*, the story of Fossey, her work with mountain gorillas, and her efforts to save them. Fossey herself was murdered in her cabin at her field site in Rwanda in 1985 (see Roberts 1995). The mystery of her death remains unsolved. The last entry in her diary reads: "When you realize the value of all life, you dwell less on what is past and concentrate on the preservation of the future." Through the efforts of the fund she established, the number of mountain gorillas has increased.

Chimpanzees are also vulnerable to poachers. One famous chimp, Lucy, raised by an American family and taught to use sign language, met a grim fate when she was taken to Africa to live in the wild. In 1986, soon after she had joined an island colony of chimps in The Gambia, Lucy's mutilated corpse was discovered—minus skin, hair, hands, and feet. "We can only speculate that Lucy was killed—probably shot—and skinned. Because of her confidence with humans, she was always the first to confront newcomers to the island. She might have surprised an armed intruder, with fatal consequences" (Carter 1988, p. 47).

Primates also are killed when they are agricultural pests. In some areas of Africa and Asia, baboons and macaques raid the crops on which people depend for subsistence. Between 1947 and 1962, the government of Sierra Leone held annual drives to rid farm areas of monkeys, and between 15,000 and 20,000 primates perished each year.

A final reason for the demise of the primates is the capture of animals for use in labs or as pets. Although this threat is minor compared with deforestation and the hunting of primates for food, it does pose a serious risk to certain endangered species in heavy demand. One of the species most hurt by this trade is the chimpanzee, which has been widely used in biomedical research. One especially destructive way of capturing young primates is to shoot the mother and take her clinging infant.

Human–Primate Similarities

There is a substantial gap between primate society and fully developed human culture. However, studies of primates have revealed many similarities. Scholars used to contend that learned (versus instinctive) behavior separates humans from other animals. We know now that monkeys and apes also rely on learning. Many of the differences between humans and other primates are differences in degree rather than in kind. For example, monkeys learn from experiences, but humans learn much more. Another example: Chimpanzees and orangutans make tools for specific tasks, but human reliance on tools is much greater.

LEARNING

Common to monkeys, apes, and humans is the fact that behavior and social life are not rigidly programmed by the genes. All these animals learn throughout their lives. In several cases, an entire monkey troop has learned from the experiences of some of its members. In one group of Japanese macaques, a three-year-old female monkey started washing dirt off sweet potatoes before she ate them. First her mother, then her age peers, and finally the entire troop began washing sweet potatoes, too. The direction of learning was reversed when members of another macaque troop learned to eat wheat. After the dominant males had tried the new food, within four hours the practice had spread throughout the troop. Changes in learned behavior seem to spread more quickly from the top down than from the bottom up.

For monkeys as for people, the ability to learn, to profit from experience, confers a tremendous adaptive advantage, permitting them to avoid fatal mistakes. Faced with environmental change, primates don't have to wait for a genetic or physiological response. Learned behavior and social patterns can be modified instead.

TOOLS

Anthropologists used to distinguish humans from other animals as tool users, and there is no doubt that Homo does employ tools much more than any other animal does. However, tool use also turns up among several nonhuman species. For example, in the Galápagos Islands off western South America,

Learned behavior among wild chimps includes rudimentary tool manufacture. At Tanzania's Gombe Stream National Park, chimps use specially prepared twigs to "fish" for termites.

there is a "woodpecker finch" that selects twigs to dig out insects and grubs from tree bark. Sea otters use rocks to break open mollusks, which are important in their diet. Beavers are famous for dam construction.

When it became obvious that people weren't the only tool users, anthropologists started contending that only humans make tools with foresight, that is, with a specific purpose in mind. Chimpanzees show that this, too, is debatable, as we saw at the beginning of this chapter in the news story about how chimps living in the Tai rain forest of Ivory Coast make and use stone tools to crack nuts. In 1960, Jane Goodall (1996) began observing wild chimps—including their tool use and hunting behavior—at Gombe Stream National Park in Tanzania, East Africa. From the work of Goodall and many other researchers we know that wild chimps regularly make tools. To get water from places their mouths can't reach, thirsty chimps pick leaves, chew and crumple them, and then dip them into the water. Thus, with a specific purpose in mind, they devise primitive "sponges."

The best studied form of tool making by chimps involves "termiting." Chimps make tools to probe termite hills. They choose twigs, which they modify by removing leaves and peeling off bark to expose the sticky surface beneath. They carry the twigs to termite hills, dig holes with their fingers, and insert the twigs. Finally, they pull out the twigs and dine on termites that were attracted to the sticky surface.

Termiting isn't as easy as it might seem. Learning to termite takes time, and many Gombe chimps never master it. Twigs with certain characteristics must be chosen. Furthermore, once the twig is in the hill and the chimp judges that termites are crawling on its surface, the chimp must quickly flip the twig as it pulls it out so that the termites are on top. Otherwise they fall off as the twig comes out of the hole. This is an elaborate skill that neither all chimps nor human observers have been able to master.

Chimps have other abilities essential to culture. When they are trained by humans, their skills flower, as anyone who has ever seen a movie, circus, or zoo chimp knows. Wild chimps and orangs aim and throw objects. The gorilla, our other nearest relative, lacks the chimp's proclivity for tool making. However, gorillas do build nests, and they throw branches, grass, vines, and other objects. Hominids have considerably elaborated the capacity to aim and throw, which is a homology passed down from the common ancestor of humans and apes. Without it we never would have developed projectile technology and weaponry— or baseball.

PREDATION AND HUNTING

Like tool making and language, hunting has been cited as a distinctive human activity that is not shared with our ape relatives. Again, however, primate research shows that what was previously thought to be a difference of kind is a difference of degree. The diets of other terrestrial primates are not exclusively vegetarian, as was once thought. Baboons kill and eat young antelopes, and researchers have repeatedly observed hunting by chimpanzees.

For several years John Mitani, David Watts, and other researchers have been observing chimpanzees at Ngogo in Uganda's Kibale National Park. This is the largest chimp community ever described in the wild. In 1998 it consisted of 26 adult males, 40 adult females, 16 adolescent males, 5 adolescent females, and 30 infants and juveniles (Mitani and Watts 1999). (Remember that chimp communities have a more stable male than female core membership—adolescent males tend to stay on while adolescent females tend to leave to join other troops.) The large community size permits the formation of large hunting parties, which contributes to hunting success. Hunting parties at Ngogo included an average of 26 individuals (almost always adult and adolescent males). The average hunting time was 19 minutes, varying from 2 to 91 minutes in 29 observed hunts. Most hunts (78 percent) resulted in at least one prey item being caught—a much higher success rate than that among lions (26 percent), hyenas (34 percent), or cheetahs (30 percent). In most hunts (81 percent) the Ngogo chimps managed to catch multiple prey animals (three on average). The favored prey, at Ngogo as in other chimp communities, was the red colobus monkey.

As described by Mitani and Watts (1999), hunting by chimps is both opportunistic and planned. Opportunistic hunting took place when chimps encountered potential prey as they moved about during the day. Other hunts were organized patrols, in which the chimps became silent and moved together in a single file. They would stop, look up into the trees, scan, and change direction several times. Attentive to any arboreal movement, they would stop and search whenever they detected motion. After they spotted a monkey, the chase would begin. Encountering no prey, the chimps would go on patrolling, sometimes for several hours. The Ngogo chimps also collaborate by encircling red colobus groups, blocking potential escape routes, and driving their prey down hill slopes from taller to shorter trees. Chimps may give a specific call, the hunting call, at the start of a hunt, mobilizing hunters into action. Sometimes isolated chimps that encountered a red colobus monkey would give this call, after which other chimps would rush to the site and begin to hunt.

It turns out that chimps eat meat almost as much as some human hunter-gatherers do (Kopytoff 1995; Stanford 1999; Stanford and Bunn, eds. 2001). According to University of Southern California anthropologist Craig Stanford (1999), chimps may consume a quarter pound of meat a day when they hit their hunting stride. This meat intake is comparable to that of some contemporary groups of hunter-gatherers. According to Stanford, male chimps often hunt as a way to gain access to sexually receptive females. Stanford repeatedly observed male chimps dangling monkey meat in front of a sexually swollen female, sharing only after copulation. When in estrus ("heat," or heightened sexual receptivity), female chimps copulate with more than a dozen males each day. The presence of meat in the diet of a female chimpanzee may enhance her offspring's survival chances (Kopytoff 1995). Meat sharing also could increase male reproductive success by making it easier to mate. Stanford found hunting to be seasonal at Gombe—occurring during the dry summer months, precisely the season when females tend to be sexually receptive, and when fruits, leaves, and nuts are scarce.

There appear to be political as well as sexual reasons for meat sharing by chimps. In 1992 the Japanese zoologist Toshisada Nichida described how, in Tanzania's Mahale Mountains, a high-ranking chimp male gave out pieces of meat to allies, while denying them to his enemies (Kopytoff 1995). Stanford observed a similar use of meat to cement alliances at Gombe. Archeological evidence indicates that humans hunted by at least 2.5 million years ago, based on stone meat-cutting tools found at Olduvai Gorge in Tanzania. Given our current understanding of chimp hunting and tool making, we can infer that hominids may have been hunting much earlier than the first archaeological evidence attests. Since chimps seem to devour the monkeys they kill, leaving few remains after their meal, we may never find archaeological evidence for the first hominid hunt, especially if it was done without stone tools.

AGGRESSION AND RESOURCES

The potential for predation and aggression may be generalized in monkeys and apes, but its expression seems to depend on the environment. Jane Goodall specifically linked chimpanzee aggression and predation to human encroachment on their natural habitat. The Gombe chimps are divided into a northern group and a smaller group of southerners. Parties from the north have invaded the southern territory and killed southern chimps. Infant victims were partially eaten by the assailants (Goodall 1986).

John MacKinnon's research (1974) among orangutans on the Indonesian islands of Kalimantan (Borneo) and Sumatra showed that orangutans also have suffered as a result of human encroachment, particularly farming and timbering. On Borneo, in response to nearby human activities, orangs have developed a pattern of extreme sexual antagonism that may further endanger their survival. During MacKinnon's field work, Bornean orangs rarely had sex. Their limited sexual encounters were always brief forced copulations, often with screaming infants clinging to their mothers throughout the ordeal.

As MacKinnon did his field work, logging operations were forcing orangs whose territory was destroyed into his research area, swelling the population it had to support. The response to this sudden overpopulation was a drastic decline in the local orang birth rate. Primates respond in various ways to encroachment and to population pressure. A change in sexual relationships that reduces the birth rate is one way of easing population pressure on resources.

We see that primate behavior is not rigidly determined by the genes. It is plastic (flexible), capable of varying widely as environmental forces change. Among humans, too, aggression increases when resources are threatened or scarce. What we know about other primates makes it reasonable to assume that early hominids were neither uniformly aggressive nor consistently meek. Their aggression and predation reflected environmental variation (see Silverberg and Gray 1992; Wrangham and Peterson 1996).

Human–Primate Differences

The preceding sections have emphasized similarities between humans and other primates. Homo has elaborated substantially on certain tendencies shared with the apes. A unique concentration and combination of characteristics make humans distinct. However, the savanna or open grassland niche in which early humans evolved also selected certain traits that are not so clearly foreshadowed by the apes.

SHARING AND COOPERATION

Early humans lived in small social groups called bands, with economies based on hunting and gathering (foraging). Until fairly recently (12,000 to 10,000 years ago), all humans based their subsistence on hunting and gathering and lived in bands. Some such societies even managed to survive into the modern world, and ethnographers have studied them. From those studies we can conclude that in such societies, the strongest and most aggressive members do not dominate, as they do in a troop of terrestrial monkeys. Sharing and curbing of aggression are as basic to technologically simple humans as dominance and threats are to baboons.

We've seen that bonobos use sex to curb aggression and reduce conflict, and that male chimps cooperate in hunting. But as we saw from the brain response study described in Chapter 3, humans appear to be the most cooperative of the primates—in the food quest and other social activities. Except for meat sharing by chimps, the ape tendency is to forage individually. Monkeys also fend for themselves in getting food. Among human foragers, men generally hunt and women gather. Men and women bring resources back to the camp and share them. Older people who did not engage in the food quest get food from younger adults. Everyone shares the meat from a large animal. Nourished and protected by younger band members, elders live past the reproductive age and are respected for their knowledge and experience. The amount of information stored in a human band is far greater than that in any other primate society. Sharing, cooperation, and language are intrinsic to information storage. Through millions of years of adaptation to an omnivorous diet, hominids have come to rely, more than any other primate, on hunting, food sharing, and cooperative behavior. These are universal features in human adaptive strategies.

MATING AND KINSHIP

Another difference between humans and other primates involves mating. Among baboons, chimpanzees, and bonobos, most mating occurs when females enter estrus, during which they ovulate. Receptive females form temporary bonds with, and mate with, males. Human females, by contrast, lack a visible estrus cycle, and their ovulation is concealed. Neither a woman's sexual receptivity nor her readiness to conceive is physically evident, as it is in chimps and bonobos. Not knowing when ovulation is occurring, humans maximize their reproductive success by mating throughout the year. Human pair bonds for mating tend to be more exclusive and more durable than are those of chimps or bonobos. Related to our more constant sexuality, all human societies have some form of marriage. Marriage gives mating a reliable basis and grants to each spouse special, though not always exclusive, sexual rights in the other.

Marriage creates another major contrast between humans and nonhumans: exogamy and kinship systems. Most cultures have rules of exogamy requiring marriage outside one's kin or local group. Coupled with the recognition of kinship, exogamy confers adaptive advantages. It creates ties between the spouses' groups of origin. Their children have relatives, and therefore allies, in two kin groups rather than just one. The key point here is that ties of affection and mutual support between members of different local groups tend to be absent among primates other than Homo. There is a tendency among primates to disperse at adolescence. Among chimps and gorillas, females tend to migrate, seeking mates in other groups. Both male and female gibbons leave home when they become sexually mature. Once they find mates and establish their own territories, ties

Through millions of years of adaptation to an omnivorous diet, hominids have come to rely on gathering, hunting, and food sharing. These three Batak women from Palawan Island, the Philippines, share wild honeycombs. Locate the Philippines in your atlas.

with their natal groups cease. Among terrestrial monkeys, males leave the troop at puberty, eventually finding places elsewhere. The troop's core members are females. They sometimes form uterine groups made up of mothers, sisters, daughters, and sons that have not yet emigrated. This dispersal of males reduces the incidence of incestuous matings. Females mate with males born elsewhere, which join the troop at adolescence. Although kin ties are maintained between female monkeys, no close lifelong links are preserved through males.

Humans choose mates from outside the natal group, and usually at least one spouse moves. However, *humans maintain lifelong ties with sons and daughters*. The systems of kinship and marriage that preserve these links provide a major contrast between humans and other primates.

Behavioral Ecology and Fitness

According to evolutionary theory, when the environment changes, natural selection starts to modify the *population*'s pool of genetic material. Natural selection has another key feature: the differential reproductive success of *individuals* within the population. **Behavioral ecology** studies

the evolutionary basis of social behavior. It assumes that the genetic features of any species reflect a long history of differential reproductive success (that is, natural selection). In other words, biological traits of contemporary organisms have been transmitted across the generations because those traits enabled their ancestors to survive and reproduce more effectively than their competition.

Natural selection is based on *differential* reproduction. Members of the same species may compete to maximize their reproductive fitness—their genetic contribution to future generations. *Individual fitness* is measured by the number of direct descendants an individual has. Illustrating a primate strategy that may enhance individual fitness are cases in which male monkeys kill infants after entering a new troop. Destroying the offspring of other males, they clear a place for their own progeny (Hausfater and Hrdy 1984).

Besides competition, one's genetic contribution to future generations also can be enhanced by cooperation, sharing, and other apparently unselfish behavior. This is because of *inclusive fitness*—reproductive success measured by the genes one shares with relatives. By sacrificing for their kin—even if this means limiting their own direct reproduction—individuals actually may increase their genetic contributions (their shared genes) to the future. Inclusive fitness helps us understand why a female might invest in her sister's offspring, or why a male might risk his life to defend his brothers. If self-sacrifice perpetuates more of their genes than direct reproduction does, it makes sense in terms of behavioral ecology. Such a view can help us understand aspects of primate behavior and social organization.

Maternal care always makes sense in terms of reproductive fitness theory because females know their offspring are their own. But it's harder for males to be sure about paternity. Inclusive fitness theory predicts that males will invest most in offspring when they are surest the offspring are theirs. Gibbons, for example, have strict male–female pair bonding, which makes it almost certain that the offspring are those of both members of the pair. Thus we expect male gibbons to offer care and protection to their young, and they do. However, among species and in situations in which a male can't be sure about his paternity, it may make more sense to invest in a sister's offspring than in a mate's because the niece or nephew definitely shares some of that male's genes.

Summary

1. Humans, apes, monkeys, and prosimians are primates. The primate order is subdivided into suborders, superfamilies, families, genera, species, and subspecies. Organisms in any subdivision (taxon) of a taxonomy are assumed to share more recent ancestry with each other than they do with organisms in other taxa. But it's sometimes hard to tell the difference between homologies, which reflect common ancestry, and analogies, biological similarities that develop through convergent evolution.

2. Prosimians are the older of the two primate suborders. Some 40 million years ago, anthropoids displaced prosimians from niches their ancestors once occupied. Tarsiers and lorises are prosimians that survived by adapting to nocturnal life. Lemurs survived on the isolated island of Madagascar.

3. Anthropoids include humans, apes, and monkeys. All share fully developed primate trends, such as depth and color vision. Other anthropoid traits include a shift in tactile areas to the fingers. The New World monkeys are all arboreal. Old World monkeys include both terrestrial species (e.g., baboons and macaques) and arboreal ones. The great apes are orangutans, gorillas, and chimpanzees. The lesser apes are gibbons and siamangs.

4. Gibbons and siamangs live in Southeast Asian forests. These apes are slight, arboreal animals whose mode of locomotion is brachiation. Sexual dimorphism, slight among gibbons, is marked among orangutans, which are confined to two Indonesian islands. Sexually dimorphic gorillas, the most terrestrial apes, are vegetarians confined to equatorial Africa. Two species of chimpanzees live in the forests and woodlands of tropical Africa. Chimps are less sexually dimorphic, more numerous, and more omnivorous than gorillas are. Terrestrial monkeys (baboons and macaques) live in troops. Baboon males, the troop's main protectors, are twice the size of females.

5. Deforestation poses a special risk for the primates. Most of the 190 living primate species are in tropical forests—in Africa, Asia, South America, and Central America. Primates also are endangered as humans hunt them for food (bush meat) and capture them for zoos and research.

6. There are significant differences between humans and other primates. But similarities are also extensive, and many differences are of degree rather than of kind. A unique concentration and combination of ingredients make humans distinct. Some of our most important adaptive traits are foreshadowed in other primates, particularly in the African apes. Primate behavior and social organization aren't rigidly programmed by the genes. The ability to learn, which is the basis of culture, is an adaptive advantage available to many nonhuman primates. Chimpanzees make tools for several purposes. They also hunt and share meat.

7. Important differences between humans and other primates remain. Aggression and dominance are characteristic of terrestrial monkeys. Sharing and cooperation are equally significant in human bands. Connected with sharing among humans is a traditional division of subsistence labor by age and gender. Only humans have systems of kinship and marriage that permit us to maintain lifelong ties with relatives in different local groups.

8. From the perspective of behavioral ecology, individuals in a population compete to increase their genetic contribution to future generations. Maternal care makes sense from this perspective because females can be sure their offspring are their own. Because it's harder for males to be sure about paternity, evolutionary theory predicts they will invest most in offspring when they are surest the offspring are theirs.

KEY TERMS

analogies Similarities arising as a result of similar selective forces; traits produced by convergent evolution.

anthropoids Members of Anthropoidea, one of the two suborders of primates; monkeys, apes, and humans are anthropoids.

arboreal Tree-dwelling; arboreal primates include gibbons, New World monkeys, and many Old World monkeys.

behavioral ecology Study of the evolutionary basis of social behavior.

bipedal Two-footed; upright bipedalism is the characteristic human mode of locomotion.

brachiation Under-the-branch swinging; characteristic of gibbons, siamangs, and some New World monkeys.

convergent evolution Independent operation of similar selective forces; the process by which analogies are produced.

estrus Period of maximum sexual receptivity in female baboons, chimpanzees, and other primates, signaled by vaginal area swelling and coloration.

gibbons The smallest apes, natives of Asia; arboreal.

hominids Members of the zoological family that includes fossil and living humans; many scientists now include chimpanzees and gorillas in this family.

hominoids Members of the superfamily including humans and all the apes.

homologies Traits that organisms have jointly inherited from a common ancestor.

opposable thumb A thumb that can touch all the other fingers.

primatology The study of fossil and living apes, monkeys, and prosimians, including their behavior and social life.

prosimians The primate suborder that includes lemurs, lorises, and tarsiers.

sexual dimorphism Marked differences in male and female anatomy and temperament.

taxonomy Classification scheme; assignment to categories (*taxa;* singular, *taxon*).

terrestrial Ground-dwelling; baboons, macaques, and humans are terrestrial primates; gorillas spend most of their time on the ground.

CRITICAL THINKING QUESTIONS

1. Give three examples of homologies between humans and apes. Can you think of behavioral as well as biological homologies?

2. Among the primates, give an example of an analogy produced through convergent evolution. Can you think of analogies involving animals other than primates?

3. What are the main trends in primate evolution? Compare a cat or dog with a monkey, ape, or human. What are the main differences in the sensory organs—those that have to do with vision, smell, and touch, for example?

4. Which seems most similar to human social organization, that of baboons, gorillas, or chimpanzees?

5. What are some examples of ways in which nonhuman primates rely on learning to adapt to their environment?

6. How do tools differ with respect to humans and other animals?

7. What environmental conditions might trigger predatory behavior among primates? How about humans?

8. Give three examples of major behavioral differences between humans and other primates.

9. Why is it significant that among primates, only humans maintain ties of affection and mutual support between different local groups?

10. How do behavioral ecology and fitness theory help us understand differences between female and male parental investment strategies?

Atlas Questions

Look at Map 5, "Major Primate Groups."

1. On what continents are there nonhuman primates today? How does this differ from the past? What primate thrives today in North America?

2. What nonhuman primates live on the island of Madagascar? Are they monkeys or what? Where do other members of their suborder live?

3. On what continents can you find apes in the wild today? What continent that used to have apes lacks them today (except, of course, in zoos).

SUGGESTED ADDITIONAL READINGS

Burton, F. D., and M. Eaton

1995   *The Multimedia Guide to Non-Human Primates.* Upper Saddle River, NJ: Prentice-Hall. A CD-ROM combining photos, illustrations, video, sound, and text—presenting over 200 species of nonhuman primates.

De Waal, F. B. M.

1997   *Bonobo: The Forgotten Ape.* Berkeley: University of California Press. Field-based study of rare and remote apes noted for their similarities to humans and their sexual behavior.

1999   *Chimpanzee Politics: Power and Sex among Apes,* rev. ed. Baltimore: Johns Hopkins University Press. Hierarchy, sex, and alliance among apes, mainly based on zoo observations.

Fedigan, L. M.

1992   *Primate Paradigms: Sex Roles and Social Bonds.* Chicago: University of Chicago Press. Focuses on sex roles in primate social organization.

Fossey, D.

1983   *Gorillas in the Mist.* Boston: Houghton Mifflin. Social organization of the mountain gorilla; basis of the popular film.

Goodall, J.

1996   *My Life with the Chimpanzees.* New York: Pocket Books. Popular account of the author's life among the chimps.

Hinde, R. A.

1983   *Primate Social Relationships: An Integrated Approach.* Sunderland, MA: Sinaeur Associates. Theoretical implications of aspects of social life among various primates.

Montgomery, S.

1991   *Walking with the Great Apes: Jane Goodall, Dian Fossey, Birutá Galdikas.* Boston: Houghton Mifflin. The stories of three primatologists who have worked with, and to preserve, chimpanzees, gorillas, and orangutans.

Morbeck, M. E., A. Galloway, and A. L. Zihlman, eds.

1997   *The Evolving Female: A Life-History Perspective.* Princeton, NJ: Princeton University Press. Primatology and human evolution from a female perspective.

Napier, J. R., and P. H. Napier

1985   *The Natural History of Primates.* Cambridge, MA: The MIT Press. Readable and well-illustrated introduction to the primates.

Roberts, J. L.

1995   *Dian Fossey.* San Diego, CA: Lucent Books. Biography of the gorilla researcher and protector.

Russon, A. E., K. A. Bard, and S. Taylor Parker, eds.

1996   *Reaching into Thought: The Minds of the Great Apes.* New York: Cambridge University Press. Papers examining the intelligence of the apes.

Small, M. F.

1993   *Female Choices: Sexual Behavior of Female Primates.* Ithaca, NY: Cornell University Press. Sexual behavior and characteristics of female apes and monkeys.

Small, M. F., ed.

1984   *Female Primates: Studies by Women Primatologists.* New York: Liss. Differences in female strategies in various primate groups.

Smuts, B. B.

1989   *Sex and Friendship in Baboons.* Cambridge, MA Harvard University Press. Pair bonding, mutual support, and parental investment in baboon social organization, with implications for early human evolution.

Stanford, C. B.

1999   *The Hunting Apes: Meat Eating and the Origins of Human Behavior.* Princeton, NJ: Princeton University Press. The role of meat and hunting in sex and alliance among wild chimps.

Stanford, C. B., and H. T. Bunn, eds.

2001   *Meat-Eating and Human Evolution.* New York: Oxford University Press. Compendium of various recent studies.

Strum, S. C., and L. M. Fedigan, eds.

2000   *Primate Encounters: Models of Science, Gender, and Society.* Chicago: University of Chicago Press. The roles of males and females in primate social organization.

Swindler, D. R.

1998   *Introduction to the Primates.* Seattle: University of Washington Press. Up-to-date survey.

Wrangham, R. W., ed.

1994   *Chimpanzee Cultures.* Cambridge, MA: Harvard University Press.

INTERNET EXERCISES

1. Primate Conflict: Go to the Living Link's video collection at Emory University's Center for the Advanced Study of Ape and Human Evolution website, **http://www.emory.edu/LIVING_LINKS/a/video.html,** and watch the Chimpanzee Conflict Movie, **http://www.emory.edu/LIVING_LINKS/sounds/ram_text/conflict_28k.ram.**

   a. What different kinds of aggression are presented in the movie?

   b. What are the different responses to aggression? Did these responses tend to escalate or terminate the aggressive behavior?

   c. Is aggressive behavior restricted to adults? Does it take on different forms in juveniles?

   d. Which of these aggressive behaviors and responses do humans share with the chimpanzees? For example, do humans use Bluff Display?

2. Endangered Primates: Go to the Living Link's video collection at Emory University's Center for the Advanced Study of Ape and Human Evolution website, **http://www.emory.edu/LIVING_LINKS/a/video.html,** and watch the African Bushmeat Crisis Movie, **http://www.emory.edu/LIVING_LINKS/sounds/ram_text/bushmeat.ram.**

   a. The filmmakers argue that killing primates is similar to murder. Do you agree?

   b. The filmmakers suggest that the roots of the problem lie in those who hunt gorillas, not in those who buy and consume them. Do you think that if Joseph stopped hunting, people would stop eating gorillas?

   c. What other steps would you suggest to help preserve the mountain gorilla populations in Africa?

See Chapter 5 at your McGraw-Hill Online Learning Center for additional review and interactive exercises.

Bringing It All Together

See your OLC *Bringing It All Together* links

Saving the Forests

Deforestation, a problem that faces the world, is also a topic that has attracted the attention of anthropology's four subfields and two dimensions. Anthropology has always been concerned with how environmental forces influence humans and primates and how human activities affect the biosphere and the earth itself. As we saw in Chapter 4, biological anthropologists have examined the relation between farming, deforestation, and the spread of malaria and the gene that causes sickle-cell anemia. Other physical anthropologists—primatologists—see deforestation as a major threat to the animals they study. Paleoanthropologists have suggested a link between climate change, shrinking of forests, and the origin of hominids. Archaeologists have viewed deforestation in the context of resource use by ancient farmers and herders. Linguistic anthropologists have studied how people name and classify plants and forest resources. Cultural anthropologists have documented the varied uses people make of the forest and its products. From the fairy tales of Western Europe (e.g., Hansel and Gretel) to recent Hollywood films (e.g., The *Blair Witch Project*, *AI*), the forest plays a potent symbolic role as a place of mystery, danger, and enchantment. Today applied anthropologists are working to devise culturally appropriate and effective strategies to curb deforestation and preserve biodiversity.

Deforestation is a global concern. Forest loss contributes to greenhouse gas production (CO_2), which has been implicated in global warming. The destruction of tropical forests is also a major factor in the loss of global biodiversity. This is the case because of the many species, often of limited distribution, in forests, especially in the tropics. Tropical forests may contain more than half of earth's species while covering just 6 percent of the planet's land surface. Yet tropical forests are disappearing at the rate of 10 million to 20 million hectares per year (the size of New York state).

Among the tropical animals whose natural habitats are threatened, primates, most of which are forest dwellers, are especially at risk. Consider the Democratic Republic of the Congo (DRC), the country that ranks fourth in the world in terms of greatest biodiversity. Its threatened species include gorillas and bonobos. The major threat to the bonobo, which is found only in the DRC, is forestry and loss of the hardwood forests where most bonobos live (Stern 2000). In Indonesia, deforestation threatens the orangutan. Contact with humans after the opening of a road for loggers and miners proved fatal to hundreds of orangs. Recent Indonesian policy has promoted plantations rather than forest preservation. Government policy has shifted from selective logging, which permits some animals to survive, to clear-cutting of the forest, which destroys the habitat (Dreifus 2000). As we hear regularly on the news, forests also have suffered from ancient and modern forest fires.

Cultural factors, including politics, affect the use of the forest and its perceived value to humans. Some governments and administrations are more environment-friendly than others are. And even if a country has strict environmental laws, those laws require enforcement. Consider Brazil's Amazon rain forest, where dozens of primate species live. Brazilian national deforestation policy has to be implemented at the local level, but many local political systems are controlled by ranching and mining interests that oppose environmental regulation.

Physical, archaeological, and cultural anthropologists have all examined how human strategies of adaptation, including economic activities, affect the environment, including use of the forest. The historic shift from foraging (hunting and gather-

Applied anthropology uses anthropological perspectives to identify and solve contemporary problems that affect humans. Deforestation is one such problem. Here children carrying saplings participate in a reforestation project in Sri Lanka.

ing) to food production (farming and herding) first took place in the Middle East some 10,000–12,000 years ago, and again in the Western Hemisphere 5,000 years later. With food production, the rate at which human beings degrade their environments increased. Population increase and the need to expand farming caused deforestation in many parts of the ancient Middle East and Mesoamerica (Mexico, Guatemala, Belize, and Honduras). People cut down trees to plant crops such as wheat in the Middle East and maize (corn) in Mesoamerica. Even today, many farmers think of trees as giant weeds to be removed and replaced with productive fields. Many farmers burn vegetation to remove weeds, then use the ashes for fertilizer. Herders burn to promote the growth of young tender shoots for their livestock. If done too often, as may happen when population grows, these activities result in deforestation. The use of fuel wood by early smelters also took its toll on the forests.

As we'll see in Chapter 11, located in what is now western Honduras, Copán was once a thriving Maya royal center. Its collapse some 1,400 years ago was linked to deforestation, erosion, and soil exhaustion due to overpopulation and overfarm-

ing. Archaeologists have reconstructed hillside farmhouses with debris from erosion at Copán. The erosion started around 750 AD and continued for generations, until the farm sites were abandoned. Some of them eventually were buried by erosion debris. Studies of Copán's paleopathology reveal food stress and malnutrition. Most (80 percent) of the corpses buried there had anemia, due to iron deficiency. Even Copán's nobles were malnourished. One noble skull, known to be such from its carved teeth and cosmetic deformation, has telltale signs of anemia: spongy areas at its rear.

What about forests, their uses and value, and threats to them today? In many parts of the world, forests supply medicinal plants; food products such as honey, game, and fruits; and wood—used to build houses, fences, and animal pens. Forests are also vital parts of watersheds—regions drained by river systems; trees take up and conserve water. By conserving water, forests impede erosion and siltation (mineral deposits) in irrigation canals.

Glen Green (a geologist) and Robert Sussman (a biological anthropologist) (1990) used remote sensing (as discussed in Chapter 3) to study deforestation in the eastern rain forests of Madagascar.

In this area are found several endangered species, including the lemurs discussed in "Beyond the Classroom" in Chapter 5. Green and Sussman found deforestation there to be correlated both with topographic relief (the slope or steepness of the land) and with human population density. Sparsely populated areas and very hilly areas had less forest loss than did densely populated and flat to moderately hilly areas. More than half the forest cover in the sparsely populated regions had survived, compared with just 19 percent in the high-density areas. The Green–Sussman study exposed an important fact for policy makers: Although low relief areas need protection the most, nearly all of Madagascar's forest reserves had been established in hilly areas. What recommendation would an applied anthropologist make for the location of future protected areas?

Often, as in eastern Madagascar, in the ancient Middle East, and at Copán, deforestation is demographically driven—caused by population pressure. Madagascar's population is growing at a rate of 3 percent annually, doubling every generation. Population pressure leads to migration, including rural–urban migration. Madagascar's capital, Antananarivo, had just 100,000 people in 1967, but over 1 million by 1990. Urban growth promotes deforestation if city dwellers rely on fuel wood from the countryside, as has been true in Madagascar.

As forested watersheds disappear, crop productivity declines, as happened at Copán. Madagascar is known as the "great red island," after the color of its soil. On that island, the effects of erosion and runoff are visible to the naked eye. Looking at its rivers, Madagascar appears to be bleeding to death. Increasing runoff of water no longer trapped by trees causes erosion of low-lying rice fields near swollen rivers, as well as siltation in irrigation canals (Kottak, Gezon, and Green 1994).

Besides population pressure, another prominent cause of deforestation is commercial logging, which can degrade forests in several ways. Obviously, logging deforests because it removes trees. Less evident are the destructive effects of road building, tree dragging, and other features of commercial logging. A logging road may cut a swath for erosion. In one village in Madagascar, whose forest had recently been invaded by loggers from outside, villagers told an ethnographer that the loggers killed a dozen trees for every log they dragged out (Kottak, Gezon, and Green 1994).

The global scenarios of deforestation include demographic pressure (from births or immigration) on subsistence economies, commercial logging, road building, cash cropping, fuel wood needs associated with urban expansion, and clearing and burning associated with livestock and grazing. The fact that forest loss has several causes has a policy implication: Different deforestation scenarios require different conservation strategies.

What can be done? On this question applied anthropology weighs in (see Kottak and Costa 1993), spurring policy makers to think about new conservation strategies. The traditional approach has been to restrict access to forested areas designated as parks, then employ park guards and punish violators. Modern strategies are more likely to consider the needs, wishes, and abilities of the people (often impoverished) living in and near the forest. Since effective conservation depends on the cooperation of the local people, their concerns must be addressed in devising conservation strategy.

Typically, forests have substantial economic and cultural utility for the

The causes of deforestation are diverse. In this example from Madagascar, the rain forest has been cut back to enlarge a cattle ranch. What are some other causes of deforestation?

Forests supply medicinal plants, food products, and wood. This woman is collecting medicinal plants in Sarawak, Malaysia.

communities in and near them. Forests supply firewood and wood for house and granary construction, fences, and technology (e.g., oxcarts and mortars and pestles—for pounding grain). Some forests are used for food production, including slash-and-burn or shifting cultivation. Tree crops such as bananas, fruits, and coffee do well in the forest, where foraging for wild products also proceeds. Forests also contain vital cultural products. In Madagascar, for example, these products include medicinal plants and pastes considered essential for the proper growth of children. In one ethnic group rice from a forest field is part of the ceremony used to ensure a successful and fertile marriage. Another ethnic group has its most sacred tombs in the forests. Traditionally, these cul-

turally vital areas of the forest have been tabooed for burning and wood cutting. They are part of a local conservation system that has been in place for generations.

What happens when activities are banned not by the traditional culture but by an external agency? Government-imposed conservation policies may require people to change the way they have been doing things for generations to meet the goals of outside planners rather than those of local people. When communities are asked to give up traditional activities on which they depend for their livelihood, they usually resist. To be successful, conservation schemes must involve local people in planning and implementing the policies and programs that will affect them.

Effective environmentalism requires culturally informed negotiation with political and economic interests at the local, regional, national, and international levels. Here is an arena in which anthropology is fruitfully applied. Conservationists must learn to recognize and build on diverse systems of environmental values—different "ethnoecologies." (An *ethnoecology* is any society's traditional set of environmental perceptions, its ideas about the environment in relation to people and society.) Effective conservation strategy requires extensive and ongoing knowledge of affected areas and the socioeconomic and cultural practices of the local people.

To curb the global deforestation threat, we need conservation strategies that work. Laws and enforcement may help reduce commercially driven deforestation caused by burning and clear-cutting. But local people also use and abuse forested lands. A challenge for the environmentally oriented applied anthropologist is to find ways to make forest preservation attractive to local people and to ensure their cooperation. Successful conservation must be based on culturally appropriate policies, which applied anthropologists can help devise for specific places. To provide locally meaningful incentives, we need good anthropological knowledge of each affected area. Governments and international agencies are likely to fail if they try to impose their goals without considering the practices, customs, rules, laws, beliefs, and values of the people to be affected. Applied anthropologists work to make "good for the globe" good for the people.

6

PRIMATE EVOLUTION

Overview

The primate order evolved by exploiting new opportunities that arose at the end of the Mesozoic era. The age of reptiles yielded to the age of mammals—the Cenozoic era, which began some 65 million years ago. Flowering plants proliferated, along with the insects attracted to them and the animals that preyed on those insects. Primate traits like grasping hands and depth perception aided in the capture of insects and were adaptive in an arboreal environment.

By the Eocene epoch, primates had spread and diversified, mainly in Europe and North America, which were connected at that time. Among primates, the Eocene was the age of prosimians. By the end of the Eocene, the anthropoids had emerged; they eventually displaced the prosimians in most places. In the next

epoch, the Oligocene, the New World monkeys split off from the catarrhines, the ancestors of Old World monkeys, apes, and humans.

The ensuing Miocene epoch, divided into Early, Middle, and Late, witnessed a fluorescence of proto-apes, an amazing variety unlike anything that survives in the contemporary world. Some 16 million years ago, Africa collided with Eurasia. The new land connection allowed African fauna, including apes, to spread into Europe and Asia, where the apes proliferated. The lines leading to the orangutan, on the one hand, and the African apes, on the other, split during the middle Miocene. The common ancestor of humans, chimps, and gorillas—as yet unidentified—lived during the late Miocene, some five to eight million years ago.

Suddenly, Primate Ancestors Pushed Back to Time Dinosaurs Roamed

WASHINGTON POST NEWS BRIEFS

by Guy Gugliotta

April 18, 2002

Fossil evidence confirms that a variety of primates lived, mainly in Europe and North America, during the geological epoch known as the Eocene (54–38 m.y.a.—million years ago). On that basis, many paleontologists suspect that the earliest primates appeared during the previous epoch, the Paleocene (65–54 m.y.a.). The status of several Paleocene fossils as possible primates has been debated, but not resolved. Based on the current *fossil* evidence, it's difficult to believe the first primates might date back even farther—to the age of the dinosaurs, the Mesozoic era, which ended 65 million years ago. Despite what we've seen in the movies, early *humans* did *not* coexist with the dinosaurs. But maybe primates did. Paleontology isn't the only scientific field that studies evolution. For example, significant evolutionary trees have been drawn on the basis of similarities and differences in DNA. As you read this news brief, consider the different techniques scientists use to interpret the past. What analytic techniques support the unorthodox idea that primates may date back 85 million years?

Primates—the mammals from which humans evolved—emerged on Earth much earlier than had been thought, originating perhaps 85 million years ago during the age of the dinosaurs, according to a new analysis. The findings should add fuel to the debate between paleontologists, who place the origin of primates at 55 million years ago, and molecular biologists, who use DNA sequencing to suggest they may be as old as 90 million years.

Paleontologist Robert D. Martin, vice president of academic affairs at Chicago's Field Museum, acknowledged that his team's new research supported the views of the "molecular clock" school, even though the method used by his team did not involve DNA analysis. Instead, the researchers developed a statistical model that builds an evolutionary tree based on the number of primate species alive today (235) and the number of recorded fossil species (396) and their ages. By assuming that each primate species would live approximately 2.5 million years, the team was able to estimate the length of time that elapsed between the oldest known fossil primate, which is 55 million years old, and a hypothetical "last common ancestor" of all primates, 80 million to 85 million years ago. The findings were reported in today's issue of the journal *Nature*. [See Figure 6.1.]

"I've been arguing for years that there's so many gaps in the fossil record that [primates are] probably much older than we thought," Martin said. "You look at how many species there are, and you can estimate the time of the original."

The implications of these findings, if shown to be accurate, could be profound. A primate ancestor 85 million years old would have shared the world with the dinosaurs, which went extinct 65 million years ago, probably in an ecological disaster caused by a meteor hitting the Earth . . . Martin said the earliest primate was probably a lemur-like tree dweller that weighed perhaps two pounds and dined on insects and fruit. Finally, an earlier date for primates would mean that continental drift (in which huge, ancient

A tarsier from Sumatra, Indonesia, on a human thumb. The first primates were also tiny.

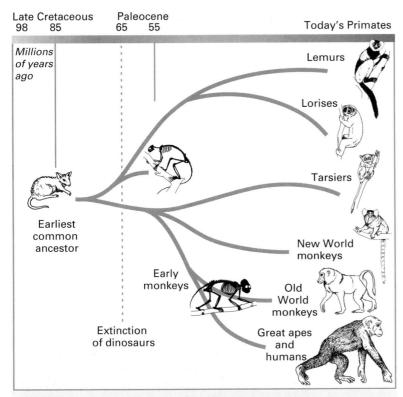

Figure 6.1   A New Evolutionary Tree for Primates, Based on Calculations Reported in This Story.

Source: BBC News, SCI/TECH, "Primate Ancestor Lived with Dinos," http://news.bbc.co.uk/hi/english/sci/tech/newsid_1935000/1935558.stm.

land masses broke up to form what are today's continents) had a significant effect in creating different primate species.

The new findings, however, drew criticism from several paleontologists, who noted that there is little fossil evidence from the dinosaur period that points to primates or indicates that mammals in general were flourishing.

"The primates are a successful group of animals," said K. Christopher Beard, curator of vertebrate paleontology at Pittsburgh's Carnegie Museum of Natural History. . . . "If primates were around and doing well, I suspect we would have found their fossils," Beard continued. "What I would do is issue a challenge and ask them to say where these animals are hiding."

What the fossil record shows is that before the dinosaur extinction, mammals were neither particularly diverse, nor particularly large. Most were rodent-like creatures, and "the biggest was about the size of a beaver," said Johns Hopkins University paleontologist Kenneth Rose. "There was an explosive radiation of mammals after [the dinosaur] extinction," Rose continued. "It took very little time before we get an animal the size of a steer, and soon we had some truly impressive creatures. With no dinosaurs in the way, there was a lot of open ecological space."

But while everyone agrees that the first unequivocal fossil primate did not appear until 55 million years ago, Martin argues that the record is too skimpy to conclude that the order began only a few million years prior to that.

"Primate paleontologists read the fossil record as if it told us everything," Martin said. "That's reasonable if you have a dense record, but our calculations show we have fossil evidence for only about 5 percent of the extinct primates."

By contrast, molecular biologists analyze DNA to calculate the amount of genetic difference in related species, creating an evolutionary tree that can be projected backward in time to the earliest common ancestor. "Our results actually fit the molecular trees, and they're always much earlier," Martin said. "Several people have generated the tree for mammals," and have come up with dates "around 90 million years." But "there are no fossils that say that," said Michael Novacek, provost and curator of paleontology at New York's American Museum of Natural History, even though "it could be that the record is incomplete." "So what's the truth?" Novacek asked. "I don't know."

Source: *Washington Post* (http://www.washingtonpost.com), April 18, 2002, p. A03. http://www.washingtonpost.com/ac2/wp-dyn?pagename= article&node=&contentId=A4580-2002Apr17.

The fossil record, as we've just seen, provides evidence for only 5 percent of extinct primates. With such small numbers, the fossil record gives us the merest glimpse of the diverse bioforms— living beings—that have existed on earth. In Chapter 3, in the section "Dating the Past," we learned why some areas and times are better represented in the fossil record than others are. Conditions favoring fossilization open special "time windows" for certain places and times, such as western Kenya from 18 to 14 **m.y.a.**—million years ago. Because western Kenya was geologically active then, it has a substantial fossil record. Between 12 and 8 m.y.a., the area was quieter geologically, and there are few fossils. After 8 m.y.a., another time window opens in the Rift Valley area of eastern Kenya. The East African highlands were rising, volcanoes were active, and lake basins were forming and filling with sediments. This time window extends through the present and includes many hominid fossils. Compared with East Africa, West Africa has been more stable geologically and has had few time windows (Jolly and White 1995).

In considering the primate fossil record, we'll see that different geographic areas provide more abundant fossil evidence for different time periods. This doesn't necessarily mean that primates weren't living elsewhere at the same time. The discussions of primate and human evolution must be tentative, because the fossil record is limited and spotty. Much is subject to change as knowledge increases. Recall from Chapter 1 that a key feature of science is to recognize the tentativeness and uncertainty of knowledge. Scientists, including fossil hunters, constantly seek out new evidence, and devise new methods, such as DNA comparison, to improve their understanding, in this case of primate and human evolution.

Chronology

We learned in Chapter 3 that the remains of animals and plants that lived at the same time are found in the same stratum. Based on fossils found in stratigraphic sequences, the history of vertebrate life has been divided into three main eras. The *Paleozoic* was the era of ancient life—fishes, amphibians, and primitive reptiles. The *Mesozoic* was the era of middle life—reptiles, including the dinosaurs. The *Cenozoic* is the era of recent life—birds and mammals. Each era is divided into periods, and the periods are divided into epochs. (See Figure 6.2.)

See the Virtual Exploration

mhhe
●com
/kottak

Anthropologists are concerned with the Cenozoic era, which includes two periods: Tertiary and

Era	Period	
Cenozoic	Quaternary	1.8 m.y.a.
	Tertiary	65 m.y.a.
Mesozoic	Cretaceous	146 m.y.a.
	Jurassic	208 m.y.a.
	Triassic	245 m.y.a.
Paleozoic	Permian	286 m.y.a.
	Carboniferous	360 m.y.a.
	Devonian	410 m.y.a.
	Silurian	440 m.y.a.
	Ordovician	505 m.y.a.
	Cambrian	544 m.y.a.
Proterozoic	Neoproterozoic	900 m.y.a.
	Mesoproterozoic	1,600 m.y.a.
	Paleoproterozoic	2,500 m.y.a.
Archaean		3,800 m.y.a.
Hadean		4,500 m.y.a.

Figure 6.2   Geological Time Scales.
The geological time scale, based on stratigraphy. Eras are subdivided into periods, and periods, into epochs. In what era, period, and epoch did *Homo* originate?

Era	Period	Epoch		Climate and Life Forms
Cenozoic	Quaternary	Holocene	11,000 B.P.	Transition to agriculture; emergence of states
		Pleistocene	1.8 m.y.a.	Climatic fluctuations, glaciation; *Homo, A. boisei*
	Tertiary	Pliocene	5 m.y.a.	*A. robustus, A. africanus, A. afarensis, A. anamensis, Ardipithecus ramidus*
		Miocene	23 m.y.a.	Cooler and drier grasslands spread in middle latitudes; Africa collides with Eurasia (16 m.y.a.); *Afropithecus, Ramapithecus, Sivapithecus*
		Oligocene	38 m.y.a.	Cooler and drier in the north; anthropoids in Africa (Fayum); separation of catarrhines and platyrrhines; separation of hylobatids from pongids and hominids
		Eocene	54 m.y.a.	Warm tropical climates become widespread; modern orders of mammals appear; prosimianlike primates; anthropoids appear by late Eocene
		Paleocene	65 m.y.a.	First major mammal radiation

Figure 6.2   **Geological Time Scales—Concluded.**
Periods and Epochs of the Cenozoic Era.

Quaternary. Each of these periods is subdivided into epochs. The Tertiary had five epochs: Paleocene, Eocene, Oligocene, Miocene, and Pliocene. The Quaternary includes just two epochs: Pleistocene and Holocene, or Recent. Figure 6.2 gives the approximate dates of these epochs. Sediments from the Paleocene epoch (65 to 54 m.y.a.) have yielded fossil remains of diverse small mammals, some possibly ancestral to the primates. Prosimian-like fossils abound in strata dating from the Eocene (54 to 36 m.y.a.). The first anthropoid fossils date to the middle to late Eocene and the early Oligocene (36 to 23 m.y.a.). Hominoids became widespread during the Miocene (23 to 5 m.y.a.). Hominids first appeared in the late Miocene or early Pliocene (5 to 2 m.y.a.) (Figure 6.2).

See your OLC Internet Exercises

mhhe ●com /kottak

Early Primates

When the Mesozoic era ended, and the Cenozoic began, some 65 million years ago, North America was connected to Europe, but not to South America. (The Americas joined some 20 million years ago.) Over millions of years, the continents have "drifted" to their present locations, carried along by the gradually shifting plates of the earth's surface (Figure 6.3).

During the Cenozoic, most land masses had tropical or subtropical climates. The Mesozoic era had ended with a massive worldwide extinction of plants and animals, including the dinosaurs. Thereafter, mammals replaced reptiles as the dominant large land animals. Trees and flowering plants soon proliferated, supplying arboreal foods for the primates that eventually evolved to fill the new niches.

According to the arboreal theory, primates became primates by adapting to arboreal life. The primate traits and trends discussed in the last chapter developed as adaptations to life high up in the trees. A key feature was the importance of sight over smell. Changes in the visual apparatus were adaptive in the trees, where depth perception facilitated leaping. Grasping hands and feet were used to crawl along slender branches. Grasping feet anchored the body as the primate reached for foods at the ends of branches. Early

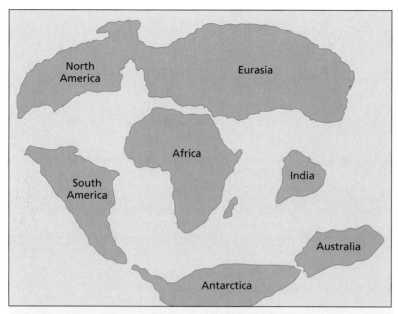

Figure 6.3   Placement of Continents at the End of the Mesozoic.   When the Mesozoic era ended, and the Cenozoic began, some 65 million years ago, North America was connected to Europe, but not to South America.

According to one theory, binocular vision and manipulative hands developed among primates because they facilitated the capture of insects. What is this theory called? Here a Colombian squirrel monkey uses its hands and eyes to eat a katydid.

primates probably had omnivorous diets based on foods available in the trees, such as flowers, fruits, berries, gums, leaves, and insects. The early Cenozoic era witnessed a proliferation of flowering plants, attracting insects that were to figure prominently in many primate diets.

Matt Cartmill (1974, 1992) notes that although primate traits work well in the trees, they aren't the only possible adaptations to arboreal life. Squirrels, for example, do just fine with claws and snouts and without binocular vision. Something else must have figured in primate evolution, and Cartmill suggests a **visual predation theory**. This is the idea that binocular vision, grasping hands and feet, and reduced claws developed because they facilitated the capture of insects, which figured prominently in the early primate diet. According to this theory, early primates first adapted to bushy forest undergrowth and low tree branches, where they foraged for fruits and insects. Particularly in pursuing insects, early primates would have relied heavily on vision. Close-set eyes permitted binocular vision and depth perception. Such a visual apparatus would have allowed early primates to judge the distance to their prey without moving their heads. They would have hunted like cats and owls. The snout would have been reduced, with a less acute sense of smell, as the eyes came closer together. Early primates would have held on with their grasping feet as they snared their prey with their hands. Several living prosimians retain the small body size and insectivorous diet that may have characterized the first primates. Jurmain (1997) suggests that although key primate traits might have evolved first for life in the lower branches, such traits would have become even more adaptive when bug snatching was done higher up in the trees.

EARLY CENOZOIC PRIMATES

There is considerable fossil evidence that a diversified group of primates lived, mainly in Europe and North America, during the second epoch of the

Compare this line drawing reconstruction of Shoshonius, a member of the Eocene omomyid family, with a modern tarsier from Mindanao in the Philippines. What similarities and differences do you notice?

Cenozoic, the Eocene. On that basis it is likely that the earliest primates lived during the first epoch of the Cenozoic, the Paleocene (65–54 m.y.a.). The status of several fossils as possible Paleocene primates has been debated. As there is no consensus on this matter, such fossils are not discussed here.

The first fossil forms clearly identified as primates lived during the Eocene epoch (54–38 m.y.a.) in North America, Europe, Africa, and Asia. They reached Madagascar from Africa late in the Eocene. The ancestral lemurs must have traveled across the Mozambique Channel, which was narrower then than it is now, on thick mats of vegetation. Such naturally formed "rafts" have been observed forming in East African rivers, then floating out to sea.

In primate evolution, the Eocene was the age of the prosimians, with at least 60 genera in two main families (*Omomyidae* and *Adapidae*). The widely distributed **omomyid** family lived in North America, Europe, and Asia. The omomyids, such as *Shoshonius*, portrayed in the drawing on this page, were squirrel-sized. But unlike squirrels they had grasping hands and feet, used to manipulate objects and to climb by encircling small branches. Early members of the omomyid family may be ancestral to all anthropoids. Later ones may be ancestral to tarsiers.

The **adapid** family was probably ancestral to the lemur–loris line. The only major difference between the Eocene adapids, such as *Smilodectes*, shown in the photo on page 151, and today's lemurs and lorises is that the latter have a dental comb (see Figure 6.4). This structure is formed from the incisor and canine teeth of the lower jaw.

Sometime during the Eocene, ancestral anthropoids branched off from the prosimians by becoming more diurnal (active during the day) and by strengthening the trend favoring vision over smell. Some Eocene prosimians had larger brains and eyes, and smaller snouts, than others did. These were the ancestors of the anthropoids. Anthropoid eyes are rotated more forward when compared with lemurs and lorises. Also, anthropoids have a fully enclosed bony eye socket, which lemurs and lorises lack. And unlike lemurs and lorises, anthropoids lack a rhinarium, a moist nose continuous with the upper lip. Anthropoids have a dry nose, separate from the upper lip. Another distinguishing anthropoid feature has to do with molar cusps—bumps on the teeth. The primitive number of cusps on mammalian lower molars is six. The anthropoids have lost one or two cusps on their lower molars, so as to have four or five.

The oldest probable anthropoid discovered so far is *Eosimias*, from the Eocene of China. The oldest definite anthropoid is *Catopithecus*, from the late Eocene of Egypt. By the end of the Eocene, many prosimian species had become extinct, reflecting competition from the first anthropoids.

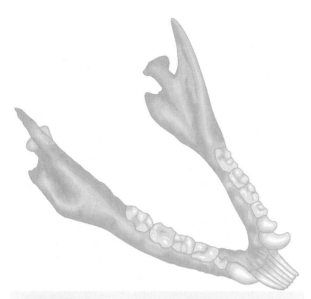

Figure 6.4   A Dental Comb.
A dental comb is a derived trait present among
contemporary lemurs and lorises but absent in
Eocene adapids such as *Smilodectes*.
SOURCE: Robert Jurmain and Harry Nelson, *Introduction
to Physical Anthropology*, 6th ed. (Minneapolis: West
Publishing, 1994), p. 210.

OLIGOCENE ANTHROPOIDS

During the Oligocene epoch (38–23 m.y.a.), anthropoids became the most numerous primates. Most
of our knowledge of early anthropoids is based on
fossils from Egypt's Fayum deposits. This area is a
desert today, but 36–31 million years ago it was a
tropical rain forest.

The anthropoids of the Fayum lived in trees
and ate fruits and seeds. Compared with prosimians, they had fewer teeth, reduced snouts, larger
brains, and increasingly forward-looking eyes. Of
the Fayum anthropoid fossils, the *parapithecid* family is the more primitive and is perhaps ancestral
to the New World monkeys. The parapithecids
were very small (two to three pounds), with similarities to living marmosets and tamarins, small
South American monkeys. One genus of this
group, *Apidium*, is one of the most common fossils
in the Fayum beds.

The *propliopithecid* family seems ancestral to the
catarrhines—Old World monkeys, apes, and
humans. This family includes *Aegyptopithecus*,
which, at 13–18 pounds, was the size of a large
domestic cat. The propliopithecids share with the

later catarrhines a distinctive dental formula:
2.1.2.3, meaning two incisors, one canine, two premolars, and three molars. (The formula is based on
one-fourth of the mouth, either the right or left side
of the upper or lower jaw.) The more primitive primate dental formula is 2.1.3.3. Most other primates,
including prosimians and New World monkeys,
have the second formula, with three premolars
instead of two. Besides the Fayum, Oligocene
deposits with primate bones have been found in
North and West Africa, southern Arabia, China,
Southeast Asia, and North and South America.

The Oligocene was a time of major geological
and climatic change. North America and Europe
separated and became distinct continents. The
Great Rift Valley system of East Africa formed.
India drifted into Asia. A cooling trend began,
especially in the Northern Hemisphere, where primates disappeared.

Miocene Hominoids

The earliest hominoid fossils date to the Miocene
epoch (23–5 m.y.a.), which is divided into three
parts: lower, middle, and upper or late. The early
Miocene (23–16 m.y.a.) was a warm and wet period,
when forests covered East Africa. Recall from the
last chapter that *Hominoidea* is the superfamily that
includes fossil and living apes and humans. For simplicity's sake, the earliest hominoids are here called
proto-apes, or simply apes. Although some of these
may be ancestral to living apes, none is identical, or
often even very similar, to modern apes.

PROCONSUL

The superfamily known as *Pliopithecoidea* includes
several species of the genus *Proconsul*. The *Proconsul* group represents the most abundant and successful anthropoids of the early Miocene. This
group lived in Africa and includes three species:
Proconsul (*P.*) *africanus*, *P. nyanzae*, and *P. major*.
Possibly descended from the Oligocene propliopithecids, these early Miocene proto-apes had teeth
with similarities to those of living apes. But their
skeleton below the neck was more monkeylike.
Some *Proconsul* species were the size of a small
monkey; others, the size of a chimpanzee, usually
with marked sexual dimorphism. Their dentition
suggests they ate fruits and leaves.

Smilodectes was a member of the lemurlike adapid family, which lived during the Eocene. Compare this drawing reconstructing a *Smilodectes* from Wyoming with a modern black lemur (*Eulemur macaco*) from Madagascar.

Their skulls were more delicate than those of modern apes, and their legs were longer than their arms—more like monkeys. *Proconsul* probably moved through the trees like a monkey—on four limbs—and lacked the capacity for suspension and brachiation displayed by modern apes. *Proconsul* probably contained the last common ancestor shared by the Old World monkeys and the apes. By the middle Miocene, *Proconsul* had been replaced by Old World monkeys and apes.

Fossils of Miocene monkeys and prosimians are rare; ape fossils are much more common. Like many living apes, those of the Miocene were forest dwellers and fruit eaters. They lived in areas that, as the forests retreated, monkeys would eventually colonize. By the late Miocene (10–5 m.y.a.) the age of the apes had ended, and monkeys had become the most common anthropoid in the Old World (except for humans, eventually).

Why did the Old World monkeys thrive as the Miocene apes faded? The probable answer was the monkeys' superior ability to eat leaves. Leaves are easier to get than fruits, which are typical ape foods. As the forests retreated at the end of the Miocene, most apes were restricted to the remaining tropical rain forests in areas of (mainly West) Africa and Southeast Asia. Monkeys survived over a wider area. They did so because they could process leaves effectively. Monkey molars developed *lophs*: ridges of enamel that run from side to side between the cusps of the teeth. Old World monkeys have two such lophs, so their molars are called *bilophodont*. Such lophs slice past each other like scissor blades, a good way to shear a leaf.

Some species of *Proconsul* may have been ancestral to the living African apes. *Proconsul* also may be ancestral to the Old World monkeys. *Proconsul* had all the primitive traits shared by apes and Old World monkeys and none of the derived traits of either. *Primitive* traits are those passed on unchanged from an ancestor, such as the five-cusped molars of the apes, which are inherited from an old anthropoid ancestor. *Derived* traits are those that develop in a particular taxon after they split from their common ancestor with another taxon. Examples are bilophodont molars among Old World monkeys. The Old World monkeys have derived bilophodont molars and primitive quadrupedal bodies. The apes have primitive molars and derived brachiating bodies. Proconsul had both primitive teeth and a primitive quadrupedal body.

AFROPITHECUS AND KENYAPITHECUS

During the early Miocene (23–16 m.y.a.), Africa was cut off by water from Europe and Asia. But during the middle Miocene, Arabia drifted into Eurasia, providing a land connection between Africa, Europe, and Asia. Migrating both ways—out of and into Africa—after 16 m.y.a. were various animals, including hominoids. Proto-apes were the most common primates of the middle Miocene (16–10 m.y.a.). Over 20 species have been discovered. (See Figure 6.5.) Their teeth retain the primitive anthropoid five-cusped molar pattern.

During the middle Miocene, the hominoids spread widely, in Europe, Asia, and Africa. East African apes of the middle Miocene include *Afropithecus*, *Equatorius*, and two species of *Kenyapithecus*, one earlier, one later. *Afropithecus* is a large Miocene hominoid from northern Kenya, dated to 18 to 16 m.y.a. (Leakey, Leakey, and Walker 1988). The *Afropithecus* remains consist of skull, jaw, and postcranial (below the head) fragments. *Afropithecus* seems to have been a slow-moving arboreal

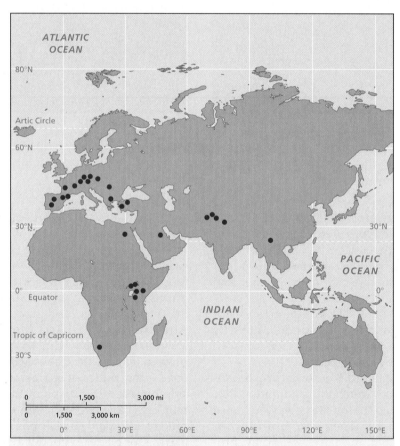

Figure 6.5 **The Geographic Distribution of Known Miocene Apes.**

SOURCE: Robert Jurmain and Harry Nelson, *Introduction to Physical Anthropology*, 6th ed. (Minneapolis: West Publishing, 1994), p. 302.

ape, with large projecting front teeth (similar to those of the modern African apes).

A recent discovery is a 15-million-year-old partial skeleton assigned to a new genus, *Equatorius africanus*. The find, from Kenya, consists of upper incisors, a lower jaw with teeth, and bones from the arm, shoulder, collarbone, chest, wrists, fingers, and vertebrae, all belonging to a single male. In its skeleton *Equatorius* is more modern than earlier hominoids, suggesting that it used the ground more frequently than earlier hominoids did.

There are clear similarities between *Equatorius* and the earlier of the two species of *Kenyapithecus*. Based on these similarities, the discoverers of *Equatorius* have suggested that the earlier *Kenyapithecus* species should be reclassified as *Equatorius*. The two *Kenyapithecus* species that have been recognized traditionally are *K. africanus* (earlier) and *K. wickeri* (later). *Equatorius* and *K. africanus* represent an older pattern. *K. wickeri* illustrates a more modern pattern—more like today's great apes. *K. wickeri*'s dental pattern also is found in the teeth of an unnamed ape from a middle Miocene site in Turkey (Ward et al. 1999).

Equatorius and *Afropithecus* are probable *stem hominoids*: species somewhere on the evolutionary line near the origins of the modern ape group. Stem hominoids are considered too primitive to be the direct ancestors of living apes and humans.

SIVAPITHECUS

Middle and late Miocene apes are often grouped in two families: *Ramapithecidae* and *Dryopithecidae*. The ramapithecids lived during the middle and late Miocene in Europe, Asia, and Africa. There are at least two ramapithecid genera: *Sivapithecus* and *Gigantopithecus*.

Sivapithecus fossils were first found in the Siwalik Hills of Pakistan. They include specimens formerly called "*Ramapithecus*" from that region, along with fossil apes from Turkey, China, and Kenya. A late Miocene find with an almost complete face from Pakistan's Potwar Plateau shows many similarities to the face of the modern orangutan. Because of facial and dental similarities, *Sivapithecus* of the late Miocene is now seen as ancestral to the modern orangutan. The orangutan line appears to have separated from the one leading to the African apes and humans more than 13 million years ago.

Hominids undoubtedly originated from a Miocene ape, but it is unclear which one it might be. "*Ramapithecus*" fossils from Asia and Africa were once viewed as a possible hominid ancestor, based on dental similarities with early hominids: thick tooth enamel, broad molars, and robust jaws. But scientists no longer see a close link between "*Ramapithecus*" or *Sivapithecus* and hominids.

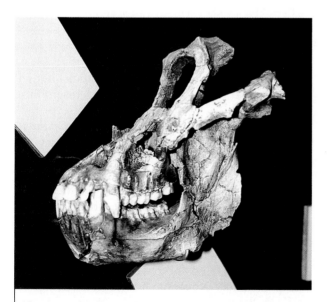 

Compare this *Sivapithecus* side view with a contemporary female orangutan.

These dental and jaw characteristics are widely shared with several other middle and late Miocene hominoids, including *Gigantopithecus*.

GIGANTOPITHECUS

Gigantopithecus is almost certainly the largest primate that ever lived. Confined to Asia, it persisted for millions of years, from the Miocene until 400,000 years ago, when it coexisted with members of our own genus, *Homo erectus*. Some people think *Gigantopithecus* is not extinct yet, and that we know it today as the yeti and bigfoot (Sasquatch).

Gigantopithecus was discovered in an unlikely place. In China, druggists sell fossils known as "dragon's" teeth and bones, which are ground up to be used medicinally. In 1935 the anthropologist G. H. R. von Koenigswald recognized that a "dragon's tooth" being sold by a Hong Kong druggist was actually that of an extinct ape. Since then, three jaw bones and more than 1,000 teeth have been recovered, some in drugstores, some at geological sites in China and Vietnam (Pettifor 1995). Some such sites have *Gigantopithecus* remains associated with those of *Homo erectus* (Ciochon et al. 1990), who may have hunted the ape into extinction.

With a fossil record consisting of nothing more than jaw bones and teeth, it is difficult to say for sure just how big *Gigantopithecus* was. Based on ratios of jaw and tooth size to body size in other apes, various reconstructions have been made. One has *Gigantopithecus* weighing 1,200 pounds and standing 10 feet tall (Ciochon et al. 1990). Another puts the height at 9 feet and cuts the weight in half (Simons and Ettel 1970). All agree, however, that *Gigantopithecus* was the largest ape that ever lived. There have been at least two species of *Gigantopithecus*: *G. blacki*, the one that coexisted with *H. erectus* in China and Vietnam, and the much earlier (5 m.y.a.) *G. giganteus*, from northern India.

Given its size, *Gigantopithecus* must have been a ground-dwelling ape rather than an arboreal brachiator. Based on its jaw and dental patterns, it probably ate grasses, fruits, seeds, and especially bamboo. Very large animals, including China's giant panda, need an abundant food source such as bamboo. *Gigantopithecus* molars were adapted to a diet demanding cutting, crushing, and grinding of tough, fibrous matter. The molars are mas-

A reconstruction of *Gigantopithecus* by Russell Ciochon and Bill Munns. Munns is shown here with "Giganto." What would be the likely environmental effects of a population of such large apes?

sive and flat, with low crowns and thick enamel. The premolars are also broad and flat, resembling molars.

See your OLC Internet Exercises

mhhe ●com /kottak

Could it be that *Gigantopithecus* did not go extinct, but survives today as the yeti ("abominable snowman" of the Himalayas) or Sasquatch (reportedly sighted in the Pacific Northwest)? Probably not. These creatures are based on legend, not fact. Survival of a species requires a sufficiently large breeding population. Given its dietary demands, *Gigantopithecus* would surely be detectable and have an observable environmental effect. Never have *Gigantopithecus* fossils or teeth been discovered in the Western Hemisphere. Nor are the areas of yeti and Sasquatch sightings ones in which *Gigantopithecus* would fit adaptively.

DRYOPITHECUS

The dryopithecids lived in Europe during the middle and late Miocene. This group probably includes the common ancestor of the lesser apes (gibbons and siamangs) and the great apes. The first fossil member of the *Dryopithecus* group (*Dryopithecus fontani*) was found in France in 1856. The five-cusp and fissure pattern of its molar teeth, known as the Y-5 arrangement, is typical of the dryopithecids and of hominoids in general. Other dryopithecids have been found in Hungary, Spain, and China.

The continental drift that created the land bridge between Africa and Eurasia as the middle Miocene began also triggered mountain building and climatic change. With a cooler, drier climate, forest patches, dry woodlands, and grasslands replaced extensive tropical forests in East Africa and South Asia. The cooling trend continued through the late Miocene (10–5 m.y.a.). As grasslands spread, the stage was set for the divergence of the lines leading to humans, gorillas, and chimps.

OREOPITHECUS

Is upright bipedalism unique to hominids? A recent reanalysis of the fossil remains of an ancient Italian ape suggests otherwise. *Oreopithecus bambolii*, which lived seven to nine million years ago, apparently spent much of its time standing upright and shuffling short distances to collect fruit and other foods. This mode of locomotion contrasts with those of other fossil and living apes, which climb, brachiate, or knuckle-walk. The first *Oreopithecus* fossils were found more than 100 years ago in central Italy. The taxonomic placement and evolutionary significance of *Oreopithecus* have been debated for decades. Similarities have been noted between this Italian ape and both the ramapithecid and the dryopithecid families.

Meike Kohler and Salvador Moya-Sola (1997) recently reanalyzed *Oreopithecus* remains in the Natural History Museum in Basel, Switzerland. These skeletal pieces represented the lower back, pelvis, leg, and foot. The scientists found the creature's lower body to be intermediate between those of apes and early hominids. Like early hominids, *Oreopithecus* had a lower back that arched forward, a vertically aligned knee joint, and a similar pelvis. All these features are significant for upright walking. However, *Oreopithecus* had a unique foot. Its big toe splayed out 90 degrees from the other toes, all of which were shorter and straighter than those of modern apes. The foot's birdlike, tripod design was probably associated with a short, shuffling stride. Considering the entire postcranium (the area behind or below the head—the skeleton), there are substantial similarities between *Oreopithecus*, *Dryopithecus*, and the living great apes and hominids.

Interpret the World
Atlas Map 6

Look at Map 6, "Evolution of Primates" in your atlas. This map shows the world picture of primate evolution, indicating major sites with taxa and dates. Note that primates at some time have inhabited all the continents except Australia. When did the first primates appear in Asia? Map 6 shows that the geographic distribution of primates has changed through time, with North America prominent during the Eocene, Europe during the Eocene and Miocene, and Africa from the Oligocene through the present. Which of the continents that has wild primates today has the poorest fossil record. Why do you think that is?

A Missing Link?

The idea of "the missing link" goes back to an old notion called the "Great Chain of Being." This was the theological belief that various entities could be placed in a progressive chain. Among life forms, humans were at the top of the chain. Above them stood only angels and divinity. Below them were the apes, most clearly the African apes. But humans seemed too exalted, too different from those apes, to be directly linked to them. Between humans and the apes, there needed to be some form more progressive than the apes—some sort of missing link in the Great Chain of Being. Although modern science does not endorse the Great Chain of Being, it does recognize that our ancestor was a life form that differed from contemporary gorillas and chimps. Humans are not descended from gorillas or chimps. Rather, humans and the African apes share a common

The Great Chain of Being—a powerful visual metaphor for a divinely inspired universal hierarchy ranking all forms of higher and lower life. From Didacus Valades, *Rhetorica Christiana* (1579). What can you tell about the levels in the hierarchy?

orangutan and the gibbon) or with any monkey. All the apes are more closely related to each other—and more physically alike—than they are to monkeys. So why is it human parents at zoos go on saying to their kids "look at the monkey" when they are seeing a chimp, gorilla, or orang? It must be the old idea of our exalted status. We easily detect the monkey in the ape but not the ape in ourselves. Still, the apes fascinate us, to some degree because of their human-like qualities. Gorillas are popular at zoos from San Diego to Atlanta, especially when they are displayed in "family" groups. The antics of orangutans and especially of chimps have been featured in movies and TV shows. The stories of Washoe the chimp and Koko the gorilla, apes that have been taught sign language, have been featured in magazines and on TV. Even the national tabloids on display in the grocery store often turn to apes for their animal stories. Invariably such stories continue the confusion with comments about "monkeying around" or "monkey see, monkey do." Apes aren't monkeys. Apes are a lot closer to humans than they are to monkeys. Imagine a live-action film called *Planet of the Monkeys*. Where could they find actors who could locomote on four legs for an entire movie?

Human ancestors almost certainly diverged from those of chimps and gorillas late in the Miocene epoch, between eight and five million years ago. The evolutionary line leading to orangutans probably split from the one leading to humans, chimps, and gorillas around 13 m.y.a. Around eight million years ago, the common ancestors of humans, chimps, and gorillas started diverging (Fisher 1988*a*). They split up by occupying different environmental niches. Separated in space, they became reproductively isolated from one another—leading to speciation. Ancestral gorillas split off first. They eventually occupied forested zones of the mountains and lowlands of equatorial Africa. They developed a diet based on leaves, shoots, bulk vegetation, and fruits. Humans and chimps share a more recent common ancestor with each other than either does with the gorilla. Chimps evolved into frugivores (fruit eaters) in Africa's forests and woodlands. Ancestral hominids spent more time in Africa's open grasslands, or savannas. Ancestral chimps and humans, like their contemporary

ancestor—a creature that was like chimps and gorillas in some ways, like humans in others. Over time all three species have evolved and have diverged from one another. Is there reason to believe that a chimp ancestor living millions of years ago would look more like a hominid than a contemporary chimp does?

Understanding Ourselves   The idea of a huge gap between humans and the apes persists—despite evidence that humans and chimps share about 98.7 percent of their DNA. There's no doubt that humans, chimps, and gorillas share a more recent common ancestor with each other than they do with other apes (e.g., the

descendants, may well have added meat to their diet by hunting.

As we have seen, Miocene deposits in Africa, Asia, and Europe have yielded an abundance of hominoid fossils (see Figure 6.5). Some of these may have evolved into modern apes and humans, but others became extinct. Formerly, as was mentioned, certain Asian fossils such as *Sivapithecus* and *"Ramapithecus"* were analyzed as possible common ancestors of humans and the apes. Most scientists have now excluded these Miocene hominoids from the family tree of humans, chimps, and gorillas, considering *Sivapithecus* a probable ancestor of orangs. Discovered in Greece in 1989, the middle to late Miocene ape *Ouranopithecus* lived in Europe some 9–10 m.y.a. This find may be linked to the living African apes and even to hominids (Begun, Ward, and Rose 1997). One distinctive trait that *Ouranopithecus* shares with the modern African apes and humans is the *frontal sinus* (a cavity in the forehead, one of the areas where we get sinus infections and headaches).

On the basis of Miocene finds reported and analyzed during the last decade, some scientists have pondered a new scenario for ape and human evolution. As mentioned, during the middle Miocene, a land bridge connected Africa and Eurasia. This connection enabled hominoids to spread from Africa into Asia and Europe, where they diversified into the groups discussed previously. At the same time, the apes' forest habitat was shrinking in East Africa, and the number of ape species there shrank along with it. In the middle and late Miocene, there appears to have been much more ape diversity in Europe and Asia than there was in Africa. During the late Miocene, Old World monkeys took over from the dwindling African apes in many areas they once inhabited. The new hominoid evolutionary scenario, proposed but hardly established, is that the line leading to the African apes and hominids may have emerged in Europe, with a hominoid such as *Ouranopithecus*. Then there would have been a return migration to Africa, where diversification of ancestral gorillas, chimps, and hominids started around 8 m.y.a. Continued work by fossil hunters, analysts, and taxonomists eventually may reconcile the main issues involving the Miocene apes in relation to their living successors.

Back to Africa for an important recent discovery. In July 2001 anthropologists working in Cen-

tral Africa—in northern Chad's Djurab desert (Figure 6.6)—unearthed the 6–7-million-year-old skull of the oldest probable or possible human ancestor yet found. This discovery consists of a nearly complete skull, two lower jaw fragments, and three teeth. It dates to the time period when humans and chimps would have been diverging from a common ancestor. "It takes us into another world, of creatures that include the common ancestor, the ancestral human and the ancestral chimp," George Washington University paleobiologist Bernard Wood said (quoted in Gugliotta 2002).

The discovery was made by a 40-member multinational team led by the French paleoanthropologist Michel Brunet. The actual discoverer

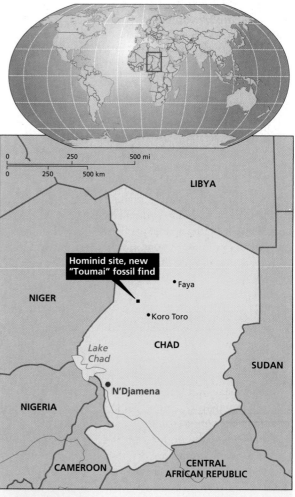

Figure 6.6   Location of Toumai: Discovery.

Background Information

STUDENT: Barbara Hewitt
SUPERVISING PROFESSOR: Ariane Burke
SCHOOL: University of Manitoba
YEAR IN SCHOOL/MAJOR: Graduated in spring 2000/Anthropology
FUTURE PLANS: Graduate school in forensic archaeology and osteology in England
PROJECT TITLE: Maceration of a Canadian Lynx

What is maceration? How might it be useful to archaeologists and biological anthropologists? Would the ethical issues involved be different with primates versus the lynx described here?

In January 2000 I took a Practicum in Archaeology class. We were each to conduct our own research project. I chose to complete a maceration project for our faunal laboratory. The carcass I chose to work with was that of an infirm Canadian lynx, which had been euthanized and donated by the zoo. My objective was to examine the condition of its bones, to determine how its former health would be reflected in its skeleton.

By macerating an animal of known age, with a documented medical history and stable diet, we could compare this animal with one reared in the wild and look at differences in health. To macerate an animal, you remove the pelt and musculature from the bones, then soak the skeleton in chemicals to remove the grease. Once the bones are dry, they are dipped in preservative to keep them from decaying. I examined the bones and teeth for indications of ill health. In this particular lynx,

advanced age had resulted in the ossification of many joints. This would have made extended movement quite painful. I was surprised by the damage to her joints. The excessive development of bone around the joints was like that in humans with osteoarthritis, which gave me a good idea of how painful and debilitating that disease can be. I detected a completely healed break in the right front humerus (upper arm bone), indicating that the animal had been healthy and well nourished when the break happened for the break to have healed so well. Only four teeth remained; this lynx could not eat solid food when she died.

The most challenging aspect of this project was that I worked unassisted. With only an instruction manual to follow, and an occasional consultation with my supervisor, I learned how to most effectively skin and deflesh an animal. The processing and analysis of the skeleton took far longer than I expected. A mistake during processing gave me a deeper appreciation for the people who analyze faunal remains in an archaeological context. The bones had been processed, and were laid out for drying, when another student moved them without moving the

labels as well. After that, each bone had to be indentified again and laid out for relabeling.

The best part of this project was what it taught me about the development of bones and the talent of people who identify and work with them. In trying to reidentify the elements of the lynx skeleton, I realized exactly how tough it would be to pick up a bone (or fragment of a bone) from an archaeological site and determine which bone it is, what species it comes from, and the pathology of that particular animal or person. I think I learned more about the inherent difficulties of faunal identification in an archaeological context from that error than from any other aspect of the project.

The bones of the lynx that I macerated and processed have already proved useful to several faunal analysis classes, and to our zooarchaeologists when asked to identify bones brought to the department for identification.

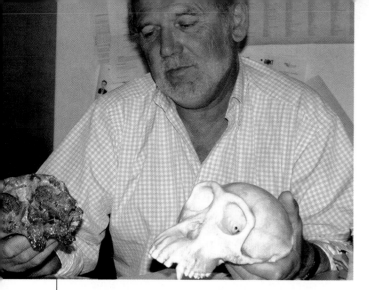

French paleoanthropologist Michel Brunet holds *Sahelanthropus tchadensis*, nicknamed "Toumai" (on the left) and a modern chimpanzee skull (on the right). If Toumai isn't a human ancestor, what else might it be?

crocodiles, fish, and rodents. The animal species enabled the team to date the site where Toumai was found (by comparison with radiometrically dated sites with similar fauna).

Was Toumai the "missing link," a common ancestor, a gorilla ancestor (as Wolpoff, Senut, Pickford, and Hawks [2002] suggest), or the earliest hominid known to science? The discovery of Toumai moves scientists close to the time when humans and the African apes diverged from a common ancestor. As we would expect in a fossil so close to the common ancestor, Toumai blends apelike and human characteristics. Although the brain was chimp-sized, the tooth enamel was thicker than a chimp's enamel, suggesting a diet that included not just fruits, but also tougher vegetation of a sort typically found in the savanna. Also, Toumai's snout did not protrude as far as a chimp's—making it more humanlike, and the canine tooth was shorter than those of other apes. "The fossil is showing the first glimmerings of evolution in our direction," according to University of California at Berkeley anthropologist Tim White (quoted in Gugliotta 2002).

The Toumai find is also important because it suggests that human ancestry was not confined to eastern and southern Africa, as had been thought. "To study human origins, you need places where the animals lived," White said. "First you had the South African caves and the East African Rift Valley, and now Brunet has found the Chad Basin and opened up a new area with huge potential" (quoted in Gugliotta 2002). What of the hominids after Toumai? We'll see in the next chapter.

was the university undergraduate Ahounta Djimdoumalbaye, who spied the skull embedded in sandstone. The new fossil was dugged *Sahelanthropus tchadensis*, referring to the northern Sahel region of Chad where it was found. The fossil is also known as "Toumai," a local name meaning "hope of life."

The discovery team identified the skull as that of an adult male with a chimp-sized brain (320–380 cubic centimeters), heavy brow ridges, and a relatively flat, human-like face. Toumai's habitat included savanna, forests, rivers, and lakes—and abundant animal life: elephants, antelope, horses, giraffes, hyenas, hippopotamuses, wild boars,

Summary

1. Primates have lived during the past 65 million years, the Cenozoic era, with seven epochs: Paleocene, Eocene, Oligocene, Miocene, Pliocene, Pleistocene, and Recent. The arboreal theory states that primates evolved by adapting to life high up in the trees. The visual predation theory suggests that key primate traits developed because they facilitated the capture of insects.

2. The first fossils clearly identified as primates lived during the Eocene (54–38 m.y.a.), mainly in North America and Europe. The omomyid family

may be ancestral to the anthropoids and the tarsier. The adapid family was probably ancestral to the lemur–loris line.

3. During the Oligocene (38–23 m.y.a.), anthropoids became the most numerous primates. The parapithecid family may be ancestral to the New World monkeys. The propliopithecid family, including *Aegyptopithecus,* seems ancestral to the catarrhines—Old World monkeys, apes, and humans.

4. The earliest hominoid fossils are from the Miocene (23–5 m.y.a.). Africa's *Proconsul* group contained the last common ancestor shared by the Old World monkeys and the apes. Since the middle Miocene Africa, Europe, and Asia have been connected. Proto-apes spread beyond Africa and became the most common primates of the middle Miocene (16–10 m.y.a.). East African apes of the middle Miocene include *Afropithecus*, *Equatorius*, and *Kenyapithecus*. Middle and late Miocene apes are often grouped in two families: *Ramapithecidae* and *Dryopithecidae*. The ramapithecids included at least two genera: *Sivapithecus* and *Gigantopithecus*. *Sivapithecus* was ancestral to the modern orangutan. Asia's *Gigantopithecus*, the largest primate ever to live, persisted for millions of years, finally coexisting with *Homo erectus*.

5. The dryopithecids, found mainly in Europe, probably include the common ancestor of the lesser apes (gibbons and siamangs) and the great apes. *Oreopithecus bambolii*, which lived 7–9 m.y.a., was an ape that stood upright while collecting fruit and other foods. There are skeletal similarities between *Oreopithecus*, *Dryopithecus*, and the living great apes and hominids.

6. *Ouranopithecus*, which lived in Europe some 9–10 m.y.a., may be linked to chimps, gorillas, and humans. Anthropologists have yet to identify the fossils of the common ancestors of humans, gorillas, and chimps. However, biochemical evidence strongly suggests that the diversification into ancestral gorillas, chimps, and hominids began in Africa during the late Miocene. A skull found in 2001 in northern Chad, dated at 6–7 m.y.a., officially named *Sahelanthropus tchadensis*, more commonly called "Toumai," may or may not be the earliest hominid yet known.

KEY TERMS

adapids Early (Eocene) primate family ancestral to lemurs and lorises.

arboreal theory Theory that the primates evolved by adapting to life high up in the trees, where visual abilities would have been favored over the sense of smell, and grasping hands and feet would have been used for movement along branches.

dryopithecids Zoological ape family living in Europe during the middle and late Miocene; probably includes the common ancestor of the lesser apes (gibbons and siamangs) and the great apes.

m.y.a. Million years ago.

omomyids Early (Eocene) primate family found in North America, Europe, and Asia; early omomyids may be ancestral to all anthropoids; later ones may be ancestral to tarsiers.

postcranium The area behind or below the head; the skeleton.

Proconsul Early Miocene genus of the pliopithecoid superfamily; the most abundant and successful anthropoids of the early Miocene; the last common ancestor shared by the Old World monkeys and the apes.

Sivapithecus Widespread fossil group first found in Pakistan; includes specimens formerly called *"Ramapithecus"* and fossil apes from Turkey, China, and Kenya; early *Sivapithecus* may contain the common ancestor of the orangutan and the African apes; late *Sivapithecus* is now seen as ancestral to the modern orang.

visual predation theory Theory that the primates evolved in lower branches and undergrowth by developing visual and tactile abilities to aid in hunting and snaring insects.

CRITICAL THINKING QUESTIONS

For more self testing, see the self quizzes

mhhe
●**com**
/kottak

1. What are the pluses and minuses of relying on the fossil record to reconstruct evolution? Besides fossils, what are other lines of evidence for primate and human evolution?

2. What are some unanswered questions about early primate evolution? What kinds of information would help provide answers?

3. Watch a squirrel move about. How do its movements compare with a monkey's movements? With a cat's movements? With your own? What do these observations suggest to you about that animal's ancestral habitat?

4. What is your opinion about the merits of the arboreal theory versus the visual predation theory of primate origins?

5. There have been reported sightings of "bigfoot" in the Pacific Northwest of North America and of the yeti (abominable snowman) in the Himalayas. What facts about apes lead you to question such reports?

6. Who were the common ancestors of humans, chimps, and gorillas? When and where did they probably live, and what is the fossil evidence for their existence?

7. What's the likelihood that Toumai, the 6–7-million-year-old skull found in 2001 in northern Chad, is a hominid? What else could it be? You might want to check the Internet for the latest on "Toumai."

Atlas Questions

Look at Map 6, "Evolution of Primates."

1. What continent(s) had the earliest primates? What kinds of primates were those?

2. On what continent has the evolution of primates been most continuous? Does this have implications for human evolution?

3. Which continent with several of the earliest primates has the fewest nonhuman primates today?

SUGGESTED ADDITIONAL READINGS

Begun, D. R., C. V. Ward, and M. D. Rose
1997   *Description: Function, Phylogeny, and Fossils: Miocene Hominoid Evolution and Adaptations.* New York: Plenum. A collection of very up-to-date scientific articles on the Miocene apes.

Boaz, N. T.
1999   *Essentials of Biological Anthropology.* Upper Saddle River, NJ: Prentice-Hall. Basic text in physical anthropology, with information on primate evolution and paleoanthropology.

Ciochon, R. L., J. Olsen, and J. James
1990   *Other Origins: The Search for the Giant Ape in Human Prehistory.* New York: Bantam Books. In search of *Gigantopithecus.*

Eldredge, N.
1997   *Fossils: The Evolution and Extinction of Species.* Princeton, NJ: Princeton University Press. What fossils tell us about the natural history of species.

Fleagle, J. G.
1999   *Primate Adaptation and Evolution*, 2nd ed. San Diego: Academic Press. Excellent introduction to adaptation of past and present primate species.

Hrdy, S. B.
1999   *The Woman That Never Evolved*, rev. ed. Cambridge, MA: Harvard University Press. Revised edition of a well-known contribution to primate and human evolution.

Kemp, T. S.

1999   *Fossils and Evolution*. New York: Oxford University Press. Interpreting the fossil record.

Kimbel, W. H., and L. B. Martin, eds.

1993   *Species, Species Concepts, and Primate Evolution*. New York: Plenum. The evolution of primate species.

MacPhee, R. D. E., ed.

1993   *Primates and Their Relatives in Phylogenetic Perspective*. New York: Plenum. Discussion of the primate family tree and its evolution.

Napier, J. R., and P. H. Napier

1985   *The Natural History of the Primates*. Cambridge, MA: MIT Press. The adaptations of primates, past and present.

Park, M. A.

2002   *Biological Anthropology*, 3rd ed. Boston: McGraw-Hill. A concise introduction, with a focus on scientific inquiry.

Wade, N., ed.

2001   *The New York Times Book of Fossils and Evolution*, rev. ed. New York: Lyons Press. Articles on fossils and evolution from the *New York Times*.

INTERNET EXERCISES

1. View Christopher R. Scotese's animation of continental drift **(http://www.scotese.com/pangeanim.htm)**.

    a. When did primates first appear?

    b. At that time, which continents were connected? Which continents were isolated?

    c. The article that starts this chapter says that most of the discoveries of the earliest primates were in North America and Europe. Based on the map, does it make sense that similar specimens are being found in both places? Where else can we expect to find fossil evidence of early primates? Which continents are unlikely to have the earliest primates?

2. Bigfoot: Read Lorraine Ahearn's article "Bigfoot Theory: Reality Is What You Make of It," which is a report about a 1999 bigfoot conference **(http://www.n2.net/prey/bigfoot/articles/greens.htm)**.

    a. This chapter states that some people (but few scientists) believe bigfoot is a living descendant of *Gigantopithecus blackei*. What are the arguments for and against this claim?

    b. What are some other bigfoot theories presented in this article? How could you go about testing them?

    c. What is your opinion about bigfoot? How would you go about testing it?

See Chapter 6 at your McGraw-Hill Online Learning Center for additional review and interactive exercises.

7

EARLY HOMINIDS

Overview

Who were the first hominids? Where did they live? What were they like? Did they have big brains? Did they make tools? Did they walk upright? Did they still seek refuge in the trees? How have hominids changed over several million years?

Hominids appeared during the late Miocene, a million or more years before the start of the Pliocene epoch, which began some five million years ago. Most hominid fossils have been dated to the Pliocene, and to the Pleistocene epoch, which began two million years ago. Early hominid remains come mainly from eastern and southern Africa. The first hominids, discovered in Ethiopia, have been assigned to the genus and species *Ardipithecus ramidus*. The australopithecines, members of the hominid genus *Australopithecus*, had evolved by four million years ago. *Ardipithecus* and the early australopithecines shared many features with the apes. The australopithecines had small apelike skulls, slashing front teeth, and marked sexual

dimorphism. Yet they walked on two legs. Upright bipedalism is a fundamental human characteristic that goes back more than five million years.

Remains of two groups, *A. africanus* and *A. robustus*, have been found in South Africa. Both had a powerful chewing apparatus, with large back teeth and robust faces, skulls, and muscle markings. The basis of their diet was savanna vegetation, but these early hominids also hunted small animals and scavenged the kills of predators.

By two million years ago, there were two distinct hominid groups: early *Homo* and *A. boisei*, the "hyperrobust" australopithecines, which became extinct a million years ago. Stone tools dating back 2.5 million years have been found in eastern Africa. Did early *Homo* make them? Or, more likely, did the australopithecines also make and use tools? This chapter examines early human evolution through the advent of *Homo* and the extinction of the australopithecines.

Fossils May Be Earliest Human Link

NEW YORK TIMES NEWS BRIEF

by John Noble Wilford

July 12, 2001

The fossil record grows constantly. Discoveries of possible or probable hominid fossils, such as the Toumai remains discussed in Chapter 6, regularly make the news. The year 2001 was especially good for fossil hunters. "Toumai," also known as *Sahelanthropus tchadensis*, was found that year in northern Chad. Also, fossils that are accepted more generally as hominids, assigned to the genus and species *Ardipithecus ramidus*, were found that year in Ethiopia. A key aspect of the *Ardipithecus* discovery (echoed by the find in northern Chad) is that the earliest hominids didn't live in open grassland (savanna) country, but in wooded areas. As you read this chapter, think about what life in a forested habitat would have been like for early hominids. For what purposes do you imagine they would have used the trees, and the ground? Do you think *Ardipithecus* was more like a modern chimp or more like a modern human? Why?

> An Ethiopian fossil hunter has found the bones and teeth of forest-dwelling creatures who lived as much as 5.8 million years ago, a discovery that appears to . . . extend knowledge of the [human] family tree back close to its roots.
>
> The fossils are the remains of creatures who apparently walked upright. They are more than one million years older than any other fossils definitively established as those of hominids, the group of species that includes humans, their direct ancestors and close relatives.
>
> The new find . . . is especially intriguing . . . because the bones appear to be so . . . apelike and their ages, 5.2 million to 5.8 million years old, put them close to the fateful evolutionary split between the lineage leading to modern humans and the one that produced chimpanzees. . . .
>
> Of particular importance . . . is . . . that these early hominids lived in a relatively wet and cool forest because the prevailing theory had been that hominids evolved in grasslands after forests disappeared. The forest was a hostile environment of shifting terrain, exploding volcanoes and menacing lava flows. . . . The scientist—Yohannes Haile-Selassie . . . —said the state of development of the

fossil teeth included strong clues that the individuals were indeed hominids. And a toe bone, he said, provided evidence that the creature was "a biped when on the ground."

> But the presence of primitive dental and bone characteristics, Mr. Haile-Selassie said, indicated that the species "was phylogenetically close to the common ancestor of chimpanzees and humans." Dr. C. Owen Lovejoy, a paleontologist at Kent State University in Ohio who has examined the fossils, said that he was "in full overall agreement" with the interpretations of Mr. Haile-Selassie and other members of the research project.
>
> Speaking of the relationship between the ancestors of humans and chimpanzees, called pongids, Dr. Lovejoy said: "We are indeed coming very close to that point in the fossil record where we simply will not be able to distinguish ancestral hominids from ancestral pongids because they were so anatomically similar. . . ."
>
> Working with Dr. Tim D. White of Berkeley, one of the most experienced hominid hunters, Mr. Haile-

Yohannes Haile-Selassie of the University of California at Berkeley holds the canine tooth of *Ardipithecus ramidus kadabba*, discovered in 1998.

Selassie and colleagues found the fossils in the Middle Awash River Valley badlands of Ethiopia, about 50 miles from where the "Lucy" skeleton, which is 3.2 million years old, was uncovered 30 years ago. The new find includes 11 specimens, including a jawbone with teeth, hand and foot bones, fragments of arm bones and a piece of collarbone. They represent at least five individuals.

Dr. White said an accurate portrayal of these creatures was not yet possible because an intact skull or limb bones had not been found. The size of the lower jaw and some bones of the skeleton suggests that one of these individuals was about the size of a modern chimpanzee. Until more diagnostic specimens are found, preferably including a skull, the fossils have been tentatively classified as a primitive subspecies, *Ardipithecus ramidus kadabba*. *Kadabba* means "basal family ancestor" in the local language, Afar. The *ramidus* species was discovered in 1994 in 4.4-million-year-old sediments, also in Ethiopia.

The evidence that these creatures lived in forests, as opposed to grasslands, is especially intriguing to scientists. In a separate report on the environmental history of the discovery site, Dr. Giday Wolde Gabriel, a geologist at Los Alamos National Laboratory in New Mexico, and his colleagues concluded that it "seems increasingly likely that early hominids did not frequent open habitats" until after 4.4 million years ago. The *Ardipithecus* hominids at that time also appeared to live in woodlands.

Dr. Stanley H. Ambrose, an anthropologist at the University of Illinois at Urbana, analyzed the chemistry of ancient soil mixed with the fossils. "The expectation was that we would find hominids in savanna grassland sites that date back to about eight million years ago, but that hasn't happened," Dr. Ambrose said. "All older hominids have been found in forested environments."

In that case, the development of upright walking, considered a definitive characteristic of hominids, presumably occurred in a wooded habitat and not as an adaptation to life on the treeless savanna, as had been supposed. . . .

Source: *New York Times*, July 12, 2001, late edition—final, section A, p. 12, column 1, and www.nytimes.com.

Although these *Ardipithecus* discoveries push the hominid lineage back to almost six million years, humans actually haven't been around too long when the age of the earth is considered.

Chronology of Hominid Evolution

If we compare earth's history to a 24-hour day (with one second equaling 50,000 years),

> Earth originates at midnight.

> The earliest fossils were deposited at 5:45 A.M.

> The first vertebrates appeared at 9:02 P.M.

> The earliest mammals, at 10:45 P.M.

> The earliest primates, at 11:43 P.M.

> The earliest hominids (the australopithecines), at 11:58 P.M.

> And *Homo sapiens* arrives 36 seconds before midnight (Wolpoff, 1999, p. 10).

For the study of hominid evolution, the Pliocene (5 to 2 m.y.a.), Pleistocene (2 m.y.a. to 10,000 B.P.), and Recent (10,000 B.P. to the present) epochs are most important. Until the end of the Pliocene, the main hominid genus was *Australopithecus*, which lived in sub-Saharan Africa. By the start of the Pleistocene, *Australopithecus* had evolved into *Homo*.

The **Pleistocene** is traditionally and correctly considered the epoch of human life. Its subdivisions are the Lower Pleistocene (2 to 1 m.y.a.), the Middle Pleistocene (1 m.y.a. to 130,000 B.P.), and the Upper Pleistocene (130,000 to 10,000 B.P.). These subdivisions refer to the placement of geological strata containing, respectively, older, intermediate, and younger fossils. The Lower Pleistocene extends from the start of the Pleistocene to the advent of the ice ages in the Northern Hemisphere around one million years ago.

Each subdivision of the Pleistocene is associated with a particular group of hominids. Late *Australopithecus* and early *Homo* lived during the Lower Pleistocene. *Homo erectus* spanned most of the Middle Pleistocene. *Homo sapiens* appeared late in the Middle Pleistocene and was the sole hominid of the Upper Pleistocene. We consider the hominids of the Middle and Upper Pleistocene in the next chapter.

During the second million years of the Pleistocene, there were several ice ages, or **glacials,** major advances of continental ice sheets in Europe and North America. These periods were separated by **interglacials,** long warm periods between the major glacials. (Scientists used to think there were four main glacial advances, but the picture has grown more complex.) With each advance, the world climate cooled and continental ice sheets—massive glaciers—covered the northern parts of Europe and North America. Climates that are temperate today were arctic during the glacials.

During the interglacials, the climate warmed up and the *tundra*—the cold, treeless plain—retreated north with the ice sheets. Forests returned to areas, such as southwestern France, that had had tundra vegetation. The ice sheets advanced and receded several times during the last glacial, the *Würm* (75,000 to 12,000 B.P.). Brief periods of relative warmth during the Würm (and other glacials) are called *interstadials*, in contrast to the longer interglacials. Hominid fossils found in association with animals known to occur in cold or warm climates, respectively, permit us to date them to glacial or interglacial (or interstadial) periods.

The Earliest Hominids

Recent discoveries of fossils and tools have increased our knowledge of early human evolution. The most significant recent discoveries have been made in Africa—Kenya, Tanzania, Ethiopia, and Chad. These finds come from different sites and may be the remains of individuals who lived hundreds of thousands of years apart. Furthermore, geological processes operating over thousands or millions of years inevitably distort fossil remains. Table 7.1 summarizes the major stages of hominid evolution. You should consult it throughout this chapter and the next one.

Climates that are temperate today were arctic during the glacials. The ice-age tundra in Western Europe may have looked like the cold, treeless plain shown here, where Russian Eskimos count on a reindeer herd for their subsistence. Would you expect to find many vegetarians in such an environment?

Table 7.1 Dates and Geographic Distribution of the Major Hominoid and Hominid Fossil Groups

Fossil Group	Dates, m.y.a.	Known Distribution
Hominoids		
Afropithecus	18–16	East Africa
Common ancestor	8–5	East Africa
"Toumai"	7–6	Chad
Hominids		
Ardipithecus ramidus	5.8–4.4	Ethiopia
Australopithecines		
A. anamensis	4.2	Kenya
A. afarensis	3.8–3.0	East Africa (Laetoli, Hadar)
Robusts	2.6–1.2	East and South Africa
A. robustus	2.6?–2.0?	South Africa
A. boisei	2.6?–1.2	East Africa
Graciles		
A. africanus	3.0–2.5?	South Africa
Homo		
H. habilis/H. rudolfensis	2.4?–1.7?	East Africa
H. erectus	1.7?–0.3	Africa, Asia, Europe
Homo sapiens	0.3–present	
Archaic *H. sapiens*	0.3–0.03 (300,000–30,000)	Africa, Asia, Europe
H. sapiens neanderthalensis	0.13–0.03 (130,000–30,000)	Europe, Middle East
H. sapiens sapiens	0.1?–present (100,000–present)	Worldwide (after 25,000 B.P.)

ARDIPITHECUS AND KENYANTHROPUS

As we saw in the news story at the beginning of this chapter, early hominids assigned to *Ardipithecus ramidus* lived during the late Miocene, between 5.2 and 5.8 million years ago. Our Miocene ancestors eventually evolved into a varied group of Pliocene–Pleistocene hominids known as the australopithecines—for whom we have an abundant fossil record. This term reflects their former classification as members of a distinct subfamily, the "Australopithecinae." Today the distinction between the **australopithecines** and later hominids is made on the genus level. The australopithecines are assigned to the genus *Australopithecus* (*A.*); later humans, to *Homo* (*H.*).

Ardipithecus ramidus is generally considered ancestral to early *Australopithecus* and, ultimately, to *Homo*. *Ardipithecus* fossils were first discovered at Kanapoi in Ethiopia by Berhane Asfaw, Gen Suwa, and Tim White. Dating to 4.4 m.y.a., these fossils consisted of the remains of some 17 individuals, with cranial, facial, dental, and upper limb bones. The 2001 news account at the beginning of this chapter discusses even older *Ardipithecus* fossils, dating back as long as 5.8 m.y.a., very near the time of the common ancestor of humans and the African apes. This find consists of 11 specimens, including a jaw bone with teeth, hand and foot bones, fragments of arm bones, and a piece of collarbone. They represent at least five individuals. These creatures were apelike in size, anatomy, and habitat, living in a wooded area rather than the open grassland or savanna habitat where later hominids proliferated. As of this writing, *Ardipithecus ramidus* is recognized as the earliest known hominid, with the Toumai find from Chad, dated to 6–7 m.y.a., possibly an even older hominid.

Presumably, *Ardipithecus ramidus* evolved into *A. anamensis*, a bipedal hominid from Aramis in Kenya, whose fossil remains were first reported by

Maeve Leakey and Alan Walker in 1995. *A. anamensis* consists of 78 fragments from two sites—pieces of skull, jaw bone, teeth, and long bones (Rice 2002). *A. anamensis* then evolved into *A. afarensis*, which usually is considered ancestral to all the later australopithecines (*africanus, robustus*, and *boisei*) as well as to *Homo* (Figure 7.1).

Complicating the picture is another recent discovery, which Maeve Leakey has named *Kenyanthropus playtops*, or flat-faced "man" of Kenya. (Actually, the sex hasn't been determined.) This 1999 fossil find—of a nearly complete skull and partial jaw bone—was made by a research team led by Leakey, excavating on the western side of Lake Turkana in northern Kenya. They consider this 3.5-million-year-old find to represent an entirely new branch of the early human family tree.

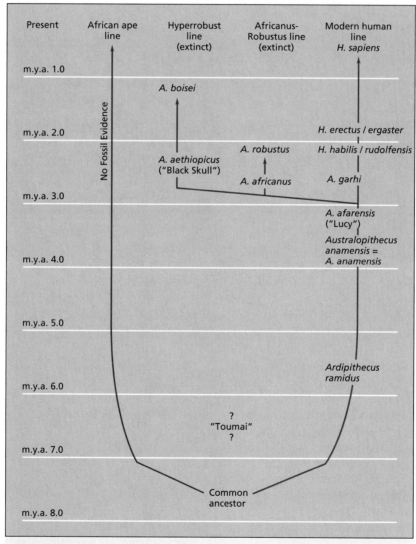

Figure 7.1   Phylogenetic Tree for African Apes and Hominids.   Their presumed divergence date was between 6 and 8 m.y.a. Branching in later hominid evolution is also shown. For more exact dates, see text.

Maeve Leakey and *Kenyanthropus platyops*, which she discovered in 1999 by Lake Turkana in northern Kenya. What's the significance of *Kenyanthropus*?

Leakey views *Kenyanthropus* as showing that at least two hominid lineages existed as far back as 3.5 million years. One was the well-established fossil species *Australopithecus afarensis* (see below), best known from the celebrated Lucy skeleton. With the discovery of *Kenyanthropus* it would seem that Lucy and her kind weren't alone on the African plain. According to Leakey, Lucy may not be a direct human ancestor after all. The hominid family tree, once drawn with a straight trunk, is beginning to look more like a bush, with branches leading in many directions (Wilford 2001).

Kenyanthropus has a flattened face and small molars that are strikingly different from those of *afarensis*. Ever since its discovery in Ethiopia in 1974 by Donald Johanson, *afarensis* has been regarded as the most likely common ancestor of all subsequent hominids, including humans. In the absence of other hominid fossils between 3.8 million and 3 million years ago, this was the most reasonable conclusion scientists could draw. Undoubtedly, as a result of the *Kenyanthropus* discovery, the place of *afarensis* in human ancestry will now be debated. Taxonomic "splitters" (those who stress diversity and divergence) will focus on the differences between *afarensis* and *Kenyanthropus* and see it as representing a new taxon (genus and/or species), as Maeve Leakey has done. Taxonomic "lumpers" will focus on the similarities between *Kenyanthropus* and *afarensis* and may try to place them both in the same taxon—probably *Australopithecus*, which is well established.

The Varied Australopithecines

In the scheme followed here, *Australopithecus* had at least five species:

1. *A. anamensis* (4.2 m.y.a.)

2. *A. afarensis* (3.8? to 3.0 m.y.a.)

3. *A. africanus* (3.0? to 2.5? m.y.a.)

4. *A. robustus* (2.6? to 2.0 m.y.a.)

5. *A. boisei* (2.6? to 1.2 m.y.a.)

Before the *Kenyanthropus* discovery, most scholars considered *A. anamensis* and *A. afarensis* to be ancestral to all the later *Australopithecus* species, as well as to *Homo*, which had appeared by 2 m.y.a. Early *Homo* then coexisted for almost a million years with *A. boisei*, which became extinct around 1.2 m.y.a. Thereafter *H. erectus*, our direct ancestors—creators of complex tools, cooperative hunters and gatherers—multiplied, expanded, and eventually colonized the world.

The dates given for each species are approximate because an organism isn't a member of one species one day and a member of another species the next day. Nor could the same dating techniques be used for all the finds. The South African australopithecine fossils (*A. africanus* and *A. robustus*), for example, come from a nonvolcanic area where radiometric dating could not be done. Dating of those fossils has been based mainly on stratigraphy. The hominid fossils from the volcanic regions of East Africa usually have radiometric dates.

AUSTRALOPITHECUS AFARENSIS

The early hominid species known as *A. afarensis* includes fossils found at two sites, Laetoli in northern Tanzania and Hadar in the Afar region of

Ethiopia. Laetoli is earlier (3.8 to 3.6 m.y.a.). The Hadar fossils probably date to between 3.3 and 3.0 m.y.a. Thus, based on the current evidence, *A. afarensis* lived between about 3.8 and 3.0 m.y.a. Research directed by Mary Leakey was responsible for the Laetoli finds. The Hadar discoveries resulted from an international expedition directed by D. C. Johanson and M. Taieb. The two sites have yielded significant samples of early hominid fossils. There are two dozen specimens from Laetoli, and the Hadar finds include the remains of between 35 and 65 individuals. The Laetoli remains are mainly teeth and jaw fragments, along with some very informative fossilized footprints. The Hadar sample includes skull fragments and postcranial material, most notably 40 percent of the complete skeleton of a tiny hominid female, dubbed "Lucy," who lived around 3 m.y.a.

Although the hominid remains at Laetoli and Hadar were deposited half a million years apart, their many resemblances explain their placement in the same species, *A. afarensis*. These fossils, along with the more recently found *Ardipithecus ramidus* and *A. anamensis*, have forced a reinterpretation of the early hominid fossil record. *A. afarensis*, although clearly a hominid, was so similar in many ways to chimps and gorillas that our common ancestry with the African apes must be very recent, certainly no more than 8 m.y.a. *Ardipithecus ramidus* and *A. anamensis* are even more apelike. These discoveries show that hominids are much closer to the apes than the previously known fossil record had suggested. Studies of the learning abilities and biochemistry of chimps and gorillas have taught a valuable lesson about homologies that the fossil record is now confirming.

The *A. afarensis* finds, which have been more completely described than *Ardipithecus ramidus* and *A. anamensis*, make this clear. The many apelike features are surprising in definite hominids that lived as recently as 3 m.y.a. Discussion of hominid fossils requires a brief review of dentition. Moving from front to back, on either side of the upper or lower jaw, humans (and apes) have two incisors, one canine, two premolars, and three molars. Our dental formula is 2.1.2.3, for a total of eight teeth on each side, upper and lower—32 teeth in all—if we have all our "wisdom teeth" (our third molars). Now back to the australopithecines. Like apes, and unlike modern humans, *A. afarensis* had sharp canine teeth that projected

beyond the other teeth. Also like apes, their lower premolar was pointed and projecting to sharpen the upper canine. It had one long cusp and one tiny bump that hints at the bicuspid premolar that eventually developed in hominid evolution.

There is, however, evidence that powerful chewing associated with savanna vegetation was entering the *A. afarensis* feeding pattern. When the coarse, gritty, fibrous vegetation of grasslands and semidesert enters the diet, the back teeth change to accommodate heavy chewing stresses. Massive back teeth, jaws, and facial and cranial structures suggest a diet demanding extensive grinding and powerful crushing. *A. afarensis* molars are large (see Figure 7.2). The lower jaw (mandible) is thick and is buttressed with a bony ridge behind the front teeth. The cheekbones are large and flare out to the side for the attachment of powerful chewing muscles.

Understanding Ourselves What makes us human? When we try to determine whether a fossil is a human ancestor, should we look for traits that make us human today? Maybe; maybe not. Sure, we look for DNA similarities, including mutations shared by certain lineages but not others. But what about our bipedal locomotion, our big brains, our long periods of childhood dependency, and our use of language and tools? Some of those key markers of humanity are fairly recent—or have origins that are impossible to date. Ironically, some of the physical markers that have led scientists to identify certain fossils as hominids rather than apes are features that humans have lost. One example is big back teeth. As they adapted to the savanna, with its gritty, tough, and fibrous vegetation, it was adaptively advantageous for early hominids to have large back teeth and thick tooth enamel. This permitted thorough chewing of tough fibrous vegetation and mixture with salivary enzymes to permit digestion of foods that otherwise would not have been digestible. The churning, rotary motion associated with such chewing also favored reduction of the front teeth, especially the canines and first premolars. These front teeth are much sharper and longer in the apes than in early hominids. The apes use their sharp self-honing teeth to pierce fruits. Males also flash their big sharp canines to intimidate and impress others, including potential mates. Bipedalism seems to have characterized the human lineage since it split from the line

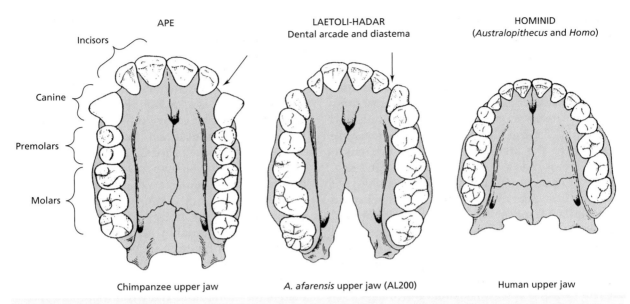

Figure 7.2 Comparison of Dentition in Ape, Human, and *A. afarensis* Palates.

leading to the African apes, but many other "human" features came later. Yet other diagnostic features, such as large back teeth and thick enamel—which we don't have now—offer clues about who was a human ancestor back then.

The skull of *A. afarensis* contrasts with those of later hominids. The brain case is very small. The cranial capacity of 430 cm³ (cubic centimeters) barely surpasses the chimp average (390 cm³). The form of the *A. afarensis* skull is like that of the chimpanzee, but the brain/body size ratio was probably larger.

Below the neck, however—particularly in regard to locomotion—*A. afarensis* was unquestionably human. Early evidence of striding bipedalism comes from Laetoli, where volcanic ash, which can be directly dated by the K/A technique, covered a trail of footprints of two or three hominids walking to a water hole. These prints leave no doubt that a small striding biped lived in Tanzania by 3.6 m.y.a. The structure of the pelvic, hip, leg, and foot bones also confirms that upright bipedalism was *A. afarensis*'s mode of locomotion.

See the Internet Exercises at your OLC

/kottak

More recent finds show that bipedalism predated *A. afarensis*. *A. anamensis* (4.2 m.y.a.) was bipedal. Relevant postcranial material from the even older *Ardipithecus ramidus* (5.8–4.4 m.y.a.)

also suggests a capacity for upright bipedal locomotion. Indeed, it was the shift toward this form of moving around that led to the distinctive hominid way of life.

Bipedalism—upright two-legged locomotion—is the key feature differentiating early hominids from the apes. African fossil discoveries suggest that hominid bipedalism is more than five million years old. This mode of locomotion generally is considered an adaptation to an open grassland or savanna habitat. Scientists have suggested several advantages of bipedalism in such an environment: the ability to see over long grass, to carry items back to a home base, and to reduce the body's exposure to solar radiation. The fossil and archaeological records confirm that upright bipedal locomotion preceded tool manufacture and the expansion of the hominid brain. However, although the earliest hominids could move bipedally through open country during the day, they also preserved enough of an apelike anatomy to make them good climbers. They could take to the trees to sleep at night and to escape terrestrial predators.

One explanation for bipedalism centers on environmental changes that swept Africa more than five million years ago. As the global climate became cooler and drier, grasslands in sub-Saharan Africa expanded. The rain forests contracted, shrinking the habitat available to arboreal primates

The Varied Australopithecines **173**

(Wilford 1995). Also, at about the same time, a geological shift deepened the Rift Valley, which runs through Ethiopia, Kenya, and Tanzania. The sinking of the valley thrust up mountains. This left the land west of the valley more humid and arboreal, while the east became more arid and dominated by savanna. The common ancestors of hominids and chimpanzees were divided as a result. Those adapting to the humid west became the chimpanzee family. Those in the east had to forge a new life in an open environment (Coppens 1994). At least one branch of the eastern primates ventured more and more into open country, looking for food but retreating to the trees to escape predators and to sleep at night. To move about more efficiently, and perhaps also to keep a lookout above the grasses for food or predators, these primates started standing up and walking on two legs. Presumably, this adaptation enhanced their chances of surviving and passing on genes that favored this stance and gait, leading eventually to bipedal hominids (Wilford 1995).

Yet another factor may have contributed to bipedalism. Early hominids might have found the tropical heat of open country very stressful. Most savanna-dwelling animals have built-in ways of protecting their brains from overheating as their body temperatures rise during the day. This isn't true of humans, nor is it likely to have been true of early hominids. The only way we can protect our brains is by keeping our bodies cool. Could it be that early hominids stood up to cool off? Studies with a scale model of the Lucy skeleton suggest that quadrupedalism exposes the body to 60 percent more solar radiation than does bipedalism. And the upright body could also catch the cooler breeze above the ground (Wilford 1995).

Although bidepal, *A. afarensis* still contrasts in many ways with later homininds. Sexual dimorphism is especially marked. The male–female contrast in jaw size in *A. afarensis* was more marked than in the orangutan. There was a similar contrast in body size. *A. afarensis* females, such as Lucy, stood between three and four feet (91 and 120 centimeters) tall; males might have reached five feet (152 centimeters). *A. afarensis* males weighed perhaps twice as much as the females did (Wolpoff 1999). Table 7.2 below summarizes data on the

Table 7.2   Facts about the Australopithecines

Species	Dates (m.y.a.)	Known Distribution	Important Sites	Body Weight (Mid-sex)	Brain Size (Mid-Sex) (cm³)
Homo sapiens sapiens	100,000 to present			60 kg/132 lbs	1,350
Pan troglodytes (chimpanzee)	Modern			42 kg/93 lbs	390
A. boisei	2.6? to 1.2	E. Africa	Olduvai, East Turkana	39 kg/86 lbs	490
A. robustus	2.6? to 2.0?	S. Africa	Kromdraai, Swartkrans	37 kg/81 lbs	540
A. africanus	3 to 2.5?	S. Africa	Taung, Sterkfontein	36 kg/79 lbs	490
A. afarensis	3.8 to 3.0	E. Africa	Hadar, Laetoli	35 kg/77 lbs	430
A. anamensis	4.2	E. Africa	Aramis	Insufficient data	No published skulls
Ardipithecus ramidus	5.8 to 4.4	E. Africa	Kanapoi	Insufficient data	No published skulls

various australopithecines, including mid-sex body weight and brain size. Mid-sex means midway between the male average and the female average.

Lucy and her kind were far from dainty. Lucy's muscle-engraved bones are much more robust than ours are. With only rudimentary tools and weapons, early hominids needed powerful and resistant bones and muscles. Lucy's arms are longer relative to her legs than are those of later hominids. Here again her proportions are more apelike than ours are. Although Lucy neither brachiated nor knuckle-walked, she was probably a much better climber than modern people are, and she spent some of her day in the trees.

The *A. afarensis* fossils show that as recently as 3.0 m.y.a., our ancestors had a mixture of apelike and hominid features. Canines, premolars, and skulls were much more apelike than most scholars had imagined would exist in such a recent ancestor. On the other hand, the molars, chewing apparatus, and cheekbones foreshadowed later hominid trends, and the pelvic and limb bones were indisputably hominid (Figure 7.3 on page 176). The hominid pattern was being built from the ground up.

Hominids walk with a striding gait that consists of alternating swing and stance phases for each leg and foot. As one leg is pushed off by the big toe and goes into the swing phase, the heel of the other leg is touching the ground and entering the stance phase. Four-footed locomotors such as Old World monkeys are always supported by two limbs. Bipeds, by contrast, are supported by one limb at a time.

The pelvis, the lower spine, the hip joint, and the thigh bone change in accordance with the stresses of bipedal locomotion. Australopithecine pelvises are much more similar (although far from identical) to *Homo*'s than to apes' and show adaptation to bipedalism (Figure 7.4 on page 177). The blades of the australopithecine pelvis (iliac blades) are shorter and broader than are those of the ape. The sacrum, which anchors the pelvis's two side bones, is larger, as in *Homo*. With bipedalism, the pelvis forms a sort of basket that balances the weight of the trunk and supports this weight with less stress. Fossilized spinal bones (vertebrae) show that the australopithecine spine had the lower spine (lumbar) curve characteristic of *Homo*. This curvature helps transmit the weight of the

upper body to the pelvis and the legs. Placement of the *foramen magnum* (the "big hole" through which the spinal cord joins the brain) farther forward in *Australopithecus* and *Homo* than in the ape also represents an adaptation to upright bipedalism (Figure 7.5 on page 177).

In apes, the thigh bone (femur) extends straight down from the hip to the knees. In *Australopithecus* and *Homo*, however, the thigh bone angles into the

An ancient trail of hominid footprints fossilized in volcanic ash. Mary Leakey found this 70-meter trail at Laetoli, Tanzania, in 1979. It dates from 3.6 m.y.a. and confirms that *A. afarensis* was a striding biped.

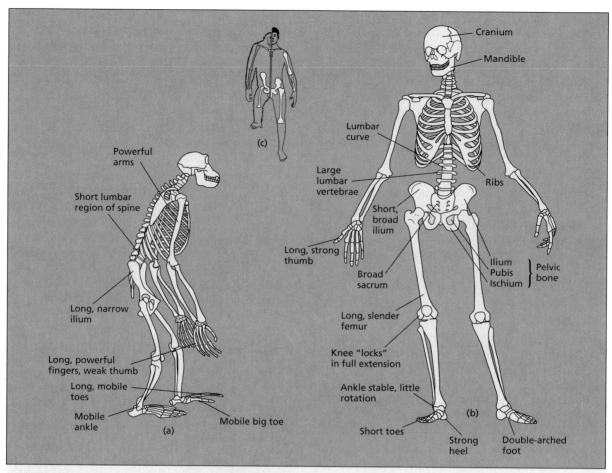

Figure 7.3 **Comparison of *Homo sapiens* and *Pan troglodytes* (the Common Chimp).** (a) Skeleton of chimpanzee in bipedal position; (b) skeleton of modern human; (c) chimpanzee and human "bisected" and drawn to the same trunk length for comparison of limb proportions. The contrast in leg length is largely responsible for the proportional difference between humans and apes.

hip, permitting the space between the knees to be narrower than the pelvis during walking. The pelvises of the australopithecines were similar but not identical to those of *Homo*. The most significant contrast is a narrower australopithecine birth canal (Tague and Lovejoy 1986).

Expansion of the birth canal is a trend in hominid evolution. The width of the birth canal is related to the size of the skull and brain. *A. afarensis* had a small cranial capacity. Even in later australopithecines, the average brain size did not exceed 600 cubic centimeters. Undoubtedly, the australopithecine skull grew after birth to accommodate a growing brain, as it does (much more) in *Homo*. However, the brains of the australop-

ithecines expanded less than ours do. In the australopithecines, the cranial sutures (the lines where the bones of the skull eventually come together) fused relatively earlier in life.

Their patterns of molar eruption (Mann 1975) suggest that australopithecine children, like our own, had a slower maturation rate than do the apes. Young australopithecines must have depended on their parents and kin for nurturance and protection. Those years of childhood dependency would have provided time for observation, teaching, and learning. This may provide indirect evidence for a rudimentary cultural life.

For a quiz on early hominids, see the Interactive Exercise

mhhe ● com /kottak

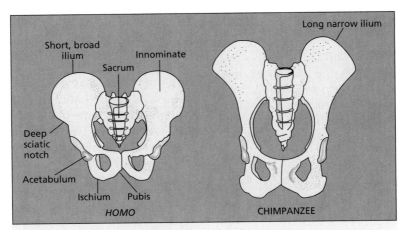

Figure 7.4   A Comparison of Human and Chimpanzee Pelvises.   The human pelvis has been modified to meet the demands of upright bipedalism. The blades (*ilia*; singular, *ilium*) of the human pelvis are shorter and broader than those of the ape. The sacrum, which anchors the side bones, is wider. The australopithecine pelvis is far more similar to that of *Homo* than to that of the chimpanzee, as we would expect in an upright biped.

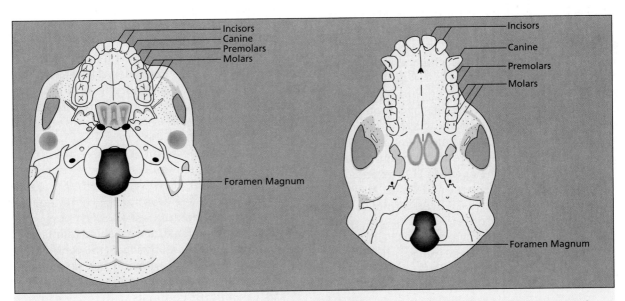

Figure 7.5   A Comparison of the Skull and Dentition (Upper Jaw) of *Homo* and the Chimpanzee.   The *foramen magnum*, through which the spinal cord joins the brain, is located farther forward in *Homo* than in the ape. This permits the head to balance atop the spine with upright bipedalism. The molars and premolars of the ape form parallel rows. Human teeth, by contrast, are arranged in rounded, parabolic form. What differences do you note between human and ape canines? Canine reduction has been an important trend in hominid evolution.

GRACILE AND ROBUST AUSTRALOPITHECINES

The fossils of *A. africanus* and *A. robustus* come from South Africa. In 1924, the anatomist Raymond Dart coined the term *Australopithecus africanus* to describe the first fossil representative of this species, the skull of a juvenile that was found accidentally in a quarry at Taung, South Africa. Radiometric dates are lacking for this non-volcanic region, but the fossil hominids found at the five main South African sites appear (from stratigraphy) to have lived between 3 and 2 m.y.a.

There were two groups of South African australopithecines: **gracile** (*A. africanus*) and robust (*A. robustus*). "Gracile" indicates that members of *A. africanus* were smaller and slighter, less robust, than were members of *A. robustus*. There were also very robust—*hyperrobust*—australopithecines in East Africa. In the classification scheme used here, these have been assigned to *A. boisei*. However, some scholars consider *A. robustus* and *A. boisei* to be regional variants of just one species, usually called *robustus* (sometimes given its own genus, *Paranthropus*).

The relationship between the graciles and the robusts has been debated for generations but has not been resolved. Graciles and robusts probably descend from *A. afarensis* or from a South African version of *A. afarensis*. Some scholars have argued that the graciles lived before (3 to 2.5? m.y.a.) and were ancestral to the robusts (2.6? to 2.0? m.y.a.). Others contend that the graciles and the robusts were separate species that may have overlapped in time. (Classifying them as members of different species implies they were reproductively isolated from each other in time or space.) Other paleoanthropologists view the gracile and robust australopithecines as different ends of a continuum of variation in a single *polytypic species*—one with considerable phenotypic variation. The range of *Australopithecus* sites in East and South Africa is shown in Figure 7.6 (on page 179).

The trend toward enlarged back teeth, chewing muscles, and facial buttressing, which is already noticeable in *A. afarensis*, continues in the South African australopithecines. However, the canines are reduced, and the premolars are fully bicuspid. Dental form and function changed as dietary needs shifted from cutting and slashing to chewing and grinding. The mainstay of the aus-

tralopithecine diet was the vegetation of the savanna.

These early hominids also might have hunted small and slow-moving game. Archaeological analyses of animal remains at australopithecine camps suggest that these hominids scavenged, bringing home parts of kills made by large cats and other carnivores. The camp sites of early hominids in East Africa include the remains of small animals and scavenged parts of carnivores' kills. However, the ability to hunt large animals was an achievement of *Homo* and is discussed later.

The skulls, jaws, and teeth of the australopithecines leave no doubt that their diet was mainly vegetarian. Natural selection modifies the teeth to conform to the stresses associated with a particular diet. Massive back teeth, jaws, and associated facial and cranial structures confirm that the australopithecine diet required extensive grinding and powerful crushing.

In the South African australopithecines, both deciduous ("baby") and permanent molars and premolars are massive, with multiple cusps. The later australopithecines had bigger back teeth than did the earlier ones. However, this evolutionary trend ended with early *Homo*, which had much smaller back teeth, reflecting a dietary change that will be described later.

Contrasts with *Homo* in the front teeth are less marked. But they are still of interest because of what they tell us about sexual dimorphism. *A. africanus*'s canines were more pointed, with larger roots, than *Homo*'s are. Still, the *A. africanus* canines were only 75 percent the size of the canines of *A. afarensis*. Despite this canine reduction, there was just as much canine sexual dimorphism in *A. africanus* as there had been in *A. afarensis* (Wolpoff 1999). Sexual dimorphism in general was much more pronounced among the early hominids than it is among *Homo sapiens*. *A. africanus* females were about four feet (120 centimeters), and males five feet (150 centimeters), tall. The average female probably had no more than 60 percent the weight of the average male (Wolpoff 1980a). (That figure contrasts with today's average female/male weight ratio of about 88 percent.)

Teeth, jaw, face, and skull changed to fit a diet based on tough, gritty, fibrous grasslands vegetation. A massive face housed large upper teeth and provided a base for the attachment of powerful chewing muscles. Australopithecine cheekbones were elongated and massive structures (Figure 7.7

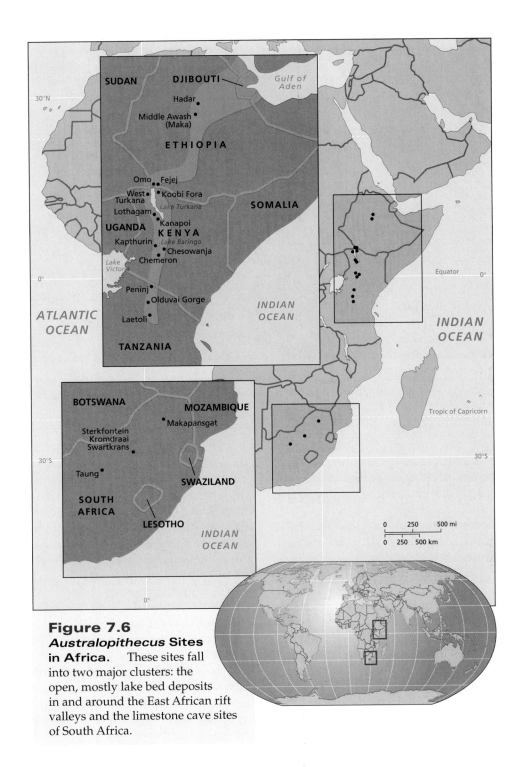

Figure 7.6
***Australopithecus* Sites in Africa.**   These sites fall into two major clusters: the open, mostly lake bed deposits in and around the East African rift valleys and the limestone cave sites of South Africa.

Members of an *A. robustus* band brandish limbs to defend their territory. This painting imagines a time of drying, with forests turning to grassland. What was the basis of the *A. robustus* diet? What kind of social organization is suggested by this image?

on page 181) that anchored large chewing muscles running up the jaw. Another set of robust chewing muscles extended from the back of the jaw to the sides of the skull.

In the more robust australopithecines (*A. robustus* in South Africa and *A. boisei* in East Africa), these muscles were strong enough to produce a *sagittal crest*, a bony ridge on the top of the skull. Such a crest forms as the bone grows. It develops from the pull of the chewing muscles as they meet at the midline of the skull.

Overall robustness, especially in the chewing apparatus, increased through time among the australopithecines. This trend was most striking in *A. boisei*, which survived through 1.2 m.y.a in East Africa. Compared with their predecessors, the later australopithecines tended to have larger overall size, skulls, and back teeth. They also had thicker faces, more prominent crests, and more rugged muscle markings on the skeleton. By contrast, the front teeth stayed the same size.

Brain size (measured as cranial capacity, in cubic centimeters—cm^3) increased only slightly between *A. afarensis* (430 cm^3), *A. africanus* (490 cm^3), and *A. robustus* (540 cm^3) (Wolpoff 1999).

These figures can be compared with an average cranial capacity of 1,350 cm^3 in *Homo sapiens*. The modern range goes from less than 1,000 cm^3 to more than 2,000 cm^3 in normal adults. The cranial capacity of chimps (*Pan troglodytes*) averages 390 cm^3 (see Table 7.2). The brains of gorillas (*Gorilla gorilla*) average around 500 cm^3, which is within the australopithecine range, but gorilla body weight is much greater.

Casts of the inside of a skull (endocranial casts) provide information about the brain's size, proportions, and shape, and the areas devoted to particular functions—such as motor activities, speech, memory, sensory integration, and vision. Australopithecine endocranial casts are more human than apelike, as we would expect in an organism that relied more on learning, memory, and intellectual association.

Given the tool-making abilities of the apes, there is no reason to doubt that the australopithecines relied on rudimentary cultural means of adaptation. Animal bones that are sharpened and scratched, as they might have been if used for digging, were found at one South African australopithecine site. The earliest known stone tools come

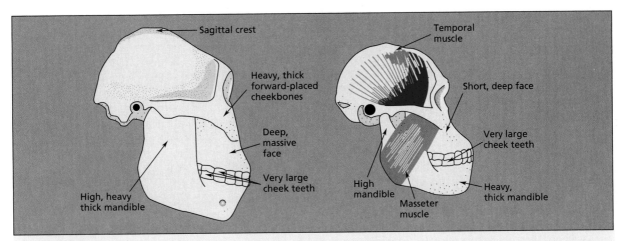

Figure 7.7 **Skulls of Robust (Left) and Gracile (Right) Australopithecines, Showing Chewing Muscles.** Flaring cheek arches and, in some robusts, a sagittal crest supported this massive musculature. The early hominid diet—coarse, gritty vegetation of the savanna—demanded such structures. These features were most pronounced in *A. boisei.*

from East Africa, with radiometric dates of 2 to 2.5 m.y.a. (Asfaw, White, et al. 1999; Jolly and White 1995). Additional evidence for early hominid tool use and manufacture is discussed below.

The Australopithecines and Early *Homo*

Between 3 and 2 m.y.a., the ancestors of *Homo* split off and became reproductively isolated from the later australopithecines, such as *A. boisei*, which coexisted with *Homo* until around 1.2 m.y.a. The first evidence for speciation is dental. The fossil sample of hominid teeth dated to 2 m.y.a. has two clearly different sizes of teeth. One set is huge, the largest molars and premolars in hominid evolution; these teeth belong to *A. boisei*. The other group of (smaller) teeth belonged to our probable ancestor, *H. habilis*, the first exemplar of the genus *Homo*.

By 1.7 m.y.a., the difference was even more evident. Two hominid groups occupied different environmental niches in Africa. One of them, *Homo*—by then *Homo erectus*—had a larger brain and a reproportioned skull; it had increased the areas of the brain that regulate higher mental functions. These were our ancestors, hominids with greater capacities for culture than the australopithecines had. *H. erectus* hunted and gathered,

made sophisticated tools, and eventually displaced its sole surviving cousin species, *A. boisei*.

A. boisei of East Africa, the hyperrobust australopithecines, had mammoth back teeth. *A. boisei* females had bigger back teeth than did earlier australopithecine males. *A. boisei* became ever more specialized with respect to one part of the traditional australopithecine diet, concentrating on coarse vegetation with a high grit content.

The separation that led to speciation between *A. boisei* and early *Homo* took time. And why, if two new *species* were forming, is one of them assigned to a new genus, *Homo*? This classification is done in retrospect, since we know that one species survived and evolved into a contemporary descendant whereas the other one became extinct. Hindsight shows us their very different lifeways, which suggest their placement in different genera.

We still don't know why, how, and exactly when the split between *Australopithecus* and *Homo* took place. Scholars have defended many different models, or theoretical schemes, to interpret the early hominid fossil record. Because new finds have so often forced reappraisals, most scientists are willing to modify their interpretation when given new evidence.

The model of Johanson and White (1979), who coined the term *A. afarensis*, proposes that *A. afarensis* split into two groups. One group, the ancestors of *Homo*, became reproductively isolated

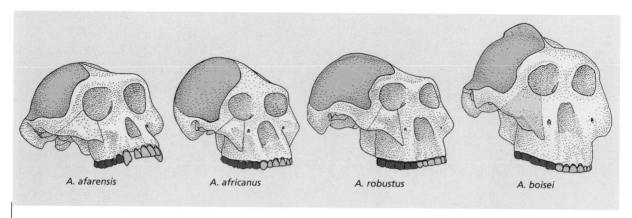

Shown from left to right are *A. afarensis*, *A. africanus*, *A. robustus*, and *A. boisei*. What are the main differences you notice among these four types of early hominids?

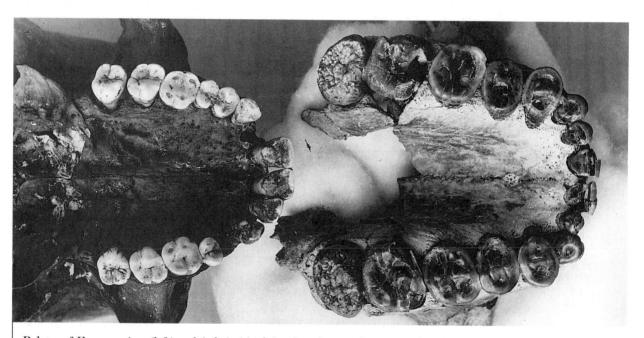

Palates of *Homo sapiens* (left) and *A. boisei* (right), a late, hyperrobust australopithecine. In comparing them, note the australopithecine's huge molars and premolars. What other contrasts do you notice? The large back teeth represent an extreme adaptation to a diet based on coarse, gritty savanna vegetation. Reduction in tooth size during human evolution applied to the back teeth much more than to the front.

from other hominids between 3 and 2 m.y.a. This group appeared as *Homo habilis*, a term coined by L. S. B. and Mary Leakey for the first members of the genus *Homo* and the immediate ancestors of *H. erectus*. *H. habilis* lived between 2 m.y.a. and about 1.7 m.y.a., by which time it had evolved into *H. erectus*. Other members of *A. afarensis* evolved into the various kinds of australopithecines (*A.*

africanus, A. robustus, and hyperrobust *A. boisei*, the last member to become extinct).

In 1985, the paleoanthropologist Alan Walker made a significant find near Lake Turkana in northern Kenya. Called the "black skull" because of the blue-black sheen it bore from the minerals surrounding it, the fossil displayed a "baffling combination of features" (Fisher 1988a). The jaw was ape-

The "black skull," dated to 2.6 m.y.a., was discovered by Alan Walker in 1985 near Lake Turkana. It gets its name from the blue-black sheen it acquired from the minerals surrounding it. The jaw is apelike and the brain is small, and there is a massive bony sagittal crest, as in *A. boisei*. Some consider the black skull to be a very early hyperrobust *A. boisei*. Others assign it to its own species, *A. aethiopicus*.

like and the brain was small (as in *A. afarensis*), but there was a massive bony crest atop the skull (as in *A. boisei*). Walker and Richard Leakey (Walker's associate on the 1985 expedition) view the black skull (dated to 2.6 m.y.a.) as a very early hyperrobust *A. boisei*. Others (e.g., Jolly and White 1995) assign the black skull to its own species, *A. aethiopicus*. The black skull shows that some of the anatomical features of the hyperrobust australopithecines (2.6? to 1.2 m.y.a.) did not change very much during well over one million years.

Interpret the World Map 7, "Early Hominids," in your atlas shows African sites from Chad to East and South Africa. Map 7 is accompanied by a time line running from 6 million to 10,000 years ago. How might you use the data in Map 7 and the time line to interpret human evolution? Can you detect patterns of origin and dispersal? Some areas, such as Tanzania, appear to have been occupied more continuously than others. However, lack of fossil evidence for continuous occupation may reflect deficiencies in the fossil record rather than absence of occupation. What factors favor or hinder the preservation and discovery of fossils, and thus produce a map like this?

Atlas Map 7

Regardless of when the split between *Homo* and *Australopithecus* occurred, there is good fossil evidence that *Homo* and *A. boisei* coexisted in East Africa. *A. boisei* seems to have lived in very arid areas, feeding on harder-to-chew vegetation than had any previous hominid. This diet would explain the hyperrobusts' huge back teeth, jaws, and associated areas of the face and skull.

H. RUDOLFENSIS AND *H. HABILIS*

In 1972, in an expedition led by Richard Leakey, Bernard Ngeneo unearthed a skull designated KNM-ER 1470. The name comes from its catalogue number in the Kenya National Museum (KNM) and its discovery location (East Rudolph—ER)—east of Lake Rudolph, at a site called Koobi Fora. The 1470 skull attracted immediate attention because of its unusual combination of a large brain (775 cc) and very large molars. Its brain size was more human than australopithecine, but its molars recalled those of a hyperrobust australopithecine. Some paleoanthropologists attributed the large skull and teeth to a very large body, assuming that this had been one *big hominid*. But no postcranial remains were found with 1470, nor have they been found with any later discovery of a 1470-like specimen.

How to interpret KNM-ER 1470? On the basis of its brain size, it seemed to belong in *Homo*. On the basis of its back teeth, it seemed more like *Australopithecus*. There are also problems with dating. The best dating guess is 1.8 m.y.a., but another estimate suggests that 1470 may be as old as 2.4 m.y.a. Originally, some paleoanthropologists assigned 1470 to *H. habilis*, while others saw it as an unusual australopithecine. In 1986, it received its own species name, *Homo rudolfensis*, from the lake near which it was found. This label has stuck—although it isn't accepted by all paleoanthropologists. Those who find *H. rudolfensis* to be a valid species emphasize its contrasts with *H. habilis*. Note the contrasts in the two skulls in the photos on page 184. KNM-ER 1813, on the left, is considered *H. habilis*; KNM-ER 1470, on the right, is *H. rudolfensis*. The *habilis* skull has a more marked brow ridge and a depression behind it, whereas 1470 has a less pronounced brow ridge and a longer, flatter face. Some think that *rudolfensis* lived earlier than and is ancestral to *habilis*. Some think that *rudolfensis* and *habilis* are simply male and female members of the same

Meet two kinds of early *Homo*. On the left KNM-ER 1813. On the right KNM-ER 1470. The latter (1470) has been classified as *H. rudolfensis*. What's the classification of 1813?

species—*H. habilis*. Some think they are separate species that coexisted in time and space (from about 2.4 m.y.a. to about 1.7 m.y.a.). Some think that one or the other gave rise to *H. erectus* (also known in Africa as *H. ergaster*). The debate continues. The only sure conclusion is that several different kinds of hominid lived in Africa before and after the advent of *Homo*.

Tools

It may have been *Homo*'s increasing hunting proficiency that forced *A. boisei* into becoming an ever-more-specialized vegetarian. Tool making also might have had something to do with the split. The simplest obviously manufactured tools were discovered in 1931 by L.S.B. and Mary Leakey at Olduvai Gorge. This site gave the tools their name—**Oldowan pebble tools.** The oldest tools from Olduvai are about 1.8 million years old. Richard Leakey also has found tools that old at East Turkana. Still older (2.5 to 2 m.y.a.) tools have been found in Ethiopia, Zaire, and Malawi (Asfaw, White, et al. 1999; Lemonick and Dorfman 1999).

Oldowan pebble tools (Figure 7.8) are pieces of stone about the size of a tennis ball. Flakes were struck off both sides to form a cutting edge. Stone is more durable than bone, horn, and wood are. Although there were probably early tools made of those materials, these substances are less likely to survive than stone is. Early hominids probably also used tools they did not make, for example, naturally chipped or cracked rocks or flakes. We can tell that early pebble tools were manufactured because their cutting edges are flaked on both sides, whereas rocks that are fractured by natural forces usually have flakes removed from just one side. Other evidence for manufacture is that some tools were made from rocks that were not locally available. They must have been brought to the site from elsewhere (Isaac 1978).

For more information on stone tool production, see the Virtual Exploration

mhhe
●com
/kottak

A. *GARHI* AND EARLY STONE TOOLS

In 1999 an international team reported the discovery, in Ethiopia, of a new species of hominid, along with the earliest traces of animal butchery (Asfaw, White, et al. 1999). These new fossils, dating to 2.5 m.y.a., may be the remains of a direct human

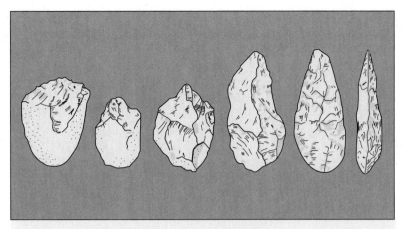

Figure 7.8   Evolution in Tool Making.   Finds at Olduvai Gorge and elsewhere show how pebble tools (the first tool at the left) evolved into the Acheulian hand ax of *H. erectus*. This drawing begins with an Oldowan pebble tool and moves through crude hand axes to fully developed Acheulian tools. The oldest tools date back to about 2.5 m.y.a. With the split between *Homo* (*habilis*, then *erectus*) and *A. boisei*, stone-tool manufacture rapidly grew more sophisticated. The Acheulian techniques of *H. erectus* are described in the following chapter.

ancestor and an evolutionary link between *Australopithecus* and the genus *Homo*. At the same site was evidence that antelopes and horses had been butchered with the world's earliest stone tools. When scientists excavated these hominid fossils, they were shocked to find a combination of unforeseen skeletal and dental features. They named the specimen *Australopithecus garhi*. The word *garhi* means "surprise" in the Afar language.

For more on early stone tools, see the Internet Exercises at your OLC

mhhe
● **com**
/kottak

Tim White, coleader of the research team, viewed the discoveries as important for three reasons. First, they add a new potential ancestor to the human family tree. Second, they show that the thigh bone (femur) had elongated by 2.5 million years ago, a million years before the forearm shortened—to create our current human proportions. Third, evidence that large mammals were being butchered shows that early stone technologies were aimed at getting meat and marrow from big game. This signals a dietary revolution that eventually may have allowed an invasion of new habitats and continents (Berkleyan 1999).

In 1997 the Ethiopian archaeologist Sileshi Semaw announced he had found the world's ear-

liest stone tools, dating to 2.5 m.y.a., at the nearby Ethiopian site of Gona. But which human ancestor had made these tools, he wondered, and what were they used for? The 1999 discoveries by Asfaw, White, and their colleagues provided answers, identifying *A. garhi* as the best candidate for toolmaker (Berkleyan 1999).

Is it surprising that australopithecines made stone tools? A series of anatomic features strongly suggest the existence of australopithecine culture. These features include upright locomotion and evidence of a long period of infant and childhood dependency. Upright bipedalism would have permitted the use of tools and weapons against predators and competitors in an open grassland habitat. Bipedal locomotion also allowed early hominids to carry things, such as scavenged parts of carnivore kills. We know that primates have generalized abilities to adapt through learning. It would be amazing if the australopithecines, who are much more closely related to us than the apes are, didn't have even greater cultural abilities than contemporary apes have.

The association, in the same area at the same time, of *A. garhi*, animal butchery, and the earliest stone tools suggests that the australopithecines were

Beyond the *Classroom*
Hydrodynamic Sorting of Avian Skeletal Remains

Background Information

STUDENT:	Josh Trapani
SUPERVISING PROFESSOR:	Peter Stahl
SCHOOL:	State University of New York at Binghamton
YEAR IN SCHOOL/MAJOR:	Senior/Anthropology
FUTURE PLANS:	Graduate school
PROJECT TITLE:	Hydrodynamic Sorting of Avian Skeletal Remains

People have dietary preferences for particular animal parts. Archaeologists typically encounter remains of animals that humans may have hunted and eaten. At a given site, certain kinds of bones may be more common than others are. How can we know whether humans choose some preferred parts to take away, while leaving others, or whether natural processes were responsible? This project examines the effects of water current in sorting avian (bird) bones. Some parts (e.g., skulls) are more likely than others are to have been moved by water, and this helps to determine whether humans played a role in the selection of animal parts at the site.

Taphonomy is the study of the processes that affect preservation of organic remains. Specific taphonomic factors may bias (i.e., alter the preservation, condition, and identifiability of) archaeological and paleontological faunal assemblages in specific ways. It is necessary to understand the taphonomic biases an assemblage has been subjected to so that accurate interpretations about that assemblage can be made.

One important taphonomic agent is sorting by current. Many archaeological sites are located near water, and current action may alter their faunal assemblages. Currents sort bones in the same way they sort sediment: by selectively removing certain bones from a site while leaving others behind. Archaeologists often attribute relative frequencies of different skeletal elements at a site to human agency (e.g., dietary preference for certain parts of an animal over others). But if the assemblage has been subjected to sorting by current (or any of a number of other taphonomic factors), such interpretations may be erroneous.

Previous studies examined the way mammal and turtle bones sort in a current. However, a study with avian material had never been done before. Bird bones are structurally different from bones of other vertebrates and they often comprise an important component of human diet. I partially and completely skele-

toolmakers, with some capacity for culture. Nevertheless, cultural abilities developed exponentially with *Homo*'s appearance and expansion. With increasing reliance on hunting, tool making, and other cultural abilities, *Homo* eventually became the most efficient exploiter of the savanna niche. The last surviving members of *A. boisei* may have been forced into ever-more-marginal areas. They eventually became extinct. By 1 m.y.a., a single species of hominid, *H. erectus*, not only had rendered other hominid forms extinct but also had expanded the hominid range to Asia and Europe. An essentially human strategy of adaptation, incorporating hunting as a fundamental ingredient of a generalized foraging economy, had emerged. Despite regional variation, it was to be the basic economy for our genus until 11,000 years ago. We turn now to the fossils, tools, and life patterns of the various forms of *Homo*.

tonized several domestic pigeons (*Columba livia*) and studied the way their bones sorted in a current.

I conducted the experiments in a flume, which is a large tank that simulates conditions inside a natural channel but allows for control of many variables. The bottom may be lined with sediment, and an adjustable current flows from one end to another. I examined the order that the bones moved in, how they moved, and how likely they were to be buried. I also examined transport of partially skeletonized birds to compare behavior of individual bones with articulated skeletal units. Repeated observations under a number of different flow conditions (e.g., current velocities, bed-form types) allowed me to determine a general order in which bones were expected to move.

This "sorting sequence" is useful as a general guide to whether an avian assemblage has been sorted by a current. For example, an assemblage containing skulls (most likely to be moved) and scapulae or shoulder blades (least likely to be moved) was probably not subjected to sorting. However, if an assemblage contains many easily-moved bones and few "lag" bones (or vice versa), it becomes necessary to rule out current sorting before attributing observed relative frequencies to human (or other) agency.

I also attempted to establish correlations between sorting behavior and bone size, shape, and density. Finally, I noted similarities and differences between sorting sequences for the pigeon and already-published sequences for other vertebrates.

Hopefully, this research constitutes a small step in the direction of understanding how current sorting operates as a taphonomic bias. This knowledge may aid our interpretations of site formation and thus allow greater insight into past human behavior and practices.

SUMMARY

1. Hominids lived during the late Miocene, Pliocene (5 to 2 m.y.a.), and Pleistocene (2 m.y.a. to 10,000 B.P.) epochs. The australopithecines had appeared by 4.2 m.y.a. The five species of *Australopithecus* were *A. anamensis* (4.2 m.y.a.), *A. afarensis* (3.8 to 3.0 m.y.a.), *A. africanus* (3.0 to 2.5 m.y.a.), *A. robustus* (2.5? to 2 m.y.a.), and *A. boisei* (2.6 to 1.0 m.y.a.). The earliest identifiable hominid remains date to between 7 m.y.a. and 5.8 m.y.a. The "Toumai" find from northern Chad is a possible early hominid. More generally accepted hominid remains from Ethiopia are classified as *Ardipithecus ramidus.* Next comes *A. anamensis,* then a group of fossils from Hadar, Ethiopia, and Laetoli, Tanzania, classified as *A. afarensis.*

2. These early finds suggest that the common ancestor of humans and the African apes lived more recently than had been thought. These earliest hominids shared many primitive features, including slashing canines, elongated premolars, a small apelike skull, and marked sexual dimorphism. Still, *A. afarensis* and its recently discovered predecessors were definite hominids. In *A. afarensis* this is confirmed by large molars and, more important, by skeletal evidence (e.g., in Lucy) for upright bipedalism.

3. Remains of two later groups, *A. africanus* (graciles) and *A. robustus* (robusts), were found in South Africa. Both groups show the australopithecine trend toward a powerful chewing apparatus. They had large molars and premolars and large and robust faces, skulls, and muscle markings. All these features are more pronounced in the robusts than they are in the graciles. The basis of the australopithecine diet was savanna vegetation. These early hominids also hunted small animals and scavenged the kills of predators.

4. Early *Homo, H. habilis* (2? to 1.7 m.y.a.), evolved into *H. erectus* (1.7 m.y.a. to 300,000 B.P.). By 2 m.y.a. there is ample evidence for two distinct hominid groups: early *Homo* and *A. boisei,* the hyperrobust australopithecines. The latter eventually became extinct around 1 m.y.a. *A. boisei* became increasingly specialized, dependent on tough, coarse, gritty, fibrous savanna vegetation. The australopithecine trend toward dental, facial, and cranial robustness continued with *A. boisei,* but these structures were reduced as *H. habilis* evolved into *H. erectus.*

5. Pebble tools dating to between 2.5 and 2 m.y.a. have been found in Ethiopia, Zaire, and Malawi. Scientists have disagreed about their maker, some arguing that only early *Homo* could have made them. Evidence has been presented that *A. garhi* made pebble tools around 2.5 m.y.a. Cultural abilities developed exponentially with *Homo*'s appearance and evolution.

KEY TERMS

See the flash cards

mhhe
com
/kottak

australopithecines Varied group of Pliocene–Pleistocene hominids. The term is derived from their former classification as members of a distinct subfamily, the Australopithecinae; now they are distinguished from *Homo* only at the genus level.

glacials The four or five major advances of continental ice sheets in northern Europe and North America.

gracile Opposite of robust; "gracile" indicates that members of *A. africanus* were a bit smaller and slighter, less robust, than were members of *A. robustus.*

Homo habilis Term coined by L. S. B. and Mary Leakey; immediate ancestor of *H. erectus;* lived from about 2 to 1.7 m.y.a.

interglacials Extended warm periods between such major glacials as Riss and Würm.

Oldowan pebble tools Earliest (2 to 2.5 m.y.a.) stone tools; first discovered in 1931 by L. S. B. and Mary Leakey at Olduvai Gorge.

Pleistocene Epoch of *Homo*'s appearance and evolution; began 1.8 million years ago; divided into Lower, Middle, and Upper.

robust Large, strong, sturdy; said of skull, skeleton, muscle, and teeth; opposite of gracile.

For more self testing, see the self quizzes

mhhe
com
/kottak

CRITICAL THINKING QUESTIONS

1. What are some of the unanswered questions about early hominid evolution? What kinds of information would help provide answers?

2. If you found a new hominoid fossil in East Africa, dated to five million years ago, would it most likely be an ape ancestor or a human ancestor? How would you tell the difference?

3. What was the first species of *Australopithecus*? Where and when did it live? What hominid lived before it?

4. What are some different ways of interpreting the relationships among the early hominids, from *Australopithecus* to *Homo*? That is, which were ancestral to *Homo,* and which were sidelines in human evolution?

5. What is the significance of the black skull?

6. Do you think that *Australopithecus* or *Homo* made the first tools? What's the basis of your opinion?

Atlas Questions

Look at Map 7, "Early Hominids: Origins and Diffusion"

1. How many African countries have hominid sites? How many have sites from the Miocene? From the Pliocene? And from the Pleistocene?

2. Compare the African distribution of nonhuman primates in Map 6 (discussed in Chapter 6) with the distribution of early hominids in Map 7. Which fossil record is better—the one for nonhuman primates or the one for hominids?

3. Compare the distribution of the African apes, as shown in Map 5 (Chapter 5) with the distribution of early hominid sites in Map 7. Also look at the distribution of extinct African apes in Map 6 (Chapter 6). What patterns do you notice? Where did early hominids overlap with the African apes (extinct and contemporary)? Where were there apes but no known early hominids, and vice versa?

SUGGESTED ADDITIONAL READINGS

Boaz, N. T.
1999   *Essentials of Biological Anthropology.* Upper Saddle River, NJ: Prentice-Hall. Basic text in physical anthropology, with information on paleoanthropology.

Bogin, B.
2001   *The Growth of Humanity.* New York: Wiley. Human growth in relation to human evolution.

Brace, C. L.
1995   *The Stages of Human Evolution*, 5th ed. Englewood Cliffs, NJ: Prentice-Hall. Brief introduction to the hominid fossil record.

2000   *Evolution in an Anthropological View.* Walnut Creek, CA: AltaMira. Essays on human evolution.

Campbell, B. G.
1998   *Human Evolution: An Introduction to Man's Adaptations*, 4th ed. New York: Aldine de Gruyter. Basic paleoanthropology text.

Campbell, B. G., and J. D. Loy, eds.
2000   *Humankind Emerging*, 8th ed. New York: Longman. Well-illustrated survey of physical anthropology, particularly the fossil record.

Cole, S.
1975   *Leakey's Luck: The Life of Louis Bazett Leakey, 1903–1972.* New York: Harcourt Brace Jovanovich. The personal and professional life of anthropology's greatest fossil finder, written by an archaeologist.

Johanson, D. C., and B. Edgar
1996   *From Lucy to Language.* New York: Simon & Schuster. Popular account of human evolution by a prominent contributor to understanding the fossil record.

Lewin, R.
1999   *Human Evolution: An Illustrated Introduction*, 4th ed. Malden, MA: Blackwell Science. Readable and well-illustrated introduction.

Park, M. A.

2002   *Biological Anthropology*, 3rd ed. Boston: McGraw-Hill. A concise introduction, with a focus on scientific inquiry.

Poirier, F. E., and J. K. McKee

1999   *Understanding Human Evolution*, 4th ed. Upper Saddle River, NJ: Prentice-Hall. Principles of human evolution.

Relethford, J. H.

2000   *The Human Species: An Introduction to Biological Anthropology*. 4th ed. Boston: McGraw-Hill. Up-to-date text in biological anthropology.

Wolpoff, M. H.

1999   *Paleoanthropology*, 2nd ed. Boston: McGraw-Hill. Thorough introduction to the hominid and pre-hominid fossil record.

INTERNET EXERCISES

1. Early Hominid Skulls: Visit Philip L. Walker and Edward H. Hagen's "Human Evolution: The Fossil Evidence in 3D" **(http://www.anth.ucsb.edu/projects/human/#).**

   Then click the link to enter the gallery.

   a. Click on the human figure labeled "Human origins" and then click on the skull labeled "Australopithecine radiation." You now have a three-dimensional view of an *Australopithecus afarensis* skull, and you can use the mouse to rotate the skull. Compare it with a modern human skull. What are some of the differences you notice? What do these differences mean about diet, environment, and brain size?

   b. Go back and view the *Paranthropus boisei* (equivalent to *Australopithecus boisei* in this text) and *Australopithecus africanus* skulls. What are the major differences between the two, and what do these differences say about diet, environment, and brain size?

2. Paleoanthropologist Fieldwork in Kenya: Go to the Human Origins Field Projects in Kenya page of the Human Origins Program at the Smithsonian, **http://www.mnh.si.edu/anthro/humanorigins/aop/aop_ken.html.**

   Explore the pages describing the field work and methods (press Continue to Next Page).

   a. The site shows pictures of the modern environment of Kenya. How much has the environment changed since early hominids lived there?

   b. Did the field work just involve excavating fossils? What other types of data are researchers gathering to understand early hominids?

   c. Make sure to read the dispatches from the researchers working at Olorgesailie in 1999, **http://www.mnh.si.edu/anthro/humanorigins/aop/Olorgesailie/dispatch/start.html.**

   Read some of the diary entries. What is a day in the field of a paleoanthropologist like?

See Chapter 7 at your McGraw-Hill Online Learning Center for additional review and interactive exercises.

8 MODERN HUMANS

Overview

This chapter begins around two million years ago, with the advent of the genus *Homo*. It ends with the much more recent past, when anatomically modern people were painting artistic masterpieces on cave walls in France and Spain. We focus here on the biological and cultural changes that led from early *Homo*, through intermediate forms, to anatomically modern humans—*Homo sapiens sapiens*.

The earliest member of our genus, *Homo habilis*, evolved into *Homo erectus* around 1.8 million years ago. With *H. erectus*, average cranial capacity doubled, compared with the australopithecines. *H. erectus* extended the human range out of Africa. Complex tools and cooperative hunting suggest a long period of enculturation and learning. Fire permitted expansion into cooler areas, as well as cooking and cave life. *H. erectus* had evolved into archaic *H. sapiens* by 300,000 years ago.

The Neandertals were a form of archaic *H. sapiens* that lived in Western Europe (and elsewhere) early in the last glacial period. Scientists tend to exclude the Neandertals as ancestors of modern humans. The ancestry of modern humans lies among other archaic *H. sapiens* groups, most probably those in Africa. Modern people had reached Western Europe by 31,000 years ago.

As glacial ice melted, the Western European food quest was generalized to include fish, fowl, and plants, in addition to the diminishing herds of big game. The start of such a diversified economy coincided with an intensification of Upper Paleolithic cave art. On limestone cave walls, prehistoric hunters painted animals important in their lives. Explanations of such cave paintings link them to hunting magic, ceremonies, and initiation rites.

Skulls in Caucasus Linked to Early Humans in Africa

NY TIMES NEWS BRIEF

by John Noble Wilford

May 12, 2000

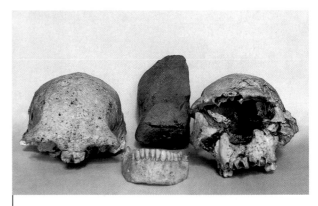

The contrasting skulls of *H. erectus* or *H. ergaster* found at Dmanisi, Republic of Georgia.

Without doubt, the origins of all humans can be traced to Africa. But when did hominids first leave that continent, and what kind of creatures were those first colonists? This account tells of the discovery of an early form of human, here dubbed *Homo ergaster* but usually called early *Homo erectus*, that had reached the former Soviet Republic of Georgia by 1.7 million years ago. The *H. ergaster* or *erectus* skulls described here are remarkably similar to comparably dated fossils found in East Africa, which have been identified as being either *H. ergaster* or an early form of *H. erectus*. Other finds at the Georgian town of Dmanisi show that the hominids living there around 1.7 m.y.a. were remarkably varied. Besides the two skulls discussed in this news story, a large jaw bone (mandible) had been found previously. The most recent (2001) discovery was of a skull with some very primitive characteristics—such as large canine teeth and a small cranial capacity (Vekua and Lordkipanidze 2002). This skull may be that of a teenage girl whose skull had not yet reached full size—but whose canines had. The simplest explanation for the anatomical differences observed at Dmanisi is that *Homo erectus* was at least as variable a species as is *Homo sapiens*. In terms of size and anatomy, who are the two most different people you can think of? Imagine the interpretations that might be offered if they were found as fossils in the same stratigraphic layer.

In a discovery with profound implications for the study of early human history, scientists digging in the nation of Georgia have found 1.7-million-year-old fossil human skulls that show clear signs of African ancestry and so may represent the species that first migrated out of Africa.

The two relatively complete skulls, being described today in the journal *Science*, begin to put a face, in a sense, to the ancestors who responded to opportunity and necessity by leaving Africa and spreading out over much of the rest of the world.

Many paleoanthropologists hailed the discovery as a major advance in their field, and said the skulls were probably the most ancient undisputed human fossils outside Africa . . . .

The international discovery team, led by Dr. Leo Gabunia of the Georgia National Academy of Sciences, concluded that the age and skeletal characteristics of the skulls linked them to the early human species *Homo ergaster*, who lived from 1.9 million to 1.4 million years ago and who some researchers think is the African version of *Homo erectus* . . . .

Dr. Susan C. Anton, . . . a member of the discovery team, said that by this time human ancestors had become more carnivorous and their diets pushed them to expand their home range to match the wider ranges of the animals they preyed on.

"With the appearance of *Homo*, we see bigger bodies that require more energy to run, and therefore need these higher quality sources of protein as fuel," Dr. Anton said of the adaptation to meat-rich diets.

As long as early human ancestors had smaller bodies and brains . . . they lived mainly on plants and confined themselves to a limited range at the edge of forests, not too deep in or too exposed far out on the savanna.

Once they had stronger bodies and high-protein meat diets, they were able to spread out geographically and ecologically.

Dr. Alan Walker, a paleoanthropologist at Pennsylvania State University who specializes in searching for human fossils in Kenya, said he agreed with the interpretation of the Georgian skulls. "The new fossils look exactly like early *Homo* skulls from Kenya," Dr. Walker said.

He said the implications of the new findings for human dispersal from Africa supported an idea he and his wife, Dr. Pat Shipman, an anthropologist, proposed in 1989.

They suggested that once the more apelike *australopithecines* evolved into the genus *Homo* and became carnivorous, they were forced to expand their home territory.

"Herbivores are restricted to where the plants are that they eat," Dr. Walker said. "Carnivores are not so restricted. Meat is meat, and you often have to travel far to find it."

The two skulls were uncovered last summer at Dmanisi, on a slope of the Caucasus Mountains 55 miles southwest of Tbilisi, the Georgian capital. At the same site in 1991, paleontologists found a jawbone of what was identified as a *Homo erectus*.

Finding the craniums—one of a young adult male and the other of a female adolescent—has seemed to quiet skeptics who had disputed the jawbone dating.

The discovery team included scientists from France, Germany and the United States, as well as Georgia . . . .

Dr. Philip Rightmire, a specialist in *Homo erectus* at the State University of New York at Binghamton, said he was impressed by the new discovery's implications for "a pretty quick, really wholesale dispersal of these people, along with other animals," from the time the new species emerged in East Africa . . . .

Unlike some scientists, Dr. Rightmire classifies the African ergaster together with the Asian erectus in the same species. To him and many others, they are regional variants of the same species . . . .

The fact that *Homo* was living and hunting in Africa by 1.7 million years ago isn't newsworthy; it's been known for decades. What's interesting here is evidence for the spread of early *Homo* beyond Africa by such an early date. As we saw in Chapter 7, at two million years ago there is African evidence for two distinct hominid groups: early *Homo* and *A. boisei*, the hyperrobust australopithecines, which became extinct around 1.2 m.y.a. *A. boisei* became increasingly specialized, dependent on tough, coarse, gritty, fibrous savanna vegetation. The australopithecine trend toward dental, facial, and cranial robustness continued with *A. boisei*. However, these structures were reduced as early forms of *Homo* evolved into *H. ergaster* (or early *H. erectus*) by 1.8–1.7 m.y.a. By that date *Homo* had generalized the subsistence quest to the hunting of large animals to supplement the gathering of vegetation and scavenging.

Early *Homo*

L.S.B. and Mary Leakey gave the name *Homo habilis* to the earliest members of our genus, first found at Olduvai Gorge in Tanzania. Olduvai's oldest layer, Bed I, dates to 1.8 m.y.a. This layer has yielded both small-brained *A. boisei* (average 490 cm^3) fossils and *H. habilis* skulls, with cranial capacities between 600 and 700 cm^3.

Another important *habilis* find was made in 1986 by Tim White of the University of California, Berkeley. OH62 (Olduvai Hominid 62) is the partial skeleton of a female *H. habilis* from Olduvai Bed I. This was the first find of a *H. habilis* skull with a significant amount of skeletal material. OH62, dating to 1.8 m.y.a., consists of parts of the skull, the right arm, and both legs. This fossil was surprising because of its small size and its apelike limb bones. Scientists had assumed that *H. habilis* would be taller than Lucy (*A. afarensis*), moving gradually in the direction of *H. erectus*. According to expectations, even a female *H. habilis* should have stood somewhere between Lucy's three feet and the five to six feet of *H. erectus*. However, not only was OH62 just as tiny as Lucy, its arms were longer and more apelike than expected. The limb proportions suggested greater tree-climbing ability than later hominids had. *H. habilis* may still have sought occasional refuge in the trees.

The small size and primitive proportions of *H. habilis* were unexpected given what was already known about early *H. erectus* in East Africa. (Some paleoanthropologists use the term *Homo ergaster* to refer to the earliest *H. erectus* fossils in Africa. Here I follow the more traditional scheme of calling them *Homo erectus*.) In deposits near Lake Turkana, Richard Leakey had uncovered two *H. erectus* skulls dating to 1.6 m.y.a. By that date, *H. erectus* had already attained a cranial capacity of 900 cm^3, along with a modern body shape and height. An

Drawing of a *Homo habilis* band, as it might have existed some two million years ago. Besides gathering and hunting small, slow animals, early *Homo* probably scavenged the prey of stronger, faster carnivores such as leopards. What's going on in this photo? Is there any evidence of rudimentary culture?

"What a find, Williams! The fossilized footprint of a brachiosaurus! ... And a *Homo habilus* thrown in to boot!"

What's wrong with this picture, besides the spelling of habilis?

amazingly complete young male *H. erectus* fossil (WT15,000) found at West Turkana in 1984 by Kimoya Kimeu, a collaborator of the Leakeys, has confirmed this. WT15,000, also known as the Nariokotome boy, was a 12-year-old male who had already reached 168 cm (5 feet 5 inches). He might have grown to six feet had he lived.

The sharp contrast between the OH62 *H. habilis* (1.8 m.y.a.) and early *H. erectus* (1.7–1.6 m.y.a.) suggests an acceleration in hominid evolution during that 100,000–200,000-year period. This fossil evidence may support a punctuated equilibrium model of the early hominid fossil record. In this view, long periods of equilibrium, during which species change little, are interrupted (punc-

tuated) by sudden changes—evolutionary jumps. Apparently hominids changed very little below the neck between Lucy (*A. afarensis*) and *H. habilis*. Then, between 1.8 and 1.6 m.y.a., a profound change—an evolutionary leap—took place. *H. erectus* looks much more human than *H. habilis* does.

GRADUAL AND RAPID CHANGE

Charles Darwin saw life forms as arising from others gradually over time, in a slow and orderly fashion. Small modifications, accumulating over many generations, add up to major changes after thousands of years. Gradualists like Darwin cite intermediate or "mixed-trait" fossils as evidence for

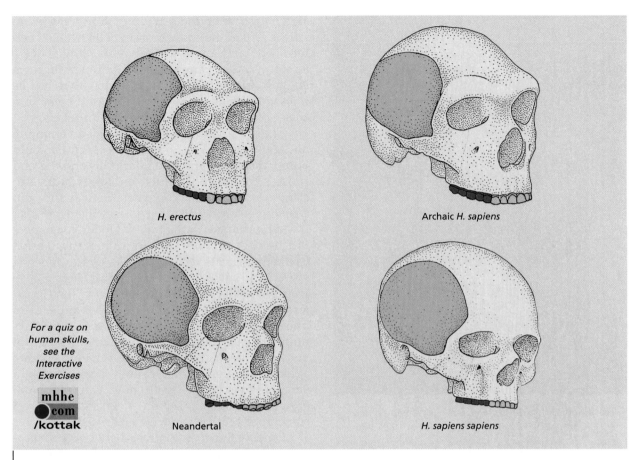

H. erectus

Archaic *H. sapiens*

Neandertal

H. sapiens sapiens

Compare these drawings (left to right) of *H. erectus*, archaic *H. sapiens*, Neandertal, and *H. sapiens sapiens*. What are the main differences you notice? Is the Neandertal more like *H. erectus* or *H. sapiens sapiens*?

their position. They contend we would see even more transitional forms if it weren't for gaps in the fossil record.

Advocates of the punctuated equilibrium model (see Eldredge 1985; Gould 1999) believe that long periods of stasis (stability), when species change little, are interrupted by evolutionary leaps. One reason for such jumps in the fossil record may be extinction followed by invasion by a closely related species. For example, a sea species may die out when a shallow body of water dries up, while a closely related species survives in deeper waters. Later, when the sea reinvades the first locale, the protected species will extend its range to the first area. Another possibility is that when barriers are removed, a group may replace, rather than succeed, a related one because it has a

trait that makes it adaptively fitter in the environment they now share.

When there is a sudden environmental change, one possibility is for the pace of evolution to increase. Another possibility is extinction. The earth has witnessed several mass extinctions—worldwide catastrophes affecting multiple species. The biggest one divided the era of "ancient life" (the Paleozoic) from the era of "middle life" (the Mesozoic). This mass extinction occurred 245 m.y.a., when 4.5 million of the earth's estimated 5 million species (mostly invertebrates) were wiped out. The second biggest extinction, around 65 million years ago, destroyed the dinosaurs. One explanation for the extinction of the dinosaurs is that a massive, long-lasting cloud of gas and dust arose from the impact of a giant meteorite. The cloud blocked solar

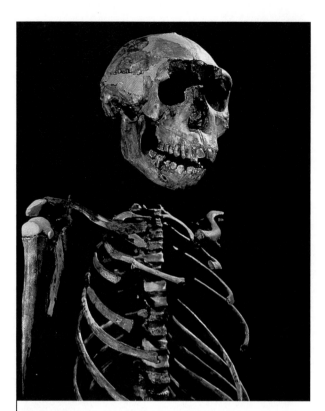

This photo shows the early (1.6 m.y.a) *Homo erectus* WT15,000, or Nariokotome boy, found in 1984 near Lake Turkana, Kenya. This is the most complete *Homo erectus* ever found.

cated soon after the advent of *Homo erectus* in Africa. Out of the crude tools in Bed I evolved better-made and more varied tools. Edges were straighter, for example, and differences in form suggest functional differentiation—that is, the tools were being made and used for different jobs, such as smashing bones or digging for tubers.

The more sophisticated tools aided in hunting and gathering. With the new tools, *Homo* could obtain meat on a more regular basis and dig and process tubers, roots, nuts, and seeds more efficiently. New tools that could batter, crush, and pulp coarse vegetation also reduced chewing demands.

With changes in the types of foods consumed, the burden on the chewing apparatus eased. Chewing muscles developed less, and supporting structures, such as jaws and cranial crests, also were reduced. With less chewing, jaws developed less, and so there was no place to put large teeth. The size of teeth, which form before they erupt, is under stricter genetic control than jaw size and bone size are. Natural selection began to operate against the genes that caused large teeth. In smaller jaws, large teeth now caused dental crowding, impaction, pain, sickness, fever, and sometimes death (there were no dentists).

Some of the main contrasts between *Australopithecus* and early *Homo* are in dentition. *H. erectus* back teeth are smaller; and the front teeth, relatively larger than australopithecine teeth. *H. erectus* used its front teeth to pull, twist, and grip objects. A massive ridge over the eyebrows (a *superorbital torus*) provided buttressing against the forces exerted in these activities.

As hunting became more important to *H. erectus*, encounters with large animals increased. Individuals with stronger skulls had better-protected brains and better survival rates. Given the dangers associated with larger prey, and without sophisticated spear or arrow technology, which developed later, natural selection favored the thickening of certain areas for better protection. The base of the skull expanded dramatically, with a ridge of spongy bone (an *occipital bun*) across the back, for the attachment of massive neck muscles. The frontal and parietal (side) areas of the skull also increased, indicating expansion in those areas of the brain. Finally, average cranial capacity expanded from about 500 cm^3 in the australopithecines to 1,000 cm^3 in *H. erectus*, which is within the modern range of variation.

radiation and therefore photosynthesis, ultimately destroying most plants and the chain of animals that fed on them.

The hominid fossil record exemplifies both gradual and rapid change. Evolution can be slow or fast depending on the rate of environmental change, the speed with which geographic barriers rise or fall, and the effectiveness of the group's adaptive response. There is no doubt that the pace of hominid evolution sped up around 1.8 m.y.a. This spurt resulted in the emergence (in less than 200,000 years) of *H. erectus*. This was followed by a long period of relative stability. One possible key to the rapid emergence of *H. erectus* was a dramatic change in adaptive strategy: greater reliance on hunting through larger body size, along with improved tools and other cultural means of adaptation.

Significant changes in technology occurred during the 200,000-year evolutionary spurt between Bed I (1.8 m.y.a.) and Lower Bed II (1.6 m.y.a) at Olduvai. Tool making got more sophisti-

Out of Africa

Biological and cultural changes enabled *Homo erectus* to exploit a new adaptive strategy—gathering and hunting. *H. erectus* pushed the hominid range beyond Africa—to Asia and Europe. Small groups broke off from larger ones and moved a few miles away. They foraged new tracts of edible vegetation and carved out new hunting territories. Through population growth and dispersal, *H. erectus* gradually spread and changed. Hominids were following an essentially human life style based on hunting and gathering. This basic pattern survived until recently in marginal areas of the world, although it is now fading rapidly.

This chapter begins around two million years ago, with the transition to *Homo*. It ends in the less distant past, when anatomically modern humans were painting artistic masterpieces on cave walls in France and Spain. We focus in this chapter on the biological and cultural changes that led from early *Homo*, through intermediate forms, to anatomically modern humans—*Homo sapiens sapiens*.

PALEOLITHIC TOOLS

For more on Oldowan tools see the Virtual Exploration

mhhe
com
/kottak

The stone-tool-making techniques that evolved out of the Oldowan, or pebble tool, tradition and that lasted until about 15,000 years ago are described by the term **Paleolithic** (from Greek roots meaning "old" and "stone"). The Paleolithic, or Old Stone Age, has three divisions: Lower (early), Middle, and Upper (late). Each part is roughly associated with a particular stage in human evolution. The Lower Paleolithic is roughly associated with *H. erectus*; the Middle Paleolithic with archaic *H. sapiens*, including the Neandertals of Western Europe and the Middle East; and the Upper Paleolithic with early members of our own subspecies, *H. sapiens sapiens*, anatomically modern humans.

The best stone tools are made from rocks such as flint that fracture sharply and in predictable ways when hammered. Quartz, quartzite, chert, and obsidian are also suitable. Each of the three main divisions of the Paleolithic had its typical *tool-making traditions*—coherent patterns of tool manufacture. The main Lower Paleolithic tool-making tradition used by *Homo erectus* was the **Acheulian**, named after the French village of St. Acheul, where it was first identified.

Like Oldowan tools, the characteristic Acheulian tool, the hand ax, consisted of a modified core of rock. Flakes removed from the core when it was struck with a hammerstone also were used as tools. Flakes, smaller tools with finer cutting edges, became progressively more important in human evolution, particularly in Middle and Upper Paleolithic tool making.

Acheulian tools were an advance over pebble tools in several ways. Early hominids had made simple tools by picking up pebbles the size of tennis balls and chipping off a few flakes from one end to form a rough and irregular edge. They used these pebble tools (and probably some of the flakes as well) for a variety of purposes, such as smashing animal bones to extract marrow. The Acheulian technique involved chipping the core all over rather than at one end only. The core was converted from a round piece of rock into a flattish oval hand ax about 15 centimeters (6 inches) long. Its cutting edge was far superior to that of the pebble tool.

Hand axes, along with digging sticks made of bone, horn, and wood, were used to dig edible roots and other foods from the ground. Hunters made tools with a sharper cutting edge to skin and cut up their prey. Cleavers—core tools with a straight edge at one end—were used for heavy chopping and hacking at the sinews of larger animals. Flakes were used to make incisions and for finer work. The Acheulian tradition illustrates trends in the evolution of technology: greater efficiency, manufacture of tools for specific tasks, and an increasingly complex technology. These trends became even more obvious with the advent of *H. sapiens*.

ADAPTIVE STRATEGIES OF *HOMO ERECTUS*

Interrelated changes in biology and culture have increased human adaptability—the capacity to live in and modify an ever-wider range of environments. Acheulian tools helped *H. erectus* increase its range. Biological changes also increased hunting efficiency. *H. erectus* had a rugged but essentially modern skeleton that permitted long-distance stalking and endurance during the hunt. The *H. erectus* body was much larger and longer-legged than those of previous hominids, permitting longer-distance hunting of large prey. There is archaeological evidence of *H. erectus*'s success in hunting elephants, horses, rhinos, and giant baboons.

An increase in cranial capacity has been a trend in human evolution. The average *H. erectus* brain (about 1,000 cm³) doubled the australopithecine average. The capacities of *H. erectus* skulls range from 800 to 1,250 cm³, well above the *H. sapiens sapiens* minimum.

Understanding Ourselves   Now we can understand why our children, compared with the young of other primates, are so dependent for so long—it's because of our big brains and our bipedal locomotion. As was noted in Chapter 7, larger skulls demand larger birth canals. However, the requirements of upright bipedalism impose limits on the expansion of the pelvic opening. If the opening is too large, the pelvis doesn't provide sufficient support for the trunk. Locomotion suffers, and posture problems develop. If, by contrast, the birth canal is too narrow, mother and child (without the modern option of Caesarean section) may die. Natural selection has struck a balance between the structural demands of upright posture and the tendency toward increased brain size—the birth of immature and dependent children whose brains and skulls grow dramatically after birth.

The interrelation between immature birth, childhood dependency, and social nurturance applies with greater force to *H. erectus* than it did to the australopithecines. During a long period of dependence, growth, and maturation, children can absorb the traditions and cultural directives of parents and other members of the group. Extended enculturation helps explain increasing complexity in tool manufacture and increasingly efficient coordination of hunting among *H. erectus*. These observations, of course, apply even more strongly to—and help us understand—our own systems of cultural transmission, as modern members of *Homo sapiens*.

H. erectus had an essentially modern, though very robust, skeleton with a brain and body closer in size to *H. sapiens* than to *Australopithecus*. Still, several anatomical contrasts, particularly in the cranium, distinguish *H. erectus* from modern humans. Compared with moderns, *H. erectus* had a lower and more sloping forehead accentuated by

a large brow ridge above the eyes. Skull bones were thicker, and, as noted, average cranial capacity was smaller. The braincase was lower and flatter than in *H. sapiens*, with spongy bone development at the lower rear of the skull. Seen from behind, the *H. erectus* skull has a broad-based angular shape that has been compared to a half-inflated football (Jolly and White 1995) (Figure 8.1). The *H. erectus* face, teeth, and jaws were larger than those in contemporary humans but smaller than those in *Australopithecus*. The front teeth were especially large, but molar size was well below the australopithecine average. Presumably, this reduction reflected changes in diet or food processing.

Taken together, the *H. erectus* skeleton and chewing apparatus provide biological evidence of a fuller commitment to hunting and gathering,

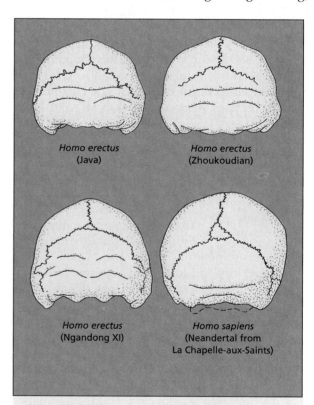

Homo erectus
(Java)

Homo erectus
(Zhoukoudian)

Homo erectus
(Ngandong XI)

Homo sapiens
(Neandertal from
La Chapelle-aux-Saints)

Figure 8.1   Rear Views of Three Skulls of *H. erectus* and One of "Archaic" *Homo sapiens* (a Neandertal).   Note the more angular shape of the *H. erectus* skulls, with the maximum breadth low down, near the base.
SOURCE: From *Physical Anthropology and Archaeology*, 5th edition, by C. J. Jolly and R. White (New York: McGraw-Hill, 1995), p. 271.

which was *Homo*'s only adaptive strategy until plant cultivation and animal domestication emerged some 10,000 to 12,000 years ago. Archaeologists have found and studied several sites of *H. erectus* activity, including cooperative hunting. At one of these sites, Terra Amata, overlooking Nice in southern France, archaeologists have documented activities of late *H. erectus* (or more probably, early archaic *H. sapiens*) populations from around 300,000 years ago. Small bands of hunters and gatherers consisting of 15 to 25 people made regular visits during the late spring and early summer to Terra Amata, a sandy cove on the coast of the Mediterranean.

Archaeologists determined the season of occupation by examining fossilized human excrement, which contained pollen from flowers that are known to bloom in late spring. There is evidence for 21 such visits. Four groups camped on a sand bar, 6 on the beach, and 11 on a sand dune. Archaeologists surmise that the 11 dune sites represent that number of annual visits by the same band (deLumley 1969/1976).

From a camp atop the dune, these people looked down on a river valley where animals were abundant. Bones found at Terra Amata show that their diet included red deer, young elephants, wild boars, wild mountain goats, an extinct variety of rhinoceros, and wild oxen. The Terra Amata people also hunted turtles and birds and collected oysters and mussels. Fish bones also were found at the site.

The arrangement of postholes shows that these people used saplings to support temporary huts. There were hearths—sunken pits and piled stone fireplaces—within the shelters. Stone chips inside the borders of the huts show that tools were made from locally available rocks and beach pebbles. Thus, at Terra Amata, hundreds of thousands of years ago, people were already pursuing an essentially human life style, one that survived in certain coastal regions into the 20th century.

The hearths at Terra Amata and other sites confirm that fire was part of the human adaptive kit by this time. Fire provided protection against cave bears and saber-toothed tigers. It permitted *H. erectus* to occupy cave sites, including Zhoukoudian, near Beijing in China, which has yielded the remains of more than 40 specimens of *H. erectus*. Fire widened the range of climates open to human colonization. Its warmth enabled people to survive winter cold in temperate regions. Human

control over fire offered other advantages, such as cooking, which breaks down vegetable fibers and tenderizes meat. Cooking kills parasites and makes meat more digestible, thus reducing strain on the chewing apparatus.

Could language (fireside chats, perhaps) have been an additional advantage available to *H. erectus*? Archaeological evidence confirms the cooperative hunting of large animals and the manufacture of complicated tools. These activities might have been too complex to have gone on without some kind of language. Speech would have aided coordination, cooperation, and the learning of traditions, including tool making. Words, of course, aren't preserved until the advent of writing. However, given the potential for language-based communication—which even chimps and gorillas share with *H. sapiens*—and given brain size within the low *H. sapiens* range, it seems plausible to assume that *H. erectus* had rudimentary speech. For contrary views, see Binford (1981), Fisher (1988b), and Wade (2002).

THE EVOLUTION AND EXPANSION OF *HOMO ERECTUS*

The archaeological record of *H. erectus* activities can be combined with the fossil evidence to provide us with a more complete picture of our Lower Paleolithic ancestors. We now consider some of the fossil data, whose geographic distribution is shown in Figure 8.2. Early *H. erectus* remains, found by Richard Leakey's team at East and West Turkana, Kenya, and dated to around 1.6 m.y.a., including the Nariokotome boy, have been discussed previously.

One fairly complete skull, one large mandible, and two partial skulls—one of a young adult male (780 cm^3) and one of an adolescent female (650 cm^3)—have been found recently at the Dmanisi site in the former Soviet Republic of Georgia (see the news story at the start of this chapter). They have been assigned a date of 1.7–1.75 m.y.a. There are notable similarities between the two partial skulls and that of the Narikotome boy (1.6 m.y.a.) found near Kenya's Lake Turkana. Tools of comparable age associated with the Kenyan and Georgian fossils also are similar. Some paleoanthropologists assign the Nariokotome and Dmanisi finds to a new species, *Homo ergaster*, intermediate between *H. habilis* and *H. erectus*. The most recent

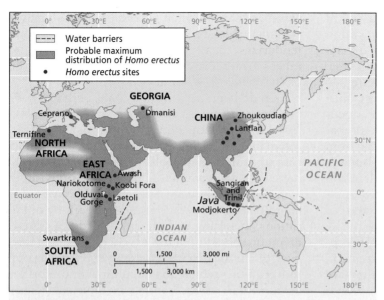

Figure 8.2   The Sites of Discovery of *Homo erectus* and Its Probable Maximum Distribution.

SOURCE: From *Physical Anthropology and Archaeology*, 5th edition, by C. J. Jolly and R. White (New York: McGraw-Hill, 1995), p. 268.

Later *H. erectus* remains come from Upper Bed II at Olduvai, Tanzania. Those fossils, about a million years old, were associated with Acheulian tools. Besides Kenya and Tanzania, African *H. erectus* fossils have been found in Ethiopia, Eritrea, and South Africa. The time span of *H. erectus* in East Africa was long. *H. erectus* fossils also have been found in Bed IV at Olduvai, dating to 500,000 B.P.

In 1891, the Indonesian island of Java yielded the first *H. erectus* fossil find, popularly known as "Java man." Eugene Dubois, a Dutch army surgeon, had gone to Java to discover a transitional form between apes and humans. Of course, we now know that the transition to hominid had taken place much earlier than the *H. erectus* period and occurred in Africa. However, Dubois's good luck did lead him to the most ancient human fossils discovered at that time. Excavating near the village of Trinil, Dubois found parts of a *H. erectus* skull and a thigh bone. During the 1930s and 1940s, excavations in Java uncovered additional remains.

The Indonesian *H. erectus* fossils date back at least 700,000, and maybe more than a million, years. Fragments of a skull and a lower jaw found in northern China at Lantien may be about the same age.

(2001) skull find, with its large canines and small brain size, looks more like *H. habilis* than do the other fossils from Dmanisi. Others simply consider all these Dmanisi fossils early *H. erectus*. The Dmanisi finds suggest a rapid spread, by 1.7 m.y.a., of early *Homo* out of Africa and into Eurasia (Figure 8.3).

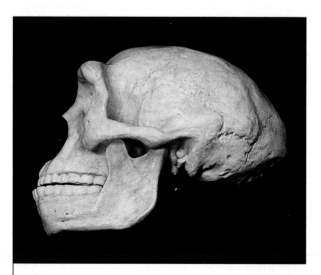

Meet *Homo erectus*. On the left is a reconstruction of one of the *H. erectus* skulls from Zhoukoudian, China. On the right, an attempt to render *H. erectus* in the flesh.

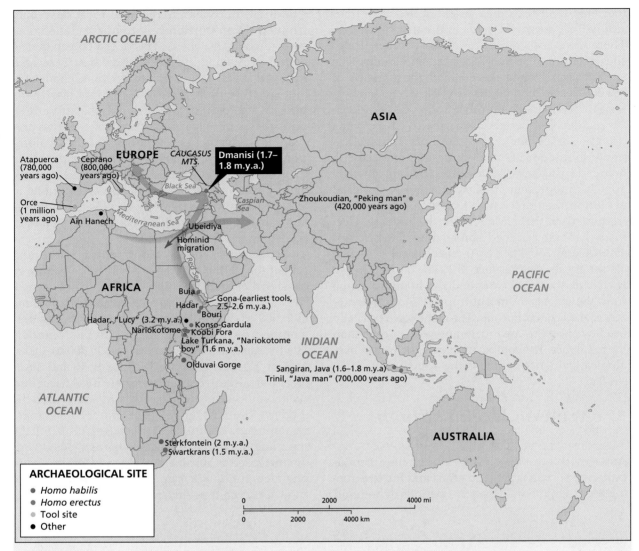

Figure 8.3　The Expansion of *H. erectus* out of Africa around 1.7 m.y.a.

Other *H. erectus* remains, of uncertain date, have been found in Algeria and Morocco in North Africa.

The largest group of *H. erectus* fossils was found in the Zhoukoudian cave in China. The Zhoukoudian ("Peking"—now Beijing—"man") site, excavated from the late 1920s to the late 1930s, was a major find for the human fossil record. Zhoukoudian yielded remains of tools, hearths, animal bones, and more than 40 hominids, including five skulls. The analysis of these remains led to the conclusion that the Java and Zhoukoudian fossils were examples of the same broad stage of human evolution. Today they are commonly classified together as *H. erectus*.

The Zhoukoudian individuals lived more recently than did the Javanese *H. erectus*, between 500,000 and 350,000 years ago, when the climate in China was colder and moister than it is today. The inference about the climate has been made on the basis of the animal remains found with the human fossils. The people at Zhoukoudian ate venison, and seed and plant remains suggest they were both gatherers and hunters.

What about Europe? A cranial fragment found at Ceprano, Italy, in 1994, has been assigned a date of 800,000 B.P. Other probable *H. erectus* remains have been found in Europe, but their dates are uncertain. All are later than the Ceprano skull, and they are usually classified as late *H. erectus*, or transitional between *H. erectus* and early *H. sapiens*. There have been recent fossil discoveries at two sites in northern Spain's Atapuerca mountains. The site of Gran Dolina has yielded the remains of 780,000-year-old hominids that Spanish researchers see as a possible common ancestor of *H. sapiens sapiens* and the Neandertals. At the nearby cave of Sima dos Huesos a team led by Juan Luis Arsuaga has found thousands of fossils representing at least 33 hominids of all ages. Almost 300,000 years old, they appear to represent an early stage of Neandertal evolution (Lemonick and Dorfman 1999). A jaw from a gravel pit at Mauer near Heidelberg, Germany, has been assigned a broad time span between 450,000 and 250,000 B.P. Archaeological evidence also suggests the presence of *H. erectus* in Europe. *H. erectus* therefore extended the hominid range from the tropics to the subtropical and temperate zones of Asia and Europe. The stone tools typically used by *H. erectus* are much more widespread than the fossils are. The combination of fossil and archaeological evidence confirms the adaptability of *H. erectus*.

Archaic *Homo sapiens*

Africa, which was center stage during the australopithecine period, is joined by Asia and Europe during the *H. erectus* and *H. sapiens* periods of hominid evolution. European fossils and tools have contributed disproportionately to our knowledge of early (archaic) *H. sapiens*. This doesn't mean that *H. sapiens* evolved in Europe, that most early *H. sapiens* lived in Europe, or that comparable changes in biology and culture were not occurring elsewhere. Indeed, the fossil evidence suggests that parallel physical changes and cultural advances were proceeding in Asia and especially in Africa (Wolpoff 1999). There were probably many more people in the tropics than in Europe during the ice ages. We merely *know more* about recent human evolution in Europe because archaeology and fossil hunting—not human evolution—have been going on longer there than in Africa and Asia.

Recent discoveries, along with reinterpretation of the dating and the anatomical relevance of some earlier finds, are filling in the gap between *H. erectus* and archaic *H. sapiens*. **Archaic H. sapiens** (300,000 to 30,000 B.P.) encompasses the earliest members of our species, along with the **Neandertals** (*H. sapiens neanderthalensis*—130,000 to 30,000 B.P.) of Europe and the Middle East and their Neandertal-like contemporaries in Africa and Asia. Brain size in archaic *H. sapiens* was within the modern human range. (The modern average, remember, is about 1,350 cm^3.) (See Table 8.1.) A rounding out of the brain case was associated with the increased brain size. As Jolly and White (1995) put it, evolution was pumping more brain into the *H. sapiens* cranium—like filling a football with air.

Table 8.1 **Summary of Data on *Homo* Fossil Groups.** Fossil representatives of the genus *Homo*, compared with modern humans (*Homo sapiens sapiens*) and chimps (*Pan troglodytes*).

Species	Dates	Known Distribution	Important Sites	Brain Size (in cm^3)
Homo sapiens sapiens	100,000 B.P. to present	Worldwide	Beijing, New York, Paris, Nairobi	1350
Homo sapiens neanderthalensis	130,000 to 30,000 B.P.	Europe, southwestern Asia	La Chapelle-aux-Saints	1430
Archaic *Homo sapiens*	300,000 to 30,000 B.P.	Africa, Europe, Asia	Kabwe, Arago, Dali, Mount Carmel caves	1135
Homo erectus	1.7 m.y.a. to 300,000 B.P.	Africa, Asia, Europe	East + West Turkana, Olduvai, Zhoukoudian, Java, Ceprano	900
Pan troglodytes	Modern	Central Africa	Gombe, Mahale	390

Archaic *H. sapiens* lived during the last part of the *Middle Pleistocene*—during the *Mindel* (second) glacial, the interglacial that followed it, and the following *Riss* (third) glacial. The distribution of the fossils and tools of archaic *H. sapiens*, which have been found in Europe, Africa, and Asia, shows that *Homo*'s tolerance of environmental diversity had increased. For example, the Neandertals and their immediate ancestors managed to survive extreme cold in Europe. Archaic *H. sapiens* occupied the Arago cave in southeastern France at a time when Europe was bitterly cold. The only Riss glacial site with facial material, Arago, was excavated in 1971. It produced a partially intact skull, two jaw bones, and teeth from a dozen individuals. With an apparent date of about 200,000 B.P., the Arago fossils have mixed features that seem transitional between *H. erectus* and the Neandertals.

The Neandertals

See the Internet Exercises at your OLC

/kottak

Neandertals were first discovered in Western Europe. The first one was found in 1856 in a German valley called Neander Valley—*tal* is the German word for valley. Scientists had trouble interpreting the discovery. It was clearly human and similar to modern Europeans in many ways, yet different enough to be considered strange and abnormal. This was, after all, 35 years before Dubois discovered the first *Homo erectus* fossils in Java and almost 70 years before the first australopithecine was found in South Africa. Darwin's *On the Origin of Species*, published in 1859, had not yet appeared to offer a theory of evolution through natural selection. There was no framework for understanding human evolution. Over time, the fossil record filled in, along with evolutionary theory. Subsequent discoveries of Neandertals in Europe and the Middle East and of archaic human fossils with comparable features in Africa and Asia confirmed this stage of human evolution as geographically widespread. With the discovery of earlier and later hominid fossils, the similarities and differences between Neandertals and other members of *Homo sapiens* have become clearer.

Fossils that are not Neandertals but that have similar features (such as large faces and brow ridges) have been found in Africa and Asia. The Kabwe skull from Zambia (130,000 B.P.) is an archaic *H. sapiens* with a Neandertal-like brow ridge. Archaic Chinese fossils with Neandertal-like features have been found at Maba and Dali. Neandertals have been found in Central Europe and the Middle East. For example, Neandertal fossils found at the Shanidar cave in northern Iraq date to around 60,000 B.P., as does a Neandertal skeleton found at Israel's Kebara cave (Shreeve 1992). At the Israeli site of Tabun on Mount Carmel, a Neandertal female skeleton was excavated in 1932. She was a contemporary of the Shanidar Neandertals, and her brow ridges, face, and teeth show typical Neandertal robustness.

COLD-ADAPTED NEANDERTALS

By 75,000 B.P., after an interglacial interlude, Western Europe's hominids (Neandertals, by then) again faced extreme cold as the Würm glacial began. To deal with this environment, they wore clothes, made more elaborate tools, and hunted reindeer, mammoths, and woolly rhinos.

The Neandertals were stocky, with large trunks relative to limb length—a phenotype that minimizes surface area and thus conserves heat. Another adaptation to extreme cold was the Neandertal face, which has been likened to a *H. erectus* face that has been pulled forward by the nose. This extension increased the distance between outside air and the arteries that carry blood to the brain and was adaptive in a cold climate. The brain is sensitive to temperature changes and must be kept warm. The massive nasal cavities of Neandertal fossils suggest long, broad noses. This would expand the area for warming and moistening air.

Neandertal characteristics also include huge front teeth, broad faces, and large brow ridges, and ruggedness of the skeleton and musculature. What activities were associated with these anatomical traits? Neandertal teeth probably did many jobs later done by tools (Brace 1995; Rak 1986). The front teeth show heavy wear, suggesting that they were used for varied purposes, including chewing animal hides to make soft winter clothing out of them. The massive Neandertal face showed the stresses of constantly using the front teeth for holding and pulling.

Comparison of early and later Neandertals shows a trend toward reduction of their robust features. Neandertal technology, a Middle Pale-olithic tradition called **Mousterian**, improved considerably during the Würm glacial. Tools assumed many burdens formerly placed on the anatomy. For example, tools took over jobs once done by the front teeth. Through a still imperfectly understood mechanism, facial muscles and supporting structures developed less. Smaller front teeth—perhaps because of dental crowding—were favored. The projecting face reduced, as did the brow ridge, which had provided buttressing against the forces generated when the large front teeth were used for environmental manipulation.

THE NEANDERTALS AND MODERN PEOPLE

Scientists disagree about whether the Neandertals were ancestral to modern Western Europeans. The current prevailing view, denying this ancestry, proposes that *H. erectus* split into separate groups, one ancestral to the Neandertals and the other ancestral to *H. sapiens sapiens*—**anatomically modern humans (AMHs)** who appeared in Western Europe after 40,000 B.P. (Early AMHs in Western Europe often are referred to as *Cro-Magnon*, after the earliest fossil find of an anatomically modern human, in France's Les Eyzies region, Dordogne Valley, in 1868.) In different versions of this view, modern humans evolved in Africa, Asia, Central Europe, or the Middle East. They eventually colonized Western Europe, displacing the Neandertals there. In this interpretation, the Neandertals who lived in Western Europe during the Ice Age were too anatomically specialized to evolve into modern Europeans.

What were the contrasts between the Neandertals and AMHs? Like *H. erectus* before them, the Neandertals had heavy brow ridges and slanting foreheads. However, average Neandertal cranial capacity (more than 1,400 cm^3) exceeded the modern average. Neandertal jaws were large, providing support for huge front teeth, and their faces were massive. The bones and skull were generally more rugged and had greater sexual dimorphism—particularly in the face and skull—than do those of AMHs. In some Western European fossils, these contrasts between Neandertals and AMHs are accentuated—giving a stereotyped, or *classic Neandertal*, appearance.

Some scientists believe only the classic Neandertals were too different to be ancestors of AMHs. They contend that outside Western Europe, the anatomical differences were fewer and the people who lived there were not really Neandertals but merely Neandertal-like in some respects. Actually, the European Neandertals were variable, and many lacked the "classic" constellation of features.

Doubt about the Neandertal ancestry of Western Europeans is partly due to the history of fossil discoveries. As mentioned, the first Neandertal remains were found in 1856; and the first *H. erectus* ("Java man"), in 1891. The inclusion of "Java man" in the human evolutionary tree was debated for decades. Nor was the first australopithecine skull, uncovered in 1924, immediately accepted as a hominid. Without these earlier hominids, which were much more different from AMHs than the Neandertals were, the differences between Neandertals and moderns stood out and were emphasized.

The interpretation of one fossil contributed most to the scientific rejection of Neandertal ancestry (and to the popular stereotype of the slouching caveman). This was the complete human skeleton

In a wilderness survival school in the mountains of central Spain, Mikel Aguirre flakes a flint knife. Manufactured in four minutes, the razor-sharp blade will be used to butcher a goat.

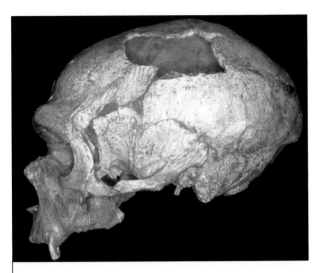

The skull of the classic Neandertal found in 1908 at La Chapelle-aux-Saints. This was the first Neandertal to be discovered with the whole skull, including the face, preserved. Later finds showed that La Chapelle wasn't a typical Neandertal but an extreme form. What was atypical about this fossil?

What images would you have if you heard someone described as "a Neandertal"? The European Neandertals were a variable population, but they have been stereotyped as subhuman brutes. The Neandertal Museum in Erkrath, Germany, near the original fossil discovery site, offers different representations of Neandertals, from a beast to "just a guy in a suit."

discovered in 1908 at La Chapelle-aux-Saints in southwestern France, in a layer containing the characteristic Mousterian tools made by Neandertals. This was the first Neandertal to be discovered with the whole skull, including the face, preserved.

The skeleton was given for study to the French paleontologist Marcellin Boule. His analysis of the fossil helped create the stereotype of Neandertals as brutes who had trouble walking upright. Boule argued that La Chapelle's brain, although larger than the modern average, was inferior to modern brains. Further, he suggested that the Neandertal head was slung forward like an ape's. To round out the primitive image, Boule proclaimed that the Neandertals were incapable of straightening their legs for fully erect locomotion. However, later fossil finds show that the La Chapelle fossil wasn't a typical Neandertal but an extreme one. Also, this much-publicized "classic" Neandertal turned out to be an aging man whose skeleton had been distorted by osteoarthritis. Hominids, after all, have been erect bipeds for millions of years. European Neandertals were a variable population. Other Neandertal finds lack La Chapelle's combination of extreme features and are more acceptable ancestors for AMHs.

Advocates of the Neandertal ancestry of modern Europeans cite certain fossils to support their view. For example, the Central European site of Mladeč (31,000 to 33,000 B.P.) has yielded remains of several hominids that combine Neandertal robustness with modern features. Wolpoff (1999) also notes modern features in the late Neandertals found at l'Hortus in France and Vindija in Croatia. A recently reported (1999) find of a four-year-old boy in Portugal, dated to 24,000 B.P., also shows mixed Neandertal and modern features.

Fossils from Israel's Mount Carmel site of Skhūl also combine archaic and modern features. But most analyses stress the "modernness" of the Skhūl fossils, which date to 100,000 B.P. Another group of modern-looking and similarly dated (92,000 B.P.) skulls comes from the Israeli site of Qafzeh. The Skhūl and Qafzeh fossils would seem to cast serious doubt on the Neandertal ancestry of AMHs in Europe and the Middle East. The skulls from Skhūl (Figure 8.4) and Qafzeh have a modern, rather than a Neandertal, shape and are classified as AMHs. Their brain cases are higher, shorter, and rounder than Neandertal skulls. There

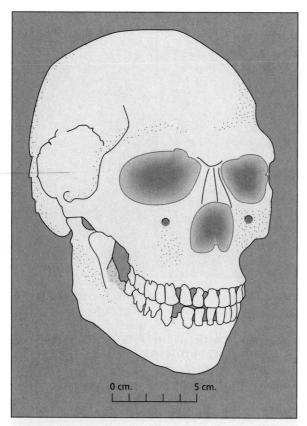

Figure 8.4 Skhūl V.

This anatomically modern human with some archaic features was recently redated to 100,000 B.P. This is one of several fossils found at Skhūl, Israel. Formerly dated to 32,000 B.P., this fossil group once seemed transitional between Neandertals and *H. sapiens sapiens*.

is a more filled-out forehead region, which rises more vertically above the brows. A marked chin is another modern feature. Still, these early AMHs do retain distinct brow ridges, though reduced from their archaic *H. sapiens* ancestor.

Dated to 100,000 and 92,000 B.P., the Skhūl and Qafzeh findings suggest that archaic *H. sapiens* was evolving directly into AMHs in the Middle East more than 50,000 years before the demise of the Western European Neandertals. Neandertals and AMHs, therefore, overlapped in time rather than being ancestor and descendant. AMHs even may have inhabited the Middle East before the Neandertals did. Ofer Bar-Yosef (1987) suggests that during the last (Würm) glacial period, which began around 75,000 B.P., Western European Nean-

dertals spread east and south (and into the Middle East) as part of a general southward expansion of cold-adapted fauna. AMHs, in turn, followed warmer-climate fauna south into Africa, returning to the Middle East once the Würm ended.

Most current interpretations of the fossil evidence and dating favor the replacement hypothesis, which denies the Neandertal ancestry of AMHs in Western Europe and the Middle East. AMHs seem likely to have evolved from an archaic *H. sapiens* African ancestor. In Africa, as in the Middle East and Asia, the archaic *H. sapiens* fossils generally had flatter, less projecting faces than the Neandertals did. Eventually, AMHs spread to other areas, including Western Europe, where they replaced, or interbred with, the Neandertals, whose robust traits eventually disappeared (Figure 8.5).

About Eve In 1987 a group of molecular geneticists at the University of California at Berkeley offered support for the idea that *H. sapiens sapiens* (anatomically modern humans or AMHs) arose fairly recently in Africa, then spread out and colonized the world. Rebecca Cann, Mark Stoneking, and Allan C. Wilson (1987) analyzed genetic markers in placentas donated by 147 women whose ancestors came from Africa, Europe, the Middle East, Asia, New Guinea, and Australia.

The researchers focused on mitochondrial DNA (mtDNA). This genetic material is located in the cytoplasm (the outer part—not the nucleus) of cells. Ordinary DNA, which makes up the genes that determine most physical traits, is found in the nucleus and comes from both parents. But only the mother contributes mitochondrial DNA (cloned from her own mtDNA) to the fertilized egg. The father plays no part in mtDNA transmission, just as the mother has nothing to do with the transmission of the Y chromosome, which comes from the father and determines the sex of the child. Because mtDNA is cloned, its genetic pattern is usually an exact replica of the mother's, except when mutations occur.

To establish a "genetic clock," the Berkeley researchers measured the variation in mtDNA in their 147 tissue samples. They cut each sample into segments to compare with the others. By estimating the number of mutations that had taken place in each sample since its common origin with the 146 others, the researchers drew an evolutionary tree with the help of a computer.

That tree started in Africa and then branched in two. One group remained in Africa, while the other one split off, carrying its mtDNA to the rest of the world. The variation in mtDNA was greatest among Africans. This suggests that they have been evolving the longest. In fact, some of the earliest dated AMH fossils have been found on the African continent. AMH fossils and associated tools that may date back 100,000 years have been found at two South African cave sites, as well as at Qafzeh and Skhūl, Israel, as described previously.

The Berkeley researchers concluded that everyone alive today has mtDNA that descends from a woman (dubbed "Eve") who lived in sub-Saharan Africa around 200,000 years ago. Eve was not the only woman alive then; she was just the only one whose descendants have included a daughter in each generation through the present. Because mtDNA passes exclusively through females, mtDNA lines disappear whenever a woman has no children or has only sons. The details of the Eve theory suggest that her descendants left Africa no more than 135,000 years ago. They eventually displaced the Neandertals in Western Europe and went on to colonize the rest of the world.

Recent DNA Evidence Additional DNA comparisons have been used to support the view that the Neandertals and AMHs were distinct groups, rather than ancestor and descendant. In 1997, ancient DNA was extracted from one of the Neandertal bones originally found in Germany's Neander Valley in 1856. This DNA, from an upper arm bone (humerus), has been compared with the DNA of modern humans. The kinds of matches we would expect in closely related humans did not occur. Thus, there were 27 differences between the Neandertal DNA and a reference sample of modern DNA. By contrast, samples of DNA from modern populations worldwide show only five to eight differences with the reference sample.

See the Internet Exercises at your OLC

mhhe
●com
/kottak

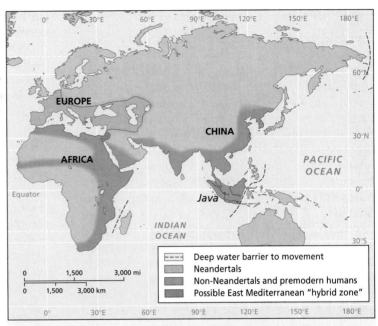

Figure 8.5 **The Known Distribution of Human Populations Approximately 130,000 to 28,000 B.P.** According to some scholars, Neandertals and moderns may have mixed in the East Mediterranean hybrid zone. In your opinion, would that have been possible?

SOURCE: From *Physical Anthropology and Archaeology*, 5th edition, by C. J. Jolly and R. White (New York: McGraw-Hill, 1995), p. 277.

This was the first time that DNA of a premodern human had been recovered. The original analysis was done by Svante Pääbo of the University of Munich. The findings were then duplicated by Mark Stoneking and Anne Stone at Pennsylvania State University. The researchers again focused on mitochondrial DNA. Using a "genetic clock" again, these scientists interpreted their results to mean that Neandertals and moderns separated over 550,000 years ago.

We know that the Neandertals coexisted with modern humans in the Middle East for thousands of years. At certain Israeli sites, modern humans date back 100,000 years. Middle Eastern Neandertals date back 40,000 to 60,000 years. In Western Europe, Neandertals survived perhaps through 28,000 years ago. To what extent did Neandertals and AMHs interact? Did they trade or interbreed? Were the Neandertals outcompeted by modern humans or killed off by them? Were they absorbed into the AMH population and genetically swamped (Rose 1997)?

MULTIREGIONAL EVOLUTION

There are two competing theories about the origin of anatomically modern humans. One is the **Eve theory** (based on the molecular study discussed previously). The other is **multiregional evolution**. According to the first theory, a small group of modern people arose recently in one place (Africa), then spread out and occupied the rest of the world. Somehow they replaced the native, and more archaic, populations of all other regions. The multiregional model (Wolpoff 1999; Wolpoff and Caspari 1997) proposes that the evolution was more inclusive. Ever since *H. erectus* spread beyond Africa, human bands have always maintained relations with their neighbors, including interbreeding. Linked by gene flow, humans in every region could and would share any beneficial mutation that arose in any one place. If a genetic change conferred a substantial selective advantage, it would spread rapidly from one group to all the others—across the entire human range. In this way human groups in Africa, Asia, and Europe would have come to share the features and behaviors of modern humans.

Advocates of multiregional evolution believe the fossil evidence contradicts the theory of an Eve who lived as recently as 200,000 B.P. Fossils show that certain physical features have persisted in particular regions for hundreds of thousands of years. For example, there are striking similarities between fossils dating back 750,000 to 500,000 years in Australasia (Indonesia and Australia), China, and Europe and the people who live in each of those regions today. One example is the facial similarity between modern Chinese people and the "vertical flat face" (Fenlason 1990) of *H. erectus* fossils found near Beijing. Another example is the "protruding face with large teeth and heavy brows," which is characteristic of both Indonesian *H. erectus* fossils and modern Native Australians. A third example is the prevalence among both ancient and modern Europeans of "angular faces with large projecting noses."

These unique regional features appeared (in *H. erectus*) long before the proposed migration of Eve's descendants. These traits probably arose through the founder effect (random genetic drift). By chance, the ancient founders of each regional population happened to have flat, protruding, or angular faces. After the founders settled each region, some of their unique physical features became common among their descendants.

If Eve's descendants arrived later than these fossils lived, and wiped out the previous inhabitants of China, Australasia, and Europe, these specific physical similarities between the fossils and the modern people of each region wouldn't exist. Rather than the Eve hypothesis, Milford Wolpoff proposes a model of multiregional evolution, in which *H. erectus* evolved into modern *H. sapiens* in each region (Africa, Europe, northern Asia, and Australasia). As the regional populations evolved, gene flow always connected them, so that beneficial mutations would spread rapidly from one group to all the others since they always belonged to the same species. Wolpoff agrees that a mitochondrial Eve might have existed, but much earlier than the Berkeley researchers suggest. Many anthropologists doubt that Eve could have lived as recently as 200,000 B.P. However, most anthropologists would have no trouble accepting a *H. erectus* Eve. Assuming the mtDNA mutation rate was much slower than the Berkeley researchers estimated, our common African mother could have been a member of one of the first hominid groups to migrate out of Africa more than 1.7 million years ago.

Advances in Technology

Early *H. sapiens sapiens* (AMHs) made tools in a variety of traditions, collectively known as **Upper Paleolithic** because of the tools' location in the upper, or more recent, layers of sedimentary deposits. Some cave deposits have Mousterian tools (made by Neandertals) at lower levels and increasing numbers of Upper Paleolithic tools at higher levels.

Although the Neandertals are remembered more for their physiques than for their manufacturing abilities, their tool kits were sophisticated. Mousterian technology included at least 14 categories of tools designed for different jobs. The Neandertals elaborated on a revolutionary technique of flake-tool manufacture invented in southern Africa around 200,000 years ago, which spread widely throughout the Old World. Uniform flakes were chipped off a specially prepared core of rock. Additional work on the flakes produced such special-purpose tools as those shown in Figure 8.6.

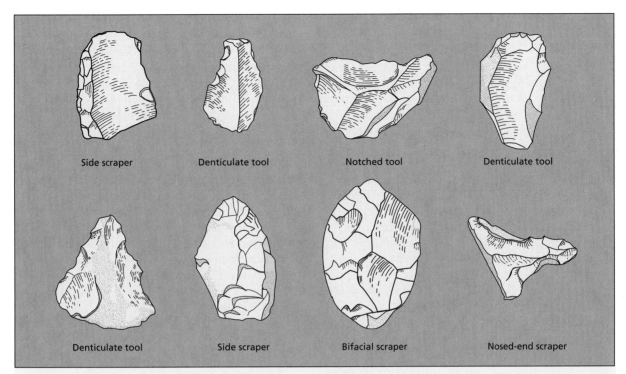

Figure 8.6   Middle Paleolithic Tools of the Mousterian Tool-Making Tradition.
The manufacture of diverse tool types for special purposes confirms Neandertal sophistication.

Scrapers were used to prepare animal hides for clothing. And special tools also were designed for sawing, gouging, and piercing (Binford and Binford 1979).

The Upper Paleolithic traditions of early *H. sapiens sapiens* all emphasized **blade tools**. Blades were hammered off a prepared core, as in Mousterian technology, but a blade is longer than a flake—its length is more than twice its width. Blades were chipped off cores four to six inches high by hitting a punch made of bone or antler with a hammerstone (Figure 8.7). Blades were then modified to produce a variety of special-purpose implements. Some were composite tools that were made by joining reworked blades to other materials.

The blade-core method was faster than the Mousterian and produced 15 times as much cutting edge from the same amount of material. More efficient tool production might have been especially valued by people whose economy depended on cooperative hunting of mammoths, woolly rhinoceroses, bison, wild horses, bears, wild cattle, wild boars, and—principally—reindeer. It has been estimated that approximately 90 percent of

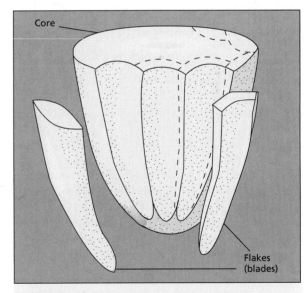

Figure 8.7   Upper Paleolithic Blade-Tool Making.   Blades are flakes that are detached from a specially prepared core. A punch (usually a piece of bone or antler) and a hammerstone (not shown here) were used to knock the blade off the core.

the meat eaten by Western Europeans between 25,000 and 15,000 B.P. came from reindeer.

Trends observable throughout the entire archaeological record also mark the changeover from the Mousterian to the Upper Paleolithic. First, the number of distinct tool types increased. This trend reflected functional specialization—the manufacture of special tools for particular jobs. A second trend was increasing standardization in tool manufacture. The form and inventory of tools reflect several factors: the jobs tools are intended to perform, the physical properties of the raw materials from which they are made, and distinctive cultural traditions about how to make tools. Furthermore, accidental or random factors also influenced tool forms and the proportions of particular tool types (Isaac 1972). However, Mousterian and Upper Paleolithic tools were more standardized than those of *H. erectus* were.

Other trends include growth in *Homo*'s total population and geographic range and increasing local cultural diversity as people specialized in particular economic activities. Illustrating increasing economic diversity are the varied special-purpose tools made by Upper Paleolithic populations. Scrapers were used to hollow out wood and bone, scrape animal hides, and remove bark from trees. Burins, the first chisels, were used to make slots in bone and wood and to engrave designs on bone. Awls, which were drills with sharp points, were used to make holes in wood, bone, shell, and skin.

Upper Paleolithic bone tools have survived: knives, pins, needles with eyes, and fishhooks. The needles suggest that clothes sewn with thread—made from the sinews of animals—were being worn. Fishhooks and harpoons confirm an increased emphasis on fishing.

Different tool types may represent culturally distinct populations that made their tools differently because of different ancestral traditions. Archaeological sites also may represent different activities carried out at different times of the year by a single population. Some sites, for example, are obviously butchering stations, where prehistoric people hunted, made their kills, and carved them up. Others are residential sites, where a wider range of activities was carried out. The major fossils and hominid types found in the Old World through the Upper Paleolithic are summarized in Figure 8.8.

Interpret the World
Atlas Map 8

With increasing technological differentiation, specialization, and efficiency, humans have become increasingly adaptable. Through heavy reliance on cultural means of adaptation, *Homo* has become (in numbers and range) the most successful primate by far. The hominid range expanded significantly in Upper Paleolithic times with the colonization of two new continents—North America and South America—a story told in Chapter 10. (Australia was colonized by at least 50,000 B.P.) Look at Map 8, "Origins and Distribution of *Homo sapiens sapiens*," in your atlas. The map shows water, land, and glacial ice cover and indicates the major finds of *H. sapiens sapiens* (AMHs), with dates of sites and fossils and approximate dates of migrations. On Map 8 can you locate three major migrations and their dates?

Glacial Retreat

Consider now one regional example, Western Europe, of the consequences of glacial retreat. The Würm glacial ended in Europe between 17,000 and 12,000 years ago, with the melting of the ice sheet in northern Europe (Scotland, Scandinavia, northern Germany, and Russia). As the ice retreated, the tundra and steppe vegetation grazed by reindeer and other large herbivores gradually moved north. Some people moved north, too, following their prey.

Shrubs, forests, and more solitary animals appeared in southwestern Europe. With most of the big-game animals gone, Western Europeans were forced to use a greater variety of foods. To replace specialized economies based on big game, more generalized adaptations developed during the 5,000 years of glacial retreat.

As water flowed from melting glacial ice, sea levels all over the world started rising. Today, off most coasts, there is a shallow-water zone called the *continental shelf*, over which the sea gradually deepens until the abrupt fall to deep water, which is known as the *continental slope*. During the ice ages, so much water was frozen in glaciers that most continental shelves were exposed. Dry land extended right up to the slope's edge. The waters right off-

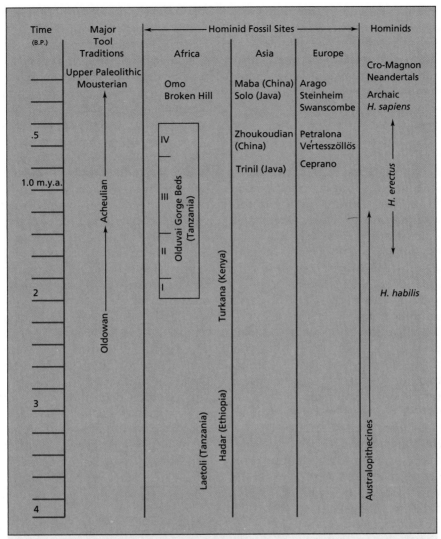

Figure 8.8 *Chronology of Evolution in Human Biology and Tool Making over the Past Four Million Years.*
See the text for particular fossils found at the different sites.

shore were deep, cold, and dark. Few species of marine life could thrive in this environment.

How did people adapt to the postglacial environment? As seas rose, conditions more encouraging to marine life developed in the shallower, warmer offshore waters. The quantity and variety of edible species increased tremendously in waters over the shelf. Furthermore, because rivers now flowed more gently into the oceans, fish such as salmon could ascend rivers to spawn. Flocks of birds that nested in seaside marshes migrated across Europe during the winter. Even inland

Europeans could take advantage of new resources, such as migratory birds and springtime fish runs, which filled the rivers of southwestern France.

Although hunting remained important, southwestern European economies became less specialized. A wider range, or broader spectrum, of plant and animal life was being hunted, gathered, collected, caught, and fished. This was the beginning of what anthropologist Kent Flannery (1969) has called the *broad-spectrum revolution*. It was revolutionary because, in the Middle East, it led to food production—human control over the reproduction of plants and animals. In a mere 10,000 years—after more than a million years during which hominids had subsisted by foraging for natural resources—food production based on plant cultivation and animal domestication replaced hunting and gathering in most areas.

Cave Art

It isn't the tools or the skeletons of Upper Paleolithic people but their art that has made them most familiar to us. Most extraordinary are the cave paintings, the earliest of which dates back some 30,000 years. More than a hundred cave painting sites are known, mainly from a limited area of southwestern France and adjacent northeastern Spain. The most famous site is Lascaux, found in 1940 in southwestern France by a dog and his young human companions.

The paintings adorn limestone walls of true caves located deep in the earth. Over time, the paintings have been absorbed by the limestone and thus preserved. Prehistoric big-game hunters painted their prey: woolly mammoths, wild cattle and horses, deer, and reindeer. The largest animal image is 18 feet long (see "Interesting Issues").

Most interpretations associate cave painting with magic and ritual surrounding the hunt. For example, because animals are sometimes depicted with spears in their bodies, the paintings might have been attempts to ensure success in hunting. Artists might have believed that by capturing the animal's image in paint and predicting the kill, they could influence the hunt's outcome.

Another interpretation sees cave painting as a magical human attempt to control animal reproduction. Something analogous was done by Native Australian (Australian aboriginal) hunters and gatherers, who held annual *ceremonies of increase* to honor and to promote, magically, the fertility of the plants and animals that shared their homeland. Australians believed that ceremonies were necessary to perpetuate the species on which humans depended. Similarly, cave paintings might have been part of annual cere-

monies of increase. Some of the animals in the cave murals are pregnant, and some are copulating. Did Upper Paleolithic people believe they could influence the sexual behavior or reproduction of their prey by drawing them? Or did they perhaps think that animals would return each year to the place where their souls had been captured pictorially?

Paintings often occur in clusters. In some caves, as many as three paintings have been drawn over the original, yet next to these superimposed paintings stand blank walls never used for painting. It seems reasonable to speculate that an event in the outside world sometimes reinforced a painter's choice of a given spot. Perhaps there was an especially successful hunt soon after the painting had been done. Perhaps members of a social subdivision significant in Upper Paleolithic society customarily used a given area of wall for their drawings.

Cave paintings also might have been a kind of pictorial history. Perhaps Upper Paleolithic people, through their drawings, were reenacting the hunt after it took place, as hunters of the Kalahari Desert in southern Africa still do today. Designs and markings on animal bones may indicate that Upper Paleolithic people had developed a calendar based on the phases of the moon (Marshack 1972). If this is so, it seems possible that late Stone Age hunters, who were certainly as intelligent as

Landscape of the Dordogne region of southwestern France. In this town, Les Eyzies, you can stay at the Cro-Magnon Hotel. You can also visit nearby sites of cave painting. Note the limestone cliffs. What is the significance of this area for prehistory?

In the mountains of southern France, where human beings have habitually hunted, loved and produced art, explorers have discovered an underground cave full of Stone Age paintings, so beautifully made and well preserved that experts are calling it one of the archeological finds of the century.

The enormous underground cavern [see Figure 8.9], which was found on Dec. 18, 1994, in a gorge near the town of Vallon-Pont-d'Arc in the Ardèche region, is studded with more than 300 vivid images of animals and human hands that experts believe were made some 20,000 years ago.

In this great parade of beasts appear woolly-haired rhinos, bears, mammoths, oxen and other images from the end of the Paleolithic era, creatures large and small and variously drawn in yellow ochre, charcoal and hematite. The murals have surprised specialists because they also include a rare image of a red, slouching hyena and the era's first-ever recorded paintings of a panther and several owls. Specialists say this ancient art gallery surpasses in size that of the famous caves of Lascaux and Altamira, which are widely held to be Western Europe's finest collection of Stone Age art.

Archeologists said they were thrilled not only by the number and the quality of the images but also by the discovery that the great underground site, sealed by fallen debris, appears to have been left undisturbed for thousands of years. They see this as tantamount to finding a time capsule full of hidden treasures.

One remarkable find, they said, was the skull of a bear, placed on a large rock set in the middle of one gallery against a backdrop of bear paintings.

"Is this some kind of altar? Someone placed the skull there for a reason," said Jean Clottes, France's leading rock art specialist. Many other skulls and bones of cave-bears were found in the underground warren, along with bones, flint knives, footprints and remains of fireplaces, all of which archeologists hope will provide important clues to the questions: What was the purpose of these paintings? What did their makers have in mind? . . .

The known part of the cavern consists of four great halls, up to 70 yards long and 40 yards wide, which are connected by smaller galleries roughly five by four yards, according [to] a report issued by the Ministry of Culture. The more than 300 paintings and engravings vary in size between 2 feet and 12 feet long. Some stand alone, while others are clustered in panels or painted with some cohesion, such as two rhinos head-to-head as if in a fight. As Mr. Clottes showed a videotape revealing a panel with four horses' heads close together, drawn in charcoal, he said: "These are one of the great marvels of prehistoric art." The artist or artists, he continued, made use of the natural colors of the rock

Figure 8-9   Location of Chauvet Cave.
Source: From *The New York Times*.

and of natural stone relief to give form and bulges to the animals.

Archeologists have long believed that the deep prehistoric caves were used not as habitats, because they were too dark, but for religious services or cults about which next to nothing is known. Some specialists believe that initiation rites were held in the caves and that the drawings of the humans' hands from the Paleolithic found here and elsewhere were a token of membership in a cult or community . . .

SOURCE: Marlise Simons, "Prehistoric Art Treasure Is Found in French Cave," *New York Times*, January 19, 1995, pp. A1, A5.

Aboriginal wall painting by the Tjapukal people of Kuranda, Queensland, Australia. Like Upper Paleolithic Europeans, Native Australians made both cave painting and petroglyphs, carvings on stone.

we are, would have been interested in recording important events in their lives.

It is worth noting that the *late* Upper Paleolithic, when many of the most spectacular multicolored cave paintings were done and Paleolithic artistic techniques were perfected, coincides with the period of glacial retreat. An intensification of cave painting for any of the reasons connected with hunting magic could have been caused by concern about decreases in herds as the open lands of southwestern Europe were being replaced by forests.

The Mesolithic

The broad-spectrum revolution in Europe includes the late Upper Paleolithic and the **Mesolithic**, which followed it. Again, because of the long history of European archaeology, our knowledge of the Mesolithic (particularly in southwestern Europe and the British Isles) is extensive. According to the traditional typology that distinguishes between Old, Middle, and New Stone Ages, the Middle Stone Age, the Mesolithic, had a characteristic tool type—the *microlith* (Greek for "small stone"). Of interest to us is what an abundant inventory of small and delicately shaped stone tools can tell us about the total economy and way of life of the people who made them.

By 12,000 B.P., there were no longer subarctic animals in southwestern Europe. By 10,000 B.P. the glaciers had retreated to such a point that the range of hunting, gathering, and fishing populations in Europe extended to the formerly glaciated British Isles and Scandinavia. The reindeer herds had gradually retreated to the far north, with some human groups following (and ultimately domesticating) them. Europe around 10,000 B.P. was forest rather than treeless steppe and tundra. Europeans were exploiting a wider variety of resources and gearing their lives to the seasonal appearance of particular plants and animals.

People still hunted, but their prey were solitary forest animals, such as the roe deer, the wild ox, and the wild pig, rather than herd species. This led to new hunting techniques: solitary stalking and trapping, similar to more recent practices of many American Indian groups. The coasts and lakes of Europe and the Middle East were fished intensively. Some important Mesolithic sites are Scandinavian shell mounds—the garbage dumps of prehistoric oyster collectors. Microliths were used as fishhooks and in harpoons. Dugout canoes were used for fishing and travel. The process of preserving meat and fish by smoking and salting grew increasingly important. (Meat preservation had been less of a problem in a subarctic environment since winter snow and ice, often on the ground nine months of the year, offered convenient refrigeration.) The bow and arrow became essential for hunting water fowl in swamps and marshes. Dogs were domesticated, as retrievers, by Mesolithic people (Champion and Gamble 1984). Woodworking was important in the forested environment of northern and Western Europe. Tools used by Mesolithic carpenters appear in the archaeological record: new kinds of axes, chisels, and gouges.

Big-game hunting and, thereafter, Mesolithic hunting and fishing were important in Europe, but

Beyond the *Classroom*
Paleolithic Butchering at Verberie

Background Information

STUDENT:	**Kelsey Foster**
SUPERVISING PROFESSOR:	**Dr. James G. Enloe**
SCHOOL:	**University of Iowa**
YEAR IN SCHOOL/MAJOR:	**Senior/Anthropology**
FUTURE PLANS:	**Marine Archaeology**
	Internship/Graduate School
PROJECT TITLE:	**Meat and Marrow: Paleolithic**
	Butchering at Verberie

How can the analysis of animal bones provide evidence for specific kinds of human activity? What kinds of animals were hunted at this Paleolithic site? What kind of eating behavior went on at the site?

The Paleolithic archaeological site of Verberie le Buisson Campin is located along the banks of the Oise River in Northern France. It was the site of repeated occupation by a small band of Paleolithic hunters to mass-kill reindeer, which make up over 98% of the faunal assemblage. Examinations of the faunal material indicate that the reindeer were killed during the fall of the year, which corresponds with the yearly migration of the reindeer herds. Dental analysis and postcranial measurements served to determine that the majority of the reindeer remains were from sub-adult males. This shows great selectivity on the part of the Paleolithic hunters for large, healthy prey.

My research focuses on furthering the existing knowledge of Verberie by attempting to determine the butchering pattern used by the Paleolithic hunters at the site. I examined the faunal remains from the entire upper occupation level (Level II1) for any indication of human modification of bone, which is indicated by the presence of stone tool cut marks and/or impact cones. Stone tool cut marks are produced during the filleting of meat from the bones and during the dismemberment of the carcass. The impact cones are the result of the cracking of bones in order to remove the marrow.

During my research I examined 1,133 specimens of reindeer bone fragments to investigate butchering practices at Verberie. Using Lewis Binford's Meat Utility Index and Marrow Utility Index numbers for the nutritive value of reindeer limb elements, I found that the elements with high marrow index values composed a greater percentage of the assemblage, while the elements with high meat index values were much less represented.

I then compared the numbers and degree of human modification between each element and found that the higher marrow utility elements showed a higher degree of exploitation for marrow cracking than did the lower marrow utility elements. This identified the systematic processing of marrow at Verberie. Conversely, the stone tool cut marks present on the assemblage were predominately the result of dismemberment and not the result of meat removal.

I finally compared the percentages of the elements with a similar ethnoarchaeologic study performed on the remains from a known marrow processing event at a Nunamuit (Alaskan Eskimos, or Inuit) residential site. The extreme similarity between these two assemblages solidified the claim of extensive marrow processing at Verberie.

When all this information is taken together, the butchering sequence at Verberie becomes clear. The butchering practice of Verberie consisted of primary dismemberment of the carcass into smaller units, with intentional snacking on the high marrow utility elements. The lack of filleting marks indicates that minimal, if any, meat exploitation occurred at the hunting camp. Therefore, if the high meat utility elements were not eaten at Verberie, they were transported to a larger residential camp for later consumption.

other foraging strategies were used by prehistoric humans in Africa and Asia. Among contemporary foragers in the tropics, gathering is the dietary mainstay (Lee 1968/1974). Although herds of big-game animals were more abundant in the tropics in prehistory than they are today, gathering has probably always been at least as important as hunting for tropical foragers (Draper 1975).

Generalized, broad-spectrum economies persisted about 5,000 years longer in Europe than in the Middle East. Whereas Middle Easterners had begun to cultivate plants and breed animals by 10,000 B.P., food production came to Western Europe only around 5000 B.P. (3000 B.C.) and to northern Europe 500 years later. In Chapter 10, we will shift our focus to the Middle East, where the origin of food production took place.

SUMMARY

1. Dental, facial, and cranial robustness was reduced as *H. habilis* evolved into *H. erectus*, who extended the hominid food quest to the hunting of large animals. *H. erectus*, with a much larger body, had smaller back teeth but larger front teeth and supporting structures, including a massive eyebrow ridge. The Lower Paleolithic Acheulian tradition provided *H. erectus* with better tools. *H. erectus*'s average cranial capacity doubled the australopithecine average. Tool complexity and archaeological evidence for cooperative hunting suggest a long period of enculturation and learning. *H. erectus* extended the hominid range beyond Africa to Asia and Europe.

2. The oldest *H. erectus* skulls yet found come from Kenya and Georgia (in Eurasia) and date back some 1.75–1.6 million years. At Olduvai Gorge, Tanzania, geological strata spanning more than a million years demonstrate a transition from Oldowan tools to the Archeulian implements of *H. erectus*. *H. erectus* persisted for more than a million years, evolving into archaic *H. sapiens* by the Middle Pleistocene epoch, some 300,000 years ago. Fire allowed *H. erectus* to expand into cooler areas, to cook, and to live in caves.

3. The classic Neandertals, who inhabited Western Europe during the early part of the Würm glacial, were among the first hominid fossils found. With no examples of *Australopithecus* or *H. erectus* yet discovered, the differences between them and modern humans were accentuated. Even today, anthropologists tend to exclude the classic Neandertals from the ancestry of Western Europeans. The ancestors of AMHs (anatomically modern humans) were other archaic *H. sapiens* groups, most probably those in Africa. AMH fos-

sil finds such as Skhūl (100,000 B.P.) and Qafzeh (92,000 B.P.) are cited to support the contention that the Neandertals (130,000 to 30,000 B.P.) and AMHs were contemporaries, rather than ancestor and descendant.

4. The classic Neandertals adapted physically and culturally to bitter cold. Their tool kits were much more complex than those of preceding humans. Their front teeth were among the largest to appear in human evolution. The Neandertals manufactured Mousterian flake tools. *H. sapiens sapiens* made Upper Paleolithic blade tools. The changeover from Neandertal to modern appears to have occurred in Western Europe by 28,000 B.P.

5. As glacial ice melted, foraging patterns were generalized, adding fish, fowl, and plant foods to the diminishing big-game supply. The beginning of a broad-spectrum economy in Western Europe coincided with an intensification of Upper Paleolithic cave art. On limestone cave walls, prehistoric hunters painted images of animals important in their lives. Explanations of cave paintings link them to hunting magic, ceremonies of increase, and initiation rites.

6. By 10,000 B.P., people were pursuing broad-spectrum economies in the British Isles and Scandinavia. Tool kits adapted to a forested environment included small, delicately shaped stone tools called microliths. The Mesolithic, or Middle Stone Age, had begun. The broad-spectrum revolution, based on a wide variety of dietary resources, began in the Middle East somewhat earlier than in Europe. As we will see in Chapter 10, it culminated in the first food-producing economies in the Middle East around 10,000 B.P.

KEY TERMS

See the flash cards

Acheulian Derived from the French village of St. Acheul, where these tools were first identified; Lower Paleolithic tool tradition associated with *H. erectus*.

anatomically modern humans (AMHs) Including the Cro-Magnons of Europe (31,000 B.P.) and the older fossils from Skhūl (100,000) and Qafzeh (92,000); continue through the present; also known as *H. sapiens sapiens*.

archaic *Homo sapiens* Early *H. sapiens*, consisting of the Neandertals of Europe and the Middle East, the Neandertal-like hominids of Africa and Asia, and the immediate ancestors of all these hominids; lived from about 300,000 to 30,000 B.P.

blade tool The basic Upper Paleolithic tool type, hammered off a prepared core.

Eve theory Theory that a small group of anatomically modern people arose recently, probably in Africa, from which they spread and replaced the native and more archaic populations of other inhabited areas.

Mesolithic Middle Stone Age, whose characteristic tool type was the microlith; broad-spectrum economy.

Mousterian Middle Paleolithic tool-making tradition associated with Neandertals.

multiregional evolution Theory that *H. erectus* gradually evolved into modern *H. sapiens* in all regions inhabited by humans (Africa, Europe, northern Asia, and Australasia). As the regional populations evolved, gene flow always connected them, and so they always belonged to the same species. This theory opposes replacement models such as the Eve theory.

Neandertals *H. sapiens neanderthalensis*, representing an archaic *H. sapiens* subspecies, lived in Europe and the Middle East between 130,000 and 30,000 B.P.

Paleolithic Old Stone Age (from Greek roots meaning "old" and "stone"); divided into Lower (early), Middle, and Upper (late).

punctuated equilibrium Model of evolution; long periods of equilibrium, during which species change little, are interrupted by sudden changes—evolutionary jumps.

Upper Paleolithic Blade-tool-making traditions associated with early *H. sapiens sapiens*; named from their location in upper, or more recent, layers of sedimentary deposits.

CRITICAL THINKING QUESTIONS

For more self testing, see the self quizzes

1. What were the main differences between the two earliest species of *Homo*? Was *Homo habilis* more like *Homo erectus*, or more like the australopithecines?

2. How do you evaluate the evidence for a punctuated equilibrium model of hominid evolution?

3. How do you evaluate the evidence for a gradualist model of hominid evolution?

4. What were the main trends in the evolution of technology during the Paleolithic? Do these trends continue today?

5. How does the geographic distribution of *H. erectus* differ from that of the australopithecines? What did culture have to do with this difference?

6. Was *Homo erectus* more like *Homo habilis* or more like *Homo sapiens sapiens*? What evidence do you offer for your opinion?

7. Do you think *H. erectus* had language? Why or why not? How about the Neandertals?

8. Do you think that *Homo sapiens sapiens* has Neandertal ancestry? Why? Can you think of ways in which the different theories about the origin of *H. sapiens sapiens* might be reconciled?

9. What cultural changes accompanied glacial retreat in Europe during the late Upper Paleolithic and the Mesolithic? Does anything happening today remind you of the effects of glacial retreat?

Atlas Questions

Look at Map 8, "Origins and Distribution of *Homo sapiens sapiens*,"

1. When and from where was Australia first settled?

2. When and from where was North America first settled? How many migrations are shown as figuring in the settlement of North America? How were these migrations related to the glacial ice cover? Did they all follow the same route?

3. What and when are the earliest *Homo sapiens sapiens* sites in Europe? How about Asia? How about Africa? Which continent has the oldest sites?

Suggested Additional Readings

Cunliffe, B., ed.
1998 *Prehistoric Europe: An Illustrated History*. New York: Oxford University Press. An Oxford illustrated history book.

Dibble, H. L., S. P. McPherron, and B. J. Roth
2000 *Virtual Dig: A Simulated Archaeological Excavation of a Middle Paleolithic Site in France*. Boston: McGraw-Hill. Interactive computer excavation of a Middle Paleolithic site.

Fagan, B. M.
2000 *People of the Earth: A Brief Introduction to World Prehistory*, 10th ed. Upper Saddle River, NJ: Prentice-Hall. Prehistoric peoples and civilizations.

2002 *World Prehistory: A Brief Introduction*, 5th ed. New York: Longman. From the Paleolithic to the Neolithic around the world.

Gamble, C.
1999 *The Palaeolithic Societies of Europe*. New York: Cambridge University Press. Survey mainly of the Middle and Upper Paleolithic in Europe.

Klein, R. G.
1999 *The Human Career: Human Biological and Cultural Origins*, 2nd ed. Chicago: University of Chicago Press. Hominid fossils, origins, and evolution.

Klein, R. G., with B. Edgar
2002 *The Dawn of Human Culture*. New York: Wiley. Becoming modern, physically and culturally.

Knecht, H., A. Pike-Tay, and R. White, eds.
1993 *Before Lascaux: The Complex Record of the Early Upper Paleolithic*. Boca Raton, FL: CRC Press. Before cave art.

Lieberman, P.
1998 *Eve Spoke: Human Language and Human Evolution*. New York: W. W. Norton. Language and behavior in human evolution.

Oakley, K. P.
1976 *Man the Tool-Maker*, 6th ed. Chicago: University of Chicago Press. Classic, brief introduction to tool making.

Rightmire, G. P.
1990 *The Evolution of* Homo erectus: *Comparative Anatomical Studies of an Extinct Human Species*. New York: Cambridge University Press. Thorough review of the fossil evidence for the H. erectus period of human evolution.

Tattersall, Ian
1998 *Becoming Human: Evolution and Human Uniqueness*. New York: Harcourt Brace. Human evolution, including primates, fossil hominids, and social evolution.

1999   *The Last Neandertal: The Rise, Success, and Mysterious Extinction of Our Closest Human Relatives*, rev. ed. Boulder, CO: Westview. One view of what happened to the Neandertals.

Ucko, P., and A. Rosenfeld
1967   *Paleolithic Cave Art*. London: Weidenfeld and Nicolson. A survey, including finds and interpretations.

Wenke, R. J.
1996   *Patterns in Prehistory: Mankind's First Three Million Years*, 4th ed. New York: Oxford University Press. Very thorough survey of fossil and archaeological reconstruction of human evolution.

INTERNET EXERCISES

1. Visit the home page of the Chauvet-Pont-d'Arc cave **(http://www.culture.gouv.fr/culture/arcnat/chauvet/en/index.html)**. Read about the discovery and authentication of the cave (under "The Cave Today") and about the archaeological context, dating, and significance of the cave (under "Time and Space").

   a. How was the cave found? How do they know the paintings are as old as they claim?

   b. When was the cave occupied? What kind of hominids were using the cave?

   c. What makes the Chauvet-Pont-d'Arc cave different from other caves used during a similar time period? What do archaeologists know about the people who occupied the cave and made the paintings?

2. Modern Hominid Origins: Visit Philip L. Walker and Edward H. Hagen's "Human Evolution: The Fossil Evidence in 3D" **(http://www.anth.ucsb.edu/projects/human/#)**. Then click the link to enter the gallery.

   a. Click on the human figure labeled "Human origins" and then click on the skull labeled "Homo erectus." You now have a three-dimensional view of a *Homo erectus* skull, and you can use the mouse to rotate the skull. Compare it with a modern human skull. What are some of the prominent features that differentiate a *Homo erectus* skull from a modern human skull? From the image, is it clear who has the bigger brain?

   b. Go back and look at the *Homo neanderthalensis* skull. Rotate the skulls to look at a profile or side view. Which skull has a large brow ridge; a low, elongated skull; and a bun on the back of the skull? From the image, is it clear who has the bigger brain? Some people have argued that modern Europeans descended from Neanderthals. Based on these skulls, do you think this is possible?

See Chapter 8 at your McGraw-Hill Online Learning Center for additional review and interactive exercises.

BRINGING IT ALL TOGETHER

See your OLC Bringing It All Together links

mhhe com /kottak

When Did Humans Start Acting Like Humans?

Let's summarize what we've learned in the last few chapters and try to bring it all together. As you read this account, note how anthropologists draft hypotheses and use evidence from artifacts, art, language, and other aspects of culture, as well as genetics, anatomy, and animal remains, to reconstruct our past.

Scientists agree that (1) between 7 and 5 million years ago, our hominid ancestors originated in Africa, as apelike creatures became habitual bipeds; (2) by 2.5 million years ago, still in Africa, hominids were making crude stone tools; and (3) by 1.7 million years ago, hominids had spread from Africa into Asia and eventually into Europe.

Most scientists agree on those three points. A smaller majority—but still a majority—of scientists think that anatomically modern humans (AMHs, or *H. sapiens sapiens*) had evolved by 130,000 years ago from ancestors who had remained in Africa. Like earlier hominids (*H. erectus* or *ergaster*), they too spread out from Africa. Eventually they replaced—perhaps in some cases interbreeding with—nonmodern human types, such as the Neandertals in Europe and parts of Asia and the successors of *H. erectus* in the Far East.

Disagreement remains about when, where, and how these early AMHs achieved *behavioral modernity*—relying on symbolic thought, elaborating cultural creativity, and, as a result, becoming fully human in behavior as well as in anatomy. Was it 90,000 or 40,000 years ago? Was it in Africa, the Middle East, or Europe? Was it population increase, competition with nonmodern humans, or a genetic mutation that triggered the change? The traditional view has been that modern behavior originated fairly recently, around 40,000 years ago, and only after *H. sapiens* had pushed into Europe. This theory of a "creative explosion" is based on evidence such as the impressive cave paintings at Lascaux and Chauvet (Wilford 2002).

Some researchers think this theory reflects Eurocentrism, in that anthropologists were more likely to believe evidence for early creativity in Western Europe. But when they found signs of early behavioral complexity in Africa or the Middle East, they discounted it. In fact, recent discoveries outside Europe do suggest an older, more gradual evolution of modern behavior, rather than its sudden appearance in Europe.

British archaeologist Clive Gamble observes, "Europe is a little peninsula that happens to have a large amount of spectacular archaeology. But the European grip of having all the evidence is beginning to slip. We're finding wonderful new evidence in Africa and other places. And in the last two or three years, this has changed and widened the debate over modern human behavior" (quoted in Wilford 2002).

Uncertainty about the origin of modern behavior reflects the long lag between the time when the species first looked modern (130,000–100,000 B.P.) and the time when it started acting modern (90,000–40,000 B.P.) (Wilford 2002). Did the capacity for behavioral modernity lie latent in early *H. sapiens* until it was needed for survival? According to archaeologist Sally McBrearty of the University of Connecticut, "the earliest *Homo sapiens* probably had the cognitive capability to invent Sputnik, but they didn't yet have the history of invention or a need for those things" (quoted in Wilford 2002). Did the need for behavioral modernity arise gradually, in the context of new social conditions, environmental change, or competition with other early human types? Or did the capacity for modern behavior develop late, reflecting some kind of genetic transformation? Mary Stiner of the University of Arizona reduces the matter to one key question: "Was there some fundamental shift in brain wiring or some change in conditions of life?" (quoted in Wilford 2002).

According to John Noble Wilford (2002), Richard G. Klein, a Stanford archaeologist, is the main advocate for the idea that human creativity dawned suddenly, in Europe around 40,000 years ago. Before this "dawn of human culture" (Klein with Edgar 2002), *Homo* had changed very slowly—and more or less simultaneously in anatomy and behavior. After this "dawn of culture," human anatomy changed little, but behavior started changing dramatically. The pace of cultural change has been accelerating ever since 40,000 B.P.

In this traditional view, it was in Europe that modern *H. sapiens* made the first tools that confirm a pattern of abstract and symbolic thought. There, humans who were behaviorally, as well as anatomically, modern also buried their dead with ceremonies, adorned their bodies with pigments and jewelry, and fashioned figurines of fertile females. Their cave paintings expressed images from their minds, as they remembered the hunt and events and symbols associated with it.

To explain such a flowering of creativity, Klein proposes a neurological hypothesis. About 50,000 years ago, he thinks, a genetic mutation acted to rewire the human brain, possibly allowing for an advance in language. Improved communication, in Klein's view, could have given people "the fully modern ability to invent and manipulate culture" (quoted in Wilford 2002). Klein thinks this genetic change probably happened in Africa and then allowed "human populations to colonize new and challenging environments" (quoted in Wilford 2002). Reaching Europe, the rewired modern humans, the AMH Cro-Magnons, met and eventually replaced the resident Neandertals.

Klein recognizes that his genetic hypothesis "fails one important measure of a proper scientific hypothesis—it cannot be tested or falsified by experiment or by examination of relevant human fossils" (quoted in Wilford 2002). AMH skulls from the time period in question show no change in brain size or function. According to Wilford (2002), Klein's critics object that his concepts of "the dawn of creativity" and of an abrupt "human revolution" are too simplistic, as well as unprovable.

Other archaeologists think it inappropriate and outdated to link the origin of human behavioral modernity so closely to the European evidence. Such thinking was more understandable when few relevant sites were known elsewhere.

But in the last 30 years, archaeologists working in Africa and the Middle East have found considerable evidence for early modern behavior, in the form of finely made stone and bone tools, long-distance trade, dietary changes, self-ornamentation, and abstract carvings.

In a survey of African archeological sites dating to between 300,000 and 30,000 years ago, Sally McBrearty and Alison Brooks (2000) conclude that artifacts thought to indicate the "human revolution" of the Upper Paleolithic in Europe—where they appear abruptly about 40,000 years ago—are found in Africa, much earlier but not all at the same time. In other words, what might appear to be a sudden event outside Africa was a slow process of accumulation within Africa. Given the genetic evidence that AMHs came from Africa, this makes good sense. There was a period of gradual cultural development in Africa for thousands of years, followed by migration out of Africa with a fairly developed culture. The implication is that humans were fully "human" long before the Upper Paleolithic and that we do not need to postulate a genetic change 50,000 years ago (e.g., a mutation "for language") to account for the "human revolution."

At South Africa's Blombos Cave, an archaeological team led by Christopher Henshilwood found evidence that AMHs were making bone

At South Africa's Blombos Cave, anatomically modern humans were making bone awls and weapon points more than 70,000 years ago. Shown here--some of the more than 100,000 artifacts that have been found in the cave.

awls and weapon points more than 70,000 years ago. Three weapon points had been shaped with a stone blade and then finely polished. Henshilwood thinks these artifacts indicate symbolic behavior and artistic creativity—people trying to make beautiful objects. In January 2002, Henshilwood reported additional evidence from Blombos Cave for early symbolic thought: two small pieces of ocher (a soft red iron oxide stone) with inscribed triangles and horizontal lines, dating back 77,000 years (Wilford 2002).

Earlier excavations in Congo's Katanda region had uncovered barbed bone harpoon points dating back 80,000 to 90,000 years (Yellen, Brooks, and Cornelissen 1995). Archaeologists Alison Brooks and John Yellen contend that these ancient people "not only possessed considerable technological capabilities at this time, but also incorporated symbolic or stylistic content into their projectile forms" (quoted in Wilford 2002).

Some scientists still challenge the idea of early behavioral modernity in Africa (Wilford 2002). The doubters wonder why, if the artifacts are that old and represent a basic change in human behavior, they aren't more common and widespread. John Yellen counters that AMH populations at places such as Blombos Cave and Katanda were probably small and scattered. Low population density would have been a barrier to the spread of ideas and cultural practices between groups (Wilford 2002).

In Turkey and Lebanon, Steven Kuhn, Mary Stiner, and David Reese (2001) found evidence that, around 43,000 years ago, coastal people made and wore beads and shell ornaments with repetitive designs. Some of the shells were rare varieties, white or brightly colored. The bone of a large bird was incised for use as a pendant. The Mediterranean coastal sites of Ucagizli Cave in Turkey and Ksar Akil in Lebanon are located in a corridor of ancient migrations from Africa into Europe and Asia. There the archaeologists also found remains of animal bones that offered evidence for a dietary change. Over time, the people ate fewer deer, wild cattle, and other large animals. They also hunted fewer of the slower-reproducing, easier-to-catch animals, such as shellfish and tortoises, and more of the more agile animals such as birds and hares (Kuhn, Stiner, and Reese 2001).

Body ornamentation—a sign of behavioral modernity. On the left, a man from Irian Jaya, Indonesia (island of New Guinea—see your atlas). On the right, a man photographed at Finsbury Park, England. What are the social functions of such ornamentation?

Kuhn, Stiner, and Reese (2001) suggest that population increase could have caused changes in the living conditions of these AMHs—putting pressure on their resources and forcing experimentation with diet and subsistence strategies. Even a modest increase in the population growth rate could double or triple the numbers and populations of small AMH bands, forcing people to vary their subsistence strategies. People would be living nearer to one another, with more opportunities to interact. Body ornaments could have been part of a system of communication, signaling group identity and social status. The archaeologists note that such standardized ornaments first appeared at about the same time at two other widely separated sites, in Kenya and Bulgaria. Such reliance on communication through ornamentation probably implies "the existence of certain cognitive capacities and that these evolved relatively late in prehistory" (Stiner and Kuhn, quoted in Wilford 2002; Kuhn, Stiner, and Reese 2001).

Such capacities probably were not the result of a sudden genetic mutation. "The fact that traditions of ornament making emerged almost simultaneously in the earliest Upper Paleolithic/Late Stone Age on three continents argues strongly against their corresponding to a specific event in the cognitive evolution of a single population," according to Stiner and Kuhn (quoted in Wilford 2002).

Clive Gamble attributes the rise of behavioral modernity more to increasing social competition than to population increase. Competing with neighboring populations, including, in Europe, the Neandertals, could have produced new subsistence strategies, along with new ways of sharing ideas and organizing society. Such innovations would have advantaged AMH bands as they occupied new lands and faced new circumstances, including contact with nonmodern humans.

According to archaeologist Randall White of New York University, an expert on Cro-Magnon creativity, early personal adornment in Africa and the Middle East shows that the human creative capacity was latent in AMHs long before they reached Europe (Wilford 2002). Facing new circumstances, including competition, AMHs honed their cultural abilities, which enabled them to maintain a common identity, communicate ideas, and organize their societies into "stable, enduring regional groups" (quoted in Wilford 2002). Symbolic thought and cultural advances, expressed most enduringly in artifacts, ornamentation, and art, gave them the edge over the Neandertals, with whom they may have interbred, but whom they eventually replaced in Europe.

The origin of behavioral modernity continues to be debated. We see, however, that archaeological work in many world areas suggests strongly that neither anatomical modernity nor behavioral modernity was a European invention. Africa's role in the origin and development of humanity is prominent yet again.

9

HUMAN DIVERSITY AND "RACE"

Overview

Scientists have approached the study of human biological diversity in two main ways: racial classification, an approach that has been rejected, and the current explanatory approach. It is not possible to define human races biologically. Because of a range of problems involved in classifying humans into racial categories, biologists now focus on specific biological differences and try to explain them.

Race is a cultural category, not a biological reality. "Races" derive from contrasts perceived in particular societies, rather than from scientific classification. In American culture, one acquires a racial identity at birth. But in the final analysis, race in the United States isn't based on genetics or appearance. Children of mixed unions, no matter what they look like,

are usually classified with the minority-group parent. Other cultures have different ways of assigning racial labels, of socially constructing race.

Latin American countries deal with race differently. In Brazil, for example, full siblings may belong to different races if they look different. Brazilians recognize many more races than Americans do. A person's racial identity can change during his or her lifetime. It also varies depending on who is doing the classifying.

Environmental variables involving educational, economic, and social backgrounds provide better explanations for performance on intelligence tests by races, classes, and ethnic groups than do genetic differences in learning ability.

A Hemings Family Turns from Black, to White, to Black

NEW YORK TIMES NEWS BRIEF

by Brent Staples

December 17, 2001

Descendants of Thomas Jefferson and descendants of Sally Hemings pose for a group shot in 1999 in front of Jefferson's plantation.

Race is a reality of everyday life, right? Maybe not. Are races real, and in what sense? What entitles someone to belong to one race rather than another? Genes, ancestry, physical appearance? This chapter shows that races are social categories rather than biological facts. North American racial categories are socially constructed. That is, races are defined by society and culture, not by science. Consider this account of the descendants of Eston Hemings, a son of Thomas Jefferson, who was white, and Sally Hemings, an African-American woman with light skin. What should Eston's race have been? Was he right in changing it? Are his descendants, who have intermarried with whites across several generations, white or black? All of us have African roots. How recent must those roots be to turn a "white" person into a "black" person? How do you know whether Julia Jefferson, discussed in this article, is "black" or "white"? How do you know what your race is?

The Census Bureau is poking and prodding the nearly seven million people who described themselves as belonging to more than one race in the 2000 census . . . . Are some of them about to quit one race and join another? Given the slippery history of race in the census, the answer is probably "yes."

Historians who study the 19th century commonly turn up people who appear as "black" or "mulatto" in one census and "white" in another. These judgments were made by census workers who behaved essentially as race police, counting people as either black or white depending on what they looked like or on the race of the people who lived nearest to them. White people who either lived with or married blacks were magically rendered black in the census. This came at a time when blacks were sometimes barred from voting, from public school and from testifying in court. Fair-skinned blacks escaped the penalties of race by moving to places where no one knew them and taking up lives among the white folk. They lived in terror of discovery. To protect their new identities, they often broke ties with their black families.

The number of black people who passed into whiteness is difficult to determine. A provocative 1958 study cited in Supreme Court records estimated that as many as 15,000 blacks slipped across the line to live and sometimes marry as white every year in the 1940's alone. The study, by the sociologist Robert Stuckert, concluded that by the close of that decade, one in five Americans who were recorded as white in the census had an unacknowledged black ancestor within the previous four generations. . . .

The 40's found young Julia Jefferson entering her teens in a white, suburban household with parents who admonished her to avoid black people and play only with "her own kind." When she bicycled off to meet a black friend she'd met in Bible school, her parents followed her in the car, put the bicycle in the trunk and told her never to do that again. . . .

Julia's father was descended from Eston Hemings, a son of the enslaved woman Sally Hemings and Thomas Jefferson. A genetic study in 1998 established a match on the Y chromosome markers between Thomas Jefferson's descendants and Eston Hemings's. . . . The emerging consensus is that Thomas Jefferson and Sally Hemings became lovers when she was little more than a child and remained involved for nearly 40 years. The evidence suggests that the former president fathered several, if not all, of Sally's children.

Three of the Hemings children slipped off into whiteness, leaving the family and their black identities behind. Beverly and Harriet Hemings seem to have made a clean getaway, leaving little evidence that would have allowed people to track them down. But the Hemings records and oral histories show that Eston's journey into whiteness was painful. Freed in Thomas Jefferson's will in 1827, Eston and his brother Madison lived for a time in the mixed-race community of Charlottesville, Va., but were forced to abandon the state by a vicious campaign aimed at purging Virginia of free people of color. The two brothers moved to Ohio, where Madison lived as black for the remainder of his days.

Driven perhaps by the "black codes" that forbade him from educating his children or testifying in court, Eston moved with his wife and three teenaged children to Wisconsin. There he dropped the "black" Hemings name and became the "white" E. H. Jefferson. Turning white allowed Eston's children and grandchildren to fare well professionally. But they often exhibited signs of distress, including early deaths and a possible suicide that may have been related to the stress of passing for white. . . .

Julia learned about Sally Hemings during the 1970's, after the historian Fawn Brodie published a steamy biography of Jefferson, which included speculation about the love affair. The subterfuge and deceit of the cover-up have come pouring back to Julia in recent years, as the story became steadily more public and the white and the black Jeffersons began to discover each other and make common cause.

Meeting the black Jeffersons has had a profound effect on Julia. . . . She has examined her own prejudices and found the exercise "very painful." Everyone in the family was aware of her journey. But they were probably surprised when this 67-year-old grandmother announced her plan to declare herself "black" on the 2000 census. Julia says her children are fine with the decision. But another relative said it was a bad idea to pass blackness down through the generations and said that Eston had sacrificed a lot for the advantages Julia was "throwing out the window."

Julia responded that "these are different times." When people ask her why a middle-class woman who has lived all of her life as white would check "black" on the census, Julia sometimes gives them the smart-alecky answer "Because I can." Then she tells them the real reasons. She wants the government to support affirmative action and believes that goal will be easier to achieve if more people are counted as black. Most important, she says, "I want to show people that I am not afraid to be black."

SOURCE: Brent Staples, "A Hemings Family Turns from Black, to White, to Black," *New York Times*, December 17, 2001, late edition—final, section A, p. 20, column 1.

The classification of human beings into races is arbitrary. Racial classification varies among societies, and it varies through time in the same society, as we've just seen in this discussion of American census categories. Human biological diversity is real, but discrete (separate and clearly demarcated) human races don't exist. Historically, scientists have approached the study of human biological variation from two main directions: (1) racial classification, an approach that has been rejected, and (2) the current explanatory approach, which focuses on understanding specific differences. I'll review each approach briefly, first considering the problems with racial classification and then providing an example of the explanatory approach to human biological diversity. Biological differences are real, important, and apparent to us all. Modern scientists seek to explain this diversity, rather than trying to pigeonhole humanity into discrete categories called races.

Race: A Discredited Concept in Biology

In theory, a biological race would be a geographically isolated subdivision of a species. Such a *subspecies* would be capable of interbreeding with other subspecies of the same species, but it would not actually do so because of its geographic isolation. Subspecies that remain separate and reproductively isolated long enough eventually can develop into different species. Some biologists also use "race" to refer to "breeds," as of dogs or roses. Thus, a pit bull and a chihuahua would be different races of dogs. Such domesticated "races" have been carefully bred by humans for generations. However, human populations have not been isolated enough from one another to develop into discrete races. Nor have

The photos in this chapter illustrate only a small part of the range of human biological diversity. Shown here is a Bai minority woman, from Shapin, in China's Yunnan province.

humans experienced controlled breeding like that which has created the various kinds of dogs and roses. Humans vary biologically, for example, in their genetic attributes, but there are no sharp breaks between human populations of the sort we might associate with discrete subspecies or races. We can observe gradual, rather than abrupt, shifts in gene frequencies between neighboring human populations. Such gradual shifts are called **clines**. We do not, however, find the sharp shifts in genes and other biological features we would associate with discrete races.

Racial classification has fallen out of favor in biology for several reasons. The main reason is that scientists have trouble grouping people into distinct racial units. A race is supposed to reflect shared *genetic* material (inherited from a common ancestor), but early scholars used *phenotypical* traits (usually skin color) for racial classification. **Phenotype** refers to an organism's evident traits, its "manifest biology"—anatomy and physiology. There are thousands of evident (detectable) physical traits. They range from skin color, hair form, and eye color (which are visible) to blood type, color blindness, and enzyme production (which become evident through testing).

There are several problems with a phenotypical approach to race. First, which traits should be primary in assigning people to different races? Should races be defined by height, weight, body shape, facial features, teeth, skull form, or skin color? Like their fellow citizens, early European and American scientists gave priority to skin color. The phenotypic features that were most apparent to those early scientists, for example, skin color, were also the very characteristics that had been assigned arbitrary cultural value for purposes of discrimination. Genetic variations (e.g., differences in blood types) that were not directly observable were not used in early racial classification.

Many school books and encyclopedias still proclaim the existence of three great races: the white, the black, and the yellow. This simplistic classification was compatible with the political use of race during the colonial period of the late 19th and early 20th centuries. The tripartite scheme kept white Europeans neatly separate from their African, Asian, and Native American subjects. (See "Interesting Issues" for the "American Anthropological Association [AAA] Statement on 'Race.'") Colonial empires began to break up, and scientists began to question established racial categories, after World War II.

RACES ARE NOT BIOLOGICALLY DISTINCT

History and politics aside, one obvious problem with "color-based" racial labels is that the terms don't accurately describe skin color. "White" people are more pink, beige, or tan than white. "Black" people are various shades of brown, and "yellow" people are tan or beige. But these terms have also been dignified by more scientific-*sounding* synonyms: Caucasoid, Negroid, and Mongoloid.

Another problem with the tripartite scheme is that many populations don't neatly fit into any one of the three "great races." For example, where would one put the Polynesians? *Polynesia* is a triangle of South Pacific islands formed by Hawaii to the north, Easter Island to the east, and New Zealand to the southwest. Does the "bronze" skin color of Polynesians connect them to the Caucasoids or to the Mongoloids? Some scientists, recognizing this problem, enlarged the original tripartite scheme to include the Polynesian "race." Native Americans presented a similar problem.

A Native American:
a Chiquitanos Indian woman
from Bolivia.

Were they red or yellow? Some scientists added a fifth race—the "red," or Amerindian—to the major racial groups.

Many people in southern India have dark skins, but scientists have been reluctant to classify them with "black" Africans because of their "Caucasoid" facial features and hair form. Some, therefore, have created a separate race for these people. What about the Australian aborigines, hunters and gatherers native to what has been, throughout human history, the most isolated continent? By skin color, one might place some Native Australians in the same race as tropical Africans. However, similarities to Europeans in hair color (light or reddish) and facial features have led some scientists to classify them as Caucasoids. But there is no evidence that Australians are closer genetically or historically to either of these groups than they are to Asians. Recognizing this problem, scientists often regard Native Australians as a separate race.

Finally, consider the San ("Bushmen") of the Kalahari Desert in southern Africa. Scientists have perceived their skin color as varying from brown to yellow. Some who regard San skin as "yellow" have placed them in the same category as Asians. In theory, people of the same race share more recent common ancestry with each other than they do with any others. But there is no evidence for

recent common ancestry between San and Asians. Somewhat more reasonably, some scholars assign the San to the Capoid race (from the Cape of Good Hope), which is seen as being different from other groups inhabiting tropical Africa.

Similar problems arise when any single trait is used as a basis for racial classification. An attempt to use facial features, height, weight, or any other phenotypical trait is fraught with difficulties. For example, consider the *Nilotes*, natives of the upper Nile region of Uganda and Sudan. Nilotes tend to be tall and to have long, narrow noses. Certain Scandinavians are also tall, with similar noses. Given the distance between their homelands, to classify them as members of the same race makes little sense. There is no reason to assume that Nilotes and Scandinavians are more closely related to each other than either is to shorter and nearer populations with different kinds of noses.

Would it be better to base racial classifications on a combination of physical traits? This would avoid some of the problems mentioned above, but others would arise. First, skin color, stature, skull form, and facial features (nose form, eye shape, lip thickness) don't go together as a unit. For example, people with dark skin may be tall or short and have hair ranging from straight to very curly. Dark-haired populations may have light or dark skin, along with various skull forms, facial features, and body sizes and shapes. The number of

A Native Australian.

As a result of public confusion about the meaning of "race," claims as to major biological differences among "races" continue to be advanced. Stemming from past AAA actions designed to address public misconceptions on race and intelligence, the need was apparent for a clear AAA statement on the biology and politics of race that would be educational and informational.

The following statement was adopted by the Executive Board of the American Anthropological Association in May 1998, based on a draft prepared by a committee of representative anthropologists. The Association believes that this statement represents the thinking and scholarly positions of most anthropologists.

In the United States both scholars and the general public have been conditioned to viewing human races as natural and separate divisions within the human species based on visible physical differences. With the vast expansion of scientific knowledge in this century, however, it has become clear that human populations are not unambiguous, clearly demarcated, biologically distinct groups. Evidence from the analysis of genetics (e.g., DNA) indicates that most physical variation, about 94%, lies within so-called racial groups. Conventional geographic "racial" groupings differ from one another only in about 6% of their genes. This means that there is greater variation within "racial" groups than between them. In neighboring populations there is much overlapping of genes and their phenotypic (physical) expres-sions. Throughout history whenever different groups have come into contact, they have interbred. The continued sharing of genetic materials has maintained all of humankind as a single species.

Physical variations in any given trait tend to occur gradually rather than abruptly over geographic areas. And because physical traits are inherited independently of one another, knowing the range of one trait does not predict the presence of others. For example, skin color varies largely from light in the temperate areas in the north to dark in the tropical areas in the south; its intensity is not related to nose shape or hair texture. Dark skin may be associated with frizzy or kinky hair or curly or wavy or straight hair, all of which are found among different indigenous peoples in tropical regions. These facts render any attempt to establish lines of division among biological populations both arbitrary and subjective.

Historical research has shown that the idea of "race" has always carried more meanings than mere physical differences; indeed, physical variations in the human species have no meaning except the social ones that humans put on them. Today scholars in many fields argue that "race" as it is understood in the United States of America was a social mechanism invented during the 18th century to refer to those populations brought together in colonial America: the English and other European settlers, the conquered Indian peoples, and those peoples of Africa brought in to provide slave labor.

From its inception, this modern concept of "race" was modeled after an ancient theorem of the Great Chain of Being, which posited natural categories on a hierarchy established by God or nature. Thus "race" was a mode of classification linked specifically to peoples in the colonial situation. It subsumed a growing ideology of inequality devised to rationalize European attitudes and treatment of the conquered and enslaved peoples. Proponents of slavery in particular during the 19th century used "race" to justify the retention of slavery. The ideology magnified the differences among Europeans, Africans, and Indians, established a rigid hierarchy of socially exclusive categories, underscored and bolstered unequal rank and status differences, and provided the rationalization that the inequality was natural or God-given. The different physical traits of African-Americans and Indians became markers or symbols of their status differences.

As they were constructing US society, leaders among European-Americans fabricated the cultural/behavioral characteristics associated with each "race," linking superior traits with Europeans and negative and inferior ones to blacks and Indians. Numerous arbitrary and fictitious beliefs about the different peoples were institutionalized and deeply embedded in American thought . . .

Ultimately "race" as an ideology about human differences was subsequently spread to other areas of the world. It became a strategy for dividing, ranking, and controlling colonized people used by colonial

Roma, or Gypsies, such as these women at the central market in Athens, Greece, have faced discrimination in many nations. During World War II, the Nazis led by Adolph Hitler murdered 11 million Jews, Gypsies, Africans, homosexuals, and others.

powers everywhere. But it was not limited to the colonial situation. In the latter part of the 19th century it was employed by Europeans to rank one another and to justify social, economic, and political inequalities among their peoples. During World War II, the Nazis under Adolf Hitler enjoined the expanded ideology of "race" and "racial" differences and took them to a logical end: the extermination of 11 million people of "inferior races" (e.g., Jews, Gypsies, Africans, homosexuals, and so forth) and other unspeakable brutalities of the Holocaust.

"Race" thus evolved as a world view, a body of prejudgments that distorts our ideas about human differences and group behavior. Racial beliefs constitute myths about the diversity in the human species and about the abilities and behavior of people homogenized into "racial" categories. The myths fused behavior and physical features together in the public mind, impeding our comprehension of both biological variations and cultural behavior, implying that both are genetically determined. Racial myths bear no relationship to the reality of human capabilities or behavior . . .

We now understand that human cultural behavior is learned, conditioned into infants beginning at birth, and always subject to modification. No human is born with a built-in culture or language. Our temperaments, dispositions, and personalities, regardless of genetic propensities, are developed within sets of meanings and values that we call "culture" . . .

It is a basic tenet of anthropological knowledge that all normal human beings have the capacity to learn any cultural behavior. The American experience with immigrants from hundreds of different language and cultural backgrounds who have acquired some version of American culture traits and behavior is the clearest evidence of this fact. Moreover, people of all physical variations have learned different cultural behaviors and continue to do so as modern transportation moves millions of immigrants around the world.

How people have been accepted and treated within the context of a given society or culture has a direct impact on how they perform in that society. The "racial" world view was invented to assign some groups to perpetual low status, while others were permitted access to privilege, power, and wealth. The tragedy in the United States has been that the policies and practices stemming from this world view succeeded all too well in constructing unequal populations among Europeans, Native Americans, and peoples of African descent. Given what we know about the capacity of normal humans to achieve and function within any culture, we conclude that present-day inequalities between so-called "racial" groups are not consequences of their biological inheritance but products of historical and contemporary social, economic, educational, and political circumstances.

NOTE: For further information on human biological variations, see the statement prepared and issued by the American Association of Physical Anthropologists, 1996 (*American Journal of Physical Anthropology* 101, pp. 569–70).

A man from Afghanistan. How would he look without the turban?

EXPLAINING SKIN COLOR

Traditional racial classification assumed that biological characteristics were determined by heredity and that they were stable (immutable) over long periods of time. We now know that a biological similarity doesn't necessarily indicate recent common ancestry. Dark skin color, for example, can be shared by tropical Africans and Native Australians for reasons other than common ancestry. It is not possible to *define races* biologically. Still, scientists have made much progress in *explaining* variation in human skin color, along with many other expressions of human biological diversity. We shift now from classification to *explanation*, in which natural selection plays a key role.

As recognized by Charles Darwin and Alfred Russel Wallace, **natural selection** is the process by which nature selects the forms most fit to survive and reproduce in a given environment—such as the tropics. Over the years, the less fit organisms die out, and the favored types survive by producing more offspring. The role of natural selection in producing variation in skin color will illustrate the explanatory approach to human biological diversity. Comparable explanations have been provided for many other aspects of human biological variation.

combinations is very large, and the amount that heredity (versus environment) contributes to such phenotypical traits is often unclear.

There is a final objection to racial classification based on phenotype. The phenotypical characteristics on which races are based supposedly reflect genetic material that is shared and that has stayed the same for long time periods. But phenotypical similarities and differences don't necessarily have a genetic basis. Because of changes in the environment that affect individuals during growth and development, the range of phenotypes characteristic of a population may change without any genetic change. There are several examples. In the early 20th century, the anthropologist Franz Boas (1940/1966) described changes in skull form (e.g., toward rounder heads) among the children of Europeans who had migrated to North America. The reason for this was not a change in genes, for the European immigrants tended to marry among themselves. Also, some of their children had been born in Europe and merely raised in the United States. Something in the environment, probably in the diet, was producing this change. We know now that changes in average height and weight produced by dietary differences in a few generations are common and may have nothing to do with race or genetics.

Before the 16th century, almost all the very dark-skinned populations of the world lived in the tropics, as does this Samburu woman from Kenya.

Skin color is a complex biological trait. That means it is influenced by several genes. Just how many isn't known. **Melanin**, the primary determinant of human skin color, is a chemical substance manufactured in the epidermis, or outer skin layer. The melanin cells of darker-skinned people produce more and larger granules of melanin than do those of lighter-skinned people. By screening out ultraviolet radiation from the sun, melanin offers protection against a variety of maladies, including sunburn and skin cancer.

Interpret the World
Atlas Map 9
Prior to the 16th century, most of the world's very dark-skinned peoples lived in the **tropics**, a belt extending about 23 degrees north and south of the equator, between the Tropic of Cancer and the Tropic of Capricorn. Look at Map 9, "Human Variations: Skin Color," in your atlas. Using a skin-color index (Biasutti's index), Map 9 shows the relationship between human skin color (melanin production) and ultraviolet radiation from the sun. Note that the association between dark skin color and a tropical habitat existed throughout the Old World, where humans and their ancestors have lived for millions of years. The darkest populations of Africa evolved not in shady equatorial forests but in sunny open grassland, or savanna, country.

Outside the tropics, skin color tends to be lighter. Moving north in Africa, for example, there is a gradual transition from dark brown to medium brown. Average skin color continues to lighten as one moves through the Middle East, into southern Europe, through central Europe, and to the north. South of the tropics skin color is also lighter. In the Americas, by contrast, tropical populations do not have very dark skin. This is because the settlement of the New World, by light-skinned Asian ancestors of Native Americans, was relatively recent, probably dating back no more than 20,000 years.

How, aside from migrations, can we explain the geographic distribution of skin color? Natural selection provides an answer. In the tropics, there is intense ultraviolet radiation from the sun. Unprotected humans there face the threat of severe sunburn, which can increase susceptibility to disease. This confers a selective *dis*advantage (i.e., less success in surviving and reproducing) on lighter-skinned people in the tropics (unless they stay indoors or use cultural products, like umbrellas or lotions, to screen sunlight). Sunburn also impairs the body's ability to sweat. This is a second reason why light skin color, given tropical heat, can diminish the human ability to live and work in equatorial climates. A third disadvantage of having light skin color in the tropics is that exposure to ultraviolet radiation can cause skin cancer (Blum 1961).

A fourth factor affecting the geographic distribution of skin color is vitamin D production by the body. W. F. Loomis (1967) focused on the role of ultraviolet radiation in stimulating the manufacture of vitamin D by the human body. The unclothed human body can produce its own vitamin D when exposed to sufficient sunlight. But in a cloudy environment that is also so cold that people have to dress themselves much of the year (such as northern Europe, where very light skin color evolved), clothing interferes with the body's manufacture of vitamin D. The ensuing shortage of vitamin D diminishes the absorption of calcium in the intestines. A nutritional disease known as **rickets**, which softens and deforms the bones, may

Very light skin color, illustrated in this photo of a blond, blue-eyed North Sea German fisherman, maximizes absorption of ultraviolet radiation by those few parts of the body exposed to direct sunlight during northern winters. This helps prevent rickets.

Background Information

Student:	Heather Norton
Supervising Professors:	Jonathan Friedlaender, Temple University; Andy Merriwether, University of Michigan; and Mark Shriver, Pennsylvania State University
School:	Pennsylvania State University
Year in School:/Major:	Graduated in spring 2000 with a BA in anthropology
Future Plans:	Field work in Melanesia (the Solomon Islands) tentatively in spring 2001.
Project Title:	Skin Pigmentation in Papua New Guinea.

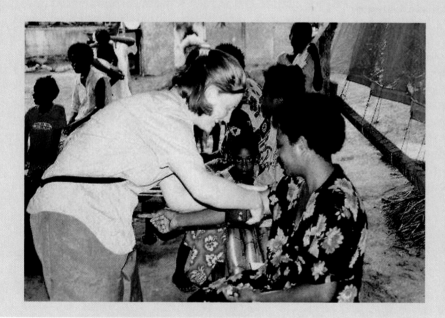

What aspects of human biological variation are addressed in this study? Are they genotypic or phenotypic?

In summer 2000, following my senior year at Penn State, I spent five weeks in Papua New Guinea studying variation in skin pigmentation. I was part of a larger research effort led by Dr. Jonathan Friedlaender and Dr. Andy Merriwether. The goal was to examine variation in mitochondrial and Y-chromosome DNA sequences in an attempt to identify patterns of migration to the islands of Melanesia. Skin pigmentation is a phenotypic trait that shows extensive variation around the world.

Skin color is primarily determined by the pigment melanin, although others, such as hemoglobin, may also contribute. One way to measure skin pigmentation is to use reflectometry, the controlled illumination of an object and the precise measurement of the light that is reflected from it. The narrow-band spectrophotometer that I used estimates the concentration of hemoglobin and melanin by taking reflectance readings. The resulting measurements are known as the melanin index (M), and the erythema index (E). The more darkly pigmented an individual, the greater their M-index measurement. I took

develop. In women, deformation of the pelvic bones from rickets can interfere with childbirth. During northern winters, light skin color maximizes the absorption of ultraviolet radiation and the manufacture of vitamin D by the few parts of the body that are exposed to direct sunlight. There has been selection against dark skin color in northern areas because melanin screens out ultraviolet radiation.

Considering vitamin D production, light skin is an advantage in the cloudy north, but a disadvantage in the sunny tropics. Loomis suggested that in the tropics, dark skin color protects the body against an *overproduction* of vitamin D by

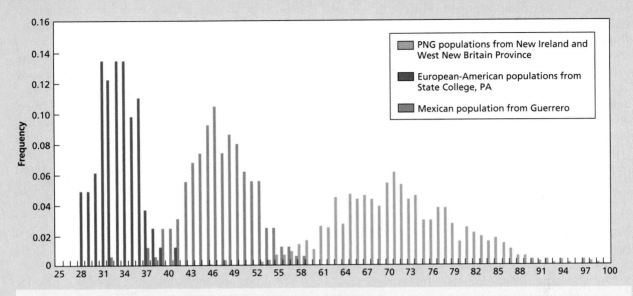

Skin Pigmentation among Various Human Groups.

M = Index of PNG, European-American, and Mexican Populations

multiple measurements on both of the inner arms of each subject, as well as measurements of their hair color.

I chose to study pigmentation in Melanesia because of its variability among individuals there. In two weeks I was able to obtain samples from Bougainvillians, whose skin contains large amounts of melanin, as well as from lighter-skinned individuals from the Sepik region of Papua New Guinea. This area of the world is also interesting from a pigmentation perspective in terms of hair color. Individuals from Papua New Guinea

and other Melanesian islands, as well as Australian aborigines, display a trait known as blondism. This refers to very blond hair, similar to someone of European descent, with darkly pigmented skin. This histogram shows the wide range of pigmentation found on the two islands—individuals at the upper end of the scale are from Bougainville, while those at the lower end are from areas such as the Sepik.

I am currently doing statistical analyses to see if differences in skin color are associated in any way with language. Although close to 1,000 languages are spoken in Papua New

Guinea, they belong to two main groups, Austronesian and non-Austronesian. The non-Austronesian speakers appear to have migrated to New Guinea first, followed by a second wave of Austronesian-speaking groups. Current mitochondrial DNA evidence supports this theory. If significant skin color differences between the two groups can be shown, it may help lend support to that argument. I hope to return to Melanesia in the spring of 2001 to continue my study of pigmentation variation, this time in the neighboring Solomon Islands.

screening out ultraviolet radiation. Too much vitamin D can lead to a potentially fatal condition (**hypervitaminosis D**), in which calcium deposits build up in the body's soft tissues. The kidneys may fail. Gallstones, joint problems, and circulation problems are other symptoms of hypervitaminosis D.

This discussion of skin color shows that common ancestry, the presumed basis of race, is not the only reason for biological similarities. We see that natural selection has made a major contribution to our understanding of human biological differences and similarities.

Social Race

Medical studies often report on different health risks and conditions of blacks and whites. Next time you see such a study, think about how the results might have differed if people had been grouped, say, as light-skinned versus dark-skinned, or assessed along a continuum of skin color, rather than simply classified as black or white. Do you imagine that blue-eyed people and brown-eyed people are prone to different health risks and medical conditions? Do they belong to different races?

We have seen that it is not possible to define races biologically. Only cultural constructions of race are possible—even though the average citizen conceptualizes "race" in biological terms. The belief that races exist and are important is much more common among the public than it is among biologists and anthropologists. Most Americans, for example, believe that their population includes biologically based "races" to which various labels have been applied. These labels include "white," "black," "yellow," "red," "Caucasoid," "Negroid," "Mongoloid," "Amerindian," "Asian-American," "African-American," "Euro-American," and "Native American."

The races we hear about every day are culturally constructed categories that may have little to do with actual biological differences. In Charles Wagley's terms (Wagley 1959/1968), they are **social races** (groups assumed to have a biological basis but actually defined in a culturally arbitrary, rather than a scientific manner). Many Americans mistakenly assume that "whites" and "blacks," for example, are biologically distinct and that these terms stand for discrete races. But these labels, like racial terms used in other societies, really designate culturally defined and perceived, rather than biologically based, groups.

HYPODESCENT: RACE IN THE UNITED STATES

How is race culturally constructed in the United States? In American culture, one acquires his or her racial identity at birth, but race isn't based on biology or on simple ancestry. Take the case of the child of a "racially mixed" marriage involving one black and one white parent. We know that 50 per-cent of the child's genes come from one parent and 50 percent from the other. Still, American culture overlooks heredity and classifies this child as black. This rule is arbitrary. From *genotype* (genetic composition), it would be just as logical to classify the child as white.

American rules for assigning racial status can be even more arbitrary. In some states, anyone known to have any black ancestor, no matter how remote, is classified as a member of the black race. This is a rule of **descent** (it assigns social identity on the basis of ancestry), but of a sort that is rare outside the contemporary United States. It is called **hypodescent** (Harris and Kottak 1963) (hypo means "lower") because it automatically places the children of a union or mating between members of different groups in the minority group. Hypodescent helps divide American society into groups that have been unequal in their access to wealth, power, and prestige.

Millions of Americans have faced discrimination because one or more of their ancestors happened to belong to a minority group. The following case from Louisiana is an excellent illustration of the arbitrariness of the hypodescent rule. It also illustrates the role that governments (federal, or state in this case) play in legalizing, inventing, or eradicating race and ethnicity (Williams 1989). Susie Guillory Phipps, a light-skinned woman with "Caucasian" features and straight black hair, discovered as an adult that she was "black." When Phipps ordered a copy of her birth certificate, she found her race listed as "colored." Since she had been "brought up white and married white twice," Phipps challenged a 1970 Louisiana law declaring anyone with at least one-thirty-second "Negro blood" to be legally black. In other words, having 1 "Negro" great-great-great-grandparent out of 32 is sufficient to make one black. Although the state's lawyer admitted that Phipps "looks like a white person," the state of Louisiana insisted that her racial classification was proper (Yetman 1991, pp. 3–4).

Cases like Phipps's are rare, because "racial" and ethnic identities are usually ascribed at birth and usually don't change. The rule of hypodescent affects blacks, Asians, Native Americans, and Hispanics differently. It's easier to negotiate Indian or Hispanic identity than black identity. The ascription rule isn't as definite, and the assumption of a biological basis isn't as strong.

To be considered "Native American," one ancestor out of eight (great-grandparents) or four (grandparents) may suffice. This depends on whether the assignment is by federal or state law or by an Indian tribal council. The child of a Hispanic may (or may not, depending on context) claim Hispanic identity. Many Americans with an Indian or Latino grandparent consider themselves "white" and lay no claim to minority-group status.

The controversy that erupted in 1990–91 over the casting of the Broadway production of the musical *Miss Saigon* also illustrates the cultural construction of race in the United States. The musical had opened a few years earlier in London, where the Filipina actress Lea Salonga had played Kim, a young Vietnamese woman. Another major role is that of the Eurasian (half-French, half-Vietnamese) pimp known as the "Engineer." For the New York production, the producer wanted Salonga to play Kim and the English actor Jonathan Pryce, who had originated the part in

London, to play the Engineer. Actors' Equity must approve the casting of foreign stars in New York productions. The union initially ruled that Pryce, a "Caucasian," could not play a Eurasian. The part had to go to an "Asian" instead. (Actors' Equity eventually reconsidered its position and allowed Pryce to open in the musical.)

In this case the American hypodescent rule was being extended from the offspring of black–white unions to "Eurasians" (in this case French–Vietnamese). Again, the cultural construction of race is that children get their identity from the minority parent—Asian rather than European. This notion also assumes that all Asians (e.g., Vietnamese, Chinese, and Filipinos) are equivalent. Thus it's okay for someone from the Philippines to play a Vietnamese (or even a Eurasian), but an Englishman can't play a half-French Eurasian.

The culturally arbitrary rule of hypodescent is behind the idea that an Asian is more appropriate to play a Eurasian than a "Caucasian" is. Hypodescent governs racial and ethnic ascription in the United States. This rule of descent channels discrimination against offspring of mixed unions, who are assigned minority status. But, as the case of *Miss Saigon* illustrates, a cultural rule that has been used against a group also can be used to promote the interests of that group. There has been a shortage of parts for Asian and Asian American actors. In this case, the hypodescent rule was used to stake a claim for Asians and Asian-Americans to have prime access to "Eurasian" as well as "Asian" parts.

RACE IN THE CENSUS

In this 1997 photo, Tiger Woods tees off at Ponte Vedra Beach, Florida. The number of interracial marriages and children is increasing, which has implications for the traditional American system of racial classification.

For more about race and the census, see the Virtual Exploration

mhhe
●com
/kottak

The U.S. Census Bureau has gathered data by race since 1790. Initially this was done because the Constitution specified that a slave counted as three-fifths of a white person and because Indians were not taxed. The racial categories specified in the U.S. census include White, Black or Negro, Indian (Native American), Eskimo, Aleut or Pacific Islander, and Other. A separate question asks about Spanish-Hispanic heritage. Check out Figure 9.1 for the racial categories in the 2000 census. What changes do you notice?

An attempt by social scientists and interested citizens to add a "multiracial" census category has

5. Is this person Spanish/Hispanic/Latino? *Mark* ☒ *the "No" box if not Spanish/Hispanic/Latino.*

☐ **No,** not Spanish/Hispanic/Latino   ☐ Yes, Puerto Rican
☐ Yes, Mexican, Mexican Am., Chicano   ☐ Yes, Cuban
☐ Yes, other Spanish/Hispanic/Latino — *Print group.* ⤵

☐☐☐☐☐☐☐☐☐☐☐☐☐☐☐☐☐☐

5. What is this person's race? *Mark* ☒ *one or more races to indicate what this person considers himself/herself to be.*

☐ White
☐ Black, African Am., or Negro
☐ American Indian or Alaska Native — *Print name of enrolled or principal tribe.* ⤵

☐☐☐☐☐☐☐☐☐☐☐☐☐☐☐☐☐☐

☐ Asian Indian   ☐ Japanese   ☐ Native Hawaiian
☐ Chinese   ☐ Korean   ☐ Guamanian or Chamorro
☐ Filipino   ☐ Vietnamese   ☐ Samoan
☐ Other Asian — *Print race.* ⤵   ☐ Other Pacific Islander — *Print race.* ⤵

☐☐☐☐☐☐☐☐☐☐☐☐☐☐☐☐☐☐

☐ Some other race — *Print race.* ⤵

☐☐☐☐☐☐☐☐☐☐☐☐☐☐☐☐☐☐

Figure 9.1 **Reproduction of Questions on Race and Hispanic Origin from Census 2000.**
SOURCE: U.S. Census Bureau, Census 2000 questionnaire.

been opposed by the National Association for the Advancement of Colored People (NAACP) and the National Council of La Raza (a Hispanic advocacy group). As the *Miss Saigon* incident demonstrates, racial classification is a political issue. It involves access to resources, including parts, jobs, voting districts, and federal funding of programs aimed at minorities. The hypodescent rule results in all the population growth being attributed to the minority category. Minorities fear their political clout will decline if their numbers go down.

But things are changing. Choice of "some other race" in the U.S. Census more than doubled from 1980 (6.8 million) to 2000 (over 15 million)—suggesting imprecision in and dissatisfaction with the existing categories (Mar 1997). In the year 2000, 274.6 million Americans (out of 281.4 million censused) reported they belonged to just one race, as shown in Table 9.1.

Hispanics totaled 35.3 million, or about 13 percent, of the total U.S. population. Nearly 48 percent of Hispanics identified as White alone, and

about 42 percent as "some other race" alone. In the 2000 census, 2.4 percent of Americans, or 6.8 million people, chose a first-ever option of identifying themselves as belonging to more than one race. About 6 percent of Hispanics reported two or more races, compared with less than 2 percent of non-Hispanics (http://www.census.gov/Press-Release/www/2001/cb01cn61.html).

The number of interracial marriages and children is increasing, with implications for the traditional system of American racial classification. "Interracial," "biracial," or "multiracial" children who grow up with both parents undoubtedly identify with particular qualities of either parent. It is troubling for many of them to have so important an identity as race dictated by the arbitrary rule of hypodescent. It may be especially discordant when racial identity doesn't parallel gender identity, for example, a boy with a white father and a black mother, or a girl with a white mother and a black father.

How does the Canadian census compare with the American census in its treatment of race? Currently, the most recent Canadian census data, gathered every five years, are for 1996. Rather than race, the Canadian census asks about "visible minorities." That country's Employment Equity Act defines such groups as "persons, other than Aboriginal peoples [a.k.a. First Nations in Canada, Native Americans in the United States], who are non-Caucasian in race or non-white in colour" (Statistics Canada 2001). The 1996 census was the first to gather systematic data on visible minorities—for the purpose of assessing employment equity. Similar to affirmative action in the United States, Canada's Employment Equity Act was a response to the political organization of diversity in that country. Table 9.2 shows that "Chinese" and "South Asian" are Canada's largest visible minorities. Note that Canada's total visible minority population of 11.2 percent contrasts with a figure of about 25 percent for the United States in the 2000 Census. In particular, Canada's Black 2 percent population contrasts with the American figure of 12.3 percent for African Americans, while Canada's Asian population is significantly higher than the U.S. figure of 3.6 percent on a percentage

Table 9.1 Americans Reporting They Belonged to Just One Race

White	75.1%
Black or African-American	12.3%
American Indian and Alaska Native	0.9%
Asian	3.6%
Native Hawaiian and Other Pacific Islander	0.1%
Some other race	5.5%

SOURCE: http://www.census.gov/Press-Release/www/2001/cb01cn61.html.

Table 9.2 Visible Minority Population of Canada, 1996 Census

	Number	Percent
Total population	**28,528,125**	**100.0**
Total visible minority population	3,197,460	11.2
Chinese	860,150	3.0
South Asian	670,590	2.4
Black	573,860	2.0
Arab/West Asian	244,665	0.8
Filipino	234,195	0.8
Southeast Asian	172,765	0.6
Latin American	176,970	0.6
Japanese	68,135	0.2
Korean	64,835	0.2
Other visible minority	69,745	0.2
Multiple visible minority	61,575	0.2
Nonvisible minority	25,330,645	88.8

SOURCE: Statistics Canada 2001.

basis. Only a tiny fraction of the Canadian population (0.2 percent) claimed multiple visible minority affiliation, compared with 2.4 percent claiming "more than one race" in the United States in 2000.

NOT US: RACE IN JAPAN

See the Internet Exercises at your OLC

mhhe.com /kottak

American culture ignores considerable diversity in biology, language, and geographic origin as it socially constructs race within the United States. North Americans also overlook diversity by seeing Japan as a nation that is homogeneous in race, ethnicity, language, and culture—an image the Japanese themselves cultivate. Thus in 1986, former Prime Minister Nakasone created an international furor by contrasting his country's supposed homogeneity (responsible, he suggested, for Japan's success in international business) with the ethnically mixed United States. To describe Japanese society, Nakasone used *tan'itsu minzoku*, an expression connoting a single ethnic-racial group (Robertson 1992).

Japan is hardly the uniform entity Nakasone described. Some dialects of the Japanese language are mutually unintelligible. Scholars estimate that 10 percent of Japan's population are minorities of various sorts. These include aboriginal Ainu, annexed Okinawans, outcast *burakumin*, children of mixed marriages, and immigrant nationalities, especially Koreans, who number more than 700,000 (De Vos et al. 1983).

Americans tend to see Japanese and Koreans as alike, but the Japanese stress the difference between themselves and Koreans. To describe racial attitudes in Japan, Jennifer Robertson (1992) uses Kwame Anthony Appiah's (1990) term *intrinsic racism*—the belief that a (perceived) racial difference is a sufficient reason to value one person less than another.

In Japan, the valued group is majority ("pure") Japanese, who are believed to share "the same blood." Thus, the caption to a printed photo of a Japanese-American model reads: "She was born in Japan but raised in Hawaii. Her nationality is American but no foreign blood flows in her veins" (Robertson 1992, p. 5). Something like hypodescent also operates in Japan, but less precisely than in the United States, where mixed offspring automatically become members of the minority group. The children of mixed marriages between majority Japanese and others (including Euro-Americans) may not get the same "racial" label as the minority parent, but they are still stigmatized for their non-Japanese ancestry (De Vos and Wagatsuma 1966).

Social Race **241**

How is race culturally constructed in Japan? The (majority) Japanese define themselves by opposition to others, whether minority groups in their own nation or outsiders—anyone who is "not us." Aspects of *phenotype* (detectable physical traits, such as perceived body odor) are considered part of being *racially different by opposition*. Other races don't smell as "we" do. The Japanese stigmatize Koreans by saying they smell different (as Europeans also do). Japanese also stereotype their minorities with behavioral and psychological traits. Koreans are stereotyped as underachievers, crime-prone, and working class. They are placed in opposition to dominant Japanese, who are positively stereotyped as harmonious, hard-working, and middle class (Robertson 1992).

The "not us" should stay that way; assimilation is generally discouraged. Cultural mechanisms, especially residential segregation and taboos on "interracial" marriage, work to keep minorities "in their place." (Still, many marriages between minorities and majority Japanese do occur.) However, perhaps to give the appearance of homogeneity, people (e.g., Koreans) who become Japanese citizens are expected to take Japanese-sounding names (Robertson 1992; De Vos et al. 1983).

In its construction of race, Japanese culture regards certain ethnic groups as having a biological basis, when there is no evidence that they do. The best example is the *burakumin*, a stigmatized group of at least four million outcasts. They are sometimes compared to India's untouchables. The *burakumin* are physically and genetically indistinguishable from other Japanese. Many of them "pass" as (and marry) majority Japanese, but a deceptive marriage can end in divorce if *burakumin* identity is discovered (Aoki and Dardess 1981).

Burakumin are perceived as standing apart from the majority Japanese lineage. Through ancestry and descent (and thus, it is assumed, "blood," or genetics), *burakumin* are "not us." Majority Japanese try to keep their lineage pure by discouraging mixing. The *burakumin* are residentially segregated in neighborhoods (rural or urban) called *buraku*, from which the racial label is derived. Compared with majority Japanese, the *burakumin* are less likely to attend high school and college. When *burakumin* attend the same schools as majority Japanese, they face discrimination. Majority children and teachers may refuse to eat with them because *burakumin* are considered unclean.

In applying for university admission or a job, and in dealing with the government, Japanese must list their address, which becomes part of a household or family registry. This list makes residence in a *buraku*, and likely *burakumin* social status, evident. Schools and companies use this information to discriminate. (The best way to pass is to move so often that the *buraku* address eventually disappears from the registry.) Majority Japanese also limit "race" mixture by hiring marriage mediators to check out the family histories of prospective spouses. They are especially careful to check for *burakumin* ancestry (De Vos et al. 1983).

The origin of the *burakumin* lies in a historic system of stratification (from the Tokugawa period: 1603–1868). The top four ranked categories were warrior-administrators (*samurai*), farmers, artisans, and merchants. The ancestors of the *burakumin* were below this hierarchy. An outcast group, they did unclean jobs, like animal slaughter and disposal of the dead. *Burakumin* still do related jobs, including work with animal products, like leather. The *burakumin* are more likely than majority Japanese to do manual labor (including farm work) and to belong to the national lower class. *Burakumin* and other Japanese minorities are also more likely to have careers in crime, prostitution, entertainment, and sports (De Vos et al. 1983).

Like blacks in the United States, the *burakumin* are class-stratified. Because certain jobs are reserved for the *burakumin*, people who are successful in those occupations (e.g., shoe factory owners) can be wealthy. *Burakumin* also have found jobs as government bureaucrats. Financially successful *burakumin* can temporarily escape their stigmatized status by travel, including foreign travel.

Today, most discrimination against the *burakumin* is *de facto* rather than *de jure*. It is strikingly like the discrimination that blacks have faced in the United States. The *burakumin* often live in villages and neighborhoods with poor housing and sanitation. They have limited access to education, jobs, amenities, and health facilities. In response to *burakumin* political mobilization, Japan has dismantled the legal structure of discrimination against *burakumin* and has worked to improve conditions in the *buraku*. Still, Japan has not instituted American-style affirmative action programs for education and jobs. Discrimination against non-majority Japanese is still the rule in companies. Some employers say that hiring *burakumin* would

Japan's stigmatized *burakumin* are physically and genetically indistinguishable from other Japanese. In response to *burakumin* political mobilization, Japan has dismantled the legal structure of discrimination against *burakumin*. This Sports Day for *burakumin* children is one kind of mobilization.

born in Japan and living there three successive years (Robertson 1992).

Like the *burakumin*, many Koreans (who by now include third and fourth generations) fit physically and linguistically into the Japanese population. Most Koreans speak Japanese as their primary language. Many of them pass as majority Japanese. Still, they tend to be segregated residentially. Often they live in the same neighborhoods as *burakumin*, with whom they sometimes intermarry. Koreans maintain strong kin ties and a sense of ethnic identity with other Koreans, especially in their neighborhoods. Most Japanese Koreans who qualify for citizenship choose not to take it because of Japan's policy of forced assimilation. Anyone who naturalizes is strongly encouraged to take a Japanese name. Many Koreans feel that to do so would cut them off from their kin and ethnic identity. Knowing they can never become majority Japanese, they choose not to become "not us" twice.

PHENOTYPE AND FLUIDITY: RACE IN BRAZIL

There are more flexible, less exclusionary ways of constructing social race than those used in the United States and Japan. Along with the rest of Latin America, Brazil has less exclusionary categories, which permit individuals to change their racial classification. Brazil shares a history of slavery with the United States, but it lacks the hypodescent rule. Nor does Brazil have racial aversion of the sort found in Japan. The history of Brazilian slavery dates back to the 16th century, when Africans were brought as slaves to work on sugar plantations in northeastern Brazil. Later, Brazilians used slave labor in mines and on coffee plantations. The contributions of Africans to Brazilian culture have been as great as they have been to North American culture. Today, especially in areas of Brazil where slaves were most numerous, African ancestry is evident.

give their companies an unclean image and thus create a disadvantage in competing with other businesses (De Vos et al. 1983).

Burakumin are citizens of Japan. Most Japanese Koreans, who form one of the nation's largest minorities (about 750,000 people), are not. As resident aliens, Koreans in Japan face discrimination in education and jobs. They lack citizens' healthcare and social-service benefits. Government and company jobs don't usually go to non-Japanese.

Koreans started arriving in Japan, mainly as manual laborers, after Japan conquered Korea in 1910 and ruled it through 1945. During World War II, there were more than two million Koreans in Japan. They were recruited to replace Japanese farm workers who left the fields for the imperial army. Some Koreans were women (numbering from 70,000 to 200,000) forced to serve as prostitutes ("comfort women") for Japanese troops. By 1952, most Japanese Koreans had been repatriated to a divided Korea. Those who stayed in Japan were denied citizenship. They became "resident aliens," forced, like Japanese criminals, to carry an ID card, which resentful Koreans call a "dog tag." Unlike most nations, Japan doesn't grant automatic citizenship to people born in the country. One can become Japanese by having one parent

The system that Brazilians use to classify biological differences contrasts with those used in the United States and Japan. First, Brazilians use many

Families migrate to the Amazon from many parts of Brazil. Notice the phenotypical diversity in this photo. How might it be reflected in racial classification?

by hypodescent and doesn't usually change. In Japan, race also is ascribed at birth, but it can change when, say, a *burakumin* or a naturalized Korean passes as a majority Japanese. In Brazil, racial identity is less automatic and more flexible. Brazilian racial classification pays attention to phenotype. A Brazilian's phenotype, and racial label, may change due to environmental factors, such as the tanning rays of the sun.

For historical reasons, darker-skinned Brazilians tend to be poorer than lighter-skinned Brazilians are. When Brazil abolished slavery in 1889, the freed men and women received no land or other reparations. They took what jobs were available. For example, the freed slaves who founded the village of Arembepe, which I have been studying since 1962, turned to fishing. Many Brazilians (including slave descendants) are poor because they lack a family history of access to land or commercial wealth and because upward social mobility is difficult. Continuing today, especially in cities, it is poor, dark-skinned Brazilians, on average, who face the most intense discrimination.

Given the correlation between poverty and dark skin, one's class status affects one's racial classification in Brazil. Thus, someone who has light skin and is poor will be perceived and classified as darker than a comparably colored person who is rich. The racial term applied to a wealthy person with dark skin will tend to "lighten" his or her skin color. This gives rise to the Brazilian expression "money whitens." In the United States, by contrast, race and class are correlated, but racial classification isn't changed by class. Because of hypodescent, racial identity in the United States is fixed and lifelong, regardless of phenotype or economic status. One illustration of the absence of hypodescent in Brazil is the fact that (unlike the United States) full siblings there may belong to different races (if they are phenotypically different).

Arembepe has a mixed and physically diverse population, reflecting generations of immigration and intermarriage between its founders and outsiders. Some villagers have dark, others light, skin color. Facial features, eye and hair color, and hair type also vary. Although physically heterogeneous, until recently Arembepe was economically homogeneous: local residents had not risen out of the national lower class. Given such economic uniformity, wealth contrasts do not affect racial classification, which Arembepeiros base on the physical

more racial labels (over 500 have been reported [Harris 1970]) than North Americans or Japanese do. In northeastern Brazil, I found 40 different racial terms in use in Arembepe, a village of only 750 people (Kottak 1999). Through their classification system, Brazilians recognize and attempt to describe the physical variation that exists in their population. The system used in the United States, by recognizing only three or four races, blinds North Americans to an equivalent range of evident physical contrasts. Japanese races, remember, don't even originate in physical contrasts. *Burakumin* are physically indistinguishable from other Japanese but are considered to be biologically different.

The system that Brazilians use to construct social race has other special features. In the United States, one's race is assigned automatically at birth

differences they perceive between individuals. As physical characteristics change (sunlight alters skin color, humidity affects hair form), so do racial terms. Furthermore, racial differences have been so insignificant in structuring community life that people often forget the terms they have applied to others. Sometimes they even forget the ones they've used for themselves. To reach this conclusion, I made it a habit to ask the same person on different days to tell me the races of others in the village (and my own). In the United States, I am always "white" or "Euro-American," but in Arembepe I got lots of terms besides *branco* ("white"). I could be *claro* ("light"), *louro* ("blond"), *sarará* ("light-skinned redhead"), *mulato claro* ("light mulatto"), or *mulato* ("mulatto"). The racial term used to describe me or anyone else varied from person to person, week to week, even day to day. My best local friend, a man with very dark skin color, changed the term he used for himself all the time—from *escuro* ("dark") to *preto* ("black") to *moreno escuro* ("dark brunet").

The North American and Japanese racial systems are creations of particular cultures. They are not scientific—or even accurate—descriptions of human biological differences. Brazilian racial classification is also a cultural construction. However, Brazilians have devised a way of describing human biological diversity that is more detailed, fluid, and flexible than the systems used in most cultures. Brazil lacks Japan's racial aversion. It also lacks a rule of descent like that which ascribes racial status in the United States (Degler 1970; Harris 1964).

The operation of the hypodescent rule helps us understand why the populations labeled "black" and "Indian" (Native American) are growing in the United States but shrinking in Brazil. North American culture places all "mixed" children in the minority category, which therefore gets all the resultant population increase. Brazil, by contrast, assigns the offspring of mixed marriages to intermediate categories, using a larger set of ethnic and racial labels. A Brazilian with a "white" (*branco*) parent and a "black" (*preto*) parent will almost never be called *branco* or *preto* but instead by some intermediate term (of which dozens are available). The United States lacks fully functional intermediate categories, but it is those categories that are swelling in Brazil. Brazil's assimilated Indians are called *cabôclos* (rather than *indíos*, or a specific tribal name, like *Kayapó* or Yanomami). With

hypodescent, by contrast, someone may have just one of four or eight Indian grandparents or great-grandparents and still "feel Indian," be so classified, and even have a tribal identity.

For centuries, the United States and Brazil each has had mixed populations, with ancestors from Native America, Europe, Africa, and Asia. Although these populations have mixed in both countries, Brazilian and North American cultures have constructed the results differently. The historic reasons for this contrast lie mainly in the different characteristics of the settlers of the two countries. The mainly English early settlers of the United States came as women, men, and families. Brazil's Portuguese colonizers, by contrast, were mainly men—merchants and adventurers. Many of these Portuguese men married Native American women and recognized their "racially mixed" children as their heirs. Like their North American counterparts, Brazilian plantation owners had sexual relations with their slaves. But the Brazilian landlords more often freed the children that resulted—for demographic and economic reasons. (Sometimes these were their only children.) Freed offspring of master and slave became plantation overseers and foremen and filled many intermediate positions in the emerging Brazilian economy. They were not classed with the slaves, but allowed to join a new intermediate category. No hypodescent rule ever developed in Brazil to ensure that whites and blacks remained separate (see Degler 1970; Harris 1964).

Stratification and "Intelligence"

See the Internet Exercises at your OLC

mhhe .com /kottak

Over the centuries groups with power have used racial ideology to justify, explain, and preserve their privileged social positions. Dominant groups have declared minorities to be *innately*, that is, biologically, inferior. Racial ideas have been used to suggest that social inferiority and presumed shortcomings (in intelligence, ability, character, or attractiveness) are immutable and are passed across the generations. This ideology defends stratification as inevitable, enduring, and "natural"—based in biology rather than society. Thus, the Nazis argued for the superiority of the "Aryan race," and European colonialists asserted the "white man's burden." South Africa institutionalized *apartheid*. Again and again, to justify the exploitation of minorities and native peoples, those in control have proclaimed the innate inferiority of the oppressed. In the United States the supposed superiority of whites was once standard segregationist doctrine. Belief in the biologically based inferiority of Native Americans has been an argument for their slaughter, confinement, and neglect.

However, anthropologists know that most of the behavioral variation among human groups rests on culture rather than biology. The cultural similarities revealed through thousands of ethnographic studies leave no doubt that capacities for cultural evolution are equivalent in all human populations. There is also excellent evidence that within any stratified (class-based) society, differences in performance between economic, social, and ethnic groups reflect their different experiences and opportunities. (Stratified societies are those with marked differences in wealth, prestige, and power between social classes.)

Stratification, political domination, prejudice, and ignorance continue to exist. They propagate the mistaken belief that misfortune and poverty result from lack of ability. Occasionally, doctrines of innate superiority are even set forth by scientists, who, after all, tend to come from the favored stratum of society. One of the best-known examples is Jensenism, named for the educational psychologist Arthur Jensen (Jensen 1969; Herrnstein 1971), its leading proponent. Jensenism is a highly questionable interpretation of the observation that African Americans, on average, perform less well on intelligence tests than Euro-Americans and Asian Americans do. Jensenism asserts that blacks are hereditarily incapable of performing as well as whites do. Writing with Charles Murray, Richard Herrnstein made a similar argument in the 1994 book *The Bell Curve*, to which the following critique also applies (see also Jacoby and Glauberman, eds. 1995). It should be noted that Jensen, Herrnstein, and Murray have no special training or expertise in genetics or evolution.

Environmental explanations for test scores are much more convincing than are the genetic arguments of Jensen, Herrnstein, and Murray. An environmental explanation does not deny that some people may be smarter than others. In any society, for many reasons, genetic and environmental, the talents of individuals vary. An environmental explanation does deny, however, that these differences can be generalized to whole populations. Even when talking about individual intelligence, however, we have to decide which of several abilities is an accurate measure of intelligence.

Psychologists have devised various kinds of tests to measure intelligence, but there are problems with all of them. Early intelligence tests required skill in manipulating words. Such tests do not measure learning ability accurately for several reasons. For example, individuals who have learned two languages as children—bilinguals— don't do as well, on average, on verbal intelligence tests as do those who have learned a single language. It would be absurd to suppose that children who master two languages have inferior intelligence. The explanation seems to be that because bilinguals have vocabularies, concepts, and verbal skills in both languages, their ability to manipulate either one suffers a bit. This would seem to be offset by the advantage of being fluent in two languages.

Understanding Ourselves   Are you bilingual? Probably not. Most Americans aren't— even many people raised in homes where two languages are spoken. Do you come from, or know someone who comes from, such a home? Is that person bilingual? What do you think of bilingual people? In public are you, or would you be, embarrassed to speak a language other than English? When you hear someone speaking a foreign language in public, what do you think?

One explanation for why bilinguals do less well on IQ tests than monolinguals do has been suggested in the text. Can you think of others? Do you think that North American culture discriminates against bilinguals—or, more generally, against people who speak foreign languages? Is American culture intolerant of, perhaps even phobic about, foreign languages? How can we learn about other cultures if we avoid learning their languages? Do American attitudes about foreign languages help us understand why American intelligence agencies did not anticipate the September 11, 2001, attacks against the World Trade Center and the Pentagon? More widespread and effective knowledge of Middle Eastern languages, such as Arabic, and of Central Asian languages, such as Persian (spoken in Iran) and Pashto (spoken in Afghanistan), would seem indicated as the United States claims interests in those world areas.

Tests reflect the experience of the people who devise them, who tend to be educated people in Europe and North America. It isn't surprising that middle- and upper-class children do best, because they are more likely to share the test makers' educational background, knowledge, and standards. Numerous studies have shown that performance on the Scholastic Achievement Test (SAT) can be improved by coaching and preparation. Parents who can afford hundreds of dollars for an SAT preparation course enhance their children's chances of getting high scores. Standardized college entrance exams are similar to IQ tests in that they have claimed to measure intellectual aptitude. They may do this, but they also measure type

and quality of high school education, linguistic and cultural background, and parental wealth. No test is free of bias based on class and culture.

Tests can only measure phenotypical intelligence, the product of a particular learning history, rather than genetically determined learning potential. IQ tests use middle-class experience as a standard for determining what should be known at a given chronological age. Furthermore, tests usually are administered by middle-class white people who give instructions in a dialect or language that may not be totally familiar to the child being tested. Test performance improves when the cultural, socioeconomic, and linguistic backgrounds of takers and examiners are similar (Watson 1972).

Links between social, economic, and educational environment and test performance show up in comparisons of American blacks and whites. At the beginning of World War I, intelligence tests were given to approximately one million American army recruits. Blacks from some northern states had higher average scores than did whites

At South Carolina's Clemson University in 1998, high school juniors take the SAT as part of a career enrichment program for minority students. How did you prepare for the SAT?

from some southern states. At that time northern blacks got a better public education than many southern whites did, and so their superior performance wasn't surprising. The fact that southern whites did better, on average, than southern blacks did also was expectable, given the unequal school systems then open to whites and blacks in the South.

Racists tried to dismiss the environmental explanation for the superior performance of northern blacks compared with southerners by suggesting selective migration, saying that smarter blacks had moved north. However, it was possible to test this hypothesis, which turned out to be false. If smarter blacks had moved north, their superior intelligence should have been evident in their school records while they were still living in the South. It was not. Furthermore, studies in New York, Washington, and Philadelphia showed that as length of residence in those cities increased, test scores also rose.

Studies of identical twins raised apart also illustrate the impact of environment on identical heredity. In a study of 19 pairs of twins, IQ scores varied directly with years in school. The average difference in IQ was only 1.5 points for the eight twin pairs with the same amount of schooling. It was 10 points for the 11 pairs with an average of five years' difference. One subject, with 14 years' more education than his twin, scored 24 points higher (Bronfenbrenner 1975).

These and similar studies provide overwhelming evidence that test performance measures background and education rather than genetically determined intelligence. For centuries, Europeans and their descendants have extended their political and economic control over much of the world. They colonized and occupied environments that they reached in their ships and conquered with their weapons. Most people in the most powerful contemporary nations—located in North America, Europe, and Asia—have light skin color. Some people in these currently powerful countries may incorrectly assert and believe that their position rests on innate biological superiority. Remember (as we saw in a previous section) that a prime minister of Japan has made such a claim.

We are living in and interpreting the world at a particular time. In the past there were far different associations between centers of power and human physical characteristics. When Europeans were barbarians, advanced civilizations thrived in the Middle East. When Europe was in the Dark Ages, there were civilizations in West Africa, on the East African coast, in Mexico, and in Asia. Before the Industrial Revolution, the ancestors of many white Europeans and North Americans were living more like precolonial Africans than like current members of the American middle class. Do you think preindustrial Europeans would excel on contemporary IQ tests?

SUMMARY

1. How do scientists approach the study of human biological diversity? Because of a range of problems involved in classifying humans into racial categories, contemporary biologists focus on specific differences and try to explain them. Biological similarities between groups may reflect—rather than common ancestry—similar but independent adaptation to similar natural selective forces.

2. Race is a cultural category, not a biological reality. "Races" derive from contrasts perceived in particular societies, rather than from scientific classifications based on common genes. In the United States, "racial" labels like "white" and "black" designate social races—categories defined by American culture. In American culture, one acquires his or her racial identity at birth. But American racial classification, gov-

erned by the rule of hypodescent, is based on neither phenotype nor genes. Children of mixed unions, no matter what their appearance, are classified with the minority-group parent.

3. Ten percent of Japan's people are minorities: Ainu, Okinawans, *burakumin*, children of mixed marriages, and immigrant nationalities, especially Koreans. Racial attitudes in Japan illustrate "intrinsic racism"—the belief that a perceived racial difference is a sufficient reason to value one person less than another. The valued group is majority ("pure") Japanese, who are believed to share "the same blood." Majority Japanese define themselves by opposition to others. These may be minority groups in Japan or outsiders—anyone who is "not us." Residential segregation and taboos on "interracial" marriage work

against minorities. Japanese culture regards certain ethnic groups as having a biological basis when there is no evidence that they do. The *burakumin* are physically and genetically indistinguishable from other Japanese, but they still face discrimination as a social race.

4. Such exclusionary racial systems are not inevitable. Although Brazil shares a history of slavery with the United States, it lacks the hypodescent rule. Full siblings who are phenotypically different can belong to different races. Brazilian racial identity is more of an achieved status. It can change during someone's lifetime, reflecting phenotypical changes. Given the correlation between poverty and dark skin, the class structure affects Brazilian racial classification. Someone with light skin who is poor will be classified as darker than a comparably colored person who is rich.

5. Some people assert genetic differences in the learning abilities of "races," classes, and ethnic groups. However, environmental variables (particularly educational, economic, and social background) provide better explanations for performance on intelligence tests by such groups. Intelligence tests reflect the life experiences of those who develop and administer them. All tests are to some extent culture-bound. Equalized environmental opportunities show up in test scores.

KEY TERMS

See the flash cards

/kottak

cline A gradual shift in gene frequencies between neighboring populations.

descent Rule assigning social identity on the basis of some aspect of one's ancestry.

hypervitaminosis D Condition caused by an excess of vitamin D; calcium deposits build up in the body's soft tissues, and the kidneys may fail; symptoms include gallstones and joint and circulation problems; may affect unprotected light-skinned individuals in the tropics.

hypodescent Rule that automatically places the children of a union or mating between members of different socioeconomic groups in the less-privileged group.

melanin Substance manufactured in specialized cells in the lower layers of the epidermis (outer skin layer); melanin cells in dark skin produce more melanin than do those in light skin.

natural selection As formulated by Charles Darwin and Alfred Russel Wallace, the process by which nature selects the forms most fit to survive and reproduce in a given environment.

phenotype An organism's evident traits, its "manifest biology"—anatomy and physiology.

rickets Nutritional disease caused by a shortage of vitamin D; interferes with the absorption of calcium and causes softening and deformation of the bones.

social race A group assumed to have a biological basis but actually perceived and defined in a social context, by a particular culture rather than by scientific criteria.

tropics Geographic belt extending about 23 degrees north and south of the equator, between the Tropic of Cancer (north) and the Tropic of Capricorn (south).

For more self testing, see the self quizzes

/kottak

CRITICAL THINKING QUESTIONS

1. If race is a discredited term in biology, what has replaced it?

2. What are the main problems with racial classification based on phenotype?

3. Besides those given in the text, can you think of other reasons why "race" is problematic?

4. What does racism mean if race has no biological basis?

5. What are three examples of ways in which the hypodescent rule affects American racial classification?

6. What are the main physical differences between majority Japanese, on the one hand, and *burakumin*, on the other?

7. What kind of racial classification system operates in the community where you grew up or now live? Does it differ from the racial classification system described for American culture in this chapter?

8. What is the difference between race and skin color in contemporary American culture? Are the social identities of Americans and discrimination against some Americans based on one or both of these attributes?

9. When medical studies find differences between blacks and whites, are those differences best explained by sociocultural or biological factors? Could such studies be more accurate if they abandoned the labels "black" and "white" in favor of other measures of biological variation, such as actual skin color or body fat?

10. If you had to devise an ideal system of racial categories, would it be more like the North American, the Japanese, or the Brazilian system? Why?

11. What kinds of environmental variables explain differential performance on intelligence tests by races, classes, and ethnic groups?

Atlas Questions

Look at Map 9, "Human Variations: Skin Color."

1. Where are the Native Americans with the darkest skin color located? What factors help explain this distribution?

2. In both western and eastern hemispheres, is the lightest skin color found in the north or the south? Outside Asia, where do you find skin color closest to northern Asian skin color? Is this surprising given what you have read about migrations and settlement history?

3. Where are skin colors darkest? How do you explain this distribution? Are there any areas that don't fit the explanations for skin color distribution given in the textbook?

SUGGESTED ADDITIONAL READINGS

Cohen, M.

1998   *Culture of Intolerance: Chauvinism, Class, and Racism.* New Haven, CT: Yale University Press. Various forms of intolerance, prejudice, and discrimination are examined.

Degler, C.

1970   *Neither Black nor White: Slavery and Race Relations in Brazil and the United States.* New York: Macmillan. The main contrasts between Brazilian and North American race relations and the historic, economic, and demographic reasons for them.

De Vos, G. A., and H. Wagatsuma

1966   *Japan's Invisible Race: Caste in Culture and Personality.* Berkeley: University of California Press. Considers many aspects of the *burakumin* (and other minorities) and their place in Japanese society and culture, including psychological factors.

Diamond, J. M.

1997   *Guns, Germs, and Steel: The Fates of Human Societies.* New York: W.W. Norton. An ecological approach to expansion and conquest in world history by a non-anthropologist.

Goldberg, D. T.

1997   *Racial Subjects: Writing on Race in America.* New York: Routledge. Survey of treatments of race in the United States.

2001   *The Racial State.* Malden, MA: Blackwell. Governments, racial policies, and racism.

Goldberg, D. T., ed.

1990   *Anatomy of Racism.* Minneapolis: University of Minnesota Press. Collection of articles on race and racism.

Harris, M.

1964 *Patterns of Race in the Americas*. New York: Walker. Reasons for different racial and ethnic relations in North and South America and the Caribbean.

Molnar, S.

2001 *Human Variation: Races, Types, and Ethnic Groups*, 5th ed. Upper Saddle River, NJ: Prentice-Hall. Links between biological and social diversity.

Montagu, A.

1981 *Statement on Race: An Annotated Elaboration and Exposition of the Four Statements on Race Issued by the United Nations Educational, Scientific, and Cultural Organization*. Westport, CT: Greenwood. United Nations positions on race analyzed.

Montagu, A., ed.

1997 *Man's Most Dangerous Myth: The Fallacy of Race*, 6th ed. Walnut Creek, CA: AltaMira. Revision of classic book.

1999 *Race and IQ*, expanded ed. New York: Oxford University Press. Revision of a classic volume of essays.

Shanklin, E.

1994 *Anthropology and Race*. Belmont, CA: Wadsworth. A concise introduction to the race concept from the perspective of anthropology.

Wade, P.

2002 *Race, Nature, and Culture: An Anthropological Perspective*. Sterling, VA: Pluto Press. A processual approach to human biology and race.

INTERNET EXERCISES

1. Go to the U.S. Census page entitled "Mapping Census 2000: The Geography of US Diversity," pp. 20–23 (**http://www.census.gov/population/cen2000/atlas/censr01-104.pdf**). Examine all four maps showing aspects of racial and ethnic diversity by county in the United States. Try to explain the historic processes that have produced, and are now producing, the patterns of diversity and density of specific groups.

   a. The first map shows the ethnic group with the highest percentage of population for all U.S. counties. What is the closest county to you with a high proportion of Native Americans? How about Hispanics?

   b. Examine Maps 1 and 2 for clusters of African Americans. Why are so many African Americans clustered in the southeastern part of the United States?

   c. Examine Map 2 for clusters of Hispanics. How do you explain high concentrations of Hispanics in the Pacific Northwest, in the Midwest, and on the East Coast?

   d. On Maps 1 and 2 determine where you find the highest concentrations of Asian Americans. Why are the concentrations of Asian Americans so different from those of other ethnic groups?

   e. Examine Map 3 to see which states were the most diverse in 2000. Examine Map 4 to see which states increased most in diversity between 1990 and 2000. Give a brief definition of the diversity index used in the map calculations.

2. Race and the Census: Read Gregory Rodriguez's article in *Salon* magazine entitled "Do the Multiracial Count?" (**http://www.salon.com/news/feature/2000/02/15/census/index.html**).

   a. What was the problem that some people had with the original census? How does this reflect American notions of race as described in this chapter?

   b. What was the compromise that the Clinton administration presented? What are its ramifications?

   c. In this case what role does the federal government play in our society's notions of race? Is the federal government merely responding to changing conceptions of race of the American people, or is it trying to shape the way the American public thinks about race?

   d. Based on this chapter, how do you think this kind of question on the census form would be handled in Brazil? In Japan?

See Chapter 9 at your McGraw-Hill Online Learning Center for additional review and interactive exercises.

10

THE FIRST FARMERS

Overview

Food production encompasses the domestication of plants and animals and the farming and herding economies that result. This new economy developed out of foraging, as people gradually added domesticates to the broad spectrum of resources used for subsistence. By 10,000 B.P. ancient Middle Easterners, the first farmers, were cultivating wheat and barley and influencing the reproduction of goats and sheep. It took a few thousand years, however, for them to become full-time food producers.

There were seven independent inventions of food production: in the Middle East, sub-Saharan Africa, northern and southern China, Mesoamerica, the south central Andes, and the eastern United States. They occurred at different times and were based on different sets of crops. In

Mexico

Mesoamerica between 7000 and 4000 B.P., maize and other domesticates were gradually added to a broad-spectrum foraging economy. The first permanent farming communities arose in the lowlands and in a few frost-free areas of the highlands. In the Valley of Mexico, quick-growing maize eventually made year-round village life possible. This paved the way for the emergence of the state and city life at Teotihuacan (A.D. 100 to A.D. 700) and Tenochtitlan, the Aztec capital (1325 to 1520).

Food production and the social and political systems it supported brought advantages and disadvantages. The advantages included many discoveries and inventions. The disadvantages included harder work, poorer health, crime, war, social inequality, and environmental degradation.

Gene Study Traces Cattle Herding in Africa

NATIONAL GEOGRAPHIC NEWS BRIEF

by Ben Harder

April 11, 2002

Plant cultivation and animal domestication, which are basic to farming and herding, respectively, are the two key forms of food production. They arose together in the Middle East, home of the world's first farmers and herders, but they don't always go together. In Mesoamerica (Mexico, Guatemala, and Belize), for example, there was farming but no herding. And in sub-Saharan Africa, where cattle have tremendous economic, social, and symbolic value, some areas had herding without farming. This news brief describes recent research showing that the domestication of cattle in Africa was independent of the domestication of cattle in the Middle East and South Asia. Where in Africa were cattle originally domesticated? Were sheep and goats also domesticated in Africa, or were they brought in through trade and migration? The article also discusses a trend in which native African cattle are being displaced by larger cattle with external origins. What subfields of anthropology help us understand the origin and significance of herding in Africa?

African herders rely on cattle for food and other basic needs, and as beasts of burden. But how cattle domestication occurred in Africa has been obscured by long-ago migrations and trade.

Now, by studying the DNA of cattle in 23 countries, an international team of scientists is filling in the picture.

An extensive new study of genetic variation in African cattle sheds light on how the domestication of cattle unfolded differently in Africa than elsewhere in the world.

Evidence suggests that sheep and goats, first domesticated in the Near East, were imported into Africa through colonization and ocean-going trade. Scientists have long speculated that the domestication of cattle also occurred first in the Near East and that the practice of herding cattle was similarly imported.

But new evidence, reported in the April 12 [2002] issue of the journal *Science*, suggests that Africans independently domesticated cattle.

Belgian geneticist Olivier Hanotte, who headed the new study, said the research "reconciles the two

A close relationship between African societies and cattle, as depicted in this rock art from Algeria, is thousands of years old. Over the centuries, indigenous African cattle have interbred with cattle from outside.

schools of thought" about how cattle domestication occurred in Africa.

"There were Near Eastern influences" on African herds, he said, "but they came after local domestication." Since then, there has been considerable mixing of African and Asian breeds . . .

In many parts of Africa, people herded cattle long before agriculture was introduced from the Near East and south Asia. Some African groups that have herded cattle for centuries have never adopted agriculture at all, or have done so only recently. One example is the Masai of eastern Africa, who rarely slaughter cattle but instead mix the milk and blood of the animals to create a staple of their diet.

Intrigued by the uncommon pattern of cattle domestication in Africa, Hanotte moved to Kenya in 1995 in an effort to explain the development. He and other researchers in Europe began untangling layers of genetic information in cattle DNA to help answer major questions about the history of herding in Africa.

Their findings offer scientists and herders a virtual history book describing how cattle, crucial to so many Africans, came to be so genetically diverse. The research also underscores why preserving that variety is essential.

[For each animal], Hanotte and his colleagues analyzed more than a dozen segments of . . . DNA [from] cattle belonging to 50 different herds in 23 African nations . . .

The samples of cattle DNA . . . revealed a telling geographic pattern [of variation among] cattle from West Africa, Central Africa, and southern Africa. The greatest amount of genetic diversity was found among herds in Central Africa. Based on the data, Hanotte and his colleagues concluded that people living in Central Africa developed cattle domestication on their own, and that the techniques—or the herders themselves—gradually migrated toward the west and the south, spreading domestication across the continent.

In looking at the wide genetic variation among African cattle, the researchers [also] found evidence of interbreeding between cattle native to Africa and an imported breed.

Most modern African herds represent mixtures of two breeds: Africa's native cattle, called taurines (*Bos taurus*), and a slightly larger Asian breed, known as zebu (*Bos indicus*), which was domesticated before it arrived in Africa.

Long-distance trade across the Indian Ocean brought many domesticated plants and animals to Africa . . . Presumably, Hanotte said, trade also brought zebu bulls that farmers interbred with domesticated taurine cows, producing the mixed herds of today . . .

For thousands of years, animal farmers have gradually improved their livestock by selectively breeding animals with . . . desired traits to endow the offspring with valuable combinations of traits.

Resistance to sleeping sickness is one trait that potentially could spread through selective breeding. Taurine cattle in one region of western Africa, unlike most livestock, are resistant to the parasite that causes the deadly disease.

But the number of animals with the protective adaptation is dwindling, as local farmers give up their taurine herds for large zebu animals.

Hanotte, along with other people, is worried by this trend. "The starting material for selective breeding is diversity," he said. "We can't afford to lose it."

SOURCE: http://news.nationalgeographic.com/news/2002/04/0411_020411_africacattle.html.

In Chapter 8 we saw that Europeans of the Upper Paleolithic painted big game, including wild cattle, on cave walls. African rock art also celebrates cattle—presumably the domesticated variety. Various cereals were domesticated in Africa some 6,000 years later than the earliest food production in the Middle East. African food production—crops and herds—was both independently invented and borrowed and differed substantially from the earliest food-producing economies in the Middle East, whose development we now examine.

In Chapter 8, we also considered the economic implications of the end of the Ice Age in Europe. With glacial retreat, foragers pursued a more generalized economy, focusing less on large animals. This was the beginning of what Kent Flannery (1969) has called the **broad-spectrum revolution**. This refers to the period beginning around 15,000 B.P. in the Middle East and 12,000 B.P. in Europe, during which a wider range, or broader spectrum, of plant and animal life was hunted, gathered, collected, caught, and fished. It was revolutionary because, in the Middle East, it led to **food production**—human control over the reproduction of plants and animals.

After 15,000 B.P., throughout the inhabited world, as the big-game supply diminished, foragers had to pursue new resources. Human attention shifted from large-bodied, slow reproducers (such as mammoths) to species such as fish, mollusks, and rabbits that reproduce quickly and prolifically (Hayden 1981).

For example, archaeologist David Lubell and his colleagues have reconstructed a pattern of intensive snail collecting at Kef Zoura, eastern Algeria. Dozens of sites in and around the Kef Zoura valley were occupied between 10,000 and 7,000 years ago by members of the Capsian culture. The *Capsians* were a Mesolithic people who based much of their subsistence on land snails, including the modern species the French call *escargot*. The Kef Zoura site has yielded millions of snail shells. The Capsians were nomadic, shifting camp sites after depleting the local snail supply. They also ate plants, including various grasses, acorns, pine nuts, and pistachio nuts (Bower and Lubell 1988).

Spirit Cave in northwestern Thailand has yielded the earliest plant remains from Southeast Asia (Gorman 1969). Between about 9200 and about 8600 B.P., the people at Spirit Cave ate wild nuts, gourds, water chestnuts, black pepper, and cucumbers. Although these plants were not yet domesticated, their association at the same site does indicate a diverse diet and a broad-spectrum pattern that eventually led to food production.

The Japanese site of Nittano (Akazawa 1980), on an inlet near Tokyo, offers additional evidence for the widespread importance of broad-spectrum foraging. Nittano was occupied several times between 6000 and 5000 B.P. by members of the *Jomon* culture, for which 30,000 sites are known in Japan. The Jomon people hunted deer, pigs, bears, and antelope. They also ate fish, shellfish, and plants. Jomon sites have yielded the remains of 300 species of shellfish and 180 species of edible plants (including berries, nuts, and tubers) (Akazawa and Aikens 1986).

We've just examined intensified and diversified resource use, in the form of broad-spectrum collecting, hunting, and gathering, in Algeria, Thailand, and Japan. Early experiments in food production illustrate another, and the most significant, form of intensified resource use in the post–Ice Age world. By 10,000 B.P., a major economic shift was under way in the Middle East (Turkey, Iraq, Iran, Syria, Jordan, and Israel). People started intervening in the reproductive cycles of the plants and animals their ancestors had foraged for generations. Middle Easterners eventually became the world's first farmers and herders (Moore 1985). No longer simply harvesting nature's bounty, they grew their own food and modified the biological characteristics of the plants and animals in their diet. By 10,000 B.P., domesticated plants and animals were part of the broad spectrum of resources used by Middle Easterners. By 7500 B.P., most Middle Easterners were moving away from a broad-spectrum foraging pattern toward more specialized economies based on fewer species, which were domesticates. They were becoming farmers and herders.

Kent Flannery (1969) has proposed a series of eras during which the Middle Eastern transition to farming and herding took place (Table 10.1). The era of seminomadic hunting and gathering (12,000 to 10,000 B.P.) encompasses the last stages of broad-spectrum foraging. This was the period just before the first domesticated plants (wheat and barley) and animals (goats and sheep) were added to the diet. Next came the era of early dry farming (of wheat and barley) and caprine domestication (10,000 to 7500 B.P.). *Dry farming* refers to farming without irrigation; such farming depended on rainfall. *Caprine* (from *capra*, Latin for "goat") refers to goats and sheep, which were domesticated during this era.

During the era of increasing specialization in food production (7500 to 5500 B.P.), new crops were added to the diet, along with more productive varieties of wheat and barley. Cattle and pigs were domesticated. By 5500 B.P., agriculture extended to the alluvial plain of the Tigris and Euphrates rivers (Figure 10.1), where early Mesopotamians lived in walled towns, some of which grew into cities. Metallurgy and the wheel were invented. After two million years of stone-tool making, *H. sapiens* was living in the Bronze Age.

The archaeologist V. Gordon Childe (1951) used the term *Neolithic Revolution* to describe the origin and impact of food production—plant cultivation and animal domestication. **Neolithic**, which means "New Stone Age," was coined to refer to techniques of grinding and polishing stone tools. However, the main significance of the Neolithic was the new total economy rather than just the tool-making techniques. *Neolithic* now

Table 10.1   The Transition to Food Production in the Middle East

Era	Dates (B.P.)
Origin of state (Sumer)	5500
Increasing specialization (cattle & pig) in food production (latter barley & wheat)	7500–5500
Early dry farming (no irrigation) and caprine domestication (goat + sheep)	10,000–7500 *(farming started)*
Seminomadic hunting and gathering (e.g., Natufians) *end of Broad Spectrum Foraging*	12,000–10,000

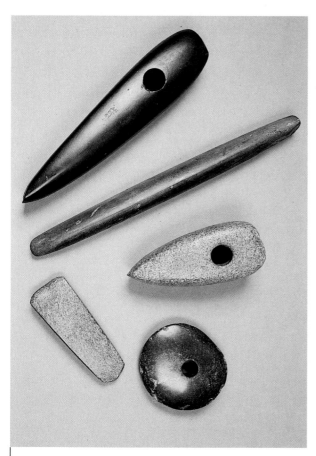

"Neolithic" was coined to refer to techniques of grinding and polishing stone tools, like these axes and hammers from Austria, Hungary, and the Czech Republic. Was the new tool-making style the most significant thing about the Neolithic?

refers to the first cultural period in a given region in which the first signs of domestication are present. The Neolithic economy based on food production produced substantial changes in human life styles. The pace of social and cultural change increased enormously.

The First Farmers and Herders in the Middle East

Middle Eastern food production arose in the context of four environmental zones. From highest to lowest, they are plateau (5,000 feet, or 1,500 meters), Hilly Flanks, steppe (treeless plain), and alluvial plain of the Tigris and Euphrates rivers (100 to 500 feet, or 30 to 150 meters). The **Hilly Flanks** is a subtropical woodland zone that flanks those rivers to the north (Figures 10.1 and 10.2).

It was once thought that food production began in oases in the alluvial plain. (*Alluvial* describes rich, fertile soil deposited by rivers and streams.) This arid region was where Mesopotamian civilization arose later. Today, we know that although the world's first civilization (Mesopotamian) did indeed develop in this zone, irrigation, a late (7000 B.P.) invention, was necessary to farm the alluvial river plain, a desert area. Plant cultivation and animal domestication started not in the arid river zone but in areas with reliable rainfall.

The archaeologist Robert J. Braidwood (1975) proposed instead that food production started in the Hilly Flanks, or subtropical woodland, zone, where wild wheat and barley would have been most abundant (see Figures 10.1 and 10.2). In 1948, a team headed by Braidwood started excavations at Jarmo, an early food-producing village inhabited between 9000 and 8500 B.P., located in the Hilly Flanks. We now know, however, that there were farming villages earlier than Jarmo (Figure 10.1) in zones adjacent to the Hilly Flanks. One example is Ali Kosh (Figure 10.1), a village in the foothills (piedmont steppe) of the Zagros mountains. By 9000 B.P., the people of Ali Kosh were herding goats, intensively collecting various wild plants, and harvesting wheat during the late winter and early spring (Hole, Flannery, and Neely 1969).

Climate change played a role in the origin of food production (Smith 1995). The end of the Ice Age brought greater regional and local variation in climatic conditions. Lewis Binford (1968) proposed that in certain areas of the Middle East (such as the Hilly Flanks), local environments were so rich in resources that foragers could adopt **sedentism**—sedentary (settled) life in villages. Binford's prime example is the widespread Natufian culture (12,500 to 10,500 B.P.), based on broad-spectrum foraging. The **Natufians**, who collected wild cereals and hunted gazelles, had year-round villages. They were able to stay in the same place (early villages) because they could harvest nearby wild cereals for six months.

Donald Henry (1989, 1995) documented a climate change toward warmer, more humid conditions just before the Natufian period. This expanded the altitude range of wild wheat and

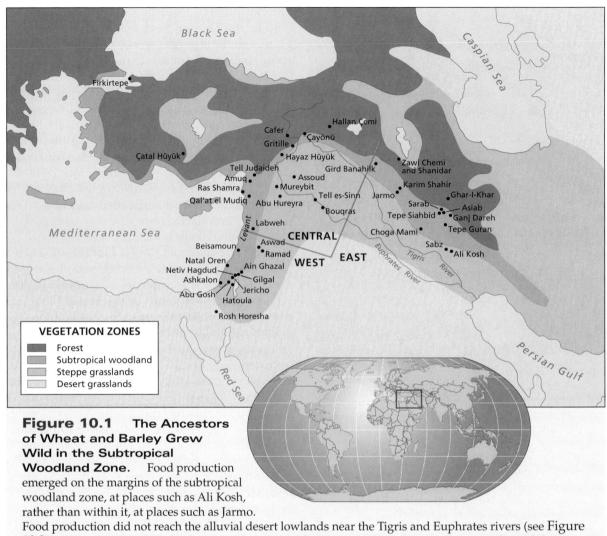

Figure 10.1 The Ancestors of Wheat and Barley Grew Wild in the Subtropical Woodland Zone.   Food production emerged on the margins of the subtropical woodland zone, at places such as Ali Kosh, rather than within it, at places such as Jarmo. Food production did not reach the alluvial desert lowlands near the Tigris and Euphrates rivers (see Figure 10.2), where Mesopotamian civilization arose around 5500 B.P., until irrigation was invented, much later.

barley, thus enlarging the available foraging area and allowing a longer harvest season. Wheat and barley ripened in the spring at low altitudes, in the summer at middle altitudes, and in the fall at high altitudes. As locations for their villages, the Natufians chose places where they could harvest wild cereals in all three zones.

Around 11,000 B.P., this favorable foraging pattern was threatened by a second climate change—to drier conditions. As many wild cereal habitats dried up, the optimal zone for foraging shrank. Natufian villages were now restricted to areas with permanent water. As population continued to grow, some Natufians attempted to maintain productivity

by transferring wild cereals to well-watered areas, where they started cultivating.

In the view of many scholars, the people most likely to adopt a new subsistence strategy, such as food production, would be those having the most trouble in following their traditional subsistence strategy (Binford 1968; Flannery 1973; Wenke 1996). Thus, those ancient Middle Easterners living outside the area where wild foods were most abundant would be the most likely to experiment and to adopt new subsistence strategies. This would have been especially true as the climate dried up. Recent archaeological finds support this hypothesis that food production began in *marginal areas*, such as the piedmont steppe, rather than in the optimal zones, such as the Hilly Flanks, where traditional foods were most abundant.

Even today, wild wheat grows so densely in the Hilly Flanks that one person working just an hour with Neolithic tools can easily harvest a kilogram of wheat (Harlan and Zohary 1966). People would have had no reason to invent cultivation when wild grain was ample to feed them. Wild wheat ripens rapidly and can be harvested over a three-week period. According to Flannery, over that time period, a family of experienced plant collectors could harvest enough grain—2,200 pounds (1,000 kilograms)—to feed themselves for a year. But after harvesting all that wheat, they'd need a place to put it. They could no longer maintain a nomadic life style, since they'd need to stay close to their wheat.

Sedentary village life thus developed before farming and herding in the Middle East. The Natufians and other Hilly Flanks foragers had no choice but to build villages near the densest stands of wild grains. They needed a place to keep their grain. Furthermore, sheep and goats came to graze on the stubble that remained after humans had harvested the grain. The fact that basic plants and animals were available in the same area also favored village life. Hilly Flanks foragers built houses, dug storage pits for grain, and made ovens to roast it.

Natufian settlements, occupied year-round, show permanent architectural features and evidence for the processing and storage of wild grains. One such site is Abu Hureyra, Syria (see Figure 10.1), which was initially occupied by Natufians around 11,000 to 10,500 B.P. Then it was abandoned—to be reoccupied later by food producers, between 9500 and 8000 B.P. From the Natufian period, Abu Hureyra has yielded the remains of grinding stones, wild plants, and 50,000 gazelle bones, which represent 80 percent of all the bones recovered at the site (Jolly and White 1995).

Prior to domestication, the favored Hilly Flanks zone had the densest human population. Eventually, its excess population started to spill over into adjacent areas. Colonists from the Flanks tried to maintain their traditional broad-spectrum foraging in these marginal zones. But with sparser resources available, they had to experiment with new subsistence strategies. Eventually, population pressure on more limited resources forced people in the marginal zones to become the first food producers (Binford 1968; Flannery 1969). *Early cultivation began as an attempt to copy, in a less favorable environment, the dense stands of wheat and barley that grew wild in the Hilly Flanks.*

The Middle East, along with certain other world areas where food production originated, is a region that for thousands of years has had a *vertical economy*. (Other examples include Peru and **Mesoamerica**—Middle America, including Mexico, Guatemala, and Belize.) A vertical economy exploits environmental zones that, although close together in space, contrast with one another in altitude, rainfall, overall climate, and vegetation (Figure 10.2). Such a close juxtaposition of varied environments allowed broad-spectrum foragers to use different resources in different seasons.

Early seminomadic foragers in the Middle East had followed game from zone to zone. In winter they hunted in the piedmont steppe region, which had winter rains rather than snow and provided

Some 12,000 to 10,000 years ago, ancient Middle Easterners followed the availability of plants and animals, from lower to higher zones. With domestication, this pattern evolved into nomadic herding (pastoralism). Contemporary Middle Eastern herders still take their flocks to grazing areas at different elevations. This 1997 photo shows a Bedouin shepherd in the hills near Bethlehem, West Bank, Israel.

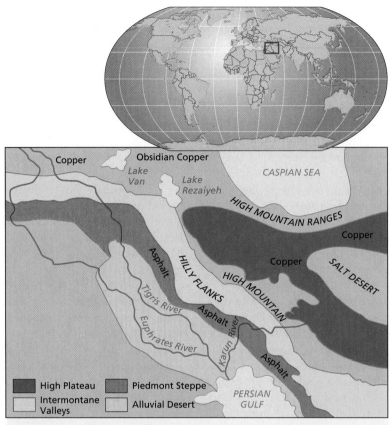

Figure 10.2   The Vertical Economy of the Ancient Middle East.   Geographically close but contrasting environments were linked by seasonal movements and trade patterns of broad-spectrum foragers. Traded resources included copper, obsidian, and asphalt, located in particular zones. As people traveled and traded, they removed plants from the zones where they grew wild in the Hilly Flanks into adjacent zones where humans became agents of selection.

winter pasture for game animals 12,000 years ago. (Indeed it is still used for winter grazing by herders today.) When winter ended, the steppe dried up. Game moved up to the Hilly Flanks and high plateau country as the snow melted. Pasture land became available at higher elevations. Foragers gathered as they climbed, harvesting wild grains that ripened later at higher altitudes. Sheep and goats followed the stubble in the wheat and barley fields after people had harvested the grain.

The four Middle Eastern environmental zones shown in Figure 10.2 also were tied together through trade. Certain resources were confined to specific zones. Asphalt, used as an adhesive in the manufacture of sickles, came from the steppe.

Copper and turquoise sources were located in the high plateau. Contrasting environments were therefore linked in two ways: by foragers' seasonal migration and by trade.

The movement of people, animals, and products between zones—plus population increase supported by highly productive broad-spectrum foraging—was a precondition for the emergence of food production. As they traveled between zones, people carried seeds into new habitats. Mutations, genetic recombinations, and human selection led to new kinds of wheat and barley. Some of the new varieties were better adapted to the steppe and, eventually, the alluvial plain than the wild forms had been.

GENETIC CHANGES AND DOMESTICATION

See the Virtual Exploration

mhhe ●com /kottak

What are the main differences between wild and domesticated plants? The seeds of domesticated cereals, and often the entire plant, are larger. Compared with wild plants, crops produce a higher yield per unit of area. Domesticated plants also lose their natural seed dispersal mechanisms. Cultivated beans, for example, have pods that hold together, rather than shattering as they do in the wild. Domesticated cereals have tougher connective tissue holding the seedpods to the stem.

Grains of wheat, barley, and other cereals occur in bunches at the end of a stalk (Figure 10.3). The grains are attached to the stalk by an *axis*, plural *axes*. In wild cereals, this axis is brittle. Sections of the axis break off one by one, and a seed attached to each section falls to the ground. This is how wild cereals spread their seeds and propagate their species. But a brittle axis is a problem for people. Imagine the annoyance experienced by broad-spectrum foragers as they tried to harvest wild wheat, only to have the grain fall off or be blown away.

In very dry weather, wild wheat and barley ripen—their axes totally disintegrating—in just three days (Flannery 1973). The brittle axis must have been even more irritating to people who planted the seeds and waited for the harvest. But fortunately, certain stalks of wild wheat and barley happened to have tough axes. These were the ones whose seeds people saved to plant the following year.

Another problem with wild cereals is that the edible portion is enclosed in a tough husk. This husk was too tough to remove with a pounding stone. Foragers had to roast the grain to make the husk brittle enough to come off. However, some wild plants happened to have genes for brittle husks. Humans chose the seeds of these plants (which would have germinated prematurely in nature) because they could be more effectively prepared for eating.

People also selected certain features in animals (Smith 1995). Some time after sheep were domesticated, advantageous new phenotypes arose. Wild sheep aren't woolly; wool coats were products of domestication. Although it's hard to imagine, a wool coat offers protection against extreme heat. Skin temperatures of sheep living in very hot areas

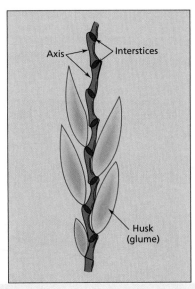

Figure 10.3   A Head of Wheat or Barley.   In the wild, the axis comes apart as its parts fall off one by one. The connecting parts (interstices) are tough and don't come apart in domesticated grains. In wild grains, the husks are hard. In domestic plants, they are brittle, which permits easy access to the grain. How did people deal with hard husks before domestication?

are much lower than temperatures on the surface of their wool. Woolly sheep, but not their wild ancestors, could survive in hot, dry alluvial lowlands. Wool had an additional advantage: its use for clothing.

What are some of the differences between wild and domesticated animals? Plants got larger with domestication, while animals got smaller, probably because smaller animals are easier to control. Middle Eastern sites document changes in the horns of domesticated goats. Such change may have been genetically linked to some other desirable trait that has left no skeletal evidence behind.

FOOD PRODUCTION AND THE STATE

The shift from foraging to food production was gradual. The knowledge of how to grow crops and breed livestock didn't immediately convert Middle Easterners into full-time farmers and herders. Domesticated plants and animals began as minor parts of a broad-spectrum economy. Foraging for fruits, nuts, grasses, grains, snails, and insects continued.

Simple irrigation systems were being used in the Middle East by 7000 B.P. By 6000 B.P., complex irrigation techniques made agriculture possible in the arid lowlands of southern Mesopotamia. Here in Sudan, we see a fairly simple, ox-powered irrigation system.

Over time, Middle Eastern economies grew more specialized, geared more exclusively toward crops and herds. The former marginal zones became centers of the new economy and of population increase and emigration. Some of the increasing population spilled back into the Hilly Flanks, where people eventually had to intensify production by cultivating. Domesticated crops could now provide a bigger harvest than could the grains that grew wild there. Thus, in the Hilly Flanks, too, farming eventually replaced foraging as the economic mainstay.

Farming colonies spread down into drier areas. By 7000 B.P., simple irrigation systems had developed, tapping springs in the foothills. By 6000 B.P., more complex irrigation techniques made agriculture possible in the arid lowlands of southern Mesopotamia. In the alluvial desert plain of the Tigris and Euphrates rivers, a new economy based on irrigation and trade fueled the growth of an entirely new form of society. This was the *state*, a social and political unit featuring a central government, extreme contrasts of wealth, and social classes. The process of state formation is examined in the next chapter.

We now understand why the first farmers lived neither in the alluvial lowlands, where the Mesopotamian state arose around 5500 B.P., nor in the Hilly Flanks, where wild plants and animals abounded. Food production began in marginal zones, such as the piedmont steppe, where people experimented at reproducing, artificially, the dense grain stands that grew wild in the Hilly Flanks. As seeds were taken to new environments, new phenotypes were favored by a combination of natural and human selection. The spread of cereal grains outside their natural habitats was part of a system of migration and trade between zones, which had developed in the Middle East during the broad-spectrum period. Food production also owed its origin to the need to intensify production to feed an increasing human population—the legacy of thousands of years of productive foraging.

Other Old World Farmers

The path from foraging to farming was one that people followed independently in at least seven world areas. As we'll see later in this chapter, three were in the Americas. Four were in the Old World, including the very first farmers and herders in the Middle East. In each of these seven centers, people independently invented domestication—albeit of different sets of crops and animals.

Food production also spread out from the Middle East and other centers of domestication. This happened through trade, through diffusion of plants, animals, products and information, and through the actual migration of farmers, who in some cases displaced native foragers. The crops and livestock that were originally domesticated in the Middle East spread westward to northern Africa, including Egypt's Nile Valley, and into Europe (Price 2000). Trade also extended eastward from the Middle East to India and Pakistan. In Egypt, an agricultural economy based on plants and animals originally domesticated in the Middle East led to a pharaonic civilization. Another early civilization eventually arose in western Pakistan.

Interpret the World
Atlas Map 10

Around 8,000 B.P., communities on Europe's Mediterranean shores, in Greece, Italy, and France, started shifting from foraging to farming, using imported species. By 7000 B.P., there were fully sedentary farming villages in Greece and Italy. By 6000 B.P., there were thousands of farming villages as far east as Russia and as far west as northern France. In your atlas, look at Map 10, "Early Neolithic Sites of the Middle East and Europe," which shows major archaeological sites there and also indicates the dates and directions of diffusion of food production from the Mediterranean and Middle East to Europe. Also note the symbols used to show plant and animal domesticates. Which plants and animals were most widely diffused in Europe? By chance, we can even meet a man from one of those European Neolithic villages. The "Iceman" discovered in the Italian Alps in 1991 (see "Interesting Issues" on pp. 264–265) came from a village of farmers who raised wheat, barley, sheep, and goats.

Compared with the Middle East, less is known about early farmers in such Old World areas as sub-Saharan Africa, South and Southeast Asia, and China. Partly this reflects the poorer preservation of archaeological remains in hot, moist habitats. Mostly it reflects the need for more archaeological research in such areas. In Pakistan's Indus River Valley, ancient cities (Harappa and Mohenjo-daro) emerged slightly later than did the first Mesopotamian city-states. Domestication and state formation in the Indus Valley were probably influenced by developments in, and trade with, the Middle East. Still, archaeological research confirms the early (8000 B.P.) presence of domesticated goats, sheep, cattle, wheat, and barley in Pakistan (Meadow 1991).

China was also one of the first world areas to develop farming, based on millet and rice. Millet is a tall, coarse cereal grass still grown in northern China. This grain, which today feeds a third of the world's population, is used in contemporary North America mainly as birdseed. By 7500 B.P., two varieties of millet supported early farming communities in northern China, along the Yellow River. Millet cultivation paved the way for widespread village life and eventually for Shang dynasty civilization, based on irrigated agriculture, between 3600 and 3100 B.P. (See Chapter 11.) The northern Chinese also had domesticated dogs, pigs, and possibly cattle, goats, and sheep by 7000 B.P. (Chang 1977).

Millet, being harvested here on a Chinese plateau, was grown in the Hwang-Ho (Yellow River) Valley by 7000 B.P. This grain supported early farming communities in northern China. What was being grown in southern China at the same time?

The glacially preserved "Iceman" found in the Italian Alps in 1991 was a Neolithic Alpine European. The find is significant because of its age, its state of preservation, and its combination of a human cadaver with clothing and possessions, including stone and metal (copper) tools. The Iceman probably came from an Alpine farming village. He was on an autumn hunting trip when he was killed and eventually frozen. DNA analysis of the contents of his stomach shows he ate red deer for his last meal (Fountain 2002). The Neolithic, which began some 10,000 years ago in the Middle East, had spread to Western Europe by 6500 B.P.

The "Iceman," who scientists now know lived about 5,300 years ago, had been in the ice 1,000 years when the Egyptians built the pyramids at Giza, more than 3,000 years when Jesus was born. Yet he was found with a remarkable array of clothing, weapons, and equipment, including some mysterious objects of types never seen before.

Some—including the man's fur hat, the oldest known in Europe—were found . . . near the Austrian–Italian border . . .

The man's body was found not in a grave, the usual source of ancient remains, but at a campsite he made during a sojourn in the mountains . . . [S]now and ice covered him and his things, preserving them almost perfectly.

His perishable belongings—items made of wood, leather, grass, and apparently even food and medicines—have come out of the ice virtually intact, providing scientists with the most intimate picture ever seen of the daily life of a prehistoric man.

For example, his ax, which has a copper head, looks and feels as new and dangerous as on the fall day in about 3300 B.C. [5,300 B.P.], when the man leaned it against a rock before bedding down for his last night. It is among the oldest copper axes known and one of the best made, dating from the dawn of the use of metals.

Archaeologists know that fateful night was in the autumn, because frozen with him was a ripe blackthorn fruit, the plumlike berry also called sloe, which grows at lower altitudes and ripens in the fall.

The man's body is startlingly well preserved—by far the most lifelike from prehistoric times. . .

The body was naturally freeze-dried and is in such good condition that pores in the skin look normal. Even his eyeballs can still be seen behind lids frozen open, and CT scans show the brain and other internal organs in place.

"We have never had a prehistoric discovery as complete as this," said Andreas Lippert, a University of Vienna archaeologist who led the expedition to the site . . . The group found more than 400 objects, most of them parts of the man's clothing.

Yet several key questions remain. What was he doing so high in the mountains? How did he die? And, most intriguing to archaeologists, did he come from one of the known prehistoric cultures of the region, or does he represent something entirely new?

What is clear is that he lived during one of the more critical transitions in the development of human culture, when stone tools were beginning to give way to metal.

Farming, which began in the Middle East about 5,000 years ear-lier, had spread to much of Eurasia by 5,300 years ago. The man probably came from a village of farmers who raised wheat, barley, and oats and herded sheep and goats.

The man in the ice was discovered Sept. 19, 1991, by Helmut and Erika Simon, a German couple hiking in the Alps. Near the 10,500-foot-high ridge that defines the Austrian–Italian border they were tramping over the snow and ice of a commonly used pass when they saw a human head and shoulders sticking out of the ice. The body was lying face down, its skin a tawny color and the head hairless. The Simons reported it to police in the Italian state of South Tirol.

The local Carabinieri, Italian police familiar with the common problem of retrieving bodies of modern climbers, insisted that this time the site was in Austria and not their problem.

Two days later the Austrian police from north Tirol arrived with a helicopter and—not realizing the site's importance—used an air hammer to hack the body out of the ice. They accidentally cut into the man's hip, but his legs stayed stuck. Forensic officials spotted the copperbladed ax on a nearby rock and, presuming foul play in the man's death, took it as "evidence."

Bad weather forced a temporary retreat. But word of the find encouraged curious hikers to trek to the body, and several tried to chop it free.

On Sept. 23, four days after the find, a forensic team from the University of Innsbruck helicoptered to the site, found that meltwater had refrozen around the body and began again to chop. When they pulled out the prone body, it was later realized,

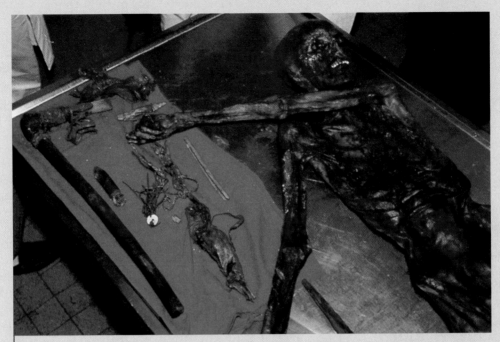

Meet the Iceman. Since his frozen body emerged from a glacier in the Italian Alps in 1991, scientists have come to realize he is the closest we may ever come to meeting a real person from the Stone Age. How would you evaluate his state of preservation?

the man's penis remained embedded in the ice.

Workers also gathered up some pieces of fur and leather clothing, string, a leather bag and a flint dagger. A long stick, apparently a bow, was still partly embedded in ice, so workers broke off part and took that, too.

Hikers and skiers had been lost in the Alps many times, but they usually emerged a few decades later when the flow of the glaciers transported them to lower altitudes where they melted out. Moreover, these "young" bodies were usually horribly transformed into misshapen blobs of "fat wax." This man in the ice, though dried and somewhat shriveled like a mummy, looked too good to be very old.

A team of glaciologists soon resolved the question with another visit to the site. They found that the body had lain at the bottom of a narrow ravine. Snow could have filled the 6-to-10-foot-deep crevice, but the resulting ice was trapped.

The glaciologists also found evidence to support the man's antiquity—his quiver, which contained 14 arrows, two of them fitted with flint arrowheads, hardly the choice of any bowman who lived since the Iron Age swept Eurasia more than 3,000 years ago.

And the glaciologists explained why the body had only just emerged. Earlier in 1991 great storms had blown dust from North Africa into the Alps, darkening the snow cover.

The dust absorbed solar heat, causing more than the usual amount of snow to melt during the summer of 1991, exposing the body.

Years after the original discovery, which turned out actually to have been in Italy rather than Austria, new imaging techniques detected an arrow point in the Iceman's shoulder. This suggests that he may have died in a weakened condition after an attack. The Iceman currently resides in Bolzano, Italy, in a museum established in his honor.

SOURCE: Boyce Rensberger, "A Man Who Lived 5,300 Years Ago," *The Washington Post*, November 26, 1992, p. E1.

Recent discoveries by Chinese archaeologists suggest that rice was domesticated in the Yangtze River corridor of southern China as early as 8400 B.P. (Smith 1995). Other early rice comes from the 7,000-year-old site Hemudu, on Lake Dongting in southern China. The people of Hemudu used both wild and domesticated rice, along with domesticated water buffalo, dogs, and pigs. They also hunted wild game (Jolly and White 1995).

China seems to have been the scene of two independent transitions to food production, based on different crops grown in strikingly different climates. Southern Chinese farming was rice aquaculture in rich subtropical wetlands. Southern winters were mild; and summer rains, reliable. Northern China, by contrast, had harsh winters, with unreliable rainfall during the summer growing season. This was an area of grasslands and temperate forests. Still, in both areas by 7500 B.P., food production supported large and stable villages. Based on the archaeological evidence, early Chinese villagers had architectural expertise. They lived in substantial houses, made elaborate ceramic vessels, and had rich burials.

At Nok Nok Tha in central Thailand, pottery made more than 5,000 years ago has imprints of husks and grains of domesticated rice (Solheim 1972/1976). Animal bones show that the people of Nok Nok Tha also had humped zebu cattle similar to those of contemporary India. Rice might have been cultivated at about the same time in the Indus River Valley of Pakistan and adjacent western India.

It appears that food production arose independently as many as seven times in different world areas. Figure 10.4 is a map highlighting those seven areas: the Middle East, north China, south China, sub-Saharan Africa, central Mexico, the south central Andes, and the eastern United States. A different set of major foods was domesticated, at different times, in each area, as we see in Table 10.2. Some grains, such as millet and rice, were domesticated more than once. Millet grows wild in China and Africa, where it became an important food crop, as well as in Mexico, where it did not. Indigenous African rice, grown only in West Africa, belongs to the same genus as Asian rice. Pigs and possibly cattle were independently domesticated in the Middle East, China, and sub-Saharan Africa. Independent domestication of the dog was virtually a worldwide phenomenon, including the Western Hemisphere. We turn now to archaeological sequences in the Americas.

The First American Farmers

Homo did not, of course, originate in the Western Hemisphere. Never have fossils of Neandertals or earlier hominids been found in North or South America. The settlement of the Americas was one of the major achievements of *H. sapiens sapiens*. This colonization continued the trends toward population increase and expansion of geographic range that have marked human evolution generally.

AMERICA'S FIRST IMMIGRANTS

See the Internet Exercises at your OLC

mhhe com /kottak

The original settlers of the Americas came from Northeast Asia. They were the ancestors of American Indians. They entered North America via the Bering land bridge, *Beringia*, which connected North America and Siberia several times during the ice ages. Beringia, which today lies under the Bering Sea, was a dry land area several hundred miles wide, exposed during the glacial advances (Figure 10.5).

Living in Beringia thousands of years ago, the ancestors of Native Americans didn't realize they were embarking on the colonization of a new continent. They were merely big-game hunters who, over the generations, moved gradually eastward as they spread their camps and followed their prey—woolly mammoths and other tundra-adapted herbivores. Other ancient hunters entered North America along the shore by boat, fishing and hunting sea animals.

This was truly a "new world" to its earliest colonists, as it would be to the European voyagers who rediscovered it thousands of years later. Its natural resources, particularly its big game, had never before been exploited by humans. Early bands followed the game south. Although ice sheets covered most of what is now Canada, colonization gradually penetrated the heartland of what is now the United States. Successive generations of hunters followed game through unglaciated corridors, breaks in the continental ice sheets. Others spread by boat down the Pacific coast.

In North America's rolling grasslands, early American Indians, *Paleoindians*, hunted horses, camels, bison, elephants, mammoths, and giant sloths. The **Clovis tradition**—a sophisticated stone

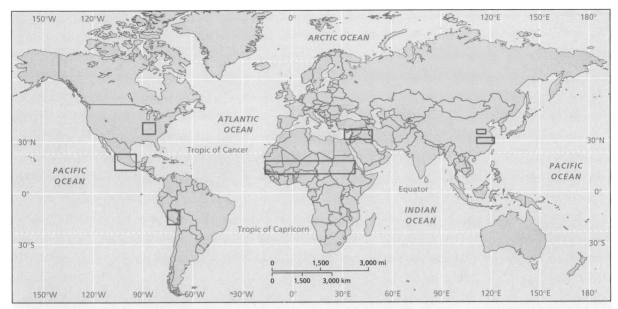

Figure 10.4 **Seven World Areas Where Food Production Was Independently Invented.** Do any of these areas surprise you?

SOURCE: B. D. Smith, *The Emergence of Agriculture* (New York: Scientific American Library, W. H. Freeman, 1995), p. 12.

See the Interactive Exercise for a quiz

mhhe
●com
/kottak

Table 10.2 **Seven World Areas Where Food Production Was Independently Invented**

World Area	Major Domesticated Plants/Animals	Earliest Date (B.P.)
Middle East	Wheat, barley Sheep, goats, cattle, pigs	10,000
South China (Yangtze River corridor)	Rice Water buffalo, dogs, pigs	8500–6500
North China (Yellow River)	Millet Dogs, pigs, chickens	7500
Sub-Saharan Africa	Sorghum, pearl millet, African rice	4000
Central Mexico	Maize, beans, squash Dogs, turkeys	4700
South Central Andes	Potato, quinoa, beans Camelids (llama, alpaca), guinea pigs	4500
Eastern United States	Goosefoot, marsh elder, sunflower, squash	4500

SOURCE: Data compiled from B. D. Smith, *The Emergence of Agriculture* (New York: Scientific American Library, W. H. Freeman, 1995).

Overland migrations from Asia ended when rising sea levels flooded Beringia, leaving a landscape of ice, ocean, and jagged peaks. How might later Asian migrants have entered North America? How might archaeologists find out more about the people who lived in Beringia?

technology based on a point that was fastened to the end of a hunting spear (Figure 10.6)—flourished between 12,000 and 11,000 B.P. in the Central Plains, on their western margins, and over a large area of what is now the eastern United States. The Monte Verde archaeological site in south central Chile has been firmly dated to 12,000 B.P. (Smith 1995). This evidence for the early occupation of southern South America suggests that the first migration of humans into the Americas may date back 20,000 years.

Reinforcing this idea is work done by archaeologist Joseph M. McAvoy, whose team has studied an early human settlement in Virginia, located on a sandy slope called Cactus Hill, 45 miles south of Richmond. McAvoy has worked since 1989 at Cactus Hill, located near the Nottoway River, where Clovis tools had been found. Beneath the Clovis-era site, McAvoy's team found tools dating back 15,000 to 17,000 years. These toolmakers, who lived in Virginia before the Clovis era, may have foraged eastern mud turtles and whitetail deer, burned remains of which were found by the archaeologists. The Americas probably were not populated by a single mass migration but rather in

spurts, perhaps starting around 20,000 years ago, as small groups of nomadic foragers made their way to North America at various times, following different routes (Todt 2000).

THE FOUNDATIONS OF FOOD PRODUCTION

As hunters benefiting from the abundance of big game, bands of foragers gradually spread through the Americas. As they moved, these early Americans learned to cope with a great diversity of environments. Thousands of years later, their descendants independently invented food production, paving the way for the emergence of states based on agriculture and trade in Mexico and Peru. New World food production emerged 3,000 to 4,000 years later than in the Middle East, as did the first states.

The most significant contrast between Old and New World food production involved animal domestication, which was much more important in the Old World than in the New World. The animals that had been hunted during the early American big-game tradition either became extinct before people could domesticate them or were not domes-

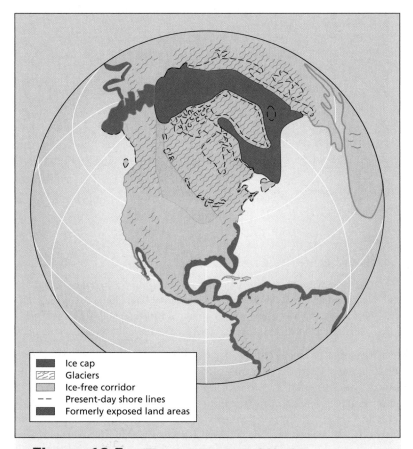

Figure 10.5 **The Ancestors of Native Americans Came to North America as Migrants from Asia.** They followed big-game herds across Beringia, an immense stretch of land exposed during the ice ages. Was their settlement of the Americas intentional? When did it probably happen? Other migrants reached North America along the shore by boat, fishing and hunting sea animals.

Legend:
- Ice cap
- Glaciers
- Ice-free corridor
- – – Present-day shore lines
- Formerly exposed land areas

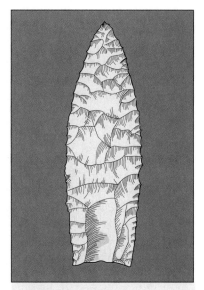

Figure 10.6
A Clovis Spear Point.
Such points were attached to spears used by Paleoindians of the North American plains between 12,000 and 11,000 B.P. Are there sites with comparable ages in South America?

ticable. The largest animal ever domesticated in the New World (in Peru, around 4,500 B.P.) was the llama. Early Peruvians and Bolivians ate llama meat and used that animal as a beast of burden (Flannery, Marcus, and Reynolds 1989). They bred the llama's relative, the alpaca, for its wool. (Llamas and alpacas are members of the *camelid* family.) Peruvians also added animal protein to their diet by raising and eating guinea pigs and ducks.

The turkey was domesticated in Mesoamerica and in the southwestern United States. Lowland South Americans domesticated a type of duck. The dog is the only animal that was domesticated throughout the New World. There were no cattle, sheep, or goats in the areas where food production

arose. As a result, neither herding nor the kinds of relationships that developed between herders and farmers in many parts of the Middle East, Europe, Asia, and Africa emerged in the precolonial Americas. The New World crops were different, although staples as nutritious as those of the Old World were domesticated from native wild plants.

Understanding Ourselves Differences in early food production between the Old World and the Americas help us understand their subsequent histories. Domesticable animals were a key ingredient in the origin of food production in the Middle East. Animals and crops thrived together in most regions of early food production in the Old World, including the Middle East, Africa, Europe, and Asia. Not so in the Americas, where wild oxen, horses, pigs, and camels once lived, but went extinct (probably due to a combination of hunting by humans and climatic changes) long before the first crops were cultivated. In the Middle East a mutually supportive relationship could develop between farming and herding. Animals could feed on stubble left in wheat fields after the crops were harvested. Crops could be grown to feed sheep, goats, and eventually cattle, pigs, horses, and donkeys. Animals could be used as beasts of burden, attached to sleds, rollers, and eventually wheeled vehicles.

The widespread use of wheeled vehicles, as diverse as oxcarts, chariots, and carriages, fueled the growth of trade, travel, and transport in the Old World. Advances in transportation led to an eventual "age of discovery" and the European conquest of the Americas. Early farmers in Mesoamerica had no trouble coming up with the idea of the wheel, which they sometimes attached to toys. But how could they have oxcarts or chariots without the appropriate animals to pull them? Dogs do pull sleds in the Arctic (never a center of food production), but dogs and turkeys can't match horses, donkeys, or oxen as beasts of burden. The lack of animal domestication in Mesoamerica is more than a textbook fact to be memorized for a test. It's a key factor in world history, helping us understand the divergent development of societies on different sides of the oceans.

Three *caloric staples*, major sources of carbohydrates, were domesticated by Native American farmers. **Maize**, or corn, first domesticated in highland Mexico, became the caloric staple in Mesoamerica and Central America; it eventually spread to coastal Peru. The other two staples were root crops: white ("Irish") potatoes, first domesticated in the Andes, and **manioc**, or cassava, a tuber first cultivated in the South American lowlands. Other crops added variety to New World diets and made them nutritious. Beans and squash, for example, provided essential proteins, vitamins, and minerals. Maize, beans, and squash were the basis of the Mesoamerican diet.

Early Peruvians and Bolivians ate llama meat, harnessed llamas as beasts of burden (as is shown here), and used llama dung to fertilize their fields. What was the largest animal domesticated in the New World?

Food production was independently invented in three areas of the Americas: Mesoamerica, the eastern United States, and the south central Andes. Mesoamerica is discussed in detail in the next section. Food plants known as goosefoot and marsh elder, along with the sunflower and a species of squash, were domesticated by Native Americans in the eastern United States by 4500 B.P. These crops supplemented a diet based mainly on hunting and gathering. They never became caloric staples like maize, wheat, rice, millet, manioc, and potatoes. Eventually maize diffused from Mesoamerica into what is now the United States, reaching both the Southwest and the eastern area just mentioned. Maize provided a more reliable caloric staple for Native North American farming. In what is now Peru and Bolivia, six species appear to have been domesticated more or less together in the highland valleys and basins of the south central Andes between 5000 and 4000 B.P. These domesticates were the potato, quinoa (a cereal grain), beans, llamas, alpacas, and guinea pigs (Smith 1995).

EARLY FARMING IN THE MEXICAN HIGHLANDS

Long before Mexican highlanders developed a taste for maize, beans, and squash, they hunted as part of a pattern of broad-spectrum foraging. Mammoth remains dated to 11,000 B.P. have been

By diffusion, manioc or cassava, originally domesticated in lowland South America, has become a caloric staple in the tropics worldwide. This young Thai farmer displays his manioc crop.

found along with spear points in the basin that surrounds Mexico City. However, small animals were more important than big game, as were the grains, pods, fruits, and leaves of wild plants.

In the *Valley of Oaxaca*, in Mexico's southern highlands, between 10,000 and 4000 B.P., foragers concentrated on certain wild animals—deer and rabbits—and plants—cactus leaves and fruits, and tree pods, especially mesquite (Flannery 1986). Those early Oaxacans dispersed to hunt and gather in fall and winter. But they came together in late spring and summer, forming larger groups to harvest seasonally available plants. Cactus fruits appeared in the spring. Since summer rains would reduce the fruits to mush and since birds, bats, and rodents competed for them, cactus collection required hard work by large groups of people. The edible pods of the mesquite, available in June, also required intensive gathering.

In fall, these early Oaxacan foragers gathered a wild grass known as **teocentli**, or *teosinte*, the wild ancestor of maize. Sometime between 7000 and 4000 B.P., teocentli-maize underwent a series of genetic changes like those described earlier for Middle Eastern wheat and barley. These changes included increases in the number of kernels per cob, cob size, and the number of cobs per stalk (Flannery 1973). Such steps toward domestication made it increasingly profitable to collect wild maize and eventually to plant maize.

Undoubtedly, some of the mutations necessary for domesticated maize had occurred in wild teocentli before people started growing it. However, since teocentli was well adapted to its natural niche, the mutations offered no advantage and didn't spread. But once people started harvesting wild maize intensively, they became selective agents. As foragers wandered during the year, they carried teocentli to environments different from its natural habitat.

Furthermore, as people harvested teocentli, they took back to camp a greater proportion of plants with tough axes and stalks. These were the plants most likely to hold together during harvesting and least likely to disintegrate on the way back home. Now teocentli depended on humans for its survival, since it lacked the natural means of dispersal—a brittle axis or stalk. If humans chose plants with tough axes inadvertently, their selection of plants with soft husks must have been intentional. Their selection of corn ears with larger cobs, more kernels per cob, and more cobs per plant was also intentional.

Eventually, people started planting maize in the alluvial soils of valley floors. This was the zone where foragers had traditionally congregated for the annual summer harvest of mesquite pods. By 4000 B.P., a type of maize had been developed that provided more food than the mesquite pods did. Once that happened, people started cutting down mesquite trees and replacing them with corn fields.

Farming triggered a population explosion and adaptive radiation throughout Mesoamerica. Yet again, changes were gradual. In the Middle East, thousands of years intervened between the first experiments in domestication and the appearance of the state. The same was true in Mesoamerica.

See the Internet Exercises at your OLC for information on the domestication of chocolate

mhhe
com
/kottak

FROM EARLY FARMING TO THE STATE

Eventually, food production led to the *early village farming community*. Permanent villages sustained by farming were occupied year-round. The earliest

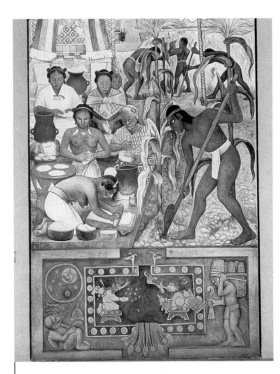

As maize cultivation spread, genetic changes led to higher yields and more productive farming. Pressures to intensify cultivation helped improve water-control systems, such as the canal irrigation shown in this mural by Diego Rivera.

such settlements in Mesoamerica developed around 3500 B.P., in two kinds of environment. One was humid lowlands, along the Gulf Coast of Mexico and the Pacific Coast of Mexico and Guatemala. Here, maize farming in rich soils was combined with gathering and hunting of several species of wild plants and animals.

Early village farming communities also emerged in one part of the Mexican highlands. In the Valley of Oaxaca in southern Mexico, winter frosts are absent, and simple irrigation permitted the establishment of early permanent villages based on maize farming. Water close to the surface allowed early farmers to dig wells right in their corn fields. Using pots, they dipped water out of these wells and poured it on their growing plants, a technique known as *pot irrigation*. The earliest year-round Mesoamerican farming depended on reliable rainfall, pot irrigation, or access to humid river bottomlands.

The subsequent spread of maize farming resulted in further genetic changes, higher yields, higher human populations, and more intensive farming. Pressures to intensify cultivation led to improvements in early water-control systems. New varieties of fast-growing maize eventually appeared, expanding the range of areas that could be cultivated. Increasing population and irrigation also helped spread maize farming.

The gradual transformation of broad-spectrum foraging into intensive cultivation laid the foundation for the emergence of the state in Mesoamerica—some 3,000 years later than in the Middle East (Table 10.3). A state is a form of social and political organization that has a formal, central government and a division of society into classes. Chiefdoms are precursors to states; they have privileged and effective leaders—chiefs—but they lack the sharp class divisions that characterize states. Evidence of what archaeologists call the *elite level*, indicating a chiefdom or a state, appears around 3500 B.P. An early example comes from Mexico's Gulf Coast, where, between 3200 and 2500 B.P., the *Olmecs* (a chiefdom) built several ritual centers. Large earthen mounds, presumably dedicated to religion, document the ability of Olmec elites to marshal labor. The Olmecs also sculpted massive stone heads, which may be representations of their chiefs.

By 2500 B.P., Olmec culture had dimmed, but the elite level was spreading throughout Mesoamerica. By A.D. 1 (2000 B.P.), the highlands, particularly the Valley of Mexico, moved to center stage in the Mesoamerican transformation. It was in the Valley of Mexico that the city and state of Teotihuacan flourished between 1900 and 1300 B.P. (A.D. 100 and A.D. 700). The Aztec state, which lasted until the Spanish conquest in 1521, arose in the valley around 1325. (The Classic Maya state thrived in Mexico's Yucatán peninsula and in neighboring areas of what are now Guatemala and Belize from A.D. 200 to 900.) The process of state formation in Mesoamerica is examined further in the next chapter.

Costs and Benefits

Food production brought advantages and disadvantages. Among the advantages were discoveries and inventions. People learned to spin and weave; to make pottery, bricks, and arched masonry; and to smelt and cast metals. They developed trade and commerce by land and sea. By 5500 B.P., Middle

Table 10.3 The Rise of Food Production and the State in Mesoamerica

These developments, from early corn domestication to the fall of the Aztec state, are organized here according to period names. Elite-level societies (beginning with the Olmecs, through the Spanish Conquest of the Aztecs) are described as Preclassic (Olmecs and Oaxaca). Next come Classic (Oaxaca continues, along with Teotihuacan and the Maya area) and Postclassic (Toltecs and Aztecs).

Period	Date (B.P.)	Area/Sites	Settlement Types	Ranking/Stratification System
Conquest (Cortez)	A.D. 1521	Mexico	Colony of Spain	Spanish domination; world system
Postclassic	1150–500 (A.D. 1000–1200) (A.D. 1325–1521)	Toltec Increased militarism Aztec	Cities, social unrest Empire More secular rule Expanded trade	State Empire
Classic	1750–1150	Teotihuacan Oaxaca Maya	Cities Trade, crafts expand	Stratification, states
Preclassic (Formative)	3500–1750	Olmec Oaxaca	Ceremonial centers Writing (by end)	Ranking, chiefdoms Stratification (by end)
Early food production	4000–3500	Oaxaca Pacific Coast Gulf Coast	Village farming community	Ranking
Earliest domestication	5000	Tehuacan Oaxaca	Seminomadic bands	Egalitarian

Easterners were living in vibrant cities with markets, streets, temples, and palaces. They created sculpture, mural art, writing systems, weights, measures, mathematics, and new forms of political and social organization (Jolly and White 1995).

Because it increased economic production and led to new social, scientific, and creative forms, food production is often considered an evolutionary advance. But the new economy also brought hardships. For example, food producers typically work harder than foragers do—and for a less adequate diet. Because of their extensive leisure time, foragers have been characterized as living in "the original affluent society" (Sahlins 1972). Certain foragers have survived into recent times and have been studied by anthropologists. Among foragers living in the Kalahari Desert of southern Africa, only part of the group needed to hunt and gather, maybe 20 hours a week, to provide an adequate diet for the entire group. Women gathered, and adult men hunted. Their labor supported older people

and children. Early retirement from the food quest was possible, and forced child labor was unknown.

With food production, yields are more reliable, but people work much harder. Herds, fields, and irrigation systems need care. Weeding can require hours of arduous bending. No one has to worry about where to keep a giraffe or a gazelle, but pens and corrals are built and maintained for livestock. Trade takes men, and sometimes women, away from home, leaving burdens for those who stay behind. For several reasons, food producers tend to have more children than foragers do. This means greater child care demands, but child labor also tends to be more needed and valued than it is among foragers. Many tasks in farming and herding can be done by children. The division of economic labor grows more complex, so that children and older people have assigned economic roles.

Not only does the new economy require hard work, so do the social and political systems supported by food production (See Chapter 11). States

Background Information

STUDENT: Maxine H. Oland

SUPERVISING PROFESSOR: Marilyn A. Masson

SCHOOL: State University of New York–Albany

YEAR IN SCHOOL/MAJOR: Senior/Anthropology

FUTURE PLANS: Graduate school in anthropology

PROJECT TITLE: Late Postclassic Economy in Northern Belize: Stone Tools and Raw Materials from the Freshwater Creek Drainage

What techniques were used to distinguish between locally made and imported tools? Does it surprise you that a food-producing state-level society such as the Maya would be using stone tools?

Laguna de On is a small archaeological site located on an island in Honey Camp Lagoon in Northern Belize. The Maya village site dates to the Postclassic Period (A.D. 900–1500). In order to better understand the economy of the region during this epoch, I sought to define patterns of local exchange regarding stone tools and raw materials. The project was funded by the National Science Foundation Research Experience for Undergraduates Award. It was completed during a field school run by the University at Albany.

It was already known that many of the tools at Laguna de On were made at Colha, a specialized lithic (stone tool) manufacturing center only 10 km away. Archaeological data at Colha indicate mass production of uniform stone tools made of highly distinctive chert. My project was concerned with the extent to which the inhabitants of Laguna de On were using local stone resources, and for what purposes.

In order to recognize those raw materials immediately available to the residents of Laguna de On, a survey was conducted of the region surrounding the lagoon. Various coarse cherts, chalcedonies, and quartz-blend materials were found outcropping naturally in sugar cane fields, road-cuts, and back yards. Every locality from which samples were collected was plotted on a map of Belize with the use of a global positioning system. The survey was purely geological, although one archaeological quarry was discovered in the process. This locality showed a surprising variety of fine chalcedonies in a concentrated area, as well as ample evidence for human modification of the materials.

In the field laboratory small samples were made of each material, using a geologist's hammer to create flakes from each nodule. These samples were labeled by locality and type (A, B, C, etc.) within the locality. They were then photographed to provide a visual record.

In the archaeology labs of the University at Albany a separate analysis of the stone tools was completed, classifying each artifact by raw material and tool type. Of the 417 stone tools examined in the study, 42 percent were made from Colha chert, which implies a heavy reliance on tools from Colha. Locally available materials made up the remaining 58 percent. An examination of tool type showed that formal tools (oval bifaces, stemmed blades) were almost exclusively acquired from Colha, while local resources were used for expedient (immediate use) tools (flakes, hammerstones).

Future work will build upon this research by comparing these findings to other nearby Postclassic sites of Northern Belize. A continuation of the raw material survey is planned, as the identification of more outcrops is essential to truly understanding procurement systems.

The labor demands of food production far exceed those associated with foraging. Here, in India's Andra Pradesh, these Banjara women are pounding grain. Such processing of food is just one step in getting the grain from the fields into people's mouths. What are some of the other steps?

States may have mathematicians, artists, astronomers, priests, and kings, but ordinary people have to sweat in the fields to grow food for the elites and specialists. Unlike foragers, food producers have bosses. The elites conscript labor to build temples and pyramids, to move stone for enduring monuments. In states, people have to pay taxes and get drafted for work or war. It is a myth that leisure time increases with civilization. For some, there is leisure and privilege; for most, there is work and obligation.

And public health declines. Diets based on crops and dairy products tend to be less varied, less nutritious, and less healthful than foragers' diets, which are usually higher in proteins and lower in fats and carbohydrates. With the shift to food production, the physical well-being of the population often declines. Communicable diseases, protein deficiency, and dental caries increase (Cohen and Armelagos 1984). Greater exposure to pathogens comes with food production.

Compared with a seminomadic foraging band, food producers tend to be sedentary. Their populations are denser, which makes it easier to transmit and maintain diseases. We saw in Chapter 4 that malaria and sickle-cell anemia spread along with food production. Population concentrations, especially cities, are breeding grounds for epidemic diseases. People live nearer other people and animals and their wastes, which also affect public health (Diamond 1997). Compared with farmers, herders, and city dwellers, foragers were relatively disease-free, stress-free, and well nourished.

Other hardships and stresses accompanied food production and the state. Social inequality and poverty increased. Elaborate systems of social stratification eventually replaced the egalitarianism of the past. Resources were no longer common goods, open to all, as they tend to be among foragers. Property distinctions proliferated. Slavery and other forms of human bondage were invented. Crime, war, and human sacrifice became widespread.

The rate at which human beings degraded their environments also increased with food production. The environmental degradation in today's world, including air and water pollution and deforestation, is on a much larger scale, compared with early villages and cities, but modern trends are foreshadowed. After food production, population increase and the need to expand farming led to deforestation in the Middle East. Even today, many farmers think of trees as giant weeds to be cut down to make way for productive fields. Previously, we saw how early Mesoamerican farmers cut down mesquite trees for maize cultivation in the Valley of Oaxaca.

Many farmers and herders burn trees, brush, and pasture. Farmers burn to remove weeds; they also use the ashes for fertilizer. Herders burn to promote the growth of new tender shoots for their livestock. But such practices do have environmental costs, including air pollution. Smelting and other chemical processes basic to the manufacture of metal tools also have environmental costs. As modern industrial pollution has harmful effluents, early chemical processes had by-products that polluted

Table 10.4 The Benefits and Costs of Food Production (Compared with Foraging)

Do the costs outweigh the benefits?

Benefits	Costs
Discoveries and inventions	Harder work
New social, political, scientific, and creative forms (e.g., spinning, weaving, pottery, bricks, metallurgy)	Less nutritious diets
	Child labor and child care demands
	Taxes and military drafts
Monumental architecture, arched masonry, sculpture	Public health declines (e.g., more exposure to pathogens, including communicable and epidemic diseases)
Writing	
Mathematics, weights, and measures	Rise in protein deficiency and dental caries
Trade and markets	Greater stress
Urban life	Social inequality and poverty
Increased economic production	Slavery and other forms of human bondage
More reliable crop yields	Rise in crime, war, and human sacrifice
	Increased environmental degradation (e.g., air and water pollution, deforestation)

air, soils, and waters. Salts, chemicals, and microorganisms accumulate in irrigated fields. These and other pathogens and pollutants, which were by and large nonissues during the Paleolithic, endanger growing human populations. To be sure, food production had benefits. But its costs are just as evident. Table 10.4 summarizes the costs and benefits of food production. We see that progress is much too optimistic a word to describe food production, the state, and many other aspects of the evolution of society.

SUMMARY

1. After 15,000 B.P., as the big-game supply diminished, foragers sought out new foods. By 10,000 B.P., domesticated plants and animals were part of a broad spectrum of resources used by Middle Easterners. By 7500 B.P., most Middle Easterners were moving away from broad-spectrum foraging toward more specialized food-producing economies. *Neolithic* refers to the period when the first signs of domestication appeared.

2. Braidwood proposed that food production started in the Hilly Flanks zone, where wheat and barley grew wild. Others questioned this: The wild grain supply in that zone already provided an excellent diet for the Natufians and other ancient Middle Easterners. There would have been no incentive to domesticate. Other scholars view the origin of food production in the context of increasing population and climate changes.

3. Ancient Middle Eastern foragers migrated seasonally in pursuit of game. They also collected wild plant foods as they ripened at different altitudes. As they moved about, these foragers took grains from the Hilly Flanks zone where they grew wild, to adjacent areas. Humans became agents of selection, preferring plants with certain attributes. Population spilled over from the Hilly Flanks into adjacent areas like the piedmont steppe. In such marginal zones people started

cultivating plants. They were trying to duplicate the dense wild grains of the Hilly Flanks.

4. After the harvest, sheep and goats fed off the stubble of these wild plants. Animal domestication occurred as people started selecting certain features and behavior and guiding the reproduction of goats, sheep, cattle, and pigs. Gradually, food production spread into the Hilly Flanks. Later, with irrigation it spread down into Mesopotamia's alluvial desert, where the first cities, states, and civilizations developed by 5500 B.P. Food production then spread west from the Middle East into North Africa and Europe and east to India and Pakistan.

5. There were seven independent inventions of food production: in the Middle East, sub-Saharan Africa, northern and southern China, Mesoamerica, the south central Andes, and the eastern United States. Millet was domesticated by 7000 B.P. in northern China; and rice, by 8000 B.P. in southern China.

6. The transition to food production took place thousands of years later in the New World. Humans entered the Americas some 20,000 years ago. Pursuing big game or moving by boat along the North Pacific Coast, they gradually moved into North America. Adapting to different environments, Native Americans developed a variety of cultures. Some continued to rely on big game. Others became broad-spectrum foragers.

7. In the New World the most important domesticates were maize, potatoes, and manioc. The llama of the central Andes was the largest animal domesticated in the New World, where herding traditions analogous to those of the Old World did not develop. Economic similarities between the hemispheres must be sought in foraging and farming.

8. The earliest New World farming was in Mesoamerica. At Oaxaca, in Mexico's southern highlands, maize was gradually added to a broad-spectrum diet between 7000 and 4000 B.P. The first permanent villages, supported by maize cultivation, arose in the lowlands and in a few frost-free areas of the highlands. In the Valley of Mexico, quick-growing maize made year-round village life possible and paved the way for the emergence of civilization and city life.

9. Food production and the social and political system it supported brought advantages and disadvantages. The advantages included discoveries and inventions. The disadvantages included harder work, poorer health, crime, war, social inequality, and environmental degradation.

KEY TERMS

See the flash cards

mhhe
●com
/kottak

broad-spectrum revolution Period beginning around 15,000 B.P. in the Middle East and 12,000 B.P. in Europe, during which a wider range, or broader spectrum, of plant and animal life was hunted, gathered, collected, caught, and fished; revolutionary because it led to food production.

Clovis tradition Stone technology based on a projectile point that was fastened to the end of a hunting spear; it flourished between 12,000 and 11,000 B.P. in North America.

food production Human control over the reproduction of plants and animals.

Hilly Flanks Woodland zone that flanks the Tigris and Euphrates rivers to the north; zone of wild wheat and barley and of sedentism (settled, nonmigratory life) preceding food production.

maize Corn; domesticated in highland Mexico.

manioc Cassava; a tuber domesticated in the South American lowlands.

Mesoamerica Middle America, including Mexico, Guatemala, and Belize.

Natufians Widespread Middle Eastern culture, dated to between 12,500 and 10,500 B.P.; subsisted on intensive wild cereal collecting and gazelle hunting and had year-round villages.

Neolithic "New Stone Age," coined to describe techniques of grinding and polishing stone tools; the first cultural period in a region in which the first signs of domestication are present.

sedentism Settled (sedentary) life; preceded food production in the Old World and followed it in the New World.

teocentli Or *teosinte*, a wild grass; apparent ancestor of maize.

CRITICAL THINKING
QUESTIONS

For more self
testing, see the
self quizzes

mhhe
com
/kottak

1. How would you explain the origin of food production? Would your explanation for the first farming in the Middle East also apply to Mesoamerica?
2. What environmental and demographic conditions contributed to the origin of food production in the Middle East? Did they also apply in Mesoamerica?
3. Is your own diet more like that of a forager or that of an early farmer? How so?
4. What were the main similarities and differences between early food production in the Middle East and in Mesoamerica?
5. For the Old World, name four caloric staples. Name three for the New World. Where was each domesticated? For each staple, is it part of your diet? What's the most important caloric staple in your diet?
6. What evidence supports the statement that transitions to food production were gradual and evolutionary?

7. Do you think it's likely that food production originated independently in south China and north China? Why?
8. Was the origin of food production good or bad? Why?

Atlas Questions

Look at Map 10, "Early Neolithic Sites of the Middle East and Europe."

1. What countries were the first to receive Middle Eastern domesticates? What countries were the last to receive these plants and animals?
2. Did Ireland receive Middle Eastern domesticates? See the text to learn the origin of the "Irish potato," which became, much later, the caloric basis of Irish subsistence.
3. Which diffused most widely, plants or animals, from the Middle East? Is the European Neolithic distribution the same for sheep, goats, cows, and pigs?

SUGGESTED ADDITIONAL
READINGS

Ashmore, W., and R. Sharer
2000   *Discovering Our Past: A Brief Introduction to Archaeology*, 3rd ed. Boston: McGraw-Hill. Good introduction.

Cohen, M. N., and G. J. Armelagos, eds.
1984   *Paleopathology at the Origins of Agriculture*. New York: Academic Press. Some of the negative consequences of food production for human health.

Diamond, J. M.
1997   *Guns, Germs, and Steel: The Fates of Human Societies*. New York: W. W. Norton. Disease, tools, and environmental forces and effects throughout human history.

Fagan, B. M.
2000   *Ancient Lives: An Introduction to Method and Theory in Archaeology*. Upper Saddle River, NJ: Prentice-Hall. How archaeologists do what they do.

2002   *World Prehistory: A Brief Introduction*, 5th ed. New York: Longman. Major events in human prehistory, including the emergence of food production and the state in various locales.

Feinman, G. M., and T. D. Price
2001   *Archaeology at the Millennium: A Sourcebook*. New York: Kluwer Academic/Plenum. Prospects and new directions in archaeology.

Gamble, C.

2000   *Archaeology, the Basics*. New York: Routledge. The title says it all.

Henry, D. O.

1995   *Prehistoric Cultural Ecology and Evolution: Insights from Southern Jordan*. New York: Plenum Press. The origin of food production in the Middle East, with reference to environmental factors.

Kent, S., ed.

1998   *Gender in African Prehistory*. Walnut Creek, CA: AltaMira Press. Women and men in the African past.

Price, T. D., ed.

2000   *Europe's First Farmers*. New York: Cambridge University Press. The expansion of farming into Europe.

Price, T. D., and G. M. Feinman

2001   *Images of the Past*, 3rd ed. Boston: McGraw-Hill. Introduction to prehistory, including the origin of food production.

Price, T. D., and A. B. Gebauer, eds.

1995   *Last Hunters, First Farmers: New Perspectives on the Prehistoric Transition to Agriculture*. Santa Fe, NM: School of American Research Press. Recent ideas on the origin of food production.

Renfrew, C., and P. Bahn

2000   *Archaeology: Theories, Methods, and Practives*, 3rd ed. New York: Thames and Hudson. Basic methods text.

Smith, B. D.

1995   *The Emergence of Agriculture*. New York: Scientific American Library, W. H. Freeman. The first farmers and herders in several world areas.

Staeck, J.

2002   *Back to Earth: An Introduction to Archaeology*. Boston: McGraw-Hill. Introduction to the field.

Wenke, R.

1996   *Patterns in Prehistory: Humankind's First Three Million Years*, 4th ed. New York: Oxford University Press. Rise of food production and the state throughout the world; thorough, useful text.

INTERNET EXERCISES

1. Read the article by Jack Challum in *The Nutrition Reporter* entitled "Paleolithic Nutrition: Your Future Is in Your Dietary Past" **(http://www.nutritionreporter.com/stone_age_diet.html)**.

   a. What kinds of foods typified the Paleolithic diet? What kinds of foods typify the modern American diet?

   b. What changes have occurred to the number and kind of foods consumed by humans? Why are our foods higher in saturated fats? What changes have occurred in vitamin intake?

   c. Despite the fact that humans may not be completely adapted to an agricultural diet, what are the physical and cultural advantages of agriculture?

2. Read the history of maize written by Ricardo J. Salvador **(http://maize.agron.iastate.edu/maizearticle.html)**.

   a. When and where was maize domesticated?

   b. Maize is a very important source of carbohydrates and is one of the top three cereal crops in the world (along with rice and wheat). However, what are its nutritional deficiencies? How did Native Americans respond to this deficiency?

   c. When did maize first arrive in Europe? How was it carried there? Where else did it spread?

See Chapter 10 at your McGraw-Hill Online Learning Center for additional review and interactive exercises.

11

THE FIRST CITIES AND STATES

Overview

The spread and intensification of food production, which was discussed in Chapter 10, paved the way for state formation. The first states developed in Mesopotamia by 5500 B.P. and in Mesoamerica some 3,000 years later. Chiefdoms were precursors to states, with privileged and effective leaders—chiefs—but lacking the sharp class divisions that characterize states. By 7000 B.P. in the Middle East and 3200 B.P. in Mesoamerica, there is evidence for what archaeologists call the elite level, indicating a chiefdom or a state. By 3200 B.P. many different chiefdoms existed in Mesoamerica, one of which was the Olmec. Chapter 10 cited the Olmec, which thrived between 3200 and 2500 B.P. on Mexico's Gulf Coast, as an example of the elite level. The Olmec were neither the first nor the most elaborate of the early Mexican chiefdoms,

and they never developed into a state. Other Mexican chiefdoms, such as the ones in Oaxaca and the Valley of Mexico, did develop into states.

Like food production, states emerged in several world areas. The very first states arose in Mesopotamia (between the Tigris and Euphrates rivers) by 5500 B.P. and in the Nile Valley by 5250 B.P. Another state flourished between 4,600 and 3,900 years ago in the Indus River Valley of Pakistan and western India. The Shang dynasty state arose in the Huang He (Yellow) River valley of northern China around 3,750 years ago. By 2200 B.P., the process of state formation had accelerated in Mesoamerica and the Andes. Early states built on the social, political, and economic hierarchies and flamboyant art styles and architecture of the chiefdoms that preceded them.

Ancient Peru Torture Deaths: Sacrifices or War Crimes?

NATIONAL GEOGRAPHIC NEWS BRIEF

by Ben Harder

April 29, 2002

Codes of conduct apply to warfare as they do to other aspects of culture. How do the perpetrators of brutality—illustrated by the possible "war crimes" described in this account—justify their behavior? Do they kill and mutilate for revenge, punishment, or desecration, or as part of a ritual? Warfare was common in ancient cities and states, as well as in the chiefdoms that preceded them. Did ancient warriors mainly kill members of their own group or members of other societies? Read this story to discover at least one way in which anthropologists go about answering this question.

Forensic anthropologist John Verano of Tulane University in New Orleans has been investigating a series of grisly executions in the arid valleys of lowland Peru. Evidence from the skeletal remains shows that the victims, who lived during the Moche civilization nearly two thousand years ago, suffered shockingly brutal deaths . . .

When the graves at a Moche temple complex in northern Peru were uncovered, the human remains showed many clear marks of violence. Various theories arose to explain it. One proposes that the Moche sacrificed some of their own people to appease the gods and improve the fertility of their land. Another suggests that the victims were . . . losers of fierce power struggles between competing prehistoric city-states . . .

So far, the scientists have unearthed more than 100 skeletons buried at different sites between about A.D. 150 and A.D. 650 . . .

The grim events revealed by the archaeological findings have long been familiar to scholars from finely rendered pottery and murals of the Moche people. Scenes embellished with abundant bloodshed show victims being humiliated, abused, and executed.

Some people have interpreted these frightening scenes as exaggerated fictions concocted by the Moche to scare enemies. The recent analysis, however, suggests that the events depicted were horrifyingly real and not figments of artists' imagination.

The revelation of gruesome forms of torture is puzzling in part because the Moche developed a vibrant and highly advanced culture. These pre-Inca Peruvians were renowned builders, artists, and warriors. Their technological advances included, for example, techniques of irrigation that made their valleys even more productive than the same land is today . . .

Combat was a prevalent theme of Moche art. The detailed scenes on pottery and murals form what UCLA anthropologist Christopher B. Donnan calls a rich "warrior narrative."

Donnan has been studying Moche art for 35 years, and his interpretation of the disturbing executions is that they were part of ritual combat among Moche elites. "From all the artistic depictions we have, these are Moche against Moche, not warfare with some other group," he said.

Combat was a prevalent theme in the life, and art—as is illustrated here—of Peru's Moche period.

In the Moche scenes of battle, each combatant wore a loincloth, patterned tunic, and conical helmet, and hung a trapezoidal metal flap from the back of his belt. Along with their other accessories, the warriors' elaborate dress suggests that they brought both wealth and pageantry to combat, which Donnan likens to medieval jousts.

Various panels show warriors squaring off, locked in combat, or in the aftermath of battle.

"A few [panels] show a warrior triumphing over another, but not striking the loser on the ground"—a sign that battles were not fought to the death, said Donnan.

Instead, the art suggests that a victorious warrior took the weapons and belongings of the loser, tied a rope around the vanquished fighter's neck, and led him away naked.

The captives were subsequently sacrificed in a bloody ritual, and their bodies—or parts of them—scattered . . . Why were the bodies . . . so mutilated and cast aside . . . ?

Verano's latest finds . . . undermine the notion that these scenes were merely a part of ritual combat. Some of the recently unearthed skeletons . . . show marks indicating that the bones were stripped of flesh . . .

Such practices of defleshing victims don't appear in Moche art, said Donnan. "This makes it extremely enigmatic," he said. "It's hard to fit it into the warrior narrative."

"These people were clearly denied proper burial," and were instead left in open pits to be preyed on by vultures and flies, Verano said. "They were desecrated. The closest analogy would be war crimes today." He thinks the victims were war prisoners, not losers of ritual combat among the elite of a particular city. "They may be Moche," he said, "but from other valleys."

One clue is that some of their wounds had time to heal before they died, perhaps an indication that they were rounded up after battle and marched back to the city where they were ultimately killed.

Other clues also hint that the victims hailed from different regions . . .

By analyzing the chemical composition of the victims' hair, Verano and his colleagues determined that some of the dead had a diet rich in seafood, indicating that they lived along the coast, while others appeared to have lived at higher elevations . . .

The victims were buried individually or in small groups, not in true mass graves. To Verano, this suggests that the victims represent "a few principal captives from each episode" of conflict between the city and its enemies . . .

Source: http://news.nationalgeographic.com/news/2002/04/0425_020426_mochekillings.html.

In coastal Peru, as in many ancient states, the population pressure triggered by productive farming fueled a pattern of warfare aimed at the acquisition of scarce resources, such as land and labor. The vanquished had to pay tribute to their conquerors. To do this, they intensified production, perfecting techniques, such as irrigation, to produce more food. Eventually, through a series of conquests, expansive states, like that of the Moche, with its famous Mochica pottery, extended their rule over entire regions. Warfare is associated with all ancient states—as, too, are impressive artistic and scientific achievements. What are other attributes of states?

Attributes of States

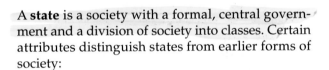

A **state** is a society with a formal, central government and a division of society into classes. Certain attributes distinguish states from earlier forms of society:

1. A state controls a specific regional territory, such as the Nile Valley or the Valley of Mexico. The regional expanse of a state contrasts with the much smaller territories controlled by kin groups and villages in prestate societies. Early states were expansionist; they arose from competition among chiefdoms, as the most powerful chiefdom conquered others, extended its rule over a larger territory, and managed to hold on to, and rule, the land and people acquired through conquest.

2. Early states had productive farming economies, supporting dense populations, often in cities. The agricultural economies of early states usually involved some form of water control or irrigation.

3. Early states used tribute and taxation to accumulate, at a central place, resources needed to support hundreds, or thousands, of specialists. These states had rulers, a military, and control over human labor.

4. States are stratified into social classes. In the first states, the non-food-producing population consisted of a tiny elite, plus artisans, officials, priests, and other specialists. Most people were commoners. Slaves and prisoners constituted the lowest rung of the social ladder. Rulers stayed in power by combining personal ability, religious authority, economic control, and force.

[handwritten margin notes: Stratification: • elites + specialists (small) • commoners (majority) • slaves & prisoners]

5. Early states had imposing public buildings and monumental architecture, including temples, palaces, and storehouses.

6. Early states developed some form of record-keeping system, usually a written script (Fagan 1996).

State Formation in the Middle East

In the last chapter we saw that food production arose in the ancient Middle East around 10,000 B.P. In the ensuing process of change, the center of population growth shifted from the zone where wheat and barley grew wild (Hilly Flanks) to adjacent areas (steppe) where those grains were first domesticated. By 6000 B.P., population was increasing most rapidly in the alluvial plain of southern Mesopotamia. (**Mesopotamia** refers to the area between the Tigris and Euphrates rivers in what is now southern Iraq and southwestern Iran.) This growing population supported itself through irrigation and intensive river valley agriculture. By 5500 B.P. towns had grown into cities. The earliest city-states were Sumer (southern Iraq) and Elam (southwestern Iran), with their capitals at Uruk (Warka) and Susa, respectively.

URBAN LIFE

The first towns arose around 10,000 years ago in the Middle East. Over the generations houses of mud brick were built and rebuilt in the same place.

Substantial tells or mounds arose from the debris of a succession of such houses. The Middle East and Asia have hundreds or thousands of such mounds, only a few of which have been excavated. These sites have yielded remains of ancient community life, including streets, buildings, terraces, courtyards, wells, and other artifacts.

The earliest known town was Jericho, located in what is now Israel, below sea level at a well-watered oasis a few miles northwest of the Dead Sea (Figure 11.1). From the lowest (oldest) level, we know that around 11,000 years ago, Jericho was first settled by Natufian foragers. Occupation continued thereafter, through and beyond biblical times, when "Joshua fit the battle of Jericho, and the walls came tumbling down."

During the phase just after the Natufians, the earliest known town appeared. It was an unplanned, densely populated settlement with round houses and some 2,000 people. At this time, well before the invention of pottery, Jericho was surrounded by a sturdy wall, with a massive tower. The wall may have been built initially as a flood barrier rather than for defense. Around 9000 B.P. Jericho was destroyed, to be rebuilt later. The new occupants lived in square houses with finished plaster floors. They buried their dead beneath their homes, a pattern seen at other sites, such as Çatal Hüyük in Turkey (see below). Pottery reached Jericho around 8000 B.P. (Gowlett 1993).

Long-distance trade, especially of obsidian, a volcanic glass used to make tools and ornaments, became important in the Middle East between 9500 and 7000 B.P. One town that prospered from this trade was Çatal Hüyük in Anatolia, Turkey (DeMarco 1997). A grassy mound 65 feet high holds the remains of this 9,000-year-old town, probably the largest settlement of the Neolithic age. Çatal Hüyük was located on a river, which deposited rich soil for crops, created a lush environment for animals, and was harnessed for irrigation by 7000 B.P. Over the mound's 32 acres (12.9 hectares), up to 10,000 people once lived in crowded mud-brick houses packed so tight that residents entered from their roofs.

Shielded by a defensive wall, Çatal Hüyük flourished between 8000 and 7000 B.P. Its individual mud-brick dwellings, rarely larger than a suburban American bedroom, had separate areas reserved for ritual and secular uses. In a given house, the ritual images were placed along the

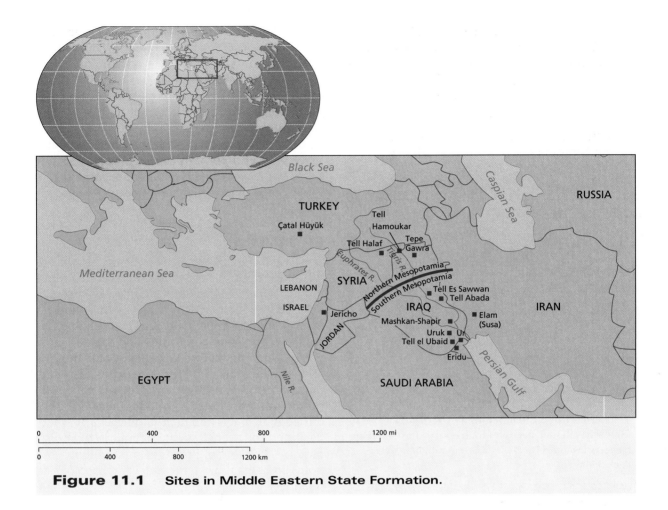

Figure 11.1   **Sites in Middle Eastern State Formation.**

walls that faced north, east, or west, but never south. That area was reserved for cooking and other domestic tasks. The ritual areas were originally identified as shrines, but ritual appears now to have been organized at the household level rather than by religious specialists. Priests appeared later in Middle Eastern history.

The ritual spaces were decorated with wall paintings, sculpted ox heads, bull horns, and relief models of bulls and rams. The paintings showed bulls surrounded by stick figures running, dancing, and sometimes throwing stones. Vultures attacked headless humans. One frieze had human hand prints painted below mounted bull horns. These images and their placement are reminiscent of Paleolithic cave art. The dwellings at Çatal Hüyük were entered through the roof, and people had to crawl through holes from room to room, somewhat like moving between chambers of a cave. The deeper down one went, the richer the art

became. The town's spiritual life seems to have revolved around a preoccupation with animals, danger, and death, perhaps related to the site's recent hunter-gatherer past.

Two or three generations of a family were buried beneath their homes. In one dwelling, archaeologists found remains of 17 individuals, mostly children. After two or three generations of family burials, the ritual art was removed; and the dwelling, burned. The site was then covered with fine dirt, and a floor laid for a new dwelling.

Çatal Hüyük's residents, though living in a town, acted independently in family groups without any apparent control by a priestly or political elite. The town never became a full-fledged city with centralized organization. Just as it lacked priests, Çatal Hüyük never had leaders who controlled or managed trade and production (Fagan 1996). Food was not stored and processed collectively, but on a smaller, domestic, scale (DeMarco 1997).

The world's earliest known town was Jericho, located in what is now Israel. Jericho was first settled by Natufian foragers around 11,000 B.P. This round tower dates back 8,000 years.

THE ELITE LEVEL

The first pottery (ceramics) dates back a bit more than 8,000 years, when it first reached Jericho. Before that date, the Neolithic is called the prepottery Neolithic. By 7000 B.P., pottery had become widespread in the Middle East. Archaeologists consider pottery shape, finishing, decoration, and type of clay as features used for dating. The geographic distribution of a given pottery style may indicate trade or alliance spanning a large area at a particular time.

An early and widespread pottery style, the **Halafian**, was first found at Tell Halaf in the mountains of northern Syria. Halafian (7500–6500 B.P.) refers to a delicate ceramic style. It also describes the period during which the elite level and the first chiefdoms emerged. The low number of Halafian ceramics suggests they were luxury goods associated with a social hierarchy.

By 7000 B.P. ranked chiefdoms had emerged in the Middle East. The Ubaid period (7000–6000 B.P.) is named for a southern Mesopotamian pottery type first discovered at a small site, Tell el-Ubaid, located near the major city of Ur in southern Iraq. Similar pottery has been discovered in the deep levels of the Mesopotamian cities of Ur, Uruk, and Eridu. Ubaid pottery is associated with advanced chiefdoms and perhaps the earliest states. It diffused rapidly over a large area, becoming more widespread than earlier ceramic styles such as the Halafian.

SOCIAL RANKING AND CHIEFDOMS

It is easy for archaeologists to identify early states. Evidence for state organization includes monumental architecture, central storehouses, irrigation systems, and written records. In Mesoamerica, even chiefdoms are easy to detect archaeologically. Ancient Mexican chiefdoms left behind stone works, such as temple complexes and the huge carved Olmec heads. Mesoamericans also had a penchant for marking their elites with durable ornaments and prestige goods, including those buried with chiefs and their families. Early Middle Eastern chiefs were less ostentatious in their use of material markers of prestige, making their chiefdoms somewhat harder to detect archaeologically (Flannery 1999).

On the basis of the kinds of status distinctions within society, the anthropologist Morton Fried (1959) divided societies into three types: egalitarian, ranked, and stratified (Table 11.1). An **egalitarian society**, most typically found among foragers, lacks status distinctions except for those based on age, gender, and individual qualities, talents, and achievements. Thus, depending on the society, adult men, elder women, talented musicians, or ritual specialists might receive special respect for their activities or knowledge. In egalitarian societies, status distinctions are not usually inherited. The child of a respected person will not receive special recognition because of his or her parent, but must earn such respect.

Ranked societies, in contrast, do have hereditary inequality. But they lack **stratification** (sharp social divisions—strata—based on unequal access to wealth and power) into noble and commoner classes. In ranked societies, individuals tend to be ranked in terms of their genealogical distance from

Table 11.1 Egalitarian, Ranked, and Stratified Societies

Kind of Status Distinction	Nature of Status	Common Form of Subsistence Economy	Common Forms of Social Organization	Examples
Egalitarian	Status differences are not inherited. All status is based on age, gender, and individual qualities, talents, and achievements.	Foraging	Bands and tribes	Inuit, Ju/'hoansi San, and Yanomami
Ranked	Status differences <u>are inherited</u> and distributed along a continuum from the highest-ranking member (chief) to the lowest without any breaks.	Horticulture, pastoralism, and some foraging groups	Chiefdoms and some tribes	Native American groups of the Pacific Northwest (for example, Salish and Kwakiutl), Natchez, Halaf and Ubaid Period polities, Olmec
Stratified	Status differences are inherited and divided sharply between distinct noble and commoner classes.	Agriculture	States	Teotihuacan, Uruk Period states, Inca, Shang dynasty, Rome, U.S., Great Britain

the chief. Closer relatives of the chief have higher rank or social status than more distant ones do. But there is a continuum of status, with many individuals and kin groups ranked about equally, which can lead to competition for positions of leadership.

Not all ranked societies are chiefdoms. Robert Carneiro (1991) has distinguished between two kinds of ranked societies, only the second of which is a chiefdom. In the first type, exemplified by some Indians of North America's Pacific Northwest, there were hereditary differences in rank, but villages were independent of one another. Exemplifying the second type were the Cauca of Colombia and the Natchez of the eastern United States. These ranked societies had become **chiefdoms**, societies in which relations among villages as well

as among individuals were unequal. The smaller villages had lost their autonomy and were under the authority of leaders who lived at larger villages. According to Kent Flannery (1999), *only those ranked societies with such loss of village autonomy should be called chiefdoms.* In chiefdoms, there is always inequality—differences in rank—among both individuals and communities.

In Mesopotamia, Mesoamerica, and Peru, chiefdoms were precursors to **primary states** (states that arose on their own, and not through contact with other state societies—see Wright 1994). Primary states emerged from competition among chiefdoms, as one chiefdom managed to conquer its neighbors and to make them part of a larger political unit (Flannery 1995).

Unlike states, such as Japan, whose emperor and empress are shown here, egalitarian societies lack inherited wealth and status and succession to political office. How are inherited status distinctions marked in your society?

Archaeological evidence for chiefdoms in Mesoamerica, where several states arose between 2,500 and 1,600 years ago, dates back more than 3,000 years. Mesoamerican chiefdoms are easy to detect archaeologically because they were flamboyant in the way they marked their aristocracy. High-status families deformed the heads of their infants and buried them with special symbols and grave goods. In burials, prestige goods show a continuum from graves with many, to less, to none, of precious materials, such as jade and turquoise (Flannery 1999).

The first Middle Eastern states developed between 6000 and 5500 B.P. The first societies based on rank, including the first chiefdoms, emerged during the preceding 1,500 years. In the Middle East, the archaeological record of the period after 7300 B.P. reveals behavior typical of chiefdoms, including exotic goods used as markers of status, along with raiding and political instability. Early Middle Eastern chiefdoms included both the Halafian culture of northern Iraq and the Ubaid culture of southern Iraq, which eventually spread north.

As in Mesoamerica, ancient Middle Eastern chiefdoms had cemeteries where chiefly relatives were buried with distinctive items: vessels, statuettes, necklaces, and high-quality ceramics. Such goods were buried with children too young to have earned prestige on their own, but who happened to be born into elite families. In the ancient village of Tell es-Sawwan, infant graves show a continuum of richness from six statuettes, to three statuettes, to one statuette, to none. Such signs of slight gradations in social status are exactly what one expects in ranked societies (Flannery 1999).

Such burials convince Flannery (1999) that hereditary status differences were present in the Middle East by 7000 B.P. But had the leaders of large villages extended their authority to the smaller villages nearby? Is there evidence for the loss of village autonomy, converting simple ranked societies into chiefdoms? One clue that villages were linked in political units is the use of a common canal to irrigate several villages. This suggests a way of resolving disputes among farmers over access to water, for example, by appeal to a strong leader. By later Halafian times in northern Mesopotamia, there is evidence for such multivillage alliances (Flannery 1999). Another clue to the loss of village autonomy is the emergence of a two-tier settlement hierarchy, with small villages clustering around a large village, especially one with public buildings. There is evidence for this pattern in northern Mesopotamia during the Halafian (Watson 1983).

HOW ETHNOGRAPHY HELPS IN INTERPRETING THE ARCHAEOLOGICAL RECORD

When they excavate sites, how do archaeologists know whether they've found a chiefdom, or some less complex form of society? Grave goods and settlement hierarchy offer clues. Also, studying ethnography helps archaeologists interpret the past.

Thus, to infer the archaeological characteristics of ancient Middle Eastern chiefdoms, Kent Flannery (1999) looks to recent chiefdoms that

This funerary chamber from Sipan, Peru (a Moche site), contains gold jewelry, pottery, and other artifacts. In chiefdoms and states, high-status families often bury their dead with distinctive symbols and grave goods.

have been studied ethnographically in that region. One example is the Basseri, a population of 16,000 migratory herders in Iran (Barth 1964). The Basseri had a large grazing territory, but some of their chiefly families also owned farming villages and city homes. Leading the Basseri was a chief, whose brothers, cousins, uncles, and nephews vied for leadership during "periods of confusion" (Barth 1964). Such political rivalry among close kin is typical of chiefdoms worldwide.

Using the Basseri as an ethnographic analogy, Flannery (1999) suggests likely characteristics of an ancient Middle Eastern chiefdom. Such an ancient confederacy of several thousand people would have had a hereditary aristocracy, but no capital city. There would have been no palace, no temples, no clear territorial boundaries. Its thousands of tents would barely leave a trace archaeologically. But by analogy with the Basseri, we might find remains of a few chiefly houses in mud-walled cities.

According to Barth (1964), a Basseri chief's home was large—to entertain visitors. The chief gave substantial gifts to his prominent subjects, who were expected to reciprocate. The chief's close kinsmen were almost as privileged as he was. By analogy, Flannery (1999) suggests, to identify an ancient Middle Eastern chiefdom, archaeologists should look not for one unique residence but also for the nearby houses of chiefly kin. Such homes would be large enough to entertain many visitors (perhaps with a spacious central court). They might have a large kitchen and storerooms for food staples and craft products used as gifts. Indeed, prehistoric houses fitting this description have been found (Jasim 1985).

According to Robert Carneiro (1991), raiding is especially common in chiefdoms. Illustrating such raiding, early chiefdoms in Mexico and Peru had public art featuring enemy corpses, mutilated prisoners, and trophy heads (Marcus 1992). Middle Eastern chiefdoms lacked this kind of art. But their sites did have defensive walls, ditches, and watchtowers comparable to those of Mesoamerica. Political alliance also offered some protection against raiding.

Despite their defenses and alliances, prehistoric chiefdoms were still raided. There is archaeological evidence that large houses, belonging to community leaders, were sacked and burned during raids in the Halafian and Ubaid periods. Consider Tepe Gawra, a site dating to the late Ubaid period (Tobler 1950). This densely packed town was defended by its position atop a mound, and by a watchtower. Its largest residence had an inner court that illustrates the kind of large, elegant reception space Flannery (1999) expects to find in the home of a chief who hosted many subordinates and visitors. There was also a large kitchen.

On the same street was a slightly less impressive residence, supporting the belief that archaeologists should look for multiple elite houses in chiefly neighborhoods. This town had been raided and partly burned. At least four victims—a baby and three youths—were left unburied in the ruins. The building hardest hit was that with the largest inner court, confirming that, as is usual, the chiefly family was the raid's main target.

From such clues—archaeological and ethnographic—we infer that chiefly families and a pattern of raiding one's rivals were present in the Middle East between 7300 and 5800 B.P.

ADVANCED CHIEFDOMS

In northeastern Syria, near the border with Iraq, archaeologists have been excavating an ancient settlement that once lay on a major trade route. This large site, Tell Hamoukar, dates back more than 5,500 years (Wilford 2000). Its remains suggest that advanced chiefdoms arose in northern areas of the Middle East independently of the better-known city-states of southern Mesopotamia, in southern Iraq (Wilford 2000).

The oldest layer yet uncovered at Tell Hamoukar contains traces of villages dating back 6,000 years. By 5700 B.P. the settlement was a prosperous town of 32 acres, enclosed by a defensive wall 10 feet high and 13 feet wide. The site had fine pottery and large ovens—evidence of food preparation on an institutional scale. The site has yielded pieces of large cooking pots, animal bones, and traces of wheat, barley, and oats for baking and brewing. The archaeologist McGuire Gibson, one of the excavators, believes that food preparation on this scale is evidence of a rank society in which elites were organizing people and resources (Wilford 2000). Most likely they were hosting and entertaining in a chiefly manner (as discussed in the preceding section).

Also providing evidence for social ranking are the seals used to mark containers of food and other goods. Some of the seals are small, with only simple incisions or cross-hatching. Others are larger and more elaborate, presumably for higher officials to stamp more valuable goods. Gibson suspects the larger seals with figurative scenes were held by the few people who had greater authority. The smaller, simply incised seals were used by many more people with less authority (Wilford 2000).

THE RISE OF THE STATE

See the Virtual Exploration for information about early writing in the Indus Valley

In southern Mesopotamia at this time (5700 B.P.), an expanding population and increased food production from irrigation were changing the social landscape even more drastically than in the north. Irrigation had allowed Ubaid communities to spread along the Euphrates River. Travel and trade were expanding, with water serving as the highway system. Such raw materials as hardwood and stone,

which southern Mesopotamia lacked, were imported via river routes. Population density increased as new settlements appeared. Social and economic networks now linked communities on the rivers in the south and in the foothills to the north. Settlements spread north into what is now Syria. Social differentials also increased. Priests and political leaders joined expert potters and other specialists. These non-food-producers were supported by the larger population of farmers and herders (Gilmore-Lehne 2000).

Economies were being managed by central leadership. Agricultural villages had grown into cities, some of which were ruled by local kings. The Uruk period (6000–5200 B.P.), which succeeded the Ubaid period, takes it name from a prominent southern city-state located more than 400 miles south of Tell Hamoukar (Table 11.2). The Uruk period established Mesopotamia as "the cradle of civilization" (see Pollock 1999).

There is no evidence of Uruk influence at Tell Hamoukar until 5200 B.P., when some Uruk pottery showed up. When southern Mesopotamians expanded north, they found advanced chiefdoms, which were not yet states. The fact that writing

Illustrating pictographic writing is this limestone tablet from the proto-urban period of lower Mesopotamia. This Sumerian script records proper names, including that of a landowner—symbolized by the hand—who commissioned the tablet.

Table 11.2 Archaeological Periods in Middle Eastern State Formation

Dates	Period	Age
3000–2539 B.P.	Neo-Babylonian	Iron Age
3600–3000 B.P.	Kassite	
4000–3600 B.P.	Old Babylonian	Bronze Age
4150–4000 B.P.	Third Dynasty of Ur	
4350–4150 B.P.	Akkadian	
4600–4350 B.P.	Early Dynastic III	
4750–4600 B.P.	Early Dynastic II	
5000–4750 B.P.	Early Dynastic I	
5200–5000 B.P.	Jemdet Nasr	
6000–5200 B.P.	Uruk	Chalcolithic
7500–6000 B.P.	Ubaid (southern Mesopotamia)– Halaf (northern Mesopotamia)	
10,000–7000 B.P.		Neolithic

Early Mesopotamian scribes used a stylus to scrawl symbols on raw clay. This writing, called *cuneiform*, left a wedge-shaped impression on the clay. What languages were written in cuneiform?

originated in Sumer, in southern Mesopotamia, indicates a more advanced, state-organized society there. The first writing presumably developed to handle record keeping for a centralized economy.

Writing was initially used to keep accounts, reflecting the needs of trade. Rulers, nobles, priests, and merchants were the first to benefit from it. Writing spread from Mesopotamia to Egypt by 5000 B.P. The earliest writing was pictographic, for example, with pictorial symbols of horses used to represent them.

Early Mesopotamian scribes used a stylus (writing implement) to scrawl symbols on raw clay. This writing left a wedge-shaped impression on the clay, called **cuneiform** writing, from the Latin word for wedge. Both the Sumerian (southern Mesopotamia) and Akkadian (northern Mesopotamia) languages were written in cuneiform (Gowlett 1993).

Writing and temples played key roles in the Mesopotamian economy. For the historic period after 5600 B.P., when writing was invented, there are temple records of economic activities. States can exist without writing, but literacy facilitates the flow and storage of information. We know that Mesopotamian priests managed herding, farming, manufacture, and trade. Temple officials allotted fodder and pasture land for cattle and donkeys, which were used as plow and cart animals. As the economy expanded, trade, manufacture, and grain

Background Information

STUDENT: Jerusha Achterberg
SUPERVISING PROFESSOR: Donald Redford
SCHOOL: The Pennsylvania State
                         University
YEAR IN SCHOOL/MAJOR: Senior/Anthropology
MINORS: Mathematics/Education Policy
                         Studies Future
PLANS: Graduate school
PROJECT TITLE: The Akhenaten Temple Project

What is the nature of the student work described here? How independent was this research?

My first archaeological field-work experience was in Egypt, where I worked as a site supervisor on the 10th round of excavations at Mendes (Tel er-Rub'a), on Middle Kingdom levels of that site in summer 2000. As a newcomer to the field, many techniques were unfamiliar to me. But the most difficult things for me to adapt to were the working conditions. Egyptian weather in July was not what my body was used to, and I was unprepared for what it would be like to work primarily with a team of native workers with whom I shared very little language. I was assigned a dig site, and a team of Egyptian workers including a Kufdi, who essentially guided the team, two pickmen and four basket-girls who removed the dirt after excavation. Rather than my primary job being the digging, as site supervisor, I recorded, measured, and mapped all our finds and loci. I was also responsible for making on-the-spot decisions about the course of our progress.

Because I had done no hands-on archeology before my arrival in Egypt, I was surprised by how quickly I learned the techniques we used. I kept constant records of every find in my site, as well as of the soil type. For those who have not worked in Egypt, it is hard to imagine the sheer volume of pottery that is found at the sites. Every piece had to be sorted and catalogued following excavation. As a result, after excavating from 6 A.M.–1 P.M., we spent the afternoons sorting and washing pottery. On occasion I was able to participate in the more specialized tasks, such as tracing the stance of representative pottery fragments and sorting through the small finds collection.

One job in which I found particular skill was rebuilding pottery vessels from the excavated fragments. This job is important, although too tedious for most people's patience. I found the repetitiveness of the work relaxing compared to the excavation work of the morning. Also, because of my past work in mathematics I found I was good at profiling the excavation site stratigraphy, and drawing spatial representations of the architecture and finds. This work was usually done with a partner. One person called out measurements from a baseline, while the other plot-

ted the information on a grid. This was later fleshed out with information about the materials involved, orientation, and presence of particular features. Prior to going to Egypt, I was concerned about handling human remains. I had never had a problem considering the idea while sitting in a classroom, but I worried that the hands-on work might be different. Recalling this worry was humorous after several hours of cleaning off a human skull. I had become so involved with the work and the satisfaction of slowly revealing the fragile bone, it hadn't occurred to me to be concerned about handling the remains. In fact, it seemed as though the care I was granting the skull was more respectful than leaving it in the ground to weather further. My reaction, or lack thereof, came as a surprise to me, but a welcome one. Overall, I'm very proud of the work I did in Egypt and the help I provided to the ongoing work at Mendes.

storage were centrally managed. Temples collected and distributed meat, dairy products, crops, fish, clothing, tools, and trade items. Potters, metal workers, weavers, sculptors, and other artisans perfected their crafts.

Prior to the invention of **metallurgy** (knowledge of the properties of metals, including their extraction and processing and the manufacture of metal tools), raw copper was shaped by hammering. If copper is hammered too long, it hardens and becomes brittle, with a risk of cracking. But once heated (annealed) in a fire, copper becomes malleable again. Such annealing of copper was an early form of metallurgy. A vital step for metallurgy was the discovery of **smelting**, the high-temperature process by which pure metal is produced from an ore. Ores, including copper ore, have a much wider distribution than does native copper, which was initially traded as a luxury good because of its rarity (Gowlett 1993).

When and how smelting was discovered is unknown. But after 5000 B.P., metallurgy evolved rapidly. The Bronze Age began when alloys of arsenic and copper, or tin and copper (in both cases known as **bronze**), became common and greatly extended the use of metals. Bronze flows more easily than copper does when heated to a similar temperature, so bronze was more convenient for metal casting. Early molds were carved in stone, as shaped depressions to be filled with molten metal. A copper ax cast from such a mold has been found in northern Mesopotamia and predates 5000 B.P. Thereafter, other metals came into common use. By 4500 B.P. golden objects were found in royal burials at Ur.

Iron ore is distributed more widely than is copper ore. Iron, when smelted, can be used on its own; there is no need for tin or arsenic to make a metal alloy (bronze). The Iron Age began once high-temperature iron smelting was mastered. In the Old World after 3200 B.P., iron spread rapidly. Formerly valued as highly as gold, iron crashed in value when it became plentiful (Gowlett 1993).

The Mesopotamian economy, based on craft production, trade, and intensive agriculture, spurred popu-lation growth and an increase in urbanism. Sumerian cities were protected by a fortress wall and surrounded by a farming area. By 4800 B.P., Uruk, the largest early Mesopotamian city, had a population of 50,000. As irrigation and the population expanded, communities fought over water. People sought protection in the fortified cities (Adams 1981), which defended themselves when neighbors or invaders threatened.

By 4600 B.P., secular authority had replaced temple rule. The office of military coordinator developed into kingship. This change shows up architecturally in palaces and royal tombs. The palace raised armies and supplied them with armor, chariots, and metal armaments. At Ur's royal cemetery, by 4600 B.P. monarchs were being buried with soldiers, charioteers, and ladies in waiting. These subordinates were killed at the time of royal burial to accompany the monarch to the afterworld.

Agricultural intensification made it possible for the number of people supported by a given area to increase. Population pressure on irrigated fields helped create a stratified society. Land became scarce private property that was bought and sold. Some people amassed large estates, and their wealth set them off from ordinary farmers. These landlords joined the urban elite, while sharecroppers and serfs toiled in the fields. By

This ziggurat, or temple tower, at Ur, Iraq, dates back to 4100 B.P. [2100 B.C.]. Temples and their officials played key roles in the Mesopotamian economy. Who handles such duties in our own society?

4600 B.P., Mesopotamia had a well-defined class structure, with complex stratification into nobles, commoners, and slaves.

Other Early States

For more on state formation in Africa, see the Internet Exercises at your OLC

mhhe
com
/kottak

In northwestern India and Pakistan, the Indus River Valley (or *Harappan*) state, with major cities at Harappa and Mohenjo-daro, takes its name from the river valley along which it extended. (Figure 11.2 maps the four great early river valley states of the Old World: Mesopotamia, Egypt, India/Pakistan, and northern China.) Trade and the spread of writing from Mesopotamia may have played a role in the emergence of the Harappan state around 4600 B.P. Located in Pakistan's Punjab Province, the ruins of Harappa were the first to be identified as part of the Indus River Valley civilization. At its peak, the Indus River Valley state incorporated 1,000 cities, towns, and villages, spanning 280,000 square miles (725,000 square kilometers). This state flourished between 4600 and 3900 B.P. It displayed such features of state organization as urban planning, social stratification, and an early writing system, which remains undeciphered. The Harappans maintained a uniform system of weights, and their cites had carefully planned residential areas with wastewater systems. An array of products from sophisticated craft industries included ceramic vessels made on potter's wheels (Meadow and Kenoyer 2000).

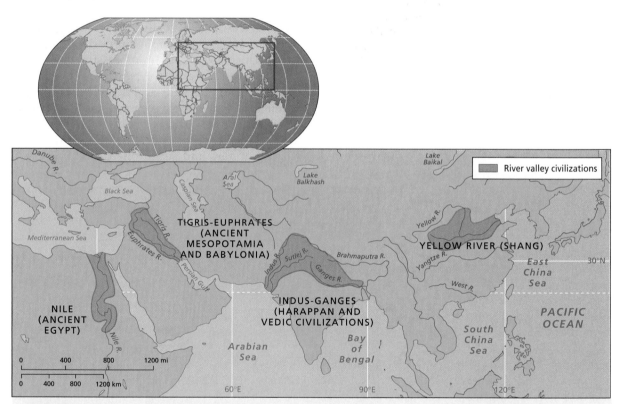

Figure 11.2   The Four Great Early River Valley States of the Old World.

By approximately 4,000 B.P. urban life had been established along the Tigris and Euphrates rivers in Mesopotamia, the Nile River in Egypt, the Indus and Ganges rivers in India/Pakistan, and the Yellow River in China.

SOURCE: Based on Map 1-1, Chapter 1, "Birth of Civilization." In Albert M. Craig, *The Heritage of World Civilizations*, *Volume I, to 1650*, 4th ed. Upper Saddle River, NJ: Prentice-Hall, 1997.

This bronze vessel was commissioned during China's Shang dynasty. The small elephant on top forms the handle of the lid. Wine was poured through the spout formed by the big elephant's trunk. Three notable features of the Shang dynasty were bronze, writing, and social stratification.

The first Chinese state, dating to 3750 B.P., was that of the Shang dynasty. It arose in the Huang He (Yellow) River area of northern China, where wheat, rather than rice, was the dietary staple. This state was characterized by urbanism, palatial (as well as domestic) architecture, human sacrifice, and a sharp division between social classes. Burials of the aristocracy were marked by ornaments of stone, including jade. The Shang had bronze metallurgy and an elaborate writing system. In warfare they used chariots and took prisoners (Gowlett 1993).

Like Mesopotamia and China, many early civilizations came to rely on metallurgy. At Nok Nok Tha in northern Thailand, metalworking goes back 6,000 years. In Peru's Andes metalworking appeared around 4000 B.P. The ancient inhabitants of the Andes were skilled workers of bronze, copper, and gold. They are also well known for their techniques of pottery manufacture. Their arts, crafts, and agricultural knowledge compared well with those of Mesoamerica at its height, to which we now turn. Note that both Mesoamerican and Andean state formation were truncated by Spanish conquest. The Aztecs of Mexico were conquered in A.D. 1519; and the Inca of Peru, in 1532.

The Indus River Valley state collapsed, apparently through warfare, around 3900 B.P. Its cities became largely depopulated. Skeletons of massacre victims have been found in the streets of Mohenjo-daro. Harappa continued to be occupied, but on a much smaller scale than previously (Meadow and Kenoyer 2000). (For more on the ongoing Harappa Archaeological Research Project, visit www.harappa.com.)

Interpret the World In your atlas, look at
Atlas Map 11 Map 11, "Ancient Civilizations of the Old World," which shows the locations of ancient civilizations (archaic states) in Europe, Africa, and Asia and also indicates the date when each state first appeared. What's the chronological order in which these states appeared? Compare Map 11 in your atlas with Figure 11.2 in the text. Figure 11.2 shows the four great early river valley states of the Old World, whereas Map 11 shows other states as well. Name some states that originated outside river valleys.

State Formation in Mesoamerica

See the Internet Exercises at your OLC

/kottak

In the last chapter we examined the independent inventions of farming in the Middle East and Mesoamerica. The processes of state formation that took place in these areas were also comparable, beginning with ranked societies and chiefdoms, and ending with fully formed states and empires.

The first monumental buildings (temple complexes) in the Western Hemisphere were constructed by Mesoamerican chiefdoms in many areas, from the Valley of Mexico to Guatemala. These chiefdoms influenced one another as they traded materials, such as obsidian, shells, jade, and pottery. (Figure 11.3 maps major sites in the emergence of Mesoamerican food production, chiefdoms, and states. See Table 10.3 on p. 273 of Chapter 10 for a chronology of Mesoamerican state formation.)

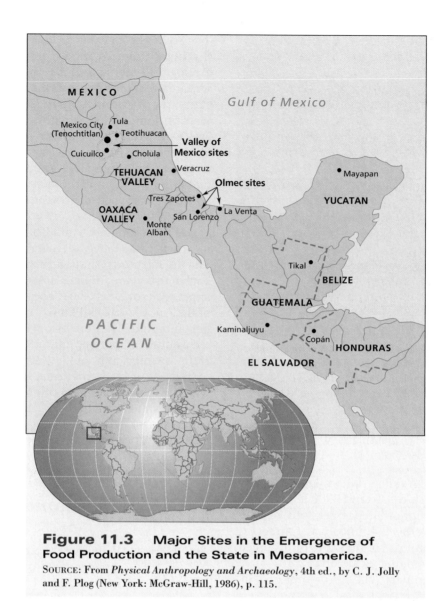

Figure 11.3 Major Sites in the Emergence of Food Production and the State in Mesoamerica.

SOURCE: From *Physical Anthropology and Archaeology*, 4th ed., by C. J. Jolly and F. Plog (New York: McGraw-Hill, 1986), p. 115.

EARLY CHIEFDOMS AND ELITES

The Olmec built a series of ritual centers on Mexico's southern Gulf Coast between 3,200 and 2,500 years ago. Three of these centers, each from a different century, are known. Earthen mounds were grouped into plaza complexes, presumably for religious use. Such centers show that Olmec chiefs could marshal human labor to construct such mounds. The Olmec were also master sculptors; they carved massive stone heads, perhaps as images of their chiefs or their ancestors, such as on Polynesia's Easter Island (see the chapter-opening photo).

There is evidence, too, that trade routes linked the Olmec with other parts of Mesoamerica, such as the Valley of Oaxaca in the southern highlands and the Valley of Mexico (see Figure 11.3). By 3000 B.P. a ruling elite had emerged in Oaxaca. The items traded at that time between Oaxaca and the Olmec were for elite consumption. High-status Oaxacans wore ornaments made of mussel shells from the coast. In return, the Olmec elite imported mirrors and jade made by Oaxacan artisans. Chiefdoms in Oaxaca developed canal and well irrigation, exported magnetite mirrors, and were precocious in their use of adobes (mud bricks), stucco, stone masonry, and architecture. Chiefdoms in the Olmec area farmed river levees, built mounds of earth, and carved colossal stone heads.

The Olmec are famous for their huge carved stone heads, but other early Mexican chiefdoms also had accomplished artists and builders, using adobes and lime plaster and constructing stone buildings, precisely oriented 8 degrees north of east.

The period between 3,200 and 3,000 B.P. was one of rapid social change in Mexico. All or almost all of Mesoamerica's chiefdoms were linked by trade and exchange. Many competing chiefly centers were concentrating labor power, intensifying agriculture, exchanging trade goods, and borrowing ideas, including art motifs and styles, from each other. Archaeologists now believe it was the *intensity of competitive interaction*—rather than the supremacy of any one chiefdom—that made social change so rapid. The social and political landscape of Mexico around 3000 B.P. was one in which 25 or so chiefly centers were (1) sufficiently separate and autonomous to adapt to local zones and conditions and (2) sufficiently interacting and competitive to borrow and incorporate new ideas and innovations as they arose in other regions (Flannery and Marcus 2000).

It used to be thought that a single chiefdom could become a state on its own. Archaeologists know now that state formation involves one chiefdom's incorporating several others into the emerging state it controls, and making changes in its own infrastructure as it acquires and holds on to new territories, followers, and goods. Warfare and attracting followers are two key elements in state formation.

Many chiefdoms have dense populations, intensive agriculture, and settlement hierarchies that include hamlets, villages, and perhaps towns. These factors pave the way for greater social and political complexity. Political leaders emerge, and military success (in raiding) often solidifies their position. Such figures attract lots of followers, who are loyal to their leader. Warfare enables leaders to incorporate new lands and people. Success in warfare leads to states' becoming even more densely occupied and in control of new lands. States, in contrast to chiefdoms, can acquire labor and land and hold on to them. States have armies, warfare, developed political hierarchies, law codes, and military force, which can be used in fact or as a threat.

The Olmec and Oaxaca were just two of many flamboyant early Mexican chiefdoms that once thrived in the area from the Valley of Mexico to Guatemala. Oaxaca went on to develop a state as early as the Teotihuacan state in the Valley of Mexico. Oaxaca and other highland areas came to overshadow the Olmec area and the Mesoamerican lowlands in general. By 2500 B.P. the Zapotec state at Oaxaca had developed a distinctive art style, perfected at its capital city of Monte Alban. The Zapotec state lasted almost 2,000 years, until it—along with the rest of Mexico—was conquered by Spain (see Blanton 1999; Marcus and Flannery 1996).

As the Olmec chiefdoms were declining, the elite level was spreading throughout Mesoamerica. By A.D. 1 (2000 B.P.), the Valley of Mexico, located in the highlands where Mexico City now stands, came to prominence in Mesoamerican state formation. In this large valley **Teotihuacan** flourished between 1900 and 1300 B.P. (A.D. 100 and 700).

STATES IN THE VALLEY OF MEXICO

The Valley of Mexico is a large basin surrounded by mountains. The valley has rich volcanic soils, but rainfall isn't always reliable. The northern part of the valley, where the huge city and state of Teotihuacan

This colossal Olmec head, carved from basalt, is displayed at the La Venta Archaeology Museum in Tabasco state, Mexico, in a setting designed to recall its original site. What is the significance of such a massive artifact?

eventually arose, is colder and drier than the south. Frosts there limited farming until quick-growing varieties of maize were developed. Until 2500 B.P., most people lived in the warmer and wetter southern part of the valley, where rainfall made farming possible. After 2500 B.P., new maize varieties and small-scale irrigation appeared. Population increased and began to spread north.

By A.D. 1 Teotihuacan was a town of 10,000 people. It governed a territory of a few thousand square kilometers and perhaps 50,000 people (Parsons 1974). Teotihuacan's growth reflected its agricultural potential. Perpetual springs permitted irrigation of a large alluvial plain. Rural farmers supplied food for the growing urban population.

By this time, a clear **settlement hierarchy** had emerged. This is a ranked series of communities that differ in size, function, and building types. The settlements at the top of the hierarchy were political and religious centers. Those at the bottom were rural villages. Such a three-level settlement hierarchy (capital city, smaller urban centers, and rural villages) provides archaeological evidence of state organization (Wright and Johnson 1975). How many levels indicate a chiefdom?

Along with state organization went large-scale irrigation, status differentiation, and complex architecture. Teotihuacan thrived between A.D. 100 and 700. It grew as a planned city built on a grid pattern, with the Pyramid of the Sun at its center. By A.D. 500, the population of Teotihuacan had

reached 130,000, making it larger than imperial Rome. Farmers were one of its diverse specialized groups, along with artisans, merchants, and political, religious, and military personnel.

After A.D. 700 Teotihuacan declined in size and power. By A.D. 900 its population had shrunk to 30,000. Between A.D. 900 and 1200, the Toltec period, the population scattered, and small cities and towns sprang up throughout the valley. People also left the Valley of Mexico to live in larger cities—like Tula, the Toltec capital—on its edge (see Figure 11.3).

Population increase (including immigration by the ancestors of the Aztecs) and urban growth returned to the Valley of Mexico between A.D. 1200 and 1520. During the **Aztec** period (A.D. 1325 to 1520) there were several cities, the largest of which—Tenochtitlan, the capital—may have surpassed Teotihuacan at its height. A dozen Aztec towns had more than 10,000 people. Fueling this population growth was intensification of agriculture, particularly in the southern part of the valley, where the drainage of lake bottoms and swamps added new cultivable land (Parsons 1976).

Another factor in the renaissance of the Valley of Mexico was trade. Local manufacture created products for a series of markets. The major towns and markets were located on the lake shores, with easy access to canoe traffic. The Aztec capital stood on an island in the lake. In Tenochtitlan, the production of luxury goods was more prestigious and

The Pyramid of the Sun, Teotihuacan's largest structure, is shown in the upper part of the photo. At its height around A.D.500, Teotihuacan was larger than imperial Rome. The mobilization of manual labor to build such structures is one of the costs of state organization.

The Aztecs played the board game of patolli, as represented here in the Codex Magliabecchiano, housed in the National Library in Florence, Italy.

more highly organized than that of pottery, basket making, and weaving. Luxury producers, such as stone workers, feather workers, and gold- and silversmiths, occupied a special position in Aztec society. The manufacture of luxury goods for export was an important part of the economy of the Aztec capital (Hassig 1985; Santley 1985).

The Origin of the State

Early states were often multivalley (extensive territorial units), whereas chiefdoms might occupy different sections of a single valley. Chiefs often could take captives from other chiefdoms and raid villages for booty. Early states, by contrast, could acquire and *hold on to* new land and people. State control is more permanent, effective, and secure than chiefly control. Early states were often extensive because they could expand against less politically developed chiefdoms. This was true of the Zapotec, Maya, and Teotihuacan states. In fact, the most extensive territorial control was achieved by some of the earliest states. Later, some of their incorporated units broke away and became independent. Some of them went on to forge new expansionist states. **Empires** are mature, territorially large, and expansive states that are typically multiethnic, multilinguistic, and more militaristic, with better developed bureaucracy than earlier states.

How and why did states originate? The state develops to handle regulatory problems encountered as the population grows and/or the economy increases in scale and diversity. Anthropologists and historians have identified the causes of state formation and have reconstructed the rise of several states. Many factors always contribute to state formation, with the effects of one magnifying those of the others. Although some contributing factors appear again and again, no single one is always present. In other words, state formation has generalized rather than universal causes.

See the Interactive Exercise for a Quiz

mhhe
com
/kottak

Furthermore, because state formation may take centuries, people experiencing the process at any time rarely perceive the significance of the long-term changes. Later generations find themselves dependent on government institutions that took generations to develop.

Understanding Ourselves State formation is the subject of numerous anthropology books. Ancient states developed out of competing chiefdoms. Chiefdoms or states conquered others and created new states in the process. Although the causes of state formation are always multiple, all states have certain features (e.g., central government, political and settlement hierarchies, stratification, taxation, a military) that define them as states. States also need economies and demographic characteristics that sustain them. Even in the modern world, can a political unit that is sparsely populated by nomadic herders be governed as easily as can one with a dense population supported by irrigation and sedentary farming? Settled farmers are easier to subject to state control than are pastoral nomads or hunters and gatherers. Given their economies, we'd expect to find more stable and enduring states in China and India than in Afghanistan, Sudan, or Somalia. We'd expect to find tighter political control in river basins with irrigated agriculture than in hilly areas of slash-and-burn farming.

The world has changed substantially since ancient times, and the pace of change has increased. Nevertheless, knowledge of a state's foundation—of the correlations between economic and political types that anthropologists study—can help us understand the stability and instability of states in today's world. Anthropological knowledge of the past, especially of political history and of economic and demographic features, supports predictions about the contemporary countries in which we'd expect nation building to be more, or less, successful. Care to offer some predictions?

HYDRAULIC SYSTEMS

One suggested cause of state formation is the need to regulate *hydraulic* (water-based) agricultural economies (Wittfogel 1957). In certain arid areas, states have emerged to manage systems of irrigation, drainage, and flood control. However, hydraulic agriculture is neither a sufficient nor a necessary condition for the rise of the state. That is, many societies with irrigation never experienced state formation, and states have developed without hydraulic systems.

But hydraulic agriculture does have certain implications for state formation. Water control increases production in arid lands, such as ancient Mesopotamia and Egypt. Because of its labor demands and its ability to feed more people, irrigated agriculture fuels population growth. This in

turn leads to enlargement of the system. The expanding hydraulic system supports larger and denser concentrations of people. Interpersonal problems increase, and conflicts over access to water and irrigated land become more frequent. Political systems may arise to regulate interpersonal relations and the means of production.

Large hydraulic works can sustain towns and cities and become essential to their subsistence. Regulators protect the economy by mobilizing crews to maintain and repair the hydraulic system. These life-and-death functions enhance the authority of state officials. Thus, growth in hydraulic systems is often (as in Mesopotamia, Egypt, and the Valley of Mexico), but not always, associated with state formation.

LONG-DISTANCE TRADE ROUTES

Another theory is that states develop at strategic locations in regional trade networks. These sites include points of supply or exchange, such as crossroads of caravan routes, and places (e.g., mountain passes and river narrows) situated so as to threaten or halt trade between centers. Here again, however, the cause is generalized but neither necessary nor sufficient. Long-distance trade has been important in the evolution of many states, including Mesopotamia and Mesoamerica. Such exchange does eventually develop in all states, but it can follow rather than precede state formation. Furthermore, long-distance trade also occurs in societies such as those of Papua New Guinea, where no states developed.

POPULATION, WAR, AND CIRCUMSCRIPTION

Carneiro (1970) proposed a theory that incorporates three factors working together instead of a single cause of state formation. (We call a theory involving multiple factors or variables a **multivariate** theory.) Wherever and whenever *environmental circumscription* (or *resource concentration*), *increasing population*, and *warfare* exist, says Carneiro, state formation will begin. Environmental circumscription may be physical or social. Physically circumscribed environments include small islands and, in arid areas, river plains, oases, and valleys with streams. Social circumscription exists when neighboring societies block expansion, emigration, or access to resources. When strategic resources are concentrated in limited areas—even when no obstacles to migration exist—the effects are similar to those of circumscription.

Coastal Peru, one of the world's most arid areas, illustrates the interaction of environmental circumscription, warfare, and population increase. Early cultivation was limited to valleys with springs. Each valley was circumscribed by the Andes Mountains to the east, the Pacific Ocean to the west, and desert regions to the north and south. The transition from foraging to food production triggered population increase (Figure 11.4). In each valley, villages got bigger. Colonists split off from the old villages and founded new ones. Rivalries and raiding developed between villages in the same valley. As villages proliferated and the valley population grew, a scarcity of land developed.

Population pressure and land shortages were developing in all the valleys. Because the valleys were circumscribed, when one village conquered another, the losers had to submit to the winners—they had nowhere else to go. Conquered villagers could keep their land only if they agreed to pay tribute to their conquerors. To do this, they had to intensify production, using new techniques to produce more food. By working harder, they managed to pay tribute while meeting their own subsistence needs. Villagers brought new areas under cultivation by means of irrigation and terracing.

Those early inhabitants of the Andes didn't work harder because they chose to do so. They were *forced* to pay tribute, accept political domination, and intensify production by factors beyond their control. Once established, all these trends accelerated. Population grew, warfare intensified, and villages were eventually united in chiefdoms. The first states developed when one chiefdom in a valley conquered the others (Carneiro 1990). Eventually, different valleys began to fight. The winners brought the losers into growing states and empires, which eventually expanded from the coast to the highlands. By the 16th century, from their capital, Cuzco, in the high Andes, the Inca ruled one of the major empires of the tropics.

Carneiro's theory is very useful, but again, the association between population density and state organization is generalized rather than universal. States do tend to have large and dense populations (Stevenson 1968). However, population increase

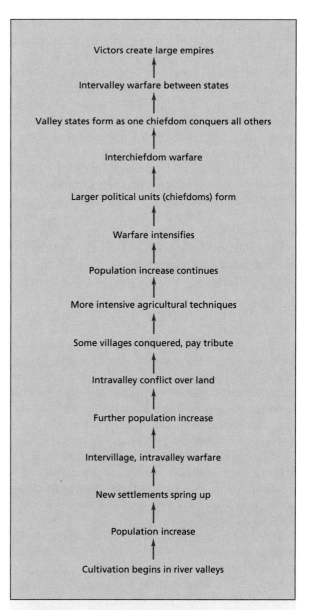

Figure 11.4 **Carneiro's Multivariate Approach to the Origin of the State as Applied to Coastal Peru.** In this very arid area, food production developed in narrow river valleys where water for cultivation was available (resource concentration). With cultivation, the population increased. Population pressure on land led to warfare, and some villages conquered others. Physical circumscription meant that the losers had no way to escape. The process accelerated as the population grew and as warfare and cultivation intensified. Chiefdoms, states, and empires eventually developed.

and warfare within a circumscribed environment did not trigger state formation in highland Papua New Guinea. Certain valleys there are socially or physically circumscribed and have population densities similar to those of many states. Warfare also was present, but no states emerged. Again we are dealing with an important theory that explains many but not all cases of state formation.

Early states arose in different areas for many reasons. In each case, interacting causes (often comparable ones) magnified each other's effects. To explain any instance of state formation, we must search for the specific changes in access to resources and in regulatory problems that fostered stratification and state machinery. The opposite of state formation is state decline.

Why States Collapse

States can be fragile and decomposable, falling apart along the same cleavage lines (e.g., regional political units) that were forged together to form the state originally. Various factors could threaten their economies and political institutions. Invasion, disease, famine, or prolonged drought could upset the balance. A state's citizens might harm the environment, usually with economic costs. For example, farmers and smelters might cut down trees. Such deforestation promotes erosion and leads to a decline in the water supply. Overuse of land may deplete the soil of the nutrients needed to grow crops.

We've just considered theories for the origin of the state. If factors such as irrigation help create states to begin with, does their decline or failure explain the fall of the state? Irrigation does have costs as well as benefits. In ancient Mesopotamia, irrigation water came from the Tigris and Euphrates rivers. Because sediment (silt) had accumulated in those rivers, their beds were higher than the alluvial plain and fields they irrigated. Canals channeled river water as it flowed down into the fields by gravity. As the water evaporated, water-borne mineral salts remained in the fields, eventually creating a poisonous environment for plants.

One of the worst droughts of the last 10,000 years, perhaps global in scale, began around 4300 B.P. and lasted three centuries. According to Richard Kerr (1998), this long dry spell contributed to the fall of northern Mesopotamia's Akkadian empire. By 4200 B.P., overall agricultural production in Mesopotamia had fallen to a fraction of what it once had been. Many fields were abandoned as useless. The drought probably played a role. So did the buildup of mineral salts in the irrigated fields.

Mashkan-shapir was a Mesopotamian city located about 20 miles from the Tigris, to which it was connected by a network of canals. This city was abandoned just 20 years after it was settled. Destruction of its fields by mineral salts seems to have been a prime factor in its collapse (see Annenberg/CPB Exhibits at http://www.learner.org/exhibits/collapse/mesopotamia.html).

One key role of the state is regulation, whether of the economy or of relations between individuals and groups. Subsistence needs must be met, and chiefdoms and states may offer greater food security than do less centralized forms of society. Political leaders often maintain storehouses or central supplies of food and other goods, which may be distributed to the people in times of need. For example, tribute collected by Mexico's Aztec rulers was used for several purposes: (1) to appease troublesome nobles and otherwise to reward the elite establishment, (2) to support royal craftsmen, and (3) to be stored in royal granaries for distribution to the urban population in times of acute food stress (Santley 1985).

States may collapse when they fail to do what they are supposed to do, such as maintain social order, protect themselves against outsiders, and allow their people to meet subsistence needs. If the economy collapses, the political structure is likely to disintegrate as well. When a state declines, basic skills typically survive, but more refined levels of knowledge, shared by fewer people, tend to be lost (Gowlett 1993).

THE MAYAN DECLINE

Generations of scholars have debated the decline of classic Mayan civilization around A.D. 900 (1700–1100 B.P.). Classic Mayan culture, featuring several competing states, flourished between A.D. 300 and 900 in parts of what are now Mexico, Honduras, El Salvador, Guatemala, and Belize. The ancient Maya are known for their monuments (temples and pyramids), calendars, mathematics, and hieroglyphic writing.

Archaeological clues to Mayan decline have been found at Copán, in western Honduras. This classic Maya royal center, the largest site in the southeastern part of the Maya area, covered 29 acres. It was built on an artificial terrace overlooking the Copán river. Its rulers inscribed their monuments with accounts of their coronation, their lineage history, and reports of important battles. The Maya dated their monuments with the names of kings and when they reigned. One monument at Copán was intended to be the ruler's throne platform, but only one side had been finished. The monument bears a date, A.D. 822, in a section of unfinished text. Copán has no monuments with later dates. The site probably was abandoned by A.D. 830.

Environmental factors implicated in Copán's demise may have included erosion and soil exhaustion due to overpopulation and overfarming. Overfarming contributes to deforestation and erosion. Hillside farmhouses in particular had debris from erosion—probably caused by overfarming of the hillsides. This erosion began as early as A.D. 750—until these farm sites were abandoned, with some eventually buried by erosion debris. For the classic Maya in general, William Sanders (1972, 1973) has attributed state decline to overfarming, leading to environmental degradation through grass invasion and erosion.

Food stress and malnutrition were clearly present at Copán, where 80 percent of the buried skeletons display signs of anemia, due to iron deficiency. One skull shows anemia severe enough to have been the cause of death. Even the nobility were malnourished. One noble skull, known to be such from its carved teeth and cosmetic deformation, also has telltale signs of anemia: spongy areas at its rear (Annenberg/CPB Exhibits).

About as many people (25,000) live in the Copán valley today as lived there in A.D. 822. Like the ancient Maya, their subsistence depends on maize farming. Today's farmers cultivate the land year after year, with no fallow or resting period, and they complain of declining harvests. That yields are falling suggests the land could use fallow time to recoup the nutrients needed for successful farming (Annenberg/CPB Exhibits).

Just as the origins of states, and their causes, are diverse, so are the reasons for state decline. The Mayan state was not as powerful as was once assumed; it was fragile and vulnerable. Increased warfare and political competition destabilized many of its dynasties and governments. Archaeologists now stress the role of warfare in Mayan state

Ruins at Copán, a center of Classic Mayan royalty in western Honduras.

The 1998 film *The X-Files* opens with a scene purportedly dating to 35,000 B.C. Two prehistoric men trek across a glacial landscape in North Texas. Soon they have an alien encounter. Who's more likely to have been in Texas back then: the humans or the aliens? The study of prehistory has spawned popular-culture creations, including movies, TV programs, and books. In these fictional works, the anthropologists (and the natives as well) usually don't bear much resemblance to their real-life counterparts. Unlike Indiana Jones, normal and reputable archaeologists don't have nonstop adventures—fighting Nazis, lashing whips, or rescuing antiquities. The archaeologist's profession isn't a matter of raiding lost arks or of going on crusades but of reconstructing lifeways through the analysis of material remains, in order to understand culture and human behavior.

Much of the popular nonfiction dealing with prehistory is also suspect. Through books and the mass media, we have been exposed to the ideas of popular writers such as Thor Heyerdahl and Erich von Daniken. Heyerdahl, a well-known diffusionist, believes that developments in one world area are usually based on ideas borrowed from another. Von

Daniken carries diffusionism one step further, proposing that major human achievements have been borrowed from beings from space who have visited us at various periods of our past. Heyerdahl and von Daniken seem to share (with some science-fiction writers) a certain contempt for human inventiveness and originality. They take the position that major changes in ancient human life styles were the results of outside instruction or interference rather than the achievements of the natives of the places where the changes took place.

In *The Ra Expeditions* (Heyerdahl 1971), for example, world traveler and adventurer Heyerdahl argued that his voyage in a papyrus boat from the Mediterranean to the Caribbean demonstrates that ancient Egyptians could have navigated to the New World. (The boat was modeled on an ancient Egyptian vessel, but Heyerdahl and his crew took along such modern conveniences as a radio and canned goods.) Heyerdahl maintained that given the possibility of ancient transatlantic voyages, Old World people could have influenced the emergence of civilization in the Americas.

What is the scientific evaluation of Heyerdahl's contention? Even if

Old World ancients had reached the New World, they couldn't have done much to propel Native Americans toward state organization because the New World wasn't yet ready for food production and the state. When Egypt became a major power capable of sending scouts across the seas, around 5,000 years ago, Mexicans were broad-spectrum foragers. Had they even started cultivating corn? (See the text for the answer.) The gradual nature of the Mesoamerican transition from foraging to food production is clearly demonstrated by archaeological sequences in such sites as Oaxaca and the Valley of Mexico. Had foreign inputs been important, they would have shown up in the material remains that constitute the archaeological record.

Beginning some 2,000 years ago, states fully comparable to those of Mesopotamia and Egypt began to rise and fall in the Mexican highlands. This occurred more than 1,000 years after the height of ancient Egyptian influence, between 3600 and 3400 B.P. Had Egypt or any other ancient Old World state contributed to the rise or the fall of Mesoamerican civilization, we would expect this influence to have been exerted during Egypt's heyday as an ancient power—not 1,500 years later.

decline. Hieroglyphic texts document increased warfare among many Mayan cities. From the period just before the collapse, there is archaeological evidence for increased concern with fortifications (moats, ditches, walls, and palisades) and moving to defensible locations. Archaeologists have evidence of the burning of structures, the

projectile points from spears, and some of the bodies of those killed. Some sites were abandoned, with the people fleeing into the forests to occupy perishable huts. (Copán, as we have seen, was depopulated after A.D. 822.) Archaeologists now believe that social, political, and military upheaval and competition had as much as or more to do

How much does Indiana Jones tell us about real archaeologists? The photo is from *Indiana Jones and the Temple of Doom.*

There is abundant archaeological evidence for the gradual, evolutionary emergence of food production and the state in the Middle East, in Mesoamerica, and in Peru. This evidence effectively counters the diffusionist theories about how and why human achievements, including farming and the state, began. Popular theories to the contrary, changes, advances, and setbacks in ancient American social life were the products of the ideas and activities of the Native Americans themselves.

There are certain unresolved issues, to be sure, in explaining why Mesoamerican civilizations rose and fell. Archaeologists are still unraveling the causes of the collapse around A.D. 900 of the Mayan culture of Mexico and Guatemala. However, there is simply no valid evidence for Old World interference before the European Age of Discovery, which began late in the 15th century. Francisco Pizzaro conquered Peru's Inca state in 1532, 11 years after its Mesoamerican counterpart, Tenochtitlan, the Aztec capital, fell to Spanish conquistadores in 1521. (We do have abundant archaeological, as well as written, evidence for this recent, historically known contact between Europeans and Native Americans.)

The archaeological record also casts doubt on contentions that the advances of earthlings came with extraterrestrial help, as Erich von Daniken argued in his book *Chariots of the Gods* (1971), and as Discovery-type TV sometimes suggests. Abundant, well-analyzed archaeological data from the Middle East, Mesoamerica, and Peru tell a clear story.

Plant and animal domestication, the state, and city life were not brilliant discoveries, inventions, or secrets that humans needed to borrow from extraterrestrials. They were long-term, gradual processes, developments with down-to-earth causes and effects. They required thousands of years of orderly change, not some chance meeting in the high Andes between an ancient Inca chief and a beneficent Johnny Appleseed from Aldebaran.

This is not to deny, by the way, that intelligent life and civilizations at a variety of technological levels—some more, some less advanced than earth—may exist throughout the galaxy or even that extraterrestrials may have occasionally ventured into this relatively isolated outer spiral arm of the Milky Way galaxy and even visited earth itself. However, even if extraterrestrials have been on earth, archaeological evidence suggests that their starship commanders observed a prime directive of noninterference in the affairs of less-advanced planets. There is no scientifically valid evidence for the rapid kind of change that sustained extraterrestrial intervention would have produced. What would constitute such evidence?

with the Mayan decline and abandonment of cities than did natural environmental factors (Marcus, personal communication).

Formerly archaeologists tended to explain state origin and decline mainly in terms of natural environmental factors, such as climate change, habitat destruction, and demographic pressure. Archaeologists now see state origins and declines more fully—in social and political terms—because we can read the texts. And the Mayan texts document competition and warfare between dynasties jockeying for position and power. Warfare was indeed a creator and a destroyer of ancient chiefdoms and states. What's its role in our own?

Summary

1. A state is a society with a formal, central government and a division of society into classes. The first cities and states, supported by irrigated farming, developed in southern Mesopotamia between 6000 and 5500 B.P. Evidence for early state organization includes monumental architecture, central storehouses, irrigation systems, and written records.

2. Towns predate pottery in the Middle East. The first towns grew up 10,000 to 9,000 years ago. The first pottery dates back just over 8,000 years. Halafian (7500–6500 B.P.) refers to a pottery style and to the period when the first chiefdoms emerged. Ubaid pottery (7000–6000 B.P.) is associated with advanced chiefdoms and perhaps the earliest states. Most state formation occurred during the Uruk period (6100–5100 B.P.).

3. Based on the status distinctions they include, societies may be divided into egalitarian, ranked, and stratified. In egalitarian societies, status distinctions are not usually inherited. Ranked societies have hereditary inequality, but they lack stratification. Stratified societies have sharp social divisions—social classes or *strata*—based on unequal access to wealth and power. Ranked societies with loss of village autonomy are chiefdoms. The first chiefdoms appeared between 7,300 and 5,800 years ago. Chiefdoms feature political instability, raiding, and exotic goods used to mark status.

4. Mesopotamia's economy was based on craft production, trade, and intensive agriculture. Writing, invented by 5600 B.P., was first used to keep accounts for trade. With the invention of smelting, the Bronze Age began just after 5000 B.P.

5. In northwestern India and Pakistan, the Indus River Valley state flourished from 4600 to 3900 B.P. The first Chinese state, dating to 3750 B.P., was that of the Shang dynasty in northern China. The major early states of the Western Hemisphere were in Mesoamerica and Peru.

6. States arose between 2500 and 1600 B.P. (500 B.C. and A.D. 400) in Mesoamerica. Previously, Olmec chiefdoms had built ritual centers on Mexico's southern Gulf Coast between 3,200 and 2,500 years ago. Between 3,200 and 3,000 B.P., intense competitive interaction among the many chiefdoms in Mesoamerica at that time fueled rapid social change. Some chiefdoms would develop into states (e.g., Oaxaca, Valley of Mexico). Others (e.g., Olmec) would not. By A.D. 1 (2000 B.P.), the Valley of Mexico had come to prominence. In this large valley in the highlands, Teotihuacan thrived between A.D. 100 and 700. Tenochtitlan, the capital of the Aztec state (A.D. 1325 to 1520), may have surpassed Teotihuacan at its height.

7. States develop to handle regulatory problems as the population grows and the economy gets more complex. Multiple factors contribute to state formation. Some appear repeatedly, but no single factor is always present. Among the most important factors are irrigation and long-distance trade. Coastal Peru, a very arid area, illustrates how environmental circumscription, population growth, and warfare may contribute to state formation.

8. Early states faced various threats: invasion, disease, famine, drought, soil exhaustion, erosion, and the buildup of irrigation salts. States may collapse when they fail to keep social and economic order or to protect themselves against outsiders. The Mayan state fell in the face of increased warfare among competing dynasties.

Key Terms

See the flash cards

/kottak

Aztec Last independent state in the Valley of Mexico; capital was Tenochtitlan. Thrived between A.D. 1325 and the Spanish Conquest in 1520.

bronze An alloy of arsenic and copper or of tin and copper.

chiefdom A ranked society in which relations among villages as well as among individuals are unequal, with smaller villages under the authority of leaders in larger villages; has a two-level settlement hierarchy.

cuneiform Early Mesopotamian writing that used a stylus (writing implement) to write wedge-shaped impressions on raw clay; from the Latin word for wedge.

egalitarian society A type of society, most typically found among hunter-gatherers, that lacks status distinctions except for those based on age, gender, and individual qualities, talents, and achievements.

empire A mature, territorially large, and expansive, state; empires are typically multiethnic, multilinguistic, and more militaristic, with better developed bureaucracy than earlier states.

Halafian An early (7500–6500 B.P.) and widespread pottery style, first found in northern Syria; refers to a delicate ceramic style and to the period when the first chiefdoms emerged.

Mesopotamia The area between the Tigris and Euphrates rivers in what is now southern Iraq and southwestern Iran; location of the first cities and states.

metallurgy Knowledge of the properties of metals, including their extraction and processing and the manufacture of metal tools.

multivariate Involving multiple factors, causes, or variables.

primary states States that arise on their own (through competition among chiefdoms), and not through contact with other state societies.

ranked society A type of society with hereditary inequality but not social stratification; individuals are ranked in terms of their genealogical closeness to the chief, but there is a continuum of status, with many individuals and kin groups ranked about equally.

settlement hierarchy A ranked series of communities differing in size, function, and type of building; a three-level settlement hierarchy indicates state organization.

smelting The high-temperature process by which pure metal is produced from an ore.

state A form of social and political organization with a formal, central government and a division of society into classes.

stratification A stratified society has sharp social divisions—*strata*—based on unequal access to wealth and power, e.g., into noble and commoner classes.

Teotihuacan A.D. 100 to 700; first state in the Valley of Mexico and earliest major Mesoamerican empire.

For more self testing, see the self quizzes

mhhe
com
/kottak

CRITICAL THINKING QUESTIONS

1. What were the main similarities and differences in the processes of state formation in the Middle East and in Mesoamerica?
2. Was the origin of the state good or bad? Why?
3. Can you think of three reasons to build walls around a town or a city? What is probably the most common reason? Does Çatal Hüyük remind you of an Upper Paleolithic cave site? Why and why not?
4. Imagine yourself transported back in time to an early chiefdom of your choice. Would it be in the Middle East or Mesoamerica? Why?
5. What would be the advantages and disadvantages of being an early chief in the Middle East? Would you rather be the chief or a chief's close relative?
6. Imagine yourself an archaeologist trying to identify ancient chiefdoms in the Middle East after excavating Mesoamerican chiefdom sites. What similar and different lines of evidence for ranking and political alliance might you find in the two hemispheres?
7. Imagine yourself transported back in time to an early state of your choice. Where would it be and why?
8. Would you feel more secure in an ancient chiefdom or an ancient state? How about those societies compared with the more egalitarian societies of prehistoric hunters and gatherers?
9. Is it harder to tell the difference between a chiefdom and a state in the ancient Middle East or in Mesoamerica. Why?

10. What kind of economic roles were available in early states, as compared with the earliest food-producing societies?

11. Why do you think the earliest states developed about 3,000 years later in Mesoamerica than in the Middle East? Imagine what might have happened if those states had developed at the same time.

12. Compare the origin of the United States or Canada with the origin of ancient states. Do any of the theories for the origin of the state apply to your country?

13. If our own state declined, what would be the most likely cause(s)? Do you view our government as stronger or weaker than it was a generation ago? How about a century ago? What is the likely reason for this strength or weakness?

14. Do you view our government as stronger or weaker than those of ancient states? What are the main reasons for this strength or weakness?

Atlas Questions

Look at Map 11, "Ancient Civilizations of the Old World."

1. What contemporary nations would you have to visit if you wanted to see all the places where ancient civilizations developed in the Old World? Would some countries be off limits for political reasons? How do you think such limitations have affected the archaeological record? Have the limitations been as substantial in the western hemisphere as in the Old World?

2. Of the ancient states shown on Map 11, which developed latest? Did other states develop even later that are not shown on Map 11? If so, give some examples, indicating where and when they appeared.

3. In which of the ancient states shown on Map 11 were Middle Eastern domesticates basic to the economy? In which states shown on Map 11 were other domesticates basic to the economy?

SUGGESTED ADDITIONAL READINGS

Blanton, R. E.
1999   *Ancient Oaxaca: The Monte Alban State*. New York: Cambridge University Press. The story of an early—and enduring—area of Mesoamerican state formation.

Blanton, R. E., S. A. Kowalewski, G. M. Feinman, and L. M. Finsten, eds.
1993   *Ancient Mesoamerica: A Comparison of Change in Three Regions*, 2nd ed. New York: Cambridge University Press. This book synthesizes research on three well-studied regions of Mesoamerica: the Valley of Oaxaca, the Valley of Mexico, and the Maya lowlands.

Diamond, J. M.
1997   *Guns, Germs, and Steel: The Fates of Human Societies*. New York: W.W. Norton. Disease, tools, and environmental forces and effects throughout human history.

Fagan, B. M.
2002   *World Prehistory: A Brief Introduction*, 5th ed. New York: Longman. Major events in human prehistory, including the emergence of the state in various locales.

Feinman, G. M., and J. Marcus, eds.
1998   *Archaic States*. Santa Fe, NM: School of American Research Press. Features of early states, in general and in particular world areas.

Joyce, R. A.
2000   *Gender and Power in Prehispanic Mesoamerica*. Austin, TX: University of Texas Press. Issues of gender and power in Mesoamerica before the Spanish Conquest.

Pollock, S.
1999   *Ancient Mesopotamia: The Eden That Never Was*. Cambridge, England: Cambridge University Press. Mesopotamia state formation—a new synthesis.

Smith, M. E., and M. A. Masson, eds.
2000   *The Ancient Civilizations of Mesoamerica: A Reader*. Malpen, MA: Blackwell. Explores the diversity of Mesoamerican chiefdoms and states.

Trigger, B. G.

1993   *Early Civilizations: Ancient Egypt in Context.* New York: Columbia University Press. Considers the Incas (Inka); the Shang and western Chou of China; the Aztecs and Mayas of Mesoamerica; the Yoruba and Benin of West Africa; Mesopotamia; and ancient Egypt.

Wenke, R.

1996   *Patterns in Prehistory: Humankind's First Three Million Years*, 4th ed. New York: Oxford University Press. Rise of food production and the state throughout the world; thorough, useful text.

INTERNET EXERCISES

1. Early Cities in Mesoamerica: Read *Archaeology* magazine's article on the New Tomb Found at Teotihuacan, **http://www.archaeology.org/online/features/mexico/index.html**.

   a. Where was the tomb found at Teotihuacan, and how old is it? Was the tomb created early or late in the history of this city? How does the tomb help us to understand the history of Teotihuacan?

   b. What was found in the tomb? What do they signify?

   c. As an example of a state, what are some of the institutions that you think may have existed at Teotihuacan? For example, do you think they had military and professional religion practitioners?

2. Indus Valley Civilization: Go to Mark Kenyoyer's "Around the Indus in 90 Slides" presentation, **http://www.harappa.com/indus/indus0.html**, and read his Essay about the Indus civilization, **http://www.harappa.com/indus/indus1.html**.

   a. Where is the Indus? When did its first cities arise? What are the names of some of the cities?

   b. What are some of the characteristics of Indus cities? Are those characteristic of a state?

   c. What are some of the common misconceptions about the origins of Indus civilization?

   d. The Indus had a form of writing. What did they write on? What are some of the common images and motifs associated with the inscriptions?

See Chapter 11 at your McGraw-Hill Online Learning Center for additional review and interactive exercises.

BRINGING IT ALL TOGETHER

The Peopling of the Pacific

On April 28, 1947, the adventurer Thor Heyerdahl and five others set out from Peru, aboard a balsa raft, on a voyage they hoped would end on Polynesia's Easter Island. (They actually reached Raroia, French Polynesia.) Contrary to scientific opinion then and now, Heyerdahl sought to prove that Native South Americans could have rafted to, and then colonized, Polynesia. No scientific evidence has ever been found to support the hypothesis that Polynesia was settled by Native Americans.

Who did settle the vast Pacific? Today, when archaeologists dig in Australia, Papua New Guinea, and the neighboring islands of the southwest Pacific (consult the map on page 311 throughout this discussion), they find traces of humankind more than 30,000 years old. Humans reached northern Australia between 50,000 and 60,000 years ago. People even reached the islands north of Australia, as far as the Solomon Islands, more than 30,000 years ago (Terrell 1998).

And there they stayed. Based on current evidence, people waited thousands of years before they risked sailing farther eastward on the open sea. Until 3000 B.P., the Solomon Islands formed the eastern edge of the inhabited Pacific. The deep-sea crossings and colonization that began around 3000 B.P. was linked to the rapid spread of the earliest pottery found in Oceania, an ornately decorated ware with geometric designs called Lapita.

The first Lapita potsherds were excavated in 1952. The name Lapita comes from the discovery site on the Melanesian island of New Caledonia. (Locate New Caledonia the map on page 311. Where does New Caledonia lie in relation to the Solomon Islands, the Bismarck Archipelago, Tonga, and Samoa?) The oldest Lapita artifacts, dating back some 3,500 years, have been found in the Bismarck Archipelago, northeast of New Guinea. Many scholars see this ornate ware as the product of an ethnically distinct people, and think the Lapita "cultural complex" was carried into the Pacific by a migration of racially distinct newcomers from Asia.

No one knows why people with Lapita pottery left home and risked sailing in deeper waters. Was it for reasons of wanderlust, a pioneering spirit, or improvements in canoe building and navigation? Some experts think the domestication of certain plants and animals thought to be of Asian origin—such as dogs, pigs, and chickens—somehow fueled Lapita's expansion (Terrell 1998).

Archaeologist John Terrell has excavated a site dated to 3000 B.P. on the Sepik (midnorthern) coast of Papua New Guinea. At that time, according to Terrell (1998), newly stabilized coastal lagoons were producing an abundance of (mainly wild) foods, fueling human population growth. Like the

Lapita pottery fragments from the Solomon Islands, dated to 3000 B.P.

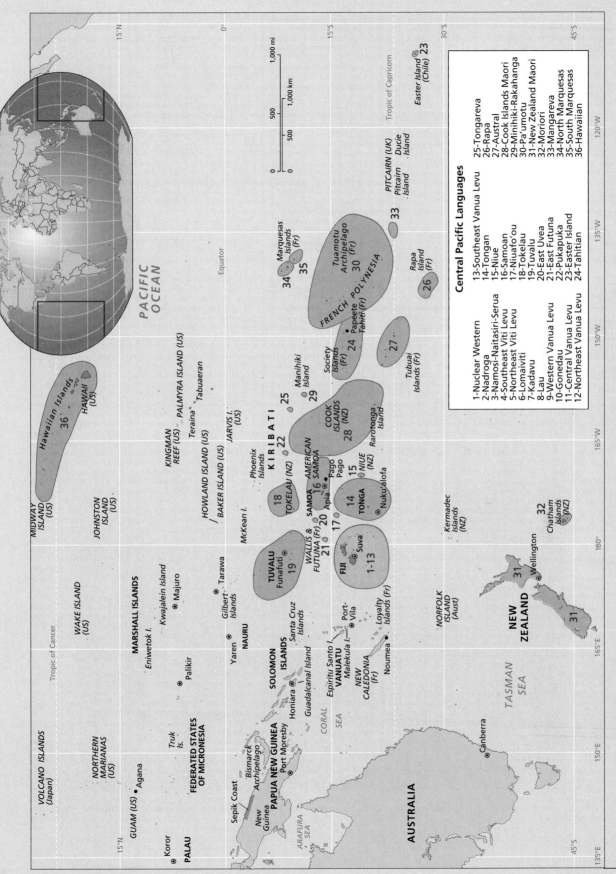

Central Pacific Languages

1-Nuclear Western
2-Nadroga
3-Namosi-Naitasiri-Serua
4-Southeast Viti Levu
5-Northeast Viti Levu
6-Lomaiviti
7-Kadavu
8-Lau
9-Western Vanua Levu
10-Gonedau
11-Central Vanua Levu
12-Northeast Vanua Levu

13-Southeast Vanua Levu
14-Tongan
15-Niue
16-Samoan
17-Niuafo'ou
18-Tokelau
19-Tuvalu
20-East Uvea
21-East Futuna
22-Pukapuka
23-Easter Island
24-Tahitian

25-Tongareva
26-Rapa
27-Austral
28-Cook Islands Maori
29-Minihiki-Rakahanga
30-Pa'umotu
31-New Zealand Maori
32-Moriori
33-Mangareva
34-North Marquesas
35-South Marquesas
36-Hawaiian

Polynesian islands are shaded orange. Other Central Pacific languages outside of Polynesia are spoken in the area shaded orange, which includes Fiji.

broad-spectrum economies discussed in Chapter 10, the resource base of the early Lapita pottery makers included diverse foods, some wild and some (e.g., yams, taro, pigs, chickens) domesticated and carefully managed.

Archaeologist David Burley uncovered early Lapita shards (potsherds) at Fanga'uta lagoon on the island of Tongatapu in the Polynesian kingdom of Tonga. Early outrigger canoes reached that lagoon after traveling hundreds, and perhaps more than a thousand, miles from the west. Radiocarbon dating of charcoal among the shards showed that seafarers reached Tonga between 2,950 and 2,850 years ago. *This is the earliest known settlement in Polynesia.* Burley thinks that Tongatapu "probably served as the initial staging point for population expansion" to other islands of Tonga, then to Samoa, and then on to the rest of Polynesia (quoted in Wilford 2002*a*).

Improvements in their outrigger canoes allowed Lapita navigators to sail across large stretches of open sea, thus propelling the Polynesian diaspora. The larger canoes could have carried dozens of people, plus pigs and other cargo. Polynesian seafarers eventually reached Tahiti to the east, and Hawaii—located more than 2,500 miles northeast of Tonga and Samoa. Later voyages carried the Polynesian diaspora south to New Zealand, and farther east to Easter Island. Covering one-fourth of the Pacific, Polynesia became the last large area of the world to be settled by humans.

The Lapita pottery found at Tongatapu offered clues about where the seafarers originated. Analyzing bits of the shards, William Dickinson, a University of Arizona geologist, found sandy minerals from outside Tonga. Some of the pots had been brought there from elsewhere. It turned out that the artifacts were made of minerals found only on the Santa Cruz Islands in Melanesia, some 1,200 miles to the west of Tonga, and just east of the Solomon Islands (Burley and Dickinson 2001). The shards from Tongatapu provided the first physical evidence linking the voyages of the Lapita people between the western and eastern parts of the Pacific. This evidence may mean that Tonga was first settled by people who came directly from central Melanesia (Wilford 2002*a*).

Anthropologists from all four subfields—archaeologists and physical, cultural, and linguistic anthropologists—have considered questions

Traditional Maori (New Zealand) oceangoing vessel. The Lapita people reached and colonized vast areas of the Pacific in their outrigger canoes.

about Polynesian origins. Who made Lapita pottery, along with the distinctive stone tools, beads, rings, and shell ornaments often found with it? Were they an ethnically distinct society of newcomers? Or did they consist of several cultural groups that came to share a handicraft style through diffusion or borrowing? How were the Lapita pottery makers linked to earlier settlers of the Pacific—the original colonists of Australia, New Guinea, and nearby islands? Did the Lapita complex originate with indigenous dark-skinned Melanesians, assumed to descend from the first settlers of the Pacific? Or was it introduced by new, lighter-skinned arrivals from Southeast Asia? Did lighter- and darker-skinned groups intermarry in Melanesia, forming a hybrid population that created the Lapita complex and eventually colonized Polynesia?

In the 18th century, the explorer Captain James Cook was struck by how similar were the appearance and customs of light-skinned Polynesians living on islands thousands of miles apart, such as Tonga, Hawaii, New Zealand, and Easter Island. Cook thought that the Polynesians originally had come from Malaysia or Micronesia. French navigators stressed the physical and cultural differences between the Polynesians and the darker-skinned Melanesians who lived near New Guinea, and who resembled the indigenous peoples of Papua New Guinea.

As in the tripartite classification of human races in vogue during the 19th century (see Chapter 9), Europeans grouped Pacific "races" into three: Polynesians ("many islands"), Melanesians ("dark islands"), and Micronesians ("little islands"). Until recently, anthropologists supposed that the ancestors of the Polynesians originated in mainland China and/or Taiwan, which they left between 3,600 and 6,000 years ago. They were seen as spreading rapidly through the Pacific, largely bypassing Melanesia. This would explain why the Polynesians are not dark-skinned and why they speak Austronesian languages, rooted in Taiwan, rather than Papuan languages, spoken in parts of Melanesia. This view now seems discredited by the fact that nothing resembling Lapita pottery has ever been found in Taiwan or southern China. Lapita features first show up in Melanesia, on islands of the Bismarck Archipelago. Recent genetic studies also suggest that ancestral Polynesians stopped off in Melanesia. Interbreeding between early Polynesians and Melanesians has

On the left, a Polynesian woman from Tahiti, Society Islands, French Polynesia. On the right, a Melanesian woman from Madang, Papua New Guinea. What differences and similarities do you notice between these two women?

left clear genetic markers in today's Polynesians. The debate now focuses on where the interbreeding took place and how extensive it was.

DNA evidence has convinced Mark Stoneking, a molecular anthropologist, that the ancestors of the Polynesians were indeed Austronesians. (The Austronesian, or Malayo-Polynesian, language family covers a large area of the world. Austronesian languages are the main languages of Polynesia [e.g., Hawaiian], Indonesia, and Malaysia, and even of Madagascar, located just off the African coast.) Stoneking thinks that the ancestral Polynesians left Southeast Asia—not necessarily Taiwan—and sailed to, then expanded along, the coast of New Guinea. They intermingled with Melanesians there and then started voyaging eastward into the Pacific. Interacting with other human groups, ancestral Polynesians exchanged genes and cultural traits (Gibbons 2001; Wilford 2002a).

Excavating in Melanesia's Bismarck Archipelago, archaeologist Patrick Kirch found evidence that newcomers from the islands of southeast Asia had reached Melanesia by 3500 B.P. They built their houses on stilts, as in houses still found in Southeast Asia. They sailed in outrigger canoes and brought agricultural plants along with them. There was mixing between the newcomers and the Melanesians. Out of their contact and interaction emerged the Lapita pottery style. Archaeologists aren't sure if Lapita pottery was first developed where the oldest specimens have been found, in the Bismarcks, or if it was introduced there by seafarers from the west (see Kirch 2000).

Why don't Polynesians resemble their presumed Melanesian cousins, or any Asian forebears? Can we explain the physical differences between Polynesians and Melanesians? Might the Polynesian population have originated in what geneticists call a founder event? In such an event, just a few people, whose physical traits do not randomly sample the larger population from which they came, happen to give rise to a very large diaspora. A very small number of people, say, a few canoeloads reaching Tonga's Fanga 'Uta Lagoon, may have given rise to the entire, geographically dispersed Polynesian population. The physical traits of such a small founding group could not fully represent the population from which they came. Whatever traits the founders happened to have, such as light skin color, would be transmitted to their descendants. This may explain why the Polynesians look so different from Melanesians, even though they share DNA in common.

Whatever their roots, the Lapita people, whose pottery marked their eastward migrations, eventually abandoned the elaborate Lapita style. On Tonga and Samoa, the decorative ceramics soon disappeared in favor of plain, functional bowls, cups, and storage vessels. Nor did the seafarers take Lapita pottery on their later voyages to the rest of Polynesia. (How might you explain this change in pottery style?)

By 2000 B.P., according to Patrick Kirch (2000), the people of Tonga had developed a significant new technology: the double-hull sailing canoe. Even though they could not spot other islands on the distant horizon, as their ancestors had been able to do in the Southwestern Pacific, the notion that the ocean was full of islands endured. Once they could more securely travel long distances—with the new canoe—they set forth. These weren't all accidental voyages and discoveries, as once was thought. These ancient sailors tacked against the prevailing east-to-west winds, knowing that, if necessary, they could ride a following wind back home. Anthropologists have learned from oral tradition that these societies had a social structure with status ranked by birth order. Many of the Polynesian island societies developed into chiefdoms, of the sort discussed in Chapter 11. According to Kirch, the Polynesian islanders "were descendants of settlers who were junior siblings and their own explorations were very often conducted by junior siblings . . . They were the ones with a reason to explore, to find new land and claim that for themselves" (quoted in Wilford 2002a). (There was a similar pattern in the early settlement of British North America.)

Long ago, the anthropologist Alexander Lesser disputed what he saw as the "myth of the primitive isolate" (quoted in Terrell 1998)—the idea that ancient peoples lived in closed societies, each one out of contact with others. It is doubtful that the human world has ever been one of distinct societies, sealed cultures, or isolated ethnic groups. Even on the small islands and atolls of the vast Pacific Ocean lived societies that contradicted the "primitive isolate." The adventurous and interconnected peoples of the Pacific and their prehistoric past reveal that human diversity is as much a product of contact as of isolation (Terrell 1998).

BIBLIOGRAPHY

Adams, R. M.
1981   *Heartland of Cities.* Chicago: Aldine.

Akazawa, T.
1980   *The Japanese Paleolithic: A Techno-Typological Study.* Tokyo: Rippo Shobo.

Akazawa, T., and C. M. Aikens, eds.
1986   *Prehistoric Hunter-Gatherers in Japan: New Research Methods.* Tokyo: University of Tokyo Press.

American Anthropological Association
         AAA Guide: A Guide to Departments, a Directory of Members. (Formerly *Guide to Departments of Anthropology.*) Published annually by the American Anthropological Association, Washington, DC.

         Anthropology Newsletter. Published 9 times annually by the American Anthropological Association, Washington, DC.

         General Anthropology: Bulletin of the General Anthropology Division.

Amick III, B., S. Levine, A. R. Tarlov, and D. C. Walsh, eds.
1995   *Society and Health.* New York: Oxford University Press.

Angier, N.
1998   When Nature Discovers the Same Design Over and Over: Lookalike Creatures Spark Evolutionary Debate. *New York Times,* December 15, pp. D1, D6.

2002   Why We're So Nice: We're Wired to Cooperate. *New York Times,* July 23, 2002. http://www.nytimes.com/2002/07/23/health/psychology/23COOP.html.

Annenberg/CPB Exhibits
2000   "Collapse, Why Do Civilizations Fall?" http://www.learner.org/exhibits/collapse/.

Aoki, M. Y., and M. B. Dardess, eds.
1981   *As the Japanese See It: Past and Present.* Honolulu: University Press of Hawaii.

Appiah, K. A.
1990   Racisms. In *Anatomy of Racism,* ed. David Theo Goldberg, pp. 3–17. Minneapolis: University of Minnesota Press.

Arensberg, C.
1987   Theoretical Contributions of Industrial and Development Studies. In *Applied Anthropology in America,* ed. E. M. Eddy and W. L. Partridge. New York: Columbia University Press.

Arnold, B., and B. Gibson, eds.
1995   *Celtic Chiefdom, Celtic State.* New York: Cambridge University Press.

Asfaw, B., T. White, *et al.*
1999   *Australopithecus garhi*: A New Species of Early Hominid from Ethiopia. *Science* 284: 629.

Ashmore, W., and R. Sharer
2000   *Discovering Our Past: A Brief Introduction to Archaeology,* 3rd ed. Boston: McGraw-Hill.

Bailey, E. J.
2000   *Medical Anthropology and African American Health.* Westport, CT: Bergin and Garvey.

Baker, P. T.
1978   *The Biology of High Altitude Peoples.* New York: Cambridge University Press.

Baker, P. T., and J. S. Weiner, eds.
1966   *The Biology of Human Adaptability.* Oxford: Oxford University Press.

Balick, M. J., and P. A. Cox
1996   *Plants, People, and Culture: The Science of Ethnobotany.* New York: Scientific American Library.

Balick, M. J., E. Elisabetsky, and S. A. Laird

1995 *Medicinal Resources of the Tropical Forest: Biodiversity and Its Importance to Human Health.* New York: Columbia University Press.

Barash, D. P.

1982 *Sociobiology and Behavior,* 2nd ed. Amsterdam: Elsevier.

Barth, F.

1964 *Nomads of South Persia: The Basseri Tribe of the Khamseh Confederacy.* London: Allen & Unwin.

Bar-Yosef, O.

1987 Pleistocene Connections between Africa and Southwest Asia: An Archaeological Perspective. *African Archaeological Review* 5: 29–38.

Batalla, G. B.

1966 Conservative Thought in Applied Anthropology: A Critique. *Human Organization* 25: 89–92.

Begun, D. R., C. V. Ward, and M. D. Rose

1997 *Description: Function, Phylogeny, and Fossils: Miocene Hominoid Evolution and Adaptations.* New York: Plenum.

Benedict, R.

1940 *Race, Science and Politics.* New York: Modern Age Books.

Berkeleyan

1999 Berkeley Researchers Head Team That Discovers New Species of Human Ancestor: Earliest Evidence of Meat-Eating, Early Beings Has Been Unearthed in Ethiopia. April 28–May 4, 1999 (27,32). http://www.berkeley.edu/news/berkeleyan/1999/0428/species.html

Binford, L. R.

1968 Post-Pleistocene Adaptations. In *New Perspectives in Archeology,* ed. S. R. Binford and L. R. Binford, pp. 313–341. Chicago: Aldine.

1981 *Bones: Ancient Men and Modern Myths.* New York: Academic Press.

Binford, L. R., and S. R. Binford

1979 Stone Tools and Human Behavior. In *Human Ancestors: Readings from Scientific American,* ed. G. L. Isaac and R. E. F. Leakey, pp. 92–101. San Francisco: W. H. Freeman.

Birdsell, J. B.

1981 *Human Evolution: An Introduction to the New Physical Anthropology,* 3rd ed. Boston: HarperCollins.

Blanton, R. E.

1999 *Ancient Oaxaca: The Monte Alban State.* New York: Cambridge University Press.

Blanton, R. E., S. A. Kowalewski, G. M. Feinman, and L. M. Finsten, eds.

1993 *Ancient Mesoamerica: A Comparison of Change in Three Regions,* 2nd ed. New York: Cambridge University Press.

Blum, H. F.

1961 Does the Melanin Pigment of Human Skin Have Adaptive Value? *Quarterly Review of Biology* 36: 50–63.

Boas, F.

1966 (orig. 1940) *Race, Language, and Culture.* New York: Free Press.

Boaz, N. T.

1993 *Quarry: Closing In on the Missing Link.* New York: Free Press.

1997 *Eco Homo: How the Human Being Emerged from the Cataclysmic History of the Earth.* New York: Basic Books.

1999 *Essentials of Biological Anthropology.* Upper Saddle River, NJ: Prentice-Hall.

Bogin, B.

1999 *Patterns of Human Growth,* 2nd ed. New York: Cambridge University Press.

2001 *The Growth of Humanity.* New York: Wiley.

Bogucki, P. I.

1988 *Forest Farmers and Stockherders: Early Agriculture and Its Consequences in North-Central Europe.* New York: Cambridge University Press.

Bolton, R.

1981 Susto, Hostility, and Hypoglycemia. *Ethnology* 20(4): 227–258.

Bond, G. C., J. Kreniske, I. Susser, and J. Vincent, eds.

1996 *AIDS in Africa and the Caribbean.* Boulder, CO: Westview.

Bower, J., and D. Lubell, eds.
1988   *Prehistoric Cultures and Environments in the Late Quaternary of Africa.* Cambridge Monographs in African Archaeology, 26. Oxford, Eng.: B.A.R.

Brace, C. L.
1964   A Nonracial Approach towards the Understanding of Human Diversity. In *The Concept of Race,* ed. A. Montagu, pp. 103–152. New York: Free Press.

1995   *The Stages of Human Evolution,* 5th ed. Upper Saddle River, NJ: Prentice-Hall.

2000   *Evolution in an Anthropological View.* Walnut Creek, CA: AltaMira.

Brace, C. L., and F. B. Livingstone
1971   On Creeping Jensenism. In *Race and Intelligence,* ed. C. L. Brace, G. R. Gamble, and J. T. Bond, pp. 64–75. Anthropological Studies, no. 8. Washington, DC: American Anthropological Association.

Braidwood, R. J.
1975   *Prehistoric Men,* 8th ed. Glenview, IL: Scott, Foresman.

Bronfenbrenner, U.
1975   Nature with Nurture: A Reinterpretation of the Evidence. In *Race and IQ,* ed. A. Montagu, pp. 114–144. New York: Oxford University Press.

Brown, P. J.
1998   *Understanding and Applying Medical Anthropology.* Boston: McGraw-Hill.

Brumfiel, E. M.
1980   Specialization, Market Exchange, and the Aztec State: A View from Huexotla. *Current Anthropology* 21(4): 459–478.

Burley, D. V., and Dickinson, W. R.
2001   Origin and Significance of a Founding Settlement in Polynesia. *Proceedings of the National Academy of Sciences* 98: 11829-11831.

Burton, F. D., and M. Eaton
1995a *The Multimedia Guide to Non-Human Primates.* Upper Saddle River, NJ: Prentice-Hall. A CD-ROM combining photos, illustrations, video, sound, and text, presenting over 200 species of nonhuman primates.

1995b *The Guide to Non-Human Primates.* Upper Saddle River, NJ: Prentice-Hall. The print version of the above.

Campbell, B. G.
1998   *Human Evolution: An Introduction to Man's Adaptations,* 4th ed. New York: Aldine de Gruyter.

Campbell, B. G., and J. D. Loy, eds.
2000   *Humankind Emerging,* 8th ed. New York: Longman.

Cann, R. L., M. Stoneking, and A. C. Wilson
1987   Mitochondrial DNA and Human Evolution. *Nature* 325: 31–36.

Carneiro, R. L.
1970   A Theory of the Origin of the State. *Science* 69: 733–738.

1990   Chiefdom-Level Warfare as Exemplified in Fiji and the Cauca Valley. In *The Anthropology of War,* ed. J. Haas, pp. 190–211. Cambridge, Eng.: Cambridge University Press.

1991   The Nature of the Chiefdom as Revealed by Evidence from the Cauca Valley of Colombia. In *Profiles in Cultural Evolution,* ed. A. T. Rambo and K. Gillogly. Anthropological Papers 85, pp. 167–190. Ann Arbor: University of Michigan Museum of Anthropology.

Carter, J.
1988   Freed from Keepers and Cages, Chimps Come of Age on Baboon Island. *Smithsonian,* June, pp. 36–48.

Cartmill, M.
1974   Rethinking Primate Origins. *Science,* April 26, pp. 436–437.

1992   New Views on Primate Origins. *Evolutionary Anthropology* 1: 105–111.

Cavalli-Sforza, L. L.
1977   *Elements of Human Genetics,* 2nd ed. Menlo Park, CA: W. A. Benjamin.

Cavalli-Sforza, L. L., P. Menozzi, and A. Piazza
1994   *The History and Geography of Human Genes.* Princeton, NJ: Princeton University Press.

Chagnon, N. A., and W. Irons, eds.
1979   *Evolutionary Biology and Human Social Behavior: An Anthropological Perspective.* North Scituate, MA: Duxbury.

Chambers, E.
1985   *Applied Anthropology: A Practical Guide.* Upper Saddle River, NJ: Prentice-Hall.

1987   Applied Anthropology in the Post-Vietnam Era: Anticipations and Ironies. *Annual Review of Anthropology* 16: 309–337.

Champion, T., and C. Gamble, eds.
1984   *Prehistoric Europe.* New York: Academic Press.

Chang, K. C.
1977   *The Archaeology of Ancient China.* New Haven, CT: Yale University Press.

Cheney, D. L., and R. M. Seyfarth
1990   In the Minds of Monkeys: What Do They Know and How Do They Know It? *Natural History,* September, pp. 38–46.

Cheney, D. L., R. M. Seyfarth, B. B. Smuts, and R. W. Wrangham
1987   The Study of Primate Societies. In *Primate Societies,* ed. B. B. Smuts, D. L. Cheney, R. M. Seyfarth, R. W. Wrangham, and T. T. Struhsaker, pp. 1–8. Chicago: University of Chicago Press.

Childe, V. G.
1951   *Man Makes Himself.* New York: New American Library.

Ciochon, R. L.
1983   Hominoid Cladistics and the Ancestry of Modern Apes and Humans. In *New Interpretations of Ape and Human Ancestry,* ed. R. L. Ciochon and R. S. Corruccini, pp. 783–843. New York: Plenum.

Ciochon, R. L., J. Olsen, and J. James
1990   *Other Origins: The Search for the Giant Ape in Human Prehistory.* New York: Bantam Books.

Clark, J. D., and S. A. Brandt
1984   *From Hunters to Farmers: The Causes and Consequences of Food Production in Africa.* Berkeley: University of California Press.

Clifton, J. A.
1970   *Applied Anthropology: Readings in the Uses of the Science of Man.* Boston: Houghton Mifflin.

Coe, M. D., and K. Flannery
1964   Microenvironments and Mesoamerican Prehistory. *Science* 143: 650–654.

Cohen, M. N., and G. J. Armelagos, eds.
1984   *Paleopathology at the Origins of Agriculture.* New York: Academic Press.

Cohen, Ronald, and E. R. Service, eds.
1978   *Origins of the State: The Anthropology of Political Evolution.* Philadelphia: Institute for the Study of Human Issues.

Cole, S.
1975   *Leakey's Luck: The Life of Louis Bazett Leakey, 1903–1972.* New York: Harcourt Brace Jovanovich.

Conkey, M., O. Soffer, D. Stratmann, and N. Jablonski
1997   *Beyond Art: Pleistocene Image and Symbol.* San Francisco: Memoirs of the California Academy of Sciences, no. 23.

Connah, G.
1987   *African Civilizations.* New York: Cambridge University Press.

Cooper, F., and A. L. Stoler, eds.
1997   *Tensions of Empire: Colonial Cultures in a Bourgeois World.* Berkeley: University of California Press.

Crick, F. H. C.
1968   (orig. 1962) The Genetic Code. In *The Molecular Basis of Life: An Introduction to Molecular Biology: Readings from Scientific American,* pp. 198–205. San Francisco: W. H. Freeman.

Crosby, A. W., Jr.
1972   *The Columbian Exchange: Biological and Cultural Consequences of 1492.* Westport, CT: Greenwood Press.

1986   *Ecological Imperialism: The Biological Expansion of Europe, 900–1900.* New York: Cambridge University Press.

1994   *Germs, Seeds & Animals: Studies in Ecological History.* Armonk, NY: M.E. Sharpe.

Cunliffe, B., ed.
1998   *Prehistoric Europe: An Illustrated History.* New York: Oxford University Press.

Dahlberg, F., ed.
1981   *Woman the Gatherer.* New Haven, CT: Yale University Press.

Darwin, C.
1958   (orig. 1859) *On the Origin of Species.* New York: Dutton.

Darwin, E.
1796   (orig. 1794) *Zoonomia, Or the Laws of Organic Life,* 2nd ed. London: J. Johnson.

De Waal, F. B. M.
1995   Bonobo Sex and Society: The Behavior of a Close Relative Challenges Assumptions about Male Supremacy in Human Evolution. *Scientific American,* March, pp. 82–88.

1997   *Bonobo: The Forgotten Ape*. Berkeley: University of California Press.

1998   *Chimpanzee Politics: Power and Sex among Apes*, rev. ed. Baltimore: Johns Hopkins University Press.

De Vos, G. A.
1971   *Japan's Outcastes: The Problem of the Burakumin*. London: Minority Rights Group.

De Vos, G. A., and H. Wagatsuma
1966   *Japan's Invisible Race: Caste in Culture and Personality*. Berkeley: University of California Press.

De Vos, G. A., W. O. Wetherall, and K. Stearman
1983   *Japan's Minorities: Burakumin, Koreans, Ainu and Okinawans*. Report no. 3. London: Minority Rights Group.

Degler, C.
1970   *Neither Black nor White: Slavery and Race Relations in Brazil and the United States*. New York: Macmillan.

Delson, E., ed.
1985   *Ancestors: The Hard Evidence*. New York: Alan R. Liss.

DeLumley, H.
1976   (orig. 1969) A Paleolithic Camp at Nice. In *Avenues to Antiquity: Readings from Scientific American*, ed. B. M. Fagan, pp. 36–44. San Francisco: W. H. Freeman.

DeMarco, E.
1997   New Dig at 9,000-Year-Old City Is Changing Views on Ancient Life. *New York Times*, November 11, www.nytimes.com.

Desjarlais, R., L. Eisenberg, B. Good, and A. Kleinman, eds.
1995   *World Mental Health: Problems and Priorities in Low-Income Countries*. New York: Oxford University Press.

Diamond, J. M.
1989   Blood, Genes, and Malaria. *Natural History*, February, pp. 8–18.

1990   A Pox upon Our Genes. *Natural History*, February, pp. 26–30.

1997   *Guns, Germs, and Steel: The Fates of Human Societies*. New York: W.W. Norton.

Dibble, H. L., S. P. McPherron, and B. J. Roth
1999   *Virtual Dig: A Simulated Archaeological Excavation of a Middle Paleolithic Site in France*. Boston: McGraw-Hill.

Dobzhansky, T., F. J. Ayala, G. L. Stebbins, and J. W. Valentine
1977   *Evolution*. San Francisco: W. H. Freeman.

Dolhinow, P., and A. Fuentes, eds.
1999   *The Nonhuman Primates*. Boston: McGraw-Hill.

Drennan, R. D., and C. A. Uribe, eds.
1987   *Chiefdoms in the Americas*. Landon, MD: University Press of America.

Earle, T. K.
1987   Chiefdoms in Archaeological and Ethnohistorical Perspective. *Annual Review of Anthropology* 16: 279–308.

1991   *Chiefdoms: Power, Economy, and Ideology*. New York: Cambridge University Press.

1997   *How Chiefs Come to Power: The Political Economy in Prehistory*. Stanford, CA: Stanford University Press.

Eddy, E. M., and W. L. Partridge, eds.
1987   *Applied Anthropology in America*, 2nd ed. New York: Columbia University Press.

Eiseley, L.
1961   *Darwin's Century*. Garden City, NY: Doubleday, Anchor Books.

Eldredge, N.
1985   *Time Frames: The Rethinking of Darwinian Evolution and the Theory of Punctuated Equilibria*. New York: Simon & Schuster.

1997   *Fossils: The Evolution and Extinction of Species*. Princeton, NJ: Princeton University Press.

Ember, M., and C. R. Ember
1997   Science in Anthropology. In *The Teaching of Anthropology: Problems, Issues, and Decisions*, eds. C. P. Kottak, J. J. White, R. H. Furlow, and P. C. Rice, pp. 29–33. Boston: McGraw-Hill.

Fagan, B. M.
1987   *The Great Journey: The Peopling of Ancient America*. London: Thames and Hudson.

1998   *Clash of Cultures*, 2nd ed. Walnut Creek, CA: AltaMira.

2000   *Ancient Lives: An Introduction to Method and Theory in Archaeology*. Upper Saddle River, NJ: Prentice-Hall.

2001   *People of the Earth: A Brief Introduction to World Prehistory,* 10th ed. Upper Saddle River, NJ: Prentice-Hall.

2002a   *Archeology: A Brief Introduction,* 8th ed. Upper Saddle River, NJ: Prentice-Hall.

2002b   *World Prehistory: A Brief Introduction,* 5th ed. Upper Saddle River, NJ: Prentice-Hall.

Falk, D.
2000   *Primate Diversity.* New York: W. W. Norton.

Farooq, M.
1966   Importance of Determining Transmission Sites in Planning Bilharziasis Control: Field Observations from the Egypt-49 Project Area. *American Journal of Epidemiology* 83: 603–612.

Fedigan, L. M.
1992   *Primate Paradigms: Sex Roles and Social Bonds.* Chicago: University of Chicago Press.

Feinman, G. M., and T. D. Price
2001   *Archaeology at the Millennium: A Sourcebook.* New York: Kluwer Academic/Plenum.

Fenlason, L.
1990   Wolpoff Questions "Eve's" Origin Date, Says It Ignores Contradictory Fossil Data. *University Record* (University of Michigan, Ann Arbor) 45(21): 12.

Fisher, A.
1988a   The More Things Change. *MOSAIC* 19(1): 22–33.

1988b   On the Emergence of Humanness. *MOSAIC* 19(1): 34–45.

Flannery, K. V.
1969   Origins and Ecological Effects of Early Domestication in Iran and the Near East. In *The Domestication and Exploitation of Plants and Animals,* ed. P. J. Ucko and G. W. Dimbleby, pp. 73–100. Chicago: Aldine.

1972   The Cultural Evolution of Civilizations. *Annual Review of Ecology and Systematics* 3: 399–426.

1973   The Origins of Agriculture. *Annual Review of Anthropology* 2: 271–310.

1995   Prehistoric Social Evolution. In *Research Frontiers in Anthropology,* eds. C. R. Ember and M. Ember, pp. 1–26. Upper Saddle River, NJ: Prentice-Hall.

1999   Chiefdoms in the Early Near East: Why It's So Hard to Identify Them. In *The Iranian World: Essays on Iranian Art and Archaeology,* eds. A. Alizadeh, Y. Majidzadeh, and S. M. Shahmirzadi. Tehran: Iran University Press.

Flannery, K. V., ed.
1986   Guila Naquitz: *Archaic Foraging and Early Agriculture in Oaxaca, Mexico.* Orlando: Academic Press.

Flannery, K. V., and J. Marcus
2000   Formative Mexican Chiefdoms and the Myth of the "Mother Culture." *Journal of Anthropological Archaeology* 19: 1–37.

Flannery, K. V., J. Marcus, and R. G. Reynolds
1989   *The Flocks of the Wamani: A Study of Llama Herders on the Punas of Ayacucho, Peru.* San Diego: Academic Press.

Fleagle, J. G.
1999   *Primate Adaptation and Evolution,* 2nd ed. San Diego: Academic Press.

Fleagle, J. G., C. H. Janson, and K. E. Reed, eds.
1999   *Primate Communities.* New York: Cambridge University Press.

Fossey, D.
1981   The Imperiled Mountain Gorilla. *National Geographic* 159: 501–523.

1983   *Gorillas in the Mist.* Boston: Houghton Mifflin.

Foster, G. M., and B. G. Anderson
1978   *Medical Anthropology.* New York: McGraw-Hill.

Fountain, H.
2002   Iceman's Last Meal. *New York Times,* September 17. http://www.nytimes.com/2002/09/17/science/17OBSE.html.

Fouts, R.
1997   *Next of Kin: What Chimpanzees Have Taught Me about Who We Are.* New York: William Morrow.

Fouts, R. S., D. H. Fouts, and T. E. Van Cantfort
1989   The Infant Loulis Learns Signs from Cross-Fostered Chimpanzees. In *Teaching Sign Language to Chimpanzees,* ed. R. A. Gardner, B. T. Gardner, and T. E. Van Cantfort, pp. 280–292. Albany: State University of New York Press.

Fox, J. W.
1987   *Maya Postclassic State Formation.* Cambridge, Eng.: Cambridge University Press.

French, H. W.
2002   Whistling Past the Global Graveyard. *New York Times,* July 14. http://www.nytimes.com/2002/07/14/weekinreview/14FREN.html.

Fried, M. H.
1960   On the Evolution of Social Stratification and the State. In *Culture in History,* ed. S. Diamond, pp. 713–731. New York: Columbia University Press.

Friedman, J., and M. J. Rowlands, eds.
1978   *The Evolution of Social Systems.* Pittsburgh: University of Pittsburgh Press.

Frisancho, A. R.
1975   Functional Adaptation to High Altitude Hypoxia. *Science* 187: 313–319.

1990   *Anthropometric Standards for the Evaluation of Growth and Nutritional Status.* Ann Arbor: University of Michigan Press.

1993   *Human Adaptation and Accommodation.* Ann Arbor: University of Michigan Press.

Futuyma, D. J.
1995   *Science on Trial,* updated ed. New York: Pantheon.

1998   *Evolutionary Biology.* Sunderland, MA: Sinauer Associates.

Gamble, C.
1999   *The Palaeolithic Societies of Europe.* New York: Cambridge University Press.

2000   *Archaeology, the Basics.* New York: Routledge.

Geertz, C.
1973   *The Interpretation of Cultures.* New York: Basic Books.

General Anthropology: Bulletin of the General Anthropology Division, American Anthropological Association.

Gibbons, A.
2001   The Peopling of the Pacific. *Science* 291(5509): 1735. http://www.eva.mpg.de/genetics/Gibbons_Science2001.pdf.

Gilchrist, R.
1999   *Gender and Archaeology: Contesting the Past.* New York: Routledge.

Gillespie, J. H.
1998   *Population Genetics: A Concise Guide.* Baltimore: Johns Hopkins University Press.

Gilmore-Lehne, W. J.
2000   Pre-Sumerian Cultures: Natufian through Ubaid Eras: 10,500–3500 B.C.E. http://www.stockton.edu/~gilbmorew/consorti/1bnear.htm.

Goldberg, D. T.
1997   *Racial Subjects: Writing on Race in America.* New York: Routledge.

Goldberg, D. T., ed.
1990   *Anatomy of Racism.* Minneapolis: University of Minnesota Press.

Goodall, J.
1968a   A Preliminary Report on Expressive Movements and Communication in Gombe Stream Chimpanzees. In *Primates: Studies in Adaptation and Variability,* ed. P. C. Jay, pp. 313–374. New York: Harcourt Brace Jovanovich.

1968b   The Behavior of Free Living Chimpanzees in the Gombe Stream Reserve. *Animal Behavior Monographs* 1: 161–311.

1986   *The Chimpanzees of Gombe: Patterns of Behavior.* Cambridge, MA: Belknap Press of Harvard University Press.

1988   *In the Shadow of Man,* rev. ed. Boston: Houghton Mifflin.

1996   *My Life with the Chimpanzees.* New York: Pocket Books.

Goodman, M., M. L. Baba, and L. L. Darga
1983   The Bearings of Molecular Data on the Cladograms and Times of Divergence of Hominoid Lineages. In *New Interpretations of Ape and Human Ancestry,* ed. R. L. Ciochon and R. S. Corruccini, pp. 67–87. New York: Plenum.

Gorman, C. F.
1969   Hoabinhian: A Pebble-Tool Complex with Early Plant Associations in Southeast Asia. *Science* 163: 671–673.

Gould, S. J.
1996   *The Mismeasure of Man.* New York: Norton.

1999   *Rock of Ages: Science and Religion in the Fullness of Life.* New York: Ballantine Books.

Gowlett, J. A. J.
1993   *Ascent to Civilization: The Archaeology of Early Humans.* New York: McGraw-Hill.

Gray, J. P.
1985   *Primate Sociobiology.* New Haven, CT: HRAF Press.

Green, E. C.
1992   (orig. 1987) The Integration of Modern and Traditional Health Sectors in Swaziland. In *Applying Anthropology,* ed. A. Podolefsky and P. J. Brown, pp. 246–251. Boston: McGraw-Hill.

Green, G. M., and R. W. Sussman
1990   Deforestation History of the Eastern Rain Forests of Madagascar from Satellite Images. *Science* 248: 212-15.

Gugliotta, G.
2002   Earliest Human Ancestor? Skull Dates to When Apes, Humans Split. *Washington Post,* July 11, p. A01.

Gwynne, M. A.
2003   *Applied Anthropology: A Career-Oriented Approach.* Boston: Allyn and Bacon

Hamburg, D. A., and E. R. McCown, eds.
1979   *The Great Apes.* Menlo Park, CA: Benjamin Cummings.

Harcourt, A. H., D. Fossey, and J. Sabater-Pi
1981   Demography of Gorilla gorilla. *Journal of Zoology* 195: 215–233.

Harlan, J. R., and D. Zohary
1966   Distribution of Wild Wheats and Barley. *Science* 153: 1074–1080.

Harris, M.
1964   *Patterns of Race in the Americas.* New York: Walker.

1970   Referential Ambiguity in the Calculus of Brazilian Racial Identity. *Southwestern Journal of Anthropology* 26(1): 1–14.

1989   *Our Kind: Who We Are, Where We Came from, Where We Are Going.* New York: Harper & Row.

Harris, M., and C. P. Kottak
1963   The Structural Significance of Brazilian Racial Categories. *Sociologia* 25: 203–209.

Harris, N. M., and G. Hillman
1989   *Foraging and Farming: The Evolution of Plant Exploitation.* London: Unwin Hyman.

Harrison, G. G., W. L. Rathje, and W. W. Hughes
1994   Food Waste Behavior in an Urban Population. In *Applying Anthropology: An Introductory Reader,* 3rd ed., ed. A. Podolefsky and P. J. Brown, pp. 107–112. Boston: McGraw-Hill.

Hartl, D. L.
1997   *Principles of Population Genetics,* 3rd ed. Sunderland, MA: Sinaeur Associates.

2000   *A Primer of Population Genetics,* 3rd ed. Sunderland, MA: Sinauer Associates.

Hartl, D. L., and E. W. Jones
2002   *Essential Genetics,* 3rd ed. Sudbury, MA: Jones and Bartlett.

Hassig, R.
1985   *Trade, Tribute, and Transportation: The Sixteenth-Century Political Economy of the Valley of Mexico.* Norman: University of Oklahoma Press.

Hausfater, G., and S. Hrdy, eds.
1984   *Infanticide: Comparative and Evolutionary Perspectives.* Hawthorne, NY: Aldine.

Heath, D. B., ed.
1995   *International Handbook on Alcohol and Culture.* Westport, CT: Greenwood Press.

Helman, C.
2001   *Culture, Health, and Illness: An Introduction for Health Professionals,* 4th ed. Boston: Butterworth-Heinemann.

Henry, D. O.
1989   *From Foraging to Agriculture: The Levant at the End of the Ice Age.* Philadelphia: University of Pennsylvania Press.

1995   *Prehistoric Cultural Ecology and Evolution: Insights from Southern Jordan.* New York: Plenum Press.

Herrnstein, R. J.
1971   I.Q. *Atlantic* 228(3): 43–64.

Herrnstein, R. J., and C. Murray
1994   *The Bell Curve: Intelligence and Class Structure in American Life.* New York: Free Press.

Heyerdahl, T.
1971   *The Ra Expeditions.* Translated by P. Crampton. Garden City, NY: Doubleday.

Heyneman, D.
1984   Development and Disease: A Dual Dilemma. *Journal of Parasitology* 70: 3–17.

Hill, C. E., ed.
1986   Current Health Policy Issues and Alternatives: An Applied Social Science Perspective. *Southern Anthropological Society Proceedings.* Athens: University of Georgia Press.

Hill, J. H.
1978   Apes and Language. *Annual Review of Anthropology* 7: 89–112.

Hill-Burnett, J.
1978   Developing Anthropological Knowledge through Application. In *Applied Anthropology in America,* ed. E. M. Eddy and W. L. Partridge, pp. 112–128. New York: Columbia University Press.

Hinde, R. A.
1983   *Primate Social Relationships: An Integrated Approach.* Sunderland, MA: Sinauer.

Hole, F., K. V. Flannery, and J. A. Neely
1969   *The Prehistory and Human Ecology of the Deh Luran Plain.* Memoir no. 1. Ann Arbor: University of Michigan Museum of Anthropology.

Holloway, R. L.
1975   (orig. 1974) The Casts of Fossil Hominid Brains. In *Biological Anthropology: Readings from Scientific American,* ed. S. H. Katz, pp. 69–78. San Francisco: W. H. Freeman.

Holtzman, J.
2000   *Nuer Journeys, Nuer Lives.* Boston: Allyn & Bacon.

Howells, W. W.
1976   Explaining Modern Man: Evolutionists versus Migrationists. *Journal of Human Evolution* 5: 477–496.

Human Organization
        Quarterly journal. Oklahoma City: Society for Applied Anthropology.

Ingold, T., D. Riches, and J. Woodburn
1991   *Hunters and Gatherers.* New York: Berg (St. Martin's).

Inhorn, M. C., and P. J. Brown
1990   The Anthropology of Infectious Disease. *Annual Review of Anthropology* 19: 89–117.

Irving, W. N.
1985   Context and Chronology of Early Man in the Americas. *Annual Review of Anthropology* 14: 529–555.

Isaac, G. L.
1972   Early Phases of Human Behavior: Models in Lower Paleolithic Archaeology. In *Models in Archaeology,* ed. D. L. Clarke, pp. 167–199. London: Methuen.

1978   Food Sharing and Human Evolution: Archaeological Evidence from the Plio-Pleistocene of East Africa. *Journal of Anthropological Research* 34: 311–325.

Jacoby, R., and N. Glauberman, eds.
1995   *The Bell Curve Debate: History, Documents, Opinions.* New York: Free Press; New York: Random House Times Books.

Janson, C. H.
1986   Capuchin Counterpoint: Divergent Mating and Feeding Habits Distinguish Two Closely Related Monkey Species of the Peruvian Forest. *Natural History* 95: 44–52.

Jasim, S. A.
1985   *The Ubaid Period in Iraq: Recent Excavations in the Hamrin Region.* BAR International Series 267 (Oxford).

Jensen, A.
1969   How Much Can We Boost I.Q. and Scholastic Achievement? *Harvard Educational Review* 29: 1–123.

Johanson, D. C., and M. Edey
1981   *Lucy: The Origins of Humankind.* New York: Simon & Schuster.

Johanson, D. C., and B. Edgar
1996   *From Lucy to Language.* New York: Simon & Schuster.

Johanson, D. C., and T. D. White
1979   A Systematic Assessment of Early African Hominids. *Science* 203: 321–330.

Johnson, A. W., and T. Earle, eds.
1987   *The Evolution of Human Societies: From Foraging Group to Agrarian State.* Stanford, CA: Stanford University Press.

2000   *The Evolution of Human Societies: From Foraging Group to Agrarian State,* 2nd ed. Stanford, CA: Stanford University Press.

Johnson, G. A.
1987   The Changing Organization of Uruk Administration in the Susiana Plain. In *The Archaeology of Western Iran,* ed. F. Hole, pp. 107–139. Washington, DC: Smithsonian Institution Press.

Johnson, T. J., and C. F. Sargent, eds.
1990   *Medical Anthropology: A Handbook of Theory and Method.* New York: Greenwood.

Jolly, A.
1985   *The Evolution of Primate Behavior,* 2nd ed. New York: Macmillan.

Jolly, C. J., and F. Plog
1986   *Physical Anthropology and Archaeology,* 4th ed. New York: McGraw-Hill.

Jolly, C. J., and R. White
1995   *Physical Anthropology and Archaeology,* 5th ed. New York: McGraw-Hill.

Jones, D.
1999   Hot Asset in Corporate: Anthropology Degrees. *USA Today,* February 18, p. B1.

Jones, G., and R. Krautz
1981   *The Transition to Statehood in the New World.* Cambridge, Eng.: Cambridge University Press.

Joralemon, D.
1999   *Exploring Medical Anthropology.* Boston: Allyn & Bacon.

Joyce, R. A.
2000   *Gender and Power in Prehispanic Mesoamerica.* Austin: University of Texas Press.

Jurmain, R.
1997   *Introduction to Physical Anthropology,* 7th ed. Belmont, CA: Wadsworth.

Katzenberg, M.A., and S. R. Saunders, eds.
2000   *Biological Anthropology of the Human Skeleton.* New York: Wiley.

Kemp, T. S.
1999   *Fossils and Evolution.* New York: Oxford University Press.

Kennedy, R. G.
1994   *Hidden Cities: The Discovery and Loss of Ancient North American Civilization.* New York: Free Press.

Kent, S.
1992   The Current Forager Controversy: Real versus Ideal Views of Hunter-Gatherers. *Man* 27: 45–70.

1996   *Cultural Diversity among Twentieth-Century Foragers: An African Perspective.* New York: Cambridge University Press.

1998   *Gender in African Prehistory.* Walnut Creek, CA: AltaMira Press.

Kent, S., and H. Vierich
1989   The Myth of Ecological Determinism: Anticipated Mobility and Site Organization of Space. In *Farmers as Hunters: The Implications of Sedentism,* ed. S. Kent, pp. 96–130. New York: Cambridge University Press.

Kerr, R. A.
1998   Sea-Floor Dust Shows Drought Felled Akkadian Empire. *Science* 279(5349): 325–326.

King, B. J., ed.
1994   *The Information Continuum: Evolution of Social Information Transfer in Monkeys, Apes, and Hominids.* Santa Fe, NM: School of American Research Press.

Kinzer, S.
2002   Museums and Tribes: A Tricky Truce. *New York Times,* December 24, 2000. Late Edition, Final, section 2, page 1, column 1; www.nytimes.com.

Kirch, P. V.
1984   *The Evolution of the Polynesian Chiefdoms.* Cambridge, Eng.: Cambridge University Press.

2000   *On the Road of the Winds: An Archaeological History of the Pacific Islands before European Contact.* Berkeley: University of California Press.

Klein, R. G.
1999   *The Human Career: Human Biological and Cultural Origins,* 2nd ed. Chicago: University of Chicago Press.

Klein, R. G., with B. Edgar
2002   *The Dawn of Human Culture.* New York: Wiley.

Kleinfeld, J.
1975   Positive Stereotyping: The Cultural Relativist in the Classroom. *Human Organization* 34: 269–274.

Klineberg, O.
1951   Race and Psychology. In *The Race Question in Modern Science.* Paris: UNESCO.

Kluckhohn, C.
1944   *Mirror for Man: A Survey of Human Behavior and Social Attitudes.* Greenwich, CT: Fawcett.

Kluge, A. G.
1983   Cladistics and the Classification of the Great Apes. In *New Interpretations of Ape and Human Ancestry,* ed. R. L. Ciochon and R. S. Corruccini, pp. 151–177. New York: Plenum.

Knecht, H., A. Pike-Tay, and R. White, eds.

1993   *Before Lascaux: The Complex Record of the Early Upper Paleolithic.* Boca Raton, FL: CRC Press.

Kohler, M., and S. Moya-Sola

1997   Ape-Like or Hominid-Like? The Positional Behavior of Oreopithecus bambolii Reconsidered. *Proceedings of the National Academy of Sciences* 94 (October 14): 11, 747.

Kopytoff, V. G.

1995   Meat Viewed as Staple of Chimp Diet and Mores. *New York Times,* June 27, pp. B5–B6.

Kottak, C. P.

1999   *Assault on Paradise: Social Change in a Brazilian Village,* 3rd ed. New York: McGraw-Hill.

1999   The New Ecological Anthropology. *American Anthropologist* 101(1): 23–35.

Kottak, C. P., L. L. Gezon, and G. Green

1994   Deforestation and Biodiversity Preservation in Madagascar: The View from Above and Below. *CIESIN Human Dimensions Kiosk.* http://www.ciesin.com.

Kretchmer, N.

1975   (orig. 1972) Lactose and Lactase. In *Biological Anthropology: Readings from Scientific American,* ed. S. H. Katz, pp. 310–318. San Francisco: W. H. Freeman.

Kuhn, S. L., M. C. Stiner, and D. S. Reese

2001   Ornaments of the Earliest Upper Paleolithic: New Insights from the Levant. *Proceedings of the National Academy of Sciences of the United States of America* 98(13): 7641-7646.

Kunitz, S. J.

1994   *Disease and Social Diversity: The European Impact on the Health of Non-Europeans.* New York: Oxford University Press.

LaBarre, W.

1945   Some Observations of Character Structure in the Orient: The Japanese. *Psychiatry* 8: 326–342.

Lamberg-Karlovsky, C. C., and J. A. Sabloff

1995   *Ancient Civilizations: The Near East and Mesoamerica.* Prospect Heights, IL: Waveland.

Larsen, C. S.

2000   *Skeletons in Our Closet: Revealing Our Past through Bioarchaeology.* Princeton, NJ: Princeton University Press.

Larson, A.

1989   Social Context of Human Immunodeficiency Virus Transmission in Africa: Historical and Cultural Bases of East and Central African Sexual Relations. *Review of Infectious Diseases* 11: 716–731.

Leakey, R. E., M. G. Leakey, and A. C. Walker

1988   Morphology of Afropithecus turkanensis from Kenya. *American Journal of Physical Anthropology* 76: 289–307.

Lee, R. B.

1974   (orig. 1968) What Hunters Do for a Living, or, How to Make Out on Scarce Resources. In *Man in Adaptation: The Cultural Present,* 2nd ed., ed. Y. A. Cohen, pp. 87–100. Chicago: Aldine.

Lee, R. B., and R. H. Daly

1999   *The Cambridge Encyclopedia of Hunters and Gatherers.* New York: Cambridge University Press.

Lee, R. B., and I. DeVore, eds.

1977   *Kalahari Hunter-Gatherers: Studies of the !Kung San and Their Neighbors.* Cambridge, MA: Harvard University Press.

Lemonick, M. D., and A. Dorfman

1999   Up from the Apes: Remarkable New Evidence Is Filling in the Story of How We Became Human. *Time* 154(8): 5–58.

Levine, L., ed.

1995   *Genetics of Natural Populations: The Continuing Importance of Theodosius Dobzhansky.* New York: Columbia University Press.

Lewin, R.

1998   *Principles of Human Evolution: A Core Textbook.* Malden, MA: Blackwell Science.

1999   *Human Evolution: An Illustrated Introduction,* 4th ed. Malden, MA: Blackwell Science.

Lewontin, R.

2000   *It Ain't Necessarily So: The Dream of the Human Genome and Other Illusions.* New York: New York Review of Books.

Lieban, R. W.

1977   The Field of Medical Anthropology. In *Culture, Disease, and Healing: Studies in Medical Anthropology,* ed. D. Landy, pp. 13–31. New York: Macmillan.

Lieberman, P.
1998   *Eve Spoke: Human Language and Human Evolution.* New York: W. W. Norton.

Livingstone, F. B.
1958   Anthropological Implications of Sickle Cell Gene Distribution in West Africa. *American Anthropologist* 60: 533–562.

1969   Gene Frequency Clines of the b Hemoglobin Locus in Various Human Populations and Their Similarities by Models Involving Differential Selection. *Human Biology* 41: 223–236.

Loomis, W. F.
1967   Skin-Pigmented Regulation of Vitamin-D Biosynthesis in Man. *Science* 157: 501–506.

Lyell, C.
1969   (orig. 1830–37) *Principles of Geology.* New York: Johnson.

MacKinnon, J.
1974   *In Search of the Red Ape.* New York: Ballantine.

Malinowski, B.
1927   *Sex and Repression in Savage Society.* London and New York: International Library of Psychology, Philosophy and Scientific Method.

Mann, A.
1975   *Paleodemographic Aspects of the South African Australopithecines.* Publications in Anthropology, no. 1. Philadelphia: University of Pennsylvania.

Mar, M. E.
1997   Secondary Colors: The Multiracial Option. *Harvard Magazine,* May–June, pp. 19–20.

Marcus, G. E., and M. M. J. Fischer
1986   *Anthropology as Cultural Critique: An Experimental Moment in the Human Sciences.* Chicago: University of Chicago Press.

1999   *Anthropology as Cultural Critique: An Experimental Moment in the Human Sciences,* 2nd ed. Chicago: University of Chicago Press.

Marcus, J.
1992   *Mesoamerican Writing Systems: Propaganda, Myth, and History in Four Ancient Civilizations.* Princeton, NJ: Princeton University Press.

Marcus, J., and K. V. Flannery
1996   *Zapotec Civilization: How Urban Society Evolved in Mexico's Oaxaca Valley.* New York: Thames and Hudson.

Marks, J.
1995   *Human Biodiversity: Genes, Race, and History.* New York: Aldine de Gruyter.

Marshack, A.
1972   *Roots of Civilization.* New York: McGraw-Hill.

Mayr, E.
1970   *Population, Species, and Evolution.* Cambridge, MA: Harvard University Press.

2001   *What Evolution Is.* New York: Basic Books.

McBrearty, S., and Brooks, A. S.
2000   The Revolution That Wasn't: A New Interpretation of the Origin of Modern Human Behavior. *Journal of Human Evolution* 39: 453–563.

McCaskie, T. C.
1995   *State and Society in Pre-Colonial Asante.* New York: Cambridge University Press.

McDonald, J. H., ed.
2002   *The Applied Anthropology Reader.* Boston: Allyn and Bacon.

McElroy, A., and P. K. Townsend
1996   *Medical Anthropology in Ecological Perspective,* 3rd ed. Boulder, CO: Westview.

McGrew, W. C.
1979   Evolutionary Implications of Sex Differences in Chimpanzee Predation and Tool Use. In *The Great Apes,* ed. D. A. Hamburg and E. R. McCown, pp. 441–463. Menlo Park, CA: Benjamin Cummings.

McGrew, W. C., L. Marchant, and T. Nishida
1996   *Great Ape Societies.* Cambridge, Eng.: Cambridge University Press.

McKusick, V.
1966   *Mendelian Inheritance in Man.* Baltimore: Johns Hopkins University Press.

1990   *Mendelian Inheritance in Man: Catalogs of Autosomal Dominant, Autosomal Recessive, and X-Linked Phenotypes,* 9th ed. Baltimore: Johns Hopkins University Press.

Meadow, R., ed.
1991   *Harappa Excavations 1986–1990: A Multi-disciplinary Approach to Third Millennium Urbanism.* Monographs in World Archeology, no. 3. Madison, WI: Prehistory Press.

Meadow, R. H., and J. M. Kenoyer
2000 The Indus Valley Mystery: One of the World's First Great Civilizations Is Still a Puzzle. *Discovering Archaeology,* March/April 2000. http://www/discoveringarchaeology.com/0800toc/8feature1-indus.html.

Miles, H. L.
1983 Apes and Language: The Search for Communicative Competence. In *Language in Primates,* ed. J. de Luce and H. T. Wilder, pp. 43–62. New York: Springer Verlag.

Miller, N., and R. C. Rockwell, eds.
1988 *AIDS in Africa: The Social and Policy Impact.* Lewiston, NY: Edwin Mellen.

Mitani, J. C., and D. P. Watts
1999 Demographic Influences on the Hunting Behavior of Chimpanzees. *American Journal of Physical Anthropology* 109: 439–454.

Mitchell, J. C.
1966 Theoretical Orientations in African Urban Studies. In *The Social Anthropology of Complex Societies,* ed. M. Banton, pp. 37–68. London: Tavistock.

Molnar, S.
1998 *Human Variation: Races, Types, and Ethnic Groups.* Upper Saddle River, NJ: Prentice Hall.

Moncure, S.
1998 Anthropologist Assists in Police Investigations. *University of Delaware Update* 17(39), August 20. http://www.udel.edu/PR/UpDate/98/39/anthrop.html.

Montagu, A.
1975 *The Nature of Human Aggression.* New York: Oxford University Press.

1981 *Statement on Race: An Annotated Elaboration and Exposition of the Four Statements on Race Issued by the United Nations Educational, Scientific, and Cultural Organization.* Westport, CT: Greenwood.

Montagu, A., ed.
1996 *Race and IQ,* expanded ed. New York: Oxford University Press.

1997 *Man's Most Dangerous Myth: The Fallacy of Race.* Walnut Creek, CA: AltaMira.

1999 *Race and IQ,* expanded ed. New York: Oxford University Press.

Montgomery, S.
1991 *Walking with the Great Apes: Jane Goodall, Dian Fossey, Biruté Galdikas.* Boston: Houghton Mifflin.

Moore, A. D.
1985 The Development of Neolithic Societies in the Near East. *Advances in World Archaeology* 4:1–69.

Moran, E. F.
1982 *Human Adaptability: An Introduction to Ecological Anthropology.* Boulder, CO: Westview.

Morbeck, M. E., A. Galloway, and A. L. Zihlman, eds.
1997 *The Evolving Female: A Life-History Perspective.* Princeton, NJ: Princeton University Press.

Morgen, S., ed.
1989 *Gender and Anthropology: Critical Reviews for Research and Teaching.* Washington, DC: American Anthropological Association.

Mowat, F.
1987 *Woman in the Mists: The Story of Dian Fossey and the Mountain Gorillas of Africa.* New York: Warner Books.

Mullings, L., ed.
1987 *Cities of the United States: Studies in Urban Anthropology.* New York: Columbia University Press.

Murphy, R. F.
1990 *The Body Silent.* New York: W. W. Norton.

Nafte, M.
2000 *Flesh and Bone: An Introduction to Forensic Anthropology.* Durham, NC: Carolina Academic Press.

Napier, J. R., and P. H. Napier
1985 *The Natural History of Primates.* Cambridge, MA: MIT Press.

Nash, D.
1999 *A Little Anthropology,* 3rd ed. Upper Saddle River, NJ: Prentice-Hall.

National Association for the Practice of Anthropology
1991 *NAPA Directory of Practicing Anthropologists.* Washington, DC: American Anthropological Association.

Nelson, H., and R. Jurmain

1991   *Introduction to Physical Anthropology,* 5th ed. St. Paul, MN: West.

New York Times

1990   Tropical Diseases on March, Hitting 1 in 10. March 28, p. A3.

Nowak, R. M.

1999   *Walker's Primates of the World.* Baltimore: Johns Hopkins University Press.

Nussbaum, M., and J. Glover, eds.

1995   *Women, Culture, and Development: A Study of Human Capabilities.* New York: Oxford University Press.

Nussbaum, M. C.

2000   *Women and Human Development: The Capabilities Approach.* New York: Cambridge University Press.

Oakley, K. P.

1976   *Man the Tool-Maker,* 6th ed. Chicago: University of Chicago Press.

Park, M. A.

1999   *Biological Anthropology,* 2nd ed. Boston: McGraw-Hill.

2002   *Biological Anthropology,* 3rd ed. Boston: McGraw-Hill.

Parsons, J. R.

1974   The Development of a Prehistoric Complex Society: A Regional Perspective from the Valley of Mexico. *Journal of Field Archaeology* 1: 81–108.

1976   The Role of Chinampa Agriculture in the Food Supply of Aztec Tenochtitlan. In *Cultural Change and Continuity: Essays in Honor of James Bennett Griffin,* ed. C. E. Cleland, pp. 233–262. New York: Academic Press.

Patterson, T. C.

1993   *Archaeology: The Historical Development of Civilizations,* 2nd ed. Upper Saddle River, NJ: Prentice-Hall.

Patterson, F.

1978   Conversations with a Gorilla. *National Geographic,* October, pp. 438–465.

Pettifor, E.

1995   From the Teeth of the Dragon— Gigantopithecus blacki. http://www.wynja.com/arch/ gigantopithecus.html.

Pfeiffer, J.

1985   *The Emergence of Humankind,* 4th ed. New York: HarperCollins.

Phillipson, D. W.

1993   *African Archaeology,* 2nd ed. New York: Cambridge University Press.

Piddington, R.

1970   Action Anthropology. In *Applied Anthropology: Readings in the Uses of the Science of Man,* ed. James Clifton, pp. 127–143. Boston: Houghton Mifflin.

Podolefsky, A., and P. J. Brown, eds.

1992   *Applying Anthropology: An Introductory Reader,* 2nd ed. Boston: McGraw-Hill.

1998   *Applying Anthropology: An Introductory Reader,* 5th ed. Boston: McGraw-Hill.

2002   *Applying Anthropology: An Introductory Reader,* 7th ed. Boston: McGraw-Hill.

Poirier, F. E., and J. K. Mckee

1998   *Understanding Human Evolution,* 4th ed. Upper Saddle River, NJ: Prentice-Hall.

Pollard, T. M., and S. B. Hyatt

1999   *Sex, Gender, and Health.* New York: Cambridge University Press.

Pollock, S.

1999   *Ancient Mesopotamia: The Eden That Never Was.* Cambridge, Eng.: Cambridge University Press.

Potts, D. T.

1997   *Mesopotamian Civilization: The Material Foundations.* Ithaca, NY: Cornell University Press.

2000   *Europe's First Farmers.* New York: Cambridge University Press.

Prag, J., and R. Neave

1997   *Making Faces: Using Forensic and Archaeological Evidence.* College Station: Texas A&M University Press.

Price, T. D., and A. B. Gebauer, eds.

1995   *Last Hunters, First Farmers: New Perspectives on the Prehistoric Transition to Agriculture.* Santa Fe, NM: School of American Research Press.

Price, T. D., and G. M. Feinman

1997   *Images of the Past,* 2nd ed. Boston: McGraw-Hill.

Quiatt, D., and V. Reynolds

1995   *Primate Behavior: Information, Social Knowledge, and the Evolution of Culture.* New York: Cambridge University Press.

Rak, Y.
1986   The Neandertal: A New Look at an Old Face. *Journal of Human Evolution* 15(3): 151–164.

Random House College Dictionary
1982   Revised ed. New York: Random House.

Reade, J.
1991   *Mesopotamia.* Cambridge, MA: Harvard University Press.

Read-Martin, C. E., and D. W. Read
1975   Australopithecine Scavenging and Human Evolution: An Approach from Faunal Analysis. *Current Anthropology* 16: 359–368.

Redfield, R.
1941   *The Folk Culture of Yucatan.* Chicago: University of Chicago Press.

Redmond, E. M.
1994   *Tribal and Chiefly Warfare in South America.* Museum of Anthropology Memoir 28. Ann Arbor: University of Michigan.

Redmond, E. M., ed.
1998   *Chiefdoms and Chieftaincy in the Americas.* Gainesville, FL: University Press of Florida Press.

Relethford, J. H.
1997   *The Human Species: An Introduction to Biological Anthropology,* 3rd ed. Boston: McGraw-Hill.

Renfrew, C., and P. Bahn
1996   *Archaeology: Theories, Methods, and Practice,* 2nd ed. London: Thames and Hudson.

2000   *Archaeology: Theories, Methods, and Practices,* 3rd ed. New York: Thames and Hudson.

Reynolds, V.
1971   *The Apes.* New York: Harper Colophon.

Rice, P.
2002   Paleoanthropology 2001—Part II. *General Anthropology.* 82: 11–14.

Richards, P.
1973   The Tropical Rain Forest. *Scientific American* 229(6): 58–67.

Ricoeur, P.
1971   The Model of the Text: Meaningful Action Considered as a Text. *Social Research* 38: 529–562.

Rightmire, G. P.
1990   *The Evolution of Homo erectus: Comparative Anatomical Studies of an Extinct Human Species.* New York: Cambridge University Press.

Rilling, J. K., D. A. Gutman, T. R. Zeh, G. Pagnoni, G. S. Berns, and C.D. Kilts
2002   A Neural Basis for Social Cooperation. *Neuron* 35: 395–405.

Roberts, D. F.
1953   Body Weight, Race and Climate. *American Journal of Physical Anthropology* 11: 533–558.

1986   *Genetic Variation and Its Maintenance: With Particular Reference to Tropical Populations.* New York: Cambridge University Press.

Roberts, J. L.
1995   *Dian Fossey.* San Diego, CA: Lucent Books.

Robertson, J.
1992   Koreans in Japan. Paper presented at the University of Michigan Department of Anthropology, Martin Luther King Jr. Day Panel, January 1992. Ann Arbor: University of Michigan Department of Anthropology (unpublished).

Rodseth, L., R. W. Wrangham, A. M. Harrigan, and B. Smuts
1991   The Human Community as a Primate Society. *Current Anthropology* 32: 221–254.

Romer, A. S.
1960   *Man and the Vertebrates,* 3rd ed., Vol. 1. Harmondsworth, Eng.: Penguin.

Rose, M.
1997   Neandertal DNA. Newsbriefs. *Archaeology* 50 (September/October): 5. http://www. archaeology.org/9709/newsbriefs/dna.html.

Rosenberg, K.R., and W.R. Trevathan
2001   The Evolution of Human Birth. *Scientific American* 285(5): 60–65.

Rushing, W. A.
1995   *The AIDS Epidemic: Social Dimension of an Infectious Disease.* Boulder, CO: Westview.

Russon, A. E., K. A. Bard, and S. Taylor Parker, eds.
1996   *Reaching into Thought: The Minds of the Great Apes.* New York: Cambridge University Press.

Sade, D.

1972 A Longitudinal Study of Social Behavior of Rhesus Monkeys. In *The Functional and Evolutionary Biology of Primates,* ed. R. Tuttle, pp. 378–398. Chicago: University of Chicago Press.

Saggs, H.

1989 *Civilization before Greece and Rome.* New Haven: Yale University Press.

Sanders, W. T.

1972 Population, Agricultural History, and Societal Evolution in Mesoamerica. In *Population Growth: Anthropological Implications,* ed. B. Spooner, pp. 101–153. Cambridge, MA: MIT Press.

1973 The Cultural Ecology of the Lowland Maya: A Reevaluation. In *The Classic Maya Collapse,* ed. T. P. Culbert, pp. 325–366. Albuquerque: University of New Mexico Press.

Sanders, W. T., J. R. Parsons, and R. S. Santley

1979 *The Basin of Mexico: Ecological Processes in the Evolution of a Civilization.* New York: Academic Press.

Santley, R. S.

1984 Obsidian Exchange, Economic Stratification, and the Evolution of Complex Society in the Basin of Mexico. In *Trade and Exchange in Early Mesoamerica,* ed. K. G. Hirth, pp. 43–86. Albuquerque, NM: University of New Mexico Press.

1985 The Political Economy of the Aztec Empire. *Journal of Anthropological Research* 41(3): 327–337.

Sargent, C. F., and C. B. Brettell

1996 *Gender and Health: An International Perspective.* Upper Saddle River, NJ: Prentice-Hall.

Sargent, C. F., and T. J. Johnson, eds.

1996 *Medical Anthropology: A Handbook of Theory and Method,* rev. ed. Westport, CT: Praeger Press.

Schaller, G.

1963 *The Mountain Gorilla: Ecology and Behavior.* Chicago: University of Chicago Press.

Scott, J.

2002 Prehistoric Human Footpaths Lure Archaeologists Back to Costa Rica. University of Colorado Press Release, May 20, 2002. http://www.eurekalert.org/pub_releases/2002-05/uoca-phf052002.php.

Sebeok, T. A., and J. Umiker-Sebeok, eds.

1980 *Speaking of Apes: A Critical Anthropology of Two-Way Communication with Man.* New York: Plenum.

Shanklin, E.

1995 *Anthropology and Race.* Belmont, CA: Wadsworth.

Shermer, M.

2002 *In Darwin's Shadow: The Life and Science of Alfred Russel Wallace.* New York: Oxford University Press.

Shore, B.

1996 *Culture in Mind: Meaning, Construction, and Cultural Cognition.* New York: Oxford University Press.

Shostak, M.

1981 *Nisa, the Life and Words of a !Kung Woman.* New York: Vintage Books.

2000 *Return to Nisa.* Cambridge, MA: Harvard University Press.

Shreeve, J.

1992 The Dating Game: How Old Is the Human Race? *Discover* 13(9): 76–83.

Sibley, C. G., and J. E. Ahlquist

1984 The Phylogeny of the Hominoid Primates, as Indicated by DNA-DNA Hybridization. *Journal of Molecular Evolution* 20: 2–15.

Silverberg, J., and J. P. Gray, eds.

1992 *Aggression and Peacefulness in Humans and Other Primates.* New York: Oxford University Press.

Simons, E. L., and P. C. Ettel

1970 Gigantopithecus. *Scientific American,* January, pp. 77–85.

Small, M. F.

1993 *Female Choices: Sexual Behavior of Female Primates.* Ithaca, NY: Cornell University Press.

Small, M. F, ed.

1984 *Female Primates: Studies by Women Primatologists.* New York: Alan R. Liss.

Smith, B. D.

1995 *The Emergence of Agriculture.* New York: Scientific American Library, W. H. Freeman.

Smith, M. E., and M. A. Masson, eds.

2000 *The Ancient Civilizations of Mesoamerica: A Reader.* Malpen, MA: Blackwell.

Smuts, B. B.

1985   *Sex and Friendship in Baboons.* New York: Aldine.

1999   *Sex and Friendship in Baboons,* with a new foreword. Cambridge, MA: Harvard University Press.

Solheim, W. G., II

1976   (orig. 1972) An Earlier Agricultural Revolution. In *Avenues to Antiquity: Readings from Scientific American,* ed. B. M. Fagan, pp. 160–168. San Francisco: W. H. Freeman.

Sonneville-Bordes, D. de

1963   Upper Paleolithic Cultures in Western Europe. *Science* 142: 347–355.

Spindler, G. D., ed.

2000   *Fifty Years of Anthropology and Education, 1950–2000: A Spindler Anthology.* Mahwah, NJ: Erlbaum Associates.

Srivastava, J., N. J. H. Smith, and D. A. Forno

1998   *Integrating Biodiversity in Agricultural Intensification: Toward Sound Practices.* Washington, DC: World Bank.

Staeck, J.

2001   *Back to the Earth: An Introduction to Archaeology,* 3rd ed. Boston: McGraw-Hill.

Steegman, A. T., Jr.

1975   Human Adaptation to Cold. In *Physiological Anthropology,* ed. A. Damon, pp. 130–166. New York: Oxford University Press.

Steponaitis, V.

1986   Prehistoric Archaeology in the Southeastern United States. *Annual Review of Anthropology* 15: 363–404.

Stern, A.

2000a   Experts Say 138 World Primate Species Endangered. Reuters. http://www.forests.org/archive/general/exsay138.htm.

2000b   More Than a Hundred Primate Species Endangered. http://www.foxnews.com/science/051200/primates.sml.

Steward, J. H.

1955   *Theory of Culture Change.* Urbana: University of Illinois Press.

Stinson, S., ed.

2000   *Human Biology: An Evolutionary and Biocultural Perspective.* New York: Wiley.

Strathern, A., and P. J. Stewart

1999   *Curing and Healing: Medical Anthropology in Global Perspective.* Durham, NC: Carolina Academic Press.

Strier, K. B.

2003   *Primate Behavioral Ecology,* 2nd ed. Boston: Allyn & Bacon.

Strum, S. C., and L. M. Fedigan, eds.

2000   *Primate Encounters: Models of Science, Gender, and Society.* Chicago: University of Chicago Press.

Susman, R. L.

1987   Pygmy Chimpanzees and Common Chimpanzees: Models for the Behavioral Ecology of the Earliest Hominids. In *The Evolution of Human Behavior: Primate Models,* ed. W. G. Kinzey, pp. 72–86. Albany: State University of New York Press.

Swindler, D. R.

1998   *Introduction to the Primates.* Seattle: University of Washington Press.

Tague, R. G., and C. O. Lovejoy

1986   The Obstetric Pelvis of A. L. 288-1 (Lucy). *Journal of Human Evolution* 15: 237–255.

Tainter, J.

1987   *The Collapse of Complex Societies.* New York: Cambridge University Press.

Tattersall, I.

1995a   *The Fossil Trail: How We Know What We Think We Know about Human Evolution.* New York: Oxford University Press.

1995b   *The Last Neanderthal: The Rise, Success, and Mysterious Extinction of Our Closest Human Relatives.* New York: Macmillan.

1998   *Becoming Human: Evolution and Human Uniqueness.* New York: Harcourt Brace.

Taylor, C.

1987   Anthropologist-in-Residence. In *Applied Anthropology in America,* 2nd ed., ed. E. M. Eddy and W. L. Partridge. New York: Columbia University Press.

Teleki, G.

1973   *The Predatory Behavior of Wild Chimpanzees.* Lewisburg, PA: Bucknell University Press.

Terrace, H. S.

1979   *Nim.* New York: Knopf.

Terrell, J. E.

1998   The Prehistoric Pacific. 51(6). *Archaeology*. Archaeological Institute of America. http://www.archaeology.org/9811/abstracts/pacific.html.

Thomson, A., and L. H. D. Buxton

1923   Man's Nasal Index in Relation to Certain Climatic Conditions. *Journal of the Royal Anthropological Institute* 53: 92–112.

Tice, K.

1997   Reflections on Teaching Anthropology for Use in the Public and Private Sector. In *The Teaching of Anthropology: Problems, Issues, and Decisions,* ed. C. P. Kottak, J. J. White, R. H. Furlow, and P. C. Rice, pp. 273–284. Boston: McGraw-Hill.

Tobler, A. J.

1950   *Excavations at Tepe Gawra,* vol. 2. Philadelphia: University of Pennsylvania Museum.

Todt, R.

2000   Western Hemisphere Inhabited at Least 15,000 Years Ago. ABCNews.Go.com News Briefs, April 7. http://abcnews.go.com/sections/science/DailyNews/first_americans000407.html.

Toth, N., and Schick, K.

1986   The First Million Years: The Archaeology of Protohuman Culture. *Advances in Archaeological Method and Theory,* pp. 1–96.

Trigger, B. G.

1993   *Early Civilizations: Ancient Egypt in Context.* New York: Columbia University Press.

Ucko, P., and A. Rosenfeld

1967   *Paleolithic Cave Art.* London: Weidenfeld and Nicolson.

Ucko, P. J., and G. W. Dimbleby, eds.

1969   *The Domestication and Exploitation of Plants and Animals.* Chicago: Aldine.

Valladas, H., J. L. Reyss, J. L. Joron, G. Valladas, O. Bar-Joseph, and B. Vandermeersch

1988   Thermoluminescence Dating of Mousterian "Proto-Cro-Magnon" Remains from Israel and the Origin of Modern Man. *Nature* 331: 614–616.

Van Schaik, C. P., and J. A. R. A. M. van Hooff

1983   On the Ultimate Causes of Primate Social Systems. *Behaviour* 85: 91–117.

Van Willingen, J.

1987   *Becoming a Practicing Anthropologist: A Guide to Careers and Training Programs in Applied Anthropology.* NAPA Bulletin 3. Washington, DC: American Anthropological Association/National Association for the Practice of Anthropology.

1993   *Applied Anthropology: An Introduction,* 2nd ed. South Hadley, MA: Bergin and Garvey.

2002   *Applied Anthropology: An Introduction,* 3rd ed. Westport CT: Bergin and Garvey.

Vekua, A., D. Lordkipanidze, et al.

2002   A Skull of Early Homo from Dmanisi, Georgia. *Science,* July 5, pp. 85–89.

Viegas, J.

2000   Planet of the Dying Apes: Conference Reveals Steep Decline in Primate Populations. http://abcnews.go.com/sections/science/DailyNews/apeconference000512.html.

Viola, H. J., and C. Margolis

1991   *Seeds of Change: Five Hundred Years since Columbus: A Quincentennial Commemoration.* Washington, DC: Smithsonian Institution Press.

Von Daniken, E.

1971   *Chariots of the Gods: Unsolved Mysteries of the Past.* New York: Bantam.

Wade, N.

1997   Testing Genes to Save a Life without Costing You a Job. *New York Times,* September 14. www.nytimes.com.

Wade, N., ed.

2001   *The New York Times Book of Fossils and Evolution,* rev. ed. New York: Lyons Press.

Wade, P.

2002   *Race, Nature, and Culture: An Anthropological Perspective.* Sterling, VA: Pluto Press.

Wagley, C. W.

1968   (orig. 1959) The Concept of Social Race in the Americas. In *The Latin American Tradition,* ed. C. W. Wagley, pp. 155–174. New York: Columbia University Press.

Ward, S., B. Brown, A. Hill, J. Kelley, and W. Downs

1999   Equatorius: A New Hominoid Genus from the Middle Miocene of Kenya. *Science EurekAlert!* August 27. http://www.eurekalert.org.

Washburn, S. L., and R. Moore

1980   *Ape into Human: A Study of Human Evolution,* 2nd ed. Boston: Little, Brown.

Watson, J. D.

1970   *Molecular Biology of the Gene.* New York: Benjamin.

Watson, P.

1972   Can Racial Discrimination Affect IQ? In *Race and Intelligence: The Fallacies behind the Race-IQ Controversy,* ed. K. Richardson and D. Spears, pp. 56–67. Baltimore: Penguin.

Watson, P. J.

1983   The Halafian Culture: A Review and Synthesis. In *The Hilly Flanks and Beyond: Essays on the Prehistory of Southwestern Asia,* ed. T. C. Young, Jr., P. E. L. Smith, and P. Mortensen. *Studies in Ancient Oriental Civilization* 36: 231–250. Oriental Institute, University of Chicago.

Webster's New World Encyclopedia

1993   College Edition. Upper Saddle River, NJ: Prentice-Hall.

Weiner, J.

1994   *The Beak of the Finch: A Story of Evolution in Our Time.* New York: Alfred A. Knopf.

Weiner, J. S.

1954   Nose Shape and Climate. *American Journal of Physical Anthropology* 12: 1–4.

Weiss, K. M.

1993   *Genetic Variation and Human Disease: Principles and Evolutionary Approaches.* New York: Cambridge University Press.

Weiss, M. L., and A. E. Mann

1990   *Human Biology and Behavior: An Anthropological Perspective,* 5th ed. Glenview, IL: Scott, Foresman.

Wenke, R. J.

1996   *Patterns in Prehistory: Mankind's First Three Million Years,* 4th ed. New York: Oxford University Press.

White, T. D., and P. A. Folkens

2000   *Human Osteology,* 2nd ed. San Diego: Academic Press.

Wilford, J.N.

1995   The Transforming Leap, from 4 Legs to 2. *New York Times,* September 5, 1995, pp. B5(N), C1(L).

2000   Ruins Alter Ideas of How Civilization Spread. *New York Times,* May 23. www.nytimes.com.

2001a   Skull May Alter Experts' View of Human Descent's Branches. *New York Times,* March 22, 2001, Late Edition, Final, section A, page 1, column 1; also www.nytimes.com.

2001b   African Artifacts Suggest an Earlier Modern Human. *New York Times,* December 2, 2001, Late Edition, Final, section 1A, page 1, column 5; also www.nytimes.com.

2002a   Seeking Polynesia's Beginnings in an Archipelago of Shards. *New York Times,* January 8, Science Desk.

2002b   When Humans Became Human. *New York Times,* February 26, 2002. Late Edition, Final, section F, page 1, column 1; also www.nytimes.com.

Wilson, C.

1995   *Hidden in the Blood: A Personal Investigation of AIDS in the Yucatan.* New York: Columbia University Press.

Wilson, D. S.

2002   *Darwin's Cathedral: Evolution, Religion, and the Nature of Society.* Chicago: University of Chicago Press.

Winslow, J. H., and A. Meyer

1983   The Perpetrator at Piltdown. *Science 83,* September, pp. 33–43.

Wittfogel, K. A.

1957   *Oriental Despotism: A Comparative Study of Total Power.* New Haven: Yale University Press.

Wolpoff, M. H.

1980a   *Paleoanthropology.* New York: McGraw-Hill.

1980b   Cranial Remains of Middle Pleistocene Hominids. *Journal of Human Evolution* 9: 339–358.

1999   *Paleoanthropology,* 2nd ed. New York: McGraw-Hill.

Wolpoff, M. H., and R. Caspari

1997   *Race and Human Evolution.* New York: Simon & Schuster.

World Almanac & Book of Facts

Published annually. New York: Newspaper Enterprise Association.

World Health Organization

1995   *World Health Report.* Geneva: World Health Organization.

Wrangham, R. W.

1980 An Ecological Model of Female-Bonded Primate Groups. *Behavior* 75: 262–300.

1987 The Significance of African Apes for Reconstructing Human Social Evolution. In *The Evolution of Human Behavior: Primate Models,* ed. W. G. Kinzey, pp. 51–71. Albany: State University of New York Press.

Wrangham, R. W., ed.

1994 *Chimpanzee Cultures.* Cambridge, MA: Harvard University Press.

Wrangham, R., W. McGrew, F. de Waal, and P. Heltne, eds.

1994 *Chimpanzee Cultures.* Cambridge, MA: Harvard University Press.

Wrangham, R. W., and D. Peterson

1996 *Demonic Males: Apes and the Origins of Human Violence.* Boston: Houghton Mifflin.

Wright, H. T., and G. A. Johnson

1975 Population, Exchange, and Early State Formation in Southwestern Iran. *American Anthropologist* 77: 267–289.

1994 Prestate Political Formations. In *Chiefdoms and Early States in the Near East: The Organizational Dynamics of Complexity,* ed. G. Stein and M. S. Rothman. *Monographs in World Archaeology* 18: 67–84. Madison, WI: Prehistory Press.

Wulff, R. M., and S. J. Fiske, eds.

1987 *Anthropological Praxis: Translating Knowledge into Action.* Boulder, CO: Westview.

Yellen, J. E., A. S. Brooks, and E. Cornelissen.

1995 A Middle Stone Age Worked Bone Industry from Katanda, Upper Semliki Valley, Zaire. *Science* 268: 553–56.

Yetman, N., ed.

1991 *Majority and Minority: The Dynamics of Race and Ethnicity in American Life,* 5th ed. Boston: Allyn & Bacon.

1999 *Majority and Minority: The Dynamics of Race and Ethnicity in American Life,* 6th ed. Boston: Allyn & Bacon.

Zeder, Melinda A.

1997 The American Archaeologist: Results of the 1994 SAA Census. *SAA Bulletin* 15(2): 12–17.

GLOSSARY

absolute dating   Dating techniques that establish dates in numbers or ranges of numbers; examples include the radiometric methods of ^{14}C, K/A, ^{238}U, TL, and ESR dating.

Acheulian   Derived from the French village of St. Acheul, where these tools were first identified; Lower Paleolithic tool tradition associated with *H. erectus.*

adapids   Early (Eocene) primate family ancestral to lemurs and lorises.

adaptation   The process by which organisms cope with environmental stresses.

adaptive   Favored by natural selection in a particular environment.

advocacy view   of applied anthropology; the belief that precisely because anthropologists are experts on human problems and social change, and because they study, understand, and respect cultural values, they should make policy affecting people.

allele   A biochemical difference involving a particular gene.

Allen's rule   Rule stating that the relative size of protruding body parts (such as ears, tails, bills, fingers, toes, and limbs) tends to increase in warmer climates.

alluvial   Pertaining to rich, fertile soil deposited by rivers and streams.

analogies   Similarities arising as a result of similar selective forces; traits produced by convergent evolution.

anatomically modern humans (AMHs)
Including the Cro-Magnons of Europe (31,000 B.P.) and the older fossils from Skhūl (100,000) and Qafzeh (92,000); continue through the present; also known as *H. sapiens sapiens.*

Anthropoidea   One of two suborders of primates; includes monkeys, apes, and humans.

anthropoids   Members of Anthropoidea, one of the two suborders of primates; monkeys, apes, and humans are anthropoids.

anthropology   The study of the human species and its immediate ancestors.

anthropology and education
Anthropological research in classrooms, homes, and neighborhoods, viewing students as total cultural creatures whose enculturation and attitudes toward education belong to a larger context that includes family, peers, and society.

anthropometry   The measurement of human body parts and dimensions, including skeletal parts (*osteometry*).

antibody   A defending protein that reacts by attacking a foreign substance; see *antigen.*

antigen   A chemical substance that triggers the production of an antibody.

applied anthropology   The application of anthropological data, perspectives, theory, and methods to identify, assess, and solve contemporary social problems.

arboreal   Tree-dwelling.

arboreal theory   Theory that the primates evolved by adapting to life high up in the trees, where visual abilities would have been favored over the sense of smell, and grasping hands and feet would have been used for movement along branches.

archaeological anthropology (prehistoric archaeology)   The study of human behavior and cultural patterns and processes through the culture's material remains.

archaic *Homo sapiens* Early *H. sapiens,* consisting of the Neandertals of Europe and the Middle East, the Neandertal-like hominids of Africa and Asia, and the immediate ancestors of all these hominids; lived from about 300,000 to 28,000 B.P.

archaic state Nonindustrial state.

artifacts Material items that humans have manufactured or modified.

Aurignacian Upper Paleolithic tradition, 35,000 to 20,000 B.P.; tools usually found in narrow valleys or near cliff walls, and thick layers suggest long occupation; may have diffused into Europe from elsewhere.

australopithecines Varied group of Pliocene–Pleistocene hominids. The term is derived from their former classification as members of a distinct subfamily, the Australopithecinae; now they are distinguished from *Homo* only at the genus level.

axis Plant part that attaches the grains to the stalk; brittle in wild grains, tough in domesticated ones.

Aztec Last independent state in the Valley of Mexico; capital was Tenochtitlan. Thrived between A.D. 1325 and the Spanish conquest in 1520.

band Basic unit of social organization among foragers. A band includes fewer than 100 people; it often splits up seasonally.

Bergmann's rule Rule stating that the smaller of two bodies similar in shape has more surface area per unit of weight and can therefore dissipate heat more efficiently; hence, large bodies tend to be found in colder areas and small bodies in warmer ones.

Beringia Area now under the Bering Sea; a dry land mass several hundred miles wide, exposed during the glacial advances.

biochemical genetics Field that studies structure, function, and changes in genetic material.

biological anthropology The study of human biological variation in time and space; includes evolution, genetics, growth and development, and primatology.

biomedicine Western medicine, which attributes illness to scientifically demonstrated agents: biological organisms (e.g., bacteria, viruses, fungi, or parasites) or toxic materials.

bipedal Two-footed.

blade tool The basic Upper Paleolithic tool type, hammered off a prepared core.

bone biology The study of bone as a biological tissue, including its genetics; cell structure; growth, development, and decay, and patterns of movement (*biomechanics*).

brachiation Under-the-branch swinging; characteristic of gibbons, siamangs, and some New World monkeys.

broad-spectrum revolution Period beginning around 20,000 B.P. in the Middle East and 12,000 B.P. in Europe, during which a wider range, or broader spectrum, of plant and animal life was hunted, gathered, collected, caught, and fished; revolutionary because it led to food production.

bronze An alloy of arsenic and copper or of tin and copper.

bush school Held in a location remote from residential areas; young people go there when they reach puberty to be instructed in knowledge viewed as essential to adult status.

caloric staple Major source of dietary carbohydrates—such as wheat, rice, or maize.

capital Wealth or resources invested in business, with the intent of producing a profit.

caprine From *capra,* Latin for "goat"; refers to goats and sheep.

Capsians Mesolithic North African foragers who based much of their subsistence on land snails.

catarrhine Sharp-nosed; anthropoid infraorder that includes Old World monkeys, apes, and humans.

catastrophism View that extinct species were destroyed by fires, floods, and other catastrophes. After each destructive event, God created again, leading to contemporary species.

Cenozoic Era of recent life—birds and mammals.

chiefdom Form of sociopolitical organization intermediate between the tribe and the state; kin-based with differential access to resources and a permanent political structure. A rank society in which relations among villages as well as among individuals are unequal, with smaller villages under the authority of leaders in larger villages; has a two-level settlement hierarchy.

chromosomes   Basic genetic units, occurring in matching (homologous) pairs; lengths of DNA made up of multiple genes.

chronology   Time frame, sequence.

civilization   A complex society with a government and social classes; synonyms are *nation-state* and *state.*

class   Zoological: Division of a kingdom; composed of related orders.

classic Neandertals   Stereotypical Neandertals of Western Europe, considered by some scholars to be too specialized to have evolved into *H. sapiens sapiens.*

cline   A gradual shift in gene frequencies between neighboring populations.

Clovis tradition   Stone technology based on a projectile point that was fastened to the end of a hunting spear; it flourished between 12,000 and 11,000 B.P. in North America.

competitive exclusion   Ecological principle that if two similar species exploit the same ecological niche, any advantage on the part of one of them, even though minor, eventually will force the other from that niche.

conspecifics   Individual members of the same species.

continental shelf   Offshore shallow-water zone over which the ocean gradually deepens until the abrupt fall to deep water, which is known as the continental slope.

continental slope   See *continental shelf.*

convergent evolution   Independent operation of similar selective forces; process by which analogies are produced.

correlation   An association between two or more variables such that when one changes (varies), the other(s) also change(s) (covaries); for example, temperature and sweating.

cranium   Skull.

creationism   Explanation for the origin of species given in Genesis: God created the species during the original six days of Creation.

cultural anthropology   The study of human society and culture; describes, analyzes, interprets, and explains social and cultural similarities and differences.

cultural ecology   The study of ecosystems that include people, focusing on how human use of nature influences and is influenced by social organization and cultural values.

cultural resource management (CRM)   The branch of applied archaeology aimed at preserving sites threatened by dams, highways, and other projects.

culture   Distinctly human; transmitted through learning; traditions and customs that govern behavior and beliefs.

culture and personality   A subfield of cultural anthropology; examines variation in psychological traits and personality characteristics among cultures.

cuneiform   Early Mesopotamian writing that used a stylus (writing implement) to write wedge-shaped impressions on raw clay; from the Latin word for wedge.

curer   Specialized role acquired through a culturally appropriate process of selection, training, certification, and acquisition of a professional image; the curer is consulted by patients, who believe in his or her special powers, and receives some form of special consideration; a cultural universal.

cytoplasm   The outer area of the cell rather than the nucleus.

diaspora   The offspring of an area who have spread to many lands.

differential access   Unequal access to resources; basic attribute of chiefdoms and states. Superordinates have favored access to such resources, while the access of subordinates is limited by superordinates.

diffusion   Borrowing of cultural traits between societies, either directly or through intermediaries.

directional selection   Long-term selection of the same trait(s); may go on as long as environmental forces remain the same.

disease   A scientifically identified health threat caused by a bacterium, virus, fungus, parasite, or other pathogen.

dominant   Allele that masks another allele in a heterozygote.

dry farming   Cultivation that is rainfall-dependent, without irrigation.

dryopithecids   Zoological ape family living in Europe during the middle and late Miocene; probably includes the common ancestor of the lesser apes (gibbons and siamangs) and the great apes.

ecology   The study of interrelationships among living things in an environment.

ecosystem   A patterned arrangement of energy flows and exchanges; includes organisms sharing a common environment and that environment.

egalitarian society   A type of society, most typically found among foragers, that lacks status distinctions except for those based on age, gender, and individual qualities, talents, and achievements.

elite level   Archaeological term for evidence of differential access to strategic resources; found in chiefdoms and states.

emotionalistic disease theories   Theories that assume that illness is caused by intense emotional experiences.

empire   A mature, territorially large and expansive state; empires are typically multiethnic, multilinguistic, and more militaristic, with a better developed bureaucracy, than earlier states.

enculturation   The social process by which culture is learned and transmitted across the generations.

estrus   Period of maximum sexual receptivity in female baboons, chimpanzees, and other primates, signaled by vaginal area swelling and coloration.

ethnography   Field work in a particular culture.

ethnology   Cross-cultural comparison; the comparative study of ethnographic data, of society, and of culture.

eugenics   Controversial movement aimed at genetic improvement by encouraging the reproduction of individuals with favored features and discouraging that of individuals with features deemed undesirable.

Eve theory   Theory that a small group of anatomically modern people arose recently, probably in Africa, from which they spread and replaced the native and more archaic populations of other inhabited areas.

evolution   Descent with modification; change in form over generations.

excavation   Digging through the layers of deposits that make up an archaeological site.

family, zoological   Group of similar genera.

food production   Cultivation of plants and domestication (stockbreeding) of animals; first developed in the Middle East 10,000 to 12,000 years ago.

foramen magnum   "Big hole" through which the spinal cord joins the brain; located farther forward in *Australopithecus* and *Homo* than in apes.

fossils   Remains (e.g., bones), traces, or impressions (e.g., footprints) of ancient life.

gametes   The sex cells: eggs (ova) and sperms.

gene   Area in a chromosome pair that determines, wholly or partially, a particular biological trait, such as whether one's blood type is A, B, AB, or O.

gene flow   Exchange of genetic material between populations of the same species through direct or indirect interbreeding.

gene pool   All the alleles and genotypes within a breeding population—the "pool" of genetic material available.

general anthropology   The field of anthropology as a whole, consisting of cultural, archaeological, biological, and linguistic anthropology.

genetic evolution   Change in gene frequency within a breeding population.

genotype   An organism's hereditary makeup.

genus (plural, *genera*)   Group of similar species.

gibbons   The smallest apes, natives of Asia; arboreal and territorial.

glacials   The four or five major advances of continental ice sheets in northern Europe and North America.

gracile   Opposite of robust.

Halafian   An early (7500–6500 B.P.) and widespread pottery style, first found in northern Syria; refers to a delicate ceramic style and to the period when the first chiefdoms emerged.

health-care systems   Beliefs, customs, and specialists concerned with ensuring health and preventing and curing illness; a cultural universal.

heterozygous Having dissimilar alleles of a given gene.

Hilly Flanks Woodland zone that flanks the Tigris and Euphrates rivers to the north; zone of wild wheat and barley and of sedentism (settled, nonmigratory life) preceding food production.

holistic Interested in the whole of the human condition: past, present, and future; biology, society, language, and culture.

Hominidae Zoological superfamily that includes fossil and living humans; according to some taxonomists, also includes the African apes.

hominids Members of the zoological family (Hominidae) that includes fossil and living humans.

Hominoidea Zoological superfamily that includes fossil and contemporary apes and humans.

hominoids Members of the superfamily including humans and all the apes.

Homo habilis Term coined by L. S. B. and Mary Leakey; immediate ancestor of *H. erectus;* lived from about 2 to 1.7 or 1.6 m.y.a.

Homo sapiens sapiens Anatomically modern humans.

homologies Traits that organisms have jointly inherited from their common ancestor.

homozygous Possessing identical alleles of a particular gene.

humanities Academic fields that study languages, texts, philosophies, arts, music, performances, and other forms of creative expression.

hybrid Mixed.

hydraulic systems Systems of water management, including irrigation, drainage, and flood control. Often associated with agricultural societies in arid and river environments.

hypervitaminosis D Condition caused by an excess of vitamin D; calcium deposits build up on the body's soft tissues and the kidneys may fail; symptoms include gallstones and joint and circulation problems; may affect unprotected light-skinned individuals in the tropics.

hypodescent Rule that automatically places the children of a union or mating between members of different socioeconomic groups in the less-privileged group.

hypoxia A body's oxygen deprivation; the difficulty of extracting oxygen from the air increases with altitude because barometric pressure decreases and molecules of air are farther apart.

illness A condition of poor health perceived or felt by an individual.

inclusive fitness Reproductive success measured by the representation of genes one shares with other, related individuals.

independent assortment Mendel's law of; chromosomes are inherited independently of one another.

independent invention Development of the same cultural trait or pattern in separate cultures as a result of comparable needs and circumstances.

indigenized Modified to fit the local culture.

indigenous peoples The original inhabitants of particular territories; often descendants of tribespeople who live on as culturally distinct colonized peoples, many of whom aspire to autonomy.

individual fitness Reproductive success measured by the number of direct descendants an individual has.

interglacials Extended warm periods between such major glacials as Riss and Würm.

interstadials Brief warm periods during a glacial; not to be confused with the longer interglacials.

ischial callosities Rough patches of skin of gibbons and Old World monkeys on the buttocks, adapted to sitting on hard rocky ground and rough branches.

ivory tower view of applied anthropology; the belief that anthropologists should avoid practical matters and concentrate on research, publication, and teaching.

Jomon Widespread (30,000 sites known) Japanese Mesolithic culture, dated to 6000 to 5000 B.P.; hunted deer, pigs, bear, and antelope, and also ate fish, shellfish, and plants.

kin-based Characteristic of many nonindustrial societies. People spend their lives almost exclusively with their relatives; principles of kinship, descent, and marriage organize social life.

kingdom, zoological Group of related classes.

knuckle-walking   A form of terrestrial locomotion in which long arms and callused knuckles support the trunk; the ape ambles around leaning forward.

lactase   See *lactose.*

lactose   A complex sugar in milk; its digestion requires an enzyme called *lactase* in the small intestine. Among most mammals, lactase production ceases after weaning, and the ability to digest milk is lost.

linguistic anthropology   The descriptive, comparative, and historical study of language and of linguistic similarities and differences in time, space, and society.

longitudinal   Long-term; refers to a study carried out over many years.

macroband   Assembly of foraging bands for intensive collecting or cooperative hunting.

maize   Corn; domesticated in highland Mexico.

maladaptive   Harmful; selected against; conferring a disadvantage with respect to survival and reproduction.

manioc   Cassava; a tuber domesticated in the South American lowlands.

medical anthropology   Field including biological and cultural, theoretical and applied, anthropologists concerned with the sociocultural context and implications of disease and illness.

meiosis   Special process by which sex cells are produced; four cells are produced from one, each with half the genetic material of the original cell.

melanin   Substance manufactured in specialized cells in the lower layers of the epidermis (outer skin layer); melanin cells in dark skin produce more melanin than do those in light skin.

Mendelian genetics   Studies ways in which chromosomes transmit genes across the generations.

Mesoamerica   Middle America, including Mexico, Guatemala, and Belize.

Mesolithic   Middle Stone Age, whose characteristic tool type was the microlith; broad-spectrum economy.

Mesopotamia   The area between the Tigris and Euphrates rivers in what is now southern Iraq and southwestern Iran; location of the first cities and states.

Mesozoic   Era of middle life—reptiles, including the dinosaurs.

metallurgy   Knowledge of the properties of metals, including their extraction and processing and the manufacture of metal tools.

microband   Small family group of foragers.

microlith   Greek for "small stone"; characteristic Mesolithic tool.

Middle Pleistocene   The period from the Mindel glacial through the Riss-Würm interglacial.

Mindel   The second major glacial advance in Europe.

mitosis   Ordinary cell division; DNA molecules copy themselves, creating two identical cells out of one.

molecular anthropology   Genetic analysis, involving comparison of DNA sequences, to determine evolutionary links and distances among species and among ancient and modern populations.

morphology   The study of form; used in linguistics (the study of morphemes and word construction) and for form in general—for example, biomorphology relates to physical form.

Mousterian   Middle Paleolithic tool-making tradition associated with Neandertals.

multiregional evolution   Theory that *Homo erectus* gradually evolved into modern *H. sapiens* in all regions inhabited by humans (Africa, Europe, northern Asia, and Australasia). As the regional populations evolved, gene flow always connected them, and so they always belonged to the same species. This theory opposes replacement models such as the Eve theory.

multivariate   Involving multiple factors, causes, or variables.

mutation   Change in the DNA molecules of which genes and chromosomes are built.

m.y.a.   Million years ago.

Natufians   Widespread Middle Eastern culture, dated to between 12,500 and 10,500 B.P.; subsisted on intensive wild cereal collecting and gazelle hunting and had year-round villages.

natural selection   Originally formulated by Charles Darwin and Alfred Russel Wallace; the process by which nature selects the forms most fit to survive and reproduce in a given environment, such as the tropics.

naturalistic disease theories Include scientific medicine; theories that explain illness in impersonal systemic terms.

Neandertals *H. sapiens neanderthalensis,* representing an archaic *H. sapiens* subspecies, lived in Europe and the Middle East between 130,000 and 28,000 B.P.

Neolithic "New Stone Age," coined to describe techniques of grinding and polishing stone tools; the first cultural period in a region in which the first signs of domestication are present.

Nilotic populations Populations, including the Nuer, that inhabit the Upper Nile region of eastern Africa.

Oaxaca, Valley of Southern Mexican valley that was an early area of food production and state formation.

Oldowan pebble tools Earliest (2 to 2.5 m.y.a.) stone tools; first discovered in 1931 by L. S. B. and Mary Leakey at Olduvai Gorge.

Olmec Elite-level society on Mexico's Gulf Coast, 3200 to 2500 B.P.

omomyids Early (Eocene) primate family found in North America, Europe, and Asia; early omomyids may be ancestral to all anthropoids; later ones may be ancestral to tarsiers.

opposable thumb A thumb that can touch all the other fingers.

order, zoological Division of a zoological class; a group of related suborders, such as the primates.

orthograde posture Straight and upright; the posture among apes and humans.

osteology The study of bones; useful to biological anthropologists studying the fossil record.

paleoanthropology The study of hominid evolution and human life as revealed by the fossil record.

paleoecology The study, often by archaeologists, of ecosystems of the past.

Paleoindians Early North American Indians who hunted horses, camels, bison, elephants, mammoths, and giant sloths.

Paleolithic Old Stone Age (from Greek roots meaning "old" and "stone"); divided into Lower (early), Middle, and Upper (late).

paleontology Study of ancient life through the fossil record.

paleopathology Study of disease and injury in skeletons from archaeological sites.

Paleozoic Era of ancient life—fishes, amphibians, and primitive reptiles.

palynology Study of ancient plants through pollen samples from archaeological or fossil sites in order to determine a site's environment at the time of occupation.

Perigordian Upper Paleolithic tradition that coexisted with the Aurignacian in Europe between 35,000 and 20,000 B.P. Perigordian tools usually are found in thin deposits and are scattered over large areas; evolved in Western Europe out of Mousterian antecedents.

personalistic disease theories Theories that attribute illness to sorcerers, witches, ghosts, or ancestral spirits.

phenotype An organism's evident traits, its "manifest biology"—anatomy and physiology.

phenotypical adaptation Adaptive biological changes that occur during the individual's lifetime, made possible by biological plasticity.

phylogeny Genetic relatedness based on common ancestry.

physical anthropology See *biological anthropology.*

plasticity The ability to change; notion that biology is affected by environmental forces, such as diet and altitude, experienced during growth.

platyrrhine Flat-nosed; anthropoid infraorder that includes the New World monkeys.

Pleistocene Epoch of *Homo*'s appearance and evolution; began two million years ago; divided into Lower, Middle, and Upper.

polity The political order.

Polynesia Triangle of South Pacific islands formed by Hawaii to the north, Easter Island to the east, and New Zealand to the southwest.

polytypic species Species with considerable phenotypic variation.

pongid Zoological family that includes orangutans.

population genetics   Field that studies causes of genetic variation, maintenance, and change in breeding populations.

postcranium   The area behind or below the head; the skeleton.

posterior   Back; for example, posterior or back dentition—premolars and molars.

pot irrigation   Simple irrigation technique used in Oaxaca; by means of pots, water close to the surface is dipped and poured on plants.

potsherds   Fragments of earthenware; pottery studied by archaeologists in interpreting prehistoric life styles.

power   The ability to exercise one's will over others—to do what one wants; the basis of political status.

practicing anthropologists   Used as a synonym for *applied anthropology;* anthropologists who practice their profession outside of academia.

prehensile   Grasping, as in the tail of the New World monkeys.

prehistory   The period before the invention of writing (less than 6,000 years ago).

prestige   Esteem, respect, or approval for acts, deeds, or qualities considered exemplary.

primary groups   Primate groups composed of a permanently bonded male and female and their preadolescent offspring.

primary states   States that arise on their own (through competition among chiefdoms), and not through contact with other state societies.

primates   Monkeys, apes, and prosimians; members of the zoological order that includes humans.

primatology   The study of the biology, behavior, social life, and evolution of monkeys, apes, and other nonhuman primates.

Proconsul   Early Miocene genus of the pliopithecoid superfamily; the most abundant and successful anthropoids of the early Miocene; the last common ancestor shared by the Old World monkeys and the apes.

prosimians   The primate suborder that includes lemurs, lorises, and tarsiers.

psychological anthropology   The ethnographic and cross-cultural study of differences and similarities in human psychology.

punctuated equilibrium   Model of evolution; long periods of equilibrium, during which species change little, are interrupted by sudden changes—evolutionary jumps.

race   An ethnic group assumed to have a biological basis.

racism   Discrimination against an ethnic group assumed to have a biological basis.

radiometric   Dating technique that measures radioactive decay.

random genetic drift   Change in gene frequency that results not from natural selection but from chance; most common in small populations.

ranked society   A type of society with hereditary inequality but not social stratification; individuals are ranked in terms of their genealogical closeness to the chief, but there is a continuum of status, with many individuals and kin groups ranked about equally.

recessive   Genetic trait masked by a dominant trait.

recombination   Following independent assortment of chromosomes, new arrangements of hereditary units produced through bisexual reproduction.

relative dating   Dating technique, e.g., stratigraphy, that establishes a time frame in relation to other strata or materials, rather than absolute dates in numbers.

relativity   Of evolution through natural selection; adaptation and fitness are in relation to specific environments, and traits are not adaptive or maladaptive for all times and places.

remote sensing   Use of aerial photos and satellite images to locate sites on the ground.

rickets   Nutritional disease caused by a shortage of vitamin D; interferes with the absorption of calcium and causes softening and deformation of the bones.

Riss   The third major glacial advance in Europe.

robust   Large, strong, sturdy; said of skull, skeleton, muscle, and teeth; opposite of gracile.

sagittal crest Bony ridge atop the skull that forms as bone grows; develops from the pull of chewing muscles as they meet at the midline of the cranium.

San Foragers of southern Africa, also known as Bushmen; speakers of San languages.

schistosomiasis Disease caused by liver flukes transmitted by snails inhabiting ponds, lakes, and waterways, often created by irrigation projects.

schizoid view of applied anthropology; the belief that anthropologists should help carry out, but not make or criticize, policy, and that personal value judgments should be kept strictly separate from scientific investigation in applied anthropology.

science A systematic field of study or body of knowledge that aims, through experiment, observation, and deduction, to produce reliable explanations of phenomena, with reference to the material and physical world.

scientific medicine As distinguished from Western medicine, a health-care system based on scientific knowledge and procedures, encompassing such fields as pathology, microbiology, biochemistry, surgery, diagnostic technology, and applications.

sedentism Settled (sedentary) life; preceded food production in the Old World and followed it in the New World.

settlement hierarchy A ranked series of communities differing in size, function, and type of building; a three-level settlement hierarchy indicates state organization.

sexual dimorphism Marked differences in male and female biology, besides the contrasts in breasts and genitals, and temperament.

sexual selection Based on differential success in mating, the process in which certain traits of one sex (e.g., color in male birds) are selected because of advantages they confer in winning mates.

sickle-cell anemia Usually fatal disease in which the red blood cells are shaped like crescents, or sickles, and increase the heart's burden by clogging the small blood vessels.

Sivapithecus Widespread fossil group first found in Pakistan; includes specimens formerly called *"Ramapithecus"* and fossil apes from Turkey, China, and Kenya; early *Sivapithecus* may contain

the common ancestor of the orangutan and the African apes; late *Sivapithecus* is now seen as ancestral to the modern orang.

smelting The high-temperature process by which pure metal is produced from an ore.

social race A group assumed to have a biological basis but actually perceived and defined in a social context, by a particular culture rather than by scientific criteria.

society Organized life in groups; typical of humans and other animals.

speciation Formation of new species; occurs when subgroups of the same species are separated for a sufficient length of time.

species Population whose members can interbreed to produce offspring that can live and reproduce.

state (nation-state) Complex sociopolitical system that administers a territory and populace with substantial contrasts in occupation, wealth, prestige, and power. An independent, centrally organized political unit; a government. A form of social and political organization with a formal, central government and a division of society into classes.

stereoscopic vision Ability to see in depth.

strategic resources Those necessary for life, such as food and space.

stratification Characteristic of a system with socioeconomic strata, sharp social divisions based on unequal access to wealth and power; see *stratum.*

stratified Class-structured; stratified societies have marked differences in wealth, prestige, and power between social classes.

stratigraphy Science that examines the ways in which earth sediments are deposited in demarcated layers known as *strata* (singular, *stratum*).

stratum One of two or more groups that contrast in regard to social status and access to strategic resources. Each stratum includes people of both sexes and all ages.

suborder Group of closely related superfamilies.

subordinate The lower, or underprivileged, group in a stratified system.

sumptuary goods Items whose consumption is limited to the elite.

superfamily Group of closely related zoological families.

superordinate The upper, or privileged, group in a stratified system.

symbiosis An obligatory interaction between groups that is beneficial to each.

systematic survey Information gathered on patterns of settlement over a large area; provides a regional perspective on the archaeological record.

systemic perspective View that changes have multiple consequences, some unforeseen.

taphonomy The study of the processes—biological and geological—by which dead animals become fossils; from the Greek *taphos,* which means "tomb."

taxonomy Classification scheme; assignment to categories (*taxa;* singular, *taxon*).

teocentli Or *teosinte,* a wild grass; apparent ancestor of maize.

Teotihuacan A.D. 100 to 700, first state in the Valley of Mexico and earliest major Mesoamerican empire.

terrestrial Ground-dwelling.

theory An explanatory framework, containing a series of statements, that helps us understand *why* (something exists); theories suggest patterns, connections, and relationships that may be confirmed by new research.

Thomson's nose rule Rule stating that the average nose tends to be longer in areas with lower mean annual temperatures; based on the geographic distribution of nose length among human populations.

traditions, in tool making Coherent patterns of tool manufacture.

tropics Geographic belt extending about 23 degrees north and south of the equator, between the Tropic of Cancer (north) and the Tropic of Capricorn (south).

tundra Cold, treeless plains.

uniformitarianism Belief that explanations for past events should be sought in ordinary forces that continue to work today.

Upper Paleolithic Blade-toolmaking traditions associated with early *H. sapiens sapiens;* named from their location in upper, or more recent, layers of sedimentary deposits.

urban anthropology The anthropological study of cities.

uterine Primate groups made up of mothers, sisters, daughters, and sons that have not emigrated.

variables Attributes (e.g., sex, age, height, weight) that differ from one person or case to the next.

vertical economy Economy based on environmental zones that, although close together in space, contrast in altitude, rainfall, overall climate, and vegetation.

visual predation theory Theory that the primates evolved in lower branches and undergrowth by developing visual and tactile abilities to aid in hunting and snaring insects.

Würm The last glacial; began around 75,000 B.P. and ended between 17,000 and 12,000 B.P.

zygote Fertilized egg, created by the union of two sex cells, one from each parent.

Glosario de antropología y arqueología física

absolute dating   fechado absoluto

Acheulian   achelense

adapids   adápidos

adaptation   adaptación

adaptive   adaptativo

advocacy view of applied anthropology
visión defensora de la antropología aplicada

allele   alelo

Allen's rule   Allen, Regla de

alluvial   aluvional o aluvial

analogies   analogías

anatomically modern humans (AMHs)
humanos anatómicamente modernos

Anthropoidea   Antropoidea

anthropoids   antropoides

anthropology   antropología

anthropology and education   antropología
y educación

anthropometry   antropometría

antibody   anticuerpo

antigen   antígeno

applied anthropology   antropología aplicada

arboreal   arbóreo

arboreal theory   teoría arbórea

**archaeological anthropology (prehistoric
archaeology)**   antropología arqueológica
(arqueología prehistórica)

archaic _Homo sapiens_   _Homo sapiens_
arcaico

archaic state   estado arcaico

artifacts   artefactos

Aurignacian   auriñacense

australopithecines   australopitecos.

axis   eje

Aztec   Azteca

band   banda

Bergmann's rule   Bergmann, Regla de

Beringia   Beringia

biochemical genetics   genética bioquímica

biological anthropology   antropología
biológica

biomedicine   biomedicina

bipedal   bípedo

blade tool   utensilio de lasca

bone biology   biología osteológica

brachiation   braquiación

broad-spectrum revolution   revolución de
amplio espectro

bronze   bronce

bush school   escuela rural (o escuela del
arbusto)

caloric staple   alimento de primera necesidad

caprine   caprino

Capsians   Capsianos

catarrhine   catarrino o catirrino

catastrophism   catastrofismo

Cenozoic   Cenozoico

ceremonies of increase   ceremonias de fertilidad

chiefdom   cacicazgo

chromosomes   cromosomas

chronology   cronología

civilization   civilización

class Zoological   clase zoológica

classic Neandertals   Neandertal clásicos

cline   clina

Clovis tradition   tradición Clovis

competitive exclusion   exclusión competitiva

complex societies Nations   sociedades complejas, naciones

conspecifics   coespecíficos

continental shelf   plataforma continental

continental slope   vertiente continental (ver continental shelf).

convergent evolution   evolución convergente

correlation   correlación

cranium   cráneo

creationism   creacionismo

cultural anthropology   antropología cultural

cultural ecology   ecología cultural

cultural learning   aprendizaje cultural

cultural resource management (CRM)   administración de recursos culturales

culture   cultura

culture and personality   cultura y personalidad

cuneiform   cuneiforme

curer   curador/a

cytoplasm   citoplasma

diaspora   diáspora

differential access   acceso diferenciado

diffusion   difusión

directional selection   selección directriz

disease   enfermedad

dominant   dominante

dry farming   cultivo seco

dryopithecids   driopitecos

ecology   ecología

ecosystem   ecosistema

egalitarian society   sociedad igualitaria

elite level   nivel de elite

emotionalistic disease theories   teorías emocionalistas de las enfermedades

empires   imperios

enculturation   culturización

estrus   estro

ethnic group   grupo étnico

ethnography   etnografía

ethnology   etnología

eugenics   eugenesia

evolution   evolución

excavation   excavación

extrasomatic   extrasomático

family, zoological   familia zoológica

fiscal   fiscal

food production   producción de alimentos

foramen magnum   foramen magnum

gametes   gametos

gene   gen

gene pool   grupo genético

general anthropology   antropología general

genetic evolution   evolución genética

genotype   genotipo

genus (plural, genera)   género (plural, géneros)

gibbons   gibones

glacials   glaciares

gracile   grácil

Halafian   Halafiense

health-care systems sistemas de atención de la salud

heterozygous heterocigótico/a

Hilly Flanks Flancos Escarpados

Hogopans Hogopanes

holistic holístico/a

Hominidae Homínidae

hominids homínidos

Hominoidea Hominoidea

hominoids hominoides

Homo habilis Homo habilis

homologies homologías

homozygous homocigótico

humanities humanidades

hybrid híbrido

hydraulic systems sistemas hidráulicos

hypervitaminosis D hipervitaminosis D

hypodescent hipodescendencia

hypoxia hipoxia

ideal types tipos ideales

illness dolencia

inclusive fitness eficacia biológica inclusiva

independent assortment Mendel's law of; Ley de Mendel de selección independiente

independent invention invención independiente

indigenous peoples pueblos indígenas

individual fitness eficacia biológica individual

interglacials interglacial

interstadials interestadial

ischial callosities callosidades isquiales

ivory tower view of applied anthropology visión de la torre de marfil de la antropología aplicada

Jomon Jomon

kin-based basado/a en el parentesco

kingdom, zoological reino zoológico

knuckle-walking locomoción sobre los nudillos

lactase lactasa (ver lactosa)

lactose lactosa

linguistic anthropology antropología lingüística

longitudinal Long-term longitudinal de largo plazo

macroband macrobanda

maize Corn cereal de maíz

maladaptive Harmful adaptativamente malo, mal adaptado, dañino

manioc Cassava mandioca Cassava

medical anthropology antropología médica

meiosis meiosis

melanin melanina

Mendelian genetics genética mendeliana

Mesoamerica Mesoamérica

Mesolithic Mesolítico

Mesopotamia Mesopotamia

Mesozoic Mesozoico

metallurgy metalurgia

microband microbanda

microlith microlito

Middle Pleistocene Pleistoceno Medio

Mindel Mindel

mitosis mitosis

molecular anthropology antropología molecular

morphology morfología

Mousterian Musteriense

multivariate multivariado

mutation mutación

m.y.a. m.a.a. (millón de años atrás)

Natufians Natufiense

natural selection selección natural

naturalistic disease theories teorías naturalistas de las enfermedades

Neandertals Neandertales

Neolithic "New Stone Age" Neolítico, "Nueva Edad de Piedra"

Nilotic populations poblaciones nilóticas

Oaxaca, Valley of Oaxaca, Valle de

Oldowan pebble tools herramientas de piedra de Olduvai

Olmec Olmeca

omomyids omómidas

opposable thumb pulgar oponible

order, zoological orden zoológico

orthograde posture postura ortógrada

osteology osteología

paleoanthropology paleoantropología

paleoecology paleoecología

Paleoindians paleoindios

Paleolithic Old Stone Age Paleolítico, Antigua Edad de Piedra

paleontology paleontología

paleopathology paleopatología

Paleozoic Paleozoico

palynology palinología

Perigordian Perigordiense

personalistic disease theories teorías personalistas de las enfermedades

phenotype fenotipo

phenotypical adaptation adaptación fenotípica

phylogeny filogenia

physical anthropology antropología física (ver antropología biológica)

plasticity plasticidad

platyrrhine platirrino

Pleistocene Pleistoceno

plural marriage matrimonio plural (ver poligamia)

polity orden político

Polynesia Polinesia

polytypic species especie politípica

pongid póngido

population genetics genética de poblaciónes

postcranium postcraneana

posterior posterior

pot irrigation riego por cántaro

potsherds fragmentos de alfarería

power poder

practicing anthropologists antropólogos practicantes

prehensile prensil

prehistory prehistoria

prestige prestigio

primary groups grupos primarios

primary states estados primarios

primates primates

primatology primatología

Proconsul Procónsul

prosimians prosimios

punctuated equilibrium equilibrio puntuado

race raza

racism racismo

radiometric radiométrica

random genetic drift flujo génico aleatorio

ranked society sociedad jerarquizada

recessive recesivo

recombination recombinación

relative dating fechado relativo

relativity relatividad

remote sensing detección remota

rickets raquitismo

Riss Riss

robust robusto/a

sagittal crest borde sagital

San San

schistosomiasis esquistosomiasis

schizoid view of applied anthropology visión esquizoide de la antropología aplicada science   ciencia

scientific medicine   medicina científica

sedentism   sedentarismo

settlement hierarchy   jerarquía de asentamiento

sexual dimorphism   dimorfismo sexual

sexual selection   selección sexual

sickle-cell anemia   anemia de células falciformes

Sivapithecus   Sivapiteco

smelting   fundición

social race   raza social

society   sociedad

speciation   especiación

species   especie

state (nation-state)   estado (estado-nación)

stereoscopic vision   visión estereoscópica

strategic resources   recursos estratégicos

stratification   estratificación

stratified   estratificado/a

stratigraphy   estratigrafía

stratum   estrato

suborder   suborden

subordinate   subordinado/a

sumptuary goods   bienes suntuarios

superfamily   superfamilia

superordinate   de rango o clase superior

symbiosis   simbiosis

systematic survey   investigación sistemática

systemic perspective   perspectiva sistémica

taphonomy   tafonomía

taxonomy   taxonomía

teocentli or teosinte   teocentli o teocintle

terrestrial   terrestre

theory   teoría

Thomson's nose rule   Thomson, Regla de la nariz de

traditions, in tool making   tradiciones en la fabricación de herramientas

tropics   trópico

tundra   tundra

uniformitarianism   uniformismo

Upper Paleolithic   Paleolítico Superior

urban anthropology   antropología urbana

uterine   uterino

variables   variables

vertical economy   economía vertical

visual predation theory   teoría de predación visual

Würm   Würm

zygote   cigoto

CREDITS

Photo Credits

Frontmatter

xxxii: (*Part 1*) Aleksander Nordahl/dagfoto@online.no

Chapter 1

2: ©Joel Gordon; **4:** ©Spencer Grant/PhotoEdit; **7:** Smithsonian Institution; **8:** ©Barton Silverman/The New York Times; **9:** (*left*) ©Roberto Candia/AP/Wide World Photos; (*right*) ©David Cannon/Getty Images; **13:** Jerald T. Milanich; **14:** J. Kyle Keener; **15:** ©Christopher J. Morris/Corbis; **17:** Courtesy Alicia Wilbur; **18:** ©Jorgen Schytte/Still Pictures/Peter Arnold, Inc.; **21:** ©National Geographic Society; **23:** William Campbell/Corbis Sygma

Chapter 2

28: (*Part 2*) ©Wesley Boxce/Photo Researchers; **30:** ©Thomas Hoepker/Magnum; **33:** ©Mike Yamashita/Woodfin Camp & Associates; **34:** ©AP/Wide World Photos; **36:** ©Corbis-Bettmann; **38:** Charles Harbutt /Actuality; **39:** ©Mark Edwards/Still Pictures/Peter Arnold, Inc.; **42:** ©Jonathan Nourok/PhotoEdit; **43:** ©Erich Lessing/Magnum; **45:** ©UNEP/Peter Arnold, Inc.; **47:** Courtesy of Ann L. Bretnall; **48:** Professor Marietta Baba, Michigan State University

Chapter 3

56: ©Victor R. Boswell/National Geographic Society; **58:** ©Kenneth Garrett/National Geographic Society; **60:** ©Joe Brockert/AP/Wide World Photos; **62:** ©Michael K. Nichols/National Geographic Society; **64:** Payson Sheets, University of Colorado, Boulder; **65:** ©Frank Lane Picture Agency/Corbis; **66:** ©Richard T. Nowitz/Corbis; **67:** ©Peter Turnley/Corbis; **69:** Dr. Jerome Rose, University of Arkansas; **72:** ©Kenneth Garrett/National Geographic; **73:** ©Jonathan Blair/Corbis; **74:** Leonardo L.T. Rhodes/Earth Scenes/Animals Animals; **75:** ©Y. Arthus/Peter Arnold, Inc.

Chapter 4

82: ©Catherine Karnow/Woodfin Camp & Associates; **84:** Jay Sand; **86:** *Noah's Ark* by Edward Hicks, 1846, 26½ × 30½, Oil on canvas, Philadelphia Museum of Art, Bequest of Lisa Norris Elkins; **91:** ©Dr. Gopal Mujrti/Phototake; **92:** ©Jean-Marc Giboux/Getty Images; **94:** ©Alfred Pasieka/Peter Arnold, Inc.; **95:** David Maxwell; **97:** ©Jean-Christian Bourcart/Newsmakers/Getty Images; **98:** ©Betty Press/Woodfin Camp & Associates; **101:** (*left*) ©Robert Caputo/Stock Boston; (*right*) ©Dennis Stock/Magnum

Chapter 5

108: ©Cyril Ruoso/Peter Arnold, Inc.; **110:** Christophe Boesch/Wild Chimpanzee Foundation; **111:** ©Mike K. Nichols/Magnum; **116:** (*left*) ©Kenneth Garrett/National Geographic Society; (*right*) ©O. Langrand/Peter Arnold, Inc.; **117:** Courtesy Jennifer Burns; **120:** ©Tom McHugh/Photo Researchers; **122:** ©Mack Henley/Visuals Unlimited; **124:** Orangutan Foundation International; **126:** ©Connie Bransilver/Photo Researchers, Inc.; **128:** ©M. Gunther/Peter Arnold, Inc.; **129:** ©Jane Goodall/National Geographic Society; **133:** ©C. Novellino/Peter Arnold, Inc.

Bringing It All Together

139: ©Mark Edwards/Still Pictures/Peter Arnold, Inc.; **140:** ©Olivier Langrand/Peter Arnold, Inc.; **141:** ©Nigel Dickinson/Peter Arnold, Inc.

Chapter 6

142: ©Michael Nichols/National Geographic Society; **144:** ©A. Compost/Bios/Peter Arnold, Inc.; **148:** ©L. & D. Klein/Photo Researchers; **149:** (*left*) Denver Museum of Nature & Science; (*right*) ©Tom McHugh/Photo Researchers; **151:** (*left*) ©Tom McHugh/Photo Researchers; (*right*) ©Roland Seitre/Peter Arnold, Inc.; **153:** (*left*) ©Science VU/Visuals Unlimited; (*right*) ©Manoj Shah/Animals Animals; **154:** Russell Ciochon, U of Iowa; **156:** From *Rhetorica Christiana*, by Didacus Valades, 1579; **159:** ©AFP/Corbis; **158:** Courtesy Barbara Hewitt

Chapter 7

164: ©Thomas Ernsting/Bilderberg/Aurora; **166:** Tim D. White/Brill Atlanta; **168:** ©Fred Mayer/Magnum; **171:** Kenneth Garrett; **175:** ©John Reader/Science Photo Library/Photo Researchers; **180:** ©Maurico Anton/National Geographic Society; **182:** (*top a,b,c,d*) ©Luba Dmytryk/National Geographic Society; **182:** (*middle*) ©Des Bartlett/Photo Researchers; **183:** Alan Walker, Johns Hopkins University/National Museums of Kenya, Kalakol Account; **184:** Kenneth Garrett; **187:** Courtesy Josh Trapani

Chapter 8

192: ©The Art Archive/Picture Desk; **194:** ©Gouram Tsibakhashvili/AP/Wide World Photos; **196:** ©Richard Schlecht/National Geographic Society;

197: ©Luba Dmytryk/National Geographic Society; 198: ©Kenneth Garrett/National Geographic Society; 202: (*left*) ©E.R. Degginger/Earth Scenes; (*right*) ©Tom McHugh/Photo Researchers; 206: ©Kenneth Garrett/National Geographic Society; 207: (*left*) Courtesy Milford H. Wolpoff; (*right*) ©Kenneth Garrett/National Geographic Society; 214: ©Kenneth Garrett/National Geographic Society; 216: ©Ernest Manewal/SuperStock; 217: Courtesy Kelsey Foster

Bringing It All Together

223: ©Kenneth Garrett/National Geographic Society; 224: (*left*) ©Lindsay Hebberd/Woodfin Camp & Associates; (*right*) ©Toby Canham/ Pressnet/Topham/The Image Works

Chapter 9

226: ©Getty Images; 228: ©Leslie Close/AP/Wide World Photos; 230: ©Paul Grebliunas/Stone/Getty Images; 231: (*top*) ©Sabine Vielmo/ Peter Arnold, Inc.; (*bottom*) ©Penny Tweedie/Woodfin Camp & Associates; 233: ©Margot Granitsas/The Image Works; 234: (*top*) ©Tom Koene/ Visuals Unlimited; (*bottom*) ©Jan Spieczny/Peter Arnold, Inc.; 236: Courtesy Heather Norton; 235: ©Hartmut Schwarzbach/ Peter Arnold, Inc.; 239: ©Chris O'Meam/AP/World Wide Photos; 243: ©P.J. Griffiths/Magnum; 244: ©Mark Edwards/Peter Arnold, Inc.; 247: ©Mary Ann Chatain/AP/Wide World Photos

Chapter 10

252: ©Jean Paul Kay/Peter Arnold, Inc.; 254: ©Erich Lessing/Art Resource; 257: ©Erich Lessing/Art Resource; 259: ©Will Yurman/The Image Works; 262: ©Mike Yamashita/ Woodfin Camp & Associates; 265: ©Hinterleitner/Gamma Presse; 263: ©Michael Andrews/Earth Scenes; 268: ©Janet Foster/Masterfile; 270: ©Phil Schermeister/Corbis; 271: ©Ron Giling/Peter Arnold, Inc.; 272: ©Schalkwijk/Art Resource; 275: ©John Isaac/Still Pictures/Peter Arnold, Inc.; 274: Courtesy Maxine N. Oland

Chapter 11

280: ©O. Louis Mazzatenta/National Geographic Society; 282: ©Nathan Been/Corbis; 286: Ancient Art and Architecture Collection Ltd./ Bridgeman Art Library; 288: ©Shizuo Kambayashi/AP/Wide World Photos; 289: ©Heinz Plenge/ Peter Arnold, Inc.; 290: ©Erich Lessing/Art Resource; 291: ©Barry Iverson/ Woodfin Camp & Associates; 292: Courtesy Jerusha Achterberg; 293: ©Georg Gerster/Photo Researchers; 295: Freer Gallery of Art; 297: ©Robert Frerck/Odyssey/Chicago; 298: ©Jacques Jangoux/Peter Arnold, Inc.; 299: ©Scala/Art Resource; 303: ©F. Stuart Westmorland/Photo Researchers; 305: ©Photofest

Bringing It All Together

310: Roger Green/Anthropology; 312: ©Arno Gasteiger/Bilderberg/Aurora; 313: (*left*) ©Gonzalez/Laif/Aurora; (*right*) ©Albrecht G. Schaefer/Corbis

Text and Illustration Credits

Front Matter

ii-iii: From *Student Atlas of World Geography*, Third Edition, by John L. Allen. Copyright © 2003 by The McGraw-Hill Companies, Inc. Reprinted by permission of McGraw-Hill/Dushkin, a division of The McGraw-Hill Companies, Guilford, CT 06437.

Chapter 1

4: Del Jones, "Hot Asset in Corporate: Anthropology Degrees," *USA TODAY*, February 18, 1999, p. B1. Copyright © 1999 USA TODAY. Reprinted with permission.

Chapter 2

30: Excerpts from Malcolm W. Browne, "Buried on a Hillside, Clues to Terror," *The New York Times*, February 23, 1999. Copyright © 1999 by The New York Times Co. Reprinted with permission. 36: AAA Code of Ethics. Adapted from http://www.aaanet.org/committees/ ethics/ethcode.htm. With permission of the American Anthropological Association.

Chapter 3

60: Excerpts from Stephen Kinzer, "Museums and Tribes: A Tricky Truce," *The New York Times*, December 24, 2000, section 2, p. 1. Copyright © 2000 by The New York Times Co. Reprinted with permission.

Chapter 4

84: Excerpts from Nicholas Wade, "DNA Backs a Tribe's Tradition of Early Descent from the Jews," *The New York Times*, May 9, 1999, section 1, p. 1. Copyright © 1999 by The New York Times Co. Reprinted with permission. 93: Figures 4.5, Adapted from Joseph B. Birdsell, *Human Evolution: An Introduction to the New Physical Anthropology*. Copyright © 1981 by Harper & Row, Publishers, Inc. Reprinted by permission of Pearson Education, Inc., Glenview, IL.

Chapter 5

110: "Chimp Tool Sites Show Evidence of Human-Like Behavior," CBC News Online, May 26, 2002. Reprinted with permission of the Canadian Broadcasting Corporation. 114: Table 5.2, Adapted from Robert Martin, "Classification of Primates," in Steve Jones, Robert Martin, and David Pilbeam, eds., *The Cambridge Encyclopedia of Human Evolution* (Cambridge: Cambridge University Press, 1992), pp. 20-21. Reprinted with the permission of Cambridge University Press. 115: Fig. 5.2, From Roger Lewin, *Human Evolution: An Illustrated Introduction*, 3rd ed. (Boston: Blackwell Scientific Publications, 1993), p. 44. Reprinted by permission of Blackwell Publishing Ltd., Oxford, UK. 123: Fig. 5.6, From Clifford J. Jolly and Fred Plog, *Physical Anthropology and Archaeology*, 4th ed., p. 115. Copyright © 1986 by The McGraw-Hill Companies, Inc. Reprinted with permission. 124: Claudia Dreifus, "Saving the Orangutan," *The New York Times*, March 21, 2000. Copyright © 2000 by The New York Times Co. Reprinted with permission. 127: Figure 5.7, From Roger Lewin, *Human Evolution: An Illustrated Introduction*, 3rd ed. (Boston: Blackwell Scientific Publications, 1993), p. 45. Reprinted by permission of Blackwell Publishing Ltd., Oxford, UK.

Chapter 6

144: Guy Gugliotta, "Suddenly, Humans Age 3 Million Years," *The Washington Post*, April 18, 2002, p. A03. Copyright © 2002 The Washington Post. Reprinted with permission. 145: Figure 6.1, Based on an original figure compiled by D. Quednau, N. Klaud, and R.D. Martin. By permission of Dr. Robert Dennis Martin, The Field Museum, Chicago, IL. **146:** Figure 6.4, From *Introduction to Physical Anthropology*, 6th edition, by Robert Jurmain and Harry Nelson, p. 210. Copyright © 1994 Wadsworth. Reprinted with permission of Wadsworth, a division of Thomson Learning: www.thomsonrights.com. Fax 800 730-2215. **152:** Figure 6.5, From *Introduction to Physical Anthropology*, 6th edition, by Robert Jurmain and Harry Nelson, p. 302. Copyright © 1994 Wadsworth. Reprinted with permission of Wadsworth, a division of Thomson Learning: www.thomsonrights.com. Fax 800 730-2215. **157:** Figure 6.6, Tom Brown/2002. Copyright © The Christian Science Monitor. Reprinted with permission.

Chapter 7

166: Excerpts from John Noble Wilford, "Fossils May Be Earliest Human Link," *The New York Times*, July 12, 2001, p. A12. Copyright © 2001 by The New York Times Co. Reprinted with permission.

Chapter 8

194: Excerpts from John Noble Wilford, "Skulls in Caucasus Linked to Early Humans in Africa," *The New York Times*, May 12, 2000. Copyright © 2000 by The New York Times Co. Reprinted with permission. **200:** Figure 8.1, From Clifford J. Jolly and Randall White, *Physical Anthropology and Archaeology*, 5th ed., p. 271. Copyright © 1995 by

The McGraw-Hill Companies, Inc. Reprinted with permission. **202:** Figure 8.2, From Clifford J. Jolly and Randall White, *Physical Anthropology and Archaeology*, 5th ed., p. 268. Copyright © 1995 by The McGraw-Hill Companies, Inc. Reprinted with permission. **209:** Figure 8.5, From Clifford J. Jolly and Randall White, *Physical Anthropology and Archaeology*, 5th ed., p. 277. Copyright © 1995 by The McGraw-Hill Companies, Inc. Reprinted with permission. **215:** Excerpts and Figure 8.9 from Marlise Simons, "Prehistoric Art Treasure Is Found in French Cave," *The New York Times*, January 19, 1995, pp. A1, A5. Copyright © 1995 by The New York Times Co. Reprinted with permission.

Chapter 9

228: Excerpts from Brent Staples, "A Hemings Family Turns from Black, to White, to Black," *The New York Times*, December 17, 2001, p. A20. Copyright © 2001 by The New York Times Co. Reprinted with permission. **232:** Excerpts from the American Anthropological Association Statement on Race. From http://www.aaanet.org/stmts/racepp.htm. Reprinted with permission of the American Anthropological Association.

Chapter 10

254: Excerpts from Ben Harder, "Gene Study Traces Cattle Herding in Africa," http://news.nationalgeographic.com (April 11, 2002). Reprinted by

permission of the National Geographic Society. **264:** Excerpts from Boyce Rensberger, "Iceman Yields Details of Stone Age Transition: Portrait of Life 5,300 Years Ago Emerges," *The Washington Post*, October 15, 1992. Copyright © 1992 The Washington Post. Reprinted with permission. **267:** Figure 10.4, From *The Emergence of Agriculture* by Bruce D. Smith, p. 12. Copyright © 1995 Scientific American Library. Reprinted by permission of Henry Holt and Company, LLC. Table 10.2, Data compiled from *The Emergence of Agriculture* by Bruce D. Smith. Copyright © 1995 Scientific American Library. Reprinted by permission of Henry Holt and Company, LLC.

Chapter 11

282: Excerpts from Ben Harder, "Ancient Peru Torture Deaths: Sacrifices or War Crimes?" http://news.nationalgeographic.com (April 29, 2002). Reprinted by permission of the National Geographic Society. **294:** Figure 11.2, Based on Map 1-1 from *Heritage of World Civilizations*: Vol. I, to 1650, 4th ed. by Craig/Graham/Kagan/Ozmant/Turner. Copyright © 1997 Prentice-Hall. Reprinted by permission of Pearson Education, Inc., Upper Saddle River, NJ. **296:** Figure 11.3, From Clifford J. Jolly and Fred Plog, *Physical Anthropology and Archaeology*, 4th ed., p. 115. Copyright © 1986 by The McGraw-Hill Companies, Inc. Reprinted with permission.

Name Index

SUBJECT INDEX

Mental illness, 44
Mesoamerica. *See also* specific
    countries
    definition of, 259, 277, 284
    state formation in, 295–299
Mesolithic, 216, 218, 219, 255
Mesopotamia
    archeological periods in, 291
    definition of, 307
    economic development,
        293–294
    food production and,
        255–256
    fortresses and, 293
    land ownership and, 293–294
    rise of state in, 290–291
    social ranking and, 286–288
    state collapse in, 302
    state formation in, 285–291
    urban life and, 284–285
    writing development and,
        290–291
Mesozoic era, 143, 144, 146, 147
Metallurgy, 256, 293, 295, 307
Mexico
    Aztec state and, 253, 272,
        295, 298, 299, 302, 306
    chiefdoms and, 296–297
    food production in, 254–255,
        266, 268, 272
    foraging and, 304
    maize production and, 253
    Maya state, 272, 274, 299,
        302–305
    modern migration and, 40
    origin of state, 299–302
    settlement hierarchy and, 298
    social development in, 289
    Spanish conquest of, 297
    Teotihuacan state and, 253,
        272, 287, 297, 299
    Valley of, 297–299
    Zapotec state and, 297, 299
Michigan State University, 48
Microbes, 98–99
Microenculturation, 48
Microlith, 216
Middle East. *See* Mesopotamia;
    specific countries
Middle Pleistocene, 167–168
Midwives, 67
Miocene epoch, 150–156, 165, 169
Miocene hominoids, 150–155
Miss Saigon 239
Missing link, 155–157, 159
Mitochondrial DNA (mtDNA),
    76, 208–209, 236
Mitosis, definition of, 90, 104
Moche period, 282–283
Mohenjo–daro city state, 263
Molecular anthropology, 59,
    67–69, 78, 145
Molecular dating, 76
Monkeys, 118–120
Morocco, 203
Motorola, 4
Mousterian tools, 206, 210,
    211, 219

mtDNA. *See* Mitochondrial
    DNA
Multiregional evolution,
    210, 219
Multivariate, definition of,
    300, 307
"Museums and Tribes: A Tricky
    Truce" (Kinzer), 60
Mutations, definition of, 88, 104
m.y.a. (million years ago),
    146, 160

NAACP. *See* National
    Association for the
    Advancement of
    Colored People
NAGPRA. *See* Native American
    Graves Protection and
    Repatriation Act
NAPA. *See* National Association
    for the Practice of
    Anthropology
Nariokotome boy, 196, 198, 201
NASA. *See* National Aeronautics
    and Space
    Administration
National Aeronautics and Space
    Administration
    (NASA), 63
National Association for the
    Advancement of
    Colored People
    (NAACP), 240
National Association for the
    Practice of
    Anthropology
    (NAPA), 32
National Council of La Raza, 240
National Institutes of Health
    Human Genome
    Project, 97
National Science Foundation, 274
Native American Graves
    Protection and
    Repatriation Act
    (NAGPRA), 60–61
Native Americans
    artifact recovery and, 60–61
    census and, 239
    culture of, 7
    food production and,
        266–268
    haplogroups and, 69
    hypodescent rule and,
        238–239
    Kennewick Man and,
        60–61, 69
    race and, 230–231
    ranked societies and, 287
    social race and, 246
Natufian culture, 257–259,
    277, 284
Natural History Museum (Basel,
    Switzerland), 155
Natural selection
    definition of, 87, 104, 234, 249
    differential reproduction
        and, 133

directional selection, 92
fitness and, 133
    genetic evolution and, 91–94
    genetic recombination and, 83
    origin of species and, 83
    sickle–cell anemia and, 92–94
Naturalistic disease theories,
    definition of, 44, 52
Nature versus nurture, 8
Navajo tribe, 61
Nazis, 233, 245–246
Neandertals
    cold–adapted Neandertals,
        205–206
    definition of, 219
    discovery of, 205
    Eve theory, 208–209
    fossil site locations for,
        204, 206
    as *H. Sapiens*, 112, 193
    H. Sapiens Sapiens and, 204
    mitochondrial DNA
        (mtDNA) testing
        and, 208–209
    modern people and, 206–209
    multiregional evolution, 210
    skull of, 197, 207
    tool use, 199
Neolithic
    Çatal Hüyük and, 284–285
    definition of, 256–257, 377
    "Iceman" and, 264
    Mesopotamia and, 291
Neolithic Revolution, 256
Netherlands, 8
New Caledonia, 310
New Guinea, 236, 310
New World monkeys, 118–120
New York University, 225
New Zealand, 312, 313
NGOs. *See* Nongovernmental
    organizations
Nigeria, 102, 122
Nile Valley, 263, 281
Nilotes people, 100, 101, 231
Nittano site, 256
Nok Nok Tha site, 266
Nongovernmental organizations
    (NGOs), 32, 50
Nutrition. *See* Diet

Oaxaca Valley, 271, 281, 296
Obsidian, 284
Oedipus complex, 20, 44
OH62 (Olduvai Hominid 62), 195
Old World monkeys, 118–120,
    151, 175
Oldowan pebble tools, 184
Olduvai Gorge site, 184, 202
Olduvai Hominid 62, 195
Olduvai site, 174
Oligocene epoch, 150
Olmec, 272, 287, 296–297
Omomyids, 149, 160
On the Origin of Species (Darwin),
    87, 205
Opposable thumb, 113–114, 118,
    135

Orangutans, 122, 124–125
Oreopithecus, 155
Oreopithecus bambolii, 155
Orthograde posture 118
Osteology, 67
    definition of, 14
Ouranopithecus, 157
Overfarming, 303
Oxfam, 50
Oxford University, 84

P. major, 150
P. nyanzae, 150
Pacific Islanders, 239
Pakistan, 153, 263, 281, 294
Paleoanthropology
    definition of, 14, 73, 78
    excavation and, 70–72
    hominid study and, 69–70
    research methods, 59, 63
    systematic surveys and,
        70–71
Paleocene era, 144
Paleoecology, definition of, 11
Paleolithic, definition of,
    199, 219
Paleolithic tools, 199
Paleontology
    definition of, 14, 73, 78
    work methods of, 59
Paleopathology, 59, 67, 78
Paleozoic era, 146
Paloindians, 266, 268
Palynology, definition of,
    63, 78
PAN. *See* "Promoting Adequate
    Nutrition"
Pan troglodytes, 174, 176, 180
Papua New Guinea, 302,
    310–311, 313
PARC. *See* Xerox Palo Alto
    (California) Research
    Center
Pastoralism, 259
Pennsylvania State University,
    194, 209, 236, 292
Personalistic disease theories,
    definition of, 44, 52
Peru
    food production and, 268
    metal working and, 295
    Moche period, 281–283
    state formation in, 302
    violence in artwork in, 289
Pharaonic civilization, 263
Phenotypes
    definition of, 89, 230, 249
    natural selection and, 91
    racial classification and,
        234, 242
Phenotypical adaptation,
    definition of, 101, 104
Philippines, 133, 149
Physical anthropology.
    See Biological
    anthropology
Pictographic writing, 290
Piedmont steppe, 262